Wissensbasierte Systeme

veranstaltet von der

Gesellschaft für Informatik e.V. (GI)

in Verbindung mit

SYSTEMS '85

Anwendungen und Perspektiven

München, Messegelände
28 29. Oktober 1985

Gesamtleitung Prof. Dr. Dr. h.c. F. L. Bauer

Organisatorische Tagungsleitung
Auskünfte Anmeldung

Prof. Dr. M. Paul
Institut für Informatik
Technische Universität München
Arcisstraße 21
D-8000 München 2
Telefon (0 89) 21 05—81 61
Telex 5 22 854 tumue d

Wissenschaftliche Tagungsleitung:

Prof. Dr. W. Brauer (Vorsitz) Universität Hamburg
Dr. H. Gallaire Europ. Comp. Industry Research Center München
Prof. Dr. B. Radig Universität Hamburg
Prof. Dr. J. W. Schmidt Universität Frankfurt
Prof. Dr. W. Wahlster Universität Saarbrücken

Informatik-Fachberichte 112

Subreihe Künstliche Intelligenz

Herausgegeben von W. Brauer in Zusammenarbeit mit dem
Fachausschuß 1.2 „Künstliche Intelligenz und
Mustererkennung" der Gesellschaft für Informatik (GI)

Springer-Verlag

Geschäftsbibliothek - Heidelberg

Titel: *Informatik-Fachberichte, Band 112*

Aufl.-Aufst.: *Neuerscheinung*

Drucker: *Weihert-Druck, Darmstadt*

Buchbinder: *"*

Auflage: *1.800*   Bindequote: *1.800*

Schutzkarton/Schuber: *./.*

Satzart: *Schreibsatz*

Filme vorhanden: *ja*

Reproabzüge vorhanden: *./.*

Preis: *DM 59,-*

Fertiggestellt: *18.10.85*

Sonderdrucke: *./.*

Bemerkungen: *./.*

Berichtigungszettel: *./.*

Hersteller: *H. Bomcaux*   Datum: *10.3.86*

Wissensbasierte Systeme

GI–Kongreß
München, 28./29. Oktober 1985

Veranstalter:
Gesellschaft für Informatik e.V.
in Zusammenarbeit mit der SYSTEMS' 85

Herausgegeben von W. Brauer
und B. Radig

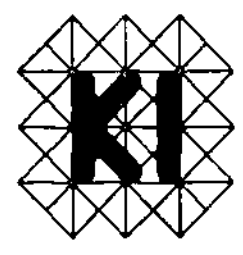

Springer-Verlag
Berlin Heidelberg New York Tokyo

Herausgeber

W. Brauer
Institut für Informatik der TU München
Arcisstr. 21, 8000 München 2

B. Radig
Universität Hamburg, Fachbereich Informatik
Schlüterstr. 70, 2000 Hamburg 13

Gesamtleitung:

F. L. Bauer, Technische Universität München

Programmkomitee:
W. Brauer (Technische Universität München), Vorsitz
H. Gallaire (ECRC München)
B. Radig (Universität Hamburg)
J. W. Schmidt (Universität Frankfurt)
W. Wahlster (Universität Saarbrücken)

Organisationsleitung:

M. Paul (Technische Universität München)

CR Subject Classifications (1982): I.2, I.2.1, I.4, I.5, I.6, I.7, I.8, I.10

ISBN-13: 978-3-540-15999-5   e-ISBN-13: 978-3-642-70840-4
DOI: 10.1007/978-3-642-70840-4

CIP-Kurztitelaufnahme der Deutschen Bibliothek. Wissensbasierte Systeme: GI-Kongress,
München, 28./29. Oktober 1985 / Veranst.: Ges. für Informatik e.V. in Zusammenarbeit mit
d. SYSTEMS '85. [Hrsg. W. Brauer ... Gesamtleitung: F. L. Bauer]. - Berlin; Heidelberg;
New York; Tokyo : Springer, 1985.
(Informatik-Fachberichte; 112 : Subreihe Künstliche Intelligenz)

NE: Brauer, Wilfried [Hrsg.]; Gesellschaft für Informatik; GT

2145/3140-543210

GELEITWORT

Ob der sogenannte *Computer* sich zum Segen der Menschheit auswirken wird, weiß heute
noch niemand. Vermutlich wird einiges durch ihn besser, anderes schlechter werden. Sicher
wird er das Bild des Menschen verändern. Das liegt daran, daß der *Computer* nicht nur mit
Zahlen rechnen kann, sondern auch derart programmiert werden kann, daß er nach außen
hin Fähigkeiten zeigt, die bei oberflächlicher Betrachtung als bezeichnend für menschliche
Intelligenz erscheinen. Das macht auf den Laien großen Eindruck, und zu den Laien gehören
auch die meisten Juristen, Politiker, Journalisten und Kaufleute.

In den USA, einer dort verbreiteten Neigung zu antropomorphen Wendungen nachkommend,
folgte auf 'Electronic Brain' 1956 der Ausdruck 'Artificial Intelligence'. Der unglücklich
gewählte Ausdruck kann vom Laien dahingehend mißverstanden werden, daß man früher oder
später auf menschliche Intelligenz verzichten könne, wolle oder müsse. Solchen Ängsten wird
durch Übertreibungen gelegentlich Vorschub geleistet (H.A.Simon 1967: A man, viewed as
a behaving system, is quite simple. The apparent complexity of his behaviour over time is
largely a reflection of the complexity of the environment in which he finds himself). Selbst
E. Feigenbaum, ein erklärter Propagandist der "Maschinellen Intelligenz", ist da viel vorsich-
tiger: "making a computer behave in ways that mimic intelligent human behaviour". Darin
liegt kein Totalitätsanspruch. H. Zemanek drückt es so aus: "the term is an abbreviation
for artificial generation of results which normally are produced by an intelligent mind". Das
braucht niemand zu veranlassen, über den Verstand hinaus den Einbezug von Bezirken des
Gefühls und des Unbewußten zu erwarten oder zu befürchten. Schließlich handelt es sich um
nichts anderes als

die Befreiung des Menschen von der Last gleichförmiger geistiger Tätigkeit,

ein Anliegen, das seit Pascal und Leibniz die Menschheit bewegt. Während aber Kraftmaschi-
nen bereits im 18. Jahrhundert industrielle Bedeutung erlangt haben, sind Informatikmaschi-
nen erst durch die Mikroelektronik handlich und erschwinglich geworden.

Die Informatikmaschine ist auf den Bezirk der Vernunft beschränkt. Sie stützt sich auf eine
Wissensbasis, die auch im Laufe der Benutzung erweitert werden kann und gibt auf geeignete
Fragen im Rahmen ihrer Fähigkeiten Antworten, die auf logisch-kombinatorischen Regeln der
Wissensverknüpfung beruhen.

Da die Wissensbasis erst einmal von Experten des jeweiligen Gebiets aufgestellt werden muß,
ist das Schlagwort "Expertensysteme" aufgekommen. Die Erfolge, die Expertensysteme in
jüngster Zeit aufweisen konnten, scheinen davon herzurühren, daß sie umso leistungsfähiger

sein können, je genauer sie auf ein eng begrenztes Gebiet zugeschnitten sind. Daß die Fortschritte anfänglich gering waren, beruht wohl darauf, daß die Ansprüche ursprünglich zu hoch gesteckt wurden und zu allgemein gehalten waren ("General Problem Solver": Newell, Shaw, Simon 1959).

Es lag also nahe, der Münchner Messegesellschaft und der Gesellschaft für Informatik e.V. vorzuschlagen, diesem aufstrebenden Gebiet mit einem Kongress im Rahmen der SYSTEMS Rechnung zu tragen. Ich hoffe, daß dieser Kongress zu einem tragenden Bestandteil auch künftiger SYSTEMS-Messen wird. Mein besonderer Dank gilt dem Vorsitzenden des Programmkomitees, Prof. W. Brauer, und dem Vorsitzenden des Organisationskomitees, Prof. M. Paul, mit ihren Mitarbeitern vom Institut für Informatik der Technischen Universität München, für ihre Bereitschaft zur Übernahme ihrer Ämter und für ihren selbstlosen Einsatz.

Nachdem wir das ominöse Jahr 1984 überstanden haben, ohne daß - wenigstens in unserem Land - Orwells Schrecken eingetreten sind, wird es Mode, vom Jahr 2030 zu reden. Es ist anzunehmen, daß der stürmische wissenschaftliche und wirtschaftliche Fortschritt auf dem Gebiet der Informatik noch eine Weile anhalten, aber noch vor 2030 in ein ruhigeres Fahrwasser übergehen wird. Gerade im Hinblick auf die "maschinelle Intelligenz" und die diesbezüglichen Versprechungen ist es beruhigend, an Nestroys Ausspruch erinnern zu können: "Überhaupt hat der Fortschritt das an sich, daß er größer ausschaut, als er ist".

August 1985   F.L. Bauer

VORWORT

Daten mit hoher Geschwindigkeit zu verarbeiten, ist heute eine Selbstverständlichkeit. Informationen über Sachverhalte aus Faktenbanken zu gewinnen und über weltweite Kommunikationsverbindungen an einen Ort zu bringen, ist mit Hilfe der heute existierenden Technik zuverlässig und routinemäßig machbar. An der Schwelle zum breiten, industriellen Einsatz stehen nun Verfahren, die die Erhebung, Strukturierung, Manipulation, Archivierung und Weitergabe von Wissen selbst zum Gegenstand haben.

Datenverarbeitung, Informationsverarbeitung und nun Wissensverarbeitung sind die Technologien, mit denen die Informatik in Industrie, Wirtschaft und Verwaltung immer intensiver hineinwirkt. Die Wissensverarbeitung eröffnet einerseits völlig neuartige Perspektiven für den Einsatz von Computern und die Anwendung der Informatik und bietet andererseits viele Möglichkeiten, bisherige Verfahren der Daten- und Informationsverarbeitung fehlertoleranter und benutzerfreundlicher zu gestalten und zu umfassenderen Systemen zu vereinigen.

Nach einer langen Phase theoretischer und experimenteller Grundlagenuntersuchungen setzt jetzt weltweit ein großes Interesse der Praxis an Wissensbasierten Systemen ein. Nicht nur in den USA und in Japan, sondern auch in immer stärkerem Maße in Europa und insbesondere auch in der Bundesrepublik Deutschland haben Forschungsteams und Hersteller beträchtliche Erfolge in diesem zukunftsträchtigen Bereich. Jetzt kommt es ganz besonders darauf an, daß potentielle Anwender dieser innovativen Technologie rechtzeitig deren Relevanz für ihre eigenen Aufgaben und Ziele erkennen. Deshalb ist es ein besonderes Anliegen der Gesellschaft für Informatik e.V. (GI), Anwender, Praktiker und Theoretiker Wissensbasierter Systeme zum Internationalen GI-Kongress '85 zusammenzubringen.

Daß der Kongress in München stattfindet, liegt nicht nur an der freundlichen Unterstützung durch den Bayerischen Staatsminister für Wirtschaft und Verkehr, Anton Jaumann, und am großen Engagement von Prof. F.L. Bauer als dem Initiator der Tagung. Die Veranstaltung in Zusammenarbeit mit der Münchner Messe- und Ausstellungsgesellschaft sowie dem SYSTEMS-Beirat als integraler Bestandteil der SYSTEMS'85 durchzuführen zu können, ist ein entscheidender Vorteil dieser Fachtagung.

Die SYSTEMS versteht sich als universelle internationale Fachmesse für Computer- und Kommunikationssysteme und bietet deshalb dem Kongressbesucher vielfältige Möglichkeiten, sich von den konkreten Resultaten der Forschung und Entwicklung zu überzeugen. Der GI-Kongress hingegen liefert dem Messebesucher eine wichtige Ergänzung durch umfangreiche Information über Methodologie, Entwicklung, Anwendung und Perspektiven Wissensbasierter Systeme sowie durch die Möglichkeit des Dialogs zwischen Entwicklern und Anwendern.

Obwohl diese Systeme eine im Detail heute noch schwer abschätzbare Zukunft des Computereinsatzes eröffnen und zur Bewältigung von Aufgaben der Wissensverarbeitung neue Methoden einsetzen, fußen sie doch notwendigerweise auf dem Schatz von Methoden und Verfahren, den die Informatik bisher angehäuft hat und der auf der SYSTEMS '85 präsentiert wird. Wir hoffen, daß im Spannungsfeld zwischen "Künstlicher Intelligenz" und traditioneller, noch bis in weite Zukunft dominierender, aber durch die neue Technologie beeinflußter Daten- und Informationsverarbeitung eine fruchtbare, das gegenseitige Verständnis vertiefende Diskussion zustandekommt. Aus diesem Grund hat das Programmkomitee Vortragende zu gewinnen versucht, die nicht nur über die als Expertensysteme bezeichneten speziellen neuen wissensbasierten Anwendungssysteme berichten, sondern auch über neue Ergebnisse aus benachbarten Gebieten, bei denen Wissensverarbeitung eine zunehmend wichtige Rolle spielt und die außerdem bedeutende Beiträge zur Konstruktion leistungsfähiger Wissensbasierter Systeme liefern werden.

Eine in zweifacher Hinsicht wichtige klassische Technologie ist die der Datenbanken. Einerseits können Wissensbasierte Systeme nicht nur durch Hinzunahme klassischer Datenbanken, sondern vor allem durch den Einsatz von Methoden und Verfahren aus dem Datenbankbereich beträchtlich erweitert werden. Andererseits läßt sich vorstellen, daß Datenbanken mittels Methoden und Verfahren der "Künstlichen Intelligenz" wesentlich weiterentwickelt werden können. Über den Stand der Technik und künftige Möglichkeiten eines Zusammenwachsens von Datenbanken und wissensbasierten Systemen wird in mehreren Vorträgen informiert.

Eine der interessantesten Schnittstellen zu anderen Informatikdisziplinen ergibt sich, wenn wissensbasierte Systeme Information über ihre Umwelt aus Sensorsignalen ermitteln müssen. Am Beispiel des visuellen Sensors wird der Übergang von der Bildsignalverarbeitung zum Bildverstehen erläutert.

Wichtiger Bestandteil ablauffähiger Systeme sind Algorithmen. Ihr Entwurf und ihre Integration zu Gesamtsystemen sind mit den bekannten Techniken des Software Engineering angehbar. Ein Problem bereitet jedoch die Handhabung von Wissen. Da mit diesem in wissensbasierten Systemen explizit umgegangen wird und es nicht nur als Voraussetzung des Problemlösens schlechthin notwendig ist, muß es ebenso gestaltet werden wie Information und Datensemantik. In mehreren Beiträgen wird der Übergang vom Software Engineering zum Knowledge Engineering sichtbar.

Natürlich werden auch Themen aus dem Kernbereich der Wissensverarbeitung vorgestellt, so etwa das weite Gebiet der Wissenserhebung, -formalisierung und -repräsentation. Dieser Kernbereich wird unterstützt durch Erfahrungsberichte aus Anwendungen, in denen Probleme, Vorgehensweisen und Erfolge dargestellt werden.

Einen breiten Raum nimmt die Information über die Anwendungen von wissensbasierten Systemen ein. Drei Kategorien von Beiträgen hat das Programmkomitee ausgewählt. In der ersten berichten die Vortragenden über Erfahrungen bei der Realisierung und beim Einsatz Wissensbasierter Systeme. Zuhörer und Leser sollen in die Lage versetzt werden, gleiche oder ähnliche Probleme in ihrem eigenen Anwendungsbereich in Beziehung zu prototypischen Lösungen setzen zu können. Die zweite Kategorie enthält Beiträge, in denen Hilfsmittel und Werkzeuge zur Entwicklung wissensbasierter Systeme vorgestellt werden. Ihre Existenz und Weiterentwicklung ist unabdingbare Voraussetzung dafür, daß in breiten Anwendungsbereichen eine Vielzahl von Anwendern Wissensbasierte Systeme zur Problemlösung einsetzen können. Die dritte Gruppe greift besonders den zweiten Teil des Kongress-Untertitels - Anwendungen und Perspektiven - auf. Führende Verantwortliche in der datenverarbeitenden Industrie gehen aus vom heutigen Stand des Einsatzes Wissensbasierter Systeme und schätzen die Perspektiven des industriellen Einsatzes ab. Neue Interaktionsformen und ihre Einflüsse auf die Arbeitsabläufe und die Gestaltung von Arbeitsinhalten werden dargestellt. Ergänzend werden in der Podiumsdiskussion Chancen und Perspektiven des Marktes für wissensbasierte Systeme aufgezeigt.

Die Herausgeber des Tagungsbandes danken im Namen des Programmkomitees den Vortragenden für ihren Beitrag zum Gelingen der Konferenz. Ganz besonders danken wir allen, daß sie trotz ihrer beruflichen Belastung die Zeit gefunden haben, ihren Beitrag rechtzeitig schriftlich bereitzustellen und damit auch den Interessenten, denen es nicht möglich war nach München zu kommen, die Gelegenheit geben, aus dem Internationalen GI-Kongress über wissensbasierte Systeme Nutzen zu ziehen.

September 1985   W. Brauer, B. Radig

INHALTSVERZEICHNIS

R. Bayer
Database Technology for Expert Systems 1

W. Bibel
Wissensbasierte Software-Entwicklung 17

A. Blaser, B. Alschwee, He. Lehmann, Hu. Lehmann, W. Schönfeld
Ein juristisches Expertensystem mit natürlichsprachlichem
Dialog - Ein Projektbericht 42

M. Broy
Rechnergestützte Systeme für den Programmentwurf 58

F. di Primio, D. Bungers, T. Christaller
BABYLON als Werkzeug zum Aufbau von
Expertensystemen 70

U. Hein
EPITOOL - A Development and Execution Environment
for Knowledge Systems 80

F. Herrmann, G. Hornung
INTRA - Ein Expertensystem zur Software-Unterstützung
bei Hewlett-Packard 89

U. Kastens
Anwendungen intelligenter Übersetzergeneratoren 99

P. Henne, W. Klar, K.-H. Wittur
DEX.C3 - Ein Expertensystem zur Fehlerdiagnose im automatischen
Getriebe 105

H. Haugeneder, E. Lehmann, P. Struß
Knowledge-Based Configuration of Operating Systems - Problems
in Modeling the Domain Knowledge 121

H. Marburger
Kooperativität in natürlichsprachlichen Zugangssystemen 135

H. Marchand
Objektorientierte Wissensdarstellung in industriellen
Expertensystemen 145

A. Borgida, S. Greenspan, J. Mylopoulos
Knowledge Representation as the Basis for Requirements
Specifications 152

H.-H. Nagel
Wissensgestützte Ansätze beim maschinellen Sehen:
Helfen sie in der Praxis? 170

J.-M. Nicolas
Logic Databases 199

E.S. Biagioni, K. Hinrichs, C. Muller, J. Nievergelt
Interactive deductive data management - the Smart
Data Interaction package 208

P. Pagé, P. Mossack
PREDICT: Ein wissensbasiertes Data Dictionary 221

K. Pasedach
Wissensbasierte Systeme als Bestandteile von Produkten
und Systemen der Elektro-Industrie 225

F. Puppe
Erfahrungen aus drei Anwendungsprojekten mit MED1 234

M. Rauh
Expertensysteme für Praktiker heute und morgen 246

E.M. Riseman, A.R. Hanson
A Methodology for the Development of General
Knowledge-Based Vision Systems 257

S.E. Savory
TWAICE: Die Expertensystem-Shell von Nixdorf 289

J.M. Smith
Large-Scale Knowledge Systems 294

M.-J. Schachter-Radig
Wissenserwerb und -formalisierung für den kommerziellen
Einsatz Wissensbasierter Systeme 314

D. Schieferle
Erfahrungen beim Einsatz von Expertensystemen und der
Integration in die Gesamtorganisation eines Unternehmens 333

E. Lehmann, H. Schwärtzel, H. Schweppe
Industrielle Nutzung wissensbasierter Systeme 347

R. Venken, M. Bruynooghe, L. Dekeyser, B. Krekels
    The Centralised Scheduler VS. The Distributed Specialists:
    Towards a Flexible Controller in PROLOG for Expert Systems 370

T. Wittig
    Expertensysteme in der Prozeßleittechnik 384

L.A. Zadeh
    A Formalization of Commonsense Reasoning Based on
    FUZZY Logic 398

Liste der Autoren

B. Alschwee	IBM Wissenschaftl. Zentrum, Heidelberg
R. Bayer	Technische Universität München
E.S. Biagioni	ETH Zürich, Schweiz
W. Bibel	Technische Universität München
A. Blaser	IBM Wissenschaftl. Zentrum, Heidelberg
A. Borgida	Rutgers University, New Brunswick, USA
M. Broy	Universität Passau
M. Bruynooghe	Katholieke Universiteit Leuven, Belgium
D. Bungers	G M D, St. Augustin
T. Christaller	G M D, St. Augustin
L. Dekeyser	Katholieke Universiteit Leuven, Belgium
F. di Primio	G M D, St. Augustin
S. Greenspan	Schlumberger-Doll Research, Ridgefield, USA
A.R. Hanson	University of Massachussetts, Amherst, USA
H. Haugeneder	Siemens A.G., München
U. Hein	EPITEC, Linköping, Sweden
P. Henne	G M D, St. Augustin
F. Herrmann	Hewlett-Packard, Böblingen
K. Hinrichs	ETH Zürich, Schweiz
G. Hornung	Hewlett-Packard, Böblingen
U. Kastens	Universität Paderborn
W. Klar	G M D, St. Augustin
B. Krekels	Katholieke Universiteit Leuven, Belgium
E. Lehmann	Siemens A.G., München
He. Lehmann	IBM Wissenschaftl. Zentrum, Heidelberg
Hu. Lehmann	IBM Wissenschaftl. Zentrum, Heidelberg
H. Marburger	Universität Hamburg
H. Marchand	Danet GmbH., Darmstadt
P. Mossack	Software A.G., Darmstadt
C. Muller	ETH Zürich, Schweiz
J. Mylopoulos	University of Toronto, Canada
H.-H. Nagel	Fraunhofer-Institut für Informations- und Datenverarbeitung - IITB, Karlsruhe
J.-M. Nicolas	ECRC, München
J. Nievergelt	ETH Zürich, Schweiz
P. Pagé	Software A.G., Darmstadt
K. Pasedach	Philips Forschungslab., Hamburg
F. Puppe	Universität Kaiserslautern

M. Rauh	Philips Kommunikations Industrie AG, Siegen
E.M. Riseman	University of Massachussetts, Amherst, USA
S.E. Savory	Nixdorf Computer AG., Paderborn
J.M. Smith	Computer Corporation of America, Cambridge, USA
M.-J. Schachter-Radig	S C S, Hamburg
D. Schieferle	Digital Equipment GmbH., Stuttgart
W. Schönfeld	IBM Wissenschaftl. Zentrum, Heidelberg
H. Schwärtzel	Siemens A.G., München
H. Schweppe	Siemens A.G., München
P. Struß	Siemens A.G., München
R. Venken	B.I.M., Everberg, Belgien
T. Wittig	Krupp Atlas Elektronik, Bremen
K.-H. Wittur	G M D, St. Augustin
L.A. Zadeh	University of California, Berkely, USA

Database Technology for Expert Systems

Rudolf Bayer
Institut für Informatik
Technische Universität München
XEROX PARC*

1. Knowledge Representation in Database Systems and Expert Systems

It is generally believed today that in order to be successful, expert systems must be built for a special application area [19]. Therefore they rely heavily on domain specific knowledge rather than using general problem solving techniques. Knowledge exists in two variants of considerable qualitative difference: *Facts* and *laws of thinking*. The laws of thinking are also called more formally *rules of inference*, since they are used to infer or to deduce new knowledge from known facts.

Facts like *Ludwig II. drowned on June 13, 1886* are memorized blindly and are of relatively little importance to most people and for human learning in the western hemisphere. What people really are supposed to learn is *thinking* and judgment.

Rules and Horn clauses:
Let us first consider thinking laws: in the field of expert systems they are generally represented in a semiformal way as rules like:

> *if* condition A *then* conclusion C

a concrete example being:

> *if* Father of x is z *and* Brother of z is y *then* Uncle of x is y

It is useful and interesting to memorize some facts, in particular for utilizing them to practice our thinking ability. Knowing the facts stated in A or looking them up in a dictionary, anybody familiar with that rule of inference can then deduce the new fact that C holds. It is not economical to memorize too many facts; dictionaries and computers, databases in particular are much better in storing and recalling them than humans are. We would expect just about everybody, however, to know the above rule and to be able to apply it to perform the deduction if presented with the facts in A.

In expert systems the above rule is even more formally written as a Horn clause:

$$\text{Uncle}\ (\ x\ ,\ y\ )\ \leftarrow\ \text{Father}\ (\ x,\ z\ )\ \ \text{Brother}\ (\ z\ ,\ y\ )$$

The conditions -or the antecedent- forming the righthand side of the rule, the conclusion forming the lefthand side. The formal variables -or formal parameters- x,y,z always have the same meaning, i.e. assume the same values if they appear in several different places in the rule.

Facts can also be represented as rules, they simply have empty right sides, since they obviously hold without having to be derived from other facts. The following rules represent some facts:

*Some of the research presented in this paper was performed while spending sabbatical time at XEROX PARC.

Father (Justin , Manfred)   ←
Father (Anja , Rudolf)   ←
Father (Nikolaus , Manfred)   ←
Father (Thomas , Erwin)   ←
Brother (Manfred , Rudolf)   ←
Brother (Erwin , Rudolf)   ←
Brother (Manfred , Erwin)   ←

Queries and views:
Knowledge representation in databases looks different from such rules superficially but is equivalent in essence: Facts are simply represented as relations, also called *base relations*, rules of inference are represented as query expressions or as *view* definitions [8], [1]. In the syntax of the SQL query language the above rule for Uncle would be written as:

    define view Uncle *as*
        select x , y *from* Father, Brother
        where Father.z = Brother.z

The condition Father.z = Brother.z expresses explicitly that the two attributes Father.z, and Brother.z should be instantiated identically in order to deduce that Uncle(x,y) holds. In the terminology of relational algebra this means that a natural join operation must be performed between the two database relations Father and Brother w.r. to the attribute z in order to construct the view relation Uncle. Uncle is assumed to be a virtual relation; it could be stored in the database system using various caching techniques or it could be constructed on demand. The database system may decide what to do on the basis of available resources. The above facts would be stored in two separate base relations called Father and Brother containing the tuples:

Father:	Justin	Manfred	**Brother:**	Manfred	Rudolf
	Anja	Rudolf		Erwin	Rudolf
	Nikolaus	Manfred		Manfred	Erwin
	Thomas	Erwin			

The join operation of relational algebra is the typical and most important operation for rule processing. Other forms of rules lead to expressions containing selection and projection operators of relational algebra [8] in addition to the natural join.

Thus the knowledge needed for expert systems , which is abstractly expressed as rules, is represented in database systems as follows:

1. Facts expressed as rules with empty right sides are stored in ordinary relations of a database. These relations are called *fact-relations* or *base-relations*.

2. Rules with non-empty right sides -they describe how to deduce new facts- are represented as query expressions or view definitions in a database query language. In this paper we use SQL and Q for this purpose. For more details see [1], [4], and [5].

Recursion:
Just as in rule definitions, views of databases are used to define further views, eventually arriving at complex sets of view definitions. The only fundamental difference between rules and relational expressions is the lack of recursion in the latter. We give a very simple example for recursive rules:

Ancestor (x , y) ← Parent (x , y)
Ancestor (x , y) ← Ancestor (x , y↑z) Parent (x↑z , y)

The notations y↑z and x↑z mean: the two variables y and x are both renamed to z to enforce identical instantiation or -in database terminology -a join. Syntactically this could be written in SQL as a recursive view definition:

define view Ancestor **as**
    select x , y **from** Parent
        union
    select Ancestor.x , Parent.y **from** Ancestor , Parent
    where Ancestor.y = Parent.x

It is interesting to note that the SQL syntax does not even forbid such recursive view definitions, although today's implementations cannot handle them.

Query languages and rule processing:
In the past database query languages were not targeted for rule processing. The view mechanism captures only some of the features needed. Furthermore, today's implementations of query languages probably cannot handle large sets of complex view definitions very well. There are, however, probably sparked by the extensive research on deductive database systems [11], [12], [20], several serious efforts under way to generalize database systems and to use their full potential for rule processing [5], [4], [18], [21], thus creating powerful tools for building expert systems. In this effort the first order of business is to generalize database query languages to make them suitable for expressing rules and to develop efficient rule processing algorithms by exploiting database technology.

2. Rules and Deduction Strategies

Rules and expert systems:
Knowledge in the form of basic facts and of inference rules is a very important constituent of an expert system. We have just seen, how knowledge can be represented in relational database systems. Such knowledge is used to deduce new knowledge. i.e. for drawing conclusions. for deriving new facts or -in the face of imprecise reasoning- for deriving new hypotheses or beliefs of various levels of certainty. The algorithm that deduces new knowledge is generally called the *inference engine* of an expert system. It is the third important component -besides the rules and the facts (which sometimes are also jointly called the *knowledge base*)- of an expert system.

The other components of an expert system are the *explanation module* -which explains from which facts and by what rules conclusions are reached-, the *user interface module* (both are not discussed in this paper) and the *blackboard* or the *working memory* for keeping intermediate results, which will be discussed briefly in chapter 4.

It is important to understand that there is no magic in expert systems. They are just computer programs -sometimes almost trivial as the examples in this paper, sometimes very complex- which are written in some programming language. In principle any programming language can be used for writing expert systems. In practice, however, some languages and programming environments are more suitable than others. Furthermore it must be understood, that rules and facts are just a certain model, a programming paradigm at a rather abstract level for constructing expert systems; they need not be explicit features of a language used to implement an expert system.

Support for deduction:
The various tools for building expert systems offer quite different levels of support for deduction and quite different strategies for performing it. To explain the basic concepts, consider the following example, in which the rules are expanded into a search tree, where the intermediate nodes act as subgoals to be established:

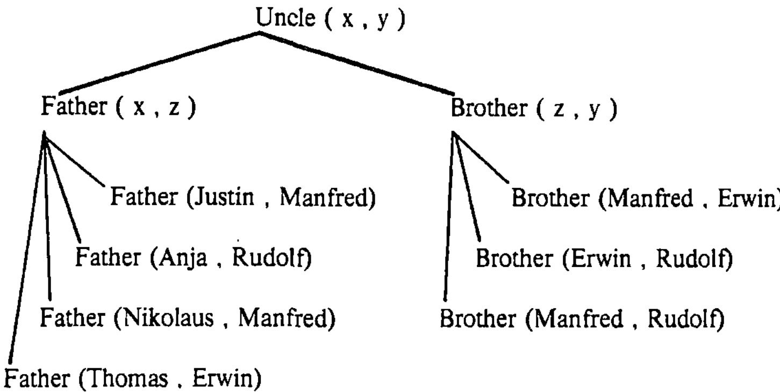

To deduce who is an uncle of Justin, this tree could be searched in a top down, left to right fashion, replacing the node Uncle(x,y) by Uncle(Justin,y) and the node Father(x,z) by Father(Justin,z), satisfying the subgoal Father(Justin,z) by the particular z instance Manfred after inspecting and rejecting the first three leaves. This then leads to searching the right subtree replacing the node Brother(z,y) by Brother(Manfred,y) and finding Brother(Manfred,Rudolf) to satisfy the subgoal Brother(Manfred,y) with the particular y instantiation Rudolf. This finally leads to the satisfaction of our top goal Uncle(Justin,y) with the instantiation y=Rudolf. Thus we have deduced the fact that Justin has an uncle named Rudolf. Backtracking from this leaf and continuing the search in the right subtree would deduce the further fact Uncle(Justin,Erwin).

Expert system tools differ considerably in how much automatic support they provide for processing the above tree. The basic tasks to be performed are:

1. Expand a rule -like that for Uncle(x,y)- whose left side has been established as a goal, and establish the predicates on the right side as subgoals, here Father(x,z) and Brother(z,y).

2. Identify and instantiate variables, here the two occurrences of z are indentified and instantiated with Manfred.

3. Search the base relations to find tuples satisfying the bound variables (resolution).

Expanding and searching the tree in a top down fashion is also called *backward chaining*. If the search leads to subgoals which cannot be satisfied or have been exhaustively searched, they must be replaced by other subgoals leading to *backtracking*. If the tree is generated in a top down fashion but evaluated in a strictly bottom up way as in database systems for classical query evaluation, one speaks of *forward chaining*. In general both depth first forward and backward chaining lead to backtracking.

Additional search variants arise, if forward and backward chaining are applied in a depth first or breadth first way or a combination of both, leading e.g. to the *best first* technique of OPS5 [16].

There is no generally superior strategy for processing search trees, the best strategy seems to depend heavily on the particular problem to be solved. To give two very simple examples, imagine two rule systems: F for computing Fibonacci numbers, and G for computing the greatest common divisor of two natural numbers. Fibonacci numbers are computed very efficiently by forward chaining leading to an algorithm of linear complexity, whereas pure backward chaining has exponential complexity for F, i.e. explodes combinatorially. On the other hand greatest common divisors are computed very effectively by backward chaining and rather awkwardly by forward chaining.

Aspects of deduction support:
In judging the support provided by expert system tools for rule processing many aspects beyond the backward/forward chaining issue are important. We just consider a few:

Variable instantiation: A variable in a rule must be set to a value of the domain of the variable before testing the rule for applicability. In some systems -like PROLOG and most relational database systems- variable instantiations are automatic, in others they must be programmed essentially by using explicit assignment statements.

Search and scope of search: Depending on the application, all or only some consequences derivable from the factbasis may be desired. All consequences are typically needed for applications having few well defined answers or optimal solutions (in a precise mathematical sense) for a problem. Some consequences are often sufficient for poorly defined problems, especially if the comparison of the quality of the solutions is a matter of taste rather than of a precisely defined measure. Reasons for a limited amount of search are among others: too large a search space to find all solutions, too large a solution space, lack of comparison techniques for solutions. Finding better solutions may be quite feasible but too costly compared to the achievable improvement in the quality of the solution.

Other aspects: In some systems deduction is data driven, i.e. triggered by changes in the fact basis, in others it is goal driven. Sometimes precise reasoning is feasible, sometimes only fuzzy reasoning with varying levels of certainty is possible as in Mycin [16], final judgment being the responsibility of the expert human user. Selecting the rules to be used for deduction is sometimes automatic, following fixed builtin strategies, sometimes very flexible and left completely to application program control. The typing of variables in predicates ranges from no typing to type hierarchies and very strong typing. Searching during deduction may proceed in parallel or sequentially. The discussion of some of these issues will be resumed briefly later in this paper.

It seems that each expert system and expert system tool developed its own strategy for rule processing according to the needs of the application it was primarily designed for.

3. Rules and Query Optimization

This chapter investigates the rule processing capabilities that database systems could provide. Basically we generalize database query processing techniques and apply them to rule systems. For the purpose of demonstration we use the following very simple rule system, which partially defines family structure:

Base relations:

        Father (x , y)   x has father y
        Mother (x , y)
        Married (x , y)
        Sex (x , s)   x has sex s in { male , female }

Rules:

$$
\begin{aligned}
\text{Parent (x , y)} \quad &\leftarrow \text{ Father (x , y) + Mother (x , y)} \\
\text{Ancestor (x , y)} \quad &\leftarrow \text{ Ancestor (x , y↑z) Parent (x↑z , y)} \\
\text{Ancestor (x , y)} \quad &\leftarrow \text{ Parent (x , y)} \\
\text{Sibling (x , y)} \quad &\leftarrow \text{ Mother (x , y↑z)   Mother (x↑y , y↑z) x≠y} \\
\text{Uncle (x , y)} \quad &\leftarrow \text{ Parent (x , y↑z) Sibling (x↑z , y)} \\
& \text{ Sex (x↑y , male)} \\
\text{Uncle (x , y)} \quad &\leftarrow \text{ Parent (x , y↑z) Sibling (x↑z , y↑u)} \\
& \text{ Married (x↑u , y) Sex (x↑y , male)}
\end{aligned}
$$

These rules are written in Q [5], which is very similar to Horn clauses w.r. to the features used in this paper, with the following main difference: In Horn clauses the domain of a variable is defined by its position within a predicate, whereas in Q unique attribute names are used instead of positions. Whenever possible attribute names are also used as variable names, they are renamed only when necessary. Thus in the rule

$$\text{Ancestor (x , y)} \quad \leftarrow \quad \text{Ancestor (x , y↑z) Parent (x↑z , y)}$$

the y attribute of Ancestor is renamed to z, using the notation y↑z, the x attribute of Parent is renamed to z with x↑z. The identical instantiation for both occurrences of z on the right side of the rule then causes automatically a join operation between Ancestor and Parent w.r. to z. In SQL this join on the right side would be written without using the renaming technique as

> *select* Ancestor.x , Parent.y *from* Ancestor, Parent
> *where* Ancestor.y = Parent.x

A further feature of Q is that renaming of relations (which is needed in SQL for the introduction of range variables whenever a relation occurs more than once in a query) is not needed. Consider the rule for Sibling, where Mother appears twice on the right side. In SQL Sibling would be defined as a view:

> *define view* Sibling *as*
> *select* M1.x , M2.x *from* Mother M1 , Mother M2
> *where* M1.y = M2.y *and*   M1.x ≠ M2.x

Note the renaming of both occurrences of Mother to M1, M2 resp.

For technical reasons it is convenient to *normalize* this rule system, distinguishing all rules by separate names for the left sides. This affects the two rules for Ancestor and Uncle introducing predicates A1, U1, U2. Then the two additional rules

$$
\begin{aligned}
\text{Ancestor (x , y)} \quad &\leftarrow \text{ A1 (x , y) + Parent (x , y)} \\
\text{Uncle (x , y)} \quad &\leftarrow \text{ U1 (x , y) + U2 (x , y)}
\end{aligned}
$$

are introduced. Here the + operator means logical disjunction, or if one thinks of predicates as being defined by their extensions, then + is the set union of two relations. Also note the introduction of rules for Father, Mother, Married, Sex with empty right sides. These rules correspond to the original base relations.

Normalized Rule System:

$$
\begin{aligned}
\text{Ancestor (x , y)} \;&\leftarrow\; \text{A1 (x , y) + Parent (x , y)}\\
\text{Uncle (x , y)} \;&\leftarrow\; \text{U1 (x , y) + U2 (x , y)}\\
\text{Parent (x , y)} \;&\leftarrow\; \text{Father (x , y) + Mother (x , y)}\\
\text{A1 (x , y)} \;&\leftarrow\; \text{Ancestor (x , y↑z) Parent (x↑z , y)}\\
\text{Sibling (x , y)} \;&\leftarrow\; \text{Mother (x , y↑z) Mother (x↑y , y↑z) x≠y}\\
\text{U1 (x , y)} \;&\leftarrow\; \text{Parent (x , y↑z) Sibling (x↑z , y)}\\
 & \qquad \text{Sex (x↑y , male)}\\
\text{U2 (x , y)} \;&\leftarrow\; \text{Parent (x , y↑z) Sibling (x↑z , y↑u)}\\
 & \qquad \text{Married (x↑u , y) Sex (x↑y , male)}\\
\text{Father (x , y)} \;&\leftarrow\;\\
\text{Mother (x , y)} \;&\leftarrow\;\\
\text{Married (x , y)} \;&\leftarrow\;\\
\text{Sex (x , s)} \;&\leftarrow\;
\end{aligned}
$$

To answer a question like "Who are the uncles of Justin?" -formally written as Uncle (Justin, y)- one could deduce all pairs of people (x,y) such that y is uncle of x, and then select those pairs for which x = Justin. This is obviously a poor algorithm. since the focusing on the subset of pairs with the property x = Justin should be done as early as possible. In database query optimization this corresponds exactly to a well known optimization heuristic: to perform selections before joins. This heuristic can be cast into a formal transformation of the rule system, which binds x to Justin and selects and expands as subgoals of our top goal Uncle(Justin,x) only those rules which are needed to answer the question Uncle(Justin,x). Note that in our example the rules for defining Ancestor, namely Ancestor, A1, A2 are eliminated from the rule system. The result of these transformations is the rule system:

Subgoals and Rules for Uncle (Justin , y) :

$$
\begin{aligned}
\text{Uncle (Justin , y)} \;&\leftarrow\; \text{U1 (Justin , y) + U2 (Justin , y)}\\
\text{U1 (Justin , y)} \;&\leftarrow\; \text{Parent (Justin . y↑z) Sibling (x↑z , y)}\\
 & \qquad \text{Sex (x↑y , male)}\\
\text{U2 (Justin , y)} \;&\leftarrow\; \text{Parent (Justin , y↑z) Sibling (x↑z , y↑u)}\\
 & \qquad \text{Married (x↑u , y) Sex (x↑y , male)}\\
\text{Parent (Justin , y)} \;&\leftarrow\; \text{Father (Justin , y) + Mother (Justin , y)}\\
\text{Sibling (x , y)} \;&\leftarrow\; \text{Mother (x , y↑z) Mother (x↑y , y↑z) x≠y}\\
\text{Sex (x , male)} \;&\leftarrow\;\\
\text{Married (x , y)} \;&\leftarrow\;\\
\text{Father (Justin , y)} \;&\leftarrow\;\\
\text{Mother (x , y)} \;&\leftarrow\;
\end{aligned}
$$

Observations:
The following relations are needed as antecedents with different variable bindings in different rules in this rule system:

$$\text{Mother (Justin , y) Mother (x↑y , y↑z)}$$

The following common subexpression, which is a join with a generally rather large relation Sibling, is needed in two places. It is joined with different expressions, which accounts for the renaming y↑u:

$$
\begin{aligned}
&\text{Parent (Justin , y↑z) Sibling (x↑z , y)}\\
&\text{Parent (Justin , y↑z) Sibling (x↑z , y↑u)}
\end{aligned}
$$

The following projection is needed twice:

Sex (x↑y , male)

These observations lead to the modified rule system to take advantage of common subexpressions:

Modified Rule System for Common Subexpressions:

ParentSibling (Justin, y) ← Parent (Justin , y↑z) Sibling (x↑z , y)
U1 (Justin , y) ← ParentSibling (Justin , y) Sex (x↑y , male)
U2 (Justin , y) ← ParentSibling (Justin , y↑u) Married (x↑u , y)
                         Sex (x↑y , male)

Note that the predicate ParentSibling now must be evaluated only once. This becomes even more visible, if we represent the rule system as an inference tree as follows:

Inference Tree:

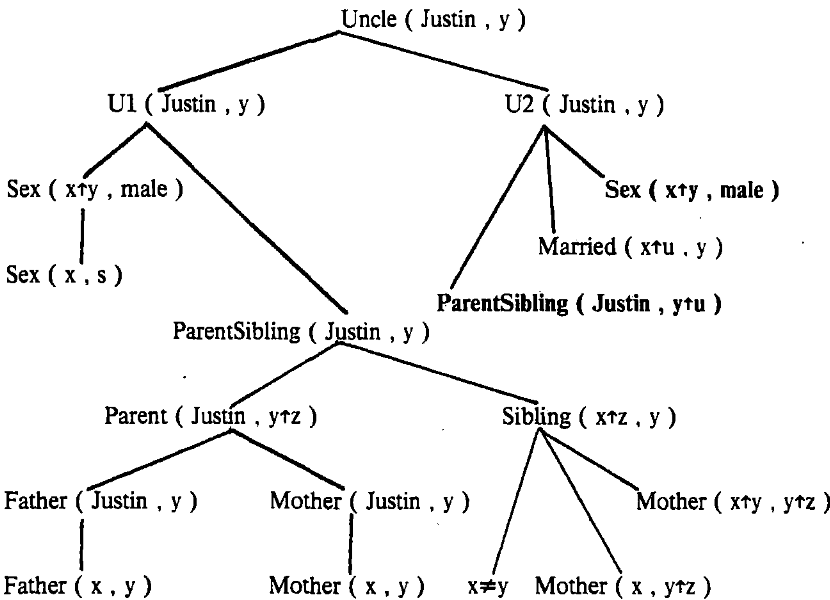

Note: A leaf of this tree is either a base relation or a common subexpression (printed bold) which -except for renaming- is identical to the root of a subtree (in our example this is Sex(x↑y,male) and ParentSibling(Justin,y).

It would certainly be an interesting exercise to take our original rule system together with a moderate size database for Father, Mother, Married, and Sex and to compare various expert system tools with respect to the following aspects:

1. How much additional design and programming effort is involved to turn this rather abstract rule system into a running program.

2. What transformations are performed on the rule system and what evaluation strategies are followed by the expert system tool to answer the question "Who are the uncles of x?"

3. How well does each system perform, i.e. how fast can it generate the answers to our question?

Such a comparison will be done, but right now we have only preliminary results on a similar experiment.

Filters:
Let us reconsider our inference tree, which is far from optimal for evaluation. Take as example the subtree for ParentSibling. This tree says: construct the relations Parent(Justin,y) and Sibling(x,y) and form a natural join with respect to the attributes y of Parent and x of Sibling, indicated by the renamings y↑z and x↑z. Obviously Sibling(x,y) will be a large intermediate relation containing few pairs of siblings which are relevant for the derivation of Uncle(Justin,y). Therefore the tree should be modified further to derive from Parent(Justin,y) a total filter -which we call ParentFilter- over y [17], which is simply a predicate satisfied only by the parents of Justin.

ParentFilter is then used analogously to variable binding to transform the rule system, in order to avoid the bulk of irrelevant derivations otherwise caused by the subgoal Sibling(x↑z,y). The method is a generalization of semijoin algorithms from database query evaluation and of the optimization heuristic to perform selections before joins. Without describing the method in more detail we present the resulting inference tree and rule system for ParentSibling after moving ParentFilter down in the tree as far as possible:

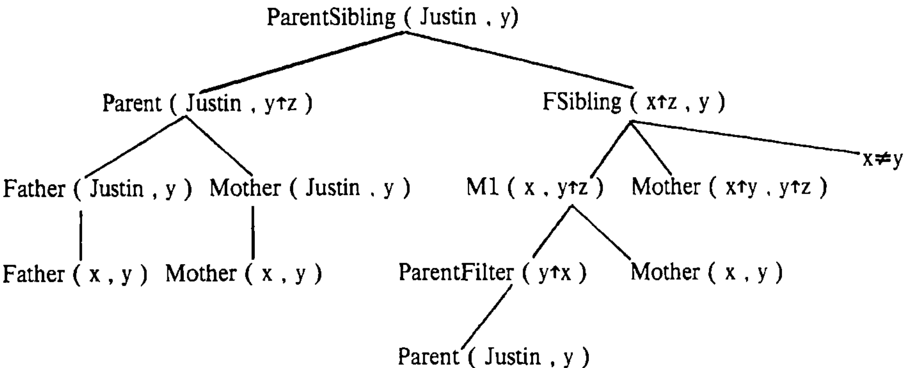

Written as a rule system this would be:

ParentSibling (Justin , y) ← Parent (Justin , y↑z) FSibling (x↑z , y)
Parent (Justin , y) ← Father (Justin , y) + Mother (Justin , y)
FSibling (x , y) ← M1 (x , y↑z) Mother (x↑y , y↑z) x≠y
M1 (x , y) ← ParentFilter (y↑x) Mother (x , y)
ParentFilter (y) ← Parent (Justin , y)

Note that the filter ParentFilter acts like a selection on the relation Mother, so now M1 is a subset of Mother and FSibling is a subset of Sibling leading to much simpler join calculations.

This example also demonstrates, that the heuristic *selections before joins* must be refined for rule processing. Because of the weak selectivity of the constant *male* in the relation Sex, it would be a poor strategy to compute the complete selection Sex(x,male) over Sex. It is much more efficient to use an index over the first attribute x of Sex in order to access the tuple (Y,S) for a ParentSibling Y of Justin in the relation Sex directly, and to check whether S=male or not.

The transformation techniques for rule systems were only demonstrated informally on a very simple example. They can be formalized and made rigorous, of course.

In addition to the transformations for rule systems other advanced query evaluation techniques, e.g. fast merge-join algorithms should be adopted to rule processing.

Evaluation of recursive rule systems:
Our example of a simple rule system demonstrates yet another challenge. Let us now assume that we would like to know all the ancestors of Justin's uncles. We ask the query

$$\text{Uncle (Justin, } y \uparrow z) \text{ Ancestor } (x \uparrow z, y)$$

and add the new rule

$$\text{UA } (x , y) \leftarrow \text{Uncle } (x , y \uparrow z) \text{ Ancestor } (x \uparrow z , y)$$

to our rule system. Expanding the top goal UA (Justin, y) then leads to the tree:

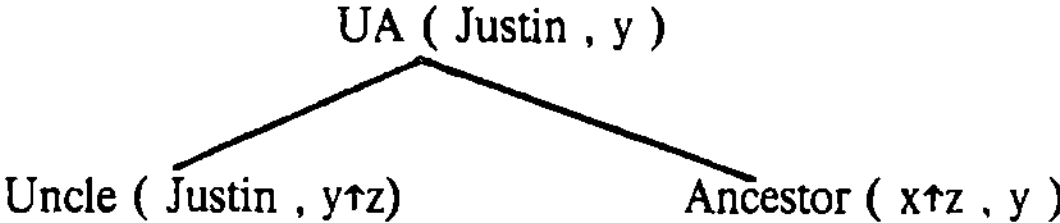

We already have the optimized tree for evaluating Uncle(Justin, y). Expansion of Ancestor(x,y) using our normalized rule system then results in the tree:

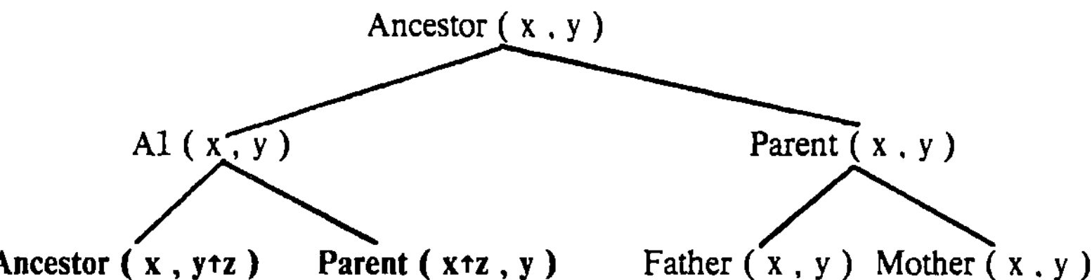

The expansion stops here, since we have already internal nodes for Parent(x,y) and for Ancestor(x,y). The complication arising now is that the node Ancestor(x,y) needed for the leaf Ancestor (x,y↑z) is in a path above that leaf, therefore needing the value of that leaf for its own evaluation. This situation is typical for a recursive definition. As a rule system this is:

$$\begin{aligned}
\text{Ancestor } (x , y) &\leftarrow \text{A1 } (x , y) + \text{Parent } (x , y) \\
\text{A1 } (x , y) &\leftarrow \text{Ancestor } (x , y \uparrow z) \text{ Parent } (x \uparrow z , y) \\
\text{Parent } (x , y) &\leftarrow \text{Father } (x , y) \text{ Mother } (x , y)
\end{aligned}$$

The recursion is apparent, since Ancestor is defined in terms of A1 which in turn is defined in terms of Ancestor, etc.

Fixpoints of rule systems:
The solution of such a recursive rule system is a fixpoint of relations which can be approached from

below by evaluating the rule system repeatedly until the fixpoint is reached. As starting values the base relations are initialized once, during the iteration they do not change. The relations derived by the rules -Ancestor, A1, Parent- are initialized as empty. The fixpoint is reached when the derived relations no longer change. In our example Parent is changed only by the first iteration, Ancestor by the second, A1 by the third and then alternately Ancestor and A1 until the fixpoint is reached.

Using such a rule system directly may be very inefficient, since many derivations are computed again and again. To avoid such redundant deductions the technique of Δ-transformations for recursive rule systems was developed. The technique is described in detail in [4] and in [15]. The basic idea is that only the real changes ΔR of a derived relation R are carried forward from one iteration step to the next. The iteration stops as soon as no changes occur, i.e. when all Δ's of derived relations remain empty. The correctness of the transformation relies mainly on the monotonicity of the operators $+$ and natural join.

Delta-transformation of rule systems:
We demonstrate the general technique on our simple example. The subset of recursive rules is:

$$
\begin{aligned}
\text{Ancestor}\,(\,x\,,y\,) \quad &\leftarrow\ \text{A1}\,(\,x\,,y\,)\,+\,\text{Parent}\,(\,x\,,y\,) \\
\text{A1}\,(\,x\,,y\,) \quad\quad &\leftarrow\ \text{Ancestor}\,(\,x\,,y{\uparrow}z\,)\ \text{Parent}\,(\,x{\uparrow}z\,,y\,)
\end{aligned}
$$

Ancestor and A1 are initially empty. Parent is obtained by a first evaluation step from Father and Mother and assigned to Ancestor.

To optimize the evaluation of this rule system we now consider it as an iteration scheme. In each iteration step all rules are evaluated once and new relations are computed for the left sides. Thus we replace $\leftarrow$ by the assignment operator $:=$ and give indices to the successive relations derived. For the following more formal calculation we use A for Ancestor and P for Parent, we leave off all the variables and write $*$ for the join operation. Our rule system then becomes:

$$
(1) \quad
\begin{aligned}
A_{i+1} \quad &:= \quad A1_i + P \\
A1_{i+1} \quad &:= \quad A_i * P
\end{aligned}
$$

Since the operators involved (set union and natural join) are monotonic, we can write $A1_i$ and A_i as expressions of the form:

$$
(2) \quad
\begin{aligned}
A_i \quad &= A_{i-1} + \Delta A_i \qquad &&\text{with } \Delta A_i = A_i - A_{i-1} \\
A1_i \quad &= A1_{i-1} + \Delta A1_i \qquad &&\text{with } \Delta A1_i = A1_i - A1_{i-1}
\end{aligned}
$$

Substituting (2) into (1) we obtain:

$$
(3) \quad
\begin{aligned}
A_{i+1} &:= (A1_{i-1} + \Delta A1_i) + P = (A1_{i-1} + P) + \Delta A1_i = A_i + \Delta A1_i \\
A1_{i+1} &:= (A_{i-1} + \Delta A_i) * P = A_{i-1} * P + \Delta A_i * P = A1_i + \Delta A_i * P
\end{aligned}
$$

We now define $AuxA_{i+1}$ and $AuxA1_{i+1}$ as:

$$
(4) \quad
\begin{aligned}
AuxA_{i+1} \quad &= \Delta A1_i \\
AuxA1_{i+1} \quad &= \Delta A_i * P
\end{aligned}
$$

Then the following hold:

$$
(5) \quad
\begin{aligned}
A_{i+1} &= A_i + AuxA_{i+1} \quad ; \quad AuxA_{i+1} \supseteq \Delta A_{i+1} \\
A1_{i+1} &= A1_i + AuxA1_{i+1} \quad ; \quad AuxA1_{i+1} \supseteq \Delta A1_{i+1}
\end{aligned}
$$

and it suffices to compute $AuxA_{i+1}$ and $AuxAl_{i+1}$ in each iteration step, which is much more efficient than evaluating (1). Together these derivation steps then result in the following incremental iteration scheme:

$$
\begin{aligned}
&1: \quad AuxA_{i+1} &&:= \quad \Delta Al_i \\
&2: \quad AuxAl_{i+1} &&:= \quad \Delta A_i * P \\
&3: \quad \Delta A_{i+1} &&:= \quad AuxA_{i+1} - A_i \\
&4: \quad \Delta Al_{i+1} &&:= \quad AuxAl_{i+1} - Al_i \\
&5: \quad A_{i+1} &&:= \quad A_i + \Delta A_{i+1} \\
&6: \quad Al_{i+1} &&:= \quad Al_i + \Delta Al_{i+1}
\end{aligned}
$$

When both ΔA_i and ΔAl_i become empty, then also $AuxA_{i+1}$, $AuxAl_{i+1}$, ΔA_{i+1}, ΔAl_{i+1} become empty, etc. Thus also $A_{i+1} = A_i$ and $Al_{i+1} = Al_i$, which means that we have reached a fixpoint of our iteration scheme and therefore of our rule system.

Note that the equations (2) and (5) are independent of the form of the particular rules (1), thus (2) and (5) can be considered as metaequations holding for every rule system with monotonic operators. Only (4) depends on the form of the rule, but (4) is easily derived for arbitrary rules by substituting (2) and expanding the rule.

It is now easy to see that the assignment pairs 1 and 2, 3 and 4, 5 and 6 may each be done in parallel and that 4 and 5 may be interchanged. This then leads to the following program to compute the fixpoint of our recursive rule system iteratively:

```
begin Parent     := Father + Mother;
      Ancestor := empty;
      Al       := empty;
      DeltaAl  := empty;
      Ancestor := DeltaAncestor := Parent;
      while DeltaAncestor ≠ empty or DeltaAl ≠ empty do
         begin
            parbegin AuxAncestor     := DeltaAl,
                     AuxAl           := DeltaAncestor * Parent
            parend;
            parbegin
               begin DeltaAncestor   := AuxAncestor - Ancestor;
                     Ancestor        := Ancestor + DeltaAncestor
               end,
               begin DeltaAl         := AuxAl - Al;
                     Al              := Al + DeltaAl
               end
            parend
         end
end
```

Now the calculation of the set difference and the set union in each compound statement can be further optimized. For details see [4].

Note: The Δ-transformation of every rule system yields a program of this structure: All rules can be evaluated in parallel to compute the AuxVariables, then for all rules the computation of their Δ's and their new values are computed in parallel. Considering the potential for parallel processing, a system of n rules yields 2n processes, of which n may alternately run in parallel.

Summary and open problems:
We demonstrated the Δ-transformation of the recursive rule system only informally on a very small example. It is applicable in general and is described in detail in [4]. Computational complexity analysis and preliminary performance measurements indicate that the technique of Δ-transformations is a very effective optimization for rule processing. In addition we have seen that a variety of classical query optimization methods can be generalized to support rule processing effectively.

The basic technique proposed for rule processing on relational database systems can be summarized as follows:

1. Backward chaining from queries or otherwise established goals is used to generate an inference tree and to bind variables as far as possible. Generalizations of database query optimization are applied to transform this tree or the rule system resp. to obtain an efficient evaluation schema. Novel techniques are: Δ-transformations and the introduction and propagation of filters like ParentFilter in our example.

2. For the evaluation of the inference tree the set oriented operators of relational algebra are used. In particular no backtracking is needed during the evaluation phase. The evaluation itself is a pure forward chaining algorithm.

We indicate briefly some additional important research issues for rule processing on database technology without presenting the solutions in this paper:

Computation of the conflict set: At any time during the deduction process one must determine which out of a potentially very large set of rules are ready to fire (conflict set) and select one or several of them -e.g. U1 or U2 for Uncle(Justin,y)- for firing (conflict resolution). Often only necessary but not sufficient conditions for firing can be checked easily. For example in the original rule for U1(Justin,y) the three relations on the right side must be nonempty; this is an easy condition to check or to remember. It is, however, not a sufficient condition for the rule to fire, since additional join conditions w.r. to variables z and y must be met, which are much harder to compute. Again a generalization of a heuristic from query optimization may be useful here: Evaluate the right sides of rules in the order of increasing expected size of the intermediate result relations.

Goal establishment: Derived relations can be established as goals -meaning that their values should be computed and kept in the system or used otherwise- in various ways. In an ordinary database system they are established by the user entering queries as in our example for Uncle(Justin,y). Subgoal expansion and inference tree optimization is caused when the goal is established. Then the evaluation is performed. On the other hand in realtime monitoring systems -e.g. for a power plant- some goals corresponding to certain control actions would remain established permanently with their optimized inference trees prepared and available for immediate evaluation. A similar mechanism is used for the preoptimized queries and view definitions of system R [1]. Deduction (forward chaining) is triggered when the base data -or their deltas in an optimized inference tree- like measurements of the state variables of the powerplant, change in certain ways, e.g. surpass thresholds.

Triggers: For certain data changes all consequences of these changes w.r. to the whole rule system may be desired. In database systems such data are called *triggers*, in LOOPS they are called *active data*, sometimes the term *data driven deduction* is used. It is interesting to observe that the propagation of triggers to other triggers (supertriggers) is entirely analogous to the propagation of goals via subgoals. Both require the transitive closure of certain relations over the rule system. In a rule system combinations of goals and triggers may be useful. Furthermore, goals and triggers may be established permanently or temporarily.

Rule control: In principle rules can be written in such a way that they are ready to fire only when they should fire. Often it is more convenient to separate the decision to fire completely from the rules themselves. There is a wide spectrum of methods to control the firing of rules, it can be done by rule ordering [7], or separate control statements [6], or by additional rules, or a combination of these techniques. Database query languages do not presently offer any such features. They must be added to the rule language or programmed in a host language from which the rule language is used.

4. Database Support for Storage Management

In expert systems dealing with large amounts of data, storage management of working memory and of peripheral memory is a critical issue. Many expert system tools are LISP based and use list structures and garbage collection for managing working memory. Peripheral memory is organized as a simple file system.

List structures are reminiscent of the techniques used in network oriented database systems typified by the CODASYL model. Navigating through the database structure is the responsibility of the application program. A semantically much higher level of programming is achieved by the relational database model, in which explicit navigation through program control is basically replaced by a sophisticated query optimizer. This separates query semantics from the navigational control structure and implementation details and leads to a considerable degree of *data independence*, i.e. the independence of an application program from the details of data representation.

Describing deduction by rules and performing high level rule optimization in combination with forward chaining for rule evaluation may have considerable benefits for storage management for the following reasons: The intermediate results corresponding to nodes of the inference tree are in principle generated by single applications of the set oriented operators of relational algebra -recursive rules are only slightly more complicated to evaluate. Therefore the intermediate results can easily be grouped together in intermediate relations. This should lead to rather compact representations in storage, since selfdescribing type information and pointers are not needed. Furthermore the inference tree indicates precisely, when intermediate result relations are no longer needed and can be discarded as a whole rather than relying on garbage collection for reclaiming storage.

If in the course of a deduction subgoals or hypotheses are established they are either reached or abandoned entirely. If they are abandoned, then all deductions performed in trying to reach such a subgoal can be given up. This is very reminiscent of the concept of an atomic transaction in database systems, which either commits successfully or aborts without leaving any traces in the state of the database. Elaborate techniques for supporting atomic transactions which are carefully integrated with synchronization, caching and storage management techniques both for main storage and peripheral storage have been developed [10]. It seems that such techniques can be generalized to become very useful for deduction over large fact bases and rule systems. To explain the issue, consider the following example:

Assume that the subgoal

$$S \leftarrow T * U$$

depending on the two antecedents T and U is established during a deduction. In a set oriented evaluation many tuples may be generated for T and U. Yet the join between T and U may yield an empty result, in which case S fails and all derivations satisfying T and U can be abandoned. Thus when establishing S, a transaction t is started. When S fails t is aborted leading to an automatic -and very efficient [10]- erasure of the intermediate results T and U. Today many expert systems use backtracking or garbage collection to accomplish this.

It may be useful to generalize the transaction concept of database systems to allow nested transactions. They seem to be needed to support deduction since subgoals are generated recursively. Considerable work on nested transactions has already been done in the setting of long transactions [13], [14].

5. Large Multiaccess and Distributed Expert Systems

Many future expert systems will have to support the following requirements:

1. Large volumes of base data and large rule systems
2. Simultaneous access by many users
3. Distribution of the expert system over many computers
4. Real time deduction to produce advice and to support decision making

Examples of such expert systems would be among many others:

a) Investment advice and management of a bank or brokerage house for a large number of clients.

b) Spare parts management including advance ordering and transportation of the spare parts for a plant in a poorly developed country.

Database systems have confronted the above requirements and have developed techniques -which by now are well established- for meeting them:

1. To deal with large volumes of extremely valuable data two general problems had to be solved:
-- how to store, access, and search data efficiently in a hierarchy of main and peripheral stores,
-- how to secure data through effective recovery and archiving techniques.

2. To support simultaneous access for many users, the concept of a transaction and synchronization methods for transactions were developed. Today these methods are fully automated and part of modern database systems to give the user the convenience and the ease of use of a single user database system.

3. The distribution issues for expert systems are very similar to those for database systems. Enumerating them would only yield a list of familiar buzz words. The point is that techniques to build distributed database systems are highly developed, though not widely applied yet [3], and can very likely be adapted to build distributed expert systems.

4. Realtime expert systems may well be the least understood of the requirements identified in this chapter. In particular it is not clear, whether data access or computation -here in the special form of deduction- will turn out to be the bottle neck. The opinions of hardware designers of highly parallel inference engines and of practitioners who have built operational expert systems are rather contradictory on this question. If computational power should indeed turn out to be a bottleneck, then deduction techniques generalized from relational algebra look very promising, since they offer the potential of a rather high degree of parallel deduction [4].

References:

1. Astrahan et al.: *System R: Relational Approach to Database Management.*
   ACM TODS. 1. 2. 97-137 (June 1976)

2. Bayer, R., Graham, R., Seegmueller, G.: *Advanced Course on Operating Systems.*
Lecture Notes in Computer Science, vol. 60. Berlin: Springer 1978

3. Bayer, R., Elhardt, K., Kiessling, W., Killar, D.: *Verteilte Datenbanksysteme.*
Informatik Spektrum **(1984)** 7, 1-19

4. Bayer, R: *Query Evaluation and Recursion in Deductive Database Systems.*
Technical report TUM-I8503, Technical University Munich 1985

5. Bayer, R.: *Q: A Recursive Query Language for Databases.*
Technical Notes, XEROX PARC, June 1985

6. Bobrow, D., Stefik, M.: *The LOOPS Manual.* Palo Alto: XEROX Corporation 1983

7. Clocksin,W., Mellish, C.: *Programming in Prolog.* Berlin: Springer 1981

8. Codd, E.F.: *A Relational Model of Data for Large Shared Data Banks.*
CACM **13**, 6, 377-387 (June 1970)

9. Date, C..J.: *An Introduction to Database Systems.* Reading, Mass.: Addison-Wesley 1977

10. Elhardt, K., Bayer, R.: *A Database Cache for High Performance and Fast Recovery.*
ACM TODS **9**, 4, 503-525 (December 1984)

11. Gallaire, H., Minker, J.: *Logic and Databases.* New York: Plenum Press 1978

12. Gallaire, H., Minker, J., Nicolas, J.-M.: *Logic and Databases: A Deductive Approach.*
ACM Computing Surveys, **16**, 2, 153-186 (June 1984)

13. Gray, J.: *Notes on Database Operating Systems.* In [2].

14. Gray, J.: *The Transaction Concept: Virtues and Limitations.*
Proc. 7th VLDB Conference 144-154, Cannes 1981.

15. Guentzer, U., Bayer, R.: *Control for Iterative Evaluation of Recursive Rules in Deductive Database Systems.* Technical report TUM-I8513, Technical University Munich 1985

16. Hayes-Roth, F., Waterman, D.A., Lenat, D.B. (eds): *Building Expert Systems.*
Reading, Mass.: Addison-Wesley 1983

17. Kiessling, W.: *Datenbanksysteme fuer Rechenanlagen mit intelligenten Subsystemen: Architektur, Algorithmen, Optimierung.* Dissertation and technical report TUM-I83007, Technical University Munich 1983

18. Lucas, P.: *On the Versatility of Knowledge Representations.*
IBM Research report RJ4573. IBM Res. Lab. San Jose 1985

19. Newell, A.: *Intellectual Issues in the History of Artificial Intelligence.*
Technical report CMU-CS-82-142. Carnegie-Mellon University 1982

20. Proceedings 1st. International Conference on Expert Database Systems. Kiawah Island, S.C.: 1984

21. Stonebraker M.: *Triggers and Inference in Data Base Systems.* Private Communication, June 1985

WISSENSBASIERTE SOFTWARE-ENTWICKLUNG

W. Bibel

Institut für Informatik

Technische Universität München

INHALT

EINLEITUNG

1. DIE SOFTWAREPROBLEMATIK

  1.1   Die Hardware / Software Dichotomie

  1.2   Die Dimensionen des Softwareraumes

  1.3   Das Fehlerspektrum

  1.4   Die Hintergrundproblematik

2. DER STAND DER TECHNIK

  2.1   Ergonomie

  2.2   Sprache

  2.3   Korrektheit im Detail

  2.4   Programmierumgebungen

  2.5   Softwareentwicklungsumgebungen

  2.6   Problemlösen

  2.7   Marktanalyse

3. ASPEKTE FÜR DIE NAHE ZUKUNFT

  3.1   Modellskizze zur prädikativen Systementwicklung

  3.2   Chancen der Realisierbarkeit

  3.3   Kurzfristige Möglichkeiten

    ZUSAMMENFASSUNG

EINLEITUNG

Der Informationstechnologie kommt in rapide zunehmendem Maße immer mehr eine Schlüsselrolle in den Industriestaaten zu. Auf dem industriellen Produktionssektor ist diese Entwicklung zum Teil bereits weit fortgeschritten, im Dienstleistungssektor kommt sie gerade auf höhere Touren, doch etwa auch im Agrarsektor wird sie nicht mehr allzu lange auf sich warten lassen.

Die mit dieser Entwicklung verbundenen gesellschaftlichen Umwälzungen werden besonders in Europa weiterhin auf tiefverwurzelte Widerstände stoßen. Letztlich werden jedoch die ökonomischen und – wenn der Wille dazu vorhanden ist – auch ökologischen Vorteile dieser Technologie die nötigen gesellschaftlichen Anpassungen in den Industriestaaten einfach erzwingen, wenn auch hier in Europa später als etwa in den USA und in Japan.

Innerhalb der Informationstechnologie wiederum spielt die Computertechnik wohl die zentrale Rolle. Dies läßt sich nicht zuletzt an den (im Vergleich zu anderen Industriezweigen) außergewöhnlichen Markterfolgen ablesen. So lag weltweit die Computer Produktion 1981 bereits bei über 50 Mrd. $, der jährliche Produktionszuwachs erreichte jahrelang im Mittel mehr als 20%, und bis 1990 prognostiziert man für diesen Markt eine Größenordnung von nahezu 200 Mrd. $ (nur für die Hardware).[1]

Die Rechner selbst sind aber nur die eine Seite der Medaille. In den letzten beiden Jahrzehnten nämlich hat sich das Verhältnis des Kostenaufwandes von Software und Hardware sehr zu ungunsten von Software und Service verlagert. So rechnet man bei einer Großrechenanlage schon heute mit einem Kostenanteil von nahezu 50% der Gesamtkosten allein für Software und Service.[1] Bei integrierten Computersystemen dürfte dieser Anteil noch höher liegen. Zudem geht man allenthalben davon aus, daß sich auch hier der Trend fortsetzt, so daß der Softwareproduktion eine mindestens ebenso große Bedeutung wie der Hardwarefertigung zukommt. "Software, often as much as hardware, sells systems".[1] Andererseits besteht Übereinstimmung darin, daß wir noch immer weit von einer professionellen "Softwarefertigung" entfernt sind. Über die geeigneten Wege hin zu einer solchen Fertigungstechnik besteht allerdings nur sehr wenig Übereinstimmung. Vielmehr stehen wir hier vor einem ganzen Bündel von Problemen grundsätzlicher Natur.

Es ist die Aufgabe dieser kurzen Studie, die Probleme aufzuzeigen, eine Übersicht über eine Vielfalt von Lösungswegen zu geben und ein längerfristiges Konzept für diesen Bereich zu skizzieren. Es erscheint der im Vorangegangenen beschriebenen, außerordentlichen Bedeutung der Softwareentwicklung für die gesamte Wirtschaft angemessen, ein solches Konzept nicht auf partikuläre ad-hoc Vorschläge zu beschränken, sondern darin auch die Möglichkeiten anzudeuten, die sich insbesondere mit fortgeschrittenen Techniken der Wissensver-

arbeitung erreichen ließen, die in dem Gebiet der Künstlichen
Intelligenz (Intellektik) erarbeitet wurden und dort experimentell
erprobt und weiterentwickelt werden.

1. DIE SOFTWAREPROBLEMATIK

Schon viel ist über die Softwareproblematik, ja die "Softwarekrise"
geschrieben worden. Gleichwohl ist es für die nachfolgenden
Überlegungen nötig, an wichtige Aspekte in diesem Zusammenhang nochmals
zu erinnern.

1.1 Die Hardware / Software Dichotomie

Die Trennung von Rechensystemen in den Hardware- und Softwareteil hat
sich bis heute trotz immer flexiblerer Hardwaretechnologie
außerordentlich bewährt. Noch immer kosten Änderungen an der Hardware
ein zigfaches entsprechender Änderungen an der Software und erfordern
viel mehr Zeit zur Durchführung. Ein Faktor 50 ist hier nicht
untypisch.[2] Ohne evolutionäre Anpassungen (also Änderungen) der
integralen Systeme an die sich ständig wandelnden Anforderung wäre der
Computermarkt jedoch wohl kaum von solcher Dynamik geprägt.

In der Praxis geht man meist von der Vorstellung einer fixierten
Hardware aus und paßt sich bei der Softwareentwicklung und -
modifikation diesen Gegebenheiten an. Dies ist jedoch eine
Idealvorstellung, denn in Wirklichkeit ist natürlich auch der
Hardwaremarkt in ständigem Fluß und erlaubt mit fortschreitender Tech-
nologie immer flexiblere Gesamtlösungen. Mehr und mehr ist daher die
Softwareproblematik tatsächlich eine Hardware/Software Problematik.
Zudem sei angemerkt, daß von den Prinzipien her die Probleme beim
Rechnerentwurf mit denen des Softwareentwurfs identisch sind.

Obwohl sich aus diesem letztgenannten Grund, sozusagen ohne
Einschränkung der Allgemeinheit, die Diskussion auf die
Softwareproblematik reduzieren läßt, ist es dennoch äußerst wichtig, im
Auge zu behalten, daß es eigentlich immer um ein Gesamtsystem bestehend
aus Soft- und Hardware geht und daß beide Teile nicht unabänderlich
sind.

1.2   Die Dimensionen des Softwareraumes

"Software" ist ein weitreichender Begriff; dementsprechend können mit "Softwareerstellung" sehr unterschiedliche Tätigkeiten gemeint sein. Zur besseren Übersicht wollen wir den Softwareraum mittels der folgenden drei (nicht ganz voneinander unabhängigen) Dimensionen strukturieren.

1.2.1 Der Lebenszyklus

Von der Idee bis zum (nie ganz) fertigen Produkt durchläuft Software eine Reihe von Verwandlungen, so daß man treffend von ihrem Lebenszyklus spricht. Er besteht zum Beispiel aus den folgenden Phasen

Idee, Marktlücke (Analyse)
Rahmenbedingungen für Gesamtsystem (Definition)
Rahmenbedingungen für den Softwareteil
Spezifikation des Softwareteils (Entwurf)
Rapider Prototyp
Detailentwurf
Algorithmisierung
Implementierung und Integration
Validierung, Tests
Installierung
Einsatz und Wartung

Diese Phasen sind begleitet von parallel erstellten Produkten, die von gleicher Wichtigkeit wie die eigentliche Software selbst sind: Testprogramme und -pläne, Dokumentation, Testmaterial für den Anwender, Wartungsanleitungen, etc. Nach aller Erfahrung wird der Lebenszyklus auch nicht in der suggerierten sequentiellen Weise durchlaufen, sondern es gibt sowohl Schleifen als auch zeitliche Überlappungen.

1.2.2 Intensive / extensive Komplexität

Die simple Umcodierung eines Programmpakets von einer Assemblersprache in eine andere wird ebenso als Softwareaufgabe betrachtet wie die Entwicklung eines Programmsynthesesystems. Letzteres ist zweifelsohne eine Aufgabe von betont **intensiver** Komplexität, bei der schwierige algorithmische Probleme zu lösen sind. Bei einer solchen Aufgabe ist Softwareerstellung vom **Problemlösen** kaum zu unterscheiden.

Natürlich ist auch die erstgenannte Aufgabe ein Prob-lem, das es zu
lösen gilt. Dort stehen einer solchen Lösung aber (wegen der großen
Extension des Problems) höchstens Schwierigkeiten hinsichtlich des
zusätzlichen Aufwandes, keineswegs jedoch grundsätzliche Probleme
entgegen. In einem solchen Fall würde man (bei großen Programmpaketen)
daher von hoher **extensiver** Komplexität sprechen. Statt vom Problemlösen
spricht man hier nur vom **Implementieren.**

1.2.3 Teamgröße

Softwareentwicklung reicht von der Einmanntätigkeit bis hin zur
Entwicklung komplexer Systeme, in die hunderte von Mannjahren an Arbeit
in großen Teams einfließen. Mit wachsender Teamgröße kommen beachtliche
Organisations- und Managementprobleme mit ins Spiel, die zweifelsohne
als Bestandteil des Softwareproblems als Ganzes einbezogen werden
müssen.

1.3   Das Fehlerspektrum

Das Spektrum möglicher Fehlschläge bei der Softwareproduktion ist
beachtlich. Zur Vermeidung solcher Fehlschläge ist es wichtig, daß man
sich der möglichen Fehlerquellen sehr bewußt ist, weshalb die wichtigsten im folgenden angeführt werden. Schon vorweg läßt sich sagen,
daß man in der Softwareproduktion in **jeder** Phase des Lebenszyklus
Entscheidendes falsch machen kann.

1.3.1 Die falschen Ideen

Das Instrumentarium heutiger Marktbeobachtung ist bei einem so
dynamischen Bereich wie der Computertechnik sicher nicht fein und
zukunftsorientiert genug, um den Erfolg einer Softwareentwicklung, die
in der Regel Jahre dauert, schon von vorneherein garantieren zu
können. So manches teuer implementierte Softwarepaket ist nie wirklich
eingesetzt worden[2], von den Klagen der Benutzer in weniger extremen
Fällen zu schweigen, in denen die Programme von den tatsächlichen
operationellen Bedürfnissen weit entfernt sind. Dieses Problem ist viel
fundamentaler als man vielleicht gemeinhin annimmt; zumindest ein wenig
davon haftet dem größten Teil aller im Einsatz befindlichen Programme
an. Zweifelsohne liegt hierin auch ein ganz wesentlicher Kostenfaktor.[2]

1.3.2 Verfälschung bei der Vervollständigung

Selbst wenn die Idee gut war und das Endprodukt mit ihr im Einklang steht, ist der Erfolg noch nicht ga-rantiert. Denn zwischen dem ursprünglichen konzentrierten Konzept und dem Endprodukt sind so viele Details zur Vervollständigung hinzuzufügen, daß das Endergebnis dem Konzept formal zwar nicht widersprechen muß aber doch "nicht in seinem Sinn ist". Jedes Konzept läßt sich auf diese Weise "legal" verfälschen.

1.3.3 Realisierbarkeitsprobleme

Nicht nur die anvisierte Marktlücke begründet eine gute Idee, vielmehr muß das Ganze mit den verfügbaren Mitteln im anvisierten Zeitraum auch realisiert werden können. Dabei mag es ja noch hingehen, daß sich die Fertigstellung gegenüber den Arbeitsplänen in der Regel erheblich verzögert und damit die Kosten ansteigen.[3] Viel kritischer ist, daß eine zeitliche Vorausplanung um so weniger möglich ist, je intensiver (vgl.1.2.2) die Komplexität der Aufgabe ist. Nicht nur bei Forschungsprojekten mußte man daher schon große Entwicklungsvorhaben abbrechen, weil der zeitliche Aufwand jeden Rahmen sprengte und sich als unabsehbar erwies.

1.3.4 Diskrepanz zwischen Idee und Resultat

Die klassischen Fehler bei der Softwarentwicklung jedoch entstehen durch **Abweichungen**, die sich beim Übergang von der einen zur nächsten Phase des Lebenszyklus einschleichen. Sagen wir, der Firmenchef formu-liert seine Idee eines zukünftigen Produktes; aber schon in den darauf folgenden Projektvorbereitungen ergeben sich Beschreibungen, die mit der Idee nicht mehr im Einklang stehen. In den Händen der Projektbe-teiligten entwickeln ferner einzelne Teile ein oft allzu selbständiges Eigenleben. Schließlich die meist untersuchte Fehlerquelle bei der Programmierung, wenn nämlich das Programm sich letztlich ganz anders verhält als der Programmierer ursprünglich beabsichtigte; dabei reicht die Palette wiederum vom kleinen "bug" bis hin zum fundamentalen Fehler im logischen Aufbau des Programmes.

1.3.5 Mängel korrekter Software

Selbst wenn alle vorgenannten Fehlerquellen ausgeschaltet wurden, so daß das Endprodukt von der Funktion her nicht nur eine echte Marktlücke schließt, sondern auch fehlerfrei läuft, selbst in einem solchen Fall ist der wirkliche Erfolg nicht garantiert. Denn die funktionale Lösung allein macht noch kein qualitativ gutes Produkt. Auch das "wie" spielt eine mitentscheidende Rolle. Besonders die **Effizienz** der Software ist natürlich ein wichtiges Erfolgskriterium. Was nützt die schönste Operation, wenn sie den Benutzer damit nervt, daß er minutenlang am Bildschirm auf den Abschluß ihrer Durchführung warten muß. Die **Flexibilität** kann zu wünschen übrig lassen, im Falle von geringfügig veränderter Randbedingungen in der Aufgabenstellung, bei der umgebenden Software oder bei der zugrundeliegenden Hardware. Schließlich hängt der Erfolg auch von der ergonomischen **Handhabbarkeit** ab, ein noch immer schwer meßbares und doch wichtiges Qualitätskriterium.

1.3.6 Kompatibilitätsmängel

Der Einsatz auch der erfolgreichsten Software kann an der mangelnden Kompatibilität mit den vor Ort vorhandenen Gegebenheiten scheitern. Genau gesagt ist dies eigentlich in der Regel der Fall, weil mangels akzeptierter Standardisierungsnormen Teile verschiedener Herkunft selten zueinander passen.

1.4   Die **Hintergrundproblematik**

Angesichts einer so reichhaltigen Fehlerpalette fragt man sich nach der tieferliegenden Problematik, die all diesen Phänomenen zugrunde liegt. Diese kann nur im Umfeld gesucht werden. Das Umfeld jedoch besteht aus den **Menschen**, den **Werkzeugen** und dem **wirtschaftlichen Problemraum**. Je nach Perspektive sieht man den Kern der Problematik bei dem einen oder anderen.

1.4.1 Die beteiligten Menschen

Allein das quantitative Personalproblem ist schon eklatant. In den USA schätzt man die Lücke zwischen Angebot und Nachfrage auf 50 – 100K (fehlender) Softwarespezialisten.[2] Ohne zusätzliche Maßnahmen erwartet man einen Anstieg dieser Zahl auf nahezu 1 Million für das Jahr 1990.[2] Bei aller Skepsis gegenüber solchen Schätzungen bleibt die unleugbare Tatsache eines gravierenden Mangels an qualifizierten Softwarespezia-listen.

Hinzu kommt das qualitative Personalproblem. Seit den Anfängen der Computertechnik paaren sich auf diesem (wie jedem) Pioniergebiet

wirkliche Kreativität, die von den neuen Aufgaben herausgefordert wird,
und Mit-telmäßigkeit, die die Gunst der Expansion nutzt, ein sicheres
Plätzchen zu ergattern. Und das Mittelmaß zeugt neues Mittelmaß,
besonders bei der Ausbildung.

1.4.2 Die einsetzbaren Werkzeuge

Aber auch an den methodologischen und technischen Werkzeugen zur
Softwareproduktion mangelt es fundamental. Im Detail ist das Angebot
äußerst reichhaltig. Der nächste Abschnitt wird darüber einen gewissen
Überblick geben. Er wird aber auch klar zu machen versuchen, daß die
meisten der Konzepte zu partikulär, zu wenig fundamental an die
Problematik herangehen. Das Zusammenwirken der verschiedenen Ansätze in
einem einheitlichen Konzept, das den gesamten Lebenszyklus im Auge hat,
ist bis heute nicht erreicht. Selbst in den partikulären Ansätzen ist
vieles noch ungelöst.

1.4.3 Der wirtschaftliche Problemraum

Mehr als bei irgendwelchen anderen Geräten oder Werkzeugen wird bei
komplexen Computersystemen die enge Verflochtenheit mit dem gesamten
wirtschaftlichen und gesellschaftlichen Gefüge deutlich. Man könnte bereits an eine "Soziologie der Software" denken. Kein Wunder, daß etwas
von der gesellschaftlichen Problematik (in anderer Form) auch bei der
Software in Erscheinung tritt.

2. DER STAND DER TECHNIK

Obwohl die im letzten Abschnitt dargelegte Problematik der
Softwareentwicklung sicher unbestreitbar ist, sollte man nicht
übersehen, daß die Werkzeuge für das klassische Programmieren schon
einen sehr hohen Entwicklungsstand erreicht haben. Daß man sich mit
diesem Stand trotzdem noch nicht zufrieden gibt, liegt an den ständig
steigenden Anforderungen durch immer komplexere Systeme. Da der Mensch
sich nur bedingt in seiner Leistung verbessern läßt, können diese
Anforderungen nur durch neue Techniken erfüllt werden, von denen im
nächsten Abschnitt die Rede sein soll.

Hier wollen wir nun den derzeitigen Entwicklungsstand skizzieren
und kritisch beurteilen, wie er durch Produkte auf dem Markt und durch

einsatzfähige Systeme aus den Laboratorien charakterisiert ist. Als Gesichtspunkte der Gliederung dienen die menschlichen Unzulänglichkeiten im Sinne einer effizienten Softwareentwicklung.

2.1   Ergonomie

Man sollte den positiven Einfluß nicht unterschätzen, den moderne Arbeitsplätze am Bildschirm auf die Produktivität bei der Programmierung haben. Die Zeiten des Stapelbetriebs sind ja noch gar nicht so lange her. Moderne Menü-, Fenster- und Zeigertechniken über Maus oder durch Berührung erhöhen zusätzlich die Bequemlichkeit, die schon von der Tastatur weitgehend unterstützt wird. Die effizienteste Kommunikationsform des Menschen ist allerdings noch nicht möglich, die zweifellos aus einer Kombination gesprochener Sprache, geschriebener Sprache und bildhafter Ausdrucksformen besteht. Bis zur Verfügbarkeit von Arbeitsplätzen mit diesen Möglichkeiten werden (nur) noch einige Jahre vergehen. In einer längerfristigen Perspektive sollte man jedenfalls ihre Möglichkeit miteinbeziehen.

2.2   Sprache

Wie hat man in den letzten 2 - 3 Jahrzehnten um Programmiersprachen und ihre Details gestritten - rückblickend ein recht belangloser Streit. Was einzig zählt ist die Erkenntnis, die sich nunmehr durchgesetzt zu haben scheint, daß bei der Softwareentwicklung die Beschreibung von Wissen in logischer oder funktionaler Form (ggfs. in graphischer Darstellung) eine mindestens ebenso große Rolle wie die imperative Darstellung von Anweisungen spielt. Auf diesem Hintergrund ist das breite Interesse an PROLOG und LISP zu verstehen, das nun auch bis in die bislang unbelehrbarsten Softwarezirkel vorgedrungen ist.

Damit soll nicht gesagt sein, daß nun mit LISP und PROLOG der Weisheit letzter Schluß erreicht ist. Das Ziel muß vielmehr zunächst sein, jedem Anfänger den Einstieg in die Programmierung über die natürliche Sprache zu ermöglichen. Je nach Fortschritt seines Abstraktionvermögens wird er dann nach und nach auch mit einem formalen Sprachsystem vertraut werden, das ihm systemseitig angeboten werden könnte, worauf wir im nächsten Abschnitt 3 zurückkommen werden.

2.3   Korrektheit im Detail

Kreative Softwareentwicklung verträgt sich nur in den seltensten
Ausnahmen mit Pedanterie im kleinen Detail wie etwa einer korrekten
Syntax. Zweifelsohne sind auf dieser Ebene des "low level debugging"
und der Syntaxprüfung die ausgereiftesten Testsysteme kommerziell
verfügbar, in der Tat eine spürbare Arbeitserleichterung für den
kreativen Entwickler.

Natürlich sind sie alle programmiersprachen- oder datenbank-
spezifisch, lokal orientiert, insgesamt in keiner Weise intelligent.
Für eine fortgeschrittenere Form der Programmierung, wie sie im
nächsten Abschnitt 3 vorgeschlagen wird, dürften sie in ihrer
bisherigen Form eher völlig obsolet werden.

2.4   Programmierumgebung

Schon in sogenannten Programmierumgebungen ist die Fehlerkorrektur, das
Debugging, meist ein dynamisch integrierter Prozeß, so daß lokale
Fehler durch die von der Umgebung ständig gegebene Anleitung einfach
nicht durchgelassen werden und also überhaupt nicht mehr entstehen.
Dies betrifft statische ebenso wie dynamische Fehler.

Als gute Beispiele solcher Programmerumgebungen nennen wir
INTERLISP[4], den Cornell Program Synthesizer[5] und Smalltalk[6]. Sie alle
basieren auf je auf einer Programmiersprache (LISP, PL/1, Smalltalk),
sind interaktiv und stellen die klassischen Hilfsmittel dem Benutzer
zur Verfügung, nämlich Editor, Compiler oder Interpreter, Linker,
Lader, Laufzeitsystem und Debugger, die alle an die betreffende
Programmiersprache angepaßt sind. Dementsprechend kann der Programmierer einheitlich über die Sprachkonzepte mit dem System
kommunizieren. Insbesondere ist es nicht nötig, von einem Kontext (z.B.
Editieren) auf einen anderen (z.B. Testen) eigens umzuschalten. Ja,
durch die modernen hochauflösenden Bildschirme ist es sogar möglich,
mittels der Fenster- und Maustechnik verschiedene Aufgaben parallel
auszuführen.

INTERLISP unterstützt die Verwaltung durchgeführter Änderungen
(mittels des "file package"). Mit dem "Masterscope" kann man die
Auswirkungen verfolgen, die durch eine beabsichtigte Änderung entstehen
würde. Dabei kann man sich die Resultate der Analyse (wie z.B.

Verweislisten) nicht nur ausdrucken lassen, sondern auch gezielte Anfragen an eine von Masterscope unterhaltene Datenbank stellen. Zudem bietet INTERLISP die Möglichkeit, über sein DWIM ("do what I mean") eine Fehlersituation vom System selbst bereinigen zu lassen.

Der Cornell Program Synthesizer hat mit Programmsynthese im klassischen Sinne kaum etwas zu tun. Man kann mit ihm gleichzeitig programmieren und testen oder fehlersuchen. Die Programmausführung wird dabei mit jeder Programmerweiterung weitergetrieben, wobei das Ausführungsergebnis auf einer, das Programm auf der anderen Seite des Bildschirmes dargestellt wird. Die Programmausführung kann man sich auf dem PL/1 Niveau anweisungsweise demonstrieren lassen. Ebenso lassen sich die Werte verfolgen, die ausgewählte Variablen bei der Ausführung annehmen.

Smalltalk ist für leistungsstarke Arbeitsplatzrechner ("personal computers") wie die Dandelion von Xerox gedacht. Smalltalk hat kein Betriebssystem im üblichen Sinne, was dem der Sprache zugrundeliegenden Modell von miteinander kommunizierenden Objekten entspricht. Auch hier kann man unter extensivem Gebrauch der Fenster-/Maus-Technik leicht zwischen Editieren, Kompilieren, Testen und Fehlersuchen beliebig umschalten.

Wir haben diese Programmierumgebungen deswegen relativ ausführlich beschrieben, weil sie besonders typisch für den gegenwärtigen Stand der beherrschten Technik sind. Damit soll nicht gesagt sein, daß diese Techniken bereits weitverbreitet seien. Vielmehr werden sie bis heute vorwiegend nur an Universitäten und Forschungslaboratorien eingesetzt. Man muß jedoch betonen, daß ohne solch komfortable Programmierumgebungen viele der komplexen Programmsysteme aus dem Gebiet der Künstlichen Intelligenz ("Intellektik") wohl schwerlich hätten entwickelt werden können. Wenn daher die Industrie sich (u.a. angeregt durch die jüngsten Förderprogramme) gleichermaßen an solch komplexe Aufgaben mit dem Ziel der professionellen Produktion heranwagen möchte, so sind derartige Umgebungen **unabdingbare Voraussetzungen** für einen späteren Erfolg.

2.5 Softwareentwicklungsumgebungen

Während Programmierumgebungen den einzelnen Programmierer in seiner Arbeit unterstützten, ist es das Ziel von Softwareentwurfs- und -

entwicklungssystemen bzw. -umgebungen (SEE - software engineering environment, auch SPU - Software-Produktionsumgebungen) einen möglichst großen Teil des Lebenszyklus auch größerer Softwaresysteme in ihrer Entwicklung zu unterstützen, d.h. angefangen von der Formulierung der Rahmenbedingungen bis hin zu den letzten Testläufen. Insbesondere zielen sie auf Systeme ab, die in Teams erstellt werden.

Es gibt bereits eine Reihe solcher im Einsatz oder in der Entwicklung befindlicher Systeme, die größtenteils in einem 1981 erschienenen Proceedingsband[7], einem Tutorial[8] und einem guten Überblickstitel[9] beschrieben werden. Die technische Reife der Programmierumgebungen ist hier jedoch noch bei weitem nicht erreicht. Zum Teil handelt es sich auch lediglich um Methodologien bzw. um Entwurfstechniken, die noch nicht von Systemen unterstützt werden. Der Grund liegt in der Tatsache, daß hier noch eine Reihe von grundsätzlichen Fragen nicht ausreichend geklärt sind.

Wegen der außerordentlich starken Förderung ist es wohl angebracht, hier an erster Stelle das ADA Programming Support Environment (APSE)[10] zu nennen, das innerhalb von STARS (siehe 1.1) entwickelt wird. Ein deutscher Ableger wird unter dem Namen SPERBER vom Bundesamt für Wehrtechnik und Beschaffung vorangetrieben. APSE ist in Schichten (Zwiebelmodell) strukturiert. Der Kern KAPSE umfaßt die Datenbank-, Kommunikations- und Laufzeitfunktionen. Die nächste Schicht MAPSE (minimal APSE) definiert (zusammen mit KAPSE) eine Programmierumgebung der Art wie sie im vorangegangenen Abschnitt 2.4 beschrieben wurde. Hierauf soll dann die oberste Schicht gebaut werden, die aus Anwendungs- und Methodensystemen bestehen wird. Derzeit sind lediglich die Funktionen der beiden unteren Schichten spezifiziert.

Das Schwergewicht bei Ansätzen wie APSE liegt insbesondere auf einer Bereitstellung einer dedizierten Datenbank, der Projektbibliothek, in der bereits eine Vielfalt von Softwareteilen in der zugrundeliegenden Programmiersprache (hier ADA) zur Verfügung steht, so daß ein wesentlicher Anteil der Systementwicklung im Zusammenbinden solch vorgefertigter Standardteile besteht.

Im Vergleich dazu besteht das System HDM (Hierarchical Development Methodology)[11] aus einer integrierten Menge von Sprachen und Hilfsmitteln, die auf gemeinsamen (zum Teil auf Parnas zurückgehenden) Konzepten des Software Engineering beruhen. Besonderen Wert wird hier auf eine formale Spezifikation und auf die Verifikation (im Sinne von Naur/Floyd/Hoare) gelegt. HDM ist natürlich wesentlich bescheidener im Gesamtansatz als APSE; dafür befindet es sich bereits im praktischen Einsatz.

Von den reinen Methoden zur Entwicklung großer Softwaresysteme, die jedoch von keinem System automatisch unterstützt werden, seien hier die bekannte Jackson Technik[12] und die von Softlab vertretene S/E/TEC Methode[13] genannt. Solche Methoden unterstützen das Verlegen der Problemteile, die Modularisierung, die Fixierung der Schnittstellen, usw. bereits in der Entwurfsphase. Ohne solchen Methoden ihre außerordentliche Bedeutung für die Praxis zum gegenwärtigen Zeitpunkt absprechen zu wollen, muß das Interesse doch dahin gehen, sie soweit zu präzisieren, daß sie der zumindest teilweisen Automatisierung zugänglich werden.

Ein solcher Ansatz zur Automatisierung der Entwurfsphase kann überhaupt nur mit einem wissensbasierten System gelingen, das in der Lage ist auch deduktive Verarbeitungsprozesse durchzuführen. Keiner der hier erwähnten Ansätze sieht eine solche Möglichkeit vor. Es läßt sich daher die kritische Frage stellen, ob das mit großem Aufwand betriebene ADA- und APSE-Projekt und vergleichbare Ansätze aus den klassischen Softwarekreisen wirklich auf der Höhe der Zeit sind.

2.6   Problemlösen

Die am Ende des letzten Abschnitts 2.5 gestellte Frage läßt sich an dem folgenden Kernpunkt kristallisieren. Alle bisher erwähnten Ansätze und Systeme zur Unterstützung der Softwareentwicklung bestehen im wesentlichen in vorgefertigten Organisationshilfen und im Anbau und der Bereitstellung von Methoden- und Verfahrensbanken. Tritt ein unvorhergesehenes, wenn auch noch so einfaches Problem auf, bleibt die Lösung völlig dem Programmierer überlassen. Über die Bereitstellung vorher eingespeicherten Wissens hinaus wird die Problemlösung nicht unterstützt.

Zugegeben, Problemlösen ist ein außerordentlich schwieriges Gebiet. Und doch erscheint es mir als verfehlt, diesen Teil von der automatisch unterstützten Softwareentwicklung vollends auszuklammern, da sonst ein solches System einfach zu starr und an kleinsten unvorhergesehenen Schwierigkeiten scheitern würde. Der Hinweis, daß in solchen Fällen ja der Mensch einspringen kann, geht zumindest insoweit fehl, als niemand sich in der Fülle automatisch erledigter Details in einem solchen Fall zurechtfinden würde.

Zu diesem Aspekt der Softwareentwicklung gibt es bislang nur experimentelle Ansätze, die ziemlich vollständig in einem gerade erschienenen Buch[14] repräsentiert sind. Einer davon ist das (dort als Kapitel 3 repräsentierte) LOPS[15]-Projekt des Autors dieser Studie, in dem die mit dem Problemlösen beim Programmieren zusammenhängenden Phänomene untersucht werden, wovon im Abschnitt 3 nochmals zu sprechen sein wird.

2.7   Marktanalyse

Ein System, das auch noch den Markt für Systeme (eigentlich das ganze gesellschaftliche Umfeld) als Problemraum mit einbezieht und damit sogar noch das Ausfindigmachen der "richtigen" Idee unterstützen könnte, ist derzeit natürlich lediglich Illusion. Zur Abrundung sollte dieser Aspekt jedoch nicht unerwähnt bleiben, weil ja nicht auszuschließen ist, daß jemand demnächst eine gute Idee für ein entsprechendes Expertensystem hat, das zumindest einzelne Aspekte klarer zu sehen hilft.

3.   ASPEKTE FÜR DIE NAHE ZUKUNFT

Im ersten Abschnitt haben wir von den wesentlichen Problemen der Softwareentwicklung gesprochen. Die kritischen Anmerkungen zu den im zweiten Abschnitt vorgestellten Lösungsansätzen haben sodann darauf hingedeutet, daß die Probleme sicher noch nicht ausreichend gelöst sind. Insbesondere sind Aspekte wie das Problemlösen in den vorrangig betriebenen Entwicklungen vergleichsweise nur wenig beachtet. Hinzu kommt der generelle Eindruck, daß die Softwaretechnik auch heute noch am Modell des tradionellen Programmierens haftet und so die neuen Perspektiven nicht wirklich ernst nimmt, die von den aus der Intellektik kommenden Techniken der Wissensverarbeitung eröffnet worden sind.

Unter diesen Gesichtspunkten soll in diesem letzten Abschnitt eine Form der rechnergestützten Systementwicklung skizziert werden, die die erkannten Probleme zu überwinden, die Mängel in den bisherigen

Ansätzen zu vermeiden sucht und vollen Gebrauch von der in den allernächsten Jahren zu erwartenden Rechenleistungen spezieller symbolverarbeitender Systeme macht.

Hinsichtlich der zu erwartender Leistungssteigerungen wurde bisher immer auf das Fifth-Generation Projekt[16] der Japaner verwiesen, deren Ziele von vielen bis heute mit Skepsis beurteilt werden. Inzwischen sind jedoch vergleichbare Ziele auch von den Amerikanern gesteckt worden. So geht man bei DARPA[17] davon aus, daß man innerhalb weniger Jahre die Leistungsfähigkeit von symbolverarbeitenden Maschinen um einen Faktor 100 und bis Anfang der 90er Jahre um einen weiteren Faktor 10 - 100 mit Techniken verbessert, von denen man bereits präzise Vorstellungen hat.

Meineserachtens muß man angesichts solcher Möglickkeiten auch den Zugang zur Softwareentwicklung von Grund auf neu überdenken. Die anschließenden Gedanken hierzu können naturgemäß nicht mehr als eine Skizze hierzu sein. Sie beginnt mit einer modellhaften Vorstellung über die Art und Weise der Systementwicklung, für die ich schon 1974 den Begriff "prädikatives Programmieren"[18] geprägt habe. (Eine jüngst unter dem gleichen Titel erschienene Arbeit[19] zielt jedoch nur in Teilen auf das Gleiche ab.)

3.1 Modellskizze zur prädikativen Systementwicklung

Die Idee zu einem System entsteht in der Regel durch Beobachtung einer konkreten, als Mangel empfundenen Situation. Mit der Beschreibung dieser Situation und des Mangels beginnt die Systementwicklung; also muß sie in unser gedachtes Systementwicklungssystem (SES) bereits aufgenommen werden. Wir können uns vorstellen, daß dies mittels gesprochener/geschriebener natürlicher Sprache, illustriert mit graphischen Skizzen geschieht. SES formalisiert diese Beschreibung im Rahmen eines logischen Formalismus und testet durch Rückfragen die semantische Übereinstimmung mit den tatsächlichen Vorstellungen des Erzählers, was gegebenenfalls noch zu Korrekturen führt.

Ein Erlebnis macht meist noch keine Idee. Zu ihr bedarf es in der Regel noch zusätzlich eines Abstraktionsprozesses, der das Erlebnis in seiner Struktur als Einzelfall unter vergleichbaren Fällen mit funktionell immer dem gleichen Mangel erweist. SES kann aufgrund seiner formalisierten Darstellung bei diesem Abstraktionsprozeß hilfreiche

Dienste leisten. Weitere Szenarien werden als Instanzen der gleichen nun in SES verfügbaren abstrakten Form erkannt und in SES mit festgehalten. Jetzt ist eine Idee vorgegeben.

Sie wird nun einem Unternehmer vorgetragen. Nehmen wir an, sie findet ein erstes Interesse bei ihm, jedoch denkt er noch an eine weitere Situation, die er gerne unter den gleichen Hut bringen möchte. Dies mag durchaus zu einer Revision des vorherigen Abstraktionsprozesses hin zu einer noch höheren, auch das neue Beispiel noch umfassenderen Abstraktion samt Instanzen (sprich Idee) führen.

Er gibt nun die Idee seiner Marktanalyseabteilung, die auf der Grundlage des so erreichten Zustandes in SES und unter Zuhilfenahme einer Datenbank systematisch reale Situationen auf ihre Kompatibilität mit der vorgegebenen abstrakten Struktur absucht, ihre Häufigkeit abschätzt und zudem die Verträglichkeit einer potentiellen Automatisierung mit den in der Gesellschaft bestehenden Wertvorstellungen und den ökologischen Randbedingungen prüft, immer unterstützt durch SES in der oben bei der Ideenfindung bereits angedeuteten Weise. Zudem werden die Entwicklungschancen und -kosten mit einer entsprechenden Datenbank durch Vergleich mit früheren tatsächlichen Entwicklungen abgeschätzt. Soweit Informationen sich für den Fall als relevant erweisen, speichert SES diese für spätere Überprüfungen.

Nehmen wir an, die Analyse fällt (möglicherweise erst nach weiterer Modifikation) günstig aus und der Unternehmer entscheidet für eine Produktion. Alle seine Anweisungen an den Entwicklungsleiter werden zusätzlich in SES aufgenommen, das diese Protokolle während der gesamten Entwicklungsphase immer wieder mit dem entstehenden Produkt vergleicht. Bei möglichen entwicklungsbedingten Abweichungen kann sich durchaus die Notwendigkeit zu neuen Entscheidungen auf höchster Firmenebene ergeben, was wegen des in SES bereits in der Vorbereitungsphase eingebrachten und sofort verfügbaren Umfeldwissens und des Wissens über den Entwicklungsstand jedoch zügig durchgeführt werden kann.

Die tatsächliche Entwicklung beginnt nun mit einer hochgradig parallel durchgeführten Suche im Raum möglicher Modularisierungen nach einer, die möglichst viele bereits entwickelte Systemteile miteinbezieht. Die Modularisierung ist in dieser Phase noch keinerlei Problem, weil es sich ja immer noch um eine System**beschreibung** handelt. Genau deshalb sprechen wir von einer prädikativen Systementwicklung, weil es sich bei jeder Beschreibung (eine möglicherweise große Menge von) Beziehungen (oder Prädikaten) unter Objekten handelt. Beschreibungen sind **prädikats-** und nicht **objekt**orientiert, weil Objekte erst durch ihre Beziehungen und Eigenschaften einen Sinn erhalten. Da diese Beschreibung in SES in formaler Form vorliegt, kann diese Modularisierung weitgehend automatisch durchgeführt werden, denn sie besteht im wesentlichen in der Erkennung syntaktischer Strukturen in einem (möglicherweise extensiv komplexen) formalen Beschreibungstext (d.h. in einer Zeichenkette).[20] Da die Beschreibung in dieser Phase eventuell noch unvollständig ist, kann sich später noch die Notwendigkeit zu einer Revision der schließlich gewählten Modularisierung ergeben, weshalb relevante Informationen aus dieser Phase ebenfalls gespeichert werden.

Nun kann der Prozess der Programmsythese in SES etwa in der Art von LOPS[15] unter der Anleitung eines im kreativen mathematischen Denken geschulten Entwicklers ablaufen. Als Ergebnis dieser prädikativen Algorithmierungsphase ergibt sich im Erfolgsfall sowohl eine Vervollständigung der ursprünglichen Modulbeschreibung als auch eine neuentwickelte, äquivalente, immer noch logische, aber implizit algorithmische Beschreibung, wie sie etwa ein heutiges PROLOG Programm darstellt.

Schlichtes Aneinanderreihen der für die einzelnen Module so erstellten Logikprogramme ergibt einen Prototyp des Systems zur Testerprobung in der realen Anwendung. Dies kann nochmals zu einer sich aus diesen praktischen Erfahrungen ergebenden Umformulierung der Beschreibung auf höchster Ebene führen. Die sich daraus als nötig erweisenden Modifizierungen des in SES natürlich gespeicherten vorher erarbeiteten Transformationsprozesses bis hin zum Logikprogramm werden in der Regel keine besonderen kreativen Ideen erfordern und dürften daher von SES weitgehend automatisch erledigt werden können.

Die Kompilierungs- und damit gekoppelte Optimierungsphase bildet dann den Abschluß der Systementwicklung. Dabei verstehe ich unter Kompilierung eine aus interpretativ erzeugten Testläufen abstrahierte, also auch verallgemeinerte Steuerungskomponente zum Logikprogramm, die beide zusammen ein auf entsprechendes hochparallel arbeitender Hardware funktional und effizient ausführbares Programm darstellen (vgl. Abschnitt V.2 in meinem Buch[21]). Auch nach diesem abschließenden Prozess ist das Programm noch verständlich, weil insbesondere der eine Teil immer noch aus einer logischen Beschreibung besteht, die notfalls sogar leicht in natürliche Sprache umformuliert werden kann.

Die Notwendigkeit zu einer konventionell nötigen Vali-dierungs-, Verifikations- oder Testphase entfällt, weil unkorrekte Schritte vom konstruktiven Ansatz her nicht überleben können.

3.2   Chancen der Realisierbarkeit

Von einem gedachten System wie SES im vorangeganen Ab-schnitt zu träumen, dies allein würde natürlich noch keinen Sinn ergeben. Vielmehr stellt sich sofort die Gretchenfrage nach der Realisierbarkeit. Genauer gefragt, könnte man sich vorstellen, daß mit den heute wenigstens im Ansatz entwickelten Techniken ein System wie SES im Verlauf einer Dekade machbar wäre, mit dem ja die in den Abschnitten 1 und 2 dargestellten Probleme weitgehend überwunden wären?

Aus meiner Sicht läßt sich diese Frage bejahen, eine Antwort, die im vorliegenden Abschnitt im einzelnen erläutert werden soll. Zuallererst sei dazu jedoch mit Nachdruck darauf hingewiesen, daß SES nicht als vollautomatisches System gedacht ist, sondern ganz im Gegenteil durch seine Betonung der Dialogfähigkeit auf allen Ebenen die menschliche Kreativität in möglichst optimaler Weise miteinbeziehen möchte. Mit diesem Hinweis sei einem weitverbreiteten Mißverständnis vorgebeugt, das die Intension zum minutiösen Gesamtverständnis mit der zur Vollautomatisierung fälschlicherweise identifiziert.

Beginnen wir gleich mit der höchsten, der Sprachebene, auf der der Benutzer mit der Maschine kommuniziert. Wir haben schon in Abschnitt 2.2 darauf hingewiesen, daß es die Kommunikations- oder Programmiersprache nie geben wird. Der Firmenchef wird sich immer einer anderen Sprache bedienen wie der Wissensingenieur. Deshalb kann die Lösung nur in einer Benützersprachpalette liegen, wobei sich zudem durch die Benutzung mit der Zeit eine dem Einzelnen sich anpassende individuelle Benutzersprache herausbilden sollte. An der Oberfläche spricht SES viele Sprachen, die intern jedoch auf einen einheitlichen Formalismus abgebildet werden.

Der Erfolg heutiger natürlichsprachlicher Systeme ist ein sicheres Indiz dafür, daß eine Sprachpalette bis zur höchsten, der natürlichen Ebene im Bereich des Möglichen liegt. Auch die für eine oben angedeutete Individualisierung nötigen Adaptionstechniken sind im

Prinzip bekannt. Eine erste definitorische Stufe ließe sich sogar
sofort verwirklichen, wo der Benutzer seine Sprache (und Werkzeuge)
definitorisch mit der Zeit selbst gestaltet, wobei wir durchaus auch an
graphische Techniken denken. Die Existenz von (wenn auch rudimentären)
Spracherkennungschips am Markt läßt zudem an der Möglichkeit künftiger
akustischer Kommunikation kaum Zweifel aufkommen.

Der nächste Aspekt hinsichtlich der Realisierbarkeit von SES sei
derjenige der internen Wissensrepräsentation. Unsere Vision geht ja
davon aus, daß eine Vielfalt von Wissen, angefangen von
Erlebnisbeschreibungen über Richtlinien von Firmenchefs bis hin zu
Massendaten aus Datenbanken miteinander in Bezug gebracht werden
sollen. Die Tatsache, daß die damit zusammenhängenden Fragen der
Wissensrepräsentation heute bereits in anwendungsorientierten Projekten
zentral behandelt werden, kann als sicheres Indiz für praktikable
Lösungen in der allernächsten Zeit herhalten.

Im einzelnen zeichnet sich für den Eingeweihten die Möglichkeit
von Formalismen mit den folgenden Fähigkeiten ab. Sie erlauben eine
einheitliche Strukturierung von deskriptivem Wissen; dabei ist zu
beachten, daß in einem Raum zeitabhängiges Wissen dann auch deskriptiv
ist, wenn die Zeit als eigene Dimension auftritt. In jedem Fall
ermöglichen sie die Einbindung von funktionalen (proceduralen)
Beziehungen. Geeignete Schnittstellen hin zu konventionellen
Datenbanken sind ohnehin schon in Bälde zu erwarten. Von der Repräsen-
tationsseite her lassen sich auch keine prinzipiellen Probleme
hinsichtlich der nötigen Vielfalt in den Abstraktionsniveaus erkennen.

Was allerdings heute noch nicht im Detail absehbar ist, betrifft
die Übergänge von einem solchen Abstraktionsniveau zum anderen. Solche
Transformationen und Beziehungen sind an verschiedenen Stellen unserer
Modellskizze erforderlich. So etwa wenn nach Erstellung eines Prototyps
sich die Notwendigkeit zur "Umformulierung der Beschreibung auf höchster Ebene" (siehe 3.1) ergibt. Die Mechanismen solch zusammenfassender
Abstraktionen sind heute mit Sicherheit noch nicht ausreichend
verstanden, worauf auch Zadeh jüngst hingewiesen hat[22].

Ähnliches gilt für die bei der Programmsynthese erforderlichen
kreativen Transformationsprozesse. Es ist sogar zu vermuten, daß die
fehlenden Prinzipien hier zum Teil die gleichen sind. Es ist meine
Überzeugung, daß der gemeinsame Hintergrund die bis heute
unzulänglichen Problemlösungssysteme sind, denen wiederum

leistungsfähige Inferenzmechanismen abgehen. Theoretisch sind solche
Mechanismen bekannt; die zu ihrer weiteren Entwicklung, Aufbereitung
und Implementierung nötigen aufwendigen Investitionen hat jedoch bisher
niemand zu erbringen für nötig gehalten, der dazu in der Lage gewesen
wäre. Selbst wenn diese Schwachstelle (die die in 1.2.2 bereits
erwähnte intensive Komplexität betrifft) in naher Zukunft nicht
allzusehr verbessert werden könnte (was aufgrund unserer Erfahrungen
mit LOPS[23] unwahrscheinlich ist), selbst dann macht SES natürlich noch
Sinn wegen der eingangs betonten Einbeziehung der menschlichen
Fähigkeiten.

Die extensive Komplexität dagegen, die ja bei SES bisher nicht
erprobte Ausmaße annehmen würde, dürfte weder von den Prinzipien noch
von den maschinellen Voraussetzungen her grundsätzliche Probleme
aufwerfen. Auch bei der Vielzahl von Einzelproblemen, die in diesem
Zusammenhang im Detail durchzuhäkeln wären, kann ich aus der hier
eingenommenen Perspektive keine unüberwindbaren Hindernisse
erkennen.

3.3   Kurzfristige Möglichkeiten

Unter den kurzfristigen Forschungen und Entwicklungsmaßnahmen sind aus
der hier vertretenen Sicht natürlich all diejenigen besonders zu
begrüßen, die einen Schritt in die soweit skizzierte Richtung gehen
(wie etwa Arbeiten zur Modellierung der Rahmenbedingungen[24], um nur ein
Beispiel zu nennen). Hier wollen wir uns jedoch abschließend darauf beschränken, einige der Möglichkeiten aufzuzeigen, Methoden aus der
Intellektik sofort bei der konventionellen Softwareproduktion nutzbar
einzubringen. Die Bedeutung solcher Sofortmaßnahmen sollte man nicht an
der Länge dieses Abschnitt messen. Vielmehr wäre hierzu eine eigene
Studie durchaus angemessen, die dann jedoch umfangreichere Analysen
erfordern würde als in dem vorgegebenen Rahmen möglich waren.

Der Grund für diese Bedeutung liegt darin, daß niemand an dem
Faktum vorbeigehen kann, daß es nun einmal bereits Software im Werte
von hunderten von Milliarden Mark gibt, die sich der oben entworfenen
Vision nicht ohne weiteres einordnet. Mit ihr werden wir noch auf Jahre
hinaus rechnen müssen. Ebensowenig kann man davon ausgehen, daß heutige
Softwareexperten von heute auf morgen ihren bisherigen Programmierstil
über Bord werfen. Wir müssen also Assembler-, COBOL- und FORTRAN-
Programme in die Betrachtung miteinbeziehen und haben dabei alle

Aspekte von der Entwicklung über die Fehleranalyse bis hin zur Wartung im Auge.

Als erstes sollte man erwarten, daß auch im konventionellen Programmieren in Sprachen wie FORTRAN und COBOL die in Abschnitt 2.4 beschriebenen Entwicklungstechniken Eingang finden, soweit sie sprachunabhängig sind. Sheil[25] erwartet sich davon eine Entwicklung, die schließlich den Boden für einen SES-artigen Zugang bereiten könnte. Eine Reihe von Arbeiten, die in diesem Zusammenhang relevant sind, finden sich etwa in [26].

Eine klassische Anwendung von Methoden der Intellektik besteht in der Programmverifikation. In einer guten konventionellen Programmierumgebung sollte man sich ihrer bedienen können. Als vorbildliche Beispiele seien das Boyer-Moore System[27] und der Standford Verifier[28] genannt. Wie in Abschnitt 3.1 bereits erwähnt, würde diese Form der Verifikation in dem von uns favorisierten Zugang jedoch obsolet.

Eine naheliegende Idee besteht in der Einbeziehung wissensbasierter Systeme in den Entwicklungsprozess von konventioneller Software. Als paradigmatisches Beispiel eines solchen Expertensystems nennen wir CHI[29] (das Nachfolgerprojekt zu PSI). Es soll den gesamten Prozess von der Spezifikation bis hin zur Wartung, ja sogar den der evolutionären Weiterentwicklung unterstützen. Von den Zielen her kommt es daher unserem SES schon relativ nahe.

All diese vorerwähnten Anwendungen bezogen sich auf die Neuentwicklung von Software. Ein Löwenanteil aller Softwareinvestitionen wird jedoch von Modifikationen bestehender Software verschlungen. Im typischen Fall handelt es sich um im Endeffekt recht triviale Änderungen. Trotzdem sind sie oft unrealisierbar, weil niemand verfügbar ist, der sich im System auskennt, und weil die Zeit für die zu einer solchen Einsicht nötige Analyse einfach nicht vorhanden ist.

Es ist abzusehen, daß sich hier schon in allernächster Zukunft ein weites Feld der Anwendung der PROLOG Programmierung und möglicherweise auch bestimmter Programmsynthesemethoden[30] auftun wird. Ein überzeugendes Experiment hierzu wurde bei IBM durchgeführt[31]. Die Aufgabe bestand darin, die IMS Cross Memory Local Storage Option in einem Prototyp zu testen (IMS - Information Management System - ist IBM's populärstes DBMS). Dies erforderte jedoch eine Anpassung von MVS

(Multiple Virtual memory System), IBM´s größtes Betriebssystem neuesten Stands, an diese neue "cross memory" Architektur. Es ging um nicht weniger als zehntausende von Instruktionen, die unter Terminzwang anzupassen waren.

Die Projektgruppe entschied sich für den "Umweg" über PROLOG und ersparte sich damit einen beträchtlichen Teil der andernfalls nötigen stumpfsinnigen Kleinarbeit. Nämlich es wurde erst ein PROLOG Programm SCAN (Semantic Code ANalysis) entwickelt, das Assembler Code "versteht" und so zur interaktiven Modifizierung von Programmen in S370 Assemblersprache herangezogen werden kann, was solche Modifizierungen um ein Vielfaches vereinfacht. Man kann mutmaßen, daß die dann dem Programmierer noch verbleibenden Programmieraufgaben einfachster Natur mittels wohlbekannter Programmsynthesetechniken ebenfalls noch automatisiert werden können.

So verliert vielleicht in Bälde die Halde an zum Teil chaotischer Software doch zunehmend an Schrecken, weil sich in solcher Weise bestehende Pakete in moderne Systeme einbinden lassen und weil sich eine solche Technik offensichtlich gleichermaßen für die Fehleranalyse und für die Systemwartung einsetzen läßt.

Dies hat unseren Blick nochmals auf PROLOG gerichtet. Es sei daher abschließend die herausragende Bedeutung von PROLOG als ein (beinahe revolutionärer) Schritt in die in Abschnitt 3.1 anvisierte Richtung betont. Jede mit PROLOG zusammenhängende Entwicklung wie eine Verbesserung seiner funktionalen Möglichkeiten, eine Anhebung der PROLOG Programmierumgebungen etwa auf den INTERLISP-Standard, die Entwicklung von Schnittstellen hin bis zu konventioneller Software oder Datenbanken, eine weitergehende PROLOG Kompilierung, dies und vieles andere mehr kann aus der Sicht dieser Studie nur allzu begrüßt werden.

ZUSAMMENFASSUNG

In dieser Studie wurden den üblichen Ansätzen zur Bewältigung der immensen Probleme bei der Softwareproduktion und Wartung eine Modellskizze zur prädikativen Systementwicklung gegenübergestellt. Da es sich hier zweifelsohne um einen längerfristigen Prozess des Uebergangs handeln wird, sind abschließend noch eine Reihe von Anwendungen einzelner Methoden aus der Intellektik (d.i. dem Gebiet der

Künstlichen Intelligenz) auf die Softwareentwicklung zusammengestellt worden, die kurzfristig diesen Prozess günstig beeinflussen könnten. Alle Anzeichen deuten jedoch bereits heute schon darauf hin, daß ein solcher Prozess bereits in vollem Gange ist, der die Softwareproduktion von der Ebene des klassischen Programmierens auf die der Verarbeitung von Wissen in all seinen Manifestationen anheben wird.

DANK

Herrn Professor E. Jessen bin ich für eine Reihe von Anregungen und Bemerkungen dankbar, die aus Zeitnot leider nur noch zum Teil in der vorliegenden Fassung berücksichtigt werden konnten. Die Studie selbst geht auf eine Anregung von Herrn Dr. D. Schütt zurück und wurde von der Firma Siemens AG großzügig unterstützt, wofür ich meinen herzlichen Dank aussprechen möchte.

---

[1] A study of the competitive position of the US Computer Industry. US Department of Commerce, March 10, 1983

[2] Software technology for adaptable, reliable systems (STARS) program stategy. US department of defense, 15 March 1983.

[3] B.W. Bochum, Software Engineering Economics, Prentice Hall 1981

[4] W.Teitelbaum, L.Masinter, The INTERLISP programming environment, Computer April 1981

[5] W.Teitelbaum, T.Reps, S.Horwitz, The why and wherefore of the Cornell Program Synthesizer, ACM SIGPLAN Notices, Bd.16, Nr.6, S.8-16, Juni 1981

[6] A series on Smalltalk, BYTE, Bd.6, Nr.8, August 1981

[7] H.Hünke (Hrsg.), Software Engineering Environments, Pro-ceedings, North Holland, Amsterdam, 1981

[8] A.I.Wassermann, Tutorial: Software development environ-ments, IEEE Cat.No.EHO 187-5

[9] W.Hesse, Methoden und Werkzeuge zur Softwareentwicklung, Informatik Spektrum 4, 229-245, 1981

[10] J.N.Baxton, L.E.Druffel, Requirements for an ADA Program-ming Support Environment, siehe Hünke[7]

[11] Silverberg, B.A., An overview of the hierarchical development methodology, siehe Hünke[7]

[12] M.A.Jackson, Constructive methods of program design, LNCS 44, 1976

[13] S/E/TEC - Die Software Engineering Technologie von Soft-lab, Softlab, München, 1981

[14] A.Biermann et al. (Hrsg.), Automatic program construction methods, MacMillan, New York, 1984

[15] W.Bibel u. K.M.Hörnig, LOPS-A system based on a stragical approach to programm sythesis, in A.Biermann[14], Kap.3, 1984

[16] T.Moto-oka, Proceedings Intern. Conference on Fifth Generation Computer Systems, North Holland, 1982

[17] Point paper - DARPA Strategic Computing Program, Washington, 7.Nov.1983

[18] W.Bibel, Prädikatives Programmieren, LNCS 33, Springer, Berlin, 274-283, 1975

[19] E.Hehner, Predicative Programming, CACM 27, 134-151, 1984

[20] W.Bibel, Logical program sythesis, in: T.Moto-oka[16]

[21] W.Bibel, Automated theorem proving, Vieweg Verlag, Wies-baden, 1982

[22] L.Zadeh, Coping with the imprecision of the real world, CACM 27, 304-311, 1984

[23] W.Bibel an K.M.Hörnig, LOPS - A System baced on a strategical

approach to program sythesis, chapter 3 in Biermann[14]

24 S.J.Greenspan, Requirements modeling: A knowledge representation approach to Software requirements definition, TR CSRG-155, U. Toronto 1984

25 B.Sheil, Power tools for programmers, Datamation, 131-144, 1983

26 P.Degano and E.Sandewall (Eds.), Integrated Interactive Computing Systems, North-Holland, 1983

27 R.S.Boyer and J S.Moore, A computational logic, Academic Press, New York, 1979

28 W.Polak, Program Verification at Stanford: Past, Present, Future, In: GWAI-81, Informatik-FB 47, Springer, Berlin, 1981

29 C.Green and T.T.Pressburger, CHI, Kestrel Institute, Palo Alto, CA

30 K.M.Hörnig, Can logical program synthesis cope with real life problems? Bericht ATP-11-XII-81, FGKI Inst. f. Informatik, TUM, 1981

31 W.G.Wilson and C.C.John, Semantic Code Analysis, IJCAI-83, 520-525, Kaufmann, Los Altos, 1983

*EIN JURISTISCHES EXPERTENSYSTEM
MIT NATÜRLICHSPRACHLICHEM DIALOG
- EIN PROJEKTBERICHT -*

Albrecht Blaser, Brigitte Alschwee,
Hein Lehmann, Hubert Lehmann,
Wolfgang Schönfeld
IBM Wissenschaftliches Zentrum
6900 Heidelberg

Zusammenfassung

Es wird der Entwurf eines Expertensystems vorgestellt, bei dem die natürliche Sprache sowohl für den Erwerb von Wissen als auch für den Dialog mit dem Benutzer bei Konsultationen verwendet wird. Für die Wissensrepräsentation wird die Diskursrepräsentationstheorie verwendet, eine Variante der Prädikatenlogik, die sich besonders für die systematische Übersetzung von Texten in logische Form eignet. Das Expertensystem wird gemeinsam von Wissenschaftlern der Universität Tübingen und des Wissenschaftlichen Zentrums der IBM Deutschland in Heidelberg entwickelt und soll in einem Bereich der Rechtswissenschaft, dem deutschen Straßenverkehrsstrafrecht, eingesetzt werden.

Einleitung

Expertensysteme sind Hilfsmittel für Experten eines Anwendungsbereichs. Ein wesentliches Problem bei der Konstruktion von Expertensystemen ist deshalb die Gestaltung des Dialogs mit den Anwendern des Systems, aber auch mit den Experten, die an der Erstellung der Wissensbasis mitwirken. Da die Anwender zwar Experten auf ihrem Gebiet, aber keine Computerwissenschaftler sind, entstehen häufig Barrieren, wenn eine Konsultation des Expertensystems nicht auf ähnliche Weise wie ein Fachgespräch mit einem Kollegen geführt werden kann. In solchen Fällen strebt man an, den Dialog mit dem Anwender in natürlicher Sprache zu führen. Der weitere Schritt zur interaktiven, teilweise automatischen Extraktion von Wissen aus Texten liegt dann für solche Anwendungen nahe, bei denen große Teile des Wissens in natürlichsprachlichen Texten vorliegen.

Beides setzt voraus, daß Expertensysteme eingegebene Texte analysieren, systematisch in eine formale Repräsentation übersetzen und als Wissen verwenden können. Ansätze hierzu scheiterten in der Vergangenheit vor allem am Fehlen ausgereifter Verfahren zum systematischen Übersetzen von Texten in eine geeignete Repräsentationssprache. Fortschritte verspricht hier die von Kamp (1981) eingeführte Diskursrepräsentationstheorie (DRT), die wir in einem Teilgebiet der Rechtswissenschaft, dem deutschen Straßenverkehrsstrafrecht, anwenden wollen, wo das Wissen im wesentlichen aus Gesetzen, Verordnungen, Kommentaren und Urteilen, die schriftlich niedergelegt sind, besteht.

Wir stellen hier das juristische Expertensystem vor, das seit einiger Zeit im Rahmen eines gemeinsamen Forschungsprojektes des Wissenschaftlichen Zentrums der IBM in Heidelberg und der Universität Tübingen entwickelt wird. Ziel des Projekts ist die Entwicklung des Prototyps eines Expertensystems für das Straßenverkehrsstrafrecht, mit dessen Hilfe Juristen, etwa Rechtsanwälte, ihre Klienten beraten und sich auch selbst über die bestehende Rechtsprechung informieren können. Der Dialog des Systems mit dem Juristen soll so weit wie möglich in natürlicher Sprache stattfinden. Ein großer Teil der Wissensbasis soll durch die Analyse von Gesetzen, Kommentaren und Gerichtsurteilen gewonnen werden. Überlegungen dazu, wie etwa Gerichtsurteile, die schriftlich vorliegen, halbautomatisch in die Wissensbasis integriert werden können, finden sich in Alschwee / Grundmann (1985).

Im folgenden wird zunächst anhand eines Beispiels beschrieben, wie ein Jurist einen Fall mit dem Expertensystem behandeln möchte. Aus der Vielzahl von Problemen, die beim Aufbau eines Expertensystems zu lösen sind, wollen wir danach zwei für unser Projekt besonders wichtige herausgreifen. Zunächst werden wir eine Einführung in die von uns gewählte *Wissensrepräsentationssprache* , die Diskursrepräsentationsstrukturen , und die Algorithmen zur Erzeugung dieser Strukturen aus natürlichsprachlichen Texten geben. Danach stellen wir das *Beweisverfahren* vor, das wir für die Verarbeitung der Diskursrepräsentationsstrukturen einsetzen wollen. Der folgende Abschnitt zeigt dann die *Architektur* des gesamten Systems und erläutert die Interaktion der Komponenten anhand des Beispiels aus dem ersten Abschnitt. Wir schließen mit einem Überblick über *Pläne und Stand des Projekts*.

Beispiel einer Fallbehandlung mit dem juristischen Expertensystem

Juristen soll das Expertensystem einerseits die Möglichkeit bieten, Fälle zu behandeln, d.h. Fragen zu konkreten Unfallbeschreibungen zu stellen. Das sind typischerweise Fragen nach Gesetzen, die auf den Fall anwendbar sind, und danach, ob der Beschuldigte einen bestimmten Paragraphen verletzt hat. Andererseits sollte das System auch in der

Lage sein, allgemeine Fragen der Juristen zu beantworten. Es sollte Texte von gespeicherten Gesetzen und Gerichtsurteilen anzeigen und auch Fragen zu den gespeicherten Regeln, wie etwa 'Muß jeder Unfallbeteiligte auf das Eintreffen der Polizei warten?' beantworten können.

Eine Konsultation zum §142 StGB (Unerlaubtes Entfernen vom Unfallort) könnte wie folgt ablaufen:

Jurist:

Der Beschuldigte fuhr in der Nacht zum 15.1.1985 in der Hauptstraße um 0.30 Uhr in ein am Straßenrand parkendes fremdes Fahrzeug, dessen Kotflügel dabei beschädigt wurde. Der Beschuldigte verließ die Unfallstelle sofort.

Hat der Beschuldigte den Tatbestand von §142 StGB erfüllt ?

System:

Entstand ein Sachschaden über 30 DM ?

Jurist:

Warum diese Frage ?

System:

Es ist zu klären, ob der Vorfall ein Unfall im Straßenverkehr ist. Er ist es nur, wenn ein Sachschaden von mehr als 30 DM oder ein nicht geringer Personenschaden entstand.

Jurist:

Der· Sachschaden betrug 200 DM.

System:

Waren feststellungsbereite Personen anwesend ?

Jurist:

Nein.

System:

Der Beschuldigte hat den Tatbestand von §142 erfüllt, denn:

1. Es liegt ein Unfall im Strassenverkehr vor.
2. Der Beschuldigte war Unfallbeteiligter.
3. Der Beschuldigte hat niemandem die Feststellungen ermöglicht.
4. Der Beschuldigte hat nicht eine angemessene Zeit an der Unfallstelle gewartet.

Der Jurist gibt die Fakten über den Unfall, die er für wichtig hält, sowie eine Frage in natürlicher Sprache ein. Das Expertensystem versucht, die Frage durch Anwendung seines Wissens zu beantworten. Dazu analysiert es Unfallbeschreibung und Frage und fügt diese mit Aussagen aus seiner Wissensbasis zu einer Argumentationskette zusammen.
Fehlen Fakten über den Unfall, so fragt das System den Juristen nach diesen Fakten. Der Jurist kann seinerseits fragen, warum das System diese Frage stellt und erhält

daraufhin eine Erklärung der bisher durchgeführten Schritte zur Beantwortung der Frage. Ist die Erklärung nicht ausreichend, so kann der Jurist zu einzelnen Unterpunkten nachfragen.
Ist die Antwort auf die Frage gefunden, so wird sie zusammen mit Erklärungen der wesentlichen Schritte ausgegeben. Der Jurist kann auch hier detailliertere Erklärungen zu einzelnen Unterpunkten anfordern. Danach kann er weitere Fragen zu dem Fall stellen oder die Fallbehandlung beenden.

Zufriedenstellende Techniken zur Implementierung eines Systems, das in der Lage ist, einen solchen Dialog zu führen, sind noch nicht verfügbar. In unserem Projekt arbeiten wir insbesondere an Lösungen für folgende Fragen:

1. Wie können Texte systematisch in eine formale Repräsentationssprache übersetzt werden?
2. Wie kann man einen "natürlichen" Dialog führen?
3. Wie kann das Wissen erworben und in der Wissensbasis dargestellt werden?
4. Wie kann man dieses Wissen anwenden?

Unsere Ansätze zur Lösung der beiden letzten Fragen werden wir in den folgenden Kapiteln vorstellen.

Darstellung und Erwerb des juristischen und sonstigen Wissens

Das juristische Wissen gliedert sich in 1. Gesetze, Verordnungen, 2. Kommentare, 3. Urteile, wobei Kommentare vor allem auf Urteilen gründen. Dieses Wissen muß bei der Behandlung von Fällen in unterschiedlicher Weise eingesetzt werden. Versuche, Aspekte des Rechts im Rahmen von Expertensystemen zu formalisieren, finden sich auch bei McCarty (1983), McCarty / Sridharan (1981), Fiedler (1966), Herberger / Simon (1980), Sergot (1980) und Stamper(1978).

Für das oben angegebene Fallbeispiel benötigen wir aus dem § 142 StGB die Sätze (1) und (4):

(1) Ein Unfallbeteiligter, der sich nach einem Unfall im Straßenverkehr entfernt, bevor er

1. zugunsten der anderen Unfallbeteiligten und der Geschädigten die Feststellung seiner Person, seines Fahrzeugs und der Art seiner Beteiligung durch

seine Anwesenheit und durch die Angabe, daß er an dem Unfall beteiligt ist, ermöglicht hat oder

2. eine nach den Umständen angemessene Zeit gewartet hat, ohne daß jemand bereit war, die Feststellungen zu treffen,

wird mit Freiheitsstrafe bis zu drei Jahren oder mit Geldstrafe bestraft.

(4) Unfallbeteiligter ist jeder, dessen Verhalten nach den Umständen zur Verursachung des Unfalls beigetragen haben kann.

Daneben ist eine Reihe weiterer Begriffe zu definieren, die in diesen Sätzen des Paragraphen vorausgesetzt werden und von denen unter anderem folgende in Kommentaren zu finden sind:

1. Ein Unfall im Straßenverkehr (Verkehrsunfall) ist ein plötzliches Ereignis, dessen Ursache Gefahren des Straßenverkehrs sind und das einen nennenswerten Schaden verursacht.
2. Gefahren des Straßenverkehrs sind Ereignisse, die auf einer öffentlichen Verkehrsfläche stattfinden.
3. Ein nennenswerter Schaden ist ein nicht belangloser Personenschaden oder ein Sachschaden über 30 DM.
4. Eine feststellungsbereite Person ist jemand, der bereit ist festzustellen, daß ein anderer an einem Unfall beteiligt ist, auch bereit ist, die Person dieses anderen und das in den Unfall verwickelte Fahrzeug festzustellen, und der diesem anderen nicht nahesteht.

In einem ersten Ansatz haben wir das notwendige Wissen in Form eines Prolog-Programms formalisiert. Die Ausdrucksmöglichkeiten von Prolog sind insofern beschränkt, als die Prolog-Regeln und -Fakten universelle Hornformeln sind. Umgekehrt kann man zeigen (vgl. Volger, 1985), daß nur universelle Horntheorien die folgende zentrale Eigenschaft von Prolog besitzen: Die durch das Prolog-Programm erzeugte (d.h. mit Hilfe der Prolog-Resolution definierte) deduktive Datenbank ist gerade das minimale Termmodell. Man kann zwar auch deduktive Kalküle für ausdrucksstärkere Formelklassen in Prolog simulieren, da Formelanalyse und Deduktionsverfahren in einem Prolog-Programm beschrieben werden können. Hierbei ergeben sich jedoch Laufzeitprobleme, da die Prolog-Resolution in vielfacher Weise eingeht.

Kamp hat 1981 eine Theorie der semantischen Diskursanalyse entwickelt, die die systematische Transformation von Texten in eine logische Struktur in Form von Bedingungen über Individuen erlaubt. Mit dieser Theorie können eine Reihe sprachlicher Probleme behandelt werden, die die linguistische Forschung seit langem beschäftigt haben, wie etwa die logisch adäquate Erfassung relativ komplizierter anaphorischer Beziehungen (cf. Guenthner / Lehmann, 1983). Ebenso ist es möglich, temporale Beziehungen sowie Ereignisstrukturen zu charakterisieren (cf. Partee, 1984).

Der zentrale Begriff der Diskursrepräsentationstheorie ist der der *Diskursrepräsentationsstruktur (DRS)*. Eine DRS für einen Text T ist ein Paar <U,Kon>, wobei Kon eine Menge von Bedingungen ist und U die Menge der vom Text eingeführten Individuen, der Diskursreferenten. Für diese sind mehrere Sorten vorgesehen, z.B. ui für Individuen, ei für Ereignisse, etc. Bedingungen sind

- atomar   Prädikat(t1,...,tn)
- konditional   (->,K1,K2)
- disjunktiv   (v,K1,K2)
- negativ   (¬,K1)

wobei t1,...,tn Terme sowie K1 und K2 DRSen sind.

Für die Erzeugung von DRSen aus Texten ist ein sogenannter *DRS-Konstruktionsalgorithmus* formuliert worden, der zu jeder syntaktischen Konstruktion angibt, wie die Übersetzung in DRSen aussieht. Eine Prolog-Implementierung für ein Fragment der deutschen Sprache ist in Kolb, 1985 beschrieben. Näheres zur automatischen Erzeugung von DRSen auf der Grundlage des User Speciality Languages (USL) Systems, einer natürlichsprachlichen Schnittstelle zu einer relationalen Datenbank, findet sich in (Guenthner / Lehmann, 1984) und ausführlicher in (Guenthner / Lehmann / Schönfeld, 1985), zu USL selbst in Ott / Zoeppritz (1979), Lehmann (1978 und 1980) und Zoeppritz (1984). Wir wollen die Erzeugung einer DRS anhand des Beispiels der folgenden Definition eines Unfalls erläutern (siehe Abb. 1):

Ein plötzliches Ereignis, dessen Ursache keine vorsätzliche Handlung ist und das einen Schaden verursacht, ist ein Unfall.

Der Übersetzung in die DRS liegen u.a. folgende Regeln zugrunde:

1. Nominalphrasen werden so analysiert, daß ein neuer, bisher nicht vorgekommener Diskursreferent einer passenden Sorte eingeführt wird. Dieser kann als eine existentiell quantifizierte Variable angesehen werden; es sei denn, er wird auf der linken Seite einer konditionalen Bedingung eingeführt. Dann ist der Diskursreferent als universell quantifiziert zu betrachten. Die Nomina *Ereignis,*

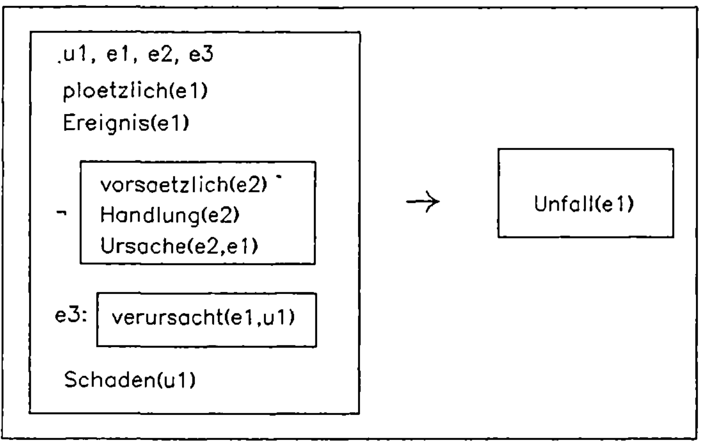

Abb. 1

Ursache, *Handlung*, *Unfall* werden als Prädikate dargestellt, die Ereignisse bezeichnen, *Schaden* als ein Prädikat, das für einen Zustand steht.

2. Attributive Adjektive wie *plötzlich* werden als Prädikate dargestellt mit dem Diskursreferenten des regierenden Nomens als Argument.

3. Die durch *kein* ausgedrückte Negation bewirkt die Negation der betreffenden DRS.

4. Relativsätze werden wie Hauptsätze analysiert, wobei das Relativpronomen durch den Diskursreferenten des regierenden Nomens ersetzt wird.

5. Verben, die Ereignisse wie *verursachen* ausdrücken, werden in eine eigene DRS eingebettet, die mit einer Ereignisreferenz versehen wird.

Um Texte in eine adäquate logische Form zu überführen, ist es zusätzlich notwendig, Hintergrundwissen zu verwenden, das insbesondere bei der Auflösung kontextueller Referenzen zum Tragen kommt. Im obigen Beispiel wäre es daneben sinnvoll, den Begriff *verursachen* durch *Ursache* zu ersetzen. Dazu braucht man eine Regel, die umgangssprachlich lauten müßte:

Wenn ein Ereignis etwas verursacht, dann ist es seine Ursache.

Dieses Hintergrundwissen setzt sich zusammen zum einen aus *Allgemeinwissen*, zum anderen aus *bereichsspezifischem* Wissen, d.h. in unserem Falle juristischem Wissen. Das hinzuzuziehende Allgemeinwissen ist teilweise reines Sprachwissen, zum Beispiel, daß ein Unfallort und eine Unfallstelle dasselbe sind, oder daß ein Unfallort der Ort ist, an dem ein Unfall stattgefunden hat. Davon zu unterscheiden ist Weltwissen: daß ein Ford Fiesta ein PKW ist, ein PKW ein Fahrzeug, ein Fahrzeug ein physisches Objekt, etc. Es würde hier zu weit führen, selbst für das obige einfache Beispiel alles in Frage kommende Wissen vollständig anzuführen, geschweige denn seine Formalisierung. Selbst wenn die Fragen der geeigneten Repräsentation des Wissens und seiner effizienten Speicherung befriedigend gelöst wären, müßte deshalb heute jeder Versuch, ein System zur vollautomatischen Analyse von Texten eines größeren Anwendungsbereichs zu realisieren, am fehlenden formalisierten Hintergrundwissen scheitern. Systeme mit überschaubarem Anwendungsbereich und interaktivem Wissenserwerb auch für das Hintergrundwissen werden aber schon bald zumindest prototypisch implementiert werden können. Dazu hoffen wir mit unserem Projekt beizutragen.

Das Beweisverfahren

Unter den vielen existierenden logischen Kalkülen eignen sich im wesentlichen nur zwei zur Automatisierung: Gentzen-Kalküle und Resolutionskalküle (s.a. Richter 1978). Das von uns entwickelte Beweisverfahren (korrekter eigentlich: Beweissuchverfahren) orientiert sich an einem speziellen Gentzen-Kalkül, dem Tableau-Kalkül (cf. Guenthner / Lehmann / Schönfeld 1985). Dies erscheint uns aus zwei Gründen sinnvoll. Einmal sind für Verfahren vom Gentzen-Typ am leichtesten die wichtigsten Eigenschaften *Korrektheit* und *Vollständigkeit* zu untersuchen (gerade dazu wurde der Tableau-Kalkül entwickelt). Des weiteren eignen sie sich, ganz im Gegensatz zu Verfahren vom Resolutions-Typ, zur Beantwortung von offenen Fragen: Im Fall der Nicht-Beweisbarkeit liefern sie brauchbare Information darüber, warum etwas nicht beweisbar ist. Da der Tableau-Kalkül aber nur *eine* spezielle (auch im täglichen Leben benutzte) Schlußweise widerspiegelt, muß man daran denken, andere Kalküle zu integrieren.

Das Beweisverfahren (mit der von uns vorerst gewählten Strategie) wird durch ein Anfrage des Benutzers an das System aktiviert, z.B. durch
   Hat der Beschuldigte den Tatbestand von §142 StGB erfüllt ?
Selbstverständlich arbeitet es nur mit der internen DRS-Darstellung. Der Verständlichkeit halber wird es hier aber mit natürlich-sprachlichen Formulierungen erläutert. Einen Überblick über die Vorgehensweise in diesem Beispiel gibt Abb. 2 unten. Der Ausgangspunkt für die Beantwortung der eingegebenen Frage ist:
   Ist es unter Einbeziehung des gesamten vorhandenen Wissens denkbar, daß er den Tatbestand nicht erfüllt hat? Oder führt diese Annahme in jedem Fall zu einem Widerspruch?
Das Beweisverfahren fügt also die Aussage

Der Beschuldigte hat den Tatbestand von §142 StGB nicht erfüllt.
vorübergehend zur Wissensbasis hinzu und schließt von ihr ausgehend weiter.

Hätte er den Tatbestand nicht erfüllt, so müßte aufgrund der Formulierung des Paragraphen eine der folgenden Aussagen gelten.
1. Es liegt kein Unfall vor.
2. Er ist an dem Unfall nicht beteiligt.
3. Er ist der einzige Unfallbeteiligte und der einzige Geschädigte.
4. Er hat die Feststellungen ermöglicht.
5. Er hat lange genug gewartet, weil keine feststellungsbereite Person anwesend war.
Diese Aussagen sind natürlich nicht als voneinander unabhängig zu betrachten. So meint z.B. 2.
2'. Es liegt zwar ein Unfall im Straßenverkehr vor,
     der Beschuldigte ist aber gar nicht daran beteiligt.
und
5'. Es war keiner da, dem gegenüber er hätte Feststellungen ermöglichen können.
     Er hat aber wenigstens lange genug gewartet.
Die Fälle können in der angegebenen Reihenfolge abgearbeitet werden. In einer ersten Version wird unser Beweisverfahren (genauso wie ein PROLOG-Interpretierer) dies tun. Beobachtungen der juristischen Praxis zeigen jedoch, daß der Rechtsanwalt meist nicht so 'schulmäßig' vorgeht, sondern intuitiv schneller zum Ziel führende Strategien anwendet. Wie dies im Rechner nachgespielt werden kann, ist noch Gegenstand weiterer Forschungen.

Im 1. Fall müßte aufgrund der Definition von 'Verkehrsunfall' gelten (alternativ):
1.1. Das Ereignis ist kein Unfall.
1.2. Es wurde nicht von Gefahren des Straßenverkehrs verursacht.
1.3. Es hatte keinen nennenswerten Schaden.
Man geht der Reihe nach vor. Liest man die Unfallbeschreibung genau, so stellt man bez. 1.1. fest, daß man das folgende Hintergrundwissen ausnützen kann:
     Heißt der Ort eines Ereignisses 'Unfallstelle', so ist das Ereignis ein Unfall.
Dies führt zu einem Widerspruch, der Ereignisort dürfte nicht 'Unfallstelle' heißen. Auch 1.2 führt zu einem Widerspruch, denn das Fahren auf der Hauptstraße hat die Kollision mit dem fremden Fahrzeug verursacht.

Dies kann hier leider nicht systematisch fortgeführt werden, da eine Fülle von Wissen über die Begriffe 'Fläche', 'Verkehr', 'öffentlich', 'fahren', 'verursachen' usw. benötigt wird. Dieses Wissen wird im Einzelfall auf ganz unterschiedliche Weise bereitgestellt. Für die zentralen Begriffe hat das System das gesamte erforderliche Hintergrundwissen von Anfang an zur Verfügung. Für alle Begriffe ist das aber nicht

zu erreichen (genauso wie beim Wissen über ein spezielles Unfallgeschehen, vgl. di
Bemerkungen zu 1.3.1. weiter unten). Also gibt das System dem Benutzer die
Möglichkeit, Wissen nachzuliefern. Das läuft einerseits auf eine Umformulierung der
anfänglich gegebenen Beschreibung, andererseits (für das System wegen möglicher Inkonsistenzen sehr viel kritischer) auf allgemeine Regeln zur Interpretation der verwendeten Begriffe hinaus. Inwieweit der Endbenutzer letzteres tun sollte, muß noch
geklärt werden.

Im Fall 1.3. müßte gelten (alternativ):

1.3.1. Es liegt überhaupt kein Schaden vor.

1.3.2. Es liegt ein belangloser Schaden vor,

   d.h. ein Sachschaden unter 30 DM oder geringer Personenschaden.

1.3.1. steht im Widerspruch zur Tatsache, daß der Kotflügel beschädigt wurde. (Eigentlich braucht man auch hier noch eine Hintergrundregel.) Zu 1.3.2. läßt sich kein
widersprechendes Faktum finden. Abb. 2 zeigt den jetzt erreichten Zustand der
Beweissuche in Form eines Tableau.

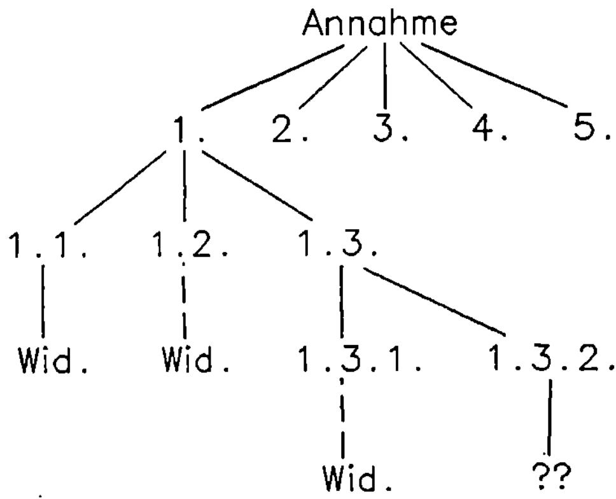

Abb. 2

Man könnte hier die Beweissuche beenden und ausgeben:

   Allein aufgrund der vorliegenden Tatsachen läßt sich kein Nachweis führen, daß der
   Tatbestand des §142(i) StGB erfüllt ist.

Als Begründung könnte das System eine Situation beschreiben, in der die o.a. Annahme
zutrifft, indem es die Aussagen 1., 1.3. und 1.3.2 auflistet. Das ist aber hier nicht
sinnvoll, denn die eingegebene Unfallbeschreibung ist ja mehr oder weniger zufällig
entstanden. Es könnte sein (und ist i.a. sehr wahrscheinlich), daß wesentliche Details
vergessen wurden. Diese nachzuliefern muß man dem Benutzer ermöglichen. Daher fragt
das System gemäß 1.3.2.:

War der Sachschaden über 30 DM ?

Mit dem dann vom Benutzer eingegebenen Wissen kann das Beweissuchverfahren weiter arbeiten. Nach einer Reihe von weiteren Schlüssen stellt es fest, daß alle Möglichkeiten, unter denen unsere Annahme wahr sein könnte, zum Widerspruch führen. Daher ist die Annahme zu verwerfen, und das System gibt aus:

Der Beschuldigte hat den Tatbestand von §142 erfüllt.

Damit ist das Prinzip einer Beweissuche vom Gentzen-Typ erklärt.

Mit der hier benutzten Strategie ist der Tableau-Kalkül eine echte Erweiterung von PROLOG, d.h. wenn das Beweisverfahren mit einer PROLOG-Wissensbasis und einer in PROLOG zulässigen Abfrage arbeitet, so arbeitet es genauso wie jeder PROLOG-Interpretierer. (Dies ist in Schönfeld (1985) ausgeführt.)

Es gibt dazu einige Variationen. Einmal ist es durchaus denkbar, daß man nicht mit der (als Annahme verneinten) Benutzerfrage anfängt, also nach 'backward chaining' verfährt, sondern von den Unfall-Fakten aus weiter schließt ('forward chaining'). Das ist vor allem dann sinnvoll, wenn das System Wissen über mehrere Tatbestände enthält, unter die der gegebene Sachverhalt subsumiert werden kann. Des weiteren kann man sich überlegen, ob man wirklich alle Teilfragen strikt der Reihenfolge nach abarbeiten will – vielleicht führt eine andere Reihenfolge schneller zum Ziel. Eine entsprechende Vorausschau könnte z.B. durch eine Heuristik geleistet werden, die aus der Konstellation der in der Unfallbeschreibung vorkommenden Begriffe einen Satz von dazu passenden Regeln auswählt. Es ist aber sehr schwierig zu entscheiden, ob sich eine solche Vorausschau lohnt. Viel wichtiger als dies ist unserer Ansicht nach, das Vorgehen bei der Suche nach einem formalen Beweis so auszulegen, daß es dem Benutzer als natürlich erscheint, er mitdenken kann. Wir glauben, daß das o.a. Beispiel zeigt, wie gut der Tableau-Kalkül diese Forderung erfüllt. (Vgl. auch Herberger / Simon 1980.)

Die Architektur des Systems

Abb. 3 zeigt die Komponenten des Expertensystems, deren Aufgaben und Zusammenwirken anschließend kurz erläutert werden.

Die Dialog-Komponente steuert den Dialog mit dem Benutzer. Zunächst gibt der Benutzer dem System bekannt, daß er einen neuen Fall behandeln möchte, und gibt dann die zugehörigen Fakten ein. Zu jeder Zeit kann er die Schilderung des Falles durch Fragen unterbrechen bzw. abschließen. Die eingegebenen Sätze werden an die Übersetzungskomponente zur Generierung von DRSen übergeben. Im Falle von Mehrdeutigkeiten erhält die Dialog-Komponente die für die entsprechenden Lesarten erzeugten DRSen, die zur

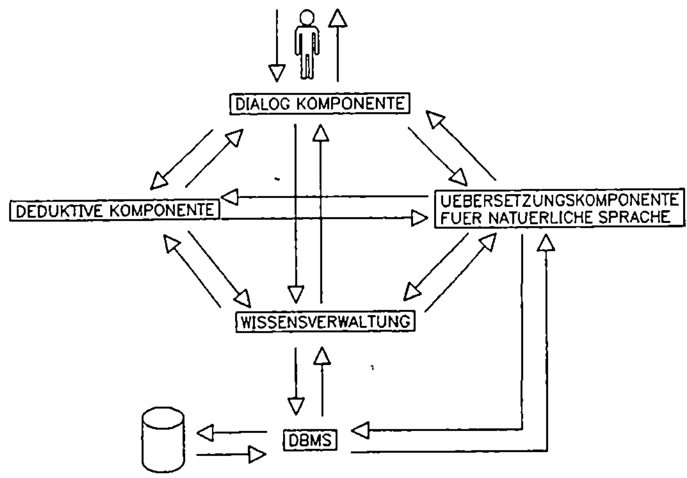

Abb. 3

Generierung einer Frage an den Benutzer dienen. Wenn kontextuelle Referenzen nicht aufgelöst werden können, werden dem Benutzer die entsprechenden Kandidaten im Eingabetext angezeigt.

Rückfragen des Benutzers auf Antworten des Systems werden durch die Erklärungskomponente, die Teil der Dialog-Komponente ist, behandelt. Zu ihrer Beantwortung benutzt die Erklärungskomponente den von der deduktiven Komponente erstellten Beweisbaum, Texte zu den darin vorkommenden DRSen sowie lexikalische und syntaktische Informationen.

Wenn Regeln automatisch aus natürlich-sprachlichen Texten erzeugt werden, sollten sinnvollerweise auch die Formulierungen für Fragen, Antworten und Erklärungen des Systems weitgehend automatisch generiert werden. Dabei ergeben sich eine Reihe von Problemen, die bisher noch nicht zufriedenstellend gelöst sind, z.B. die Generierung von Beschreibungen für Objekte, die keine Eigennamen haben. Es muß ein Verfahren entwickelt werden, um aus der Menge der Prädikate, die das Objekt beschreiben, ein Teilmenge auszuwählen, die das Objekt eindeutig beschreibt, möglichst redundanzfrei ist und das Objekt in "natürlicher" Weise benennt.

Die Übersetzungskomponente generiert aus den natürlichsprachlichen Benutzereingaben DRSen. Dabei wird die Benutzereingabe satzweise zunächst syntaktisch und semantisch analysiert. Die Komponenten zur syntaktischen und semantischen Analyse werden auf der Grundlage des USL-Systems implementiert. Die Syntaxanalyse wird ergänzt durch den Zugriff auf ein Lexikon, das in der Datenbank gespeichert ist. Das Lexikon umfaßt die

notwendigen morphologischen und syntaktischen Merkmale zu dem für die Anwendung benötigten Wortschatz (etwa 20.000 Wörter).
Nach der Syntaxanalyse wird eine sogenannte Zwischenstruktur erzeugt, auf die der DRS-Konstruktionsalgorithmus angewendet wird, wobei die entstehenden Bedingungen in die DRS des Textes eingebettet werden. Die Einbettung umfaßt die Auflösung der kontextuellen Referenzen sowie die zeitliche Einordnung in den Kontext. Dabei wird die deduktive Komponente benötigt, wenn semantische Kriterien herangezogen werden müssen (näheres hierzu siehe Guenthner / Lehmann 1983).

Die deduktive Komponente implementiert - wie im vorigen Abschnitt beschrieben - ein Beweisverfahren für DRSen, das auf dem Tableau-Kalkül aufbaut. Die abgeleiteten Fakten werden als Baum (Beweisbaum, Tableau) angeordnet, auf den auch andere Komponenten lesend zugreifen können. So würde es in unserem Beispiel nicht ausreichen, daß die deduktive Komponent nur 'ja' ausgibt. Vielmehr muß die Erklärungs-Komponente aus dem Beweisbaum eine sinnvolle Erklärung kontruieren, z.B. indem sie die Fakten der Tiefe 1 ausgibt (im vorigen Abschnitt die Aussagen 1.,...,5.). Es ist im allgemeinen noch offen, wie man sinnvolle Begründungen gibt. Erste Überlegungen dazu finden sich in Alschwee / Grundmann (1985).

Die Wissensbasis mit dem juristischen und Allgemeinwissen ist wie das Lexikon in der Datenbank gespeichert. Ihr Umfang, insbesondere aufgrund der Gerichtsurteile und der großen Mengen von Allgemeinwissen, das zum Verstehen von Unfallbeschreibungen notwendig ist, erlaubt es nicht, alle Regeln im Arbeitsspeicher zu halten. Als Datenbanksystem wird das relationale Datenbanksystem SQL/DS verwendet (cf. IBM, 1983). Sowohl die formale Repräsentation als auch die Texte des juristischen Wissens sind dort abgelegt. Alle Komponenten, außer der natürlichsprachlichen Analyse, die direkt das Lexikon abfragen kann, haben nur über die Wissensverwaltung dazu Zugriff.

Pläne und Stand des Projektes

Die Zusammenarbeit zwischen der Universität Tübingen und der IBM zur Durchführung dieses Projekts begann offiziell im Oktober 1984 und ist zunächst auf 3 Jahre befristet. Im gemeinsamen Projektteam sind die Fachrichtungen Computerlinguistik, Logik, Informatik und Rechtswissenschaften vertreten.

Die Aufbauphase diente der Etablierung der Zusammenarbeit und Definition der Projektpläne uud wurde im Frühjahr 85 mit der Spezifikation des geplanten Prototyps LEX1 abgeschlossen. Gleichzeitig wurde die Forschung auf verschiedenen Gebieten vorangetrieben und erste Ergebnisse wurden veröffentlicht.

In der laufenden Phase 1, die etwa ein Jahr dauern soll, wird ein erster Prototyp des juristischen Expertensystems implementiert werden. Da wir für die natürlichsprachliche Komponente Teile des existierenden USL-Prototyps verwenden können, da einige andere Teilkomponenten wie die DRS-Generierung, die halbautomatische Thesauruserweiterung oder die Dialogkontrolle schon kodiert sind und da wir als Implementierungssprache Prolog verwenden, glauben wir relativ schnell ein erstes lauffähiges System erstellen zu können. Seine linguistischen und juristischen Fähigkeiten werden allerdings sehr begrenzt sein. Wir werden uns beschränken auf die Behandlung von Fällen zum §142,1 StGB. Das Lexikon, die Grammatik, die Semantikroutinen und die Wissensbank sollen soweit ausgebaut sein, daß ein vorgegebener Korpus von Unfallbeschreibungen behandelt werden kann.

In der zweiten und vorläufig letzten geplanten Phase des Projekts soll dieser Prototyp zunächst an der Universität Tübingen ausgewertet werden. Die Ergebnisse dieses Tests und parallel dazu durchgeführter weiterer Forschung sollen dann Eingang finden in einen zweiten, wesentlich verbesserten Prototyp, der abschließend ebenfalls einer Auswertung unterzogen werden soll.

Wir versprechen uns von diesem Projekt u.a. die folgenden Ergebnisse:

- zunächst die beiden Prototypen, die aber nicht Selbstzweck sind, sondern in erster Linie dem Studium offener Probleme und hierfür entwickelter Lösungen dienen,
- die Entwicklung einer Wissensrepräsentationssprache, die besonders geeignet ist, Texte wiederzugeben,
- die Entwicklung von Algorithmen zur weitgehend automatischen Übersetzung von natürlichsprachlichen Texten in diese formale Sprache,
- die Entwicklung geeigneter Beweisverfahren,
- Verfahren zur halbautomatischen Erweiterung einer Wissensbank,
- Methoden zur Strukturierung und Verwaltung großer Wissensbanken,
- Aussagen über Formalisierbarkeit des Rechts,
- etc.

Einige Resultate liegen schon vor:

- Spezifikation, Grob-Design und Teile des Codes für den ersten Prototyp sind fertig (cf. Alschwee/Grundmann, 1985).
- Die Wissensrepräsentationssprache ist definiert (cf. Guenthner/Lehmann/Schönfeld, 1985), aber für notwendige Ergänzungen offen.
- Für ein Fragment der deutschen Sprache ist der Algorithmus zur systematischen Erzeugung der DRSen entwickelt (cf. Guenthner/Lehmann, 1983 und 1984).

- Das Beweissuchverfahren ist entworfen (cf. Schönfeld, 1985) und Teile davon sind implementiert.
- Möglichkeiten zur halbautomatischen Erweiterung des Thesaurus wurden vorgeschlagen und einige davon wurden implementiert (cf. Wirth, 1984).
- Ein in Prolog implementiertes Experimentiersystem zeigt am Beispiel des § 142,1 StGB, wie juristische Tatbestände formal repräsentiert werden können.

Wir gehen nicht davon aus, daß wir für alle Fragen komplette Antworten finden werden. Wir hoffen aber, weitere Fortschritte erzielen zu können. Sicher werden wir aber am Ende des Projekts die Chancen solcher Verfahren besser beurteilen können. Unsere Einschätzung heute ist, daß erfolgversprechende Ansätze vorhanden sind, daß aber viel Arbeit in den Aufbau von linguistischen und allgemeinen Wissensbanken gesteckt werden muß, bevor Expertensysteme mit natürlichsprachlichem Dialog und Wissenserwerb für den praktischen Einsatz in größerem Umfange implementiert werden können.

Literatur

* Alschwee, B., S. Grundmann (1985), "Systemdesign für ein computergestütztes juristisches Expertensystem", in: D. Fiedler, B. Traunmüller (Hrsg.), *Proc. GI Workshop "Formalisierung und formale Modelle im Recht"* , Schweizer, Bonn, München (erscheint).

* Fiedler, H. (1966), "Juristische Logik in mathematischer Sicht", in: *Archiv für Rechts- und Sozialphilosophie*, Bd. 52, S. 93.

* Guenthner, F., H. Lehmann (1983), "Rules for Pronominalization", *Proc. 1st Conference and Inaugural Meeting of the European Chapter of the ACL*, Pisa, 1983.

* Guenthner, F., H. Lehmann (1984), "Automatic Construction of Discourse Representation Structures", *Proc. COLING'84*, p. 398.

* Guenthner, F., H. Lehmann, W. Schönfeld (1985): "A Theory for the Representation of Knowledge", *IBM J. Res. Develop* (erscheint).

* Herberger, M., D. Simon (1980), *Wissenschaftstheorie für Juristen*, Metzner, Frankfurt.

* IBM (1983), *SQL/Data System General Information*, GH24-5013, IBM Corp., Endicott, USA

* Kamp, H. (1981), "A Theory of Truth and Semantic Representation", in Groenendijk, J. et al. *Formal Methods in the Study of Language*, MC TRACT 135, Univ. Amsterdam.

* Kolb, H.-P. (1985), "Aspekte der Implementation von DRT". Magisterarbeit Univ. Tübingen, FNS Skript 85-1, Forschungsstelle für natürlich-sprachliche Systeme, Tübingen.

* Lehmann, H. (1978), "Interpretation of Natural Language in an Information System", *IBM J. Res. Develop*, vol. 22, p. 533.

* Lehmann, H. (1980), "A System for Answering Questions in German", Vortrag bei 6th International Symposium of the ALLC, Cambridge, England.

* McCarty, L. T. (1983), "Permissions and Obligations", *Proc. 8th IJCAI*, p. 287.

* McCarty, L. T., N. S. Sridharan (1981), "A Computational Theory of Legal Argument", Manuskript.

* Ott, N., M. Zoeppritz (1979), "USL - an Experimental Information System Based on Natural Language", in L. Bolc (ed): *Natural Language Based Computer Systems*, Hanser, München.

* Partee, B. H. (1984), "Nominal and Temporal Anaphora", *Linguistics and Philosophy*, vol. 7, p. 243.

* Richter M. (1978), *Logikkalküle*, Teubner Studienbücher Informatik, Stuttgart.

* Schönfeld, W. (1985), "PROLOG Extensions Based on Tableau Calculus", *Proceedings IJCAI'85*, International Joint Conferences on Artificial Intelligence, Inc., (erscheint).

* Sergot, M. (1980), "Programming Law: LEGOL as a Logic Programming Language", Dept. of Computing and Control, Imperial College, London.

* Stamper, R. (1978), "Towards a Semantic Model for the Analysis of Legislation", A. Martino, E. Maretti, C. Ciampi (eds.): *Informatica e Diritto, Anno IV*, Le Monnier, Florenz.

* Volger, H. (1985), "On Theories which Admit Initial Structures", FNS-Bericht 85-1, Forschungsstelle für natürlich-sprachliche Systeme, Tübingen.

* Wirth, R. (1984), "Halbautomatische Erweiterung eines bestehenden Thesaurus", Diplomarbeit, Univ. Heidelberg/FHS Heilbronn.

* Zoeppritz, M. (1984), *Syntax for German in the User Specialty Languages System*, Niemeyer, Tübingen.

Rechnergestützte Systeme für den Programmentwurf[*]

Manfred Broy
Fakultät für Mathematik und Informatik
Universität Passau
Postfach 2540
839 Passau

Zusammenfassung

Der Entwurf von Programmen entspricht in weiten Teilen der Modellierung und
Deduktion in formalen Kalkülen. Sowohl die Programmfragmente, als auch die
Umformungsregeln können als formale Objekte verstanden werden. Damit sind
sie formaler (deduktiver) Manipulation zugänglich, die durch rechnergestützte
Systeme unterstützt werden kann. Konzeption, Einsatzmöglichkeiten und die
Leistungsfähigkeit rechnergestützter Systeme für den Programmentwurf
werden diskutiert.

1. Einleitung

Der Entwurf von Programmsystemen, von der Erarbeitung der Anforderungen, über die
Validierung, die Konzeption der Lösungen und die Wahl der konkreten Algorithmen und
Repräsentationen der Datenstrukturen bis hin zur Codierung, Optimierung und
Systempflege, stellt eine komplexe Aufgabe dar. Es ist naheliegend, diese Aufgabe einer
Rechnerunterstützung zugängig zu machen.

Dies erfordert allerdings eine genaue Einsicht in und ein volles Verständnis für den
Programmentwurfsprozeß: Die Gestaltung eines Systems für den rechnergestützten
Entwurf von Programmen muß selbst auch den klassischen Prinzipien des
Programmentwurfs folgen.

So besteht der erste Schritt bei der Gestaltung eines solchen Systems in einer genauen
Erarbeitung der Anforderungen an ein rechnergestütztes System für den
Programmentwurf. Wichtig sind dabei die speziellen Motivationen und Zielvorgaben für
die Einbeziehung von Rechnerunterstützung. Entscheidende Gründe für einen Einsatz von
Rechnerunterstützung können sein:

- die Verbesserung der Zuverlässigkeit und Erhöhung der Standards,

- die Steigerung der Programmiereffizienz.

---

* Diese Arbeit entstand teilweise im Rahmen des Sonderforschungsbereich 49,
Programmiertechnik und der ESPRIT Projekte Meteor und Prospectra

Diese Ziele scheinen auf den ersten Blick in einem gewissen Gegensatz zu sein: Zur Steigerung der Zuverlässigkeit und der Standards ist im allgemeinen ein erhöhter Aufwand zu treiben, was im Gegensatz zur Programmiereffizienz zu stehen scheint. Hier ist jedoch zu beachten, daß eine Erhöhung der Zuverlässigkeit gleichzeitig eine Verringerung des Aufwands bei der Wartung und Fehlerbeseitigung bedeutet. Darüberhinaus kann man auch auf Effizienzsteigerung durch verstärkte Wiederverwendung von Entwurfsarbeit hoffen.

Die allgemeinen Ziele der Steigerung von Zuverlässigkeit und Programmiereffizienz können beim Einsatz von Systemen für den rechnergestützten Programmentwurf in folgender Weise spezifisch unterstützt werden: Eine Rechnerunterstützung erlaubt den konsequenteren Einsatz von fortgeschrittenen Methoden des Programmentwurfs (einschließlich einer besseren Dokumentation) kann eine Reihe trivialer, bei manuellem Arbeiten auftretenden Fehler vermeiden helfen und durch die Automatisierung einer Reihe einfacher, aber arbeitsintensiver Tätigkeiten auch den Zeitaufwand des Programmentwicklers reduzieren.

Dabei ist insbesondere zu klären, welche Schritte der Programmerstellung in welcher Form unterstützt werden sollen. Im folgenden diskutieren wir zuerst einige allgemeinen Aspekte der Rechnerunterstützung des Programmentwurfsprozesses und wenden uns dann der Frage zu, in welcher Weise jeweils die einzelnen Phasen des Programmentwurfsprozesses unterstützt werden können. Bewußt verzichten wir hier vollständig darauf auf die Vielzahl der bereits existierenden Einzelwerkzeuge einzugehen (hierfür sei auf [ER 85] verwiesen) und konzentrieren uns auf Fragen der Konzeption und Integration.

2. Aspekte rechnergestützter Programmiersysteme

Beim Entwurf von rechnergestützten Programmentwurfssystemen sind natürlich die allgemeinen Prinzipien für die Gestaltung und Konstruktion dialogorientierter Systeme gültig. Darüberhinaus sind jedoch noch eine Reihe spezifischer Punkte zu beachten. Wir behandeln im weiteren weniger Fragen der Unterstützung des Softwareprojektmanagements oder spezielle Implementierungstechniken, sondern konzentrieren uns stärker auf die qualitativen programmiertechnischen Aspekte des rechnergestützten Programmentwurfs.

2.1 Benutzerschnittstelle

Da der Programmentwurf eine komplexe Tätigkeit darstellt, ist es um so wichtiger, dem Programmentwickler eine Benutzerschnittstelle anzubieten, die ihn von allen unnötigen Schwierigkeiten und zusätzlichen Belastungen freihält und es ihm gestattet, sich voll auf die Entwicklungsaufgabe zu konzentrieren. Dies betrifft die ergonomische Ausgestaltung der Benutzschnittstelle im physischen Bereich wie Bildschirm, Tastatur, Maus etc. Dies betrifft aber auch die Ausgestaltung der konzeptionellen Bereiche der Benutzerschnittstelle wie Graphik, Fenstertechniken und spezielle Systemfunktionen für die Gewinnung von Informationen aus dem System.

Grundsätzlich ist zu betonen, daß alle bekannten Prinzipien für die Ausgestaltung einer

Dialogschnittstelle auch und insbesondere hier gelten (vgl. [Nievergelt 83]), daß aber der Verzahnung von speziellen Systemfunktionen mit einer komfortablen Benutzeroberfläche besondere Bedeutung zukommt.

2.2 Verwaltung der Informationseinheiten

In einem System für die die rechnerunterstützte Programmierung fallen eine Vielzahl von verschiedenartigen Informationseinheiten an, die im System gehalten werden müssen und auf die nach sehr spezifischen Gesichtspunkten zugegriffen wird. Dies erfordert die Verwaltung einer Datenbank, die allerdings in einer sehr spezifischen Weise organisiert sein sollte, um dem Programmentwickler in möglichst guter Weise über den jeweiligen Stand der Entwicklung und die weiteren möglichen Entwicklungsschritte informieren zu können.

Dabei ist zu beachten, daß neben Daten für das Projektmanagement, der Versionsverwaltung, Projektbibliotheken etc. auch Programmierregeln und -methoden abgespeichert werden müssen. Hier ist eine Unterstützung des Benutzers bei der Auswahl der Regeln und Methoden besonders wichtig.

2.3 Einbeziehung von Programmiermethoden

Es gibt Bestrebungen, rechnergestützte Systeme für den Programmentwurf unabhängig von bestimmten Programmentwurfsmethoden und Programmiersprachen zu halten. Dies scheint primär auch durch die kommerzielle Überlegung motiviert zu sein, die Einsatzmöglichkeiten eines System möglichst breit zu halten. Umgekehrt kann jedoch nur eine möglichst weitgehende Einbeziehung von Methoden in ein System eine spezifische Unterstützung auch des Einsatzes der Methoden umfassend gewährleisten.

Dieser Konflikt zwischen universellen Einsatzmöglichkeiten und methodikspezifischer Unterstützung läßt sich lösen, indem man zwischen der Bereitstellung einer Schnittstelle und einer Reihe allgemeiner, für die rechnerunterstützte Programmentwicklung typischerweise benötigter Systemfunktionen zum einen, und der Ausgestaltung eines solchen Systemrahmens im Sinn einer Programmiermethodik und spezieller Programmiersprachen zum anderen unterscheidet. Man unterscheidet also einen Systemkern für ein rechnergestütztes Programmiersystem, und dessen Erweiterung im Sinn gewisser Programmiermethoden.

Hierbei ist es wichtig, noch einmal zu betonen, daß ein Systemkern selbst, auch wenn er eine Vielzahl von Werkzeugen vorsieht, noch nicht ausreicht, ein effektiv einsetzbares Werkzeug für den Programmentwurf zu schaffen. Erst die Integration der Werkzeuge im Sinn einer Programmiermethode schafft ein durchgängiges Instrument.

Nicht jede Programmiermethode ist in der gleichen Weise für den Einsatz in rechnergestützten Systemen geignet. Viele der gebräuchlichen Programmiermethoden müssen dazu noch weiterentwickelt werden und an die Erfordernisse eines rechnergestützten Einsatzes angepaßt werden. Eine besondere Bedeutung kommt hier einmal der Formalisierung zu.

2.4 Einbeziehung von Sprachen

Sollen sich Programmierumgebungen an bestimmten Programmiersprachen orientieren? Dies hängt natürlich von der Funktion ab, die man rechnergestützten Systemen für den Programmentwurf zuordnet. Will man im System entwickeln, unter Einschluß der Codierungsphase, bis eine lauffähige Programmeinheit vorliegt, so ist es sicher erforderlich, bestimmte Programmiersprachen konkret mit in das System einzubeziehen. Sei es durch Einbeziehung von Programmen, die die systemspezifische Darstellung in die gewünschte Programmiersprache umsetzen, sei es durch die explizite Entwicklung der Programme in der spezifischen Programmiersprache.

In jedem Fall es natürlich wünschenswert, daß auch die Umsetzung in lauffähige Programmsysteme noch mit Systemunterstützung vorgenommen wird. Geschieht dies nicht und müssen in dieser Phase noch im größeren Umfang manuelle Arbeiten ausgeführt werden, so gehen entscheidende Vorteile rechnergestüzter Programmentwicklung verloren. Darüberhinaus stellt sich ohnehin die Frage nach der adäquaten externen (Benutzer-orientierten) Repräsentation der im System gespeicherten Programmeinheiten. Der Programmentwickler benötigt solch eine externe Repräsentation (oder gar mehrere externe Repräsentationen, die unterschiedliche Sichten erlauben) für die interaktive Entwicklung. Viele der gängigen Programmiersprachen sind weder von ihrer Lesbarkeit, noch von ihren semantischen Eigenschaften besonders gut für diesen Zweck geeignet.

2.5 Formen der Unterstützung des Programmentwurfs

Rechnergestützte Systeme können den Programmentwurf in folgenderen Bereichen unterstützen:

- Dokumentation und Versionsverwaltung (Projektmanagement)

- Syntaktische Überprüfungen (z.B. der Schnittstellen von Modulen)

- Konsistenzüberprüfungen

- Anwendung von Entwicklungsregeln im Dialog (einschl. Verifikationsregeln)

- Interpretations- und Analysehilfen (einschl. Testhilfen)

- Entscheidungsunterstützung

- Automatische Durchführung gewisser Entwurfsschritte

Man beachte, daß die Liste der aufgeführten Bereiche gewissermaßen von relativ einfachen, primär syntaktischen, in vielen existierenden Systemen bereits realisierten Unterstützungsmöglichkeiten zu immer komplexeren, im Augenblick weniger oder noch garnicht beherrschten Bereichen der rechnerunterstützten Programmentwicklung übergeht.

2.6 Die Bedeutung von Formalisierung

Programmentwicklung bedeutet immer Modellierung und letztendlich Modellierung in einem formalen Modell. Die Erstellung von Programmen in "maschinennaher" oder doch zumindest effizienzorientierter Form (z.B. unter Verwendung von Geflechtstrukturen und selektiven, destruktiven Zuweisungen) stellt auch eine formale (wenn auch maschinennahe) Modellierung dar. Allerdings sind hier die grundlegenden Modellstrukturen eines Programmsystems allgemein durch die Fülle der Implementierungsdetails schwer zu isolieren.

Für einige Programmentwickler in der Praxis stellen "formale Methoden" Reizworte dar. Andere trivialisieren den Einsatz formaler Methoden auf eine rein syntaktische Ebene, z.B. auf die Verwendung formaler Sprachen, d.h. auf die Definition der syntaktischen Eigenschaften von Schnittstellen. Ein typisches Beispiel stellt die Definition der sogenannten "Packages" in der Programmiersprache Ada dar. In den sichtbaren Teilen werden nur Namen und Funktionalitäten der verwendeten Sorten und Operationen aufgelistet. Eine Beschreibung der Semantik unterbleibt völlig. Aber nur wenn auch die Semantik der Operationen in irgendeiner Form formal beschrieben ist, können rechnergestützte Systeme auch in diesem Bereich Hilfestellungen geben.

Es ist sicher wichtig zu betonen, daß Formalisierung für die Programmentwicklung nie einen Wert an sich darstellt. Vielmehr ist eine Formalisierung nur soweit von Bedeutung, wie sie für die weitere Durchführung der Programmentwicklungsaufgabe notwendig ist, oder für deren methodische Unterstützung.

Als Faktoren für den Grad der Formalisierung sind insbesondere Verfügbarkeit und Entwicklungsstand von Methoden und der Ausbildungsstand des Entwicklungsteams von Bedeutung. Es ist zu erwarten, daß Programmierer erst durch ausreichende Rechnerunterstützung mit einer Reihe fortgeschrittener Programmiermethoden in Berührung kommen werden, bzw. erst dadurch der Einsatz dieser Methoden praktisch möglich wird.

In diesem Zusammenhang ist es sicher nötig, auch kurz die Frage der Einbeziehung natürlicher Sprache zu diskutieren. Häufig hört man die Äußerung, daß eine Beschreibung in natürlicher Sprache völlig ausreichend für die Spezifikation sei. Dies mag stimmen, soweit man die Rolle von Spezifikationen auf die reine Wiedergabe der Anforderungen beschränkt sieht, obwohl auch hier Zweifel anzumelden sind, ob die Präzision der Sprache ausreicht. Versteht man jedoch Spezifikationen als zentralen Bestandteil in der Programmentwicklung, wichtig für die Validierung, die Konstruktion einer Entwurfsspezifikation bis hin zur Verifikation und Dokumentation, so wird der Wert formaler Spezifikation deutlich.

Manchmal wird die Hoffnung geäußert, daß es auch möglich werden könnte, in natürlicher Sprache abgfaßte semantische Charakterisierungen maschinell zu behandeln. Soll natürliche Sprache in einem rechnergestützten System eingesetzt werden, und sollen auch semantische Inhalte analysiert und manipuliert werden, so bedeutet das stets eine Formalisierung der natürlichen Sprache. Damit wird die natürliche Sprache zur formalen Sprache gemacht, die lediglich syntaktisch mit einer Teilmenge der natürlichen Sprache übereinstimmt. Die große Stärke natürlicher Sprache für die menschliche Verständigung, das Zulassen von Mehrdeutigkeiten und intuitivem Verständnis geht hierbei zwangsläufig weitgehend verloren.

2.7 Dokumentation und Unterstützung von Entwurfsentscheidungen

Die Durchführung einer Programmentwicklung umfaßt eine Vielzahl von Entwurfsentscheidungen. Dies beginnt bei der Erarbeitung der Anforderungsspezifikation, geht weiter bei der Erstellung der Entwurfsspezifkation und setzt sich fort in den implementierungsspezifischen Entscheidungen bei der Wahl der Algorithmen und der Repräsentation der Datenstrukturen. Naturgemäß müssen viele dieser Entscheidungen vom Programmentwickler getroffen werden und können nicht vom System übernommen werden.

Besonders wichtig ist dabei eine adäquate Aufbereitung und Darstellung der im Entwicklungssystem vorhandenen Information, so daß der Programmentwickler eine möglichst umfassende Sicht und Einsicht in den Stand der Programmentwicklung erhält. Dabei sind Methoden für die graphische Aufbereitung von besonderer Bedeutung.

2.8 Bedeutung von Regeln

Soll das Programmunterstützungssystem mehr sein als eine Mischung aus Dokumentationssystem und Textverarbeitungssystem, d.h. soll die Programmentwicklung qualifiziert auch im Bereich des Schließens über Programmeigenschaften und der Weiterentwicklung und Modifikation von Programm(teil)en unterstützt werden, so ist die Einbeziehung semantischer Information unumgänglich. Dies gilt gleichermaßen für Systemprogramme, die Programmteile als Eingabe erhalten und bearbeiten (Interpreter, symbolische Auswerter), wie für stärker regelorientierte Ansätze. Insbesondere die Einbeziehung regelhafter Information, das Sammeln, Speichern, Anwenden, Verifizieren und Klassifizieren von Regeln ist für leistungsfähige Programmentwicklungssysteme entscheidend.

2.9 Weiterentwicklung des Systems

Ein Programmentwicklungssystem kann nur dann ein flexibles Instrument in der Hand eines Systementwicklers darstellen, wenn es auch möglich ist, das Unterstützungssystem weiterzuentwickeln, und den speziellen Anwendungssituationen anzupassen. Dies kann erfolgen durch die Eingabe neuer anwendungsspezifischer Entwichlungsregeln ins System, bis hin zur Definition neuer spezifischer Entwicklungsunterstützungsprozeduren.

2.10 Grenzen der Automatisierung

Es ist äußerst schwierig, die Grenzen der Möglichkeiten für Automatisierung des Programmentwicklungsprozesses auszuloten. Es liegt auf der Hand, daß gewisse Grenzen durch die Grenzen der Berechenbarkeit bzw. der Entscheidbarkeit feststehen. Weitere, vielleicht entscheidendere Grenzen ergeben sich aus komplexitätstheoretischen Betrachtungen. Sind viele Ableitungen im Prinzip automatisch möglich, so ist sicher oft die kombinatorische Vielfalt der zu verwendenden Kalküle häufig so hoch, daß dies praktisch unmöglich ist.

Zusätzlich stellt die effizienzspezifische Bewertung von Programmversionen ein weitgehend ungelöstes Problem dar: Selbst wenn die Ableitung einer hocheffizienten Programmversion automatisch möglich wäre, um diese Programmversion als (im Gegensatz zu anderen) besonders effizient zu erkennen, wäre eine automatische Bewertung des Effizienzverhaltens von Programmen nötig. Dies stößt wieder an Grenzen der Berechenbarkeit und ist auch in einer mehr pragmatischen Form nach heutigem Stand des Wissens in absehbarer Zeit nicht automatisch möglich.

3. Phasen des Programmentwurfs

Wie bereits mehrfach angedeutet, erfolgt der Programmentwurf in Phasen. Dabei ist zu fragen, in welcher Form die einzelnen Phasen des Programmentwurfs unterstützt werden können. Wir wollen im einzelnen folgende Phasen unterscheiden:

- Erarbeitung der Anforderungsbeschreibung (Requirement Engineering)

- Validierung (durch schnelle Prototyperstellung)

- Systementwurf (Strukturierung und Dekomposition)

- Systemimplementierung

- Adaption und Optimierung

- Wartung und Weiterentwicklung

Diese Aufteilung in Phasen findet sich in vielen Ansätzen von Programmiermethoden in gewissen Variationen. In der Praxis sind diese einzelnen Phasen allgemein nicht klar getrennt. Insbesondere können in gewissen Entwicklungsstadien unterschiedliche Systemkomponenten zur gleichen Zeit in verschiedenen Phasen sein. Man beachte, daß hier bewußt die Validierungsphase sehr früh angesetzt ist. Erfolgt der Übergang zu einer formalsierten Fassung bereits in der Anforderungsbeschreibung, und kann diese durch Prototypen illustriert werden, so kann bereits auf dieser Ebene eine Validierung erfolgen.

Für ein rechnergestütztes System für die Programmentwicklung ist es wichtig, nicht nur die einzelnen Phasen zu unterstützen, sondern auch die Übergänge zwischen den Phasen. Das generelle Ziel ist die Schaffung eines kohärenten formalen Rahmens. Dies ist entscheidend für die Flexibilität der Vorgehensweise.

3.1 Erarbeitung der Anforderungen

Der Übergang von informellen Beschreibungen und Vorstellungen zu einer formalen Modellbildung und Beschreibung stellt einen der entscheidenden Schritte, wenn nicht den entscheidenden Schritt in der Programmentwicklung dar. In der heutigen Praxis wird dieser Schritt relativ spät vorgenommen. Häufig erfolgt eine endgültige Formalisierung erst durch die Codierung. Vielfach setzt sich aber heute die Überzeugung durch, daß dieser Schritt in einer erheblich früheren Phase auf einer bedeutend abstrakteren Ebene vollzogen werden sollte.

Die Erarbeitung der Anforderungen stellt nämlich insoweit einen besonders kritischen Schritt dar, als in diesem Schritt im allgemeinen nicht nur die informell beim Benutzer bereits dezidiert vorhandenen Vorstellungen vollständig erfaßt werden, sondern in weiten Bereichen diese Vorstellungen erst entwickelt werden müssen. Dies beinhaltet eine Vielzahl weitreichender Entscheidungen, deren Konsequenzen im ersten Augenblick nur unvollständig oder garnicht erkannt werden.

3.2 Validierung

Jene Phase der Programmentwicklung, in der von einer informellen, verbalen Beschreibung zu einer formalen Beschreibung übergegangen wird, ist also besonders entscheidend. Hier werden Mißverständnisse, Unzulänglichkeiten, Unvollständigkeiten und Inkonsistenzen der Anforderungsbeschreibung entweder entdeckt und beseitigt, oder sie bleiben bestehen und wirken sich später verheerend aus.

Was kann nun die Rechnerunterstützung in dieser ersten wichtigen Phase des Programmentwurfs an Hilfestellung geben? In jedem Fall können Systeme Dokumentationshilfen anbieten. Sie können gewisse syntaktische Eigenschaften überprüfen. Aber was ist darüber hinaus möglich.

An der Nahtstelle zwischen informeller Beschreibung und formaler Beschreibung ist jede (im engeren Sinn) formale Behandlung naturgemäß ausgeschlossen. Trotzdem kann durch die Formalisierung eine besondere Hilfestellung gegeben werden: Ist nämlich die formale Spezifikation von einer Form, die eine automatische Auswertung unmittelbar oder doch nach geringfügigen Änderungen gestattet, so kann durch die so erreichte schnelle Erstellung eines (wenn auch äußerst ineffizienten) Prototyps die Validierungsphase effektiv unterstützt werden (vgl. [Hussmann 85]).

3.3 Systementwurf (Strukturierung und Dekomposition)

Die Erarbeitung eines Systementwurfs aus einer Anforderungsspezifikation kann in vielfältiger Weise durch Rechner im Dialog unterstützt werden. Viele der anfallenden Schritte sind schematisch, bedeuten die Anwendung gewisser Regeln und Schemata.

So kann beispielsweise die Dekomposition der Anforderungsspezifikation in Modulspezifikationen unterstützt werden. In vielen Fällen können aus der Anforderungsspezifikation Teile der Schnittstellenbeschreibungen für die Subkomponenten automatisch generiert werden.

Weiter können gewisse zustandsorientierte oder auch kontrollflußorientierte Systementwurfsspezifikationen systematisch, das heißt durch Anwendung von Regeln und Schemata oder gar von Umsetzungsprogrammen aus den Anforderungsbeschreibungen gewonnen werden.

3.4 Systemimplementierung

Eine Systemimplementierung besteht in der Wahl der Repräsentationen für die einzelnen Rechenstrukturen und in der Wahl der Algorithmen zur Berechnung der zu implementierenden Funktionen auf den Repräsentationen. Hier kann die Systemunterstützung eine Familie von Standardimplementierungen bereitstellen. Zusätzlich kann das System Hilfestellungen für die Konstruktion und Verifikation von

Implementierungen anbieten.

Analoges gilt für die Konstruktion von Algorithmen für spezifizierte Systemfunktionen. Je abstrakterer und allgemeinerer algorithmische Prinzipien in Regeln zu repräsentiert werden können, um so effektiver kann die Systemunterstützung in dieser Phase sein.

3.5 Adaption und Optimierung

Auch Optimierungsschritte und Adptionsschritte können in ähnlicher Weise wie eben angedeutet unterstützt werden. Hier ist jedoch noch eine stärkere Einbeziehung halb- und vollautomatischer Optimierungs- und Umsetzungsverfahren, wie man sie auch in optimierenden Übersetzern findet, denkbar.

Es ist jedoch wünschenswert, daß der Programmentwickler die Anwendung solcher Optimierungsübergänge genau kontrollieren kann. Dazu gehört, daß er die optimierten Fassungen gegebenenfalls überprüfen und im Dialog nachverbessern kann. Dies erfordert eine benutzerfreundliche externe Repräsentationsmöglichkeit auch für optimierte Programmversionen.

3.6 Wartung und Weiterentwicklung

Archiviert man zu einem entwickelten Programmsystem die wichtigsten Zwischenversionen der Entwicklungsgeschichte, so können nach Bedarf daraus neue Versionen erzeugt werden. Insbesondere können gewisse Entwurfsentscheidungen revidiert werden, es kann auf abstraktere Systemversionen zurückgesetzt werden, und neue Entwicklungslinien können verfolgt werden. Darüberhinaus ergeben die Zwischenversionen wichtige Bestandteile der Programmdokumentation.

Nachdem wir die wichtigsten Aspekte von Systemen für die rechnergestützte Programmentwicklung in ihren Grundzügen grob beschrieben haben, wollen wir abschließend kurz skizzieren, wie ein System, das zumindest einen Teil der beschriebenen Anforderungen erfüllt, konzeptionell aussehen könnte.

4. Ein integriertes System zur Programmentwicklung

Mit der Untersuchung und der Konstruktion von Kalkülen für die Programmentwicklung und ihrer Integration in ein System für den rechnergestützten Programmentwurf beschäftigt sich mittlerweile seit etwa 10 Jahren das Projekt CIP (Computer-aided Intuition-guided Programming, vgl. [CIP-L 85]) an der Technischen Universität München und seit kurzem auch an der Universität Passau.

Für das Projekt CIP stand und steht die Integration aller Phasen des Programmentwurfs speziell im Vordergrund. Dies schließt die verwendete Programmiersprache ein. Konsequenterweise wurde deshalb eine auf alle Phasen der Programmentwicklung eingerichtete Sprache, eine sogenannte Breitbandsprache, im Rahmen des Projekts entworfen, da sich existierende Programmiersprachen als für den Zweck nicht besonders geeignet erwiesen haben.

Im folgenden wird kurz der im Projekt CIP verfolgten Ansatz für ein rechnergestütztes

Programmentwicklungssystem beschrieben. Weite Teile der beschriebenen Unterstützungsmöglichkeit sind in Prototypversionen implementiert und befinden sich in der Erprobungsphase.

Unterstützung der Erarbeitung der Anforderungsspezifikation: In der ersten Phase einer Programmentwicklung ist eine Anforderungsbeschreibung zu erarbeiten. Prinzipien von Anforderungsbeschreibungen sind: Präzision, Abstraktheit und Lesbarkeit. Die Sprache CIP-L enthält für die Formulierung von Spezifikationen und von dokumentierenden Annotationen folgende Spezifikationskonzepte: Hierarchische abstrakte algebraisch spezifizierte Datentypen unter Einbeziehung von partiellen Funktionen und (rekursiver) Artvereinbarungen, prädikatenlogische Konstrukte der Logik erster Ordnung unter Einbeziehung von Kennzeichnungs- und Auswahloperator und Formalismen der Mengenlehre.

Insbesondere stehen eine Reihe von vordefinierten generischen algebraischen Spezifikationen zur Verfügung, die direkt in die algebraische Spezifikation des Benutzers mit einbezogen werden können.

Validierung: Für die Validierung insbesondere algebraischer Spezifikationen wurde ein System enwickelt. Dieses System erlaubt die Auswertung von Anfragen, die in Form von Gleichungen über algebraischen Spezifikationen formulierter sind. Dies erlaubt algebraische Spezifikationen direkt als Prototypen einzusetzen.

Entwurfsspezifikation: Der wichtigste Aspekt einer Entwurfsspezifikation betrifft die Modularisierung (Definition der Schnittstellen). Für die Formulierung einer Entwurfsspezifikation aufbauend auf der validierten Anforderungsspezifkation stehen neben den bereits erwähnten Konstrukten alle Elemente einer applikativen Programmiersprache zur Verfügung. Die methodische Einbeziehung von Konstrukten für die Spezifikation verteilter Systeme ist in Entwicklung.

Implementierung: Liegt eine Entwurfsspezifikation vor, so ist der nächste konsequente Schritt die Erarbeitung einer Implementierung. Dies umfaßt die Wahl konkreter Repräsentationen für die auftretenden Rechenstrukturen, die Entwicklung von Algorithmen für die spezifizierten Funktionen und deren Darstellung in einer angestrebten Implementierungssprache. Man beachte: Ist die Entwurfsspezifikation voll formal, so ist der gesamte Implementierungs- vorgang vollständig formal durchführbar, d.h. insbesondere verifizierbar oder gar rein deduktiv im Kalkül durchführbar. Die Implementierung der algebraischen Spezifikationen durch die Definition von Datenstrukturrepräsentationen und die Implementierung der Funktionen durch (rekursive) Rechenvorschriften wird unterstützt durch eine Vielzahl von Programmentwicklungsregeln (Implementierungsrelation für abstrakte Datentypen, Programmtransformationsregeln etc.).

Programmentwicklungsregeln ("Transformationsregeln") unterstützen insbesondere folgende Schritte:

- Umformungen von Spezifikationen durch Regeln der Prädikatenlogik

- Ableitung von Gleichungen für die Gewinnung von rekursiven Rechenvorschriften

- Transformation rekursiver Funktionen auf repetitive Form

- Übergang zu iterativen, zuweisungsorientierten Stilen

- Einbeziehung selektiven Änderns und von Geflechtstrukturen (Zeigern)

Optimierung: Um schließlich effiziente Implementierungen erzielen zu können, wird ein zuweisungsorientierter Sprachstil angeboten, der auch Zeigerkonzepte zur Definition von Geflechtstrukturen einschließt. Auch dieser Stil wird durch Transformationsregeln unterstützt.

Die im Projekt CIP entwickelte Methodik ist speziell auf eine rechnergestützte Programmentwicklung im Dialog ausgerichtet. Dabei wird bewußt eine sehr weitgehende Automatisierung der Entwicklung nicht angestrebt. Vielmehr soll die eigentliche Entwicklungsarbeit wie das Treffen der Entwurfsentscheidungen und die Wahl der Implementierungstechniken ausschließlich dem Programmentwickler überlassen bleiben. Das System bietet nur Hilfe an bei der Dokumentation, bei der Aufbereitung der im System vorhandenen Information, bei der Verifikation von Anwendungsbedingungen und bei der Anwendung von Entwicklungsregeln.

Dabei zeigen sich auch die momentanen Schwächen des verfolgten Ansatzes: Häufig sind die Entwicklungsregeln viel zu schwach, es ist eine Vielzahl von kleinen Schritten auszuführen, bis ein spürbarer Entwicklungsfortschritt erzielt werden kann. Darunter leidet auch die Klarheit, mit der eine bestimmte Entwicklungslinie verfolgt werden kann. Es ist sicherlich notwendig, Regeln einzusetzen, die größere Entwicklungssprünge realisieren. Darüberhinaus sollten ganze Implementierungstechniken unterstützt werden, so daß der Programmentwickler mit gezielter Systemunterstützung eine bestimmte Implementierungsstrategie verfolgen kann.

Um solche Vorstellungen stärker realisieren zu können sind allerdings noch intensive Forschungsanstrengungen in allen Bereichen der Grundlagen der Programmentwicklung nötig, angefangen von Untersuchungen über Datenstrukturschemata und ihre Implementierung, über Algorithmen und Algorithmenklassen, Entwicklungsregeln und Entwicklungstechniken, bis hin zu Programmiersprachen und Programmierstilen und sogar zu Rechnerarchitekturen.

5. Abschließende Bemerkungen

Das Ziel der Grundlagenforschung im Bereich von rechnergestützten Programmentwurfssystemen ist eine vollständig funktionale formale Behandlung und Beherrschung des Programmentwicklungsprozesses als Voraussetzung für eine weitergehende Rechnerunterstützung und teilweise Automatisierung, wobei die Wiederverwendbarkeit von Entwurfsarbeit ein wichtiges Anliegen ist.

Literatur

[CIP-L 85]
F.L. Bauer, R. Berghammer, M. Broy, W. Dosch, F. Geiselbrechtinger, R. Gnatz, E. Hangel, W. Hesse, B. Krieg-Brückner, A. Laut, T. Matzner, B. Möller, F. Nickl, H. Partsch, P. Pepper, K. Samelson, M. Wirsing: The Munich Project CIP, Volume I: The Wide Spectrum Language CIP-L. Lecture Notes in Computer Science 183, Berlin-Heidelberg-New York-Tokyo: Springer 1985

[ER 85]
P. Rechenberg (Gasthrg.): Schwerpunktthema: Werkzeuge der Softwaretechnik. Elektronische Rechenanlagen 27:2, 1985

[Hussmann 85]
H. Hussmann: Rapid Prototyping for Algebraic Specifications – RAP System User's Manual. Universität Passau, Fakultät für Mathematik und Informatik, MIP 8504, 1985

[Nievergelt 83]
J. Nievergelt: Die Gestaltung der Mensch-Maschine Schnittstelle. In: I. Kupka (Hrsg.): GI – 13. Jahrestagung. Informatik-Fachberichte 73, Berlin- Heidelberg-New York-Tokyo: Springer 1983, 41-50

[Pepper 84]
P. Pepper (ed.): Program Transformation and Programming Environments. Berlin-Heidelberg-New York-Tokyo: Springer 1984

BABYLON als Werkzeug zum Aufbau von Expertensystemen

F. di Primio, D. Bungers, T. Christaller

Forschungsgruppe Expertensysteme
Institut für Angewandte Informationstechnik
Gesellschaft für Mathematik und Datenverarbeitung mbH
Postfach 1240
D-5205 St. Augustin 1
Tel. 02241-14-2679

Zusammenfassung

Das System **BABYLON** basiert auf der Hypothese, daß unter Verwendung heterogener Repräsentationsformalismen Expertenwissen adäquat dargestellt werden kann. Es unterscheidet sich von vergleichbaren Systemen durch eine extrem modulare Architektur, mit der eine problemorientierte Auswahl der einzusetzenden Formalismen unterstützt wird. Zur Zeit befindet sich **BABYLON** in der Erprobung und erste Erfahrungen dazu liegen vor. Sie erlauben es, Perspektiven über die Nützlichkeit allgemeiner Werkzeugsysteme zu formulieren.

BABYLON: Ein Softwarewerkzeug für den Wissensingenieur

Mit steigender Popularität von Expertensystemen kommen zunehmend auch Knowledge-Engineering-Werkzeuge für deren Entwicklung auf den Markt - vor allem aus den USA, wo sie meist von Spin-off-Firmen im Umfeld der großen KI-Zentren vertrieben werden. Die Zielgruppe solcher Systeme ist nicht mehr der *Programmierer*, sondern der *Wissensingenieur*, dessen Aufgabe es ist, das Wissen von Experten abzufragen und so aufzubereiten, daß es in vordefinierte Formalismen gegossen und von mit diesen verbundenen Inferenztechniken verarbeitet werden kann.

Das von der Forschungsgruppe *Expertensysteme* der Gesellschaft für Mathematik und Datenverarbeitung entwickelte System **BABYLON** stellt eines der wenigen deutschen Systeme dieser Art dar. Der Wissensingenieur findet mit **BABYLON** eine komfortable Arbeitsumgebung vor, in der er das Wissen mit den Formalismen darstellen kann, die der jeweiligen Problemstellung und seinem Ausdrucksstil angemessen sind. Das Funktionsangebot von **BABYLON** umfaßt grob gesagt

- die heute einschlägigen Formalismen zur Wissensrepräsentation

- Hilfen zum Wissensbasis-Management und

- Erklärungen für die ablaufenden Problemlösungsprozesse.

All dies wird dem Wissensingenieur über eine benutzerfreundliche Oberfläche angeboten, die auf modernen Rasterdisplays einer LISP-Machine (graphische Visualisierungen, maussensitiven Menüs und Fenstertechnik) basiert.

Allgemeine vs. spezielle Werkzeugsysteme

Bei Knowledge-Engineering-Werkzeugen kann man grob unterscheiden zwischen zwei Arten von Systemen. Die einen sind für den Einsatz in engen Problemfeldern gedacht. Ein in diesem Sinne *spezielles* System ist z.B. MED 1 [PUPPE 83], das stark auf die Modellierung diagnostischer Aufgaben im medizinischen Bereich abgestimmt ist. Die zweite Art sind Systeme, die vom methodischen Funktionsumfang her betrachtet verschiedene Repräsentationsformen unterstützen, und damit den Anspruch erheben, unabhängig von einzelnen Anwendungsfeldern allgemein einsetzbar zu sein, z.B. Systeme wie KEE [KEE 83] und LOOPS [BOBROW/STEFIK 83].

Diese Systeme werden als *hybride* Systeme bezeichnet [KUNZ/KEHLER/WILLIAMS 84], da sie zum Aufbau von Wissensbasen die Möglichkeit bieten, verschiedene Wissensrepräsentationsformalismen alternativ bzw. komplementär zueinander zu gebrauchen. Das bedeutet, daß zur Wissensrepräsentation neben PRODUKTIONS-REGELN (das *FORTRAN* der Expertensystemtechnik), auch beispielsweise noch objektorientierte Darstellungsmöglichkeiten (FRAMES) oder ein logischer Formalismus zur Verfügung stehen. Dafür gibt es keine zwingende theoretische oder technische Notwendigkeit, denn alle Formalismen sind gleichmächtig, d.h. jedes repräsentierbare Wissen läßt sich in jedem Formalismus darstellen. So hat z.B. Hayes [HAYES 80] nachgewiesen, daß objektorientierte Konstrukte sich leicht in eine prädikatenlogische Darstellung überführen lassen, und Frames damit keine qualitative Steigerung der Wissensrepräsentationsmächtigkeit bedeuten.

Der Grund für die Bereitstellung verschiedener Formalismen liegt vielmehr in der Absicht, die unterschiedlichen Wissenstypen einer Anwendung jeweils in der *natürlichsten* Form darstellen zu können, z.B. Erfahrungsregeln des Experten in Form von Produktionsregeln (WENN *dies vorliegt* DANN *ist folgendes zu tun*), definitorische Zusammenhänge des Gegenstandsbereiches in Prädikatenlogik und die Zustandsbeschreibungen der Objekte in Form von Frames. Bezweckt wird damit, daß sowohl Benutzer als auch Systementwickler ihre Problemlösungen bzw. das Verhalten des Expertensystems nicht in einen uniformen Formalismus zwingen bzw. interpretieren müssen. Dadurch soll erreicht werden, daß auch komplexe Wissensbasen transparent bleiben und ihr Entwicklungs- und Wartungsaufwand reduziert wird.

Geschlossene vs. offene Systeme

Allgemeine Werkzeugsysteme werden wie die speziellen letztlich immer für die Realisierung konkreter Anwendungen gebraucht und müssen daher eine problemorientierte

Darstellung des betreffenden Gegenstandsbereichs erlauben. Entscheidend sind in dem Zusammenhang die Mittel, die vom allgemeinen Werkzeugsystem bereitgestellt werden, um es an das anvisierte Problemfeld anzupassen. Diese Mittel können nicht allein die Basis-Wissensrepräsentationsformalismen sein, denn das würde bedeuten, daß jeder einzelne Formalismus ein *spezielles* System wäre und damit das *allgemeine* Werkzeugsystem nichts Anderes als ein Nebeneinander von spezialisierten Systemen. Aber auch die Integration der gegebenen Formalismen, wie auch immer gestaltet, reicht im allgemeinen nicht aus, um die Anforderungen einer beliebigen speziellen Anwendung zu erfüllen.

Das wichtigste Kriterium, um zu beurteilen, ob ein allgemeines System angepaßt und damit praktisch eingesetzt werden kann, ist der *Grad der Offenheit* des Systems. Darunter verstehen wir die Spezialisierungsmöglichkeiten, die das System bietet (Offenheit), und der dazu notwendige Realisierungsaufwand (Grad). Die Offenheit alleine ist ja nicht entscheidend, sonst wäre z.B. LISP, die Programmiersprache, in welcher die meisten Werkzeugsysteme implementiert sind, bzw. jede andere Programmiersprache auch ein geeignetes Expertensystemwerkzeug, weil sie sich für jede Anwendung gebrauchen läßt.

Entscheidend ist beides, die Basis-Ausdrucksmächtigkeit des Systems und der Aufwand, mit dem sie sich für den jeweiligen Bereich adäquaten Darstellungsformen anpassen lassen. Wenn man sich den Weg, der von einer Basissprache wie LISP zu einer konkreten Expertensystemanwendung führt, bildlich vorstellt, so sollte ein *gutes* allgemeines Werkzeugsystem irgendwo in der Mitte sein, nicht zu nah der Basissprache und nicht zu weit von den Anwendungsfeldern. Je näher ein Werkzeugsystem einer konkreten Anwendung ist, um so spezieller und geschlossener ist er.

Architekturkonzept von BABYLON

Die meisten allgemeinen Werkzeugsysteme haben sich aus früheren speziellen Expertensystem-Shells entwickelt, die ihrerseits aus einzelnen Expertensystementwicklungen hervorgegangen waren, und denen zunächst nur ein Repräsentationsformalismus zugrunde lag. Das gilt z.B. für S.1 [S.1 84], das auf dem produktionsregelbasiertem EMYCIN [van MELLE 80] basiert, das als Verallgemeinerung der im Expertensystem MYCIN [SHORTLIFFE 76] benutzten Techniken hervorging.

In **BABYLON** dagegen [DI PRIMIO/BREWKA 85] konnte die Forderung nach multipler Wissensrepräsentation bereits dem Architekturkonzept von vornherein zugrundegelegt werden. Dies war deshalb möglich, weil kein spezielles Werkzeugsystem existierte, zu dem ein aufwärtskompatibles allgemeines System entwickelt werden mußte, noch gab es eine unmittelbar bevorstehende Anwendung. So konnte die Architektur ohne Abstriche entwickelt werden.

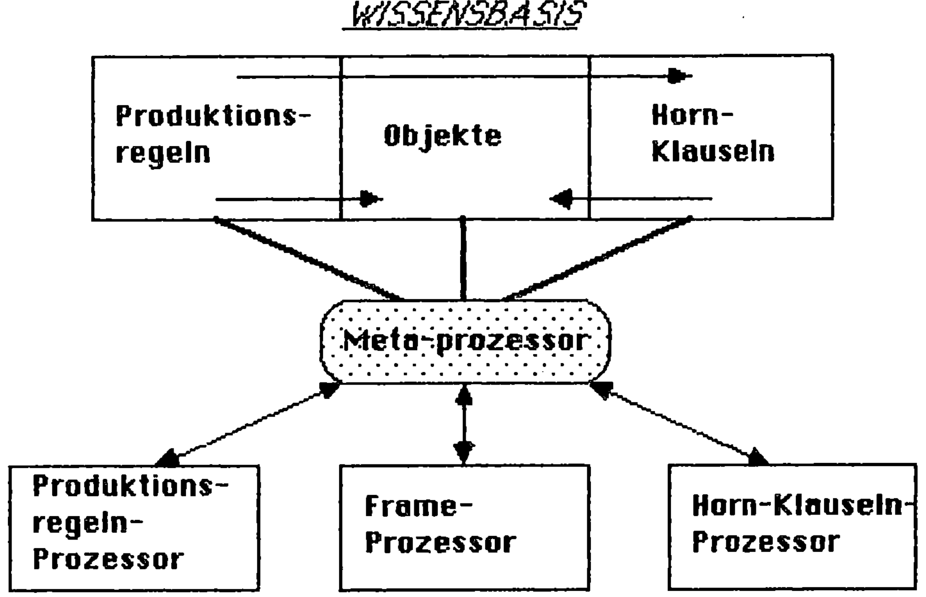

Die Richtung der Pfeile in der Wissensbasis deutet auf die Referenzen, die innerhalb eines Formalismus auf die anderen gemacht werden.

Abbildung 1: **Die BABYLON-Architektur**

Das System verarbeitet eine Wissensbasis, die aus unterschiedlich repräsentiertem Wissen (z.B. in Form von Produktionsregeln, Frames oder Horn-Klauseln) besteht, nach dem Prinzip des verteilten Problemlösens. Für jeden der Formalismen gibt es einen eigenständigen Sprachprozessor. Der *Frame-Prozessor* interpretiert die Objektkonstrukte, der *Horn-Klauseln-Prozessor* die Horn-Klauseln usw.. Ein sogenannter *Meta-Prozessor* koordiniert die einzelnen Sprachprozessoren dadurch, daß er die Referenzen verwaltet, die innerhalb von Ausdrücken eines Formalismus auf solche gemacht werden, die in einem der anderen Formalismus dargestellt sind (s. folgende Abbildung).

Eine ähnliche modulare Organisation des Wissens, die das Prinzip der verteilten Verarbeitung realisiert [ERMAN/LESSER 75], lag dem HEARSAY-II-System zugrunde, in welchem verschiedene Typen von Wissen in Modulen (*Knowledge Sources*) zusammengefaßt waren, die bei der Analyse gesprochener Sprache miteinander kooperierten, indem sie Ergebnisse über eine globale (aber passive) Datenstruktur (*Blackboard*) austauschten.

Die Integration der Wissensrepräsentationsformalismen wird dadurch erreicht, daß Prämissen von Produktionsregeln Referenzen auf Objektzustände (Frame-Formalismus) bzw. Relationsausdrücke (Horn-Klausel-Formalismus) sein können. Innerhalb von Horn-Klauseln (als Prämissen) kann schließlich auch auf Objekte referiert werden. D.h., daß sowohl bei der Auswertung von Produktionsregeln als auch von Horn-Klauseln die Vererbungsmechanismen des Frame-Formalismus eingesetzt werden können (für eine ähnlich gestaltete Integration von Produktionsregeln und Frames s. [ENGELMANN/STANTON 84]). Einen Relationsausdruck als Produktionsregelprämisse zu gebrauchen, bedeutet schließlich, daß die Resolutionsstrategie des Horn-Klausel-Formalismus auch innerhalb der Produktionsregeln zur Verfügung steht.

Aufgrund der verschiedenen syntaktischen Struktur der Formalismen erkennt der Meta-Prozessor z.B. ob innerhalb einer Produktionsregel eine Referenz auf Objektzustände oder ein prädikatenlogischer Ausdruck zur Auswertung ansteht, und delegiert die Bearbeitung an den jeweils zuständigen Basis-Prozessor, der sie dann durchführt. Die Architektur ist streng hierarchisch. Die Basis-Prozessoren wissen nichts voneinander. Sie sind lediglich in der Lage zu erkennen, ob im Rahmen einer ihnen gestellten Aufgabe eine Teilaufgabe entsteht, die nicht in ihre Kompetenz fällt. In einem solchen Fall schalten sie den Meta-Prozessor ein, der den Typ der Teilaufgabe bestimmt und sie an einen der anderen Basis-Prozessoren bzw. an seine eigene Meta-Instanz (den Benutzer) weiterleitet.

Da jeder Basis-Prozessor nur mit dem Meta-Prozessor direkt kommuniziert, ist es relativ einfach, einen Basis-Prozessor auszutauschen bzw. einen neuen hinzuzufügen. Man braucht nur den Meta-Prozessor zu verändern oder zu ergänzen. Wir sprechen hier vom Vorteil der *Offenheit in der Breite.* Der Meta-Prozessor verwendet zur Unterscheidung der verschiedenen Formalismen eine eigene Wissensbasis, die mit Hilfe des Horn-Klausel-Formalismus aufgebaut ist und die ihre syntaktischen Definitionen enthält (wissensbasierte Selbstverwaltung des Werkzeugsystems). Deshalb besteht der Aufwand für die Anbindung eines neuen Sprachprozessors darin, die Horn-Klausel-Basis um geeignete Horn-Klauseln zu erweitern.

Alle übrigen derzeit existierenden hybriden Systeme verfolgen einen anderen Ansatz. Sie erlauben entweder eine direkte Kommunikation zwischen den für die verschiedenen Formalismen zuständigen Prozessoren (heterarchische Architektur), übersetzen die Formalismen ineinander [BRACHMAN/LEVESQUE 82] oder in einen tiefer liegenden Formalismus. So werden in LOOPS [BOBROW/STEFIK 83] Produktionsregeln in Ausdrücke der Systemsprache LISP übersetzt.

Sowohl der heterarchisch interpretierende als auch der compilierende Ansatz bieten nicht den Vorteil einer einfachen Erweiterung in der Breite wie **BABYLON**. Verglichen mit unserem Ansatz sind die erwähnten Architekturkonzepte vielleicht etwas effizienter bezüglich der Ausführungszeiten. Wir glauben jedoch, daß dieses nur ein scheinbarer Vorteil ist. So sind Rechnerarchitekturen vorstellbar (und teilweise schon in der Realisierung begriffen), die auf mehreren Hardware-Prozessoren basieren und auf denen das **BABYLON**-Konzept viel effizienter implementiert werden kann. Nicht zufällig sprechen wir von Basis-*Prozessoren*, wenn wir die Interpreter für die jeweiligen Wissensrepräsentationsformalismen meinen.

Für die Arbeitsweise der verschiedenen Prozessoren in **BABYLON** ist es vollkommen irrelevant, daß sie zur Zeit vollständig in LISP implementiert sind. Der Meta-Prozessor macht keinen Gebrauch von dieser Tatsache. Die Kommunikation erfolgt aufgrund eines festgelegten Protokolls mit Mitteln des objektorientierten Programmierstils (message passing), und das ist das einzige, was die Prozessoren einzuhalten haben. Falls die technischen Voraussetzungen vorliegen, können also die Prozessoren von der jetzigen Einbettung in einer Einprozessor-LISP-Welt in andere spezialisierte Software-/Hardware-Umgebungen verlagert werden. Das nennen wir den Vorteil der *Offenheit in der Tiefe* (Richtung Hardware).

Schließlich ist **BABYLON**, wie die meisten Systeme, auch *offen in der Höhe*. D.h., man kann das System selbst durch Bootstrapping-Techniken erweitern. Ein Beispiel dafür (Aufwand 3 Mannwochen, 3 Seiten Code) ist die Realisierung einer Wissensbasis, die eine *Top-Down-Refine*-Problemlösungsstrategie [BYLANDER et al. 83] darstellt [DI PRIMIO 85]. Diese (allgemeine) **BABYLON**-Wissensbasis kann von allen anderen (konkreten) Wissensbasen benutzt werden, die Gebrauch von der entsprechenden Interpretationsstrategie machen wollen.

Probleme bei der Portierung von Expertensystemen

Die Entwicklung allgemeiner Werkzeugsysteme wie **BABYLON** dient dazu, unterschiedliche Expertensysteme mit möglichst geringem Aufwand zu entwickeln. Das ist allerdings nur ein erster notwendiger Schritt, damit mehr Expertensysteme entstehen können. Solange dasselbe Werkzeugsystem und dieselbe Hardware-/Software-Basis verwendet wird, mag er genügen. Es ist allerdings absehbar, daß, vergleichbar zu anderen Leistungssystemen wie Datenbankverwaltungssysteme, auch Expertensysteme portierbar sein müssen.

Es gibt zwei verschiedene Gründe, die dazu zwingen sowohl das Werkzeugsystem als auch die damit erstellten Wissensbasen portierbar zu machen. Da ist zum einen zwischen Entwicklungs- und Einsatzumgebung eines Expertensystems zu unterscheiden. Im Augenblick ist es gängige Praxis, die Strukturierung des Anwendungsbereiches und den ersten Wissenserwerb auf leistungsfähigen aber teuren Spezialrechnern, z.B. LISP-Maschinen, durchzuführen.

Ein Grund für die ökonomische Relevanz von Expertensystemen ist, daß mit ihnen Wissen leicht vervielfältigt werden kann, das bisher nur wenige Experten besitzen. Damit ein Expertensystem einsetzbar wird, muß es in entsprechend vielen Kopien verfügbar sein. Erfordert jede Kopie die Anschaffung eines solchen Spezialrechners, wird der geplante Einsatz unrentabel. Es kann aber auch möglich sein, daß aus organisatorischen (infrastrukturellen) Gründen beim Einsatz andere Rechnersysteme verwendet werden müssen.

Die Portierbarkeit des Werkzeugsystems garantiert auch die Portierbarkeit der damit erstellten Wissensbasen und ist mit bekannten Mitteln des Software-Engineering realisierbar. Die Definition funktionaler Schnittstellen zum Graphiksystem und Betriebssystem der fraglichen Gastrechner gehört z.B. dazu.

Schwieriger ist das Problem der Basissoftware, die Programmiersprache, in der das Werkzeugsystem realisiert wurde. Sie muß möglichst als Standard in der Entwicklungs- und Einsatzumgebung verfügbar sein. Diese Forderung wird z.Z. weder von LISP noch von PROLOG erfüllt. In den USA versuchte man in den vergangenen Jahren, COMMONLISP als Standard zu definieren [STEELE 84]. Das ist aber bislang noch nicht gelungen. Es bleibt abzuwarten, ob durch die Implementierung unterschiedlicher COMMONLISP-Systeme ohne Standardisierungskomitee und Überprüfung die wünschenswerte Standardisierung bewirkt werden kann.

Will man unabhängig von derartigen Standardisierungsbemühungen sein, ist ein anderer Weg denkbar, der bei der Implementierung von S.1 beschritten wurde. Als Basissoftware wird hier eine in INTERLISP-D eingebettete Programmiersprache, GLISP, verwendet [GORDON 83]. Der GLISP-Compiler ist mit Hilfe eines einfachen Übersetzungsprogramms in jeden beliebigen LISP-Dialekt portierbar. Dasselbe Programm ist in der Lage, den vom GLISP-Compiler erzeugten INTERLISP-D-Code zu übersetzen. Damit sind auch in GLISP geschriebene Programme, z.B. Werkzeugsysteme, unabhängig von den Eigenheiten der verschiedenen LISP-Dialekte.

Noch vollkommen ungelöst ist das Problem, Wissensbasen unabhängig von ihren Werkzeugsystemen zu portieren. Für die dort verwendeten Repräsentationsformalismen ist keine Standardisierung in Aussicht und bisher gibt es auch noch keine Übersetzungsprogramme, um z.B. LOOPS-Ausdrücke in äquivalente **BABYLON**-Ausdrücke abzubilden. Die Konsequenz ist, daß ein einmal gewähltes Werkzeugsystem solange unterstützt werden muß, wie man damit erstellte Wissensbasen verwenden will.

Es ist geplant, **BABYLON** in den nächsten Jahren auf vielen verschiedenen Rechnersystemen verfügbar zu machen. Zuerst werden Portierungen nach Dialekten vorgenommen, die ähnlich zu COMMONLISP sind. Wir hoffen, daß sich dadurch einerseits ein leicht portierbarer Kern definieren läßt und andererseits klarer wird, welche Eigenschaften die Benutzerschnittstelle haben muß.

Perspektiven

Die Zeit für abgeschlossene *Black-Box*-Werkzeuge ist noch nicht reif: Der Bedarf für Expertensysteme ensteht erst und neue Anwendungen werden erschlossen, während gleichzeitig die KI-Forschung weiter Methoden und Techniken der Wissensverarbeitung findet und die Hardware-Architekten neue Rechner entwickeln. **BABYLON** scheint gute Voraussetzungen zu haben, um mit diesen Entwicklungen Schritt zu halten: Die Erweiterung um neue Formalismen der Wissensrepräsentation und um neue Inferenztechniken ist ebenso möglich, wie das Verlagern von jetzt noch durch Software realisierten Funktionen auf Hardware.

Die F&E-Arbeiten an **BABYLON** in verschiedenen Verbundvorhaben dienen neben der Portierung auf unterschiedliche Rechner dem Nachweis der Erweiterbarkeit bezüglich der Repräsentationsformalismen und Schlußfolgerungstechniken, etwa um Constraints, damit Abhängigkeiten zwischen Fakten berücksichtigt werden können (Anwendungsbeispiel: Schnittstellenerfordernisse bei Konfigurationsaufgaben), oder um nicht-monotone Inferenztechniken, mit denen auch solche Fakten handhabbar werden, deren Gültigkeit während des Problemlösungsprozesses durch Einflüsse einer sich zeitlich verändernden Umwelt verändert werden können (Anwendungsbeispiel: Prozeßkontrolle).

Als sehr nützlich könnte sich die **BABYLON**-Architektur künftig auch bei der Kopplung von Expertensystemen mit anderen vorhandenen informationstechnischen Systemen erweisen. Bis heute können nämlich Expertensysteme mit Datenbanken, Simulationsmodellen oder CAD/CAM-Systemen wenn überhaupt nur schwer kommunizieren. Über eine abstrakte Schnittstelle könnte **BABYLON**s Meta-Prozessor Aufgaben auch nach außen delegieren, so daß Expertensysteme und Fremdsystem ein Anwendungsproblem arbeitsteilig lösen können. Diese Schnittstelle gilt es freilich noch zu schaffen.

BABYLON repräsentiert den heutigen *State-of-the-Art* von Knowledge Engineering Werkzeugen; und dieser ist von den Erfordernissen der Praxis stark mitgeprägt. Auch die künftigen Weiterentwicklungen werden in engem Zusammenhang mit ernsthaften Anwendungen durchgeführt. Zu diesem Zweck ist **BABYLON** zur Erprobung mehreren Institutionen aus Industrie und Forschung für Anwendungsarbeiten auf dem Gebiet der Expertensysteme zur Verfügung gestellt worden - zunächst im Rahmen eines ein- bis dreijährigen Beta-Tests. Ihr Feedback wird gewährleisten, daß sich **BA-BYLON** auch künftig am Bedarf einer noch im Entstehen befindlichen Knowledge-Engineering-Praxis orientiert.

Stand der Implementierung

BABYLON ist vollständig in ZetaLisp auf einer LISP-Maschine implementiert. Es hat einen Umfang von ca. 2000 Blöcken. Enthalten sind Basis-Prozessoren für Frames, Horn-Klauseln und Produktionsregeln, der Metaprozessor, spezielle Editierhilfen und graphische Präsentation von Abhängigkeiten von Wissenselementen. Eine erste interne Evaluierung basierte auf einer Portierung der Wissensbasis des DEX.C3 Expertensystems (siehe [KLAR/WITTUR/HENNE 85]).

Literatur

[BOBROW/STEFIK 83]
Bobrow, D. G.; Stefik, M.
The LOOPS Manual.
XEROC PARC, 1983

[BRACHMAN/LEVESQUE 82]
Brachman, R.J.; Levesque, A.J.
Competence in Knowledge Representation.
In: Proc. of AAAI-82, 189-192

[BYLANDER et al. 83]
Bylander, T.; Mittal, S.; Chandrasekaran, B.
CSRL: A Language for Expert Systems for Diagnosis.
In: Proc. of JICAI-83, 218-221

[ENGELMANN/STANTON 84]
Engelmann, C.; Stanton, W.M.
An Integrated Frame/Rule Architecture.
In: Elithorn, A.; Banerji, R. (Eds.)
Artificial and Human Intelligence
North-Holland, Amsterdam 1984, 141-146

[ERMAN/LESSER 75]
Erman, L.D.; Lesser, V.R.
A multi-level organization for problem solving using many diverse,
cooperating sources of knowledge.
In: Proc. of IJCAI-75, 483-490

[DI PRIMIO 85]
di Primio, F.
Bootstrapping in **BABYLON**:
Aufbau und Struktur einer Wissensbasis für die
Top-Down-Refine-Strategie.
GMD, St. Augustin, erscheint demnächst

[DI PRIMIO/BREWKA 85]
di Primio, F.; Brewka, G.
BABYLON: Kernel System of an Integrated Environment for Expert System
Development and Operation.
In: Proc. of Fifth International Workshop on Expert Systems and their Applications
Avignon 1985 , 573-583

[HAYES 80]

Hayes, P.J.
The Logic of Frames
In: Metzing, D. (Ed.):
Frame Conception and Text Understanding.
Berlin, de Gruyter, 1980, 46-61

[KEE 83]
Kee User's Manual.
Menlo Park, CA: IntelliGenetics, 1983

[KLAR/WITTUR/HENNE 85]
Klar, W.; Wittur, K.-H.; Henne, P.
Ein Expertensystem zur Fehlerdiagnose im automatischen Getriebe C 3
von Ford.
In: Proc. Systems85, Springer, Berlin, 1985

[KUNZ/KEHLER/WILLIAMS 84]
Kunz, J.C.; Kehler, T.P.; Williams, M.D.
Applications Development Using a Hybrid AI Development System.
In: The AI Magazine V(1984)3, 41-54

[NOVAK 83]
Novak, G.S.
Knowledge-based Programming Using Abstract Data Types
In: Proc. AAAI, 1983, S.288-291

[PUPPE 83]
Puppe, B.; Puppe, F.
Overview on MED1: a Heuristic Diagnostics System with an Efficient Control
Structure .
In: Informatik-Fachberichte 76, GWAI-83, 11-22, Springer-Verlag

[S.1 84]
S.1 Reference Manual.
Framentec, Monaco 1984

[SHORTLIFFE 76]
Shortliffe, E.H.
Computer-based medical consultations: MYCIN.
New York, American Elsevier, 1976

[STEELE 84]
Steele, G.L.
CommonLisp: The Language.
Digital Press, Burlington, 1984

[van MELLE 80]
van Melle, W.
A domain independent system that aids in constructing consultation
programs.
Rep. No. STAN-CS-80-820, Computer Science Dept.
Stanford University 1980

EPITOOL
- A Development and Execution Environment
for Knowledge Systems

Uwe Hein
EPITEC AB
St Larsgatan 12
58224 Linköping
Sweden

1. INTRODUCTION

The *EPITOOL Software Development System* is an advanced software package intended to be used both as a development and a run-time environment for knowledge systems. Since EPITOOL is a domain and task independent tool kit, it can be used to develop many different applications. As such EPITOOL is more than a software package: it is equally a framework for building knowledge systems. Consequently, this document also discusses methodological implications and explains why EPITOOL will make the development of knowledge systems considerably more cost effective.

Within the lifecycle of one particular application, EPITOOL will first serve as a development vehicle for the application developer. This stage is of critical importance in any project, since the process of knowledge transfer is usually quite difficult and time consuming. EPITOOL acknowledges this fact by providing the knowledge engineer with many powerful development tools, such as debugging and analysis tools, specialized editors and a variety of display tools.

A knowledge engineer develops an application by defining knowledge and inference structures and by designing communication facilities for the end user. The set of knowledge elements, termed a knowledge base, uniquely identifies a particular application. EPITOOL has been designed as a flexible tool kit with the ambition to give the knowledge engineer many degrees of freedom in the design of a knowledge base without introducing an unbearable amount of design decisions.

The resulting knowledge system system will finally be consulted by a number of end-users in order to solve some particular problem. End-users, too, will add and modify knowledge elements. The end-user, however, will be concerned with particular units of knowledge, rather than generic knowledge structures which describe the general characteristics of a problem domain.

EPITOOL has been developed by EPITEC AB in Linköping. It contains facilities for knowledge represention and problem solving, as well as powerful development tools for the knowledge engineer. EPITOOL has been designed with the objective to support the design and implementation of complex, large scale industrial and commercial applications.

This document provides an informal presentation of EPITOOL. It discusses major product characteristics, the way EPITOOL can be used to represent and manipulate domain knowledge, and the problem solving primitives provided by EPITOOL.

Since the main purpose of this document is to provide a comprehensive overview of the product, technical details have been omitted as much as possible. Examples have been included in order to make the document more legible. For the sake of readability, they have been slightly simplified.

A prototype of EPITOOL implemented on XEROX 1108 AI workstations has been in operation since May 85 and is currently being used by the EPITEC knowledge engineering group in several applications. Product release is planned for spring 86. At that time EPITOOL will be available on XEROX AI workstations and VAX systems. Further implementations of EPITOOL are currently being negotiated.

2. GENERAL CHARACTERISTICS

EPITOOL is a development and execution environment for knowledge systems. It is domain independent in the sense that the facilities for knowledge representation and problem solving do not make any commitment to a particular application domain. Thus, EPITOOL can be used to develop a medical diagnosis system as well as a computer configuration or a travel planning system. In fact, EPITOOL can be thought of as a programming language providing primitives for knowledge manipulation in the same sense that conventional programming languages provide primitives for arithmetic or string manipulation. Chapter 3 describes how knowledge is represented in EPITOOL.

The problem solving primitives are not committed either to any particular task type. Since EPITOOL is task independent, it can be used do develop diagnosis systems as well as configuration systems. This means that given EPITOOL, it is not obvious how to design and implement a diagnosis system. There are no diagnosis primitives in EPITOOL, nor are there primitives for system configuration or prospecting. We have prefered to provide more basic, hence more general primitives. On one hand we do not believe that a well-defined taxonomy for problem types exists yet, on the other hand we prefer that an EPITOOL user should be able to build several applications within the same knowledge representation framework, since the overhead of learning and adopting to new frameworks might be considerable. The impacts of this design decision are further discussed in chapter 4.

Much effort has been spent in order to achieve a high degree of machine independency. Even though EPITOOL primarily will be implemented in Interlisp-D and CommonLisp, it should be possible to adopt EPITOOL to many different environments as future needs dictate, since most parts of the systems have been specified at a sufficiently abstract level. In addition, all EPITOOL functions are available for simple TTY terminals. Therefore, applications in EPITOOL may be transfered between different environments as long as they do not escape into the host LISP system. Every environment in which EPITOOL will be implemented will provide the full EPITOOL functionality. The form in which this functionality is realized may vary, however, depending on the features provided by the host environment.

A typical EPITOOL user does not need to write any LISP programs in order to develop a knowledge system. In cases where access to LISP is required, however, EPITOOL provides a well defined interface to the host LISP system. An application which relies on LISP code cannot be guaranteed to be portable to another environment. Since EPITOOL contains its own powerful procedural language, the need to write LISP code should only arise in very special cases such as interfacing EPITOOL with other LISP software, writing special calculation programs, interfacing EPITOOL with the external world, implementing special purpose graphics etc.

Finally, the design of EPITOOL is open in the sense that we foresee a number of future extensions which we already have anticipated in the current design. One example is the general treatment of truthvalues. Even though the current implementation is build on a two valued logic, other logics could be added with minor efforts. Another example is the layered design of the access functions. At the bottom layer we have fully parameterized functions which allow us to access objects in a variety of ways. The inconvenience of complex arguments required is removed by a higher level of functions which implement a more specific functionality. Again, further additions and modifications can be made by implementing additional functions at a still higher level relying on the generality of the lower level access functions.

EPITOOL may be conceived of as consisting of two major components: the knowledge-base management system (KBMS) and the interface management system (IFMS). The KBMS consists of thoses functions which deal with the creation and manipulation of knowledge-bases, whereas the IFMS deals with those functions that manage the communication between users and EPITOOL. The IFMS provides different "interfaces" to the services of the KBMS.

The IFMS has been designed to exist in two different physical environments: one version will be supported by advanced graphics software as typically found on advanced workstations with bit-mapped displays, the other version will exist on simple display terminals as often found on mainframe computers. Both environments will provide the same services to the user, as far as the KBMS is concerned. What will differ, however, is the way those services can be requested by the user.

The IFMS consists of a complex set of functions which support a variety of services to the user, besides providing an interface to the services of the KBMS. File handling, on-line documentation, help packages, user profiles, and system development tools are part of those services.

3. FEATURES OF THE PARADIGM

The cornerstone of EPITOOLs performance is the set of knowledge representation features that it provides to the knowledge engineer. These features support an extensive range of different types of knowledge that can be used in a single application and thereby brought to bear on individual problems. The diversity of knowledge types responds to the requirement for different problem solving techniques and knowledge representation features even within a single application.

This diversity is harnessed by two important forms of integration: the synthesis of different knowledge types into a single theoretical paradigm, and the automatic translation of knowledge expressions of different types into an underlying coherent architecture. This section discusses the salient properties of EPITOOLs primary knowledge representation and problem solving facilities.

3.1. KNOWLEDGE REPRESENTATION

3.1.1 Concepts and Individuals

The basic unit used for representing knowledge is a concept. A concept describes and defines a collection of similar entities in terms of what properties may be asserted, what actions may be applied to those entities and which predicates may be tested. Much of the information in the KBMS is associated with concepts and the structure of concepts is therefore one of the most crucial, and complex parts of the system. One of the important benefits of an object oriented representation system such as EPITOOL is the way huge amounts of chunks of knowledge can be structured, facilitating the work of the knowledge engineer.

Particular objects in a problem domain are represented as individuals. Individuals are created as instances of concepts and consequently reflect the properties which have been defined for their parent concept. Each individual is a direct instance of exactly one concept. The KBMS will not allow individuals to deviate from the definition provided by their parent concept. Such situations could arise, if aspects are added to or deleted from concepts, types for aspects changed, or if the parent concept were deleted. In those cases the KBMS will invalidate the individuals in question. The definition given in a concept must yield for all instances of the concept.

> example: A drill may be defined as

concept: drill
  aspects:
     price
     max-depth
     max-diameter
     speed
     tool
  methods:
     start
     stop
     drill
  predicates:
     small
     big
     expensive

This examples shows a (simplified and informal) definition of a concept "drill". The definition states that a drill has a price, maximal depth, maximal diameter, speed and a drilling tool. In EPITOOL properties, parts and other attributes are simply called aspects. Besides the aspects, there are also three actions (called methods in EPITOOL) which may be performed with a drill: starting it, stopping it and drilling. Three predicates have been defined allowing one to ask whether a particular drill is small, big, or expensive.

3.1.2 Conceptual taxonomies

In an application there will be many concepts that are similar in some respects, different in other respects. The full power of the concept mechanism lies in the possibility to define concepts as specializations of other concepts. If a concept is defined as a specialization of another concept, then it automatically inherits everything that has been defined for the more general concept. Only those properties that are specific for the specialized system need to be defined explicitly.

In order to achieve a clear and concise semantics the concept hierarchy is a strict specialization hierarchy. A fundamental principle is therefore that if a concept A is a specialization of a concept B then everything true of B should also be true of A and every A should also be a B.

example: If we, in addition to the drill, had other types of tools in our domain such as mills, saws or lathes, each of which could have a price and an owner, then it would be more natural to define a more general concept

        concept: tool
            aspects:
                price
                owner

and thereafter to define the concept drill as a specialization of the concept "tool". In that way price and owner would be automatically inherited by all drills.

According to the basic principle mentioned above our representation will assume that whatever holds for tools holds for drills (unless modified by the drill concept) and that all drills can be considered tools.

EPITOOL also allows that a concept may be defined as a specialization of more than one concept, as long as there are no name conflicts with respect to the parent concepts. Multiple specialization can be seen as a union operation. A concept will inherit all properties of all parents.

3.1.3 Types

The concept hierarchy also provides the base for the EPITOOL type machinery. There are three different kinds of concepts: proper concepts, primitive concepts, and group concepts. Primitive concepts represent build-in, non-structured data types such as integers and strings. Proper concepts are structured, user defined data types, such as drill and tool above. Primitive concepts do not have any aspects and are restricted in terms of operations allowed on then. An EPITOOL user may not modify primitive concepts.

Any finite collection of individuals may be put together into a group which will be either a set or a sequence. A number of operations is defined on groups such as union and intersection, but also mapping operations which can be used to filter groups of individuals. Groups can be used for a variety of purposes. In particular different subsets of a given concept can in most cases be easily represented as groups, thus keeping the concept hierarchy simple and transparent.

3.1.4 Aspects and values

If an aspect has been defined for some concept, then each instance of the concept may be assigned a value for that aspect. The form of the value and the behavior of the access functions can be affected by means of facets which are used in an aspect definition. One of these is the type facet. For each aspect the user must specify a type. The type defines the set of legal values fore that aspect. Another facet is the valtype facet. A value assigned to an aspect may be shared by all instances of the concept (ComVal), or may be specific for each instance (IndVal). Default values may also be provided for an aspect.

example: in the prévios definition of "tool" the price aspect could be defined as:
concept: tool
    aspects:
        price *type*: Integer *default*: 0

the definition says that values for prices of tools must be of type integer and that in lack of better information it will be assumed that a tool is for free.

EPITOOL distinguishes three different types of values.
    - individuals (definite values)
    - restraints
    - unknown

Individuals are used to represent definite values. "Unknown" is regarded and treated as a value, i e can be returned by functions such as matching operations. Restraints allow reasoning with indefinite values. In many cases it may be known that the value for some aspects is among a number of known alternatives, or that is not among those alternatives. Restraint based reasoning is powerful, since it allows decisions based on incomplete information.

example: If it is known that a person is either a Danish or Swedish citizen, then it can be decided that it is true that the person is a citizen of the nordic countries, even if the persons citizenship is not explicitly known.

Restraints can be formed by means of a description language. Descriptions can be used to characterize individuals. They are used for expressing restraints, but also for associative access to individuals and group formation. All descriptions are based on some concept. Usually, a description will be used to add additional restrictions in addition to what has been defined for the concept.

example: given our definition of drill, we could characterize potential drill individuals by means of the following descriptions:

      - a drill with speed greater-than 2000
      - a drill with max-depth less than 50 and speed greater-than 15

- a drill with tool a MDX720 drill.

Decision knowledge is encoded with the help of rules. The left-hand side of a rule may contain any number of premises, the right hand side may contain any number of actions. Rules are organized into rulesets and associated with concepts.

Although rules are used to express much of the problem solving knowledge needed in mostapplications, EPITOOL also provides functions by means of which procedural information can be expressed in a straightforward fashion. Functions are either object oriented, i e associated with concepts, or global in which case the access to the function definition is not affected by the concept hierarchy.

3.2. PROBLEM SOLVING

EPITOOL has been designed as a task independent knowledge engineering tool. Consequently, we have been focusing on a set of useful problem solving primitives rather than on one particular problem solving paradigm. The advantage of our approach is that it is possible to use the basic EPITOOL framework for a variety of applications, rather that using a number of specialized tools which enforce their own knowledge representation conventions each. Once a user has learned the EPITOOL framework (and working environment), it will be easier for him to design his own control structures on top of the EPITOOL primitives.

Problem solving in the EPITOOL framework can be seen as infering information about objects. Thus if the task is to identify a fault in a system, then our representation of system might contain a fault aspect. This allows us to solve the fault identification problem by asking what the fault is. Naturally, there is no simple answer immediately available. Since there is not, the KBMS will attemp to deduce a value for the aspect by using all available inference sources. Asking for a "goal aspect" may therefore invoke a complex reasoning chain in order to determine a value. Of course, there are many more ways to organize a problem solving process. In all cases, however, it is a matter of deriving information about objects.

As discussed above, problem solving and decision making knowledge is mostly encoded in rules which are packaged into rulesets. Every ruleset is associated with a concept which may be considered a focus for the ruleset. Whenever a ruleset is invoked it will operate on an individual which is an instance of the associated concept. A ruleset may be associated with a concept in three different ways:

- as a method
- as a request driven method (RDIM)
- as a data-driven inference method (DDIM)

A ruleset associated with a concept as a method has to get invoked explicitly through some individual. The corresponding method is then looked up in the concept hierarchy and applied to the individual. This is the EPITOOL analog to message passing in object oriented systems.

If a ruleset is to be used as a request driven inference method, then its purpose is to deduce a value for some aspect. Each ruleset implements one particular knowledge source. Several rulesets may be associated with an aspect, if there are alternative ways to compute the value. In a RDIM ruleset the right-hand sides of the rules usually consist of a statement to conclude a value for the aspect to which the concept has been attached.

A ruleset to be used as a data-driven inference method will prescribe actions to be executed as soon as a value for some aspect has been changed. Thus, DDIMs are typically used to implement forward chaining control structures.

A ruleset is always defined in the context of some concept. The exact indexing of the rule set is, however, automatically taken care of by the KBMS. Thus, if the user defines a data-driven inference method, the system will automatically advice the relevant aspects to trigger the ruleset on every change that occurs.

A ruleset may contain any number of rules. In addition a ruleset has a number of attributes by which the behavior of the ruleset can be specified. Among those are formal parameters in case of method invocation, local parameters, initialization sequence, and control structure. There are several predefined control structures available, determining what should happen once a rule has executed successfully.

In EPITOOL rulesets are evaluated by a ruleset interpreter. The advantage of working with explicit representations for rules is the possibility to implement functions for static analysis and indexing. This approach also allows more advanced control structures (such as dynamic priorities or meta-rules which could control.the order of rule invokation)

A Rule consists of a left-hand side, a right-hand side, and a rule descriptor. The left hand side consists of any number of premises. The right hand side varies depending on the type of ruleset. In a RDIM ruleset, the RHS will usually be a statement to conclude a value.

A LHS premise consists, in turn, of a modality and a proposition. The modality is responsible of mapping truthvalues as returned by the proposition into a 2-valued logic. Naturally, the top-level decision whether to execute the rule or not must be "2-valued". There may be many different modalities, however, depending on the underlying logic. In EPITOOL (alpha) , a proposition may have three different truth values: true, false or unknown, where false(p) means that it is definitely known that p is not the case.

4. METHODOLOGICAL IMPLICATIONS

Knowledge engineering is concerned with the transfer of knowledge and expertise from a human expert into a computer program. The process of knowledge transfer confronts the knowledge engineer with two important problems. Firstly, what is the knowledge that the expert uses? Secondly, how can that knowledge be formalized in a computer program?

The task of the knowledge engineer would be considerably easier, if there was a coherent and unified theory of what human knowledge is. Unfortunately, there is no such theory and a lot of work remains to be done, before such a theory will exist. Results from artificial intelligence have, however, led to a number of formalisms, or paradigms, that may be considered simple and primitive theories of how knowledge may be organized. Indeed, for many practical applications such simple formalisms have been proven sufficient.

The formalism provided by EPITOOL may be considered as such a primitive theory. It contains a few primitive elements, such as concepts, rules, groups and descriptions with which knowledge may be represented in a variety of ways. Even though the EPITOOL framework is a primitive systems compared with the complexity of human knowledge in general, it facilities the task of the knowledge engineer tremendously, since it provides a framework which can be used by the kowledge engineer when identifying knowledge structures.

Instead of asking, what knowledge is used by the expert, a knowledge engineer using EPITOOL will ask more specific questions: what domain concepts are there? What aspects are relevant? Which aspects could be infered from which aspects? How could we define such inferences in terms of rules and rulesets?

Even though these questions are already more tractable than the question what knowledge is involved, the knowledge engineer will still have to consider alternative ways of organizing knowledge structures, since there is sufficient redundancy in the representation formalism to allow a knowledge engineer to find a convenient, not just a possible representation.

Asked as a number of concrete questions the process of eliciting the knowledge from the human expert becomes already more feasible. In addition, the second question, how to represent these structures in a computer programs, also finds a simpler answer. Units such as concepts, rules, descriptions and functions can be directly represented in an EPITOOL program. They are executable specifications.

By using the built in representation and inference facilities the task of the knowledge engineer becomes much more efficient, since she or he may think and program at a much higher level of abstraction. There is no need to define one's own data structures for facts, concepts or rules. This saves many hours of design and programming work, eliminating also the risk of a poorly designed knowledge system.

INTRA

Ein Expertensystem zur Software-Unterstützung
bei Hewlett-Packard

Feodora Herrmann, Günter Hornung

Administrative Productivity Operation (APO)

Hewlett-Packard GmbH, D-7030 Böblingen

1. Einleitung

Ein typisches Anwendungsgebiet für Expertensysteme ist die Fehlersuche; auf Grund
von Symptomen, die fehlerhaftes Verhalten beschreiben, wird eine Diagnose erstellt
und darauf aufbauend eine entsprechende Therapie zur Behebung des Fehlers vorgeschlagen. Für eine erfolgreiche Fehlersuche muß ein Experte - und damit auch ein
Expertensystem - neben fundiertem Sach- und Faktenwissen über das Anwendungsgebiet
auch über persönliches, manchmal vages, schwierig zu formulierendes, in langer Zeit
erworbenes Erfahrungswissen verfügen.

Ein guter Experte für die Fehlersuche zeichnet sich dadurch aus, daß er nicht nur
die Ursache eines Fehlers findet und entsprechende Aktionen in seiner Therapie
vorschlägt, sondern darüber hinaus Begründungen und Erklärungen für seine Vorschläge
gibt und somit den Lösungsprozeß transparent macht (Hayes-Roth et al. 1983). Von
einem Experten können wir nicht für alle Fehler eine vollständige Diagnose und
Therapie zur Behebung erwarten. In solchen Fällen kann er aber zumindest Hinweise
geben oder auch Teillösungen anbieten.

Das bekannteste Expertensystem für die Fehlersuche ist MYCIN (Buchanan und Shortliffe 1984), das bakteriologische Infektionskrankheiten diagnostiziert und eine
Behandlung dafür vorschlägt. Außerhalb des medizinischen Bereichs werden zur Zeit
viele Expertensysteme zur Fehlersuche für den technischen Bereich entwickelt. Bei
Hewlett- Packard werden bereits zwei Expertensysteme zur Hardwarewartung und
-unterstützung in der Praxis eingesetzt. Diese befassen sich zum einen mit der Fehlersuche bei Plattenlaufwerken, zum anderen mit der Fehlersuche bei der
Datenübertragung.

Ein weiteres Expertensystem auf dem Gebiet der Fehlersuche - es analysiert Fehler in
einem Softwarepaket und schlägt Aktionen für deren Vermeidung vor - soll hier näher
beschrieben werden.

2. Probleme bei der Software-Unterstützung

Anwender haben üblicherweise beim Einsatz ihrer Software mit verschiedenen Problemen zu kämpfen. Insbesondere während der Einführungszeit tauchen gehäuft Fragen über eine korrekte Handhabung des Programms auf. Beim täglichen Einsatz treten Probleme einer optimalen Systemnutzung und -auslastung sowie Wünsche nach zusätzlichen Leistungseigenschaften und Verbesserungsvorschläge in den Vordergrund. Weitergehend benötigt der Anwender Unterstützung, falls er Fehlermeldungen erhält, die beispielsweise durch Fehler bei der Handhabung der Applikation, durch Ressourcenprobleme oder auch durch Fehler bei der Anpassung des Programmpakets an die speziellen Bedürfnisse des Kunden verursacht wurden. Schließlich hat die Software-Unterstützung noch die Aufgabe, dem Anwender bei Programmabbrüchen schnellstens Vorschläge und Aktionen zur Vermeidung und Behebung des Fehlers anzubieten.

Üblicherweise erfolgt die Software-Unterstützung telefonisch, d.h. der Kunde ruft eines der sog. Kundenbetreuungszentren von Hewlett-Packard an, die für die Softwarewartung und -unterstützung verantwortlich sind. Er schildert sein Problem und erwartet möglichst sofort einen Lösungsvorschlag. Handelt es sich um einen Fehler, den der Kunde selbst beheben kann, muß der Support-Ingenieur im Kundenbetreuungszentrum die dafür notwendigen Aktionen beschreiben. Ansonsten (z.B. bei Programmfehlern) muß er Vorschläge für eine zeitweise Umgehung des Problems anbieten, auf die bis zur endgültigen Behebung des Fehlers ausgewichen werden kann. Dazu braucht er - abhängig von der Art des Fehlers - verschiedene Informationen über das Kundensystem und die Fehlerumgebung (Abbruch-Trace, Fehlermeldungen, Inhalte von Datenbanken, Systemkonfiguration, Quellcode usw.).

Die Probleme, die nicht im Kundenbetreuungszentrum gelöst werden können, werden an die Abteilungen delegiert, die für die Entwicklung und die direkte Software-Unterstützung verantwortlich sind. Bei solchen schwierigen und komplexen Problemen kann also nicht sofort eine Lösung angeboten werden; vielmehr ist der Fehlerfindungsprozess dadurch gekennzeichnet, daß erst nach und nach alle dafür notwendigen Informationen beschafft werden können und mehrere Ingenieure daran beteiligt sind.

Unsere Abteilung hat die weltweite Verantwortung für die Entwicklung sowie die Wartung und Unterstützung der Finanzbuchhaltungs-Software. Der Zeitaufwand und auch die notwendige Informationsmenge für die Unterstützung dieses FiBu-Pakets steigen mit der Komplexität des zu lösenden Problems. In unserem Fall können die Probleme mit jeweils steigender Komplexität wie folgt kategorisiert werden:

1. Fehler, die zum Programmabbruch führen und die ohne Quellcode lösbar sind.

   Eine entsprechende Diagnose und Behebung kann auf Grund eines Abbruch-Trace, Wissen über die Konfiguration des Kundensystems und oft auch aus Erfahrungen ähnlicher Fehler geliefert werden. Ungefähr ein Drittel aller Probleme, die von den Kundenberatungszentren selbst gelöst werden können, fallen in diese Kategorie.

2. Fehler, die zum Programmabbruch führen und die nur mit Hilfe des Quellcodes lösbar sind.

   Die Ursache des Fehlers muß im Quellcode lokalisiert werden. Dazu muß die Abbruchstelle im Code gefunden, sowie die Anweisungen überprüft werden, die vor dem Abbruch durchlaufen wurden.

3. Fehlermeldungen ohne Abbruch

   Solche Fehler sind dadurch charakterisiert, daß entweder ein Benutzer auf seinem Bildschirm eine Fehlermeldung erhält und/oder eine Fehlermeldung auf dem zentralen sog. Systemverwalterbildschirm angezeigt wird. Zur Behebung dieser Fehler müssen diese meist dupliziert und dabei ein Trace zur Verfolgung des Systemverhaltens eingeschaltet werden.

4. Falsche Reaktion des Systems

   Die Behandlung solcher Probleme erfordert unbedingt einen Trace. Oft dauert deren Lösung mehrere Tage, auch wenn alle Information bereits beschafft ist und mehrere Anwendungsprogrammierer und Support-Ingenieure eingeschaltet werden. Erfahrungen haben gezeigt, daß Fehler dieser Kategorie nur durch die Support-Ingenieure in der Entwicklungsabteilung gelöst werden können.

5. Verbesserungsvorschläge und Forderungen nach zusätzlichen Leistungseigenschaften

   Diese Probleme sind keine Fehler im eigentlichen Sinne und somit keine Aufgabe der Software-Unterstützung. Erweiterungen in der Anwendung werden durch die Entwicklungsabteilung vorgenommen.

3. Software-Unterstützung mit INTRA

Es war unser Ziel, ein Expertensystem zu entwickeln, das zunächst Probleme der Kategorie 1 lösen kann. INTRA (INtelligent TRace Analyzer) kann dadurch die Qualität der Software-Unterstützung in den Kundenbetreuungszentren verbessern und somit die Support-Ingenieure entlasten.

INTRA befragt zunächst den Benutzer nach Informationen auf dem Abbruch-Trace, der automatisch bei jedem Abbruch der Finanzbuchhaltungs-Software erzeugt wird. Falls dieser in maschinenlesbarer Form verfügbar ist, wird diese Information direkt aus dem Trace gelesen. In den meisten Fällen muß der Benutzer noch Fragen nach der Systemkonfiguration und der Umgebung, in der das FiBu-Paket läuft, beantworten. Zu jeder Frage des Systems kann eine ausführliche Hilfe angefordert werden. Jede Antwort auf eine Frage kann zu einem beliebigen späteren Zeitpunkt wieder revidiert werden.

Das folgende Beispiel zeigt einen Dialog mit INTRA. Benutzereingaben sind unterstrichen, Erklärungen stehen in Klammern.

```
INtelligent TRace Analyzer, XG.00


My name is INTRA. I will try to help you solve your HPFA problem. Currently,
I can only analyze normal HPFA abort dumps (no RF/IF dumps).
Please, get your dump ready.

Please, enter an ID for your problem:

Example-1

____________________________________________________________________________


What is the 'Possible Class of Abort'?

  Customizer Intrinsic Failure
  Application Transaction Failure
  Driver Segment Failure
  Monitor Intrinsic Failure
  V/3000 Intrinsic Failure
  Image Intrinsic Failure
  CT procedure failure
  Workfile procedure failure
  File System Abort
  MPE intrinsic abort
  other

  <Benutzer drückt HELP-Taste>


____________________________________________________________________________
```

INTRA has asked you to provide the abort class of your HPFA problem.
The abort class is listed on the first page of your dump under
   'Possible Class of abort:'

<Benutzer drückt CONTINUE-Taste, dadurch wird die letzte Frage erneut gestellt.
 Dann wählt er 'File System Abort' aus.>

What is the 'File System Error'?

   Out of Disc Space (FSERR 46)
   Nonexistent Group (FSERR 51)
   Nonexistent Permanent File (FSERR 52)
   Too many files (FSERR74)
   Exclusive Violation: File being accessed (FSERR 90)
   other

<Benutzer wählt 'Out of Disc Space (FSERR 46)' aus>

Do you have any unnecessary files on the system?

No

Did you recently encounter a system failure which was not properly recovered?

No

How is the free disc space distributed over the discs?

   Fragmented
   Unfragmented
   No free disc space left

<Benutzer drückt HELP-Taste>

In order to assess the disc free space distribution, run FREE5.PUB.SYS.
Generally, there is enough disc space available if
   Subystem Total Free Space > 30000.

The free disc space is considered FRAGMENTED if there is a disc with
   Largest Free Area < (Total Free Space / 2).

<Benutzer drückt CONTINUE-Taste, dadurch wird die letzte Frage erneut gestellt.
 Dann wählt er 'Fragmented' aus.>

Has a CONDENSE recently been performed on the discs?

<u>Yes</u>

<Nun bietet INTRA folgende Problemanalyse an:>

User Problem Example-1

The following possible cause of your problem could be identified.

Diagnosis:

  FOPEN failed to open a file.

  The system does not have sufficient contiguous disc space to build
  or extend a file.

Possible Actions:

  Take a SYSDYUMP of the whole system and make a RELOAD from this backup.
  After this, the unused space on each disc will be contiguous.

If you have any further questions, please contact APO Online Support
in Boeblingen.

---

4. Die Entwicklungsumgebung für INTRA

4.1 Software

In den Forschungslaboratorien von Hewlett-Packard wurde HPRL (Heuristic Programming and Representation Language) (Rosenberg 1982), eine Sprache zur Konstruktion von Expertensystemen entwickelt. HPRL ist in dem LISP-Dialekt PSL (Portable Standard Lisp) implementiert. HPRL enthält Sprachmittel zur Darstellung und Verarbeitung von Wissen.

Das Wissen wird mit Hilfe sog. Frames dargestellt. Frames sind komplexe Datenstrukturen, die hierarchisch organisiert sind. Hierarchisch niedrigere Frames sind dabei Spezialisierungen der jeweils höheren. Innerhalb von Frames wird Information in sog. Slots abgespeichert. Hierarchisch höhere Frames können diese Information an niedrigere "vererben". Das Hinzufügen oder Löschen von Information kann den Aufruf von Prozeduren auslösen.

Schlußfolgern und damit die Generierung von neuem Wissen aus bereits vorhandenem geschieht mit Hilfe von Regeln der Form

```
(rule   <Regel-Name>   <Regel-Typ>
    (premise      <Wenn-Teil>)
    (conclusion   <Dann-Teil>))
```

Der Wenn-Teil einer Regel beschreibt eine Menge von Aussagen. Rückwärtsverkettete (zielgesteuerte) Regeln beschreiben in ihrem Dann-Teil Aussagen, die aus den Aussagen im Wenn-Teil geschlossen werden können. Sie erlauben somit, nach Bedarf neues Wissen aus vorhandenem abzuleiten. Vorwärtsverkettete (datengesteuerte) Regeln geben in ihrem Dann-Teil Aktionen an, die ausgeführt werden, wenn eine Aussage aus dem Wenn-Teil wahr wird. Durch sie können z.B. Konsistenzprüfungen angestoßen werden.

HPRL ist in eine benutzerfreundliche Programmierumgebung eingebettet, die neben einem sehr komfortablen auf EMACS basierenden Editor Hilfsmittel zum Formulieren von Regeln und Testen des Interpretationsprozesses umfaßt.

4.2 Hardware

HPRL und damit auch INTRA laufen auf den technischen Rechnern HP 9000 mit mindestens 4 MByte Hauptspeicher. Die Finanzbuchhaltungs-Software ist auf dem Rechner HP 3000 verfügbar, einem kommerziellen Computersystem der mittleren Leistungsklasse. INTRA kann über eine Datenkommunikationsschnittstelle direkt auf FiBu-Daten der HP 3000 zugreifen.

4.3 Implementierung von INTRA

INTRA umfaßt zur Zeit etwa 100 Frames und 150 Regeln. Dabei wird die Heterarchie der
möglichen Fehlerursachen in Frames dargestellt. Das folgende Beispiel zeigt einen
Auszug aus dem Frame für die Fehlerursache FSERR46:

```
(deframe FSERR46
    (ako ($value (PROBLEM)))
    (unnecessary-files ($ask (first))
                       ($type (affirmative))
                       ($prompt ("Do you have any unnecessary files on the
                                 system?"))
                       ($help (("In order to find out about any unnessary files"
                               "you should check for"
                               " "
                               "- unused groups or accounts"
                               "- obsolete log files"
                               "- old spoolfiles which can be deleted or"
                               " printed out"))))
    (recent-system-fails ($ask (first))
                         ($type (affirmative))
                         ($prompt ("Did you recently encounter a system failure"
                         ;        "which was not properly recovered?"))
                         ($help ... ))
    ... )
```

Der Slot ako (a kind of) gibt den in der Frame-Heterarchie übergeordneten Frame von
FSERR46 an. Die Werte für die Slots UNNECESSARY-FILES und RECENT-SYSTEM-FAILS werden
direkt vom Benutzer erfragt (gesteuert durch den Wert FIRST unter $ASK). Dabei ist
jeweils unter $PROMPT der Text angegeben, der dem Benutzer als Fragetext angeboten
wird. Der unter $TYPE spezifizierte Wert schränkt die Eingabemöglichkeiten des
Benutzers ein, in diesem Fall wird nur "YES" oder "NO" als Eingabe akzeptiert. Der
zu $HELP gehörige Text wird ausgegeben, wenn der Benutzer die HELP-Taste drückt.

Wenn INTRA ein neues Problem bearbeitet, wird zunächst eine neue Instanz des Frames
PROBLEM (Wurzel der Frame-Heterarchie) erzeugt. Vorwärtsverkettete Regeln sorgen
dann dafür, daß bei jeder Instantiierung Informationen in bestimmten Slots gesammelt
werden. Aufgrund dieser Information ist es möglich, das Problem immer weiter zu
spezialisieren. Wenn z.B. für ein PROBLEM die ABORTCLASS bekannt geworden ist, so
sorgt die folgende Regel dafür, daß PROBLEM nun eine Instanz dieser ABORTCLASS in
der Frame-Heterarchie wird.

```
(rule CREATE-ABORTCLASS forward-chain-rule
    (premise (?PROBLEM abortclass ?ABORTCLASS))
    (conclusion (?ABORTCLASS instance ?PROBLEM)))
```

Rückwärtsverkettete Regeln werden zur Deduktion benutzt. Die folgende Regel wird
angewandt, wenn die möglichen Aktionen zur Fehlerbehebung gefunden werden sollen.
Die gefolgerte Aktion wird vorgeschlagen, falls die Werte "FRAGMENTED" bzw. "YES"

für die Slots "SCATTERED-SPACE" bzw. "RECENT-CONDENSE" entweder vom Benutzer eingegeben oder durch andere Regeln zugewiesen werden:

```
(rule FSERR46-RELOAD backward-chain-rule
   (premise (and (?FSERR46 scattered-space fragmented)
                 (?FSERR46 recent-condense yes)))
   (conclusion (?FSERR46 action ("Take a SYSDUMP of the whole system and make"
                                 "a RELOAD from this backup."
                                 "After this, the unused space on each disc"
                                 "will be contiguous."))))
```

5. Einsatz in der Praxis und Zukunftsperspektiven

Zur Zeit wird INTRA (Version 1) in unserer Abteilung von den Support-Ingenieuren verwendet. Sie bearbeiten mit dem Expertensystem alle eintreffenden Probleme, die durch einen Abbruch der FiBu-Software auftreten. Durch diesen Testeinsatz erwarten wir uns Fortschritte bei der Klärung folgender Fragen:

Akzeptanz

Wird INTRA von den Support-Ingenieuren überhaupt benutzt?

Inwieweit ist INTRA geeignet, Ingeniere bei der Softwarewartung und -unterstützung zu entlasten?

Wie ist die Handhabbarkeit und Benutzerfreundlichkeit von INTRA?

Leistungsfähigkeit

Für wieviele und welche Probleme findet INTRA eine Lösung?

Sind diese Lösungsvorschläge korrekt und vollständig?

Wie muß INTRA verbessert werden, damit ein Problembereich vollständig abgedeckt wird?

Erweiterungen

Wie sollte INTRA erweitert werden?

Das entscheidende Problem bei der Entwicklung von INTRA war, im Gespräch mit Experten die Expertise für die Software-Unterstützung zu gewinnen. Diese Erkenntnis wurde auch bei Entwicklung zweier prototypischer Expertensysteme auf dem Gebiet der Software-Konfiguration gewonnen (Herrmann und Hornung 1985). Um die große Bandbreite der Fehlerursachen abzudecken, war es notwendig, sehr viele Spezialisten zu befragen: Anwendungsprogrammierer, Support-Ingenieure sowie Systemspezialisten. Um ein Expertensystem zu entwickeln, ist es unbedingt notwendig, innerhalb kurzer Zeit einen Prototyp für den internen Einsatz zur Verfügung zu stellen. Nur so ist die notwendige Rückkopplung der Anwender und damit eine kontinuierliche Leistungsverbesserung überhaupt möglich.

Es ist geplant, INTRA nach dem internen Testeinsatz zu den Kundenbetreuungszentren zu transferieren. Nach der Erprobungsphase kann entschieden werden, wie das Expertensystem erweitert wird. Zum einen denken wir daran, daß mit INTRA (Version 2) auch Abbrüche analysiert werden können, die nur mit Hilfe des Quellcodes möglich sind. Zum anderen kann INTRA dadurch verbessert werden, daß es Fehler in der FiBu-Software analysiert, die nicht zum Programmabbruch führen.

6. Zusammenfassung

INTRA ist ein Expertensystem zur Unterstützung der HP-Finanzbuchhaltungs-Software. INTRA analysiert Programmabbruchsituationen und schlägt Möglichkeiten zur Fehlerbehebung und -umgehung vor. Dadurch kann die Unterstützung der Kunden beschleunigt und qualitativ verbessert werden.

Literaturverzeichnis

Buchanan, B.G.; Shortliffe, E.H. (eds.) (1984): "Rule-Based Expert Systems: The MYCIN Experiments of the Stanford Heuristic Programming Project", Addison-Wesley

Hayes-Roth, F.; Waterman, D.A.; Lenat, D.B. (eds.) (1983): "Building Expert Systems", Addison-Wesley

Herrmann, F.; Hornung, G. (1985): "Expertensysteme zur Software-Konfiguration", in: Proceedings der GI-OCG-ÖGI Jahrestagung 1985, Springer

Rosenberg, S. (1982): "HPRL - A Language for Building Expert Systems", in: Proceedings of the 8th ICJAI, Vol. 1, p. 215ff

<u>Anwendungen intelligenter Übersetzergeneratoren</u>

U. Kastens

Fachbereich Mathematik / Informatik
Universität-GH Paderborn

Programmsysteme, die aus Übersetzerspezifikationen automatisch Übersetzeralgorithmen
erzeugen sollen hier aus der Sicht intelligenter, wissensbasierter Systeme betrachtet werden. Im folgenden stellen wir dar, worin wir die Intelligenz von Übersetzergeneratoren sehen, wie ihre Wissensbasis weiter verbreitert werden könnte, und wie
sie auch für Anwendungen außerhalb des Übersetzerbaus einsetzbar sind.

<u>Einführung</u>

Die Automatisierung der Herstellung von Übersetzern für Programmiersprachen hat eine für die Informatik lange Tradition, die bis in die 50er Jahre zurückreicht. Der
wissenschaftliche und technische Fortschritt vollzog sich dabei im wesentlichen in
zwei sich gegenseitig beeinflussenden Bereichen: Methoden zur Spezifikation des Über-
setzungsproblems und Übersetzungsalgorithmen.

Die Übersetzung wird durch die Quellsprache (Programmiersprache) und die Transformation ihrer Elemente in die Zielsprache (Maschinensprache) spezifiziert. Formale
und damit präzise Spezifikationsmethoden sind Voraussetzung für die automatische Übersetzer-Erzeugung. Ihr Einsatz im Übersetzerbau begann bei der Spezifikation der strukturellen Sprachoberfläche (Symbol- und Syntaxspezifikation durch kontextfreie Grammatiken), schritt fort über die Beschreibung von Kontextabhängigkeiten (durch attributierte Grammatiken und vergleichbare Methoden) und umfaßt heute auch die formale
Spezifikation optimierender Abbildungen auf die Zielsprache (Spezifikation der Code-
Erzeugung).

Parallel zu den Spezifikationsmethoden wurden die Übersetzungsalgorithmen weiterentwickelt: Systematische Verfahren entstanden, mit denen Algorithmen aus der Spezifikation erzeugt werden können (Parser-Generatoren für kontextfreie Grammatiken z.B.
[De 77, Jo 77], Attributauswerter-Generatoren für attributierte Grammatiken z.B.
[GRW 77, Fa 82, KHZ 82, RST 78], Code-Erzeuger-Generatoren z.B. [Ca 80, GG 78]. Die
Mächtigkeit der Erzeugungsverfahren wurde erhöht (größere Grammatikklassen bei kon-
textfreien und attributierten Grammatiken), so daß der Entwurf von Spezifikationen be-
freit wurde von algorithmischen Einschränkungen. Die Speicher- und Zeiteffizienz der
Algorithmen wurde so verbessert, daß sie in Produktionsübersetzern einsetzbar sind.

Prinzipien und Einsatz dieser Techniken werden z.B. in [AU 77, Lo 84, WG 84] beschrieben.

Was begründet die Intelligenz von Übersetzergeneratoren?

Während die früheren sogenannten "Translator Writing Systems" Werkzeuge zur mehr oder weniger komfortablen Programmierung von Übersetzern waren, sind beim heutigen Stand der Technik die Voraussetzungen für intelligente Übersetzergeneratoren gegeben. Der Entwurf der Spezifikation des Übersetzerproblems ist von der automatisierbaren Konstruktion der Übersetzungsalgorithmen abtrennbar. Die Eigenschaften von Programmiersprachen und ihre Abbildung auf Maschinen werden durch Regeln beschrieben, aus denen Analyse- und Synthesealgorithmen automatisch erzeugt werden.

Solch ein intelligentes System basiert auf einer Menge von Algorithemn, die das Know-How des Übersetzerbaus repräsentieren. Für das spezielle Übersetzungsproblem werden Regeln als Spezifikation entworfen: z.B. eine kontextfreie Grammatik zur Spezifikation der Quellsprachstruktur, Regeln einer attributierten Grammatik, welche kontextabhängige Spracheigenschaften wie Typisierung, Definitionen und Gültigkeitsbereiche beschreiben, und schließlich Abbildungen von Ausschnitten des attributierten Strukturbaumes auf Operationen der Zielmaschine, wobei durch Fallunterscheidungen über Kontextbedingungen Codeoptimierungen erzielt werden können.

Solche Regelsätze akkumulieren das Wissen über die Quellsprache und die Zielmaschine. Modifikationen des Problems (Änderungen der Quellsprache oder der Zielmaschine) können dann durch Fortentwicklung der Spezifikation sicherer und kostengünstiger behandelt werden als durch Änderuungen des Übersetzerprogramms. Insbesondere wird der Herstellungsaufwand mehrerer Übersetzer für verschiedene Quell- und Zielsprachen drastisch reduziert durch Kombination der entsprechenden Spezifikationsteile. - Ein Ziel, das schon seit den 60er Jahren (UNCOL-Konzept) verfolgt wird.

In dem dargestellten Sinne kann man einen Übersetzergenerator als ein wissensbasiertes System auffassen. Aus diesem Blickwinkel wird die Übersetzer-Erzeugung z.B. auch in [Fr 85] betrachtet. Prinzipielle Unterschiede zum üblichen Konzept von Expertensystemen resultieren jedoch aus der speziellen Aufgabe der Übersetzergenerierung. So werden für die einzelnen Übersetzeraufgaben (Symbolentschlüsslung, kontextfreie, kontextabhängige Analyse, Code-Erzeugung und Optimierung) verschiedene Spezifikationsmethoden eingesetzt und verschiedene Algorithmen generiert.

Anders als bei allgemeinen Experten Systemen, für die eine gewisse Unvollständigkeit und Unschärfe des Regelsatzes typisch ist, werden an eine Übersetzerspezifikation strengere Anforderungen gestellt: Sie muß die Quellsprache eindeutig und vollständig beschreiben und die Syntheseregeln müssen hinreichend sein zur Übersetzung jedes Programms. Diese Bedingungen werden üblicherweise von einem Übersetzergenerator als Voraussetzung für die Generierung geprüft. (Ein Übersetzer, der die Übersetzung abbricht, weil das Quellprogramm eine unvorhergesehene Konstruktion enthält, ist nicht akzeptabel.)

Heute sind einige automatische Verfahren zur optimierenden Code- Erzeugung im Einsatz, die dem Konzept der Expertensysteme sehr nahe kommen: Formuliert man die Übersetzung einzelner Quellsprachelemente (die üblicherweise durch einen Ausschnitt des attributierten Struktur-Baumes repräsentiert werden) in Maschinensprachbefehle, so sind insbesondere zur Code-Verbesserung (z.B. durch Einsatz von Spezialbefehlen) umfangreiche Fallunterscheidungen nötig. Dieses Problem wird elegant durch Anwendung von Pattern-Matching Verfahren auf Bäumen gelöst: Eine Regel beschreibt ein Baummuster zusammen mit dem dafür zu erzeugenden Befehl. (Solch eine Spezifikation kann man auch als Beschreibung der Zielmaschine in Termen des Strukturbaums ansehen.) Ziel des mit diesen Regeln parametrisierten Code-Erzeugungsalgorithmus ist es, eine passende Überdeckung des Baumes mit solchen Mustern zu finden, die dann den Ziel-Code beschreibt. Geht man von einem minimalen Satz von Regeln aus, mit dem jeder Strukturbaum übersetzt werden kann (- diese Frage ist für Verfahren wie [GG 78] überprüfbar), so kann die Übersetzungsqualität verbessert werden, indem man sukzessive weitere Regeln hinzufügt, die durch Einbeziehen größeren Kontextes Spezialfälle berücksichtigen. Praktisch einsetzbare Verfahren für diese Code-Erzeugungsmethode sind z.B. in [GG 78,Ca80] präsentiert worden, wobei die Methode von Graham-Glenville auf einer sehr effizienten Syntaxanalysetechnik basiert.

Auch die Technik der Peephole-Optimierung basiert auf Pattern Matching Methoden: Über die generierte Folge von Maschinenbefehlen wird ein Fenster geschoben, durch das nur einige aufeinanderfolgende Befehle sichtbar sind. Ein Satz von Regeln definiert Muster für kurze Befehlssequenzen, die zusammengefaßt und z.B. durch einzelne Spezialbefehle ersetzt werden können. (Diese Technik eliminiert insbesondere Ineffizienzen, die durch baumorientierte Code-Erezugngung entstehen.) Auch hier kann man die Wissensbasis in Form des Regelsatzes sukzessive erweitern und damit die Qualtität der Übersetzung verbessern.

Übersetzergeneratoren könnten intelligenter sein

Trotz der bisher erreichten Systematisierung und Automatisierung lassen heutige übersetzererzeugende Systeme einige Wünsche an ihre "Intelligenz" offen: Viele Systeme sind auf die Generierung eines Übersetzerteils konzentriert (z.B. Parser-Generator [De 77, Jo 77], Attributierungs-Generator [KHZ 82, RST 78], Code-Erzeugungsgenerator [LJG 82]). Bei Verwendung mehrerer solcher Werkzeuge müssen die Spezifikationen aufeinander abgestimmt und die Übersetzerteile integriert werden, was erheblichen Auf-

wand erfordern kann. Wünschenswert wären integrierte Generatoren mit aufeinander ab-
gestimmten Spezifikationen, die den Übergang von einem Werkzeug zum anderen vereinfachen oder gar transparent machen. (Dieser Ansatz wurde z.B. im PQCC-Projekt [Le 79]
verfolgt.) Ein solches System könnte auch weitergehende Unterstützung bei Entwurfsentscheidungen leisten, die Konsequenzen auf Spezifikationen mehrerer Übersetzeraufgaben haben (z.B. Strukturbaumänderungen).

Trotz des erreichten Abstraktionsgrades der Übersetzerspezifikation ist zu ihrer Entwicklung ein erheblicher Aufwand erforderlich: Z.B. umfassen sowohl die attributierte Grammatik für Pascal in [KHZ 82] als auch die Code-Erzeugungsspezifikation für den
M68000 in [LJG 82] jeweils mehr als 2000 Zeilen. Ohne den offensichtlichen Wert solcher Spezifikationen zu schmälern, kann man feststellen, daß sie umfangreiche Teile
enthalten, deren Konzepte in vielen Sprach-, Maschinen- und Übersetzungsbeschrei-
bungen ähnlich auftreten (z.B. Behandlung von Definitionen, Gültigkeitsbereichen,
Typregeln in Programmiersprachen oder Registerzuordnung für Maschinen). Dafür könnten
standardisierte Spezifikationsteile mit dazu passenden Algorithmen von dem Übersetzer-
erzeugenden System angeboten werden. Eine so verbreiterte Wissensbasis würde den Entwicklungsaufwand für Übersetzer wesentlich reduzieren.

Anwendungen außerhalb der Übersetzergenerierung

Übersetzergeneratoren sind keine Universalwerkzeuge. Aber es ist eine Binsenweisheit,
daß Softwaresysteme in den Händen von Benutzern auch für Zwecke eingesetzt werden, für
die sie nicht entwickelt wurden. Dies ist kein Mißbrauch sondern nützlich für den Anwender, falls die Struktur des gestellten Problems mit der für das System intendierten
übereinstimmt. Für Übersetzer-erzeugende Systeme, die wie oben beschrieben durch Sätze
von Regeln gesteuert werden bieten sich auch Anwendungen außerhalb der Übersetzung von
Programmiersprachen an. Sie sind dann sinnvoll, wenn die Problemstellung die zentralen
Charakteristika der Sprachübersetzung enthält: Die zentrale Datenstruktur ist ein Baum
(beschrieben durch eine kontextfreie Grammatik). Darin findet nach gewissen Regeln
(Attributierung) ein Informationsfluß statt, der die Transformation des Baumes in das
Ergebnis steuert. Als Beispiele für solche Probleme wollen wir Textaufbereitung und
hierarchische Entwurfssysteme betrachten.

Betrachten wir das Problem der Herstellung einer Druckvorlage aus einem mit Forma-
tieranweisungen versehenen Textes ohne interaktive Eingriffe. Einem solchen Manuskript unterliegt eine hierarchische Struktur aus geschachtelten Abschnitten und Text-
blöcken verschiedener Typen (Paragraphen, Tabellen, Abbildungen, usw.). Sie kann durch
eine kontextfreie Grammatik vorgegeben werden. Die Formatierangaben bestimmen Attribute dieser Strukturelemente (z.B. Einrückung, Zentrierung, Schrifttyp, usw.). Infor-

mationsfluß durch die Baumstruktur ist notwendig zur Numerierung von Abschnitten, für Referenzen auf Abschnitte, Literaturstellen, Fußnoten, und für die Plazierung der Textstücke im Druckbild. Dies kann z.B. durch Regeln einer attributierten Grammatik beschrieben werden. Aus einer solchen Spezifikation kann ein Übersetzer-erzeugendes System einen Algorithmus generieren, der als Ergebnis eine Folge von Anweisungen zur Ausgabe des formatierten Textes produziert.

Hierarchische Entwurfssysteme finden in verschiedenen Bereichen Anwendung, z.B. technische Konstruktionen, Schaltpläne, hochintegrierte Schaltungen, Grobentwurf von Programmsystemen. Die hierarchische Struktur ist durch die Verfeinerung und Abstraktion der Konstruktionselemente gegeben. Ihnen werden Attribute zur Beschreibung ihrer Eigenschaften zugeordnet. Regeln zur Zusammensetzung der Komponenten beschreiben Konsistenzbedingungen für die Konstruktion, z.B. die Verbindungen von Schaltelementen oder die Schnittstellen von Programmmoduln. Entwurfsentscheidungen für einzelne Komponenten beeinflußen nach bestimmten Regeln Eigenschaften in der Struktur benachbarter Elemente wie Form, Plazierung und Verbindung von Schaltungselementen. Zur Berechnung solcher Eigenschaften ist dann ein Informationsfluß durch den Baum erforderlich. Einen Algorithmus dafür kann ein Übersetzer-erzeugendes System automatisch aus den spezifizierten Regeln konstruieren, falls die Spezifikation den vom System geforderten Randbedingungen genügt.

Für hierarchische Entwurfssysteme ist im allgemeinen eine interaktive Konzeption wünschenswert. Hier könnten Wechselwirkungen zu der Entwicklung interaktiver Übersetzer für beide Bereiche befruchtend wirken.

Literatur

AU 77   Aho, A.V., Ullman, J.D.: Principles of Compiler Design, Addison-Wesley, 1977

Ca 80   Cattell, R.G.G.: Automatic Derivation of Code Generators from Machine Descriptions, ACM TOPLAS 2,2, 1980

De 77   Dencker, P.: Ein neues LALR-System, Institut für Informatik, Universität-Karlsruhe, Diplomarbeit, 1977

Fa 82   Farrow, R.: LINGUIST-86 Yet Another Translator Writing System Based on Attribute Grammars, Proc. SIGPLAN Symp. on Compiler Construction, Boston 1982, SIGPLAN Not. 17, 6, 1982

Fr 85   Frenkel, K.A.: Toward Automating the Software-Development Cycle, CACM 28,6, 1985

GRW 77   Ganzinger, H., Ripken, K., Wilhelm, R.: Automatic Generation of Optimizing Multi-Pass Compilers, Proc. IFIP 1977, Toronto 1977

GG 78   Glanville, R.S., Graham, S.L.: A New Method for Compiler Code Generation 5th ACM Symp. on Principles of Progr. Lang., 1978

Jo 77   Johnson, S.C.: YACC - Yet Another Compiler Compiler, Bell Labs. Murray Hill, 1977

KHZ 82 Kastens, U., Hutt, B., Zimmermann, E.: GAG: A Practical Compiler Generator, LNCS 141, Springer, 1982

LJG 82 Landwehr, R., Jansohn, H.S., Goos, G.: Experience with an Automatic Code Generator Generator, Proc. SIGPLAN Symp. on Compiler Construction, Boston 1982, SIGPLAN Not. 17, 6, 1982

Le 79 Leverett, B.W., et.al.: An Overview of the Production Quality Compiler-Compiler Project, Comp. Sc. Dep., Carnegie-Mellon University, 1979

RST 78 Räihä, K-J., Saarinen, M., Soisalon-Soininen, E., Tienari, M.: The Compiler Writing System HLP, Dep. of Comp., University of Helsinki, 1978

WG 84 Waite, W.M., Goos, G.: Compiler Construction, Springer, 1984

-DEX.C3-
Ein Expertensystem zur Fehlerdiagnose
im automatischen Getriebe

Peter Henne, Walter Klar, Karl-Heinz Wittur
Gesellschaft für Mathematik und Datenverarbeitung
Forschungsgruppe Expertensysteme

1. Einleitung

In jüngster Zeit finden Expertensysteme in der Industrie – und zwar gerade
auch in der Automobilindustrie – immer stärkeres Interesse. DEX.C3 ist das
erste von der Forschungsgruppe Expertensysteme in der GMD entwickelte
Expertensystem. Es dient zur Diagnose von Fehlverhalten im automatischen
Getriebe C3 der Firma Ford. Die Firma Ford Europa prüft zur Zeit die Frage,
in welchen Firmenbereichen und für welche Aufgaben Expertensysteme
nutzbringend eingesetzt werden können.
Dabei muß man berücksichtigen, daß die Nutzung solcher Systeme in der
betrieblichen Praxis einer Automobilfirma noch weitgehend Neuland ist. Gerade
der Kundendienstbereich mit seiner organisatorisch und regional dezentralen
Struktur bedeutet für die praktische Implementation dieser neuen Technik eine
besondere Herausforderung [THOME83], [REITMA84]. Eine Fülle von Problemen
müssen gelöst werden, bevor dort der praktische Nutzen spürbar werden kann.
Bei der Einführung der Expertensysteme im Kundendienst ist daher ein
sorgfältig geplantes Vorgehen in mehreren Einzelschritten erforderlich.
Mit der Entwicklung des Expertensystems zur Diagnose von Fehlern im
automatischen Getriebe C3 wurde nun der erste Schritt gemacht. Dieser Schritt
hatte in hohem Maße Versuchscharakter: Es ging darum, Arbeitsweise und
Einsatzmöglichkeiten eines Expertensystems anhand eines konkreten
Anwendungsbeispiels zu illustrieren und die prinzipielle Machbarkeit
nachzuweisen. DEX.C3 gehört zu einem der wenigen Systeme in der
Bundesrepublik, das einem Feldtest unterzogen wird.
Im Vergleich zu dem DEX.C3-Überblick in [KLAWIT85] sollen in diesem Papier
die Aspekte Wissensakquisition und Erklärungsfähigkeit des Systems stärker
betont werden.

2. Identifikation des Problembereichs

Wenn es mit Hilfe eines Expertensystems gelingt, einen relativ unerfahrenen
Kfz-Mechaniker selbst zum Expertem zu machen, böte das enorme Möglichkeiten
für den Kundendienstbereich der Automobilindustrie [BUNGER85a].
Beispielsweise bei der Markteinführung von elektronischen Steuer- und
Kontrollsystemen im Auto: Obwohl solche Systeme heute prinzipiell machbar
sind, geht deren Markteinführung nicht zuletzt deshalb so langsam voran, weil
sich die Kundendienstwerkstätten in der Wartung vor kaum lösbare Probleme
gestellt sehen. Grund: Für Fehlerdiagnose und Reparatur fehlt es am nötigen
Know-how auf breiterer Basis. Expertsysteme könnten helfen, die Lücke zu
schließen, denn sie ermöglichen es, Wissen beliebig zu vervielfältigen und
breiter verfügbar zu machen [MICHIE79]. Wenn es mit Hilfe solcher Systeme
gelingt, Wissen in der Werkstatt zielgerichtet einzusetzen, das bisher nur
bei wenigen erfahrenen Kfz-Meistern und Experten in Entwicklung und Fertigung
vorliegt, so ist eine erhebliche Steigerung der Qualität und Effizienz des

Kundendienstes zu erwarten.

2.1 Fehlerdiagnose im C3-Getriebe

Mit DEX.C3 galt es nachzuweisen, daß das Wissen und die Vorgehensweise eines C3-Experten bei der Fehlerdiagnose mit einem Expertensystem korrekt und umfassend nachgebildet werden können. Desweiteren sollte das System im Falle des Gelingens für Demonstrationszwecke bereitgestellt werden, mit dem Ziel, auch andere Bereiche der Firma über diese neue Anwendungsmöglichkeit der Informationstechnik anhand eines aussagekräftigen Beispiels zu informieren.

Für die Auswahl des C3-Getriebes als Anwendungsfeld waren mehrere Punkte ausschlaggebend:

1. Die Expertise über Fehlerdiagnose im C3-Getriebe ist nicht bei jedem
   Mechaniker vorhanden.

2. Es handelt sich um ein überschaubares Feld, so daß die Entwicklung
   in verhältnismäßig kurzer Zeit abgeschlossen werden konnte.

3. Es kommt vor, daß Fehler im automatischen Getriebe nicht
   richtig erkannt werden, wodurch unnötig hohe Kosten entstehen.

Das automatische Getriebe C3 ist im wesentlichen ein in sich abgeschlossenes System, welches mechanische und hydraulische Komponenten in sich vereinigt. Aus diesem Grund stellt die Fehlersuche im C3-Getriebe ein komplexes Problem dar. Speziell ist hier die Mehrfachfunktion des Öls angesprochen (siehe auch Abb. 3), welches für die Steuerung des Getriebes, die Schmierung seiner Bauteile, sowie die Kühlung verantwortlich ist. Damit kann es die Ursache unterschiedlicher Störfälle sein, die sich durch verschiedenartige Symptome erkennbar machen und schwer zu diagnostizieren sind.

Die Problematik der korrekten Diagnosestellung in den Werkstätten liegt darin, daß die möglichen Ursachen für einen Defekt oft nicht systematisch überprüft werden. Dies führt dann teilweise zur Durchführung unnötiger Reparaturen, die den Defekt nur kurzzeitig beseitigen. Zu spätes oder zu frühes Schalten in den Gängen kann z.B durch Auffüllen des Ölstandes auf die korrekte Füllhöhe korrigiert werden, wird aber die Ursache für den zu geringen Ölstand nicht erforscht, z.B. äußere Undichtigkeit durch Ölaustritt am Entlüfter-Ventil, dann wird der beanstandete Mangel nach kurzer Zeit wieder auftreten und evtl. noch Folgefehler verursachen.

Abgesehen von Fehlern, die durch Undichtigkeit des Getriebes verursacht werden, handelt es sich bei dem C3-Getriebe um ein wenig störanfälliges Bauteil. Hinzu kommt, daß in Europa nur wenige Fahrzeuge mit automatischen Getrieben ausgestattet sind. In Deutschland treten jährlich im Durchschnitt pro Ford-Werkstatt zwei Störfälle an automatischen Getrieben auf. Aus diesen Gründen gibt es in den Werkstätten nur wenig Erfahrung mit der Fehlerfindung in defekten Getrieben, so daß eine korrekte Diagnose, die in den meisten Fällen die Voraussetzung für eine kostengünstige Reparatur bildet, nicht immer die Regel ist. Zwar stehen in den Werkstätten die Werkstatthandbücher zur Verfügung, welche pro Automodell erstellt und verteilt werden, sie können jedoch in der Praxis durch den Automechaniker nicht immer adäquat genutzt werden. So ergeben sich zum einen Probleme mit der Aktualisierung der Handbücher, zum anderen ist der Mechaniker oft nicht in der Lage, die im Handbuch enthaltenen Informationen und Hinweise gezielt auszunutzen, wenn er mit einem konkreten C3-Störfall konfrontiert ist. Ein intelligentes 'aktives

Werkstatthandbuch' in Form des C3-Expertensystems unterstützt das konsequente Verfolgen einer Diagnosesystematik und könnte so den Erfordernissen einer zielgerichteten Informationsbereitstellung bei der Kundenreparaturdiagnose gerecht werden.

3. Wissensakquisition für DEX.C3

Praktische Erfahrungen mit dem Wissenserwerb, so wie er in dem FORD-GMD-Projekt geplant und durchgeführt wurde, gab es in Deutschland noch nicht. Die Demonstrations-Entwicklung hatte insoweit ausgesprochenen Pilotcharakter und war speziell von diesem Gesichtspunkt her von erheblichem Nutzen.
Dem Aufbau der Getriebe-Wissensbasis durch die Wissensingenieure der GMD gingen intensive Befragungen und Gespräche mit einem Getriebe-Experten von Ford voraus, die sich später bei der Validation der Enddiagnosen und der Vorgehensweise des Systems fortsetzten. Diese intensive Mitwirkung eines erfahrenen C3-Getriebeexperten von FORD, der der GMD während der gesamten Projektdauer zur Verfügung stand, war für die Entwicklung von DEX.C3 unverzichtbar. Der Ford-Getriebe-Experte verfügte über langjährige Erfahrung in der Praxis und als Schulungsleiter für das automatische Getriebe C3 an der Ford-Kundendienstschule in Köln-Porz. Diese Konstellation, einerseits Fach-Experte in dem zu bearbeitenden Problembereich und andererseits Lehrerfahrung in der Vermittlung von Wissen, begünstigte die Wissensakquisitionsphase. Das Problem bei der Wissensakquisition ist es gerade, daß ein Experte in einem bestimmten Problembereich, der in der Regel keine Lehrerfahrung über dieses Gebiet besitzt, sein Fachwissen und seine Diagnosestrategie meist nur sehr schlecht weitervermitteln kann [MICAMI83], weil er sich seines für die Problemlösung verwendeten Wissens oft gar nicht bewußt ist.

Die Wissensakquisition, der Transfer des Expertenwissens in das Computerprogramm, erfolgte in mehreren Phasen (siehe dazu auch [BUNGER85b]):
In einer Orientierungsphase machten sich alle Projektmitarbeiter mit dem Aufbau und der Funktionsweise des Getriebes vertraut. In der Interviewphase wurde der Experte gezielt nach möglichen Fehlern im Getriebe und deren Ursachen befragt. Das in dieser Phase gewonnene Wissen wurde in eine Kernversion des Expertensystems umgesetzt. In der Tuningphase wurde der Experte mit dieser Kernversion am Rechner konfrontiert, damit die auftretenden Mängel in direkter Zusammenarbeit mit dem Experten behoben werden konnten.

Die Orientierungsphase begann mit dem Studium von Techniker-Informationen ([TECHC382]), die für das Getriebe existierten, um die Getriebe-Aggregate, deren korrekte Funktion und deren Zusammenspiel im Getriebe zu verstehen. Zu der Orientierungsphase gehörten aber auch mehrere Besuche des Ford-Schulungszentrums in Köln, wo wir einerseits Einblick in Schulung und Fortbildung von Mechanikern erhielten, andererseits zusammen mit dem Getriebespezialisten ein reales Getriebe zerlegten und uns Funktion und mögliche Defekte 'in natura' erläutern ließen.

Eine in der Techniker-Information enthaltene Fehlersuchtabelle war in einer vorherigen Auflage baumartig strukturiert. Diese Struktur erwies sich aber als schwer handhabbar, weil die Mechaniker kaum in der Lage waren, diszipliniert einem Prüfschema zu folgen. Laut Aussage des Ford-Experten müßte der Mechaniker immer den Fehler im Getriebe finden, wenn er sich an die Fehlersuchtabelle und ein dazugehöriges Testblatt halten würde.

Ziel der Interviewphase mußte es nun also sein, die Art und Weise des 'daran haltens', die Heuristiken des Experten, zu ergründen. Durch gezieltes Fragen nach möglichen Getriebedefekten wurde versucht, anhand von Symptomen das Fehlverhalten zu klassifizieren und einen Zusammenhang zwischen Symptomen und Diagnosen herzustellen, der sich dann später in Diagnoseregeln niederschlagen sollte. Ein weiteres Ziel dieser Phase war es, die Problemlösungsstrategie des Experten zu explizieren: wie geht er an das Problem heran, welche Fragen stellt er, etc. Gerade in dieser Phase kam der Vorteil zum tragen, daß der Experte auch Ausbilder bei FORD war. Er war fast jederzeit in der Lage zu begründen, aus welchem Grund bestimmte Informationen in dieser Situation wichtig oder unwichtig waren.

Die Interviewphase bestand aus sieben Interviews (Dauer je Interview: vier bis sechs Stunden). Teilnehmer waren jeweils der Ford-Experte und drei Wissensingenieure der GMD. Die Nachbereitung der Interviews erfolgte anhand von Tonbandmitschnitten und Protokollen, die wiederum mit dem Experten abgeglichen wurden. Ziel der Nachbereitung war es, eine Spezifikation der Wissensstruktur und des genauen Wissensrepräsentationsformalismus zu erhalten und die verbliebenen Unklarheiten zu erkennen. Den Abschluß dieser zweiten Phase bildete die Umsetzung des bis dahin extrahierten Wissens in die Implementation einer Kernversion mit 70 Regeln, dem halben Umfang der Endversion.

Die dritte Phase (Tuningphase) zeichnete sich durch ein ständiges Feedback zwischen Getriebe-Experten und Wissens-Ingenieuren aus, indem die Anmerkungen des Experten in die jeweils nächste verfeinerte Version mit aufgenommen wurden, teilweise direkt während der Dialogsitzung. Ziel dieser letzten und noch einmal sehr intensiven Kooperationsphase war es, die bis dahin erstellte Wissensbasis des Systems sukzessive solange zu erweitern und zu verfeinern, bis das Vorgehen des Systems und seine Enddiagnosen möglichst gut mit der Strategie des menschlichen Experten übereinstimmte.
Anhand der ersten Kernversion wurden gemeinsam mit dem Getriebe-Experten in einer Reihe von Dialogsitzungen konkrete Fallbeispiele zur Fehlerdiagnose durchgespielt. Bei der Demonstration dieser Kernversion stellten sich sowohl Mängel in der gewählten Problemlösungsstrategie als auch in den Regeln heraus. Das System stellte zu viele Fragen und kam nur auf Umwegen zur Lösung.
Hauptaugenmerk in dieser Phase war es nun, diese Kritik durch Änderungen der Fragestrategie und der Inferenztechnik soweit wie möglich zu entkräften. Der Unterschied zwischen menschlichem Experten und dem Expertensystem war der, daß das System davon ausging, soviel wie möglich Information zu verarbeiten und Schlüsse zu ziehen, bevor man an dem Getriebe reparieren muß. Der Getriebe-Experte war der Meinung, daß bei einem Defekt, der innerhalb des Getriebes lokalisiert wurde, nicht weiter spezialisiert werden muß, da das Getriebe in diesem Fall ja sowieso demontiert werden muß und dann alles offen sichtbar ist. Dieser unterschiedlichen Auffassung wurde dadurch Rechnung getragen, daß das System in solchen Situationen den Benutzer fragt, ob es im Diagnoseprozeß fortfahren oder abbrechen soll.
Am Abschluß der Entwicklung (während der Tuningphase prägte sich bei uns der Begriff vom 'Knowledge Engineering nach dem Radio-Eriwan-Prinzip') sagte der Experte, daß er sich in dem System wiederfinde, sowohl sein Diagnosewissen als auch seine Vorgehensweise bei der Problemlösung wären jetzt angemessen repräsentiert. Überhaupt hat sich der Experte sehr kooperativ gezeigt und war nicht skeptisch eingestellt, wie man sonst teilweise hören kann, bezüglich Ersatz des Experten durch ein eben solches System.

4. Formalisierung und Implementation

4.1 Funktionsweise von DEX.C3

Das Getriebe-Expertensystem DEX.C3 versucht im Prinzip die Vorgehensweise eines menschlichen Getriebe-Experten zu simulieren. Dies wird durch das Zusammenwirken von Fragestrategie und Ableitungsmechanismen bei der Diagnosefindung erreicht.
DEX.C3 ist ein rein regelgesteuertes System, alles Wissen ist in Form von Produktionsregeln repräsentiert.

- Übersichtsfragen
- Getriebewissen
- Diagnosen
- Regeln

Nach einer kurzen Selbsteinführung des Systems beginnt eine erste Phase, in der Wissen über den Zustand eines defekten C3-Getriebes erfragt wird. Das System stellt zunächst eine Reihe von Übersichtsfragen über den Zustand des vorliegenden Getriebes. Die Antworten des Benutzers auf die Übersichtsfragen dienen als Basisfakten für die Diagnosestellung des Expertensystems. Durch die Übersichtsfragen wird die dynamische Wissensbasis initialisiert. Getriebewissen und mögliche Diagnosen sind in der Form

$$(\langle Objekt \rangle \ \langle Attribut \rangle \ \langle Wert \rangle)$$

dargestellt, wobei <Objekt> und <Attribut> normalerweise Getriebebauteilen entsprechen und <Wert> deren Zustand, (nicht) in Ordnung (I.O/N.I.O), bezeichnet.

Den Kern des Expertensystems bildet der Regelinterpreter. Er bestimmt den Ableitungsmechanismus, nach dem eine Diagnose aufgrund der Basisfakten, weiterer Antworten und bereits abgeleiteter Fakten erstellt wird. Der DEX.C3 zugrundeliegende Interpreter basiert auf einem Hin- und Herwechseln zwischen 'forward-' und 'backward-chaining', um soweit wie möglich der Diagnosemethodik des menschlichen Experten nahezukommen. Basierend auf den Benutzerantworten auf die Orientierungsfragen über den Zustand des aktuellen Getriebes wird ein Verdacht auf einen Defekt an einem bestimmten Bauteil generiert (Verdachtsgenerierung durch 'forward-chaining'). Anschließend wird dieser Verdacht durch logische Schlußfolgerungen über den bekannten oder noch zu erfragenden Fakten gezielt überprüft (Verdachtsüberprüfung durch 'backward-chaining'), bis der Verdacht genügend gesichert erscheint oder nicht (Evidenzverstärkung, Evidenzverminderung). Läßt sich ein bestehender Verdacht nicht hinreichend bestätigen, dann wird der gleiche Prozeß für eine andere Diagnosehypothese gestartet, wobei durch den vorherigen Prozeß die Wissensbasis evtl. um neue Fakten erweitert worden ist.

Etwas formaler notiert , sieht der Ableitungsprozeß des Regelinterpreters wie folgt aus:

- (1) Stelle die in der Wissensbasis spezifizierten Übersichtsfragen und trage die Antworten in die dynamische Wissensbasis ein.

- (2) Werte alle Informationen in der dynamischen Wissensbasis mit Hilfe aller Regeln 'forward' aus. Sind keine Informationen mehr ableitbar, gehe nach 3.
  Bei der 'forward'-Auswertung der Regeln werden i.a. sowohl neue Fragen gestellt (Steuerregeln), als auch Verdächte bezüglich eines Defekts von

Getriebebauteilen erzeugt (Diagnoseregeln).

- (3) Sind alle verdächtigen Bauteile überprüft, dann gehe nach 4, ansonsten
überprüfe gezielt die aussichtsreichste in (2) erzeugte Hypothese, danach
gehe nach 2.
Bei der gezielten Überprüfung werden die relevanten Regeln 'backward'
abgearbeitet. Dabei werden i.a. neue Fragen gestellt und Informationen in
die dynamische Wissensbasis eingetragen.

- (4) Gebe die Resultate aus und stoppe.

DEX.C3 wurde noch von Grund auf entwickelt. Der Regelinterpreter, sowie alle
Werkzeuge zur Erklärung des Systemverhaltens wurden in INTERLISP-D [INTERL83]
auf einer XEROX-1108 [XEROX84] entwickelt. BABYLON [PRIBRE85] war noch nicht
verfügbar und LOOPS bot keinen 'backward-chainer' an und war noch nicht
robust genug. Der Regelinterpreter wurde völlig losgelöst von der
Wissensbasis implementiert, so daß er auch für andere Problembereiche als
Shell benutzt werden kann.

4.2 Getriebewissen

Die Wissensbasis enthält das für C3-Reparaturen relevante Erfahrungswissen
des Kundendienst-Fachmannes bzw. Kfz-Meisters und ist im wesentlichen durch
die potentiellen Fehlerfälle bestimmt, auf die sich die Diagnosen beziehen.
Es wurde Wert darauf gelegt, das Getriebe nur so detailliert darzustellen,
wie es in bezug auf die Fehlerfindung sinnvoll ist. Die Inferenzmaschine
arbeitet auf einer Repräsentation der Wissensbasis, in der das Wissen als
Fakten in der bereits erwähnten internen TRIPLE-Form (<Objekt> <Attribut>
<Wert>) dargestellt ist, wobei <Attribut> optional ist. Z.B.: (OEL STAND
ZU-NIEDRIG), (REGLER-DICHTRINGE I.O). Dieses implizit in den Regeln
vorhandene Faktenwissen wird bei der Initialisierung des Systems und während
der Arbeit der Inferenzmaschine (-> 4.1) in der dynamischen Wissensbasis
explizit gemacht.
Die in den folgenden Abbildungen suggerierte frame-artige Darstellung dient
lediglich der besseren Lesbarkeit und klareren Strukturierung.

Am Beispiel des Getriebebauteils Steuerkasten (siehe Abb. 2) erläutert,
bedeutet das oben Gesagte, daß z.B. nicht alle 21 Ventile eine separate
Darstellung in der Wissensbasis haben, sondern nur die Schalt- und
Hauptleitungsdruck-Ventile, die auch speziell als Ursache eines Störfalles
aufgrund von Symptomen diagnostizierbar sind.

```
STEUERKASTEN
Hauptleitungsdruck-Regulierventil:      <i.O/n.i.O>
Hauptleitungsdruck-Verstärkerventil:    <i.O/n.i.O>
Schaltventil-1-2:                       <i.O/n.i.O>
Schaltventil-2-3:                       <i.O/n.i.O>
Restliches Steuergehäuse:               <i.O/n.i.O>
Schaltventil-2-3:                       <i.O/n.i.O>
Restliches Steuergehäuse:               <i.O/n.i.O>
```

Abb. 1: Steuerkasten in der DEX.C3-Wissensbasis

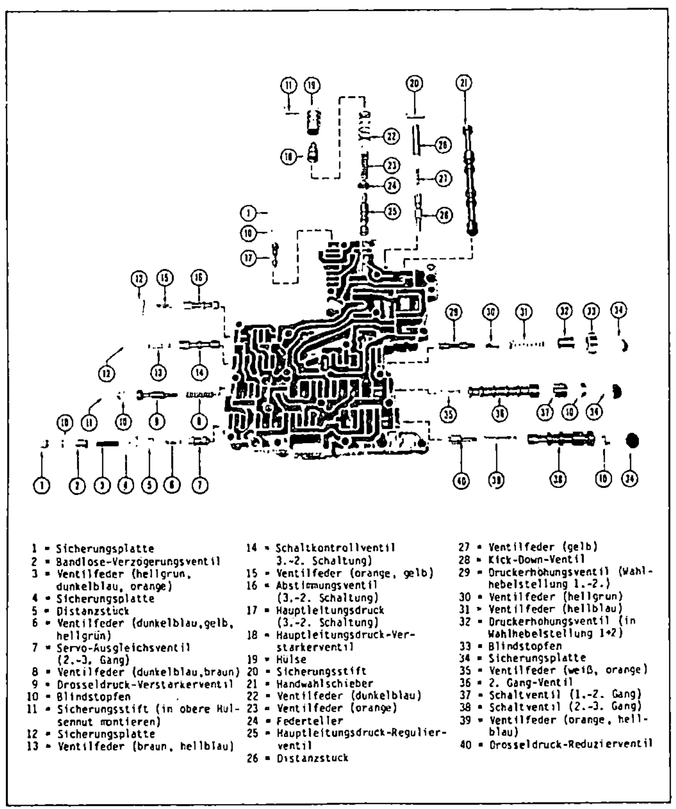

Abb. 2: Steuerkasten im C3-Getriebe (aus [REPGRA81])

Aus dem Vergleich der beiden Abbildungen 2 des realen Steuerkastens und 1 des Steuerkastenmodells in der Wissensbasis des Getriebe-Expertensystems läßt sich unschwer erkennen, daß DEX.C3 den restlichen Steuerkasten genauso wie eins seiner speziellen Ventile behandelt. Bei der systeminternen Darstellung dieser Ventile ist wiederum soweit abstrahiert, daß nur die entscheidende Eigenschaft, Funktionsfähigkeit in Ordnung (Gängigkeit 'i.O') oder nicht in Ordnung (Gängigkeit 'n.i.O'), in der Wissensbasis abgebildet ist.

Als potentielle Fehlerquelle nimmt das Öl eine Sonderstellung ein (Abb.3). Die Aufgaben des Getriebeöls sind so vielschichtig, daß es die unterschiedlichsten Störfälle verursachen kann, die sich durch verschiedenartige Symptome erkennbar machen.

Das Getriebeöl dient als Hydraulik-Steuerflüssigkeit für das Schalten der Gänge und wird gleichzeitig zur Wärmeabsorbierung und zur Schmierung von Lagern und Zahnrädern benutzt. Der Öldruck kann in den einzelnen Gangpositionen zwischen 3,4 und 19 kp/qcm variieren, die Öltemperatur kann über 70 Grad ansteigen und die Ölmenge darf nicht wesentlich unter 6,3 Liter sinken (Angaben für Ford Granada aus [REPGRA81]). Ein Defekt im Ölversorgungssystem, im Regelsystem mit Hauptleitungsdruck-(HLD)-Regulier- und Verstärker-Ventil oder im Steuerkasten (Abb. 2) haben direkte

Auswirkungen auf den Öldruck und somit auf die gesamte Steuerung des Getriebes. Andere Fehlerfaktoren bezüglich des Öls, die ebenfalls eine breite Auswirkung auf Fehlfunktionen des Getriebes haben, sind ein falscher Ölstand und die Verwendung nicht vorgeschriebenen Getriebeöls. Die Diagnosen, die als Ursache die Fehlerquelle Öl haben, und die für Öl existierenden Regeln zur Herleitung dieser Diagnosen machen insgesamt 24 Prozent der gesamten Regelbasis von 170 Regeln aus.

```
GETRIEBEÖL
Stand:               <normal/zu hoch/zu niedrig>
Farbe:               <normal-rot/dunkel-verbrannt/schwarz>
Beschaffenheit:      <normal/schaumig/verharzt>
Rückstände:          <keine/Metallabrieb/Belagabrieb>
Druck-insgesamt:     <normal/zu hoch/zu niedrig>
Druck-in-1:          <normal/zu hoch/zu niedrig>
Druck-in-2:          <normal/zu hoch/zu niedrig>
Druck-in-D:          <normal/zu hoch/zu niedrig>
Druck-in-R:          <normal/zu hoch/zu niedrig>
Druck-in-N-P:        <normal/zu hoch/zu niedrig>
```

Abb. 3: Öl-Objekt in DEX.C3-Wissensbasis

4.3 Diagnosen

Eine Diagnose im Sinne des C3-Getriebe-Expertensystems DEX.C3 ist die Bezeichnung einer Komponente des C3-Getriebes und der damit verbundene Vermerk 'i.O' (in Ordnung) oder 'n.i.O' (nicht in Ordnung). Beispiele für Diagnosen im Sinne von DEX.C3 sind:

        (Vorderes Bremsband n.i.O)   (Ölkühlung i.O).

Insgesamt ergeben sich 33 für das System relevante Diagnosen.

- Kraftübertragung
  - Kraftschlüssig
  - Formschlüssig
- Hydraulik
  - Ölversorgung, Ölzustand
  - Stellhydraulik
  - Schalthydraulik
- Verschiedenes

Die Diagnosen werden grob in die drei Kategorien 'Kraftübertragung' (11 Diagnosen), 'Hydraulik' (17) und 'Verschiedenes' (5) unterteilt. Unter die Kategorie 'Kraftübertragung', die ihrerseits nochmals in 'kraftschlüssig' (6) und 'formschlüssig' (5) aufgeteilt wird, fallen z.B. die Kupplungen und Bremsbänder. Die Kategorie 'Hydraulik' spaltet sich auf in 'Ölversorgung,Ölzustand' (5), 'Stellhydraulik' (5) und 'Schalthydraulik' (7). In ihr werden z.B. die Ventile und Dichtringe zusammengefaßt. Diese 33 Enddiagnosen spiegeln nicht die Gesamtzahl aller möglichen Fehler im Getriebe wieder. Vielmehr sind die Diagnosen, ähnlich wie das Getriebewissen, nur bis zu einem bestimmten Detaillierungsgrad im System vorhanden, da eine Verfeinerung nur bis zu diesem Grad sinnvoll ist.

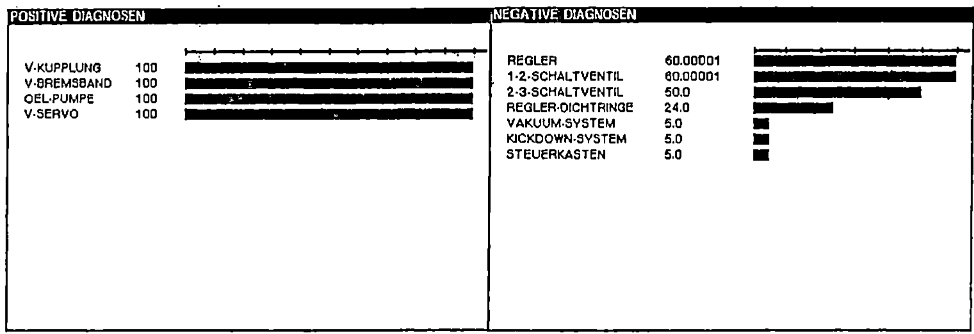

Abb. 4: Enddiagnosen in DEX.C3

Die Enddiagnosen werden in positive und negative Diagnosen aufgeteilt und
aufgelistet, grafisch unterstützt durch ein Balkendiagramm (siehe Abb. 4).
Zusätzlich werden die Bauteile aufgelistet, für die ein bestimmter Verdacht
generiert wurde, der aber für eine Diagnose als Fehlerursache nicht
ausreichte. Verdächtige Bauteile sollten bei einer Demontage des Getriebes
speziell auf Fehler untersucht werden. Alle Bauteile die von DEX.C3 nicht
gesondert aufgeführt werden, gelten implizit als unverdächtig.

4.4 Regeln

DEX.C3 enthält insgesamt 170 Regeln. Diese lassen sich aufteilen in:

- Steuerregeln
- Konsistenzregeln
- Diagnoseregeln

Die Struktur al.er Regeln ist einheitlich, d. h. eine Regel besteht immer aus
Bedingungs- und Aktionsteil. Insgesamt sind 50 Steuerregeln im System
vorhanden. Sie dienen zur Kontrolle des Systemverhaltens, legen z.B. die
Fragestrategie fest (z.B. RULE12A3), bestimmen die Reihenfolge zu prüfender
Hypothesen oder unterdrücken unsinnig gewordene Tests.

```
(RULE12A3 IF (AND (ANFAHREN IN-D I.O)
                  (ANFAHREN IN-1 I.O)
                  (ANFAHREN IN-2 I.O))
          THEN
          (ASK (VERHALTEN BEI-FAHRT I.O)))
```

"Wenn das Anfahren in allen Vorwärtsgängen, d.h. in 'D', '1' und '2' in
Ordnung ist, dann frage als nächstes nach dem Verhalten während der Fahrt!"

In DEX.C3 sind 30 Konsistenzregeln vorhanden. Konsistenzregeln beschreiben
logische Zusammenhänge allgemeiner Art. So folgert z.B. eine dieser Regeln
(RULE4):

"Wenn der Ölstand nicht zu niedrig und nicht in Ordnung ist, dann ist der
Ölstand zu hoch!"

```
(RULE04 IF (AND(NOT(OEL STAND I.0))
               (NOT(OEL STAND ZU-NIEDRIG)))
        THEN
        (LET (OEL STAND ZU-HOCH)))
```

Die Diagnoseregeln schließlich sind die Regeln, welche zur Herleitung von
End- und Zwischendiagnosen aus Symptomen benötigt werden. Die Gesamtzahl der
Regeln von diesem Typ beläuft sich auf 90. Ein Beispiel für eine
Diagnoseregel (RULE61) stellt z.B. folgende Verdachtshypothesen auf:

"Wenn der Hauptleitungsdruck im Rückwärtsgang in Ordnung und in allen
Vorwärtsgangpositionen nicht in Ordnung ist, dann besteht Verdacht auf
Undichtigkeiten an der Vorwärtskupplung, am hinteren Servo und an den
Reglerdichtringen!"

```
(RULE61 IF (AND (HL-DRUCK IN-R I.0)
                (NOT (HL-DRUCK IN-D I.0))
                (NOT (HL-DRUCK IN-1 I.0))
                (NOT (HL-DRUCK IN-2 I.0)))
        THEN
        (LET (SET-CF .5)
             (NOT (DICHTRINGE V-KUPPLUNG I.0))
             (NOT (H-SERVO I.0))
             (NOT (REGLER-DICHTRINGE I.0)))))
```

4.5 Behandlung von unsicherem Wissen

Die Informationen, mit denen ein Experte arbeiten muß, sind häufig ungenau
und vage. Deshalb muß auch ein Expertensystem mit unsicherem Wissen umgehen
können. Die Behandlung von Unsicherheit in DEX.C3 geschieht intern durch
numerische Werte (certainty factors), die mit Fakten assoziiert werden und
den Grad ihrer Bestätigung angeben. Jedem Fakt ist mittels des CF-Wertes ein
Evidenzwert zugeordnet. Dieser gibt ein Maß für die Sicherheit an, mit der
die im Tripel des Fakts formulierte Aussage, z.B. (OEL STAND I.0), gilt. Er
kann zwischen -100 (= trifft ganz bestimmt nicht zu) und +100 (= trifft ganz
bestimmt zu) liegen. Der Initialwert für jedes Fakt ist 0 (= unbekannt). Der
Evidenzwert erlaubt die Behandlung von Unsicherheiten in Bezug auf die
Gültigkeit eines Fakts. So kann der Benutzer auf eine für ein Fakt
formulierte Frage mit 'VIELLEICHT', 'UNBEKANNT', 'WAHRSCHEINLICH-NICHT'
antworten (siehe auch Abb. 6). Diese Antworten werden in entsprechende
CF-Werte für das Fakt umgewandelt und vom System auf plausible Weise
verwertet. Bei der Abarbeitung der Wissensbasis werden die CF-Werte der
Diagnosen, aufgrund der Antworten des Benutzers und einer entsprechenden
Weiterverwertung bei der Regelauswertung, entsprechend propagiert.

5. Dialog mit DEX.C3

5.1 Benutzerschnittstelle von DEX.C3

Bei der Entwicklung des C3-Getriebe-Expertensystems wurde in Hinblick auf Demonstrationszwecke und einen potentiellen Einsatz in der Werkstatt großer Wert auf eine transparente Benutzeroberfläche gelegt. Dies konnte einerseits durch extensive Ausnutzung der Möglichkeiten der Entwicklungsmaschine (Windows, Maus) und andererseits durch eigene Entwicklung spezieller Browser und Graphiken erreicht werden.
Die Benutzerschnittstelle ist weitgehend durch die interaktive Auswahl von Alternativen mit Hilfe der Menütechnik realisiert. Der Bildschirm ist in verschiedene Fenster aufgeteilt, in denen Fragen, Erklärungen, Ergebnisse und die graphische Darstellung des Systems erscheinen (siehe Abb. 5).

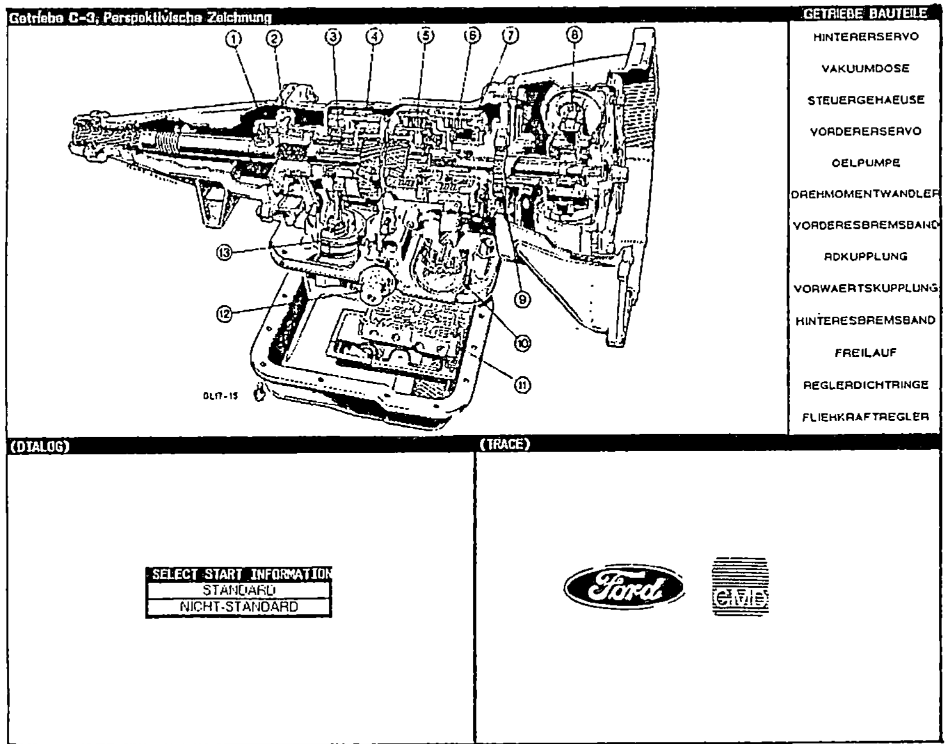

Abb. 5: Start-Menü des Expertensystems

Das Vorhandensein von maussensitiven Feldern ist Grundbestandteil des Systems: Die möglichen Antworten auf Fragen sind jeweils in Menüs zusammengestellt, die Auswahl der richtigen Antwort geschieht durch 'Klicken' einer Taste auf der Maus.

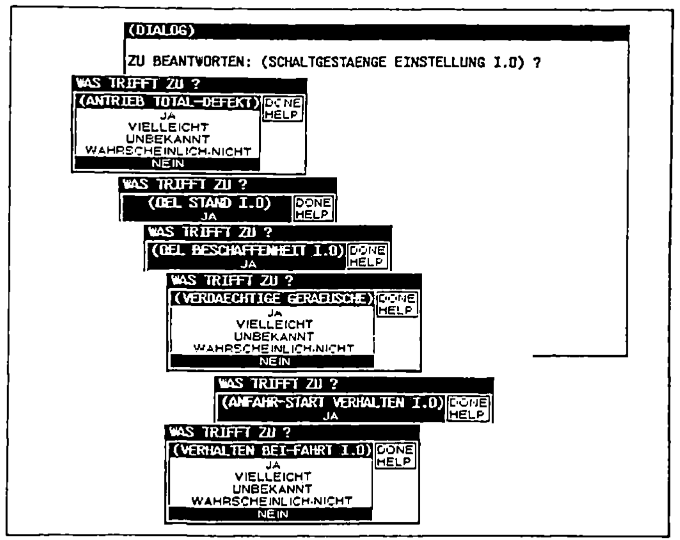

Abb. 6: Beispiel für ein Dialogmenü

Das Fenster, in dem die Dialogmenüs angezeigt und mit Hilfe der Maus bedient werden, ist mit 'DIALOG' betitelt. Das System zeigt hier mit Fortschreiten des Dialogs jeweils die gestellte Frage an. Eine der angezeigten Antwortalternativen wird durch 'Anklicken' ausgewählt. Die Antwortmenüs (siehe Abb. 6), die am Bildschirm nacheinander einzeln erscheinen und nach Beantwortung wieder verschwinden, sind hier synoptisch abgebildet, d.h. sie sind alle auf einer Abbildung in der Reihenfolge ihres Erscheinens wiedergegeben.

5.2 Erklärungskomponente

Das Verhalten von Expertensystemen muß für den Benutzer transparent und kontrollierbar bleiben [HAWALE83]. Deshalb spielt die Erklärungskomponente in jedem dieser Systeme eine wesentliche Rolle. DEX.C3 bietet dem Benutzer während des gesamten Dialogs folgende Möglichkeiten, Erklärungen zu verlangen:

- der Wissensstand des Systems (Zustand der dynamischen Wissensbasis) kann zu jeder Zeit erfragt werden.

- Why-Fragen: Das System erklärt den Kontext der aktuell gestellten Frage. Es werden die Regeln aufgelistet, aus denen zusammen mit dem erfragten Faktum die untersuchte Hypothese abzuleiten ist.

- How-Fragen: Der Benutzer kann erfragen, wie das System ein Faktum abgeleitet hat. Der Benutzer erhält die graphische Repräsentation eines Ableitungsbaums für ein gewähltes Faktum, z.B. (EINSCHALT-RUCK IN-R VORHANDEN). Der Baum (siehe Abb. 7) stellt die Verknüpfung von Fakten dar, die zur Ableitung geführt haben. Die Knoten des Baums sind maussensitiv, wodurch ein weiteres 'browsen' durch den Fakt- und Regelbaum ermöglicht wird.

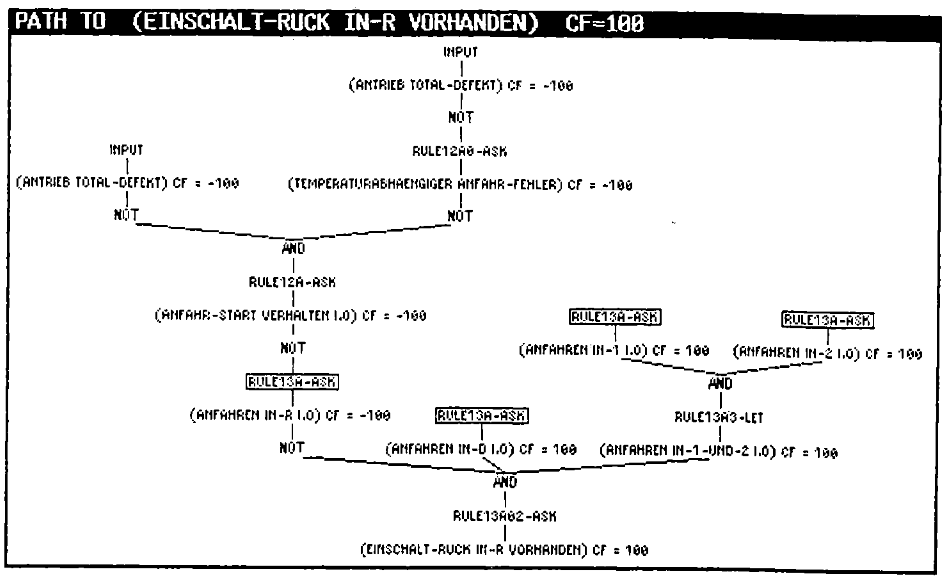

Abb. 7: Beispiel für Ableitungsbaum

- der Benutzer kann gezielt durch die Regeln 'browsen'. Er kann sich z.B. alle Regeln, in denen ein bestimmtes Faktum als Prämisse/Konklusion auftritt, listen lassen. Diese Möglichkeit ist mit der oben angeführten Möglichkeit der graphischen Repräsentation eines Ableitungsbaums dadurch gekoppelt, daß bei Selektion eines Faktknoten im Ableitungsbaum alle für dieses Faktum relevanten Regeln inspiziert werden können.

- der Trace (Abb. 5 u. 8) veranschaulicht in welchem Modus (FORWARD oder BACKWARD) der Interpreter welches Faktum bearbeitet. Dabei spiegelt der Trace zeilenweise die Ergebnisse der einzelnen Regeln wieder, wie sie sich, durch Dialogeingaben und den Regelinterpreter ('forward-/backward-chainer') gesteuert, durch Ausführen der jeweiligen Regeln ergeben; das System "denkt laut". Dabei ist auch zu erkennen, welchen aktuellen Evidenzwert (CF) das gerade betrachtete Fakt hat.

- während des gesamten Dialogs wird das Getriebe in perspektivischer Darstellung gezeigt (siehe Abb. 5). Dieser Längsschnitt durch das Getriebe gibt dem Benutzer ein sehr wichtiges Instrument an die Hand, die Eingrenzung eines Defekts zu beobachten und das entsprechende Bauteil zu lokalisieren. Während des Dialogs mit DEX.C3 werden die Bauteile, die gerade untersucht werden und als hinreichend verdächtig erscheinen, zum Blinken gebracht. Eine Legende, neben der Graphik zeigt den Namen des Bauteils an. Auf diese Weise ist der Benutzer stets über den aktuellen Fortgang der Untersuchung informiert, ohne den Text einer evtl. sehr umfassenden Agenda inspizieren zu müssen.
Wir sind insgesamt davon überzeugt, daß eine erläuternde und veranschaulichende Graphik im Zusammenhang mit Planungs-, Konstruktions- und Schulungssystemen eine zunehmend wichtige Rolle spielen wird und bald aus Expertensystem-Applikationen nicht mehr wegzudenken sein wird.

```
(TRACE)
1 FORWARD: (SCHALTGESTAENGE EINSTELLUNG I.O) CF = 100
2 FORWARD: (ANTRIEB TOTAL-DEFEKT) CF = -100
3 FORWARD: (OEL STAND I.O) CF = 100
4 FORWARD: (OEL BESCHAFFENHEIT I.O) CF = 100
5 FORWARD: (VERDAECHTIGE GERAEUSCHE) CF = -100
6 FORWARD: (ANFAHR-START VERHALTEN I.O) CF = 100
7 FORWARD: (OEL STAND ZU-NIEDRIG) CF = -100
8 FORWARD: (OEL STAND ZU-HOCH) CF = -100
9 FORWARD: (OEL AUSTRITT AN-ENTLUEFTUNG) CF = -100
10 FORWARD: (OEL AUSTRITT AM-GEHAEUSE) CF = -100
11 FORWARD: (OEL BESCHAFFENHEIT WEISSLICH.VERFAERBT) CF = -100
12 FORWARD: (OEL BESCHAFFENHEIT BRAUN.VERBRANNT) CF = -100
13 FORWARD: (OEL ENTHAELT METALLABRIEB) CF = -100
14 FORWARD: (ANFAHREN IN-D I.O) CF = 100
15 FORWARD: (ANFAHREN IN-1-UND-2 I.O) CF = 100
16 FORWARD: (ANFAHREN IN-R I.O) CF = 100
17 FORWARD: (VERHALTEN BEI-FAHRT I.O) CF = -100
18 FORWARD: (V-KUPPLUNG I.O) CF = 100
19 FORWARD: (FAHRZEUG-ZIEHT-VORWAERTS IN-R) CF = -100
20 FORWARD: (LEISTUNG I.O) CF = 100
21 FORWARD: (SCHALTVERHALTEN I.O) CF = -100
22 FORWARD: (ERSTER GANG I.O) CF = 100
23 FORWARD: (ZWEITER GANG I.O) CF = -100
24 FORWARD: (DRITTER GANG I.O) CF = -100
25 FORWARD: (REGLER I.O) CF = -5.0
26 FORWARD: (REGLER-DICHTRINGE I.O) CF = -5.0
27 FORWARD: (1-2-SCHALTVENTIL I.O) CF = -5.0
28 FORWARD: (2-3-SCHALTVENTIL I.O) CF = -5.0
29 FORWARD: (VAKUUM-SYSTEM I.O) CF = -5.0
30 FORWARD: (KICKDOWN-SYSTEM I.O) CF = -5.0
31 FORWARD: (STEUERKASTEN I.O) CF = -5.0
32 FORWARD: (ERSTER GANG VORHANDEN) CF = 100
```

Abb. 8: Trace-Beispiel

6. Abschließende Bemerkungen

Bei der vorliegenden Version von DEX.C3 stand der Demonstrationszweck im Vordergrund. Es wurde nachgewiesen, daß das Wissen und die Vorgehensweise eines Kfz-Experten bei der Fehlerdiagnose mit einem Expertensysystem korrekt und umfassend nachgebildet werden können. Zumindest nach dem Urteil des menschlichen Experten, der bei der Entwicklung von DEX.C3 mitgewirkt hat, stellt das System die richtigen Fragen im richtigen Augenblick und liefert korrekte Diagnosen, und – ein Expertensystem kann immer nur höchstens so gut sein, wie der 'angezapfte' Experte.
Die Frage, ob ein Expertensystem wie DEX.C3 im Kundendienst wirklich nutzbringend eingesetzt werden kann, kann erst nach Abschluß und Auswertung der Validierungsphase beantwortet werden. Erst wenn diese Frage positiv beantwortet ist, kann davon ausgegangen werden, daß Expertensysteme zur Qualitätssteigerung des Kundendienstes tatsächlich einen Beitrag leisten können: Für das tägliche Wartungs- und Reparaturgeschäft könnte künftig ein Wissen genutzt werden, über das nur wenige erfahrene Kfz-Meister und die Experten in Entwicklung und Fertigung verfügen. Gegenwärtig ist dieses Wissen im Kundendienst nur sehr begrenzt vorhanden.

DEX.C3 wurde von der Forschungsgruppe Expertensysteme im Projekt KNENG (KNowledge ENGineering) am Institut für Angewandte Informationstechnik der GMD im Auftrag der FORD-Werke AG Köln entwickelt. Ziel der Arbeiten im Projekt KNENG ist es, basierend auf Impulsen aus der Grundlagenforschung, prototypartige Expertensysteme für den praktischen Einsatz beim Anwender zu entwickeln und implementieren. Auf diese Weise soll die bestehende Kluft zwischen akademischer Forschung und industrieller Praxis überbrückt werden. In bezug auf die Entwicklung eines (hybriden) Werkzeugsystems wie BABYLON

[PRIMIO85] im Projekt SWENG (SoftWare ENGineering) innerhalb der Forschungsgruppe, erfüllt eine Anwendung wie DEX.C3 die Aufgabe, die schon verfügbaren Instrumente und Verfahren zu erproben und praxisrelevante Anforderungen für deren Weiterentwicklung zu liefern. In diesem Zusammenhang fand eine Re-Implementation der XEROX-Version mit BABYLON auf SYMBOLICS 36xx für die Hannover Messe 1985 statt.

Ohne die engagierte Mitwirkung von Ford - und hier ganz besonders des "Mr. Transmission" Hermann Többens - wäre dieses Expertensystem nicht zustandegekommen. Neben dem Expertenwissen, das Ford dem Projektteam der GMD für den Aufbau der Wissensbasis von DEX.C3 zur Verfügung gestellt hat, war vor allem die ausgesprochen kooperative Atmosphäre, in der das 'Knowledge Engineering' stattfand, eine wichtige Voraussetzung für das Gelingen.

7. Literatur

[BUNGER85a] D. Bungers;
Verdrängt das Expertensystem den Fachmann?, VDI-Nachrichten, Nr. 6, Februar 1985.

[BUNGER85b] D. Bungers;
Using Expert Systems for the Customer Service of Ford Europe, in: Proceedings of the Second International Conference on Artificial Intelligence, Th. Bernold (Hrsg.), Gottlieb Duttweiler Institut, Rüschlikon, Schweiz, April 1985, North Holland Pub. Co.,Amsterdam, erscheint demnächst.

[FEIGEN80] E. A. Feigenbaum;
Knowledge Engineering: The Applied Side of Artificial Intelligence, Memo HPP-80-21, Computer Science Dept., Stanford University, 1980.

[INTERL83] Interlisp-D Reference Manual;
Artificial Intelligence Ltd., Watford, England, 1983.

[HAWALE83] F. Hayes-Roth, D.A. Waterman, D.B. Lenat;
Building Expert Systems, Addison-Wesley Pub. Co., Reading, Massachusetts, 1983.

[KLAWIT85] W. Klar, K-H. Wittur;
Ein Expertensystem zur Fehlerdiagnose im automatischen Getriebe C3 von Ford, in: GMD-Jahresbericht 1984, GMD-Birlinghoven, Selbstverlag, St. Augustin, 1985.

[MICAMI83] R.S. Michalski, J.G. Carbonell, T.M. Mitchell;
Machine Learning - An Artificial Intelligence Approach, Tioga Pub. Co., Palo Alto, Californien, 1983.

[MICHIE79] D. Michie;
Expert Systems in the Micro-Electronic Age, University Press, Edinburgh ,1979.

[PRIBRE85] F. di Primio, G. Brewka;
BABYLON: Kernsystem einer integrierten Umgebung für Entwicklung und Betrieb von Expertensystemen, in: Nachrichten für Dokumentation, Jg. 36, Nr.1, Februar 1985.

[PRIMIO85] F. di Primio;
BABYLON als Werkzeug zum Aufbau von von Expertensystemen, in:
Wissensbasierte Systeme - Internationaler GI-Kongreß '85, München,
Oktober 1985, Springer-Verlag, 1985.

[REITMA84] W. Reitmann (Hrsg.);
Artificial Intelligence Applications For Business, Proceedings of
the NYU Symposium, Mai 1983, Ablex Pub. Co., Norwood, New Jersey,
1984.

[REPGRA81] Ford Granada Reparatur Anleitung;
C3-Automatik Getriebe, Reparatur Anleitung, Ford-Werke AG,
Kundendienst Selbstverlag, Köln, 1981.

[TECHC382] Ford Techniker Information;
C3-Automatik Getriebe, Arbeitsweise und Fehlerdiagnose, Ford-Werke
AG, Kundendienst Selbstverlag, Köln, 1982.

[THOME83] R. Thome (Hrsg.);
Datenverarbeitung im KFZ-Service und -Vertrieb, Anwendergespräche,
Uni Bamberg,1982, Springer-Verlag, Berlin, 1983.

[XEROX84] Rank Xerox (User's Guide);
1108 Artificial Intelligence Workstation, Artificial Intelligence
Ltd., Watford, England, 1984.

Hans Haugeneder, Egbert Lehmann, Peter Struß

Siemens AG
Zentralbereich Forschung und Technik
München

1. Introduction

The paper discusses problems of how to structure the knowledge base and to adopt the most appropriate approaches and tools for developing SICONFEX. SICONFEX is a knowledge-based system for the interactive configuration of an operation system for SICOMP computers. It was developed by the expert systems research lab of Siemens, mainly based on an object-oriented approach. The paper's aim is not to give an comprehensive overview of the system's structure and development, but rather reflects and discusses some problems we encountered during this phase. These, in our opinion, are problems of a more general character, emerging in designing an expert system in a non-trivial domain.

2. Overview of SICONFEX

SICOMP computers offered by Siemens mainly for process control applications but also for general purpose computing use configurable operating systems. These operating systems are highly flexible and can be adapted to both the users current hardware and to his specific needs. For this configuration process there is a number of implicit demands to be considered from the user's side as well as constraints and interdependencies between the hardware and software components. Above and beyond that, in order to produce an optimal operating system some discrete optimization must take place for partitioning the main storage and to assign certain software components to various storage partitions.

Up to now, in order to be able to generate his operating system, the user has to produce in a relatively low level language a set of some 40 to 200 configuration statements (the so-called parameter cards), each containing several highly interdependant parameters. These cards are then used by a generator to produce the user's specific operating system (ORG). However, these requirements have not been met properly by the inexperienced user in the past leading to operating systems produced by trial and error for each modification of the user's hardware or software. The whole procedure usually takes one to three days and is often plagued by mistakes. Even in the responsible department at Siemens, there is a shortage of experienced operating system specialists. In addition, the knowledge concerning the important interdependencies is distributed, only among several specialists and changes with time.

The project's goal was to develop an expert system to interactively support the non-specialist and to simplify the configuration of operating systems. The system should be able to conduct a conceptual intelligible dialogue with the user, during which his available hardware and his demands conerning the functionality of the software should become clear. On the basis of the results of this interaction the system should be able to configure the software as well as optimize the distribution of software in the main storage area. Finally the system should generate the set of parameter cards on the basis of the various types of information assembled during the session, to be used by the generator of the operating system. It was also considered as an important feature of the system to have a comfortable interaction modus with strong emphasis on graphical display facilities, since this aspect was continually emphasized by our client.

A configuration session with the system roughly consists of the following steps (for a more detailed description see: LEHM85): In the hardware specification phase the user becomes involved in an interactive, mouse-based dialogue with mixed user/system initiative. In the course of this interaction, he can use his naive understanding of the various hardware devices in order to arrive at a complete hardware specification. During the software specifcation phase, which is purely system driven in a menu-based style, the user is asked about his software needs until his specfication is sufficiently comprehensive to the system. The concepts and the terminology used allow him to express his functional demands on a level of description he is acquainted with and at a degree of granularity according to his knowledge. After this phase the system performs the partitioning of the main storage and generates the configuration statements . At the end of the session, all the information of the hardware and software specification phases as well as the result of the partioning and the generated "program" of configuration statements is available to the user through a set of (partially active) windows. These can be inspected and printed out easily.

After an internal Siemens decision the system should be developed within a relatively short period of time for a specific real application. The software development took place de facto from April to November 1984. The result, the first complete prototypical version, was successfully shown to the client on November 29, 1984. This considerable short time of development could only be achieved by having an appropriately equipped team of people with extensive working experience in the field of AI systems. Of course, the steady availability of two well experienced field experts contributed heavily to the sucess of the project.

SICONFEX (Sicomp CONFiguration EXpert) is a large heterogenous knowledge-based system, programmed in INTERLISP-D and LOOPS and running on a Lisp-Machine. The size of the system (not regarding the INTERLISP-D/LOOPS system code) is about 2.5 megabyte of main memory, comprising about 800 functions and methods, 1200 objects, and several rulesets. The average time for a complete session is about 20 minutes.

The SICONFEX system, which took about 5 man-years to develop, not only fulfilled the expectations of the client, but in some ways even surpassed his expectations. The first prototype version of SICONFEX after a thorough evaluation is now in the phase of being developed further in two directions firstly with respect to the completion of the knowledge base and secondly to the improvement of some of its features.

3.   Experiences and Conclusions

Broader Domains are Heterogenously Structured!

One of the first steps in designing a knowledge-based system is the specification of the general structure of the knowledge base as a model or description of the application domain and as a basis for mirroring some problem solving abilities of field experts. Decisions must be made for appropriately selecting the relevant concepts and getting a clear understanding of the ontological state of the essential pieces forming the inventory of the domain.

The goal of a more sophisticated knowledge representation is to model the application domain in a finer, more structured way independent of how these pieces of knowledge are combined for different purposes. This means, we should first investigate the inventory of possibly relevant objects and the way in which they can be named, characterized and generally related to one another. Concepts needed for characterizing the required objects should be classified, defined in terms of more primitive concepts and systematically arranged in taxonomic structures.

This modelling is relatively easy if the domain is quite homogeneous as, for example, in some systems for classifying objects characterized by feature vectors or unsophisticated medical diagnosis systems which know only manifestations (symptoms, signs, and findings), diseases and some intermediate concepts (syndroms, clinical states) and implication-like relations between them. Unfortunately, very often the domain knowledge includes a diversity of different things and relationships so that understanding and modelling them in a natural way is a nontrivial task. This has been our experience with SICONFEX. Occasionaly, important aspects become evident only in the course of working out the specification of the knowledge base and then result in a partial redesign of the whole system.

In SICONFEX we had to deal with at least three conceptually distinct areas:

1. the world of connected *physical components* of a computer configuration,
2. the abstract world of existing *computer software*, of different operating modes and rough application areas as seen from the users point of view and
3. the highly artificial world of *hypothetical* memory partitioning with more or less compatible software modules sharing the same partition.

So, as candidates for different *objects* we had to consider various different aspects:
- real technical computer devices (CPUs, disc drives, CRT terminals, memory extensions etc.) with their technical parameters
- connection cables
- addresses
- principal software modules (compilers, editors, data base management programs, ... as components of the operating system) characterized by a variety of features (storage requirerments, operational modes, need of other software modules or environments)
- explicit user wishes with respect to software modules
- expected main application areas and more or less operational modes
- (multiple) instances of software modules actually loaded in memory partitions
- patterns and parameters of configuration statements

Typical *interdependencies* between objects include the following different relationships:
- an instance or a subclass of a class
- device as part s of a computer configuration
- cable-connected (with respect to distinct connection adresses of connection units)
- hardware needed by a program
- software needed by other software modules
- considered as neccessary, important, convenient, ...   by the user

Procedures which are not naturally substitutable by descriptive means include the following:
- drawing a graphical representation of the hardware configuration or the final storage partitioning
- automatically finding the appropriate adresses for connecting devices
- interrogating the user
- computationally estimating the amount of memory required for storing the resulting operating system
- relatively simplified optimization procedures (which partially reflects routine bahavior of configuration experts)

For modelling such a heterogenous domain, a *variety of representational constructs* has been used in SICONFEX:
- frame-like object structures
- conceptual taxonomies
- inheritance mechanisms
- message passing
- IF-THEN-rules
- Global variables and attribute-value-pairs (in LISP)
- Computations (by LISP functions, LOOPS methods).

Using only rules for representing knowledge is not enough!

The degree of neccessary detail and heterogenity is dependent not only on the selected domain, but also on the intended kind of decision-making capability. Where the task is dealing with a pre-established finite set of relevant propositions (hypotheses) which have to be verified or falsified with respect to the evidence of facts characterizing each case, the most simple solution for modelling the domain is establishing the derivational structure of all relevant hypotheses as the knowledge base. Nodes of these derivation trees often will be represented as unstructured propositions (as in propositional logic) or as predicative expressions (as in predicate calculus). This is the common method to structure the knowledge base of rule-based expert systems for classification or diagnosis. This approach leads to models which more reflect some special problem-solving competence than the structure of the task domain and so may be characterized as more heuristically than epistemologically adequat (in the spirit of McCA69)).

Looking a little closer at *rules* as a paradigm for implementing and/or representing expert knowledge, we detect *two* paradigms instead of one. Firstly there are logical rules (as in PROLOG or EMYCIN) of the form

IF <premisses> THEN (with certainty n) <conclusion>

which represent (sometimes augmented) kinds of *logical implications* and therefore are well suited for modelling certain kinds of deductive or plausible reasoning (by forward or backward chaining).
Secondly we can use full-fledged *production-rules* (as in OPS) of the form

IF <pattern> THEN DO <action>

with a very different semantics. In these rules, *actions* irreversibly change the data base (which in general cannot be undone). Therefore, production rules are very procedural, providing mechanisms for pattern-directed procedure invocation and so represent an alternative opportunity for programming anything you like in a modular fashion. But it seems questionable, if we are allowed to call this knowledge representation.

As a general basis for building up knowledge-based systems, implications although well-suited and natural for judgemental tasks seem to be too special and static, while pattern-action-rules alone cannot provide for an architectural framework. It is important to understand that most statements which are true for one of these kinds of rules are not true for the other kind. Anyway, in both cases, additional structuring principles (as conceptual taxonomies with inheritance mechanisms, definitions, constraints) should be introduced for structuring complex domain knowledge in a natural and transparent way.

Beginners in expert systems and field experts often gain the impression from reading popular AI folklore, that rules are per se very powerful constructs. For instance, in the beginning period of the SICONFEX-project our field experts were convinced they had to encode their knowledge in rules and as an exercise started by writing down subsumption relations between two concepts in this form. This sometimes seemed to prevent them from describing step-by-step-procedures in a simple sequencial way.

In SICONFEX, we used LOOPS rule-sets (which are a very speciific, extremely procedural type of rules) only to a minor extent. For example we applied them to specify sets of rule-like statements for partitioning memory space and allocating software modules to memory partitions. These statements' order furthermore is of a highy sequential nature, which is a somewhat untypical feature for the use rule-based mechanisms.

In Some Cases Conventional Programming is Natural and Straightforward!

The programming methodology used in the development of a knowledge based system clearly offers the advantage of specifying as much as possible of the domain knowledge in a descriptive manner with general interpretation procedures working on it. Although the advantages of this methodology are obvious, there are classes of subproblems where a more conventional, procedural implemetation is an appropriate and satisfactory solution.

In SICONFEX, after a thorough analysis of the rules which govern that task we implemented the simulation of the component MGEN (the actual generator of the operating system) which contains a lot of computation in a purely procedural way. We came to the conclusion that this proved to be an adequate solution, with no disadvantages. Thus, to us it seems, that for some subtasks such a procedural implementation may be the natural solution. One should not try to apply the programming methodology for knowledge-based systems in an artificial, unmotivated and overgeneralized way to describe algorithmic structures. *Conventional programming* should not be considered as bad or as an old fashioned practice, but should be applied to appropriate tasks, hence treated as *one of several possible programming styles*!

Object-Oriented Programming is a Powerful Approach!

As stated above, the LOOPS programming environment provides support for object-oriented programming in a SMALLTALK-like style (see GOLD83) including message passing, a clean conceptual distinction between the class - super class relation and the class - meta class relation, and graphic tools (so-called browsers) as a good means for the interactive construction of class structures. In the SICONFEX project, as with many other tasks, the object-oriented programming paradigm within an appropriate programming environment has proved very useful for knowledge programming. From our experience this essentially concerns

- *modularity*:   the way of structuring complex programs
- *extendibility*: the power of inheritance and specialization
- *naturalness*:   the correspondence between the external view of some domain and the internal structures of the system.

Why does the object-oriented programming style provide additional power? *Modularity* in object-oriented programs is not only achieved by a clear separation of different functional aspects of the system but also by grouping the data or concepts which are manipulated by the system into sets of uniform computational behavior. This is done horizontally by distinguishing classes of objects which require essentially different functional treatment and vertically by specifying classes of objects which correspond to various specializations of the same type of functional treatment. As you can intermix the appropriate class structures of several functional aspects of the system, you are not confined to tree structures. We feel that in many cases such class structures suggest a decomposition of the system's functionality which is cleaner and of a finer granularity than that obtained in other programming styles. The programmer is forced to break the different functions into elementary pieces which have a directly inspectable context for their evaluation given by the data structure of the class these pieces are attached to.

The modularity in the sense stated above provides a good basis for *extending* a system with respect to the treated set of data as well as to its functionality. Adding new objects for which the already defined methods are sufficient only requires linking their descriptive parts to the appropriate place in the inheritance lattice. Because of the simplicity of handling the provided excellent graphic-oriented tools, this kind of extension was done occasionally in our project even by the field experts. New functional aspects of the system which are in accordance with the existing class structure can easily be added by attaching new methods to classes. They will "at once" be inherited along the existing subclass links. Specialization can be done by adding a new subclass and overriding some of the inherited methods for this class whilst not affecting the inheritance of the rest of the possibly complex functionality defined in super classes above. This applies not only to the implementation of the target system but also to the usage of tools for programming, building interfaces, etc. Because you will rarely get tools in exactly the way you need them for a specific task, it is very important to provide an easy way for modifying them. In LOOPS some of the programming and interface tools are 'objects' themselves, defined in the very same object-oriented style they support.

Choosing the object-oriented approach is a *natural* decision in cases where the domain includes physical objects and/or where people are accustomed to think in terms of entities and conceptual units. During the knowledge acquisition for the SICONFX system, a lot of the experts' static knowledge was presented to us as a collection of data about objects like devices, software systems, single programs, control cards, etc. and their relationships. Organizing these data as descriptive units in an object-centered way rather than scattering them around was obviously advantageous. It covers the "data base aspects" of this kind of knowledge and could be a strarting point for knowledge acquisition tools which mirror the familiar view of the experts.

Moreover, several types of concepts were introduced which in some sense behaved uniformly or required similar kinds of manipulation during the problem solving process. E.g. partitions of the main storage were also modelled as objects which received new programs to run in the according partition, computed their own score of "importance", extended their length if necessary, etc.

The naturalness of object-oriented programming becomes obvious in cases where interactive, mouse-based graphics are a convenient support for the manipulation of objects and relationships. For example, the hardware description component of SICONFEX offers a graphics interface which enables the user to select, arrange and connect icons. These correspond to the real world objects in his computer center like cpu, printer, disk, memory board, connection, etc.

Interdependencies between software components within the world of SICONFEX can be entered into the knowledge base by using a browser which manipulates them as relations between objects too. Using this kind of interface appears to be a strong argument for object-oriented programming because good correspondence between the manipulated graphical objects and the corresponding data and program structures makes the conceptual structure of the system transparent as well as convenient to use.

For a large project such as SICONFEX which requires the co-operation of several programmers working on different functional aspects of the same object-oriented knowledge base, there is a strong need for system support to integrate the work of several knowledge programmers. Our experience shows that these needs are only partially covered by existing programming environments. Our (rather ad hoc) approach - besides relying on a close communication among the members of the developing group - was to separate the entire structuring of the objects into clearly distinguishable non-interacting functional sections (with respect to data as well as methods).

Avoid Mixing up the Implementational Level with Knowledge Representation!

Another problem arises which appears to be much more intricate, because it occurs as a certain temptation for the knowledge programmer, namely to mix up the two levels of implementation and knowledge representation. The illusion that the object-oriented implementational level already gives you what you need for the knowledge representation has its reasons in the high level that the programming constructs have and its striking similarity to a natural, naive view of the domain. These powerful constructs are essential for rapid prototyping, because they ensure that the gap between a conceptual view of the program's task and the constructs for implementing them is not too large.

Despite of this fact, an object-oriented programming environment is far from being the same as a full-fledged (frame-based) knowledge representation language, although both in some sense deal with units of descriptions. The objects in an object-oriented language are basically *implementational constructs* which are used and organized by a programmer to create a desired behavior of the system. The conceptual objects in a knowledge representation language like KL-ONE (BRAC85) e.g. are designed in order to capture and describe domain knowledge using *epistemologically well-defined concepts*.

Knowledge Programming, Rapid Prototyping - Advantages and Dangers

"Knowledge Programming" is one of the headings which is used to characterize the impact of LOOPS, an experimental programming environment, for the development of knowledge based systems. (For a broader explanation of the ideas of knowledge programming see: STEF83!) It can be viewed as a compromise, offering a set of tools which on the one hand do not constitute a so-called expert system shell, while on the other hand enable the user to implement the necessary mechanisms starting on a relatively high level. Apart from the preparation and integration of four different paradigms, namely *object-oriented programming, procedure-oriented programming, access-oriented programming and rule-oriented programming*, one of the most prominent features of LOOPS is its powerful interactive programming tools. Both together enable the LOOPS user to develop quite sophisticated and comprehensive knowledge based systems in a relatively short time, as compared to convential programming.

Rapid prototyping using a system of this type is strongly guided by the aim of being able to quickly implement and modify computer programs that exhibit a certain desired *behavior* in terms of input-output relations rather than to develope a precise model of the *knowledge structure* of a domain. Thus rapid prototyping tries (or at least creates the possibility) to jump from a specification of the desired system's behavior to the implementation. Thus one can reach a considerably high level system development, where partial successes show up very soon. This in turn may give the system developer a too conservative attitude towards such a far reaching first step, preventing him from an often necessary phase of reconsideration and restructuring of the problem, constructing a theoretically cleaner basis.

Such an approach contradicts our guidelines for the knowledge acquisition process, which we understand as a thorough analysis of the knowledge required to solve a problem and mapping it (successively) on to a knowledge representation scheme. Only after that step should we deal with implementational issues (see WIEL84). These problems are not due to any shortcomings in LOOPS or similar systems, but rather result from a misguided use of the power of such systems.

But why should we be worried, since we have succeeded in developing an operational prototype? And is this not even more true in cases where it appears to be impossible or questionable to get a precise and consistent model of the experts' problem solving skills like in SICONFEX? We are convinced that the need for a careful analysis of the ontological and epistomological problems of a domain and for the construction of an adequate representation model not only holds for AI researchers whose primary interest is obtaining a good model for cognitive capabilities of man. It holds for all serious efforts made in building an expert system in an industrial environment. In our opinion, although the "industrial production" of expert systems typically involves deadlines and the pressure to apply rapid prototyping, it imposes a lot of requirements which stress the need for an elaborate model of the domain. This is due to the fact that an expert system as a commercial product or for internal application demands easy ways of extending and modifying its underlying knowledge base. In the case of SICONFEX this includes not only adding new devices and software components but the enhancement and completion of the set of heuristics and optimality criteria for the storage partitioning etc. Adding new problem solving steps and knowledge chunks can be hard or impossible when no explicit representation model is available serving as a conceptual framework. Such a model will express the essential features of the domain in an explicit manner and will reduce the arbitrariness of the mapping onto the implementational constructs.

Finally, since in an industrial environment the further development and support of the system may no longer be the task of the development team, there is a strong demand for comfortable tools for the extension or alteration of the knowledge base. Without a carefully designed representational model for guiding this process, the value of the best tools will be severely limited. (The problems of proceeding from a prototype to a product will be discussed more thoroughly in a forthcoming paper).

Because of the lack of strong general, domain-independent models for problem solving tasks, we in principal do not believe in any of the shiny advertisements offering "shells" for expert systems with knowledge acquisition tools that reduce the work of constructing a knowledge base into some pleasant amusement during one afternoon.

Mapping a Problem Area into a Knowledge Base is more than Pure Routine!

The mapping of the domain knowledge onto some sort of knowledge base(s) comprises - besides the design of the problem solving facilities of an expert system - the major part of the bundle of activities, which is generally subsumed under the concept "knowledge engineering". "Knowledge engineering" nowadays is often understood to be only a straightforward process of filling up the knowledge base (with respect to some given inference mechanism), resulting in an operational, knowledge based system of a nontrivia domain. Such an understanding of the concept of knowledge engineering, which has been adopted by many people especially outside the AI community, is an inadmissable oversimplification, which is highly misleading. It pretends that the application of a set of well-defined methods and procedures enable the knowledge engineer to perform this mapping in a relatively direct way as a routine task. This, however, is by no means generally true for rich empirical domains. In our configuration application, where we had to cope with a large variety of concepts, facts about these concepts, various types of heuristic information etc., we experienced knowledge engineering to be an ill-defined, adventurous activity.

The overall task of the mapping can be roughly divided into two subtasks, each of which incorporates some substantial methodological problems. The first subtask is the acquistion of the domain knowledge with the goal of understanding the domain properly. This means, being able to identify, explicate and structure the relevant facts. Unfortunately there is a *great lack of rational acquistion methods* for this complicated process which is reflected by the fact that there have been only few attempts to clarify and explore the methods of expert knowledge acquisition (as for example WIEL84). For bridging the gap between a highly skilled domain expert and a knowledge engineer who is a novice in the expert's domain, the problem emerges, how to interrogate the expert in the most efficient way. This includes the decision about a number of alternatives of the following type:

- In which order should one try to explore the subdomains?
- Should we at the beginning aim towards general principles or towards more concrete relationships?
- Should we structure the interviews very densely from the beginning or give the expert more freedom of articulation? etc.

Thereby each of the decisions may be quite critical for the further course and the possible success of the whole undertaking. In our project the field experts expected us to offer them some strict formalism for the specification of their knowledge at the very beginning. Due to our very superficial understanding of the domain at that point we were neither able nor willing to do so. To us such an a priori, unmotivated choice of a formal device seemed to lead to the risk of predeterming the process of acquiring the domain knowledge in a way, which might render the understanding and the solution of the problem more difficult.

Furthermore, after having assembled the expert's knowledge there is still the task of how to interpret these verbal and written data in such a way, that an adequate model of the domain can be specified. This task demands a considerable amount of time, serious efforts and the willingness to deal with the domain and the expert's knowledge intensively. In addition, the entire acquistion process can be very frustrating for the "knowledge engineer", even in the case of co-operative and competent field experts, which ours were. According to our experience this process seems to be very tough, often leading up blind alleys. Often we only reached viable working hypotheses after a hard long struggle. Of course, the field experts were likewise frustrated, only from a different perspective.

The second subtask is the mapping of the conceptual and structural features of the domain, as commonly understood by the field expert and knowledge engineer, onto representational and finally implementational constructs. Especially the choice of adequate representational approaches for the different sections of a heterogenous domain requires a lot of experience and creativity.

Thus the construction of a knowledge base for a rich, multidimensionally structured domain is a very demanding task. It shares some essential features with scientific research in an empirical field. That is why one has to live with a feeling, well known in this area: there is never a complete solution to the problem. Because of the nature of knowledge engineering one should not be over optimistic about reaching a better, methodologically sounder foundation soon , though various types of tools surely will help to make the process more efficient.

Epistomological Problems of the Domain Can Be Hard to Solve!

During the process of designing and implementing SICONFEX we had to cope with a couple of problems some of which are not frequently mentioned by people in AI business.

According to a wide-spread opinion the problem solving process to be modelled has some immediately recognizable global structure, which can be expressed by adeqautely organized sets of rules; thus as the main problem of knowledge acquisition remains finding the collection of correct single rules which successively are entered into the pre-specified mechanism, debugged and changed.

The situation we faced at the beginning of the project (and which we understand not to be extraordinary) was different: we were confronted with a·large amount of detailed pieces of knowledge - technical descriptions, algorithms, heuristics, ideas and intuitions - but there was no obvious global, homogeneously structured model to fit them in. So investigating the nature and structure of the overall process was the major challenge to our work. We have to admit that from our AI point of view this task was not fully accomplished.

Certainly some of the critical statements about the contradiction between rapid prototyping and a thoroughly done knowledge acquisition apply to our project. But we feel that there were additional reasons causing this problem. Our observations thus far make us believe that a single model for the process in question cannot be obtained because it does not exist.

The process of configuring the appropriate operating system for the request of the SICOMP user typically is a matter of co-operation of various experts for different subdomains (e.g. experts for compilers and debuggers, for the data management system, special modules of the operating system etc). But this does not happen in a fixed manner or using a common model for combining the fractions of knowledge, but mainly by exchanging and combining subsets of the necessary sequence of configuration statements, i.e. *results* of the reasoning processes. We found a considerable variety of types of problem solving steps and strategies depending on the subdomain and/or the person dealing with the problem.

E.g. the dicision about which programs can be run in the same partition of the main storage is obtained differently for two important classes of programs. In the case of service programs (like compilers, editors, sorting programs, etc) this decision is governed only by the degree of their necessary availlability, because they are only loosely coupled; their special sort of functionality is unimportant. So the according rule set tries to *avoid* violating the required availlability of the programs which is measured by a uniform weighting procedure.On the contrary, distributing the subsystems of the data base management system - which exhibit strong functional dependencies and interaction - a different approach appeared to be appropriate: it resulted in definite *positive* instructions for the preferrable combinations of subsystems.

Another discrepancy occured between solutions obtained by some sort of reasoning by analogy ("modify the deck of control cards stemming from a similar user system") and a "constructive approach", which step by step infers partial solutions from the investigation of the desired behavior of the computer configuration. This seems to reflect the process of "compiling knowledge" from detailled principles of reasoning to global heuristics (in the sense of CHAN83), and thus a different amount of practical experience availlable for the expert and/or the special case.

We are convinced that encountering these problems in the SICONFEX domain is not by accident. They are due to the fact that there is not a common epistomology for the domain of software systems, and that the problem solving skills of the field experts dealing with the practical problems are not mainly guided by theoretical models for the behavior and performance of very distinct multi-user operating systems.

This raises (at least) two important questions: one being *whether*, and the other *how* to construct a uniform framework for modelling and using the different fractions of expertise in such a case. While the first question could be answered by referring to the possible advantage of such a framework for the progress in *developing* the desired model, the second is still lacking a simple general answer, but states the need for further attempts and research in this area.

Acknowledgements

We would like to thank our colleagues R. Hunze, C. Johnson, and L. Schmid, who were heavily engaged in the development of the system, for their contributions to the discussions concerning the topics of this paper, as well as all people who participated in the development of SICONFEX: G. Dobner, R. Enders, E. Renner and M. Schlueter.

<u>Literature</u>

BOBR83   Bobrow, D.G. and Stefik, M.: The LOOPS Manual, Xerox Corp. 1983

BRAC85   Brachman, R.J. and Schmolze, J. G.: An Overview of the KL-ONE Knowledge Representation System. Cognitive Science 9 (2), 1985

CHAN83   Chandrasekaran, B. and Mittal, S.: Deep versus Compiled Knowledge Approaches to Diagnostic Problem Solving. International Journal of Man-Machine Studies 19, 1983

GOLD83   Goldberg, A. and Robson, D.: Smalltalk-80: The Language and its Implementation, Reading/Mass. 1983

LEHM85   Lehmann. E., Enders,R., Haugeneder,H., Hunze, R., Johnson, C., Schmid, L. and Struß, P.: SICONFEX - ein Expertensystem, für die Konfigurierung eines Betriebssystems, to appear in: GI-15. Jahrestagung, Berlin 1985

McCA69   McCarthy, J. and Hayes, P. J.: Some Philosophical Problems form the Standpoint of Artificial Intelligence, in: Meltzer, B. and Mitchie, D. (eds): Machine Intelligence 4, Edinburgh 1969

STEF83   Stefik, M., Bobrow, D.G., Mittal, S. and Conway, L.: Knowledge Programming in LOOPS: Report on an Experimental Course. AI Magazine 4 (3), 1983

WIEL84   Wielinga B. J. and Breuker, J.A.: Interpretation of verbal data for knowledge acquisition. in: O'Shea, T. (ed): ECAI-84: Advances in Artificial Intelligence, North-Holland 1984

KOOPERATIVITAET IN NATUERLICHSPRACHLICHEN ZUGANGSSYSTEMEN

HEINZ MARBURGER

Universitaet Hamburg
Fachbereich Informatik
Projektgruppe WISBER
Postfach 302762
2ooo Hamburg 36

ZUSAMMENFASSUNG

Natuerlichsprachliche Zugangssysteme muessen auf vielfaeltige Art kooperativ
reagieren koennen, um von Benutzern als angemessenes Werkzeug akzeptiert zu
werden. Deshalb ist dieser Problemkreis in den letzten Jahren mehr und mehr in
den Fordergrund der Forschung getreten. Das Papier gibt einen Ueberblick ueber
kooperative Verhaltensweisen von einigen existierenden und in der Entwicklung
befindlichen Systemen mit dem Schwerpunkt auf der Darstellung der notwendigen
Wissensquellen und Prozesse zur Generierung kooperativer Antworten.

1. EINLEITUNG

In den letzten fuenfzehn Jahren wurden eine Reihe von natuerlichsprachlichen
(nl) Zugangssystemen zu unterschiedlichen Leistungssystemen von Rechenanlagen
entwickelt. Obwohl die Konstruktion von nl Zugangssystemen zu z.B.
Bildfolgeanalysesystemen und Expertensystemen zugenommen hat, bildet der
Bereich nl Zugang zu Datenbankmanagementsystemen (DBMS) den
Forschungsschwerpunkt (vgl. [9]) und wird auch in diesem Papier
ausschliesslich behandelt. Das bedeutet jedoch nicht, dass die hier
vorgestellten Methoden nicht auch fuer den nl Zugang zu anderen
Leistungssystemen Anwendung finden (vgl. [6]); sie sind m.E. eher so
grundlegend, dass sie auch in Systemen, die nur ueber eine formalsprachliche
(fl) Schnittstelle verfuegen, einsetzbar sind.

Durch den Gebrauch von natuerlicher Sprache als Moeglichkeit zum Zugang zu
Informationen werden an nl Zugangssysteme hoehere Anforderungen als an fl
Zugangssysteme gestellt, da Benutzer davon ausgehen, dass die ueblichen
kooperativen Konventionen (vgl. [4]), die in der Mensch-Mensch-Kommunikation
befolgt werden, auch von der Maschine beachtet werden. Nl Zugangssysteme
muessen deshalb mit Faehigkeiten ausgestattet werden, die kooperatives
Verhalten realisieren.

Kooperatives Verhalten beschraenkt sich nicht auf einzelne Bereiche von nl
Systemen, sondern muss in allen Komponenten gleichmaessig entwickelt sein.
Waehrend der Analyse einer Benutzeranfrage kann sich Kooperativitaet darin
manifestieren, dass z.B. Klaerungsdialoge gefuehrt werden, um unbekannte
Woerter verarbeiten zu koennen, oder um eindeutige Referenzobjekte fuer
definite Nominalphrasen (NPs) zu identifizieren (vgl. [5]).

In Systemreaktionen kann sich Kooperativitaet ebenfalls auf vielerlei Art
aeussern; siehe die Beispiele (1a) bis (3c).

(1a)   Wieviele U-Boote gibt es?
(1b)   Keine.
(1c)   U-Boote sind nicht in der Datenbank modelliert. Folgendes paralleles
        Konzept ist modelliert: 'Schiff'.
(2a)   Welche englischen Schiffe sind laenger als das deutsche Schiff?
(2b)   Keins.
(2c)   In der Datenbank sind keine englischen Schiffe gespeichert.
(3a)   Fuhren fuenf Schiffe nach Hamburg?
(3b)   Nein.
(3c)   Nein, sechs.

Antwort (1c) auf Frage (1a) ist kooperativer als Antwort (1b), da der Benutzer
aus aus (1b) die offensichtlich falsche Schlussfolgerung ziehen kann, dass
auch U-Boote potentiell in der Datenbank (DB) gespeichert werden koennen.

Waehrend Antwort (2c) die falsche Praesupposition der Benutzerfrage (2a), dass
es in der DB englische Schiffe gibt, korrigiert, hat (2b) den Effekt, dass
implizit verstanden wird, dass es englische Schiffe gibt.

Antwort (3b) laesst nur den Schluss zu, dass keine fuenf Schiffe nach Hamburg
fuhren. Jede andere Quantitaet wird von der Antwort nicht beruehrt. (3c)
verneint ebenso wie (3b) die Proposition der Frage, bestimmt aber zusaetzlich
die tatsaechliche Anzahl der Schiffe, die nach Hamburg fuhren, und ist durch
diese Ueberbeantwortung kooperativer als (3b).

Welche Wissensquellen und Prozesse zur Realisierung dieser drei Arten von
Kooperativitaet notwendig sind, soll an Hand beispielhafter Implementationen
in den folgenden Abschnitten verdeutlicht werden. Weitere Arten von
kooperativen Verhaltensweisen werden in [16] und [17] dargestellt. Dort wird
auch der Zugang zu anderen Leistungssystemen untersucht.

2. KOOPERATIVE ANTWORTEN BEI FEHLERN

Betrachten wir noch einmal die Fragen (1a) und (2a), die moegliche Fragen an
das nl System HAM-ANS [6] sind, das u.a. Zugang zu einer DB gewaehrleistet, in
der Information ueber Schiffe, Fahrten von Schiffen und Faengen, die von
diesen Schiffen aus gemacht wurden, gespeichert sind. Da jede DB nur einen
geringen Ausschnitt der realen Welt modelliert, ist es wahrscheinlich, dass
ein Benutzer eine Frage nach Objekten, Funktionen, Eigenschaften von Objekten
oder Relationen zwischen Objekten stellen wird, die in der aktuellen DB nicht
modelliert sind. Stellt ein Benutzer eine solche Frage (z.B. (1a)), dann hat
er falsche Annahmen ueber das konzeptuelle Wissen des Systems (vgl. [3][14]),
und eine kooperative Antwort sollte diese falschen Annahmen anzeigen und
gleichzeitig, wenn es moeglich ist, unterstuetzende Information geben, so dass
der Benutzer seine Frage anders formulieren kann (vgl. [12]). Auf der anderen
Seite kann es der Fall sein, dass die Frage des Benutzers eine falsche
extensionale Praesupposition enthaelt (z.B. (2a)). Eine kooperative Antwort
sollte auf jeden Fall diese falsche Annahme korrigieren wie in (2c) (vgl.
[9]).

Um diesen Anspruechen gerecht zu werden, muss das System zum einen die
Moeglichkeit haben, Fehler zu entdecken, und zum anderen eine geeignete
Antwort auswaehlen. Dazu ist zumindest das folgende Wissen notwendig:

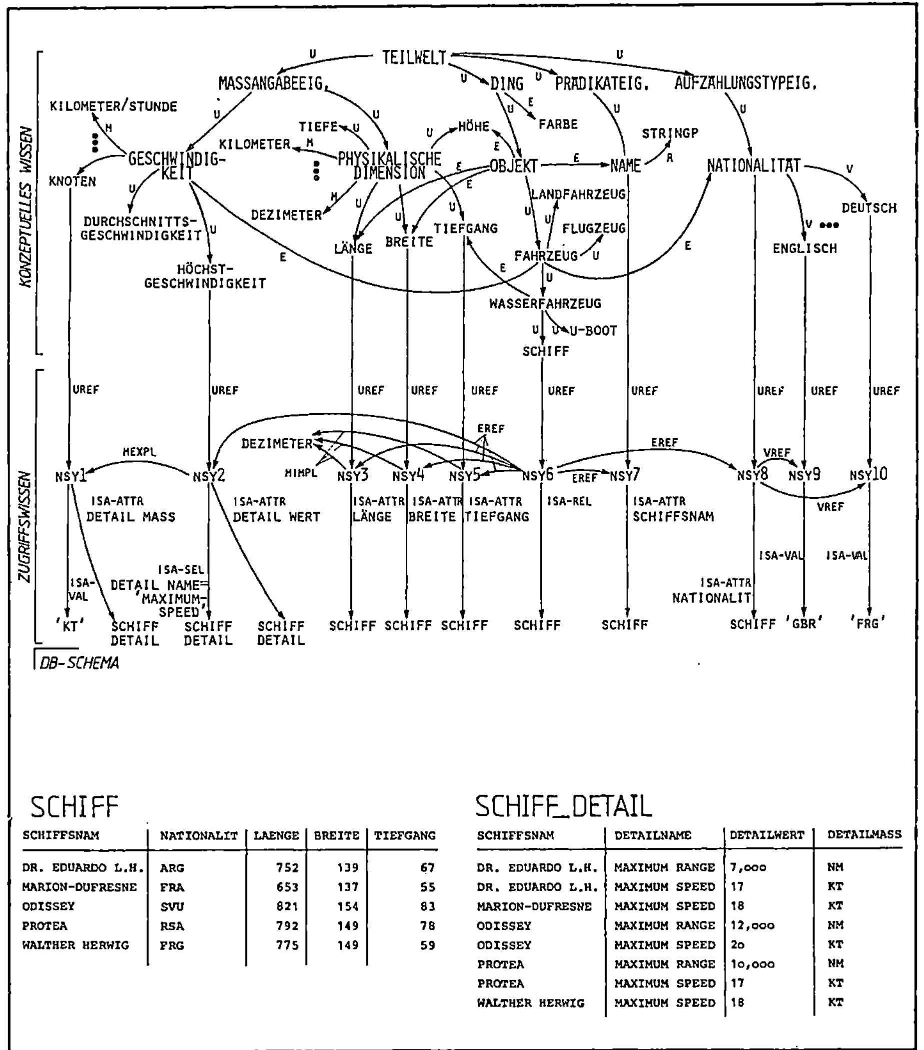

SCHIFF

SCHIFFSNAM	NATIONALIT	LAENGE	BREITE	TIEFGANG
DR. EDUARDO L.H.	ARG	752	139	67
MARION-DUFRESNE	FRA	653	137	55
ODISSEY	SVU	821	154	83
PROTEA	RSA	792	149	78
WALTHER HERWIG	FRG	775	149	59

SCHIFF_DETAIL

SCHIFFSNAM	DETAILNAME	DETAILWERT	DETAILMASS
DR. EDUARDO L.H.	MAXIMUM RANGE	7,000	NM
DR. EDUARDO L.H.	MAXIMUM SPEED	17	KT
MARION-DUFRESNE	MAXIMUM SPEED	18	KT
ODISSEY	MAXIMUM RANGE	12,000	NM
ODISSEY	MAXIMUM SPEED	2o	KT
PROTEA	MAXIMUM RANGE	1o,000	NM
PROTEA	MAXIMUM SPEED	17	KT
WALTHER HERWIG	MAXIMUM SPEED	18	KT

Abbildung 1: Konzeptuelles Wissen und Zugriffswissen
fuer zwei Relationen

- konzeptuelles Wissen: welche Konzepte, Eigenschaften und Beziehungen zwischen Konzepten kommen in dem Weltausschnit, der in der DB modelliert ist, vor
- Zugriffswissen: wie sind die Konzepte, Eigenschaften und Beziehungen in der DB dargestellt
- syntaktisches DB Wissen: welche Datentypen haben die Attribute, wieviele Attribute haben die Relationen usw.

Abbildung 1 zeigt zwei DB-Relationen, in denen Information ueber Schiffe gespeichert ist, sowie den dazu gehoerenden Ausschnitt des konzeptuellen Wissens und des Zugriffswissen, wie es in HAM-ANS dargestellt ist. Einige der

wichtigsten Kantentypen dieser Netzwerke sollen kurz beschrieben werden, da
sie fuer das weitere Vorgehen von Bedeutung sind.

U   realisiert eine Unterbegriffshierarchie fuer Konzepte und
         Eigenschaften
E   ordnet Konzepten Eigenschaften zu
V   ordnet Eigenschaften moegliche Werte zu
UREF   verbinden Knoten des konzeptuellen Wissens mit Abbildungsknoten
         des Zugriffswissen (alle Knoten, deren Name mit NSY beginnt)
EREF   ordnen einem Konzeptabbildungsknoten einen Eigenschafts-
         abbildungsknoten zu
VREF   ordnen einem Eigenschaftsabbildungsknoten einen Wertabbildungs-
         knoten zu
ISA-REL ordnet einem Abbildungsknoten einen DB-Relationsnamen zu
ISA-ATTR spezifiziert fuer einen Abbildungsknoten ein Attribut einer
         DB-Relation
ISA-VAL ordnet einem Wertabbildungsknoten einen Wert eines Attributs zu

Wie dieses Wissen das Erkennen falscher Annahmen des Benutzers unterstuetzt,
und wie kooperative Antworten ermoeglicht werden, wird im folgenden an Hand
der Verarbeitung einiger Beispielsaetze verdeutlicht. Zuerst zwei Beispiele
fuer falsche Annahmen des Benutzers ueber das konzeptuelle Wissen des Systems.

(1a) Wieviele U-Boote gibt es?

Bei der Ueberfuehrung der semantischen Repraesentation dieser nl Anfrage in
eine DB-Anfrage wird als erstes geprueft, ob fuer den Begriff 'U-Boot' eine
Verbindung zu einem Abbildungsknoten ueber eine UREF-Kante und ggf. U-Kanten
existiert. Fehlt eine solche Verbindung im konzeptuellen Wissen wie in diesem
Fall, so kann daraus geschlossen werden, dass der Begriff nicht in der DB
modelliert. ist. Nach Entdecken des Fehlers versucht das System zu
verifizieren, ob semantisch aehnliche Konzepte in der DB modelliert sind. Fuer
Schiff trifft dies zu, und die Antwort (1c) wird generiert.

(1c) U-Boote sind nicht in der Datenbank modelliert. Folgendes paralleles
     Konzept ist modelliert: 'Schiff'.

Bei Frage (4a) wird aehnlich vorgegangen. Zusaetzlich muss aber ueberprueft

(4a) Welche Farbe haben die Schiffe?

werden, ob konzeptuell eine Verbindung zwischen 'Schiff' und 'Farbe' existiert
(ueber E- und U-Kanten), und weiterhin, ob es eine Verbindung ueber einen
Konzeptabbildungsknoten und ueber einen Eigenschaftsabbildungsknoten zu
'Farbe' (ueber UREF- und EREF-Kanten) gibt. Da die letzte Ueberpruefung
scheitert, wird versucht dem Benutzer mitzuteilen, welche Eigenschaften fuer
'Schiff' modelliert sind, d.h.: Auffinden aller EREF-Kanten, die von dem
Abbildungsknoten von 'Schiff' ausgehen, und von den so gefundenen
Eigenschaftsabbildungsknoten die zugehoerigen Eigenschaften aufsuchen. Ebenso
kann in umgekehrter Reihenfolge bestimmt werden, fuer welche Konzepte 'Farbe'
modelliert ist. In dieser DB ist 'Farbe' aber fuer kein Konzept modelliert.
Die Antwort lautet also:

(4b) Farbe ist nicht fuer Schiff modelliert. Folgende Eigenschaften sind fuer
     Schiff modelliert: Laenge, Breite, Tiefgang, Hoechstgeschwindigkeit,
     und Nationalitaet. Farbe ist fuer kein Konzept modelliert.

Eine bessere Antwort ist sicherlich (4c):

(4c) Farbe ist fuer kein Konzept modelliert. Fuer Schiff sind modelliert:
     Laenge,....

Wenden wir uns jetzt der Verarbeitung von Frage (2a) zu, die die

(2a) Welche englischen Schiffe sind laenger als das deutsche Schiff?

Praesuppositionen es gibt englische Schiffe' und 'es gibt genau ein deutsches Schiff' enthaelt. Da bei der konzeptuellen Ueberpruefung keine Fehler auftreten, kann im naechsten Schritt eine DB-Anfrage formuliert werden.

Die Generierung einer DB-Anfrage fuer die gesamte Frage und deren anschliessende Auswertung durch das DBMS wuerde aber eine leere Relation liefern, da es kein englisches Schiff in der DB gibt. Die einzig moegliche Antwort ist in diesem Fall (2b).

(2b) Keins.

Um die Antwort (2c) zu erzeugen, ist es notwendig, die Ueberfuehrung von der semantischen Repraesentation in die DB-Anfrage in kleine Schritte aufzuteilen. In HAM-ANS wird zuerst versucht, die Menge der Referenzobjekte, die durch die NPs in der Frage gekennzeichnet sind, zu bestimmen. Eine Menge von Referenzobjekten zu bestimmen, heisst in einer DB-Anwendung, eine Menge von Tupeln zu finden. Fuer die beiden NPs werden die folgenden DB-Anfragen in PASCAL/R-Notation [13] generiert.

```
[EACH X1 in SCHIFF : X1.NATIONALIT = 'GBR'];
[EACH X2 in SCHIFF : X2.NATIONALIT = 'FRG'];
```

Da aber die Auswertung der ersten Anfrage eine leere Relation liefert, kann der Prozess beendet werden und die Antwort (2c) formuliert werden.

(2c) Englische Schiffe sind nicht in der Datenbank gespeichert.

Eine weitere unterstuetzende Antwort kann dem Benutzer mitteilen, welche Nationalitaeten von Schiffen gespeichert sind, z.B. (2d).

(2d) Es sind nur deutsche, argentinische, sowjetische, suedafrikanische und
     franzoesiche Schiffe gespeichert.

Antworten dieser Art koennen von dem System HAM-ANS erzeugt werden.

Die besprochenen Arten kooperativer Antworten bei Fehlern geben dem Benutzer zum einen Hinweise darauf, wo der Fehler aufgetreten ist, zum anderen darauf, welche Alternativen moeglich sind. Kooperative Dialogpartner gehen aber in der Regel noch einen Schritt weiter: Sie geben nicht nur die Information, die dem Partner die Formulierung einer neuen Frage erlauben, sondern erschliessen an Hand der Information, die waehrend des Dialogs zwischen den Partnern ausgetauscht wurde, und ihres Wissens ueber den gegenwaertigen Weltausschnitt die Ziele des Fragenden ebenso wie Plaene, wie diese Ziele erreicht werden koennen. Dieses erschlossene Wissen gibt Hinweise zur Interpretation von Aeusserungen und zur Formulierung von kooperativen Antworten. Wenn z.B. eine falsche Annahme ueber das konzeptuelle Wissen erkannt worden ist, kann der Teil der Frage, der den Fehler verursacht hat, modifiziert werden, so dass die neu entstehende Frage sowohl bedeutungsvoll als auch relevant fuer den gegenwaertigen Stand des Dialogs und damit auch fuer den Fragenden ist.

Ein System, das ein solches Verhalten realisiert, wurde von Carberry [2] entwickelt und soll im weiteren als Grundlage fuer die Ausfuehrungen dienen.

Neben dem Wissen, das in den letzten Abschnitten dargestellt worden ist, ist nun auch Wissen ueber allgemeine diskursbereichsabhaengige Plaene und Ziele sowie ueber die aus dem Dialog inferierten speziellen Plaene und Ziele des Benutzers erforderlich. Ein Plan kann Teilziele und Aktionen haben, die wiederum assoziierte Plaene besitzen. Der inferierte Plan des Benutzers wird als ein Kontextbaum dargestellt. Die Knoten in diesem Baum repraesentieren Ziele und Aktionen, die der Sprecher untersucht hat. Ihre Vorgaengerknoten repraesentieren hoehere Ziele, deren assoziierte Plaene die niedrigeren Aktionen enthalten. Der globale Kontext wird durch den gesamten Kontextbaum dargestellt. Der fokussierte Kontext ist ein Teilbaum, der den lokalen Kontext oder einen bestimmten Aspekt des Plans, auf den die Aufmerksamkeit des Benutzers gerichtet ist, repraesentiert (vgl. [1]).

Um eine kommunikativ adaequate Reformulierung der Benutzerfrage beim Auftreten eines Fehlers zu erzeugen, sind zwei weitere Prozesse notwendig. Der erste versucht unter Ausnutzung der moeglichen Expansionen des gegenwaertigen inferierten Benutzerplans, alternative Fragen vorzuschlagen. Der Prozess greift dazu auf zwei Regelmengen zurueck:

- Ersetzungsregeln bewirken eine Ersetzung von den in der Benutzerfrage spezifizierten Relationen, Funktionen, Attributen oder Objektmengen.
- Erweiterungsregeln erzeugen neue logische Joins, die in der Frage nicht spezifiziert waren.

Der zweite Prozess bewertet die moeglichen Alternativen und waehlt diejenigen aus, die am wahrscheinlichsten der Intention des Fragenden entsprechen. Drei Kriterien steuern diesen Prozess:

- Die Relevanz der revidierten Frage bezueglich der inferierten Plaene und Ziele des Benutzers.
- Die Art der Substitution bzw. Erweiterung.
- Der semantische Unterschied zwischen der revidierten Frage und der urspruenglichen Frage.

Im folgenden sollen an Hand eines Beispiels einige Aspekte dieser zwei Prozesse erlaeutert werden (fuer eine detaillierte Darstellung siehe [2]).

Angenommen ein Benutzer stellt die Frage (5a) im Diskursbereich Immobilien-

(5a) Welche Wohnungen sind zu verkaufen?

und Wohnungsmarkt, in dem einzelne Wohnungen nicht verkauft sondern nur vermietet werden. Verkauft werden Haeuser und Mietshauser. Frage (5a) enthaelt also die falsche Proposition (ZU_VERKAUFEN (WOHNUNG)).

Wenn durch den vorangegangenen Dialog deutlich wurde, dass der Benutzer nur fuer eine begrenzte Zeit Wohnraum sucht, umfasst die Expansion des Kontextmodells, das den inferierten Sprecherplan enthaelt, die moeglichen Aktionen, dass der Sprecher entweder eine Wohnung mietet oder ein Haus mietet; beides unter der Voraussetzung, dass das jeweilige Objekt zu vermieten ist (siehe Abb. 2 linke Haelfte).

Wenn in einem anderen Fall durch den vorhergehenden Dialog deutlich wurde, dass es sich beim Benutzer um einen Immobilienkaeufer handelt, der Interesse an weiteren Investitionen hat, kann die Expansion des inferierten Benutzerplans die moeglichen Aktionen andeuten, dass entweder eine Mietshaus oder ein Haus gekauft werden soll; jeweils unter der Voraussetzung, dass die Objekte zu verkaufen sind (siehe Abb. 2 rechte Haelfte).

Der Vorschlagsprozess durchsucht nun den inferierten Sprecherplan und die moeglichen Expansionen nach Propositionen, die sich mit der falschen Proposition "unifizieren" lassen. "Unifizieren" in Anfuehrungsstrichen, da bei diesem Prozess auch die semantische Naehe von verschiedenen Objektmengen, Relationen, Funktionen und Attributen beruecksichtigt wird. Die semantische

Naehe ist durch das konzeptuelle Wissen repraesentiert. In den o.g. Situationen werden jeweils zwei revidierte Fragen vorgeschlagen (siehe Abb. 2).

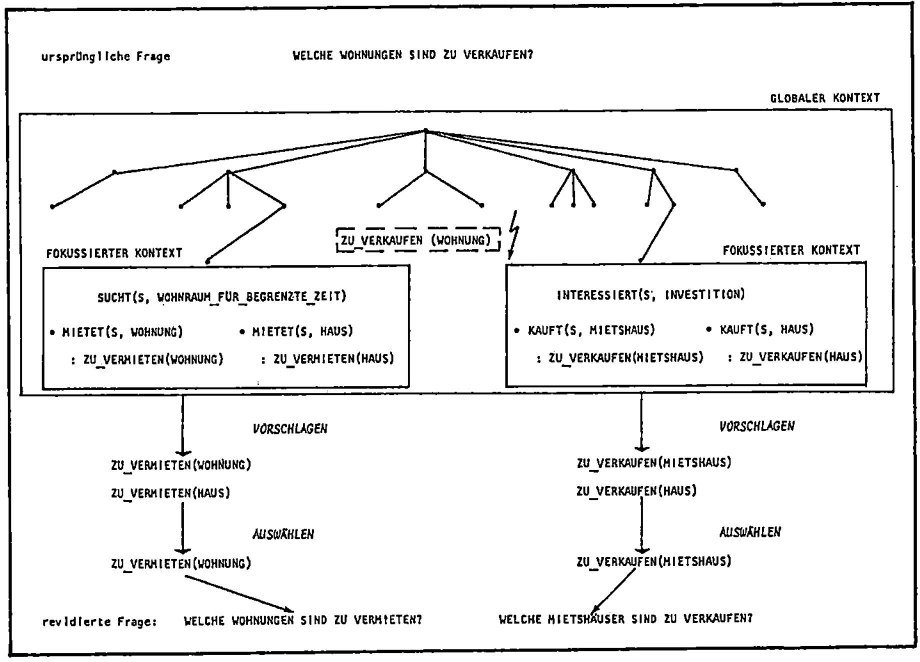

Abbildung 2: Vorschlags- und Auswahlprinzip in einem Kontextbaum

Der Auswahlprozess bestimmt anschliessend fuer jede Situation eine revidierte Frage, die die Kriterien am besten erfuellt und ausserdem einen vorher festgelegten Schwellwert erreicht. Fuer die erste Situation lautet die revidierte Frage (5b) fuer die zweite (5c).

(5b) Welche Wohnungen sind zu vermieten?
(5c) Welche Mietshaeuser sind zu verkaufen?

Sollte der Schwellwert nicht erreicht werden, werden die Prozesse von neuem angestossen: Hoeher im Kontextbaum liegende aktive Plaene werden expandiert und Propositionen in diesen Plaene wiederum mit der falschen Proposition "unifiziert"; vorgeschlagene Propositionen werden dann durch den Auswahlprozess weiterverarbeitet. Die so enstehenden revidierten Fragen sind nicht unmittelbar relevant fuer den gegenwaertigen lokalen Dialogkontext sondern relevant fuer den globalen Kontext. Werden globalere Plaene untersucht, wird der Schwellwert fuer revidierte Fragen lokalerer Plaene erniedrigt, so dass revidierte Fragen, die zuerst eine zu geringe Bewertung erhielten, waehrend des weiteren Verlaufs ausgewaehlt werden koennen. Der Prozess endet, wenn entweder eine akzeptable Frage erzeugt wurde oder alle Moeglichkeiten ausgeschoepft sind.

3. INFORMATIVE KOOPERATIVE ANTWORTEN

Kooperatives Verhalten in Frage-Antwort Dialogen wird aber nicht nur dann notwendig, wenn bei einem Partner falsche Annahmen ueber den Zustand der

Diskurswelt bestehen, sondern auch, wenn eine Frage ordnungsgemaess beantwortet werden kann. Kooperativitaet kann sich z.B. dadurch ausdruecken, dass auf eine Ja/Nein-Frage nicht nur mit ja oder nein geantwortet wird, sondern zusaetzlich speziellere Information gegeben wird. Kooperative Antworten sollen also informativ, zugleich aber nicht zu kompliziert, unverstaendlich oder unuebersichtlich sein. In diesem Abschnitt wird ein Verfahren vorgestellt, das praezisere Quantoren in Antworten generiert.

Nach Horn [7] verhaelt sich ein Sprecher kooperativ, wenn er den hoechsten Wert auf einer Skala nennt, den er als wahr erachtet. Die Skala muss der Bedingung genuegen, dass aus hoeheren Werten alle niedrigeren Werte semantisch folgen. Ein kooperativer Sprecher sagt genau so viel -bezueglich einer Skala- wie er gemaess seines Wissensstandes vertreten kann.

Betrachten wir noch einmal Frage (3a), die den numerischen Quantor 'fuenf' enthaelt, und die Antworten (3b) und (3c).

(3a) Fuhren fuenf Schiffe nach Hamburg?
(3b) Nein.
(3c) Nein, sechs.

Antwort (3c) auf Frage (3a) ist unter der Voraussetzung, dass die natuerlichen Zahlen eine Skala im o.g. Sinne darstellen, kooperativer als (3b), da, obwohl auf die Frage keine positive Antwort gegeben werden kann, der numerische Quantor 'sechs' mehr Information enthaelt als ein einfaches 'nein':

- Schiffe fuhren nach Hamburg.
- Sechs Schiffe fuhren nach Hamburg. Daraus folgt: es fuhren mehr als fuenf Schiffe nach Hamburg.
- mehr als sechs Schiffe fuhren nicht nach Hamburg.

Die Informativitaet einer Antwort wird durch den Gebrauch eines praeziseren Quantors gesteigert, ohne jedoch die Komplexitaet wesentlich zu erhoehen [15]. Ausserdem wird durch Antwort (3c) moeglichen Nachfragen des Benutzers vorgegriffen.

Fragen, die nur numerische oder vage Quantoren enthalten, machen keine Annahmen ueber die Kardinalitaet der Menge der Referenzobjekte, die durch die NPs bestimmt sind. Im Gegensatz dazu kann bei Fragen, in denen definite Quantoren oder Quantoren wie 'alle', 'jeder', 'beide' benutzt werden, davon ausgegangen werden, dass der Fragende bestimmte Annahmen hat.

Ist bei Fragen der letzten Art noch nicht durch den Dialogverlauf geklaert, welche Annahmen der Fragende hat, ist eine Antwort, die sowohl die Kardinalitaet der Menge der Objekte, fuer die das erfragte Praedikat zugetroffen hat, als auch die Kardinalitaet der Referenzobjektmenge bestimmt, kooperativer als eine Antwort, die nur die Kardinalitaet der ersten Menge

(6a) Sind die Schiffe laenger als 760 Dezimeter?
(6b) Ja, drei.
(6c) Ja, drei von den fuenf.

nennt. Antwort (6c) auf Frage (6a) bewirkt, dass der Fragende zusaetzlich zu dem Inhalt der Antwort (6b) weiss, wieviele Schiffe es im Diskursbereich gibt. Fragender und Antwortender besitzen nach dieser Antwort mehr gemeinsames Wissen und koennen den Dialog effizienter gestalten. Sollte z.B. die Auswertung von einer weiteren Frage das Ergebnis liefern, dass fuenf Schiffe das Praedikat der Frage erfuellen, so kann das System den Quantor 'alle' in der Antwort benutzen.

Im System HAM-ANS wird Kooperativitaet dieser Art realisiert. Neben dem notwendigen Wissen zur Generierung der Quantoren wurden die Ueberfuehrungsprozesse von der semantischen Repraesentation der Frage in Ausdruecke der DB-Anfragesprache so entwickelt, dass die Information ueber die Kardinalitaet der verschiedenen Mengen bereitgestellt wird. Dieses Vorgehen ist nicht so aussergewoehnlich, wie es zuerst erscheinen mag, wenn man bedenkt, dass schon fuer die Ueberpruefung von Praesuppositionsverletzungen die Kardinalitaet der Menge der Referenzobjekte, die durch eine NP bestimmt wird, berechnet werden muss.

Beispielhaft soll hier der Ueberfuehrungsprozess fuer die Frage (6a) beschrieben werden. Die Bestimmung der Kardinalitaet der Referenzobjektmenge fuer die NP 'die Schiffe' wird durch die DB-Anfrage

$$SIZE \ (SCHIFF);$$

geleistet. Das Ergebnis ist 'fuenf', und somit liegt keine Praesuppositionsverletzung vor. Nun wird die Gesamtanfrage konstruiert, aber in der Weise, dass die Tupel (Referenzobjekte), die das Praedikat erfuellen, in einer eigenen Relation gespeichert werden.

$$X:=[EACH \ X1 \ in \ SCHIFF : X1.LAENGE > 760];$$
$$SIZE(X);$$

Die Ergebnisrelation X enthaelt drei Tupel (vgl. Abb. 1). Mit dieser Information kann die Antwort (6c) gebildet werden.

4. AUSBLICK

Die Ausfuehrungen in diesem Papier sollten verdeutlichen, dass es heute schon eine Reihe von Methoden gibt, die das Verhalten von nl Zugangssystemen dem Verhalten kooperativer Dialogpartner annaehern. Untersuchungen auf diesem Gebiet befinden sich aber noch in den Kinderschuhen, so dass in den naechsten Jahren weitere Fortschritte erwartet werden koennen. Gundsaetzliche Probleme sind jedoch noch zu klaeren wie z.B. das Konzept der semantischen Naehe von Begriffen. Auch das Erkennen von Benutzerzielen waehrend eines Dialogs ist noch ein offenes Feld, in dem erst in den letzten Jahren aktiver geforscht wird.

Ich hoffe, dass durch die Beispiele deutlich wurde, dass auch fl Zugangssysteme kooperatives Verhalten zeigen muessen. Die Fehler, die in Abschnitt 2 angesprochen wurden, koennen auch bei fl Anfragen auftreten (siehe z.B. die Arbeit von Janas [8], in der gezeigt wird, wie Praesuppositionsverletzungen in DB-Anfragen erkannt werden koennen). Koennten fl Zugangssysteme Antworten erzeugen, wie sie in Abschnitt 3 besprochen wurden, wuerde die Akzeptanz der Systeme sicher erhoeht.

LITERATUR

[1] Carberry, M.S.: Tracking User Goals in an Information-Seeking Environment. In: Proc. 3rd AAAI, Washington, 1983, pp. 59-63
[2] Carberry, M.S.: Understanding Pragmatically Ill-Formed Input. In: Proc. COLING-84 and 22nd ACL, Stanford, 1984, pp. 200-206
[3] Finin, T., Goodman, B., Tennant, H.: Jets: Achieving Completeness through Coverage and Closure. In: Proc. 6th IJCAI, Tokio, 1979, pp. 275-281
[4] Grice, H.P.: Logic and Conversation. In: Cole, P., Morgan, J.L. (Hrsg): Syntax and Semantics: Speech Acts. Vol. 3. Academic Press, New York, 1975, pp. 41-58·

[5] Hoeppner, W., Jameson, A.: Kooperatives Dialogverhalten im Simulationssystem HAM-RPM. In: Proc. 4th GWAI, Bad Honnef, 1979, pp. 21-31

[6] Hoeppner, W., Christaller, T., Marburger, H., Morik, K., Nebel, B., O'Leary, M., Wahlster, W.: Beyond Domain-Independence: Experience with the Development of a German Language Access System to Highly Diverse Background Systems. In: Proc. 8th IJCAI, Karlsruhe, 1983, pp. 588-594

[7] Horn, L.R.: On the Semantic Properties of Logical Operators in English. Ph.D. Thesis, Univ. of California at Los Angeles, 1972

[8] Janas, J.M.: How to Say not Nil - Improving Answers to Failing Queries in Data Base Systems. In: Proc. 6th IJCAI, Tokio, 1979, pp. 429-434

[9] Kaplan, J.S.: Cooperative Responses from a Portable Natural Language Query System. In: Artificial Intelligence, Vol. 19, No. 2, 1982, pp. 165-187

[10] King, J.J.: Special Issue on AI and Database Research. In: SIGART Newsletter, No. 86, October 1983, pp. 32-72

[11] Marburger, H., Nebel, B.: Natuerlichsprachlicher Datenbankzugang mit HAM-ANS: Syntaktische Korrespondenz, natuerlichsprachliche Quantifizierung und semantisches Modell des Diskursbereichs. In: Schmidt, J.W. (Hrsg): Sprachen fuer Datenbanken. Springer, Berlin, 1983, pp. 26-41

[12] Mays, E.: Failures in Natural Language Systems: Applications to Data Base Query Systems. In: Proc. 1st AAAI, Stanford, 1980, pp. 327-330

[13] Schmidt, J.W., Mall, M.: PASCAL/R report. Univ. Hamburg, Fachbereich fuer Informatik, Bericht IFI-HH-B-66/80, 1980

[14] Sowa, J.F.: Conceptual Structures: Information Processing in Mind and Machine. Addison-Wesley, London 1983

[15] Wahlster, W., Marburger, H., Jameson, A., Busemann, S.: Over-Answering Yes-No Questions: Extended Responses in a NL Interface to a Vision System. In: Proc. 8th IJCAI, Karlsruhe, 1983, pp. 643-646

[16] Wahlster, W.: Cooperative Access Systems. In: Bernold, Th., Albers, G. (Hrsg): Artificial Intelligence - Towards Practical Applications. North Holland, Amsterdam, 1985, pp. 33-45

[17] Webber, B.L., Finin, T.: In Response: Next Steps in Natural Language Interaction. In: Reitman, W.R. (Hrsg): Artificial Intelligence Applications for Business, Ablex, Norwood, 1984, pp. 221-234

Objektorientierte Wissensdarstellung in industriellen
Expertensystemen

Dr. H. Marchand, DANET GmbH, Darmstadt

1. Regelorientierte und objektorientierte Wissensdarstellung

Wissensdarstellung in Regelform hat bereits eine lange Tradition
für Expertensysteme: Eine Vielzahl von Systemen benutzen Produktionsregeln als wichtigstes Mittel der Wissensrepräsentation.

Unsere Erfahrungen mit regelorientierten Expertensystemen zeigen
allerdings, daß sie, neben positiven Eigenschaften in der Proto-
typphase eine Expertensystemprojekts und als Teilaspekt der
Wissensdarstellung auch viele Nachteile mit sich bringen. Die
wichtigsten sind:

- Schwierigkeit der Verwaltung von sehr großen Regelbasen

- Schwierigkeit des Testens beim Hinzufügen neuer Regeln

- Schwierigkeit der Unabhängigkeit zwischen Inferenzsystem
  und Regelwerk

Regeln sind ein geeignetes Mittel, um Wissen, das unvollständig
und unstrukturiert ist, darzustellen.

Es zeigt sich in der Praxis, daß nur selten das darzustellende
Wissen so vorliegt. Im Gegenteil arbeiten Experten mit Konzepten,
die auf Kategorien, Klassen und Strukturen hindeuten, und die eine
zusätzliche Wissensdarstellungsform als die durch Regeln brauchen.

Dies wurde in zwei wissensbasierten Systemen deutlich, die wir
als Beispiele für die nächsten Kapitel benutzen werden: ein
Hardware/Software-Konfigurationssystem und ein Fertigungs-
planungs und -Steuerungssystem.

2. **Was sind Objekte in wissensbasierten Systemen?**

Objekte werden meistens im Zusammenhang mit Programmiersprachen
<1> erwähnt. Hier sind Objekte Pakete, die Informationen und die
Beschreibung der Verarbeitung dieser Informationen beinhalten <2>.
Aus der Sicht der Wissensdarstellung müssen andere Aspekte im
Vordergrund stehen: Objekte müssen als Wissensprimitive verstanden
werden, also für den Experten natürliche Konzepte darstellen, die
auch als solche maschinell zur Verfügung stehen.

Es werden insofern zwei Fragen zu beantworten sein:

- was sind Wissensprimitive?

- wie werden sie maschinell abgebildet?

2.1 Wissensprimitive

Expertensysteme dienen nicht nur der Sicherung und Zuverfügung-
stellung des Wissens von einzelnen Experten, sondern des Wissens
mehrerer auf eine Aufgabe spezialisierter Personen. Das gemeinsame Wissen über die Aufgabe ist für die Kommunikation und die
Kooperation zwischen diesen Personen genauso wichtig wie das
Wissen über die möglichen Lösungen dieser Aufgabe. Wissensprimitive zielen darauf ab, dieses gemeinsame Wissen im Unternehmen
explizit zu machen.

Da die Aufgabe, die man betrachtet, nicht neu ist, existiert
bereits eine Sprache, die die Kommunikation ermöglicht: linguistische Ausdrücke, Texte, Zeichnungen usw. Es empfiehlt sich,
diese Sprache genau zu analysieren, bevor man das wissensbasierte System implementiert. Ihre Semantik beinhaltet viele
Spezifika der Organisation, die zunächst kaum zu erkennen sind,
weil ihre Oberfläche die übergreifende natürliche Sprache ist
(bzw. der Teil der natürlichen Sprache, die für die Kommunikation nach außen benötigt wird). Die Erkenntnisse, die wir nach
einer solchen Analyse gewinnen konnten, sind folgende:

o Wissensprimitive betreffen konkrete Objekte und
   abstrakte Begriffe

o Wissensprimitive existieren auf mehreren Abstraktionsebenen und sind hierarchisch strukturiert.

Zunächst einige Beispiele dazu:

o Abstraktionsebenen: in einem Fertigungsunternehmen gibt es in
  der Werkstatt Maschinen, die zwischen Anschaffung und Ver-
  schrottung existent sind und deren Eigenschaften für die
  Lösung der Probleme der Werkstattsteuerung maßgebend sind.

  Diese Maschinen sind aber auch Instanzen von einem allgemeingültigen Konzept einer Maschine, nämlich eines Fertigungs-
  systems, das nach einem bestimmten Verfahren ein Produkt her-
  stellen kann. Dabei können diesem Maschinenkonzept auch all-
  gemeingültige Eigenschaften hinzugefügt werden, die z.B. Aus-

sagen der Form "jede Maschine hat eine Rüstzeit, die vom
herzustellenden Teil abhängt" entsprechen.

o Konkrete Objekte und abstrakte Begriffe: In der Konfigurationsaufgabe werden Aussagen über kausale Beziehungen
  zwischen Komponenten gemacht. Ein Satz wie "eine Zentraleinheit benötigt ein Betriebssystem" enthält auf der Ebene
  der Konzepte zwei Objekte (Zentraleinheit und Betriebssystem) und einen Begriff (benötigt), die auch in Instanzen
  dieser Formulierung (z.B. im Satz "eine 7530-B benötigt
  BS2000-GA") wiederzufinden sind. Begriffe entsprechen oft
  transitiven Verben in der natürlichen Sprache und stellen
  Beziehungen zwischen konkreten Objekten dar. Ihre Semantik
  hängt von der Aufgabe ab. Im ersten Beispiel bedeutet
  "benötigt" nicht nur "muß der Konfiguration hinzugefügt
  werden", sondern in Abhängigkeit der Eigenschaften der
  betroffenen Objekte auch Änderungen dieser Objekte.

  Ein Begriff verhält sich also genau wie ein konkretes Objekt
  was die Abstraktionsebenen betrifft: Unterschiede existieren
  zwischen der allgemeingültigen Bedeutung eines Begriffs und
  ihrer konkreten Ausprägung. Beide dienen der Kommunikation
  und müssen zu diesem Zweck auch abgebildet werden.

  (Bemerkung: Es gibt auch Wissensprimitive, die anwendungsun-
  abhängig sind. Die wichtigsten betreffen die Zeit, z.B. die
  Begriffe von Vergangenheit und Zukunft, weil alle Objekte und
  Beziehungen zwischen Objekten in einer Organisation zeitge-
  bunden sind. Siehe dazu <3> und <4>).

Zusammenfassend kann man folgende Definition geben: "Objekte"
in wissensbasierten Systemen sind Wissensprimitive, die zwei
Dimensionen haben: die Realität und ihre Abstraktion.

2.2 Maschinelle Abbildung

Abbildungen sind symbolhafte Darstellungen mit sprachlichen
oder graphischen Elementen. Eine maschinelle Abbildung ist nichts
anderes als eine von diesen Darstellungen, mit dem wichtigen
Unterschied, daß sie direkt verarbeitbar ist.

Dank der symbolverarbeitenden Programmiersprachen wie LISP oder
PROLOG ist es kaum noch notwendig, zwischen externen und internen
Abbildungen in der Maschine zu sprechen: die Symbole werden
als solche für die Verarbeitung benutzt.

o Abbildung von Objekten und Begriffen

In Anlehnung an viele Wissenspräsentationssprachen und insbesondere an Carnegie Representation Language (CRL), werden konkrete
Objekte und Begriffe als "Schemata" dargestellt.

Ein Schema hat eine Bezeichnung, Einträge ("slots") und Werte
für jeden Eintrag.

In unserem vorherigen Beispiel werden die Objekte "Zentraleinheit" und "Betriebssystem" durch folgende vereinfachte Schemata
abgebildet.

Zentraleinheit 7530

      Hauptspeicher: max. 8 MB
      anzahl_BYMUX_anschlüße: max. 13
      anzahl_BLMUX_anschlüße: max. 8

Betriebssystem BS 2000

      benötigt: hauptspeicher 4 MB

Einträge in einem Schema ermöglichen sowohl Eigenschaften als
auch Beziehungen darzustellen. Beziehungen sind aber Begriffe,
die auch in Schemata beschrieben werden:

benötigt

      definitionsbereich: < Klasse von Komponenten >
      wertbereich: < Klasse von Komponenten >
      aktion: prozedur_benötigt

wobei die Semantik des Begriffs (hier die Aktion, die mit
benötigt gemeint ist) als Funktion oder Prozedur gesondert
definiert ist.

o <u>Abbildung von Abstrationsebenen</u>

Die Hierarchie wird durch zwei Relationstypen festgelegt:

- "ist_ein" verbindet zwei abstrakte Konzepte

- "instanz_von" definiert reale Instanzen von Objekten oder
  Begriffen

So in unserem Beispiel:

Zentraleinheit 7530

      ist_ein: Zentraleinheit

Zentraleinheit 7530-B

      ist_ein: Zentraleinheit 7530

Zentraleinheit 7530-B 1

      instanz: Zentraleinheit 7530-B

wobei diese letzte Beschreibung sich auf eine konkrete bestellte
Anlage bezieht. Damit wird eine Hierarchie mit zunehmender
Abstraktion aufgebaut.

Schematisch kann man sich diese maschinelle Abbildung als eine
dritte Dimension wie folgt vorstellen:

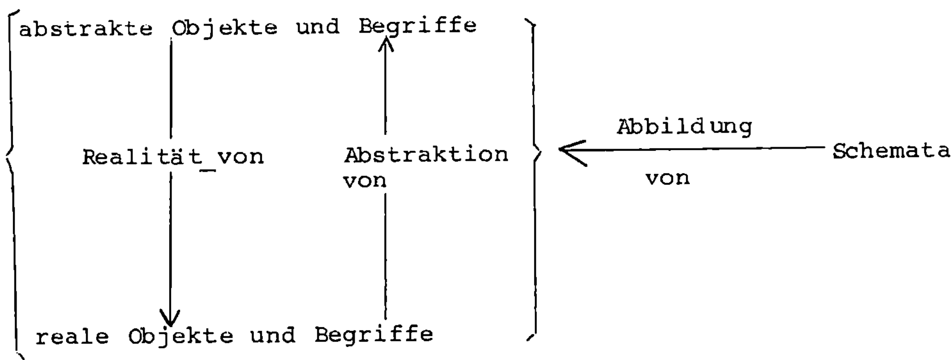

2.3 Semantische Konsistenz

Wissensbasierte Systeme müssen eine Hauptanforderung erfüllen:
die semantische Konsistenz zwischen Wissensprimitiven und ihre
Abbildung. Nur dann ist der Anspruch auf Kommunikation gewährleistet.

Informell bedeutet es, daß zwei Abbildungen konsistent sind,
wenn sie die gleiche Bedeutung haben und ein Verfahren
existiert, um die Gleichheit zu bestimmen. <3>

In den meisten praktischen Fällen bleibt es unmöglich, die Kon-
sistenzprüfung automatisch durchzuführen. Es ist daher sehr
wichtig, dem Fachmann die Möglichkeit zu geben, direkt die
maschinelle Abbildung zu kreieren.

Dies gilt selbstverständlich für Objekte (z.B. die Schemata
'Zentraleinheit 7530' oder 'NC-Maschine-1' werden genauso eingegeben als ob statt Rechner eine textuelle Beschreibung auf Papier
zu machen wäre), aber auch für Abstraktionen von Objekten und Begriffen.

3. Auswirkungen für die Inferenz in wissensbasierten Systemen

Eine objektorientierte Wissensdarstellung ermöglicht das Inferenzsystem eines Expertensystems auf wenigen Grundkomponenten zu reduzieren, die drei Merkmale des Objektsystems benutzen: die Vererbung, die prozedurale Ankoppelung und die Anwendung von Meta-wissen.

3.1 Vererbung

Die Vererbung ermöglicht Eigenschaften und Werte von Eigenschaf-ten, die in einer Abstraktionshierarchie von Schemata definiert werden, von oben (größte Abstraktion) nach unten zu übernehmen.

Die Inferenzregel, die dabei angewandt wird, heißt

        wenn etwas für ein Schema S gilt
        dann gilt es auch für alle Schemata, die
        konkreter als S sind,
        es sei denn, es ist durch einen spezielleren Eintrag
        neu definiert

Diese Inferenzregel kann sowohl vorwärts als auch rückwärts angewandt werden.

Rückwärts entspricht sie dem Lösen von Problemen durch Anwendung von allgemeingültigen Methoden. Gegeben ein Schema und eine bestimmte Fragestellung, die das Schema betrifft, aber deren Lösung nicht explizit im Schema angegeben wird, werden Lösungen aus der Hierarchie vererbt. Vorwärtsorientiert und bei einer "Breite zuerst"-Suche, ermöglicht sie schnell die richtigen Teile von einem Lösungsbaum herauszufinden.

3.2 Prozedurale Ankoppelung

Unter prozeduraler Ankoppelung versteht man die Möglichkeit, jedem Eintrag eines Schemas eine Prozedur als Wert anzugeben. Ein bestimmter Typ von Prozedur ist die Benutzung von Produktions-regeln. Die Suche in einer großen Regelmenge wird dadurch viel effizienter.

Damit erhält man die Möglichkeit, objekt-orientiert die in Expertensystemen traditionellen 'wenn....dann'-Regeln zu aktivieren.

Darüberhinaus können jede beliebige Art von sonstigen Prozeduren (einfache Funktionen, Nachrichten an andere Objekte, Aufruf von externen Programmen) angegeben werden.

Dies kommt der praktischen Feststellung entgegen, daß nicht ein einziger Typ von Inferenz in der Lage ist, die verschiedenen Problemlösungsmethoden abzudecken.

3.3 Meta-Wissen

Folgendes Beispiel aus der Konfigurierungsaufgabe faßt alle
vorhergenannten Punkte zusammen und zeigt das dritte Merkmal
eines ausgereiften Objektsystems: die Darstellung von Meta-
Wissen.

Betrachten wird folgende Regeln, die die Konfigurierung von
Schnelldruckern betreffen:

Regel 1:   wenn die Zentraleinheit bekannt ist und der Schnell-
           drucker unbekannt ist, dann konfiguriere den Schnell-
           drucker 3337

Regel 2:   wenn ein Schnelldrucker zu konfigurieren ist, dann
           konfiguriere den Schnelldrucker 3338.

Beide Regeln sind allgemein: sie gelten für alle Instanzen von
Schnelldruckern aus dem Hauptknoten der Darstellung der Objekte
"Schnelldrucker" und müssen als Wert der Eigenschaft "zu konkre-
tisieren durch:" vererbbar sein.

Meta-Wissen ermöglicht zwischen beiden Regeln auszuwählen: die
Meta-Information ist hier auch als Regel dargestellt:

Schnelldrucker

    zu konkretisieren durch: regel 1 regel 2
    [meta: wenn zentraleinheit im wenn-Teil einer Regel
           erscheint, dann wende diese Regel an]

Konklusion

Wissensbasierte Systeme in der industriellen Umgebung benötigen
mehr als nur Regeln für die Wissensdarstellung. Objektorientierte
Darstellungsmechanismen, die Vererbung, prozedurale Ankoppelung
und Meta-Wissen bereitstellen, sind heute in der Lage, die Anforderungen der Industrie zu erfüllen.

<1>   B.J. MacLennon: Values and Objects in Programming
                          Languages, SIGPLAN Notices,
                          December 1982

<2>   D. Robson: Object-oriented Software Systems, BYTE
                    August 1981

<3>   H. Marchand: Logique et coherence semantique, Ph. D.
                      e1977

<4>   M. Fox, A. Sathi, M. Greenberg: Issues in Knowledge
                          Representation for Project Management, 1984

KNOWLEDGE REPRESENTATION AS THE BASIS
FOR REQUIREMENTS SPECIFICATIONS

Alexander Borgida
Rutgers University, New Brunswick, NJ 08903, USA

Sol Greenspan
Schlumberger-Doll Research, Ridgefield, CT 06877, USA

John Mylopoulos
University of Toronto, Canada

Specification of many kinds of knowledge about the world is essential
to requirements engineering. Research on knowledge representation in
artificial intelligence provides a wealth of relevant techniques that
can be incorporated into specification languages.

What facts must be recorded during the requirements phase of a
software project? What does a language that is designed to express
such facts look like? We provide some answers to these questions in
this article.

For purposes of discussion, we define the "requirements phase" of
the software life cycle as the stage that precedes the design of software system architecture. This phase includes analysis of customer
needs, as well as specification of both the functional behavior of the
proposed system and the nonfunctional requirements that must be met.
It is clear that, to carry out these activities, the analyst must gain
an understanding of the environment in which the software will be used
and the use to which the software will be put. We contend that this
understanding should be expressed and recorded as a model of the environment, and that the various requirements should be expressed in relation to this model. Once we have made a case for this contention, we
present some features that we believe are desirable in any language
intended to support requirements engineering. In the remainder of the
article, we illustrate some features of the language RML and point out
how it arose from the confluence of two streams of thought: the representation of knowledge in artificial intelligence and the traditional
concern for abstraction found in software engineering. The article
concentrates on language-design issues and pays little attention to
such problems as the "implementation" of requirements specification
languages and their use as prototyping tools, or the semiautomatic
transformation of a specification into an effective program - problems

frequently associated with the application of artificial intelligence
to software engineering.[1]

The Need for Representing Knowledge

The requirements for a software product often describe no more
than its _functional specification_, that is, the product's behavior at
an early point in its development. However, to understand or use such
a specification requires a great deal more information than is usually
given in the specification alone. It is assumed that users of the
specification possess wide-ranging knowledge about the environment from
which the specification is drawn, and they use it to interpret the meaning of the specification. This includes knowledge of terms, technical
and scientific rules, everyday procedures and conventions, and the way
various devices work - as well as commonsense knowledge.

Consider an environment, such as a hospital, in which there may be
several computer-based systems. There may be interactive information
systems (such as those used for patient registration), real-time systems
(like those used for patient monitoring), and expert systems (such as
those used to aid in medical diagnosis).[†] Writing a requirements
specification for each of these systems is largely a matter of gathering and understanding information about patient's needs, diseases,
medical procedures, administration policies, and so on.

In current practice, the requirements specification is restricted
to describing only certain aspects of computer systems: the storage,
retrieval and manipulation of data; the computation of desired results;
the functional behavior of system tasks; and the types of information
used by the system. Features of traditional languages, such as PSL and
RSL, that are used for stating requirements reflect these limitations.
This leads to problems because system developers are not usually
experts in the application domain; therefore, the requirements specification must go beyond the limits of a strict functional specification
to capture the broader context in which the system will be placed. For
example, the rules for converting from Fahrenheit to Celsius are not
usually directly retrievable from a medical information system, yet

---

[†]
    Since our work has been primarily in the area of information sys-
tems, we draw our examples in this article from various information
systems; however, we believe that what we have to say is applicable to
any software system that is intimately related to the world outside
the computer - avionics software and office systems software, for example.

this knowledge could be quite important in writing the programs that make up the information system. To illustrate: The knowledge that a sensor reads temperatures to within an accuracy of, say, $\pm 0.5°F$ would have a direct bearing on how the program that converts degrees Fahrenheit to degrees Celsius is written (the degree of precision required in the conversion factor would be affected for instance).

We feel that even in the functional specification, the requirements statements should be written with an eye to the real world entities and activities about which information is being kept. For example, the specification statement that "the system must maintain up-to-date information about all admitted patients, including their names, ages, attending physicians, next of kin,..." is preferable to "keep a file with patient's name, age, doctor's name, next-of-kin's phone number," which makes a number of implementation decisions. We base our preference on the view that requirements specifications should talk about the "what" rather than the "how" of a software system. As we shall see, requirements specifications dealing with the world must be more powerful and expressive than requirements specifications dealing with target systems only.

While it may seem obvious that to describe a system's requirements, functional and otherwise, it is first necessary to understand the real-world concepts involved, techniques for explicitly capturing this information have yet to be adopted in software engineering. Our feeling, which is shared by several other researchers,[1-5] is that a new kind of specification is needed - one that is more world-oriented than current functional specification methods allow. We wish to view this proposed specification as forming a model of the world. In such a model, the symbols and their definitions correspond to concepts/entities in the world, and the structure of the model mirrors the structure one perceives in the world. The task of requirements specification thus has at its core the building of a <u>requirements model</u> for some portion of the world.

Perhaps the best way to understand our view of the role of this world model is to understand the relationship between the requirements model and the world, on the one hand, and the relationship between the requirements model and the software system, on the other.

<u>The model and the world</u>. The symbols in the requirements model are related to the world in that each represents some real-world entity or activity, such as a person, prescribing medication, or participating

in a clinical trial. When constructing the requirements model, one is concerned with such issues as which real-world objects should be represented, which of their properties are relevant, and how accurately and completely the model represents the world.

The value of explicitly expressing a world model is that it facilitates communication between users, can be subjected to automated aids, and can be otherwise manipulated in ways not possible with the unexpressed knowledge of a human. For example, the model can be queried to check if the represented information is correct and to derive facts not explicitly represented. The model can also be analyzed for various kinds of consistency. Furthermore, when a "context" of specific facts is provided, the model can be run as a simulation of the world being represented, and this can be used to check whether complex dynamic processes have been adequately captured. Once the requirements model has been constructed, it should, ideally, become the sole body of knowledge about the world being modeled that is used by system designers.

The model and the software system. The software system is determined by establishing "boundaries" that define what portions of the world model will be realized in a computer-based system and what portions will be considered as the environment of that system. Therefore, only some portions of the model of reality will be realized by the implemented system. While the requirements model is as true as possible to reality, the software system may be more limited. For example, the requirements model may say that a person always has a birth date, but the system may not have this on record, as in the case of patients brought unconscious into the emergency room.

Of course, the implementation of the software system will represent the knowledge about the relevant portion of the world by making use of standard techniques, such as files of records.

The use of AI knowledge representation. We have argued that capturing knowledge about the world is a significant part of requirements engineering. At the same time, one of the key conclusions of the past two decades of artificial intelligence research is that machines can exhibit intelligent behavior (that is, communicate in English, understand pictures, and so on) only when they are equipped with a great deal of knowledge about the real world. For this reason, there has been much AI research on representing and organizing knowledge with computers.[†] It is therefore natural to apply what has been learned in AI to requirements modeling. Our studies and those of Balzer[1] are among the first to meld concepts from AI knowledge representation with software engineering concerns so as to achieve better techniques and languages for software requirements specifications.

Some Principles for Requirements Modeling Languages

We feel that the central goal of a requirements specification language is to provide facilities for gathering and representing world knowledge in a natural and convenient fashion, and at the same time to organize and structure this knowledge so that it can be easily understood by system developers and by the end user. We identify the following criteria as basic to achieving these goals, though the list is clearly not exhaustive.

To begin with, a good modeling language should allow the designer to describe entities in the domain of discourse and changes (events) in the world, and to state constraints and assumptions. Some modeling languages and methods are good for describing the properties of entities (for example, languages that take entity-relationship approaches), but are weak with respect to describing change and constraints. Specification methods designed especially for processes, procedures, or events are more appropriate for describing change. Logics are the most convenient languages for stating constraints. Since a requirements modelling language must be able to describe all of these things, it is necessary to combine several kinds of modeling facilities into one language.

We believe that most information systems being developed reflect the designer's perceptions of the world. We label such perceptions concepts, whether they are about ideas, entities or activities. Most concepts are like patients and surgery, in that they arise in everyday human experience (philosophers call these "natural kinds"), as opposed to the artificially defined concepts of, say, mathematics. When we describe natural kinds, we are faced with the problem that they do not have precise definitions: Patients are sick persons, but shouldn't the class of patients also include people coming back for a checkup after they are healed? The symptoms of pneumonia include fever, but some people get pneumonia and don't have fever. And so on. It appears that descriptions of natural kinds run the risk of being either hopelessly vague or subject to contradiction. Contrast this with specifying such mathematical concepts as sets or sequences, which always

---

† The reader may find the October 1983 issue of Computer a useful survey of this area.

satisfy their constraints "by definition." Developers of languages
for requirements modeling will have to take the problem of describing
natural kinds into account.

Also, we recognize that the passing of time is a cornerstone of
our human experience and is intimately tied to the description of
dynamic aspects of the world. Therefore, a requirements modeling language must be able to talk explicitly about time and the evolution of
the world through time. A language that lacks such capabilities forces
the designer either to consider only static aspects of the world, or to
specify dynamics not by describing them, but by writing procedures.

The above concerns the kinds of knowledge that a requirements
modeling language must be able to represent. Another important concern
is a language's usefulness in organizing knowledge.

Abstraction is the foremost organizational issue. The requirements
specification for a realistic software system is likely to be very large
and detailed. Past experience in software engineering and elsewhere
suggests that the proper way to deal with many details is to abstract
out the most important ones and then introduce the others in successive
passes of a refinement process. A requirements modeling language
should support the process of abstraction both by providing guidelines
as to what are currently relevant details and by providing language
features that support the refinement process.

Languages can also help the specifier achieve more complete and
accurate descriptions. One tool for this is redundancy: If the specifier views the same situation from multiple points of view, he is less
likely to omit a significant fact. Furthermore, if multiple descriptions of the same situation do not agree, then at least one of them is
incorrect - a fact that may not be uncovered if only one description
is presented. In general, of course, we would like the language to
have an associated notion of consistency/inconsistency so that we can
recognize obviously incorrect software specifications - that is, those
for which there cannot be an implementation.

Finally, like all language designers, we would like to make the
language easy to learn and read and convenient to use.

A Language for Requirements Modeling

We have developed a language called RML that meets the above criteria.[6,7] We do not provide an in-depth description of this language
here. Instead, we highlight some of the notable features of RML and

point out their relationship to AI work on knowledge representation and to traditional software engineering concerns.

We remark that the RML language is used to state requirements and does not have an implementation per se. (Incidentally, we have used RML to specify at least one sizable example[7] - a conference organization system.) RML is part of larger information systems development project that includes the database programming language Taxis[8] and associated tools for editing, interpreting, and compiling programs. We plan to acquire computer tools that will enable us to make deductions from our requirements model and to check its consistency by translating RML into one of the AI languages for knowledge representation.

An object-oriented framework. A requirements model specified in RML consists of interrelated objects. Each object in the model stands for some entity, or activity, or, more generally, some concept in the world being modeled. For example, in a hospital information system model there are objects corresponding to each patient, room, and doctor as well as to diseases, lab tests, and so on. Objects are related to each other by properties. For example, bob hasPhysician mm, mm hasName "Dr.Mickey Mouse," mm hasSpecialty cardiology.

Objects are organized into classes for the purpose of capturing common characteristics. (Thus, "bob" belongs to the class of PATIENTS and mm is in DOCTORS.) Once this is done, we can specify relationships between generic concepts, for example, PATIENT hasPhysician DOCTOR, or DOCTOR hasSpeciality MEDICAL_SPECIALTIES. Generic information about a class restricts the relationships in which the members of the class can participate. For example, a particular patient cannot have as physician any object which is not in the class DOCTORs.

In our framework, building a requirements model consists mostly of identifying the appropriate classes and describing them in terms of applicable properties and constraints on their values. For example, a partial description of the class PATIENT is

```
PATIENT
    parts
        name: PERSON_NAMES
        address: ADDRESSES
        hasPhysician: DOCTOR
        hasDiagnosis: DISEASE
```

The chief advantage of object-oriented frameworks is that they make possible a direct and natural correspondence between the world and its model: When constructing the model, we select concepts mentioned in descriptions of the application domain and define corresponding classes of objects in the model. Each of these acts as a center around which we place information related to that concept.

Our object-oriented approach has its origins in AI knowledge representation techniques, especially semantic networks, and in programming languages such as Simula and Smalltalk.

<u>Activities and assertions are also objects</u>. We manipulate the objects in a requirements model to simulate the behavior of their counterparts in the world. In a conscious bid for uniformity, we also model as objects activities in the world, which results in the generation of activity objects, as opposed to entity objects. For example, the activity of admitting patients is modeled by the activity class ADMIT, some of whose properties are

```
ADMIT
    participants
        newPatient: PERSON
        toWard: WARD
        admitter: DOCTOR

    parts
        document: GET_INFO
                  (from ↔ newPatient)
        checkin: ASSIGN_BED
                 (toWhom ↔ newPatient,
                 onWard ↔ toWard)

    precondition
        canAdmit?: HAS_AUTHORITY
                   (who ↔ admitter,
                   where ↔ toWard)
```

ADMIT intends to convey the idea that admitting a new patient involves obtaining information from the new patient and assigning him a bed. The definition shows six properties (<u>new-Patient</u>, <u>toWard</u>, <u>admitter</u>, <u>document</u>, <u>checkIn</u>, and <u>canAdmit?</u>) that fall into three property categories (<u>participants</u>, <u>parts</u>, and <u>precondition</u>). The first three properties specify that each instance of ADMIT involves a patient, a ward, and a doctor. These three objects are participants in the activity. There are two parts: These relate each instance of ADMIT to the two named activity objects, which serve as components of the overall admit activity. The sixth property, <u>canAdmit</u>, relates each instance of ADMIT to an instance of the assertion class HAS AUTHORITY TO ADMIT. This assertion serves as a precondition, which means that at the time the activity instance starts, the related assertion instance is true.

As we have just seen, assertions, like activities, are objects that belong to classes. An assertion has properties that relate it to other objects and belong to categories such as <u>arguments</u>, <u>parts</u>, and <u>constraints</u>. Arguments are the objects that the assertion is about; parts are component formulas, and constraints are conditions that must be met for an instance of an assertion class to be true. Instances of an assertion class are true formulae in the form dictated by the containing class.

One of the distinguishing features of RML is that it combines the specification of entities, activities, and assertions into a framework in which all units of description (activities, assertions, and so on) are objects that belong to classes and have properties. It is a powerful language based on a small set of primitive concepts.

<u>Generalization hierarchies</u>. In designing RML, we followed yet another lead from semantic networks in AI: Classes in RML can be related to each other by the <u>subclass</u> or <u>IS-A</u> relationship (PATIENT IS-A PERSON, DOCTOR IS-A PERSON, and SURGEON IS-A DOCTOR, for example). One class is said to be a subclass of another only if it describes a more specialized concept and if every instance of the first class is an instance of the second class. The subclass relationship organizes the classes and their descriptions into a hierarchy, called the <u>generalization</u> or <u>IS-A</u> hierarchy. One of the important consequences of this organization is that properties of a class can be inherited by its subclasses.

For example, if we write the definition

```
PERSON
     name: HUMAN_NAMES
     age: HUMAN_AGES
     address: ADDRESS
     tel#: TELEPHONE_NUMBER
```

and then specify that PATIENT IS-A PERSON to indicate that all patients are also persons, we need not restate the fact that patients have names, ages, and so on. These facts will be inherited from the description of PERSONs. Furthermore, the same saving of effort would occur if DOCTORs, ADMINISTRATORs, or other subclasses of PERSONs were specified.

A subclass can constrain inherited properties. For example, the <u>admittingPhysician</u> property can be restricted to SURGEONs where surgical patients are involved.

The IS-A relationship organizes classes of objects into a natural taxonomy of concepts that helps to make descriptions manageable: It highlights the similarities between classes by placing them close to each other in the hierarchy. The IS-A relationship forms the basis for an abstraction mechanism called <u>generalization</u>, which is founded on the idea that it is often useful to ignore at first the detailed differences between several related classes and to present their common aspects as the description of some superclass instead. The differences between the classes can be introduced when the modeler describes how each differs as a subclass from the common superclass.

Generalization also suggests a particular methodology for developing a requirements specification. This methodology, called <u>stepwise refinement by specialization</u>,[9] prescribes that one describe first the most general classes of pertinent entities, activities and assertions occurring in the physical world. In the hospital world, these might include patients, doctors, admissions, treatments, and so on. In the next phase, important subclasses of each class are selected and described. For example, the modeler might differentiate between child and adult patients, internists and surgeons, chemotherapy and radiation therapy. Successive phases of the refinement process then introduce and describe smaller and smaller subclasses that model more and more specialized concepts. Inheritance is useful here because it allows the modeler to limit his specifications to the ways in which the subclass differs from the superclass - at each step, he need consider only information appropriate to that level.

Generalization is the appropriate abstraction principle to exploit when the difficulty of modeling is caused by a large number of details and objects that need to be captured, rather than by algorithmic complexity. After all, taxonomic hierarchies have long been used in other disciplines, such as botany and zoology, to organize numerous observations. For example, the problems of specifying the ADMIT activity are related for the most part to the many variations introduced by the persons being admitted: Children don't have their own health insurance numbers, patients undergoing surgery must be put on special diets, and so on. We claim that many software development projects, especially information systems projects, deal with precisely this kind of situation. Note that this methodology is orthogonal and complementary to the well-known <u>stepwise refinement by decomposition</u>: Variants of a class of solutions can be introduced through specialization at any level of decomposition, including the final, programming-language level.

Refinement by specialization, which we describe more fully in another work,[9] is an interesting example of the advantages to be gained

from the marriage of AI concepts (in this case, various kinds of inheritance schemes) with those of software engineering (here, abstraction).

   Representing time. Time is a very important subject in a world-
oriented modeling scheme. Time is inextricably involved in every fact
we state: an object exists at a particular time, an activity starts and
ends at particular points in time; an assertion is true at some particular time, and so on. RML captures the rich variety of references
to time that occur in everyday discourse. Designers of specification
languages typically do not include explicit references to time because
they make some grossly simplifying assumptions, such as the assumption
that events are totally ordered. Some requirements languages do supply
a handful of time-related statement types; for example, those that say
an event "happens so many times per month." However, a rich facility
for talking about time and for talking about behaviors with reference
to time is needed.

   In designing RML, we adopted a relatively simple notion of time
as an infinite and dense sequence of time points. Assertions are true
at a given time point, and the value of an object's properties as well
as its membership in a class is always evaluated with respect to a
specified time. Furthermore, every event has associated start and end
points.

   Starting from this simple foundation, we can build surprisingly
complex temporal descriptions within the object-oriented framework of
RML, including the description of time entities that correspond to
ordinary time concepts, such as dates of the year, times of the day,
and so on. The passing of a period of time can be viewed as a time
activity whose start and end points coincide with the start and end
times of a given interval. If we apply to activities the predicates
for reasoning about time intervals that were developed by Allen,[10]
we can express quite complex temporal relationships. Note that temporal predicates, such as DURING, BEFORE, and OVERLAPS, as well as classes
of concepts such as ONE_HOUR_INTERVAL, can all be defined as classes in
RML itself - they are like procedure definitions rather than extra
language features. This attests to the power of the basic ideas on
which RML is built.

   RML also makes it easy to state commonly occurring expressions
that concern time. A good example of this is the use of property
categories to abbreviate time constraints. For instance, the statement that "a new patient's location after he has been admitted is the

ward to which he is being admitted" would normally have to be written

```
ADMIT
    right_place:
        toWard of ADMIT at end(ADMIT)=
        location of (newPatient of ADMIT
            at end(ADMIT) at end(ADMIT)*
```

because it is important to know when every property (such as toWard, newPatient, or location) is to be evaluated. Property categories can be used to specify default times when properties will be evaluated. For example, final-condition evaluates all properties that lack a temporal specification at the time point corresponding to the end of the activity. Thus, the above example can be abbreviated to

```
ADMIT
    final-condition
        right-place: (toWard of ADMIT =
            location of newPatient of ADMIT)
```

Property categories are also useful for abbreviating other time constraints. They are most often used to specify property values at those times when an object is inserted into a class or removed from a class, as well as throughout the interval when an object is in a class.

We wish to point out that there are many complexities surrounding the notion of time - complexities that we believe have been successfully dealt with by RML. These include the need to represent absolute and relative time (for example, "at eight o'clock" and "one hour from now," respectively), repetitive behavior ("the motion of the earth involves one rotation around its axis every 24 hours"), and vagueness ("on Thursday"), as well as the need to give extremely detailed descriptions of events.

The representation of time and time-related information is another area where there has been almost no relevant research in software engineering and where we have benefited from work in AI.[10]

Multiple Levels of Description

We do not wish to leave the impression that artificial intelligence research has covered all the relevant problems of requirements engineering. One area of key concern for software engineering but not for AI

---

* This statement should be read as: "at the end of an ADMIT event, the value of the toWard property of the ADMIT event equals the value of the location property of the patient being admitted." The patient being admitted is the newPatient property of the ADMIT event.

is building up detailed descriptions incrementally and introducing implementation details to arrive at a final software product. We have addressed this issue in our work[7] by considering the two language levels between which an RML description is sandwiched: We use SADT as a model language for initial descriptions,[11] and the Taxis[8] programming language for implementation.

In the initial stages of requirements engineering, the chief difficulty lies in deciding what concepts and phenomena are relevant. We propose that designers will find it easier to make such decisions if they use a language created for structured analysis, such as SADT, to build a "structured lexicon" of relevant terms. SADT diagrams accomplish this by making use of boxes and connecting arrows that are labelled by English terms. However, the interpretation of SADT diagrams is dependent on the meaning of the words and phrases of the embedded language and the accompanying natural language narrative.

At this stage, RML is used to introduce classes and properties that correspond to terms in the SADT diagrams: This makes the diagrammed information precise. Thus, for each feature of a diagram (box, node, arrow, split, join, and so on), an RML concept is specified in the requirements (RML) model. For example, each activity box has a class description with the various inputs and outputs as properties belonging to appropriate property categories like input, output, etc. Essentially, the designer decides on the precise meaning of the words in the SADT model and writes them down in RML. The semantic relationships expressed in the RML model are constrained, though, by the connectivity of the SADT diagram, which the designer uses as a "road map." He then uses the RML model to specify details that are not specifiable in the SADT diagrammatic notation because of their precision (for example, whether some input is a stream of values or a single value). This scheme allows the designer to follow the SADT technique of systematically gathering terms needed for requirements so that he can build an imprecise but suggestive skeleton - another stepwise refinement process - that is fleshed out in RML.

Our melding of SADT and RML is not accidental: It was suggested by SADT's uniform treatment of data and activity diagrams, which corresponds to our uniform treatment of entities and activities as objects with properties. The narrative text accompanying SADT diagrams can be encoded in the form of properties that fall into various categories. These properties give such information as activation conditions, initial and final conditions, and constraints (for example, mutual exclusion) affecting subparts. Also, RML assertions make it possible to

capture arrow connections as general constraints (not data flow), as
suggested by Ross.[11]

Given a statement of requirements, the usual next step for the
designer is to proceed toward an implementation (possibly a prototype).
It is natural to use the programming language Taxis[8] for information
systems specified in RML, since Taxis was designed on many of the same
principles as RML: Objects are described by properties and grouped into
classes, and classes are organized along IS-A hierarchies. Taxis, however, is a procedural language with standard control constructs (loops,
conditionals, assignment) and primitive operations for data manipulation. This means, for example, that descriptions of some activities
in RML can be mapped to procedures that manipulate data objects and are
supposed to obey the constraints stated in the RML model. We are
currently developing ways to add "design decisions" features at various
points in the system so that designers can derive a Taxis program from
an RML specification.

Current Research Directions

Our current research in adapting ideas from AI knowledge representation to requirements modeling is proceeding in a number of directions.
We mention two of them here to give the reader further insight into the
usefulness of viewing knowledge representation as a basis for requirements specification.

Dealing with over-abstraction. Consistency - the absence of contradictions - is one of the most important features of a specification.
Unfortunately, in describing the natural world it is often very difficult to avoid making contradictory statements. For example, according
to medical textbooks, all patients suffering from anemia have low red-
blood-cell counts; however, a special kind of anemia - acute posthemor-
rhagic anemia - is not associated with low RBC, at least not at the
beginning. A person's heart normally beats between 70 and 90 times a
minute, but this is not so in the case of hyperthyroid patients. Situations such as these have been studied extensively in AI. The problem
of "birds fly," "penguins are birds," but "penguins don't fly" is a
classic case.

These examples appear to be cases of over-abstraction, that is,
detailed differences are ignored at the beginning in a way that doesn't
allow them to be introduced later on without destroying consistency.
This is because most concepts lack precise definitions, and almost any
rule will have exceptions.

When faced with contradictions, we can go back to the original description and make it more general - for example, we can say nothing about birds flying - so that we avoid contradictions. This has a number of disadvantages. Owing to inheritance, such a change may propagate to many other subclasses for which the original assertion was correct and useful (starlings, sparrows, storks, and so on all fly). The alternative of introducing new subclasses - for instance FLYING-BIRDS and NON-FLYING-BIRDS - can result in a combinatorial explosion of mostly uninteresting classes. A final problem is that in attempting to be as general as possible, we have no principle for deciding how far to go. Suppose we want to make an assertion about chairs. How should we characterize them? Chairs usually have four legs, but some have three, and surely carpenters have made chairs with five, six, and more legs.

From a methodological point of view, exceptions are definitely a fly in the ointment, since one can expect almost anything said at one level of refinement to be contradicted eventually at some lower level. We propose to deal with this by allowing the designer to specify exceptional classes or objects for which contradictions are explicitly acknowledged and resolved through <u>excuses</u>. (For instance, the assertion that hyperthyroid patients have high blood pressure excuses the assertion that patients in general have normal blood pressure.) Of course, we need to provide appropriate semantics for excuses so the final specification will be logically consistent. Research in AI on non-monotonic logics is one area that may provide insight on how to accomplish this.

Note that the excuse mechanism also has the advantage of supporting yet another abstraction principle, namely that of describing first the usual or normal case and then later refining this description by indicating special or exceptional cases later.[12]

<u>Relationship of world, model, and system</u>. One of the important problems confronting cognitive science is explicating the relationship, in humans and machines, between knowledge of the world and the actual state of the world. In particular, it is important to discover how one can proceed when these relationships are incomplete or even inaccurate. This is relevant to several significant distinctions that arise in requirements modeling, namely those between the world and the model of the world being built, and those between the model of the world and the model of the proposed information system, which will be part of the world. As an example, consider the distinctions between the blood

pressure of a patient at a specific time, the pressure that we can read on the sphygmomanometer or that is read by a machine, and the value recorded in a database. Our goal is to provide easy ways for designers to talk about the concepts underlying these different but related readings so that they can include in their specifications such hospital requirements as "the recorded blood pressure at any time must be within 10 of the actual blood pressure." Drawing up such nonfunctional requirements is an important part of requirements engineering. One reason for this is that they can be extremely useful during the development phase. To use the example of blood pressure readings again, nonfunctional requirements can influence how frequently blood pressure is sampled by a device that is part of a software/hardware patient-monitoring environment.

We have argued that the requirements specification of a software system should consist of a detailed model of the world, or, more accurately, of our knowledge of the world.

We have presented several features of the language RML, which was crafted to help designers build requirements models. We used these features to support the claim that requirements modeling can draw significant inspiration from work on knowledge representation in AI, but noted that this transfer must be tempered by keeping in mind the traditional concerns of software engineering.

Also, we have touched on some of the principal problems of requirements engineering: creating high-level, world-oriented descriptions that deal with the application domain of discourse rather than with system design or implementation concepts; coping with large descriptions whose details must be effectively organized; designing coherent requirements languages that are based on a small number of concepts; providing methodological guidance for incrementally constructing requirements specifications; producing provably consistent descriptions; and proceeding from requirements modeling to the design of an information system.

By basing our work on results from knowledge representation, we have reached at least partial answers to questions that have barely been addressed in software engineering. We have given several examples of how our research on requirements has been influenced by knowledge representation. This area offers ideas and techniques for both the representation of many kinds of knowledge (such as concepts from the natural world, default knowledge, exceptions, information about time, uncertainty, and incompleteness of knowledge) and the organization of such knowledge for convenient processing by humans and computers.

As a final point, we wish to note that important groundwork has been done in AI on the formal semantics of representation schemes as well as on such topics as deduction and logical consistency within knowledge bases. We have given a formal account of RML[7] that shows that an RML specification translates into a relatively standard predicate logic. An RML specification can thus be usefully viewed as a logical theory.[†] Consistency in an RML model is shown in this account to be the standard notion of logical consistency, and since this is so, deductions and inferences can be made from the model. This opens up the possibility of using computer-based theorem provers as tools in an environment for developing requirements specifications; such theorem provers could be used to decide whether a requirements model is consistent, whether a certain situation can arise or not in the world, and so on.

In conclusion, we hope we have convinced the reader that

- the requirements specification for software must be much more than a statement of the external behavior of the final system;

- it is appropriate to view the requirements specification as a model of our knowledge of the application domain and to phrase various requirements in terms of this model;

- AI research on knowledge representation provides a wealth of ideas for world modeling; and

- RML has incorporated many such ideas into a novel, powerful, yet uniform framework based on a few concepts that nevertheless supports such traditional software engineering concepts as abstraction.   ☐

Acknowledgement

The research for this article was supported in part by the National Science and Engineering Research Council of Canada and the US National Science Foundation under Grant MCS-82-1193.

References

1. R. Balzer, N. Goldman and D. Wile, "Operational Specification as the Basis for Rapid Prototyping," Proc. ACM Sigsoft Software Eng. Symp. Rapid Prototyping, Columbia, Md., in ACM Software Eng. Notes, vol.7, no.5, Dec. 1982, pp.3-16.

---

† However, RML also provides facilities for structuring descriptions, which languages based on logics alone do not.

2. M.L. Wilson, "A Requirements and Design Aid for Relational Data Bases," Proc. Fifth Int'l Conf. Software Eng., IEEE-CS Press, Los Alamitos, Calif., 1981, pp.283-293.

3. R.T. Yeh and R.T. Mittermeir, "Conceptual Modeling as a Basis for Deriving Software Requirements," Int'l Computer Symp., Taipei, Taiwan, Dec. 1980.

4. J.A. Bubenko, Jr., "On Concepts and Strategies for Requirements and Information Analysis," SYSLAB Rept. No. 4, Dept. of Computer Science, Chalmers University of Technology, 1981.

5. N. Roussopoulos, "CSDL: A Conceptual Schema Definition Language for the Design of Data Base Applications," IEEE Trans. Software Eng., vol. SE-5, no.5, Sept. 1979, pp.481-496.

6. S.J. Greenspan, J. Mylopoulos, and A. Borgida, "Capturing More World Knowledge in the Requirements Specification," Proc. Sixth Int'l Conf. Software Eng., IEEE-CS Press, Los Alamitos, Calif., 1982, pp.225-234.

7. S.J. Greenspan, "Requirements Modeling: A Knowledge Representation Approach to Software Requirements Definition," Ph.D. thesis, Dept. of Computer Science, University of Toronto, 1984.

8. J. Mylopoulos, P.A. Bernstein, and H.K.T. Wong, "A Language Facility for Designing Interactive Database-Intensive Application," ACM Trans. Database Systems, vol.5, no.2, June 1980, pp.185-207.

9. A. Borgida, J. Mylopoulos, and H.K.T. Wong, "Generalization as a Basis for Software Specification," On Conceptual Modeling: Perspectives from Artificial Intelligence, Databases, and Programming Languages, M. Brodie, J. Mylopoulos, and J. Schmidt, eds., Springer-Verlag, New York, 1984, pp.87-114.

10. J. Allen, "Maintaining Knowledge about Temporal Intervals," Comm. ACM, vol.26, no.11, Nov. 1983, pp.832-843.

11. D.T. Ross, "Structured Analysis (SA): A Language for Communicating Ideas," IEEE Trans. Software Eng., special issue on requirements analysis, vol. SE-3, no.1, Jan. 1977, pp.16-34.

12. A. Borgida, "Intelligent Handling of Exceptions in Information Systems - An Overview," Proc. First Int'l Workshop on Expert Database Systems, L. Kerscheberg, ed., Institute for Information Management, Technology and Policy, University of South Carolina, Columbia, South Carolina, Oct. 1984, pp.643-651.

Wissensgestützte Ansätze beim maschinellen Sehen:
Helfen sie in der Praxis ?

H.-H. Nagel
Fraunhofer-Institut für Informations- und Datenverarbeitung (IITB)
und
Fakultät für Informatik der Universität Karlsruhe (TH)
Karlsruhe

Abstract

Current approaches to machine vision attempt to evaluate many different kinds of knowledge, for example knowledge about shape and coloring of objects, about their illumination, and about the imaging geometry. The computer-internal representation and evaluation of these types of knowledge require mechanisms different from those employed in current expert systems. The question, which kind of knowledge is taken into account and how it is evaluated, can guide towards the true reasons for success and failure in the application of machine vision systems.

1. Einführung

Angesichts der Leistungen des menschlichen Sehsinnes fehlt es nicht an Versuchen, eine entsprechende Fähigkeit mit Hilfe von digitalen Datenverarbeitungsanlagen nachzubilden und insbesondere auch für industrielle Zwecke einzusetzen. Solche Versuche stießen zunächst auf eine Reihe von technischen Problemen bei der Aufnahme, Speicherung, Verarbeitung und Wiedergabe von Bildern, die aber in den letzten Jahren durch die schnelle technologische Entwicklung der Mikroelektronik zumindest teilweise abgebaut werden konnten. Es ist daher nicht überraschend, daß Literatur über mehrere hundert Sichtsysteme zu finden ist, von denen viele auch kommerziell angeboten werden (*Winkler 85*). Bei genauerer Nachforschung stellt man allerdings fest, daß eine ganze Reihe der bei praktischen Anwendungen zu lösenden Aufgaben durch die zur Zeit angebotenen Bildauswertungs-Systeme noch nicht befriedigend gelöst werden können (*Geißelmann 83, Radig 83, Winkler 84 + 85*). Es liegt daher nahe zu fragen, ob die in der letzten Zeit auf so positive Resonanz gestoßenen Expertensystemen es erlauben, die praktischen Einsatzmöglichkeiten von Sichtsystemen wesentlich zu erweitern.

Bevor auf diese Frage näher eingegangen wird, sollen zunächst einige Untersuchungen aus dem Fraunhofer-Institut für Informations- und Datenverarbeitung skizziert werden, an Hand derer typische Aufgabenstellungen und die zu ihrer Lösung herangezogenen Ansätze illustriert werden können. Im Anschluß daran wird der Begriff *Maschinensehen* oder *maschinelles Sehen* genauer umrissen. Die beim maschinellen Sehen abzuwickelnden Auswertungsprozesse werden anhand eines Schemas erläutert, das auch zur Strukturierung der anschließenden Diskussion über verschiedene Arten von Wissen für die Interpretation von Bildern dient.

2. Beispiele für die Bildauswertung bei industriellen Aufgabenstellungen

Beim ersten Beispiel handelt es sich um die Auswertung der Silhouetten von Teilen aus der Automobil-Industrie, die in diesem Fall durch einen Hängeförderer vor einem hell beleuchteten Hintergrund an einer Fernsehkamera vorbeitransportiert werden - siehe Abbildung 1

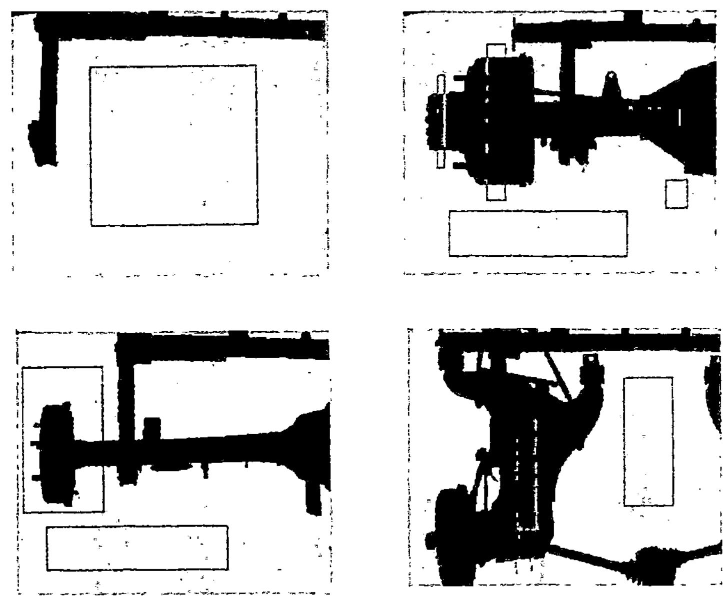

Abbildung 1: Binärbilder eines Hängeförderers vor einem homogen leuchtenden Hintergrund ohne (links oben) sowie mit verschiedenen Typen von Kraftfahrzeugachsen. Die eingeblendeten Auswertefenster dienen zur Unterscheidung der verschiedenen Achstypen. (nach *Geißelmann et al. 85*)

(*Geißelmann et al. 85*). Trotz einer großen Anzahl unterschiedlicher Bauformen muß jedes Teil erkannt werden, damit beim anschließenden Lackierprozeß das jeweils passende Spritzprogramm in den Lackierroboter geladen werden kann. Hierzu werden eine Reihe von Testfenstern im Bild so angeordnet, daß jede Silhouette eine für sie spezifische Kombination von Testfenstern vollständig überdeckt, eine andere spezifische Kombination von Testfenstern nur teilweise und die verbleibende Kombination von Testfenstern überhaupt nicht.

Jedes Testfenster entspricht einem Merkmal, dessen Wert durch die Anzahl der Bildpunkte gegeben wird, die innerhalb dieses Testfensters dunkel sind. Jede Silhouette wird durch eine spezielle Kombination von Merkmalwerten charakterisiert, ohne daß diese Merkmalkombination die Form der Silhouette vollständig oder auch nur partiell beschreiben muß. Die Bildauswertung dient hier nur der Unterscheidung von Silhouetten, nicht dagegen dem Lokalisieren eines bestimmten Teilabschnittes einer Silhouette. Dies kann zur Folge haben, daß die Merkmale - d.h. die Lage, Form und Größe der Testfenster - und ihre jeweiligen Wertekombinationen für alle Silhouetten zu überprüfen und gegebenenfalls zu ändern sind, falls die Silhouette auch nur eines einzigen weiteren Bauteiles berücksichtigt werden muß.

Der Verwendung eines Binärbildes liegt die Vorstellung zu Grunde, daß die jeweils interessierende Figur entweder heller oder dunkler ist als der Hintergrund. Folglich sollte durch Vergleich jedes Grauwertes mit einem geeignet gewählten Schwellwert unterschieden werden können, ob ein Bildpunkt zur Figur oder zum Hintergrund gehört. Obwohl viele Aufgaben existieren, bei denen durch geeignete Beleuchtungsmaßnahmen eine solche Grundvorstellung gerechtfertigt werden kann, überwiegen doch im allgemeinen die Situationen, bei denen ein solcher Ansatz nicht zum Erfolg führt. Abbildung 2 zeigt eine Beschädigung am Rande eines Porzellantellers, aufgenommen mit drei unterschiedlichen Beleuchtungen (*Stein et al. 85*). Die Erkennung einer solchen Fehlstelle mit Verfahren der Binärbildauswertung erfordert, daß man die Fehlstelle als 'Figur' vom übrigen Teil des Bildes als 'Hintergrund' abtrennen kann. Es erscheint sehr problematisch, einen Schwellwert zur sauberen Abtrennung einer solchen Fehlstelle zu finden. Statt einer reinen Figur/Hintergrund-Trennung im Binärbild sind daher direkt Grauwertübergänge zu bestimmen, d.h. man versucht, das Grautonbild in ein 'Kanten'-Bild zu überführen, das anschließend auszuwerten ist.

Die Abbildung 3 möge zur Illustration eines solchen Ansatzes dienen. Es handelt sich um ein Stanzteil mit Löchern und ausgewölbten Versteifungen, d.h. mit nicht-ebener Oberfläche. Das links darunter wiedergegebene Resultat der Bestimmung von Kantenelementen zeigt bereits, daß auch diese Operation nicht unproblematisch ist; es werden nicht alle erwarteten Kantenzüge als ununterbrochene Sequenz von Kantenelementen gefunden. Auch treten an manchen Stellen Kantenelemente auf, die nicht unmittelbar gerechtfertigt erscheinen. Wesentlich ist hier, wie nicht nur die äußere Kontur der Silhouette, sondern darüberhinaus auch innerhalb des Objektbildes liegende Kantenzüge zur Beschreibung und Erkennung herangezogen werden. Hierbei wird eine Kontur nicht als Ganzes beschrieben, sondern aus einzelnen *Formelementen* aufgebaut, die aus Teilfolgen von Kantenelementen gebildet worden sind. Solche Formelemente sind in der rechten mittleren Abbildung durch helle Geradenstücke und schwarze Kreisbogenstücke mit Mittelpunkt und Radius dargestellt. Nach Regeln, die als Produktionen formuliert sind, werden aus diesen Formelementen *Formmerkmale* aufgebaut, die auf Grund eines rechnerinternen Modells eines Werkteiles erwartet werden, z.B. die Kreise und U-förmig gebogenen Konturstücke, die in der linken unteren Abbildung gezeigt sind. Diese Formmerkmale ihrerseits sind die Bestandteile eines übergeordneten Modells des ganzen Werkteiles. Das in der rechten unteren Abbildung

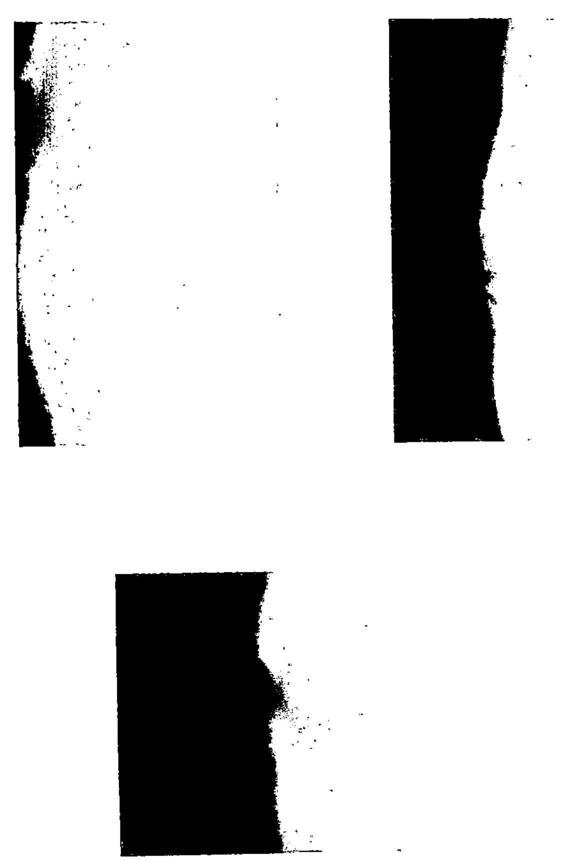

Abbildung 2: Beschädigter Rand eines Porzellantellers, aufgenommen mit drei unterschiedlichen Beleuchtungen. Sollen solche Fehler durch ein Sichtprüfsystem im Zuge einer automatischen Qualitätskontrolle zuverlässig erkannt werden, so erscheint ein Binärbildverfahren wenig geeignet, da bereits geringfügige Schwankungen der Beleuchtung die Erscheinungsform dieser Fehlstelle signifikant beeinflussen können. (nach *Stein et al. 85*)

wiedergegebene Dreieck symbolisiert die vom Programm gefundenen Beziehungen zwischen den im Erkennungsschritt herangezogenen Formmerkmalen (*Stein et al. 85*).

Im Gegensatz zum vorangehenden Beispiel, in dem das zu erkennende Werkstück nur durch ein zweidimensionales Modell - nämlich durch die alle in einer Ebene liegenden Formmerkmale - charakterisiert wird, soll jetzt ein Beispiel mit einem dreidimensionalen Modell besprochen werden. Abbildung 4 zeigt das Werkstück, ein mehrfach abgewinkeltes Blech. Das zugehörige Modell ist in zwei - relativ zum Betrachter verschiedenen - räumlichen Positionen in der letzten Reihe dieser Abbildung wiedergegeben (*Walter und Tropf 83, Tropf et al. 84*). An dieser Stelle soll bereits auf einige Details der Grauwertverteilung aufmerksam ge-

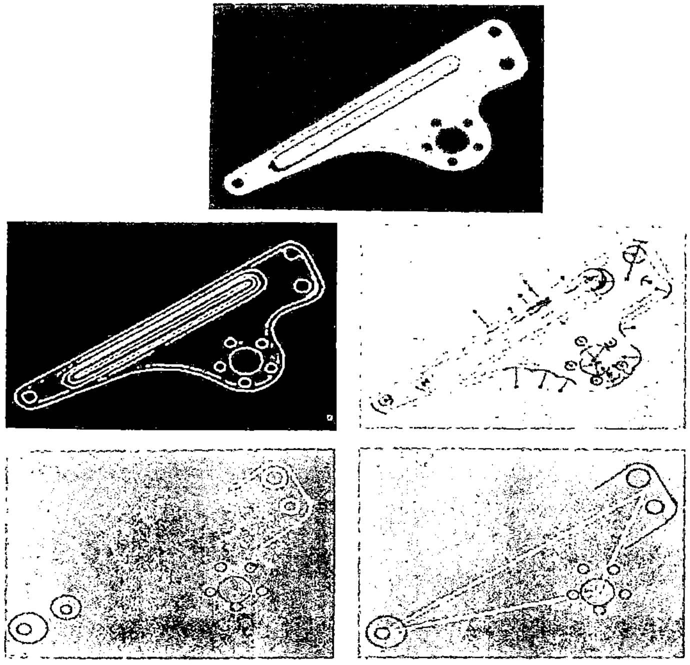

Abbildung 3: Oben in der Mitte ist die Originalaufnahme eines verhältnismäßig fla-
chen, aber nicht ganz ebenen Werkstückes wiedergegeben. In der mittleren Reihe links findet sich ein 'Kantenbild' dieses Werkstückes. Nebeneinander liegende Kantenelemente sind in der rechts daneben angeord-
neten Wiedergabe entweder zu Geraden- oder zu Kreisbogen-Stücken
zusammengefaßt worden, wobei Mittelpunkt und Radius der Kreisbo-
gen-Stücke ebenfalls angedeutet werden. Aus diesen *Formelementen*
werden anschließend *Formmerkmale* aufgebaut (links unten), die im
abschließenden Erkennungsschritt durch Vergleich mit einem Modell zu
einer - ebenen - Beschreibung des vorliegenden Werkstückes zusammengefaßt werden. (nach *Stein et al. 85*)

macht werden, auf die später zur Illustration verschiedener Gedankengänge verwiesen werden wird. Glanzlichter in den Löchern des Winkelbleches aus Abbildung 4 werden durch
Spiegelreflektion hervorgerufen. Die Intensitäts-Überhöhung auf der konvexen vorderen
Querkante des parallel zur Auflagefläche nach hinten abgewinkelten Teiles ist auf den gleichen Effekt zurückzuführen. Außerdem läßt sich ein schwacher Schatten unter diesem abgewinkelten Blechteil ausmachen, aus dem bereits auf eine Beleuchtung von rechts oben
geschlossen werden kann. Dies ist kompatibel mit der Beobachtung, daß parallel zur sichtbaren Kante der Auflagefläche ein - sehr schmaler - Schatten auftritt und daß in der Bie-
gung von der Auflagefläche zum vorderen senkrecht stehenden Blechteil ebenfalls eine auf
Schattenwurf zurückzuführende Abdunkelung vorliegt.

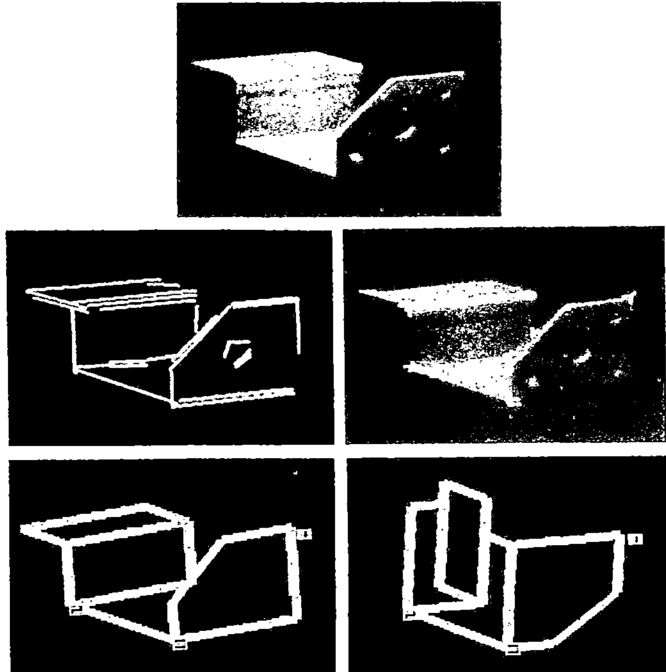

Abbildung 4: Von dem oben in der Mitte wiedergegebenen, mehrfach abgewinkelten
Blech wird das in der zweiten Reihe links dargestellte Kantenbild erzeugt. Schnittpunkte dieser Kanten liefern das in der mittleren Reihe
rechts dargestellte - allerdings unvollständige - Eckenbild. Die Aufgabe
besteht darin, ein Drahtmodell dieses Werkstückes relativ zum Betrachter so im Raum zu positionieren, daß die aus dem Drahtmodell in die
Bildebene projizierten Kanten sich möglichst gut mit den aus der Originalaufnahme ermittelten Kanten decken - z.B. links unten. In einem Zwi-
schenzustand dieses Suchprozesses können sich nach einer tentativen Zuordnung von zunächst drei Ecken Werkstückpositionen ergeben, die anschließend wegen Inkompatibilität mit gefundenen Kanten zu verwerfen sind - siehe rechts unten. (nach *Walter und Tropf 83*)

Zur Erkennung der Lage dieses Werkstückes werden zunächst Kantenelemente extrahiert
(zweite Reihe links) und Schnittpunkte zwischen den extrahierten Kanten ermittelt (zweite
Reihe rechts). Eine dieser so ermittelten Ecken wird dann versuchsweise einer Ecke des Modells zugeordnet. Dann kann aus der Lage einer zweiten Modellecke im Raum errechnet
werden, in welchem Bildausschnitt das Abbild dieser zweiten Modellecke zu suchen ist - bei
orthographischer Projektion nämlich innerhalb eines Kreises um den ersten Bildpunkt, wobei der Radius des Suchkreises durch den Abstand der zweiten Ecke von der ersten Ecke des
dreidimensionalen Modells festgelegt ist. Findet man eine passende Bildecke im Suchbe-
reich, wählt man im Modell eine dritte Ecke aus. Diese Ecke liegt im Raum auf einem Kreis
um die Verbindungslinie der ersten beiden Ecken, d.h. im Bild - je nach Orientierung des

Werkstückes relativ zum Betrachter - auf einer mehr oder weniger breiten Ellipse. Findet man auf dieser Suchellipse eine passend erscheinende Bildecke, so legt die tentative Zuordnung der gefundenen Bildecken zu den ausgewählten Modellecken eine Lage des Werkstückes relativ zum Betrachter fest. Dadurch läßt sich jetzt sehr schnell errechnen, wo andere im Modell angegebene Ecken und Kanten im Bild liegen sollten, d.h. der datengesteuerte Suchprozeß geht über in einen modellgesteuerten Verifikationsprozeß.

Im Fall des Beispiels von Abbildung 1 enthält das Erkennungsverfahren keinerlei explizites Wissen über die zu erkennenden Teile. Die aus den Binärbildern zu extrahierenden 'Merkmale' sind nur unter dem Gesichtspunkt der Trennungswirksamkeit ausgesucht, sie sollen nicht die Form der zu unterscheidenden Werkstücke beschreiben. Die 'Formmerkmale' des Beispiels von Abbildung 3 dienen im wesentlichen dem Studium der Frage, auf welche Weise sich solche bereits komplexeren lokalen Formbeschreibungen datengesteuert aus elementareren Komponenten - den Formelementen - aufbauen lassen. Im Beispiel von Abbildung 4 wurde explizit formuliertes Wissen zweier verschiedener Arten bereitgestellt: *Strukturwissen* in Form des dreidimensionalen Drahtmodells für ein zu erkennendes Objekt und *Such-* oder *Prozeßwissen* in Form eines erweiterten Übergangsnetzes zur effizienten Suche nach den Parametern, die die Lage eines abgebildeten Objektes im Raum beschreiben.

Diese Beispiele weisen darauf hin, daß eine eingehendere Diskussion des maschinellen Sehens zwischen verschiedenen Arten von Wissen unterscheiden sollte, für die auch mit unterschiedlichen internen Repräsentationsformen und Auswertungsprozeduren zu rechnen ist. Als Rahmen für eine solche Diskussion soll daher der Begriff *maschinelles Sehen* kurz umrissen und durch ein Prozeßschema gegliedert werden.

3. Der Begriff *maschinelles Sehen* oder *Maschinensehen*

Angesichts der nahezu unüberschaubaren Fülle von Assoziationen, die mit dem umgangssprachlichen Begriff *Sehen* verbunden werden können, empfiehlt es sich, einen neuen Terminus technicus *Maschinensehen* (computer vision oder machine vision) einzuführen, dessen Bedeutung auf den Kontext einer abgrenzbaren Aufgabenstellung eingeschränkt werden kann. Dieser Begriff ist eindeutiger als 'Bildauswertung', kürzer als 'algorithmische Deutung von Bildern' und bringt im Vergleich mit dem Begriff 'Bildverstehen (image understanding)' explizit zum Ausdruck, daß er sich auf ein technisches System bezieht. Die hier in drei Schritten erfolgende Einführung wird in *Nagel 85a* ausführlicher erläutert.

Schritt 1: *Maschinensehen* bezeichnet einen Prozeß, bei dem ein oder mehrere Bilder interpretiert werden und das Ergebnis dieser Interpretation in Handlungen umgesetzt wird.

In diesem ersten Schritt wird ein noch näher zu erklärender Begriff 'Interpretation von Bildern' mit Handlungen in Verbindung gebracht. Auf diesen zweiten Aspekt - daß nämlich eine Bildinterpretation letztlich in einer Handlung resultieren muß - soll zunächst eingegangen werden. Man vergleiche hierzu auch *Winkler 83, Pickett und Jha 84, Brady 85 sowie Rembold und Levi 85.*

Das mit der Fähigkeit zum 'Maschinensehen' ausgestattete technische System befindet sich in einer Umgebung, die einen begrenzten Ausschnitt der gesamten Welt darstellt. Innerhalb dieser seiner Umgebung soll das technische System eine oder mehrere Aufgaben erledigen. Dazu ist es konstruiert worden. Die Bewältigung einer bestimmten Aufgabe kann in mehrere Teilaufgaben zerlegt werden:

* Eine - zumindest näherungsweise zutreffende - Erfassung des augenblicklichen Zustandes der Umgebung sowie des technischen Systems selber. Hierzu kann u.a. eine Fernsehkamera dienen. Der auf der lichtempfindlichen Schicht der Kamera abgebildete Ausschnitt der dreidimensionalen Umgebung des technischen Systems werde Szene genannt.

* Aufbauend auf einer so ermittelten Beschreibung des aktuellen Zustandes in dem betrachteten Weltausschnitt sind eine einzelne Maßnahme oder eine Folge von Maßnahmen zu planen, mit deren Hilfe das technische System den Zustand zu erreichen versucht, der durch die zu erledigende Aufgabe explizit oder implizit vorgegeben ist.

* Umsetzung der Planung in Aktionen, z.B. Bewegung des technischen Systems in seiner Umgebung oder Beeinflussung dieser Umgebung, beispielsweise durch Greifgeräte oder ähnliches.

Die für diese Teilaufgaben vorgesehenen Subsysteme müssen miteinander Informationen austauschen können. Dazu müssen sie über eine Verständigungsgrundlage verfügen, d.h. diese Subsysteme benötigen eine gemeinsame system-interne Darstellungsform aller Zustände der Umgebung wie auch des technischen Systems selber und dessen Beziehung zu seiner Umgebung.

Schritt 2: Die system-intern darstellbaren Aussagen über den Zustand des zu berücksichtigenden Weltausschnittes bilden die *Diskurswelt*.

Wesentlich für die Definitionen dieser ersten beiden Schritte sind demnach die folgenden Überlegungen:

* Maschinensehen darf nicht getrennt werden von der Aufgabenstellung, in deren Rahmen diese Fähigkeit eines technischen Systems eingesetzt werden soll.

* Da es keine natürlichen Grenzen dafür zu geben scheint, was zur Bewältigung einer bestimmten Aufgabe gegebenenfalls in Betracht zu ziehen ist, muß eine Begrenzung der Diskurswelt durch eine explizite Entscheidung herbeigeführt werden.

Im Anschluß an die Einführung des Begriffes Diskurswelt kann jetzt der dritte Schritt der angestrebten Definition von Maschinensehen erfolgen:

Schritt 3: Die *Interpretation* eines Bildes stellt eine Beziehung zwischen jedem Pixel des digitisierten Bildes und der system-internen Darstellung der Diskurswelt her.

Der in diesem dritten Definitionsschritt angesprochene Interpretationsprozeß soll an Hand von Abbildung 5 in einen Zyklus von sechs Teilprozessen aufgegliedert werden, der im all-

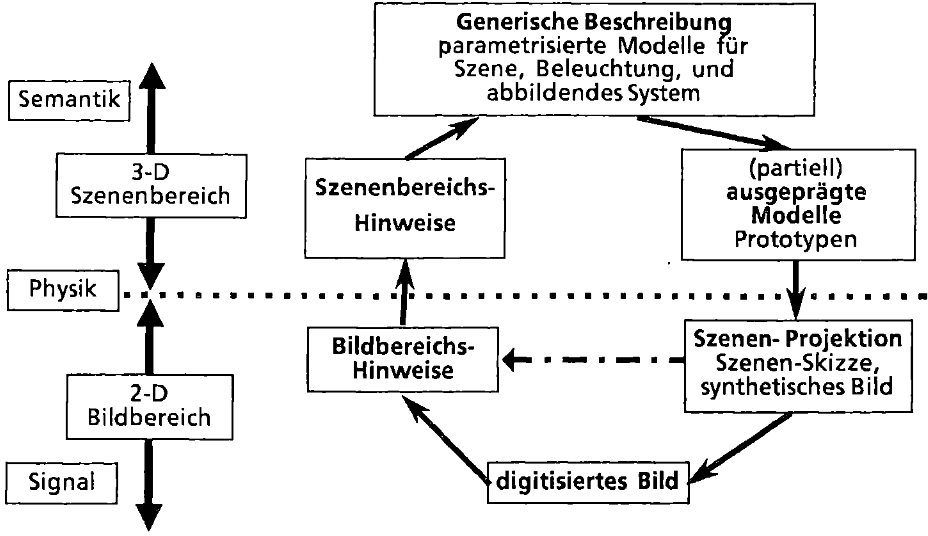

Abbildung 5: Teilprozesse des maschinellen Sehens nach *Kanade 78*, mit Modifikationen nach *Nagel 79*.

gemeinen mehr als einmal zu durchlaufen ist (*Kanade 78*, *Nagel 79*). Teile dieses Zyklus lassen sich an den Beispielen aus Abschnitt 2 illustrieren. So stellen die Ermittlung von Kantenelementen, deren Zusammenfassung zu Geraden- bzw. Kreisbogen-Stücken sowie die Ermittlung von Eckpunkten als Schnittpunkte von Geradenstücken Operationen dar, die vom digitisierten Bild zu Bildbereichs-Hinweisen führen. Das Drahtmodell von Abbildung 4 ist generisch nur im Hinblick auf seine Lageparameter. Die Auswahl zweier Ecken dieses Drahtmodells und ihre versuchsweise Positionierung im Raum können als Beispiel für die partielle Ausprägung von Lageparametern dienen. Die unter diesen Annahmen ermittelte - noch unvollständige - Szenen-Skizze wird anschließend mit Bildbereichs-Hinweisen verglichen, wodurch weitere Lageparameter festgelegt und eine nächste Iteration mit einem bereits vollständiger ausgeprägten Parametersatz vorbereitet werden. Eine ausführlichere Erläuterung dieses Schemas findet sich in *Nagel 85a*.

Dieses Schema erlaubt es, die bereits gegen Ende des zweiten Abschnittes angedeutete Unterscheidung zwischen *Struktur-* und *Prozeß*-Wissen bei der Bildauswertung zu konkretisieren. Struktur-Wissen kann assoziiert werden mit der Repräsentation von Zuständen, die durch die sechs Blöcke des Interpretationszyklus aus Abbildung 5 dargestellt werden. Es liegt nahe, einige der erforderlichen Repräsentationsformen für Zustände mehrfach zu nutzen, z.B. das synthetische Bild auf dieselbe Weise als Grauwertmatrix intern darzustellen wie das digitisierte Bild oder für die Szenen-Skizze dieselben Beschreibungs-Elemente zu verwenden wie für die Bildbereichs-Hinweise. Such- oder Prozeß-Wissen bezieht sich auf die Teilprozesse, die den Übergang zwischen diesen Zuständen des Interpretationsprozesses vermitteln.

4. Wissensgestützte Ansätze beim Maschinensehen

Maschinensehen ohne Rückgriff auf Wissen ist nach den vorangehenden Erläuterungen ein Widerspruch in sich. Der Gebrauch des Ausdruckes 'wissensgestützter Ansatz' im Zusammenhang mit Maschinensehen soll auf die *explizite* Formulierung des verwendeten Wissens hinweisen. Der Begriff *explizit* bezieht sich dabei nicht auf die Form der system-internen Repräsentation von Wissen - etwa im Sinne der Alternative zwischen einer deklarativen und einer prozeduralen Formulierung (vergleiche hierzu z.B. *Stein et al. 85*). Entscheidend ist vielmehr, daß bei der Mehrzahl der heute eingesetzten Verfahren wesentliche Voraussetzungen überhaupt nicht oder nur in sehr unvollständiger Weise definiert sind und daß das Wissen um die verschiedenen Verfahrensalternativen und die Kriterien bei der Auswahl der implementierten Verfahren nur beim Entwerfer des Systems vorliegt. Es ist daher noch nicht möglich, ein allgemeiner einsetzbares Sichtsystem in einer spezialisierenden Konfigurationsphase systematisch an die Bedingungen des jeweiligen Anwendungsfalles anzupassen - so wie es etwa neuerdings bei der Konfiguration von Betriebssystemen erfolgt (siehe z.B. *Lehmann et al. 85*). Beim Anwender macht sich dieser Mangel im Aufwand für Experimente bemerkbar, mit deren Hilfe nach noch tragbaren Kompensationsmöglichkeiten durch die Art der Gestaltung, Beleuchtung und Aufnahme der Szene oder durch die Auswahl des auszuwertenden Bildmaterials gesucht wird. Es kann auch nicht systematisch überprüft werden, ob die für den jeweiligen Einsatzfall erforderlichen Voraussetzungen vollständig erfüllt sind. Diese Schwierigkeiten bilden - zumindest teilweise - die Ursache dafür, daß der lange Zeit geradezu als prototypische Aufgabenstellung angesehene 'Griff in die Kiste' (siehe z.B. *Laethem et al. 84, Weber 84*) bei vielen Anwendern an Attraktivität verloren hat und in näherer Zukunft durch konsequenten Einsatz von Ordnungssystemen umgangen werden wird (*Brady 85, Geißelmann 83*).

Für eine angemessene Beurteilung der augenblicklichen Situation genügt es aber nicht, darauf hinzuweisen, daß bei den am Markt angebotenen (*Winkler 85*), aber auch bei den in der Literatur beschriebenen Systemen (siehe z.B. *Binford 82*) das explizit formulierte Wissen nur einen bescheidenen Umfang hat, verglichen mit den Kenntnissen, die ein menschlicher Betrachter heranzieht. Dies ist nicht nur darauf zurückzuführen, daß geeignete Repräsentationsformen für weite Bereiche des erforderlichen Wissens noch nicht hinreichend erprobt sind. Die Alternativen - insbesondere bei industriell eingesetzten Sichtsystemen - durch Gestaltung der Szene, ihrer Beleuchtung und der Aufnahmebedingungen sind zur Zeit in vielen Fällen noch kostengünstiger als bereits verfügbare Ansätze zur Auswertung explizit formulierten Wissens. Der in Abbildung 1 illustrierte Anwendungsfall möge hier als Beispiel dienen (siehe auch *Götz 85*).

Die entscheidende Frage lautet daher, welche Kosten durch den Gewinn an Flexibilität gespart werden, wenn zusätzliches Wissen explizit für maschinelles Sehen verfügbar gemacht wird. Dann läßt sich eher übersehen, bis zu welchem Grade es angesichts der raschen Weiterentwicklung auf dem Sektor auch komplexer Bausteine (siehe z.B. *Cheng et al. 85*) vorteilhaft sein kann, an Stelle einer speziellen Lösung für eine gegebene Aufgabe eine allgemeiner einsetzbare, stärker auf explizitem Wissen basierende Lösung anzustreben. Entsprechend der in Abbildung 5 angedeuteten Untergliederung in Bildbereich und Szenenbereich soll dies zunächst für den Bildbereich diskutiert werden.

5. Verfahrensentwicklungen im Bildbereich

Bei den heutigen Preisen für schnelle Arbeitsspeicher spielen Kodierungsfragen kaum eine Rolle im Hinblick auf die Repräsentation digitisierter Bilder. Die Diskussion wird sich daher auf Bildbereichs-Hinweise sowie auf die Szenen-Projektion konzentrieren. Bei den Bildbereichs-Hinweisen liegt eine Unterscheidung nahe in Primitive, die als *Bildbereichs-Elemente* bezeichnet werden sollen, und in *Bildbereichs-Strukturen*, die aus diesen Primitiven entweder nach allgemeinen oder nach aufgabenspezifischen Regeln ermittelt werden. Die Bildbereichs-Elemente sollen möglichst vollständige Aussagen über die Bildfunktion machen, d.h. über den Verlauf des Grauwertes als Funktion der Bildebenenkoordinaten. Der 'primal sketch' nach *Marr 82* kann als Entsprechung der Bildbereichs-Elemente angesehen werden (vergleiche auch *Clark und Lawrence 84*). Die Schnittstelle zwischen den Beschreibungsstufen der Bildbereichs-Elemente und der Bildbereichs-Strukturen möge als *ikonische Schnittstelle* bezeichnet werden. Damit soll zum Ausdruck gebracht werden, daß die Repräsentation der Bildbereichs-Strukturen sich nicht mehr vorwiegend an der Rasterdarstellung digitisierter Bilder orientieren muß, sondern gegebenenfalls symbolische Darstellungsformen umfassen kann (vergleiche auch *Niemann 81*).

Zunächst soll auf eine Schwierigkeit bei der weit verbreiteten Verwendung des Begriffes *Segmentation* eingegangen werden. In Verallgemeinerung des Binärbild-Ansatzes wird beim Segmentations-Ansatz davon ausgegangen, daß die Bildfunktion ein Mosaik von Regionen mit jeweils konstanten Grauwerten ist. In schlichter Extrapolation der an Binärbildern entwickelten Auswertungsansätze betrachtet man entweder den Rand oder die Innenfläche solcher Bereiche als die Quelle von Merkmalen, die eine direkte Klassifikation der beobachteten Abbildungen erlauben. Regionen konstanten Grauwertes sollten sich eindeutig einer Komponente der - meist implizit eingeführten - Diskurswelt zuordnen lassen. Diese Annahme ist nur in Ausnahmefällen erfüllt, z.B. bei Schliffbildern von ebenen Oberflächen, die aus verschieden reflektierenden Materialkomponenten bestehen (vgl. z.B. *Haralick und Shapiro 85*, Figures 1-3). Im allgemeinen trifft es nicht zu, daß ein Bildausschnitt mit einheitlicher Bedeutung auch einen einheitlichen Grauwert aufweist. Das Problem bei der gängigen Verwendung des Begriffes 'Segmentation' besteht demnach darin, daß mit der Beschreibung der Bildfunktion gleichzeitig auch die Interpretation ermittelt werden soll, was in der überwiegenden Mehrzahl der Fälle so direkt nicht möglich ist.

5.1 Bildbereichs-Elemente

Schon wegen des Kamerarauschens kann man einen wirklich konstanten Grauwert nicht erwarten. Führt man eine rein lokale Prüfung der Grauwertunterschiede unter Verwendung einer Toleranzschwelle durch, so lassen sich zufällige und systematische Grauwertvariationen nicht unterscheiden. Die Modellvorstellung einer Bildfunktion als Mosaik von Regionen konstanten Grauwertes ist eine zu starke Abstraktion von der Beobachtung, daß sich ein Bild oft gliedert in Bereiche, innerhalb derer der Grauwert nur langsam variiert, und in Übergangsbereiche mit stärkerer Grauwertvariation. Bei Segmentationsansätzen ergeben sich oft schmale Zwischenregionen, deren Grauwert im Übergangsbereich liegt und nicht klar im Toleranzintervall der an ein solches Übergangsgebiet angrenzenden größeren Regionen. Solche Übergangsregionen werden dann durch eine Heuristik der folgenden Art beseitigt:

- zu kleine Regionen werden willkürlich mit einer benachbarten größeren Region verschmolzen (siehe z.B. *Pavlidis 77*) oder

- lange und dünne Regionen zwischen zwei größeren Regionen werden mit einer der beiden anstoßenden größeren Regionen verschmolzen (*Nazif und Levine 84*).

Durch Schattenwurf hervorgerufene Feinheiten der Grauwertverteilung, die u.a. Aufschluß über die Richtung des einfallenden Lichtes geben können, sind daher bei vielen der heute verwendeten Auswerteverfahren bereits in den Bildbereichs-Hinweisen nicht mehr zu finden. Auch durch Spiegelreflektion hervorgerufene Glanzlichter - z.B. in den Löchern des Winkelbleches aus Abbildung 4 - werden meist als zu kurze Kantenstücke oder zu kleine Regionen unterdrückt. *Foster und Sanderson 84* werten dagegen ein kleines, auf Spiegelreflektion zurückzuführendes Intensitätsmaximum im Inneren eines Objektbildes aus, um die parametrische Beschreibung einer aus der Objektsilhouette gewonnenen Konturkurve zu präzisieren.

Anstatt die Bildbereichs-Hinweise auf Regionen konstanten Grauwertes und/oder die Lage sowie Orientierung von Grauwertsprüngen zu beschränken, muß die Bildfunktion beschrieben werden durch genauere Angaben auch über die *Form* und *Breite* von Grauwertvariationen. Einige der heute außer der Rechteckfunktion meist implizit angenommenen Übergangsformen sind in (*Nagel 85a*) zusammengestellt worden. Erste Ansätze zur detaillierteren Auswertung der relativen Formen von Grauwertübergängen werden z.B. bei *Kanade 81* diskutiert. Auch wird der Grauwertverlauf als bivariates Polynom erster bis dritter Ordnung in den Bildebenenkoordinaten beschrieben (siehe z.B. *Haralick et al. 83, Nagel 83, Bolle und Cooper 84, Pong et al. 84a + b*), zum Teil in der Absicht, aus einem solchen Grauwertverlauf direkt auf den Verlauf der abgebildeten Oberfläche im Raum zu schließen.

Bei der Ermittlung von Kanten machen sich unterschiedliche Formen und Breiten von Grauwertübergängen zum Teil als parallel laufende Kantenelemente bemerkbar, die meist als Artefakte des Kantendetektionsverfahrens in einer Nachbearbeitung eliminiert werden (siehe z.B. *Nazif und Levine 84*). Unausgesprochen liegt den oft verwendeten 3x3-Gradienten-Operatoren - z.B. dem Sobel- oder dem Prewitt-Operator - die Vorstellung zu Grunde, daß alle für die Interpretation wichtigen Grauwertübergänge eine große Steilheit aufweisen. Demnach sollten zu den interessierenden Grauwertübergängen auch diejenigen Ausschnitte des Ortsfrequenzspektrums beitragen, die mit einem die hohen Ortsfrequenzen besonders betonenden 3x3-Gradientenoperator erfaßt werden. Durch eine den lokalen Kontrast steigernde Beleuchtung kann dies teilweise erreicht werden. Liegt das Ergebnis einer solchen Kantendetektion innerhalb eines breiteren Bandes oberhalb der Detektions-Schwelle, so wird die Kantenposition definiert als Resultat einer zusätzlichen heuristischen Ausdünnungsoperation oder einer Suche nach dem lokalen Maximum im Anwendungsergebnis des Kantenoperators. Dabei verliert man aber die Information über die tatsächliche Breite des Grauwertüberganges, d.h. man geht davon aus, daß alle Grauwertübergänge dieselbe Breite aufweisen, eine Annahme, die im allgemeinen nicht gerechtfertigt ist. Oft wäre es sogar vorteilhaft, Angaben über die Breite eines Grauwertübergangs und deren Änderung entlang eines Kantenzuges als wichtigen Hinweis bei der Interpretation zur Verfügung zu haben, beispielsweise bei einer Holzmaserung oder einer verlaufenden Schattenkante (siehe auch *Shipman et al. 84*). Ansätze zur Ermittlung der Breite eines Grauwertüberganges finden sich z.B. bei *Korn und Erdtel 85* (siehe auch *Hartley 85*). Die Repräsentation von Bjldbereichs-Hinweisen muß demnach um Möglichkeiten zur Darstellung von Form und Breite eines Grauwertüberganges erweitert werden.

Bei der vorangehenden Diskussion wurde implizit vorausgesetzt, daß die Grauwertübergänge entlang gerader oder höchstens schwach gekrümmter Übergangsfronten zu untersuchen sind. Im Bild auftretende Eckpunkte werden als Stellen lokaler Krümmungsmaxima in einer Sequenz von Kantenelementen detektiert (siehe z.B. *Anderson und Bezdek 84, Grasmüller et al. 84, Rummel 84*) oder indirekt, als Schnittpunkt von Geradenstücken, die aus nicht zu kurzen Übergangsfronten extrahiert werden müssen - siehe z.B. Abbildung 4. Meist versagen die einfachen Kantendetektionsverfahren in der unmittelbaren Umgebung solcher Eckpunkte. Der häufig verwendete Ansatz zur Beschreibung von Grauwert-Übergangsfronten als eine dichte Folge von Kantenelementen - vergleiche Abbildung 3 - läßt sich dann nicht bis in solche Eckpunkte hinein fortsetzen. Es gibt bisher kaum Untersuchungen über den genauen Grauwertverlauf in der unmittelbaren Umgebung solcher Eckpunkte (vergleiche jedoch *Nagel 83, siehe auch Nackman 84*). Dies hängt wohl damit zusammen, daß man bisher bestrebt war, Bilder mit einer möglichst niedrigen Auflösung zu digitisieren, um den Bearbeitungsaufwand gering zu halten. Nun ist aber aus der theoretischen Analyse von - meist als perfekt vorausgesetzten - Strichzeichnungen bekannt, daß die Angabe eines Vertextyps für die Interpretation wesentliche Informationen liefern kann. Es erscheint daher sinnvoll, einen solchen Eckpunkt durch die Analyse des Grauwertverlaufes direkt zu charakterisieren und nicht nur indirekt über die Zahl und Attribute der einlaufenden Kanten. Auch der Grauwertverlauf um den Endpunkt eines Grauwertüberganges, der sich nicht fortsetzt *(Koenderink und Van Doorn 82;* siehe auch *Richards und Hoffman 84),* ist von besonderem Interesse für den Schluß von einer zweidimensionalen Grauwertverteilung auf Szenenbereichs-Hinweise im Dreidimensionalen. Bisher werden solche als 'Bruch (crack)' bezeichneten Kantenstücke meist eliminiert, wenn sie sich nicht durch oft grob-heuristische Verfahren bis zu einem geschlossenen Konturzug verlängern lassen. Die Frage ist durchaus berechtigt, ob ein höherer Aufwand zur genaueren Charakterisierung des Grauwertverlaufes an solchen - auch visuell auffälligen - Stellen im Bild sich nicht durch schnellere und zuverlässigere Verfahrensansätze in der weiteren Verarbeitung wieder auszahlt.

5.2 Bildbereichs-Strukturen

In der Ermittlung und Repräsentation von Bildbereichs-Strukturen wird Wissen darüber ausgewertet, welche Konfigurationen von Bildbereichs-Elementen sich häufiger in digitisierten Bildern finden oder auf Grund der Information aus Szenen-Skizzen erwartet werden. Im ersteren Fall handelt es sich um aufgaben-unspezifisches Wissen, das bereits von *Zucker et al. 75* als 'general purpose models' diskutiert und neuerdings von *Matsuyama 84* auch als 'perceptual (visual) knowledge' bezeichnet wurde. Gruppierungs-Algorithmen, die Bildbereichs-Elemente auf Grund gemeinsamer Nachbarschaft und/oder nahezu gleicher Orientierung zusammenfassen, werden u.a. in den Lehrbüchern von *Marr 82* und *Levine 85* behandelt.

Eine Beschreibung der strukturellen Grauwertverteilung durch eine Hierarchie von Nulldurchgängen in Bandpass-gefilterten Bildversionen wie z.B. bei *Clark und Lawrence 84* kann als Komponente einer ikonischen Schnittstelle zwischen Bildbereichs-Elementen und Bildbereichs-Strukturen angesehen werden. *Crowley und Parker 84* sowie *Crowley und Sanderson 84* gehen auch von einer symbolische Beschreibung auf der Grundlage einer Hierarchie von Bandpass-gefilterten Versionen des Original-Grauwertbildes aus, bauen daraus aber eine Strukturbeschreibung auf, die anschließend bei einem Suchverfahren nach einer Zuordnung zwischen diesen Bildbereichs-Strukturen und entsprechenden Strukturen in einer Szenen-Skizze ausgewertet wird. Die von *Hartmann 82a + b* untersuchte Hierarchie von Beschreibungsebenen betont Konturlinien und deren Kontinuität - siehe auch *Hartmann und Drüe 84*. Dies Vorgehen ist sehr viel systematischer als dasjenige von *Boyer et al. 84*, die das Binärbild eines Werkstückes an den Stellen in Komponenten zerlegen, an denen sich die Breite der Silhouette senkrecht zur Skelettachse stark ändert. Charakteristische Grauwertstrukturen werden von *Nackman 84* durch einen Konfigurationsgraphen beschrieben, der auf der symbolischen Darstellung von kritischen Punkten, Kammlinien der Bildfunktion sowie Fall-Linien aufbaut, die Grauwertmaxima voneinander separieren.

Die Charakterisierung von Kurvenzügen oder Konturlinien basiert häufig auf der Auswahl von Extremalstellen der Krümmung *(Marimont 84, Richards und Hoffman 84).* Ansätze zur Auswahl charakteristischer Punkte aus Teilen einer Konturkurve unter Bezug auf ein figurspezifisches Koordinatensystem werden von *Tejwani und Jones 85* diskutiert. *Brady und*

Asada 84 studieren lokale Symmetrien von Konturkurvenabschnitten in der Nachbarschaft von Punkten extremaler Krümmung als Elemente, aus denen charakteristische Strukturen aufgebaut werden.

Bei geschlossenen Polygonzügen verwenden *Gu und Huang 84 + 85* eine spezielle Kodierung aus alternierend konvexen und konkaven Eckpunkten, um Strukturen aufzubauen, die anschließende Zuordnungsvorgänge erleichtern. *Matsuyama et al. 84* definieren spezielle Nachbarschafts-Relationen zwischen geraden Kantenstücken und zeigen, daß solche Relationen wichtige Strukturhinweise bei der Suche nach Zuordnungen zu Szenen-Skizzen liefern können.

Eine Zusammenfassung von Bildbereichs-Elementen zu symmetrischen oder nahezu symmetrischen Konfigurationen wird ebenfalls ausgenutzt, um die Zahl der zu überprüfenden Zuordnungsmöglichkeiten drastisch einzuschränken. Ansätze hierzu werden von *Bolles und Cain 82* sowie von *Levitt 84* diskutiert, vergleiche auch *Radig und Schlieder 84*. Darüberhinaus können Symmetrien oder auch systematische Abweichungen von Symmetrien den Übergang von Bildbereichs-Strukturen zu Szenenbereichs-Hinweisen wesentlich unterstützen - siehe z.B. *Brady und Yuille 84*.

5.3 Szenen-Projektion

In vielen Fällen werden Objektbeschreibungen direkt in der Bildebene modelliert, siehe das Beispiel aus Abbildung 3 oder u.a. *(Yachida und Tsuji 75, Perkins 78 + 83, Bolles und Cain 82, Krause et al. 85)*. Expliziert wird hierbei das Wissen über die projizierte Erscheinungsform der berücksichtigten Werkstücke, allerdings mit nicht unwichtigen Einschränkungen. So wird zur Formbeschreibung auf Bildbereichs-Hinweise zurückgegriffen, z.B. Kantenelemente, deren Ermittlung mit den bereits angedeuteten Schwierigkeiten verbunden ist. Die Auswahl der für eine prototypische Szenen-Projektion heranzuziehenden Beschreibungs-Elemente bleibt dem Benutzer überlassen oder muß zumindest von ihm im Einzelnen überprüft werden. Ansätze, die für die Erkennung eines Werkstückes wichtigen Beschreibungs-Elemente ohne interaktive Eingriffe automatisch aus einem Bild auszuwählen, sind bisher noch nicht so weit gediehen, daß sie sich in der Praxis in größerem Umfange durchzusetzen beginnen. Implizit bleibt das Wissen über die Beleuchtung der Szene, über die Kameraanordnung sowie darüber, daß die Werkstücke nur wenige stabile Auflagearten aufweisen und daß sie verhältnismäßig eben sind. Da sich in vielen Fällen - insbesondere bei überlappenden Werkstücken - leichte perspektivische Verzerrungen nicht vermeiden lassen, müssen die dadurch bedingten Unterschiede zwischen den prototypischen Szenen-Skizzen und den aus einer auszuwertenden Aufnahme extrahierten Bildbereichs-Hinweisen durch hinreichend große Toleranzen berücksichtigt werden.

Auch an dieser Stelle ist zu fragen, mit welchem Aufwand man sich von solchen Randbedingungen befreien kann. Wesentlich ist in den hier angesprochenen Problemstellungen das Wissen über die durch Auflageart und Aufnahmebedingungen eingeschränkten Erscheinungsformen der Werkstück-Abbildungen. Es wäre denkbar, die Existenz von nur wenigen stabilen Auflagearten eines Werkstückes aus einem drei-dimensionalen Modell durch eine geometrische Analyse zu erschließen und dies dann zu einer Einschränkung bei der Suche nach den Parametern auszunutzen, die die in einer Aufnahme jeweils auftretende Werkstücklage beschreiben. Die Beschreibungs-Elemente für die Szenen-Skizze könnten durch Anwendung der im Auswertesystem verfügbaren Operatoren auf ein synthetisches Bild gewonnen werden, das mit Hilfe der inzwischen weit entwickelten Methoden der rechnergestützten Bilderzeugung aus dem drei-dimensionalen Modell des Werkstückes zu ermitteln ist. Da diese vorbereitenden Schritte nur einmal nach jeder Veränderung des Satzes zugelassener Werkstücke, der Kamera-Einstellung oder der Beleuchtung erforderlich sind, wäre der erforderliche größere Rechenaufwand eher tragbar. Die tatsächliche Auswertung könnte weiterhin durch Vergleich der Szenen-Skizze mit den aktuell extrahierten Bildbereichs-Hinweisen erfolgen.

Eine solche Vorgehensweise bietet die zusätzliche Möglichkeit, nach Auswahl eines Werkstückmodells und Schätzung seiner Lageparameter einen Verifikationsschritt anzuschließen, in dem ein synthetisches Bild dieses mit den geschätzten Lageparametern voll ausgeprägten Werkstückmodells unmittelbar mit dem aufgenommenen Werkstückbild verglichen wird. Dadurch sollten engere Akzeptanz-Toleranzen möglich werden. Ein grundsätzlicher methodischer Vorteil eines solchen Vorgehens wird darin liegen, daß Unterschiede in der Charakterisierung der Bildfunktion bei synthetischen und aufgenommenen Bildern desselben Werkstückes das Augenmerk gezielt auf Schwachstellen in der Extraktion der Bildbereichs-Hinweise, in der Erzeugung synthetischer Bilder sowie in der Modellierung der Aufnahme- und Beleuchtungsverhältnisse lenkt. Mit solchen Überlegungen ist aber der in Abbildung 5 als Bildbereich bezeichnete Teil des Interpretations-Zyklus bereits verlassen.

6. Verfahrensentwicklungen im Szenenbereich

Auch im Szenenbereich lassen sich Teilproblemkreise abgrenzen, bei denen eine separate Behandlung sinnvoll erscheint. Dem Strukturwissen zuordnen kann man die Repräsentation von Szenenbereichs-Hinweisen, von starren Körpern sowie der Konfigurationen von Objekten, die ihrerseits aus starren Körpern als Komponenten zusammengesetzt sein mögen. Zur Frage der Repräsentation von Körpern mit deformierbaren Oberflächen gibt es bisher kaum Veröffentlichungen im Zusammenhang mit der Interpretation von Bildern. Auch der Themenkomplex Beleuchtung wird dem Strukturwissen zugeordnet, da es sich hierbei in erster Linie um die Repräsentation der relativen Anordnung von Lichtquellen, Objektoberflächen und des bilderzeugenden Systems im Raum handelt. Zum Such- oder Prozeßwissen gehört die Frage nach dem Übergang von Szenenbereichs-Hinweisen zur Ausprägung einer Komponente der generischen Szenenbeschreibung im Rahmen einer datengesteuerten Analysephase sowie nach der Auswahl tentativer Ausprägungen der Szenenbeschreibung zur Ermittlung von Szenen-Projektionen für eine modellgesteuerte Analysephase.

6.1 Szenenbereichs-Hinweise

Umfaßt die Diskurswelt eine größere Zahl von Objekten bei nicht a priori bekannten Positionen, wird ein direkter Schluß von Bildbereichs-Hinweisen auf das abgebildete Objekt wegen der Vielzahl kombinatorischer Möglichkeiten problematisch. Es bietet sich dann an, zunächst Beschreibungs-Elemente im drei-dimensionalen Raum zusammenzustellen, die erst anschließend in einem weiteren Schritt zur Auswahl von Objektmodellen kombiniert werden. Als solche Beschreibungs-Elemente werden Geraden- und Kurvenstücke im Raum sowie Flächenstücke herangezogen. *Tomita und Kanade 84* extrahieren Stücke von Geraden oder Kreisbögen aus Aufnahmen, bei denen die Objekte mit strukturiertem Licht aufgenommen worden sind. *Silberberg et al. 84* verwenden nur Geradenstücke zur Beschreibung ihrer Objektmodelle.

Beispiele für die Verwendung von ebenen Flächenstücken finden sich u.a. bei Bhanu 84, *Brzakovic und Tou 84, Faugeras et al. 84a + b, Laethem et al. 84* und insbesondere bei *Kanade 81*, der diesen Fall ausführlicher studiert hat. Zusätzlich zu ebenen Flächenstücken werden auch Teile von quadratischen Flächen als Beschreibungs-Elemente verwendet. Hinweise auf solche Flächenstücke erschließt man entweder unter der Annahme einer speziellen Reflektionsfunktion direkt aus dem Grauwertverlauf (siehe z.B. *Bolle und Cooper 84, Cernuschi-Frias und Cooper 84, Cohen und Cayula 84, Pentland 84a, Pong et al. 84b*) oder aus Abstandsmessungen mit Laser-Abtastsystemen (siehe z.B. *Faugeras et al. 84a + b*). *Pentland 84b + c* diskutiert einen Ansatz auf der Basis einer Fraktal-Darstellung einer Oberfläche im Raum. Damit wird es möglich, nicht nur auf die Orientierung, sondern auch auf die Rauhigkeit der Oberfläche zu schließen.

6.2 Repräsentation von Objekten

Werden zur Repräsentation eines Objektes nur Punkte im Raum und gegebenenfalls eine Auswahl der sie verbindenden Kanten verwendet, so spricht man von Drahtmodellen. Zu unterscheiden ist dabei zwischen Drahtmodellen, die nur gerade Kantenstücke verwenden, und solchen, die auch gekrümmte Raumkurven enthalten (siehe z.B. *Tomita und Kanade 84*). Meist handelt es sich bei Drahtmodellen um Angaben über die Außenkanten eines Objektes. Manchmal wird ein Objekt auch nur durch Oberflächenpunkte beschrieben, die mit Attributen wie Orientierung der Körperoberfläche und Tangente einer Konturkurve ergänzt werden (*Hakalahti und Moring 84*).

Die Repräsentation von starren Körpern als Drahtmodelle (vergleiche Abbildung 4) ist unbefriedigend, wie aus der rechnergestützten Erzeugung von Bildern bekannt ist. Sie hat für einen Erkennungsprozeß allerdings den Vorteil, sich auf diejenigen Beschreibungs-Elemente zu beschränken, die als Szenenbereichs-Hinweise leichter ermittelt oder als Eckpunkte und Linien unmittelbar für eine Szenen-Projektion ausgenutzt werden können. Da sich Punkte und Kanten oft mit weniger Aufwand als Flächenbeschreibungen aus Bilder extrahieren lassen, ist die Attraktion von Drahtmodellen verständlich. Allerdings ist sie u.a.

mit dem Nachteil verbunden, daß praktisch keine Aussagen über die Beleuchtung einer
Körperoberfläche gewonnen werden können.

Es liegt daher nahe, starre Körper system-intern entweder durch Oberflächen oder durch
Volumenmodelle zu beschreiben, wie sie auch bei der rechnergestützten Konstruktion ein-
gesetzt werden (siehe z.B. *Requicha 80, Farouki und Hinds 85*). Da man glatte Oberflächen
durch die Krümmung als Funktion zweier Flächenparameter beschreiben kann, reichen
Stücke von Flächen zweiter Ordnung zur lokalen Charakterisierung von Oberflächen aus.
Sie haben aber gegenüber einer auf ebenen Flächenstücken aufgebauten Beschreibung u.a.
den Nachteil, daß ihre Manipulation mit einem größeren Aufwand verbunden ist. Beiden
Beschreibungsansätzen mit ebenen wie mit quadratischen Flächenstücken ist der Nachteil
gemeinsam, daß es bei komplexeren Objekten zu sehr unübersichtlichen Beschreibungen
kommt. Die Grobstruktur eines solchen komplexeren Objektes geht aus einer auf einem
Skelett basierenden Beschreibungsstruktur wie z.B. den sogenannten *verallgemeinerten
Zylindern* besser hervor (siehe z.B. *Binford 82*, vergleiche auch *Shafer und Kanade 83b*).
Binford und Mitarbeiter arbeiten an Verfahren, durch symbolische Manipulationen Aussagen über mögliche Szenen-Skizzen von Objekten abzuleiten, die als verallgemeinerte Zylin-
der repräsentiert werden (siehe z.B. *Binford 82* oder *Cowan et al. 84*). *Lin und Fu 84* ver-
wenden dagegen einen syntaktischen Ansatz, um die strukturellen Beziehungen zwischen
Oberflächen-Stücken anzugeben, aus denen Objektbeschreibungen aufgebaut werden.

Übersichten über einige der verwendeten Repräsentationsformen finden sich bei *Henderson 83, Boissonnat 84* sowie bei *Boult 85*. Weitgehend ungelöst ist die Frage, wie insbesondere strukturierte Objektbeschreibungen im dreidimensionalen Raum aus Beobachtungen
automatisch aufgebaut, d.h. 'gelernt' werden können - siehe hierzu aber *Faugeras et al.
84a, Huang und Chen 84, Massone et al. 84*.

Ansätze zur system-internen Beschreibung von Objekten mit gegeneinander beweglichen,
aber in sich starren Komponenten durch parametrisierte Relationen werden von *Tomita
und Kanade 84* diskutiert.

6.3 Beleuchtung

Bisher gibt es erst wenige Untersuchungen zur Frage, wie aus einer Aufnahme auf die Art,
Zahl und Position von Lichtquellen zurückgeschlossen werden kann, die zu einer konsistenten Erklärung der beobachteten Grauwertverteilungen führen. Dies hängt u.a. auch mit der
bereits erwähnten Tatsache zusammen, daß die dafür heranzuziehenden Feinheiten des
Grauwertverlaufes meist schon bei der Extraktion von Bildbereichs-Hinweisen verloren gehen. Eine genauere Analyse des jeweils vorliegenden Grauwertverlaufes kann Hinweise liefern, die sich zu einer konsistenten Schätzung der Beleuchtungsrichtung verbinden lassen.
Pentland 84a studiert Annahmen, mit deren Hilfe aus dem Grauwertverlauf sowie seiner
ersten und zweiten partiellen Ableitungen nach den Bildebenen-Koordinaten sowohl die
Oberflächen-Orientierung als auch die Lichteinfallsrichtung erschlossen werden können.

Die im Zusammenhang mit Abbildung 4 erwähnten Überlegungen zeigen allerdings, daß die Schätzung der Beleuchtungsrichtung oft eine wesentlich globalere Betrachtung vieler - zum Teil nicht sehr auffälliger - Hinweise erfordert als die lokalere Analyse, die aus einer Grauwertvariation oder einer Objektkontur auf eine gekrümmte Oberfläche schließt. Die Kenntnis der Lichteinfallsrichtung relativ zur Szene kann die Grundlage abgeben für eine weitergehende Analyse von Schattenkanten, aus der zusätzliche Hinweise zur Form und Anordnung von Oberflächen in der Szene gewonnen werden können (vergleiche *Shafer und Kanade 83a*).

Diese Diskussion bietet ein weiteres Beispiel dafür, wie durch systematisches Auswerten von im Prinzip vorhandenen Hinweisen Aussagen gewonnen werden können, die heute erst in seltenen Fällen genutzt werden. Falls die Kenntnis der Lichteinfallsrichtung für eine Auswertung erforderlich ist, muß sie heute meist durch sorgfältige Justage eingestellt oder aber interaktiv geschätzt werden.

6.4 Repräsentation nicht rein geometrischer Aspekte

Während bei der Repräsentation von Werkstücken geometrische Aspekte im Vordergrund der Überlegungen stehen, muß bei anderen Diskurswelten auch begriffliches Wissen allgemeinerer Art intern dargestellt werden können (siehe hierzu *McCalla und Cercone 83*). *McKeown 84* erläutert dies für die Interpretation von Luftaufnahmen, bei der gegebenenfalls auch Wissen über den Verwendungszweck von Bauten oder noch genereller alles Wissen, das sich in Karten kodiert findet, herangezogen werden muß (siehe auch *Ranzinger 84*). Bei der Interpretation von szintigraphischen Bildfolgen des schlagenden Herzens müssen die zwischen den Aufnahmen einer Folge detektierbaren Veränderungen in Beziehung gesetzt werden zu den diagnostischen Begriffen der Mediziner *(Bunke et al. 84, Niemann et al. 84 + 85)*.

In beiden Fällen werden semantische Netze zur Repräsentation solchen begrifflichen Wissens herangezogen. Die Strukturierung des begrifflichen Wissens kann bereits für einen noch als überschaubar gehaltenen Teilbereich erhebliche Probleme aufwerfen. Eine Hilfe dabei sind hierarchie-bildende Relationen zwischen den einzelnen zu berücksichtigenden Begriffen. Neben der Komponenten-Hierarchie (*hat-Teil* bzw. *Teil-von*) wird besonders auf die Generalisierungs-/Spezialisierungs-Hierarchie zurückgegriffen, bei der man allerdings eine Vielzahl von Auffassungen in der Literatur findet (*Brachman 83*). Eine weitere hierarchie-bildende Beziehung beginnt sich herauszuschälen, die versuchsweise als *Parameterbeeinflussung* bezeichnet werden soll: die Schätzung von Parametern in der Ausprägung eines Begriffes können beeinflußt werden durch Parameterwerte aus der Ausprägung eines anderen Begriffes, ohne daß der zweite Begriff einen Teil oder eine Verallgemeinerung bzw. Spezialisierung des ersten Begriffes bezeichnet. So können beispielsweise aus dem Schatten eines Körpers wertvolle Hinweise auf Form oder Lage des schattenwerfenden und des beschatteten Körpers gewonnen werden, ohne daß der Schatten als begrifflicher Teil oder als Ober- bzw. Unterbegriff des betreffenden Körpers angesehen werden kann. In

Bunke et al. 84 findet sich ein weiteres Beispiel für eine solche Beziehung unter der Bezeichnung 'notwendiger-Teil-von'. Eine Zusammenstellung hierarchie-bildender Relationen
zwischen Begriffen und eine saubere Festlegung, wie solche Relationen zu verwenden sind,
können eine wesentliche Hilfe bei zukünftigen Versuchen sein, die Repräsentation einer
Diskurswelt um begriffliches Wissen zu erweitern. Eine solche Erweiterung der Diskurswelt
um begriffliches Wissen, insbesondere zur Beschreibung des zeitlichen Verhaltens von Objekten in der Szene, wird bei der Verbindung von Sichtsystemen mit Robotern (*Brady und
Asada 84, Brady 85*), bei der Überwachung von Szenen mit beweglichen Objekten (*Nagel
85b*) sowie bei der Entwicklung autonom mobiler Systeme (*Giralt 84*) eine zunehmende
Rolle spielen.

6.5 Such- oder Prozeß-Wissen

Die in Abschnitt 3 verwendete Definition des Begriffes *Interpretation eines Bildes* verlangt
eine Zuordnung zwischen Pixeln eines Bildes und der in Frage kommenden Teil-Repräsenta-
tion der Diskurswelt. Im allgemeinen muß nach einer solchen Zuordnung gesucht werden.
Zuordnungen werden gesucht von Bildbereichs-Hinweisen zu Szenenbereichs-Hinweisen
und von dort nach Ausprägungen generischer Modelle. Ein anderer Suchvorgang befaßt
sich mit der Zuordnung zwischen Bildbereichs-Hinweisen und Szenen-Skizze, ein dritter mit
der Erzeugung geeigneter Szenen-Skizzen aus den generischen Beschreibungen. Um diese
Suche auch bei umfangreicheren Mengen von Bildbereichs-Hinweisen sowie komplexeren
Diskurswelten mit einem vertretbaren Aufwand durchführen zu können, müssen u.a. möglichst spezifische Bildbereichs-Hinweise ausgewählt, d.h. Bildbereichs-Elemente zu charakteristischen Bildbereichs-Strukturen zusammengefaßt werden - vergleiche Abschnitt 5.2.

Darüberhinaus kommt es aber auch darauf an, die Bildbereichs-Elemente und -Strukturen
in einer die schnelle Suche unterstützenden Weise intern darzustellen. *Bolles und Cain 82*
fassen interaktiv ausgewählte Merkmalskonfigurationen in Listen zusammen. *Boyer et al.
84* verwenden Rahmenkonstrukte (frames), um aus Bildbereichs-Elementen globalere Bildbereichs-Strukturen aufzubauen, mit deren Hilfe die Zahl der bei der Suche zu berücksichtigenden Komponenten reduziert wird. Die von *Silberberg et al. 84* verwendete verallgemeinerte Hough-Transformation stellt eine weitere Möglichkeit dar, den Suchvorgang
durch eine Auswertung der in Bildbereichs-Elementen enthaltenen Angaben zu strukturieren. *Tsai und Yu 84* erweitern Methoden zum Vergleich von Symbolketten, um Konturzüge
aus Szenen-Skizzen mit Bildbereichs-Hinweisen zu vergleichen. Ein Kurvensegment wird dabei als Symbol dargestellt, das durch Attribute wie Länge und Orientierung des Kurvenseg-
mentes ergänzt ist. Die Attributierung der Symbole macht diesen Verfahrensansatz störun-
anfälliger als Zeichenkettenvergleiche ohne Attribute.

Medioni und Nevatia 84 ziehen einen Relaxationsansatz (vergleiche auch *Bhanu und Fauge-
ras 84*) für die Zuordnung zwischen Bildbereichs-Strukturen und einer Szenen-Skizze in
Form einer Karte heran. Auch Grammatiken werden für diesen Zweck eingesetzt, siehe z.B.
Niemann 81; vergleiche auch Krause et al. 85. Tropf und Mitarbeiter studieren erweiterte

Übergangsnetze (ATN), um das a-priori-Wissen über eine geeignete Reihenfolge anzugeben, in der Bildbereichs-Hinweise bei der Auswahl von Objektpositionen und -orientierungen überprüft werden sollen (*Walter und Tropf 83, Tropf et al. 84*). *Stein et al. 84* untersuchen, inwieweit sich solches Wissen durch Produktionensysteme einfangen läßt. Diese Arbeit enthält auch Ansätze zu einem Vergleich der beiden zuletzt erwähnten Vorgehensweisen. *Lowe und Binford 85* stellen spezielle Inferenzregeln zusammen, die den Übergang von Bildbereichs- zu Szenenbereichs-Hinweisen unterstützen. Für den Fall, daß als Objektbeschreibungen nur Polyeder zugelassen sind, stehen für den Schluß vom Bildbereich zum Szenen-Bereich inzwischen ausgefeilte Regelsysteme zur Verfügung - siehe z.B. *Shapira 84 + 85*.

Eine systematische Bewertung dieser verschiedenen Ansätze steht noch aus. Zusätzlich zur Effizienz, mit der eine Methode zur Repräsentation des Suchwissens ausgewertet werden kann, spielt bei der Beurteilung auch noch die Flexibilität bei der Erweiterung oder Anpassung an neue Situationen sowie die Schwierigkeit eine Rolle, die den Suchvorgang eventuell beeinflussenden Parameter so festlegen zu können, daß die Parameterwahl unkritisch ist.

Ein langfristig fast noch wichtigeres Problem besteht in der Aufgabe, die Auswahl und Darstellung der Szenen-Skizzen nicht mehr interaktiv zu ermitteln, sondern aus der Repräsentation der Diskurswelt - einschließlich der speziellen Aufgabenstellung - automatisch zu erschließen. Von der bisher üblichen rechnergestützten Erzeugung synthetischer Bilder (computer graphics) hebt sich diese Aufgabe dadurch ab, daß die Ausprägungen von Szene und Beleuchtung nicht festliegen. Vielmehr muß innerhalb der generischen Beschreibungen nach Kombinationen von Teilbereichen freier Parameter gesucht werden, die zu charakteristischen Szenen-Skizzen führen. Dadurch wird auch von dieser Seite her der Suchaufwand bei der Zuordnung zwischen Szenen-Skizze und Bildbereichs-Hinweisen begrenzt. Ansätze in dieser Richtung werden seit Jahren im Rahmen des ACRONYM-Projektes von Binford und Mitarbeitern verfolgt (siehe z.B. *Binford 82, Cowan et al. 84*). In die gleiche Richtung, wenn auch mit wesentlich bescheidenerer Zielsetzung, weist der Ansatz von *Klinger et al. 84*, aus drei-dimensionalen Drahtmodellen von Polyedern typische Konfigurationen von Eckpunkten in Szenen-Skizzen automatisch auszuwählen, die beim Vergleich mit Bildbereichs-Strukturen eine schnelle Erkennung des betreffenden Polyeders ermöglichen sollten.

7. Diskussion

Das aktuelle Interesse an Expertensystemen - insbesondere solcher, die *Wenn-Dann*-Regeln, d.h. Produktionen zur Wissensrepräsentation verwenden (siehe z.B. *Hayes-Roth et al. 83, Horn 84, Bonnet 85*) - könnte dazu führen, die als Thema gestellte Frage in folgendem Sinne zu verstehen: welche Vorteile bietet es, 'Expertensystem-Schalen' an den Einsatz in der Bildauswertung zu adaptieren? Die vorangehende Diskussion sollte zeigen, daß bei der Interpretation von Bildern eine Fülle verschiedener Arten von Wissen berücksichtigt werden muß. Es ist daher nicht zu erwarten, daß man mit einer einzigen Repräsentationstechnik alle sich in diesem umfangreichen Problemkreis ergebenden Aufgaben gleichermaßen erfolg-

reich bearbeiten kann. Entsprechende Aussagen finden sich auch in der Literatur, z.B. bei
Brady 85 und *Mostow 85* (insbesondere pp. 23-24) oder - wenn auch indirekt - in der sehr
lesenswerten kritischen Übersicht zum Themenkomplex Expertensysteme von *Lehmann 84*.
Expertensysteme der bisher gebräuchlichen Art mögen ihre Vorteile aufweisen, wenn es darum geht, das auch bei der Bildauswertung eingesetzte heuristische Wissen expliziter zu
formulieren, um damit besser experimentieren zu können (siehe z.B. *Nazif und Levine 84,
Stein et al. 85*). Nach Abschluß einer solchen Experimentierphase kann eine stärker prozedural orientierte Formulierung wichtige Effizienzvorteile bieten.

Ein wichtiger Schritt besteht in einer sauberen Trennung zwischen der Beschreibung zulässiger struktureller Grauwertvariationen sowie der zulässigen zufälligen Störungen - d.h. des
erwarteten Rauschens - auf der einen Seite und der Interpretation dieser Grauwertstrukturen auf der anderen Seite. Die Repräsentation von Grauwertübergängen sollte nicht nur
Angaben über deren Lage und Orientierung, sondern auch über deren Form und Breite enthalten. Die bisher so betonte Dichotomie in kanten- und regionen-orientierte Verfahren
wird dabei an Bedeutung verlieren, da die Grenze zwischen einem breiteren Grauwertüber-
gang und einem kleineren Bereich langsamerer Grauwertvariation verschwimmt. Diese -
sich möglicherweise nicht gegenseitig ausschließenden und das Bild eventuell mehrfach
überdeckenden - Repräsentationen des Grauwertverlaufs könnten eine Schnittstelle zwischen der *ikonischen* Auswertung und der *symbolorientierten* Auswertung bilden. Die mit
den erwähnten Attributen ausgestatteten Bildbereichs-Elemente sollten datengesteuert zu
semi-lokalen Konfigurationen - d.h. Bildbereichs-Strukturen - erweitert werden, so daß der
Suchaufwand in den anschließenden Verarbeitungsschritten unter Kontrolle gehalten
werden kann.

Im Szenenbereich sollte man von Ecken- oder Drahtmodellen der in der Diskurswelt zu berücksichtigenden Objekte zu einer Oberflächen- oder Volumenmodellierung übergehen.
Die miteinander im Konflikt liegenden Forderungen nach schneller Erzeugung realistischer
synthetischer Bilder und nach einer möglichst automatischen Strukturierung von Szenen-
Skizzen, die eine Strukturierung der Objektbeschreibungen voraussetzt, lassen es angezeigt
scheinen, auf die Dauer im Objektbereich mit mehrfachen Repräsentationen zu rechnen
(vergleiche auch *Farouki und Hinds 85, Faugeras et al. 84a*). *Lee et al. 84* beschreiben einen
Algorithmus zur Umsetzung einer volumen-orientierten Objektdarstellung in eine solche
mit finiten Elementen. Feinmaschige Polyederbeschreibungen sind in der rechnergestützten Darstellung inzwischen so verbreitet, daß ein Subsystem zur Manipulation solcher Ob-
jektrepräsentationen in ein fortgeschrittenes Bildinterpretationssystem integriert werden
sollte. Es bleibt zu untersuchen, inwieweit Beschreibungen auf der Basis von polynomialen
Flächenstücken als Übergang zwischen den Polyeder-Repräsentationen und solchen, die
durch Kombination von Elementarvolumina erzeugt werden (constructive solid geometry),
den Interpretationsvorgang signifikant erleichtern.

Die direkte Übernahme von Ergebnissen rechnergestützter Entwurfsmethoden in die Ob-
jektrepräsentation von Sichtsystemen erscheint zwar auf den ersten Blick attraktiv. Bei der

Interpretation von Bildern gewinnen aber Aspekte an Bedeutung, die beim produktions-
bezogenen Entwurf nicht im Vordergrund stehen (vergleiche hierzu auch *Bolles et al. 84*).
So müssen nicht konkret bestimmte Objekte, sondern vielfältig parametrisierte Beziehungen zwischen Elementen von Objektbeschreibungen in der *generischen* Szenenbeschreibung repräsentiert werden. Eine solche Repräsentation muß auch die Möglichkeit bieten,
durch symbolische Manipulationen der Objektbeschreibungen Aufschlüsse über die Erscheinungsformen von Objekten in der Szenen-Skizze zu gewinnen und darüber, wie sich diese
Erscheinungsformen bei Variationen der Kamera-Position verändern.

Unabhängig von der Art der system-internen Objektbeschreibung ist der Einfluß der Beleuchtung auf die Erscheinungsform von Objekten bei der Erzeugung der Szenen-Projektion zu berücksichtigen. Dieser Teilbereich von Wissen ist systematischer als bisher in den gesamten Auswertevorgang zu integrieren.

Die Repräsentation von parametrisierten Relationen zwischen - zunächst - starren Objekt-
komponenten ist erforderlich für die Erschließung des Zusammenhangs zwischen Form und
Funktion. Eine system-interne Repräsentation von Funktionsaussagen könnte wesentliche
Erleichterungen bei der Anpassung eines Systems an neue Aufgabenstellungen sowie bei
der Interpretation multisensorieller Eingabedaten bieten.

Gelingt es, eine Rahmenrepräsentation für funktionsbedingte Zielvorstellungen verfügbar
zu machen, in die sich geometrische Standardoperationen einbetten lassen, so wären auch
wesentliche Erleichterungen bei der Realisierung von Interaktionsschnittstellen für Systementwickler und Benutzer zu erwarten (wegen entsprechender Überlegungen bei der Programmierung von Roboter siehe z.B. *Brady 85*). Entwicklungsingenieure und Facharbeiter
sind heute auf Grund langer Erfahrung damit vertraut, wie sie Werkstücke zu haltern haben. Unter Hinzuziehung von Industriephotographen lassen sich auch Beleuchtung und
Aufnahme durch Rückgriff auf vorhandenes Fachwissen bewältigen. Ohne geeignete Interaktionsschnittstellen bei Sichtsystemen dauert es aber sehr lange, bis bei dieser Gruppe von
Anwendern ausreichende Erfahrungen mit den verschiedenen Ansätzen der Bildauswertung vorliegen. Solange diese Erfahrung aber nicht zur Verfügung steht, wird man eine auf
dem Einsatz explizit formulierten Wissens beruhende Verfahrensentwicklung zugunsten
des Einsatzes vertrauter Lösungswege zu vermeiden trachten.

Eine Untergliederung des Gesamtproblems der wissensgestützten Bildauswertung in möglichst voneinander unabhängige Teilsysteme hat den zusätzlichen Vorteil, die Gestaltung
von Interaktionsschnittstellen zu vereinfachen und die Suche nach brauchbaren Parameter-
Einstellungen durch Entkopplung der verschiedenen Parametereinflüsse gerade für einen
mit den Verfahrensinterna nicht vertrauten Benutzer wesentlich zu beschleunigen.

8. Schlußfolgerungen

Maschinensehen ohne Rückgriff auf Wissen ist nach den Erklärungen des dritten Abschnittes ein Widerspruch in sich. Der Gebrauch des Ausdruckes 'wissensgestützter Ansatz' im Zu-

sammenhang mit Maschinensehen bezieht sich auf die *explizite* Formulierung des verwendeten Wissens. Maschinensehen ist heute sowohl ein Problem der Grundlagenforschung als auch ein technisches Problem bei der Erschließung des Marktes für eine neue Technologie. Speziell bei Sichtsystemen für industrielle Anwendungen muß berücksichtigt werden, daß Kostengesichtspunkte eine Minimierung des Gesamtaufwandes erzwingen. Der Datenverarbeitungsaufwand bei der Verwendung von Lösungsansätzen auf der Basis explizit formulierten Wissens muß dabei abgewogen werden gegen die Kosten von Verfahrensansätzen, die den Auswertungsaufwand durch spezielle Maßnahmen bei der Gestaltung der Szene, ihrer Beleuchtung und Aufnahme verringern. Im Rahmen einer ad-hoc Lösung für einen engumrissenen Aufgabenbereich kann ein wissensgestützter Teilansatz durchaus seine Vorteile bieten, z.B. als Modul zur Ermittlung der strukturellen Grauwertvariationen in einem Bild oder als Modul zur Beschreibung der Eigenschaften von und Beziehungen zwischen Objekten in einer Szene. Die überwiegend aus neueren Publikationen ausgewählten Zitate sollten belegen, daß selbst bei weitgehender Untergliederung des Interpretationsprozesses und der ihm zu Grunde liegenden Repräsentationen bereits auf fast allen Teilgebieten eine Fülle von Detailergebnissen vorliegen.

Größere Vorteile sind von einem wissensgestützten Ansatz aber im Rahmen eines systematischen Entwurfes von breiter einsetzbaren Sichtsystemen zu erwarten. Eine explizite Formulierung des verwendeten Wissens unterstützt die Analyse des Zusammenhanges zwischen der erwarteten und der beobachteten Kompetenz eines Lösungsansatzes, d.h. der Fähigkeit, eine Aufgabe überhaupt zu lösen. Eine solche Analyse ist die Voraussetzung für die systematische, schrittweise Verbesserung der Kompetenz von Lösungsansätzen für maschinelles Sehen. Ein weiterer, gewichtiger Vorteil einer expliziten Formulierung des herangezogenen Wissens besteht in der Möglichkeit, zusammengehöriges Wissen in einer Teilrepräsentation zusammenzufassen und dadurch das Gesamtsystem überschaubar zu gliedern. Das in Abbildung 5 dargestellte Schema und die darauf aufbauende Diskussion der anschließenden Abschnitte sollte diesen Gesichtspunkt illustrieren. In Zukunft wird dieser Aspekt bei wachsender Komplexität der zu bearbeitenden Fragestellungen noch an Gewicht gewinnen. Ein Systemansatz unter Verwendung ausgeprüfter, aber nicht notwendigerweise optimaler Teillösungen erlaubt es, Erfahrungen zu sammeln, wo weiterer Aufwand den größten Beitrag zur Verbesserung liefern kann.

Die dazu erforderlichen Entwicklungsarbeiten bilden einen Ansporn zur Kooperation zwischen Forschungsinstituten, Herstellern und Anwendern von Sichtsystemen. Prototypische Entwürfe von Sichtsystemen, die auf wissensgestützten Ansätzen aufbauen, bieten sich geradezu an als 'vermittelnde Wissensbasen (intermediary knowledge bases)' im Sinne von *Rouse 85*, die den Transfer von Einsichten und Erfahrungen zwischen Anwendern und Herstellern auf der einen Seite sowie Hochschul- und Forschungsinstituten auf der anderen Seite beschleunigen.

Anderson, I.M., *Bezdek*, J.C. (*1984*) Curvature and Tangential Deflection of Discrete Arcs: A Theory Based on the Commutator of Scatter Matrix Pairs and Its Application to Vertex Detection in Planar Shape. IEEE Trans. Pattern Analysis and Machine Intelligence **PAMI-6**, 27-40

Bhanu, B. (*1984*) Representation and Shape Matching of 3-D Objects. IEEE Trans. Pattern Analysis and Machine Intelligence **PAMI-6**, 340-350

Bhanu, B., *Faugeras*, O.D. (*1984*) Shape Matching of Two-Dimensional Objects. IEEE Trans. Pattern Analysis and Machine Intelligence **PAMI-6**, 137-156

Binford, T.O. (*1982*) Survey of Model-Based Image Analysis Systems. International Journal of Robotics Research **1**, 18-64

Boissonnat, J.-D. (*1984*) Geometric Structures for Three-Dimensional Shape Representation. ACM Transactions on Graphics **3**, 266-286

Bolle, R.M., *Cooper*, D.B. (*1984*). Bayesian Recognition of Local 3-D Shape by Approximating Image Intensity Functions with Quadric Polynomials. IEEE Trans. Pattern Analysis and Machine Intelligence **PAMI-6**, 418-429

Bolles, R.C., *Cain*, R.A. (*1982*) Recognizing and Locating Partially Visible Objects: The Local-Feature-Focus Method. International Journal of Robotics Research **1**, No. 3 (Fall 1982) 57-82

Bolles, R.C., *Horaud*, P., *Hannah*, M.J. (*1984*) 3DPO: A Three-Dimensional Part Orientation System. In "Robotics Research - The First International Symposium", M. Brady and R. Paul (eds.), pp. 413-424; Cambridge/MA London/UK: The MIT Press 1984

Bonnet, A. (*1985*) Les systèmes experts. In "Fundamentals in Computer Understanding: Speech, Vision, and Natural Language", J.P. Haton (Hrsg.), Cambridge/UK: Cambridge University Press (im Druck)

Boult, T.E. (*1985*) A Survey of some Three Dimensional Vision Systems. SIGART-Newsletter No. **92** (April 1985) 28-37

Boyer, K.L., *Safranek*, R.J., *Kak*, A.C. (*1984*) A Knowledge Based Robotic Vision System. Proc. First Conference on Artificial Intelligence Applications, pp. 45-50; Denver/Colorado, December 1984

Brachman, R.J. (*1983*) What IS-A Is and Isn't: An Analysis of Taxonomic Links in Semantic Networks. IEEE Computer **16**, No. 10 (October 1983) 30-36

Brady, M. (*1985*) Artificial Intelligence and Robotics. Artificial Intelligence **26**, 79-121

Brady, M., *Asada*, H. (*1984*) Smoothed Local Symmetries and Their Implementation. International Journal of Robotics Research **3**, No. 3 (Fall 1984) 36-61

Brady, M., *Yuille*, A. (*1984*) An Extremum Principle for Shape from Contour. IEEE Trans. Pattern Analysis and Machine Intelligence **PAMI-6**, 288-301

Brzakovic, D., *Tou*, J.T. (*1984*) Image Understanding via Texture Analysis. Proc. First Conference on Artificial Intelligence Applications, pp. 585-590; Denver/Colorado, December 1984

Bunke, H., *Feistel*, H., *Hofmann*, I., *Niemann*, H., *Sagerer*, G. (*1984*) Ein wissensbasiertes System zur automatischen Auswertung von Bildsequenzen des menschlichen Herzens. In "Mustererkennung 1984" DAGM/ÖAGM Symposium 1984, W. Kropatsch (Hrsg.), pp. 276-282. Berlin-Heidelberg-New York-Tokyo: Springer-Verlag 1984

Cernuschi-Frias, B., *Cooper*, D.B. (*1984*). 3-D location and Orientation Parameter Estimation of Lambertian Spheres and Cylinders from a Single 2-D Image by Fitting Lines and Ellipses to Thresholded Data. IEEE Trans. Pattern Analysis and Machine Intelligence **PAMI-6**, 430-441

Cheng, H.-D., *Lin*, W.-C., *Fu*, K.-S. (*1985*) Space-Time Domain Expansion Approach to VLSI and Its Application to Hierarchical Scene Matching. IEEE Trans. Pattern Analysis and Machine Intelligence **PAMI-7**, 306-319

Clark, J.J., *Lawrence*, P.D. (*1984*) A Hierarchical Image Analysis System Based upon Oriented Zero Crossings of Bandpassed Images. In "Multiresolution Image Processing and Analysis", pp. 148-168; A. Rosenfeld (ed.); Berlin Heidelberg New York Tokyo: Springer-Verlag 1984

Cohen, F.S., *Cayula*, J.-F.P. (*1984*) 3-D Object Recognition from a Single Image. Proc. Intelligent Robots and Computer Vision, Cambridge/MA, November 5-8, 1984, SPIE **521**, pp. 7-15

Cowan, C.K., *Chelberg*, D.M., *Lim*, H.S. (*1984*) ACRONYM Model Based Vision in the Intelligent Task Automation Project. Proc. First Conference on Artificial Intelligence Applications, pp. 176-183; Denver/Colorado, December 1984

Crowley, J.L., *Parker*, A.C. (*1984*) A Representation for Shape Based on Peaks and Ridges in the Difference of Low-Pass Transform. IEEE Trans. Pattern Analysis and Machine Intelligence **PAMI-6**, 156-170

Crowley, J.L., Sanderson, A.C. (1984) Multiple Resolution Representation and Probabilistic Matching of 2-D Gray Scale Shape. Proc. Workshop on Computer Vision: Representation and Control, April 30-May 2, 1984, Annapolis/MD, pp. 95-105

Farouki, R.T., Hinds, J.K. (1985) A Hierarchy of Geometric Forms. IEEE Computer Graphics and Applications **5**, No. 5 (May 1985) 51-78

Faugeras, O.D., Hébert, M., Pauchon, E., Ponce, J. (1984a) Object Representation, Identification, and Positioning from Range Data. In "Robotics Research - The First International Symposium", M. Brady and R. Paul (eds.), pp. 425-446; Cambridge/MA London/UK: The MIT Press 1984

Faugeras, O.D., Ayache, N., Faverjon, B. (1984b) A Geometric Matcher for Recognizing and Positioning 3-D Rigid Objects. Proc. First Conference on Artificial Intelligence Applications, pp. 218-224; Denver/Colorado, December 1984. See also Proc. Intelligent Robots and Computer Vision, Cambridge/MA, November 5-8, 1984, SPIE **521**, pp. 152-159

Foster, N.J., Sanderson, A.C. (1984) Determining Object Orientation Using Ellipse Fitting. Proc. Intelligent Robots and Computer Vision, Cambridge/MA, November 5-8, 1984, SPIE **521**, pp. 34-43

Geißelmann, H. (1983) Forderungen an die Bildverarbeitung in der industriellen Fertigung. 5. DAGM-Symposium Mustererkennung 1983, Karlsruhe, 11.-13. Oktober 1983, H. Kazmierczak (Hrsg.), VDE-Fachberichte **35**, pp. 72-83, Berlin-Offenbach: VDE-Verlag GmbH 1983.

Geißelmann, H., Ossenberg, K., Niepold, R., Tropf, H. (1985) Sichtsysteme in der Industrie: "Beispiele aus der Anwendung". Robotersysteme 1 (im Druck)

Giralt, G. (1984) Mobile Robots. In "Robotics and Artificial Intelligence"; Brady, M., Gerhardt, L.A., and Davidson, H.F. (eds.) NATO ASI Series F 11, pp. 365-393; Berlin Heidelberg New York Tokyo: Springer-Verlag 1984

Götz, E. (1985) Handhabungssysteme mit automatischer Bilderkennung. In "transmatic 85 Kongreß: Neue Technologien im Materialfluß und in der Fördertechnik (12.-14. April 1985)", E. Bahke (Hrsg.), pp.141-150. Schriftenreihe des Institutes für Fördertechnik der Universität Karlsruhe, Heft 8

Grasmüller, H., Hohberger, K., Köllensperger, P., Kutzer, E., Reischl, A., Rummel, P. (1984) Local Feature Extraction for Model-Based Workpiece Recognition. Proc. International Conference on Pattern Recognition, Montrèal / Quebec, July 30-August 2, 1984, pp. 886-889

Gu, W.K., Huang, T.S. (1984) Matching Perspective Views of a Polyhedron. Proc. Intelligent Robots and Computer Vision, Cambridge/MA, November 5-8, 1984, SPIE **521**, pp. 80-86

Gu, W.K., Huang, T.S. (1985) Connected Line Drawing Extraction from a Perspective View of a Polyhedron. IEEE Trans. Pattern Analysis and Machine Intelligence **PAMI-7**, 422-430

Hakalahti, H., Moring, I. (1984) Method of 2D and 3D Object Recognition in Nonoptimal Conditions. Proc. Intelligent Robots and Computer Vision, Cambridge/MA, November 5-8, 1984, SPIE **521**, pp. 24-33

Haralick, R.M., Shapiro, L.G. (1985). Image Segmentation Techniques. Computer Vision, Graphics, and Image Processing **29**, 100-132

Haralick, R.M., Watson, L.T., Laffey, T.J. (1983) The Topographic Primal Sketch. International Journal of Robotics Research **2**, No. 1 (Spring 1983) 50-72

Hartley, R. (1985) A Gaussian-Weighted Multiresolution Edge Detector. Computer Vision, Graphics, and Image Processing **30**, 70-83

Hartmann, G. (1982a) Recursive Features of Circular Receptive Fields. Biol. Cybernetics **43**, 199-208

Hartmann, G. (1982b) Recognition of Continuous Line Structures by a Hierarchical System. Proc. International Conference on Pattern Recognition, München, October 19-22, 1982, pp. 195-200

Hartmann,G., Drüe, S. (1984) Erkennungsstrategien bei Bildern mit hierarchisch codierten Konturen. In "Mustererkennung 1984" DAGM/ÖAGM Symposium 1984, W. Kropatsch (Hrsg.), pp. 120-126. Berlin-Heidelberg-New York-Tokyo: Springer-Verlag 1984

Hayes-Roth, F., Waterman, D.A., Lenat, D.B. (1983) Building Expert Systems. Reading/MA: Addison-Wesley Publishing Co., Inc. 1983

Henderson, T.C. (*1983*) Efficient 3-D Object Representations for Industrial Vision Systems. IEEE Trans. Pattern Analysis and Machine Intelligence **PAMI-5**, 609-618

Horn, W. (*1984*) Expertensysteme: Wissensrepräsentation und Inferenzprozesse. In "Mustererkennung 1984" DAGM/ÖAGM Symposium 1984, W. Kropatsch (Hrsg.), pp. 305-318. Berlin-Heidelberg-New York-Tokyo: Springer-Verlag 1984

Huang, T.S., *Chen*, H.H. (*1984*) Generating Cylindrical Representation of Solid Objects from Surface Representation. Proc. Intelligent Robots and Computer Vision, Cambridge/MA, November 5-8, 1984, SPIE **521**, pp. 316-319

Kanade, T. (*1978*) Region Segmentation: Signal versus Semantics. Proc. Int. Joint Conference on Pattern Recognition, Kyoto / Japan, November 7-10, 1978, pp. 95-105; see also Computer Graphics and Image Processing **13** (1980) 279-297

Kanade, T. (*1981*) Recovery of the Three-Dimensional Shape of an Object from a Single View. Artificial Intelligence **17**, 409-460

Klinger, A., *Bassett*, E., *Fox*, W. (*1984*) Models and Primitives from Point Nets. Proc. Intelligent Robots and Computer Vision, Cambridge/MA, November 5-8, 1984, SPIE **521**, pp. 176-183

Koenderink, J., *Van Doorn*, A. (*1982*) The Shape of Smooth Objects and the Way Contours End. Perception **11**, 129-137

Korn, A., *Erdtel*, C. (1985) Kombination verschiedener Filterkanäle zur Optimierung einer Merkmalsrepräsentation im Bildbereich. 7. DAGM-Symposium Mustererkennung, Erlangen, 24.-26.9.1985. Informatik-Fachberichte (im Druck). Berlin-Heidelberg-New York-Tokyo: Springer-Verlag 1985

Krause, P.-B., *Freytag*, R., *Hättich*, W. (*1985*) Modellgesteuerte Bildanalyse zur Erkennung und Positionsvermessung übereinanderliegender Werkstücke. Robotersysteme **1** (im Druck)

Laethem, D. Van, *Bogaert*, M., *Ledoux*, O. (*1984*) A Realistic Approach to Bin Picking. Proc. Intelligent Robots and Computer Vision, Cambridge/MA, November 5-8, 1984, SPIE **521**, pp. 98-107

Lee, Y.T., *Pennington*, A. De, *Shaw*, N.K. (*1984*) Automatic Finite-Element Mesh Generation from Geometric Models - A Point-Based Approach. ACM Transactions on Graphics **3**, 287-311

Lehmann, E. (*1984*) Expertensysteme - Überblick über den aktuellen Entwicklungsstand (1983). Siemens AG, Zentralbereich Technik, ZTI INF 131, München

Lehmann, E., *Enders*, R., *Haugeneder*, H., *Hunze*, R., *Johnson*, C., *Schmid*, L., *Struß*, P. (*1985*) SICONFEX - ein Expertensystem für die Konfigurierung eines Betriebssystems. 15. GI-Jahrestagung 1985, Informatik-Fachberichte (im Druck); Berlin Heidelberg New York: Springer-Verlag 1985

Levine, M.D. (*1985*) Vision in Man and Machine. New York etc.: McGraw-Hill Book Company 1985

Levitt, T.S. (*1984*) Domain Independent Object Description and Decomposition. Proc. National Conference on Artificial Intelligence, pp. 207-211, Austin/TX, August 6-10, 1984

Lin, W.C., *Fu*, K.-S. (*1984*) A Syntactic Approach to 3-D Object Representation. IEEE Trans. Pattern Analysis and Machine Intelligence **PAMI-6**, 351-364

Lowe, D.G., *Binford*, T.O. (*1985*) The Recovery of Three-Dimensional Structure from Image Curves. IEEE Trans. Pattern Analysis and Machine Intelligence **PAMI-7**, 320-326

Marimont, D.H. (*1984*) A Representation for Image Curves. Proc. National Conference on Artificial Intelligence, pp. 237-242, Austin/TX, August 6-10, 1984

Marr, D. (*1982*) Vision - a Computational Investigation into the Human Representation and Processing of Visual Information. San Francisco/CA: W.H. Freeman and Co. 1982

Massone, L., *Morasso*, P., *Zaccaria*, R. (*1984*) Shape from Occluding Contours. Proc. Intelligent Robots and Computer Vision, Cambridge/MA, November 5-8, 1984, SPIE **521**, pp. 114-120

Matsuyama, T. (*1984*) Knowledge Organization and Control Structure in Image Understanding. Proc. International Conference on Pattern Recognition, Montrèal / Quebec, July 30-August 2, 1984, pp. 1118-1127

Matsuyama, T., *Arita*, H., *Nagao*, M. (*1984*) Structural Matching of Line Drawings Using the Geometric Relationship between Line Segments. Computer Vision, Graphics, and Image Processing **27**, 177-194

McCalla, G., *Cercone*, N. (*1983*) Guest Editors' Introduction: Approaches to Knowledge Representation. IEEE Computer **16**, No. 10 (October 1983) 12-18

McKeown, D.M., Jr. (*1984*) Knowledge-Based Aerial Photo Interpretation. Photogrammetria

39, 91-123

Medioni, G., *Nevatia*, R. (*1984*) Matching Images Using Linear Features. IEEE Trans. Pattern Analysis and Machine Intelligence **PAMI-6**, 675-685

Mostow, J. (*1985*) Workshop on Principles of Knowledge-Based Systems: A Personal Review. ACM SIGART Newsletter No. 92 (April 1985) 15-27

Nackman, L.R. (*1984*) Two-Dimensional Critical Point Configuration Graphs. IEEE Trans. Pattern Analysis and Machine Intelligence **PAMI-6**, 442-450

Nagel, H.-H. (*1979*) Über die Repräsentation von Wissen zur Auswertung von Bildern. In "Angewandte Szenenanalyse", J.P. Foith (Hrsg.), Informatik-Fachberichte **20**, pp. 3-21. Berlin-Heidelberg-New York: Springer-Verlag 1979

Nagel, H.-H. (*1983*) Displacement Vectors Derived from Second Order Intensity Variations in Image Sequences. Computer Vision, Graphics, and Image Processing **21**, 85-117

Nagel, H.-H. (*1985a*) Principles of (Low-Level) Computer Vision. In "Fundamentals in Computer Understanding: Speech, Vision, and Natural Language", J.P. Haton (Hrsg.), Cambridge/UK: Cambridge University Press (im Druck)

Nagel, H.-H. (*1985b*) Analyse und Interpretation von Bildfolgen. Informatik Spektrum **8**, No. 4 (im Druck)

Nazif, A.M., *Levine*, M.D. (*1984*) Low Level Image Segmentation: An Expert System. IEEE Trans. Pattern Analysis and Machine Intelligence **PAMI-6**, 555-577

Niemann, H. (*1981*) Pattern Analysis. Berlin Heidelberg New York: Springer-Verlag 1981

Niemann, H., *Bunke*, H., *Hofmann*, I., *Sagerer*, G. (*1984*) Diagnostic Inferences from Image Sequences - A Knowledge Based Approach. Proc. First Conference on Artificial Intelligence Applications, pp. 610-616; Denver/Colorado, December 1984

Niemann, H., *Bunke*, H., *Hofmann*, I., *Sagerer*, G., *Wolf*, F., *Feistel*, H. (*1985*) A Knowledge Based System for Analysis of Gated Blood Pool Studies. IEEE Trans. Pattern Analysis and Machine Intelligence **PAMI-7**, 246-259

Pavlidis, T. (*1977*) Structural Pattern Recognition. Berlin-Heidelberg-New York: Springer-Verlag 1977

Pentland, A.P. (*1984a*) Local Shading Analysis. IEEE Trans. Pattern Analysis and Machine Intelligence **PAMI-6**, 170-187

Pentland, A.P. (*1984b*) Fractal-Based Description of Natural Scenes. IEEE Trans. Pattern Analysis and Machine Intelligence **PAMI-6**, 661-674

Pentland, A.P. (*1984c*) Shading into Texture. National Conference on Artificial Intelligence, Austin/TX, August 6-10, 1984, pp. 269-273

Perkins, W.A. (*1978*) A Model-Based Vision System for Industrial Parts. IEEE Trans. Computers **C-27**, 126-143

Perkins, W.A. (*1983*) INSPECTOR: A Computer Vision System that Learns to Inspect Parts. IEEE Trans. Pattern Analysis and Machine Intelligence **PAMI-5**, 584-592

Pickett, E.E., *Jha*, R. (*1984*) Task Planning and Verification Using Visual Feedback. Proc. Intelligent Robots and Computer Vision, Cambridge/MA, November 5-8, 1984, SPIE **521**, pp. 228-234

Pong, T.-C., *Shapiro*, L.G., *Watson*, L.T., *Haralick*, R.M. (*1984a*) Experiments in Segmentation Using a Facet Model Region Grower. Computer Vision, Graphics, and Image Processing **25**, 1-23

Pong, T.-C., *Haralick*, R.M., *Shapiro*, L.G. (*1984b*) The Facet Approach to Shape from Shading. Proc. IEEE Workshop on Computer Vision: Representation and Control, pp. 143-149; Annapolis/MD, April 30-May 2, 1984

Radig, B. (*1983*) 2D- und 3D-Objektbeschreibung für Sichtsysteme. 5. DAGM-Symposium Mustererkennung 1983, Karlsruhe, 11.-13. Oktober 1983, H. Kazmierczak (Hrsg.), VDE-Fachberichte **35**, pp. 300-318, Berlin-Offenbach: VDE-Verlag GmbH 1983.

Radig, B., *Schlieder*, Ch. (*1984*) Symbolische Symmetrieanalyse. In "Mustererkennung 1984" DAGM/ÖAGM Symposium 1984, W. Kropatsch (Hrsg.), pp. 283-289. Berlin-Heidelberg-New York-Tokyo: Springer-Verlag 1984

Ranzinger, H. (*1984*) Organisation von Wissen zur Fortführung von Karten mittels kenntnisgestützter Bildanalyse. In "Mustererkennung 1984" DAGM/ÖAGM Symposium 1984, W. Kropatsch (Hrsg.), pp. 270-275. Berlin-Heidelberg-New York-Tokyo: Springer-Verlag 1984

Rembold, U., *Levi*, P. (*1985*) Entwicklungstendenzen bei Expertensystemen für Roboter. In "transmatic 85 Kongreß: Neue Technologien im Materialfluß und in der Fördertechnik (12.-14. April 1985)", E. Bahke (Hrsg.), pp.125-140. Schriftenreihe des Institutes für Fördertechnik der Universität Karlsruhe, Heft 8

Requicha, A.A.G. (*1980*) Representations for Rigid Solids: Theory, Methods, and Systems.

Computing Surveys **12**, 437-464
*Richards, W., Hoffman, D.D. (**1984**)* Codon Constraints on Closed 2D Shapes. A.I. Memo 769
(May 1984); Artificial Intelligence Laboratory, Massachusetts Institute of
Technology, Cambridge/MA
*Rouse, W.B. (**1985**)* On Better Mousetraps and Basic Research: Getting the Applied World to
the Laboratory Door. IEEE Trans. Systems, Man, and Cybernetics **SMC-15**, 2-8
*Rummel, P. (**1984**)* A Model-Based Visual Sensor System for Complex Industrial Scenes.
Siemens Forschungs- und Entwicklungsberichte **13**, 151-154
*Shafer, S.A., Kanade, T. (**1983a**)* Using Shadows in Finding Surface Orientations. Computer
Vision, Graphics, and Image Processing **22**, 145-176
*Shafer, S.A., Kanade, T. (**1983b**)* The Theory of Straight Homogeneous Generalized
Cylinders. Proc. Image Understanding Workshop, pp. 210-218; L.S. Baumann (ed.),
Arlington/VA, June 23, 1983. McLean/VA: Science Applications, Inc., 1983
*Shapira, R. (**1984**)* The Use of Objects' Faces in Interpreting Line Drawings. IEEE Trans.
Pattern Analysis and Machine Intelligence **PAMI-6**, 789-794
*Shapira, R. (**1985**)* More about Polyhedra - Interpretation Through Constructions in the
Image Plane. IEEE Trans. Pattern Analysis and Machine Intelligence **PAMI-7**, 1-16
*Shipman, A.L., Bitmead, R.R., Allen, G.H. (**1984**)* Diffuse Edge Fitting and Following:
A Location-Adaptive Approach. IEEE Trans. Pattern Analysis and Machine
Intelligence **PAMI-6**, 96-102
*Silberberg, T.M., Harwood, D., Davis, L.S. (**1984**)* Object Recognition Using Oriented Model
Points. Proc. First Conference on Artificial Intelligence Applications, pp. 645-651;
Denver/Colorado, December 1984
*Stein, G., Tropf, H., Walter, I. (**1985**)* Interpretation of Industrial Scenes Using Augmented
Transition Networks and Production Systems: Procedural vs. Declarative Models.
Proc. Pattern Recognition in Practice II. Amsterdam, June 19-21, 1985 (im Druck)
*Tejwani, Y.J., Jones, R.A. (**1985**)* Machine Recognition of Partial Shapes Using Feature
Vectors. IEEE Trans. Systems, Man, and Cybernetics **SMC-15**, 504-516
*Tomita, F., Kanade, T. (**1984**)* A 3D Vision System: Generating and Matching Shape Descrip-
tions in Range Images. Proc. First Conference on Artificial Intelligence Applications,
pp. 186-191; Denver/Colorado, December 1984
*Tropf, H., Walter, I., Kammerer, H.-P. (**1984**)* Erweiterte Übergangsnetze (Augmented
Transition Networks) als prozedurale Modelle im Bereich der Bildanalyse. In
"Mustererkennung 1984" DAGM/ÖAGM Symposium 1984, W. Kropatsch (Hrsg.),
pp. 290-296. Berlin-Heidelberg-New York-Tokyo: Springer-Verlag 1984
*Tsai, W.-H., Yu, S.-S. (**1985**)* Attributed String Matching with Merging for Shape Recognition.
IEEE Trans. Pattern Analysis and Machine Intelligence **PAMI-7**, 453-462
*Walter, I., Tropf, H. (**1983**)* 3-D Recognition of Randomly Oriented Parts. Proc. International
Conference on Robot Vision and Sensory Control RoViSeC-83, Cambridge/MA,
November 1983, SPIE 449, pp. 171-178
*Weber, J. (**1984**)* Bestimmung der Greifpunkte für den Entlade-Roboter bei ungeordnet in
der Kiste liegenden zylindrischen Werkstücken. In "Mustererkennung 1984"
DAGM/ÖAGM Symposium 1984, W. Kropatsch (Hrsg.), pp. 212-221. Berlin-
Heidelberg-New York-Tokyo: Springer-Verlag 1984
*Winkler, G. (**1983**)* Erkennung industrieller Bilder mit Modellen. In "Fortschritte durch
digitale Meß- und Automatisierungstechnik", M. Syrbe und M. Thoma (Hrsg.);
Fachberichte Messen-Steuern-Regeln 10, pp. 90-99. Berlin Heidelberg New York
Tokyo: Springer-Verlag 1983
*Winkler, G. (**1984**)* Konzept für ein Visuelles Interpretationssystem für Technische Anwen-
dungen (VISTA). FhG-Berichte **2-84**, 4-7
*Winkler, G. (**1985**)* Industrielle Anwendung der digitalen Bildauswertung. Informatik
Spektrum **8**, No. 4 (im Druck)
*Yachida, M., Tsuji, S. (**1975**)* A Machine Vision for Complex Industrial Parts with Learning
Capability. Proc. Int. Joint Conference on Artificial Intelligence, Tbilisi/Georgia,
USSR, September 3-8, 1975, pp. 819-826; siehe auch IEEE Trans. Computers **C-26**,
882-894
*Zucker, S.W., Rosenfeld, A., Davis, L.S. (**1975**)* General Purpose Models: Expectations about
the Unexpected. Proc. Int. Joint Conference on Artificial Intelligence,
Tbilisi/Georgia, USSR, September 3-8, 1975, pp. 716-721

LOGIC DATABASES

Jean-Marie NICOLAS

ECRC, Munich, West Germany

Abstract:

This paper gives an introductory presentation of logic (or deductive) DBMS (Data Base Management Systems) according to three different perspectives: a functional perspective which emphasizes the new functionalities offered by such systems compared to conventional DBMS; a theoretical perspective which provides us with a logic based formal definition of deductive databases; and an implementational perspective where the various ways such systems can be implemented are briefly sketched.

1. Introduction

The field of "Logic and Databases" (GM, GMN) where databases are studied through the logic formalism is, today, the object of an increasing research effort. This is because it has now become clearer that logic can, not only be used as a framework to study database issues from a purely theoretical viewpoint, but also as a basis for the development of more powerful, and hopefully efficient, Database (management) systems. This paper gives a brief presentation of such systems which, in the literature, are quite often indifferently referred to as logic or deductive or intelligent Database systems. They are presented according to three different perspectives. Section 2 introduces them from a functional perspective pointing out in which way they extend conventional DBMS facilities. Section 3 is concerned with the theoretical viewpoint and provides us with a logic based formal definition of deductive Databases. Finally, section 4 considers the implementation aspects, and various ways such systems can be implemented are briefly sketched.

2. The Functional Perspective

A DBMS permits us to manage, i.e. to represent, manipulate and control, a set of information. Whereas a conventional system is mainly concerned with elementary information, namely facts (e.g. tuples of elements in a relational system), a deductive system will permit the handling of more general knowledge such as integrity constraints, derivation rules or generation rules. Such general knowledge can be used as meta-information (meta-facts) to improve and elaborate on fact manipulation, thus leading to systems where the database user still manipulates facts but which offer extended functionality (fact derivation, fact generation) and/or an automation of some pre-existing functionality (e.g. ad hoc programmes for integrity checking are replaced by an automatic checking based on an assertional expression of integrity constraints). Going further leads to systems which enable the user to manipulate (i.e. update, query, infer, ...) general knowledge per se. In order to make the above mentioned differences more precise, let us focus a little more on each kind of system.

2.1. Conventional (relational) DBMS

● Information Representation

In such a system information is represented at (at least) two levels. It is presented at the conceptual level in an appropriate formalism (e.g. the relational model). At this level one distinguishes the description of the information structure (e.g. relation names, attribute names, ...) which constitutes a so-called Database schema, from the set of information itself, modelled according to this structure (e.g. tuples in relations), which constitutes a (schema) instance. At the physical level (internal model) information is represented in terms of files, records and of their associated access techniques.

● Information Manipulation

Strictly speaking, only "elementary" manipulations are handled by the DBMS: namely addition, deletion, updating of facts and database querying. Queries permit the selection of information satisfying some given conditions and are expressed in an algebraic or predicate calculus based query language. More "complex" treatments are handled (outside of the DBMS) by ad hoc application programmes written in a (programming) language which constitutes a host language for the database query language (e.g. a hiring procedure).

● Information Control

In the DBMS's commercially available today (even relational ones), integrity control of information is kept out of the DBMS and ensured by adequate application programmes. As a matter of fact, one may notice that, in such systems, most of the semantics of the information of which the DBMS is in charge, resides in the application programmes and is not known by the DBMS; in this case the DBMS can certainly not ensure "by itself" any control on the information.

2.2. Logic/deductive/intelligent DBMS

The schema of such a DBMS further comprises general knowledge which expresses the semantics of information contained in the Database. This knowledge is (can be) exploited in various ways: as integrity constraints to automatically enforce fact consistency, as derivation rules for obtaining deduced facts as answer to queries, as generation rules to generate and make explicit deduced facts when database updates are carried out. Since such a system "knows" (by means of the general knowledge) the semantics of the information it is in charge of, it can automatically check for the integrity of facts and it is able to handle (through its deductive mechanism) complex treatments which in a conventional system would require the DML host programming language (thus requiring the user to be able to program).

The above mentioned functionalities rely on the utilization of general knowledge as "meta-information" to elaborate on fact manipulation: integrity constraints are used for _fact_ integrity checking, deduction rules for _fact_ deduction and queries get a set of _facts_ as answers. Facts are inferred through rules but rules are not inferred from other rules, e.g. from the two rules "cats are mammals" and "mammals are animals", new facts on "animals" will be inferred from known facts on "cats", while never explicitly inferring the rule "cats are animals". General knowledge can be further exploited so as to obtain systems which permit:

- modelling structured (complex) objects by providing structuring features in the conceptual model such as classification (which represents member/type relationships), aggregation (which represents property/type relationships) and generalization (which represents subtype/supertype relationships) (BMS). This gives a more natural representation of the world to be modelled than the flat relational model.

- operating on the schema; namely updating knowledge dynamically, checking whether a set of rules obeys some property (e.g. consistency, redundancy), retrieving rules which present some given characteristics (e.g. those rules which relate to given relations), answering queries with respect to the facts as well as with respect to the general knowledge (which implies a different semantics of answers to queries).

- providing more informative answers to queries, thus leading to answers which do not consist merely of sets of facts but also of more general statements. As an example, given the query "Who passed the exam on course CS203 this year?", the answer "Nobody, since this course was not held this year" is certainly more informative than merely an empty set of student names. As another example, answering the query "Who earns more than a given amount?" by "All those employees with an higher position than, say, group leaders" is also more informative than a list of individuals.

- manipulating meta-knowledge for improving knowledge management (e.g. such meta-knowledge may tell the system how to exploit some knowledge: as an integrity constraint or as a deduction rule; how to restore integrity when a particular constraint is violated).

- handling incomplete information such as unknown values (e.g. "John has a brother, but his name is unknown") or disjunctive information (e.g. "Felix is either black or white").

- automatically maintaining deduced information (e.g. telling the user what "basic" information he has to delete when he wants the deletion of a deduced fact to be effective).

- specifying the transactions on the database in an assertional way whilst guaranteeing integrity preservation when they are carried out.

- optimizing query evaluation on semantics ground by transforming the input query into a (semantically) equivalent one (according to the general knowledge) which is less costly to evaluate. As an example, the input query "Who are the professors who teach more than 6 hours per week?" can be reduced to "Who are the assistant professors?" if one can deduce from the general knowledge that only the assistant professors are teaching more than 6 hours per week.

Let us conclude this section with a few words on the applications which will take full advantage of the facilities offered by such systems. These are applications whose domain semantics is rather rich (i.e., where the relationships between objects, the structure of objects and the rules are not too simple), whose schema evolves a lot during the application life-time (i.e., where relationships, objects, classes of objects are often inserted, deleted or updated), and which involve a rather large set of information (i.e., more than the few hundred or so facts that Expert systems usually have to deal with). Examples of such application environments are information systems, personal databases or databases to support engineering design.

3. The Theoretical Perspective

An enumeration of the functionalities that a system should offer provides us with a certain characterization of this system but does not constitute a definition. Yet, if one wants to develop homogeneous and sound deductive DBMS a precise formal definition of a deductive Database should be given so that one has a proper understanding of what is a query, an answer to a query, an integrity constraint, a deduction rule.... . Such a definition has been obtained through a formalization of (deductive) Databases in mathematical logic which has proved to be quite useful in solving some important database issues. We just give below an intuitive idea of this definition. The interested reader is referred to (GMN, M) for more details.

There are two ways to look at a database from the viewpoint of logic. One way consists in considering a database, i.e. a set of facts, as an interpretation (of a first-order theory) and corresponds to the now so-called model theoretic approach. In this approach queries and integrity constraints are formulas which have to be evaluated on the interpretation using the semantic definition of truth. This view has been (and is being) used, either implicitly or explicitly, for studying various database aspects such as query formulation and optimization, integrity constraint formulation and enforcement, dependency formulation and derivation.

Whilst the model theoretic approach yields a quite natural formalization of conventional Databases, the second way to look at a database from the logic perspective provides us with a formal definition of both conventional and deductive databases. According to this second approach, termed the proof theoretic approach, a deductive database is defined as a particular first-order theory T (i.e. a set of axioms) associated with a set of closed logical formulas (the integrity constraints). The axioms in T are of three kinds:

1. the particularization axioms which explicitly state the usual database query evaluation assumptions:

    - The **domain closure axiom,** which states that there are no other individuals of interest than those in the database.

    - The **unique name axioms,** which state that individuals with different names are different.

    - The **completion axioms,** which state that facts not known to be true are assumed to be false.

    - The **equality axioms**, which are needed since the preceding axioms involve the equality predicate.

2. the assertions which are ground positive literals corresponding to the facts in the database.

3. the deduction rules which consist in a set of function free definite clauses.

According to this definition, the answer to a query expressed as a logical formula $W(x1, ..., xp)$ consists of those p-tuples of individuals in the database $\langle e1, ..., ep \rangle$ such that $W(e1, ..., ep)$ is derivable from T, and an integrity constraint is satisfied if it is derivable from T. Let us note that whenever the set of axioms of the third kind is empty, the deductive database reduces to a conventional database.

Clearly, due in particular to the combinatorial complexity of the particularization axioms, it would be quite inefficient to implement a deductive DBMS while sticking to the above definition; namely as a standard theorem prover which treats all the axioms of the theory T in the same way. A first step towards a more realistic implementation consists in substituting adequate meta-rules (or meta-convention) for the particularization axioms. Calling for the domain closure axiom may be avoided by dealing with range-restricted (domain independent) formulas for query, integrity constraints and deduction rule formulation. Further, the unique name and completion axioms may be removed provided that negation is interpreted as (finite) failure. Finally, since the equality axioms were needed only for the presence of the equality predicate in the above axioms, they are no longer required. A next step towards an efficient implementation of a deductive DBMS consists then in treating the axioms corresponding to deduction rules differently from those corresponding to facts. But implementation aspects are addressed in the following section.

4. The Implementational Perspective

It should now be clear that the two main components of a deductive DBMS are an inference system and,we could say, a conventional Database component. Given that both inference systems (e.g. PROLOG) and conventional DBMS (e.g. ORACLE, INGRES, ...)are available, there are three basic possibilities to built a deductive DBMS without starting from scratch: extending an inference system into a fully fledged DBMS; developing a specific deductive component on top of a conventional DBMS; coupling an inference system and a conventional DBMS. These three possibilities lead to systems aimed at different kinds of applications and/or different kinds of users and thus constitute complementary approaches rather than competing ones. They are briefly described below.

4.1. PROLOG extensions

In the same way that a COBOL program manipulating several datafiles does not constitute a (conventional) DBMS, a PROLOG program which permits a deductive manipulation of a few facts does not constitute a deductive DBMS. To achieve such a system, PROLOG should at least be extended to allow: definition and manipulation of a conceptual schema, expression and enforcement of integrity constraints, efficient access to a large set of facts.

Of course, the language permits the representation of information/knowledge as clauses or terms but it offers no organizational principles for information/knowledge structuring. Such a deficiency (from a knowledge representation point of view) can be overcome by introducing in the language standard structuring features, much as classification (or typing), aggregation - which permits the association of an object to its components or parts - or generalization (also called IS-A hierarchy) which relates a type to more generic ones. Several authors have argued convincingly (e.g. Reiter) that such structuring features can be expressed, I would say simulated, in Logic and then in PROLOG. But it does not mean that they do not have to be provided as "primitive" concepts to a (PROLOG) user; thus avoiding the user having to redefine them in each particular case and each time they are needed. Besides the simplicity of expression, the introduction of these concepts (in terms of PROLOG clauses), once and for all, on top of PROLOG, should allow the tuning of their definition so that better performances can be obtained when handling them.

Another deficiency of PROLOG with respect to knowledge conceptual modelling, is that it does not permit the definition, representation and manipulation of a conceptual schema in the database sense, i.e. there is no way to define a "frame" according to which knowledge pertinent to a particular application shall be represented. The availability of such a schema leads to a better coherence of the information which has to be described while conforming to it. Furthermore, it provides the user with a meta-description of the information he can query and modify. A schema is particularly useful then when there are various kinds of information to be presented and manipulated, which is the case in DB/KB applications.

There is a third feature which is quite important for knowledge base applications: integrity enforcement. Information is rarely independent, it is in general correlated to other information through rules (integrity constraints) which have to be enforced in order to ensure information consistency; adequate mechanisms for that purpose are then needed.

The last point we would like to make concerns the internal (physical) representation of information. In standard PROLOG, facts (i.e. ground literals) are treated in the same way as more general clauses, and the performance of the system decreases drastically when the set of facts is rather important, as is the case in knowledge base applications; adequate organization of facts (in secondary memory) and their corresponding addressing schemas must therefore be provided.

Extensions of PROLOG along the above mentioned lines are presently presently investigated in various research laboratories and some prototypes are now available (e.g. see (WD, LT)).

4.2. DBMS extension

The idea here is to extend a conventional DBMS with a specific deductive component so that the resulting system can be accessed by a casual user (who is assumed to have no competency in programming and who must be offered simple means of interacting with a system) in a similar way as a conventional system. To make the user/system interaction as easy as possible, one must first provide him with simple languages for expressing derived relation definitions and manipulations. This is in fact not a problem since standard relational languages can also be used for these purposes. But one must also, and this is the main point, hide from the user any of the problems which are related to the introduction of a deductive process (i.e. termination of this process, efficiency of deduced fact handling...). This means that the system should tackle all these problems by itself and, for this to be possible, one is led to impose some restrictions on the derived relations that can be manipulated (e.g. their definition must not contain function symbols).

Key issues in this approach are that of finding a (sound and complete) halting condition for the deductive process in presence of recursive definitions of derived relations and that of providing an efficient interface between this process and the database search process. These problems are presently the object of an important research effort and satisfactory solutions are now not far from being reached (e.g. see (V, L)).

4.3. Coupling

There are of course various ways to envisage a coupling between an inference system and a DBMS. Respective advantages and drawbacks of tight or loose coupling are, for example, discussed in (JV). One way to achieve such a coupling between PROLOG and a DBMS consists in providing PROLOG as a host language for the query language of the DBMS. A host language for a database query language is a programming language (usually PL1, COBOL, PASCAL ...) which has been interfaced with a DBMS so that programs involving database queries can be written. When one considers PROLOG to be a host language for a first order predicate calculus query language on a DBMS, one can take advantage of the similarity between the two languages to obtain a tight coupling. Both languages manipulate the same kind of elements (Predicate/Relations), both are based on Logic.

Basically, such a coupling can be done at a Predicate/Relation level and consists of admitting in PROLOG clauses some particular kind of "evaluable predicates" which are in fact relations whose definition is given in terms of a relational query. One will note that in such a case the burden of handling recursive clauses is left to the PROLOG interpretor (which means that the termination problem is left to the programmer) and that the programmer is free to decide whether a particular operation between two relations has to be handled by the PROLOG interpretor or by the DBMS evaluator. As an example of this latter point, if R1 and R2 are two relations defined by a relational query and if the clause "p<-R1, R2, Q." appears in a PROLOG program, the "join" operation between R1 and R2 will be handled by the PROLOG interpretor. If the programmer wants it to be run by the DBMS evaluator he will have to define (by a relational query) a relation R as being the join of R1 and R2 and then to write the clause as P<-R, Q.

Assuming that operation between base relations (which support a lot of facts) are better handled by the DBMS, one may try to improve the coupling by automatizing the preceding transformation.

This amounts to pre-processing the PROLOG program in order to determine those relations/predicates which are purely defined (directly or indirectly) in terms of base relations and then both to generate the adequate relational queries and modify the PROLOG clause appropriately. One should note that in such a case when recursive clauses occur in the definition of these relations, one is faced with the same problems as those mentioned in 4.2. For examples of such couplings the reader is referred to (B,OS).

5. Conclusion

An introductory presentation to Logic/deductive/intelligent DBMS has been given from three different perspectives. A functional perspective which has permitted us to point out the new functionalities that are (will be) offered by such systems. A theoretical perspective which shows that they rely on sound formal bases. An implementational perspective showing that following different implementation approaches one can achieve different types of deductive DBMS aiming at different kinds of applications and/or users.

I. References

(B)   J. Bocca "EDUCE - Design and Implementation", ECRC KB internal report No. 3, June 1985

(BMS)   M. Brodie, J. Mylopoulos and J.W. Schmidt (eds.) "On Conceptual modelling", Springer Verlag, New York, 1984

(GM)   H. Gallaire and J. Minker (eds.) "Logic and Databases", Plenum Publishing Corporation, New York, 1978

(GMN)   H. Gallaire, J. Minker and J.-M. Nicolas "Logic and Databases: a deductive approach", ACM-Computing Surveys, Vol. 16, No. 2, June 1984

(GN)   H. Gallaire and J.-M. Nicolas "How to look at deductive Databases", Proceedings, Workshop on Knowledge Base Management Systems, Xania, June 1985

(JV)   M. Jarke and Y. Vassiliou "Coupling Expert Systems with DBMS", AI application for business, ABLEX, January 1984

(L)   E.L. Lozinskii "Inference by generating and structuring Deductive Databases", Technical Report, Hebrew University of Jerusalem, June 1984

(LT)   J.W. Lloyd and R.W. Topor " A basis for Deductive Database systems", TR 85/01 University of Melbourne, April 1985

(M)   J.A. Makowsky "Model theoretical issues in theoretical computer science. Part 1: relational Databases and abstract data types", Logic Colloquium '82, North Holland, 1984

(NY)   J.-M. Nicolas and K. Yazdanian "An outline of BDGEN: a deductive DBMS", Proceedings, IFIP '83 Conference, North Holland, 1983

(OS)   I.P. Orci and D. Sahlin "Two-mode evaluation for dealing with implicit interactions between logic programs and relational Data bases", Proceedings, Workshop on KBMS, Xania, June 1985

(R)   R. Reiter "Towards a logical reconstruction of relational database theory", in (BMS)

(V)   L. Vieille "Recursive Axioms in Deductive Databases: various solutions", ECRC Technical Report No. 6, May 1985

(WD)   M. Wallace and H. Decker "PROLOG-KB prototype", ECRC Technical Report Nos. 2 and 3, February 1985

Table of Contents

1. Introduction
2. The Functional Perspective
    2.1. Conventional (relational) DBMS
    2.2. Logic/deductive/intelligent DBMS
3. The Theoretical Perspective
4. The Implementational Perspective
    4.1. PROLOG extensions
    4.2. DBMS extension
    4.3. Coupling
5. Conclusion
1. References

Interactive deductive data management -
the Smart Data Interaction package

E. S. Biagioni, K. Hinrichs, C. Muller and J. Nievergelt
ETH Zürich

Abstract

What function does a general-purpose interactive data manipulation package need to provide, and how complex does it have to be? The development of data base software has given no definitive answer to this question. The commercial packages developed during the first two decades of data base technology kept growing in size and typically require medium sized or large computers, but in recent years the proliferation of personal computers has spawned a generation of data manipulation packages that fit into half a Megabyte of memory and operate off floppy disks.

What does the sophisticated user of a data base package that runs on a personal computer really want?
- data storage that permits efficient access
- a smart query language that provides some deductive abilities and hides details of access
- effective human-computer interaction
- an escape hatch that gives him access to the system in order to handle special requirements not supported by the package.

We describe the Smart Data Interaction package designed to meet these requirements. It is based on four software building blocks that combine to provide a powerful system of modest complexity. They are:
- the Grid File data structure to provide multi-key access
- Prolog as a deductive query and manipulation package
- the Easy human-computer interface
- Modula-2 as a modern programming language that serves as implementation language for these packages, and as a language in which to write procedures that interface with the packages.

Each of the building blocks can be used alone or in various combinations. Therefore we paid particular attention to the design of the interfaces that guarantee their compatibility and the portability to other hosts (hardware and operating system). Prototype implementations on several systems, and their use in a variety of applications, have given us the experience necessary to evaluate the design.

Current address of authors:
E. S. Biagioni, K. Hinrichs, J. Nievergelt:
  Dept. Computer Science, University of North Carolina, Chapel Hill, NC 27514, USA
C. Muller: Brown Boveri Research, CH-5405 Baden, Switzerland

Contents

1 Data storage, manipulation, and interaction
2 Software building blocks
2.1 Grid file
2.2 Prolog
2.3 Easy
3 Interplay of building blocks
4 Software engineering aspects
5 Implementation, statistics, experience

1 Data storage, manipulation, and interaction

Data base technology has developed over the past two decades in response to the needs of commercial data processing. The key concepts introduced and supported by data base software mirror the reality that used to be handled manually by office clerks: Large quantities of records of a few different types, identified by a small number of attributes, mostly retrieved in response to relatively simple queries: point queries that ask for the presence or absence of one particular record, interval or range queries that ask for all records whose attribute values lie within given lower and upper bounds. More complex queries tend to be reduced to these basic types. Conventional data base technology was successful in abstracting the logical view of the data presented to the user from the physical implementation aspects that only the implementor needs to know. The user's model emphasizes *relationships among data items* rather than their intrinsic properties and their representation, and the abstraction of *access path* is introduced to hide detailed access algorithms of underlying data structures.

In recent years this picture has been changing, in response to a rapidly growing spectrum of new demands on data bases. "Non-standard data" is the catch-all phrase to denote these new applications that strain conventional data base technology: *unformatted data* in office-automation and telecommunications applications, *pictorial and geometric objects* in computer graphics and computer-aided design. The problem is not that the data to be stored requires variable-sized and variably-formatted records, but rather that the complex semantics of "non-standard" data entails entirely different access characteristics than the traditional applications of data bases. Consider the following three examples.

1) A data base system for CAD must manage "in designer real time" large collections of spatial objects in such a way that proximity queries (such as intersection, contact, minimal tolerances) are answered efficiently. In the conventional data base approach, access to these objects might be via a parts list that contains all components of a machine, and the nature of the object is not used for access. In a CAD environment, on the other hand, there are two major differences. 1) Access to the data is usually triggered by geometric queries such as *show me all the parts that get in the way*, which is answered by computation rather than by look-up. An efficient answer to this question requires that 3-dimensional space is organized, rather than the logical relatiopnship among the parts. 2) The size and shape of an object is obviously important for access in response to a geometric query such as intersection. There are many techniques for reducing the hard problem of storing spatial objects to storing (sets of) points. Common to all of them is the problem that simply formulated queries on objects turn into complex queries on points - much more complex than orthogonal range queries.

2) In knowledge-based systems the answer to most queries is not explicitly stored in the data base, but must be deduced from stored facts by applying rules of inference. The implementation of data bases to efficiently support the backtracking necessary for deduction is an open problem: traditional concepts such as "access path", developed to provide alternative sequences of memory accesses to a single data item, are insufficient for discussing the intricate and unpredictable interleaving of repeated access to the same data items that occurs during the pattern matching necessary to determine whether an inference rule applies to stored facts.

3) Many new data base installations now occur in highly interactive applications, such as CAD, where the end-user navigates visually and unpredictably through the data, instead of limiting himself to relatively few standard query types. Browsing access is highly effective if the quality of the human-computer interface is high, in particular when it uses graphic displays to visualize information. In particular, effective browsing requires that the user can at all times conveniently obtain answers to system state inquiries of the type *where am I?* and *what can I do here?*

The explosion of new demands triggered by highly interactive applications to non-standard data has spawned a new phase of *experimentation* in data bases: Traditional *modeling issues,* such as comparative evaluation of hierarchic versus relational data models, are *dwarfed by question of efficiency* - many applications become infeasible if answers are not produced in real time.

In developing experimental prototypes it is particularly important to keep software modular - a drift towards large, monolithic programs has killed many an experiment. The art is to identify components that are separately well understood and relatively small, so that the complexity of the entire package resides in well-defined interfaces, and experimentation consists in adapting these interfaces in response to new demands and accumulated experience. In order to experiment with data base software suitable for interactive deductive data management we have developed, implemented and assembled three software components that form a useful combination:

- the grid file data structure
- a Prolog interpreter that interfaces to the programming language Modula-2
- the portable human-computer interface package Easy.

We have had extensive experience with the *grid file* [NHS 84, Hi 85a,b, NH 85] for managing spatial data and geometric computation, so this component required no additional work. The published literature reports a lot of experience concerning *Prolog* and its implementation, so our work here focused mainly on an implementation that interfaces smoothly to Modula-2 [Mu 85]. The *dialog front end Easy* [Bi 85] is built on the experience collected from two earlier prototype interactive systems XS-1 [Be 82] and XS-2 [St 84, BNSS 85], so the contribution here was primarily one of turning a sizable integrated system into a portable module.

This paper describes the main characteristics of each of these three software building blocks, the considerations that determined the choice of their interfaces, and how these components fit together.

2 Software building blocks

2.1 Grid file

The *grid file* is a data structure designed to handle large amounts of multidimensional point data on disk. It adapts its shape dynamically to its contents under insertions and deletions so as to guarantee retrieval of a single record in two disk accesses. All keys (attributes) are treated symmetrically: No primary key is favored at the expense of secondary keys, thus queries that involve different attributes are processed with equal efficiency. The grid file was designed to allow the evaluation of irregularly shaped query regions in such a way that the complexity of the region affects CPU time but *not disk accesses*. The performance of data base implementations is generally limited by the latter rather than the former.

The grid file partitions space into *raster cells* and assigns data buckets to cells. The partitioning information is kept in *scales*, one for each axis of space; the assignment is recorded in an array called *grid directory*. An element of this array is a pointer to a disk block, called a *data bucket*, which contains all data points that lie in the corresponding grid cell. To avoid low bucket occupancies, several grid cells may share a bucket. Such a set of grid cells is called a *bucket region*. Bucket regions are only allowed to have the shape of a k-dimensional rectangular box. These bucket regions are disjoint, together they span the data space.

During operation of the file system the scales and the grid directory are modified in response to insertions and deletions. An overflowing bucket is split as follows. If its bucket region covers only one grid cell the grid has to be extended by a (k-1)-dimensional hyperplane that cuts the bucket region into two. This is achieved by inserting a new boundary into one of the scales and maintaining the one-to-one correspondence between the grid defined by the scales and the grid directory, i. e. inserting a (k-1)-dimensional cross-section into the grid directory. Whether or not the bucket's region originally covered only one grid cell there now exists at least one hyperplane separating the bucket region into two. To each of these two regions a new bucket is attached by updating the grid directory, and the records stored in the overflowing bucket are distributed among the new buckets as shown in Fig. 1. Conversely, if the joint occupancy of two adjacent buckets drops below a certain threshold, they may be merged into one, as long as the new bucket region remains box-shaped. If the boundary along which the two buckets have been merged is no longer needed it is removed from its scale, and the one-to-one correspondence between the grid defined by the scales and the grid directory is maintained by removing the corresponding cross-section from the grid directory.

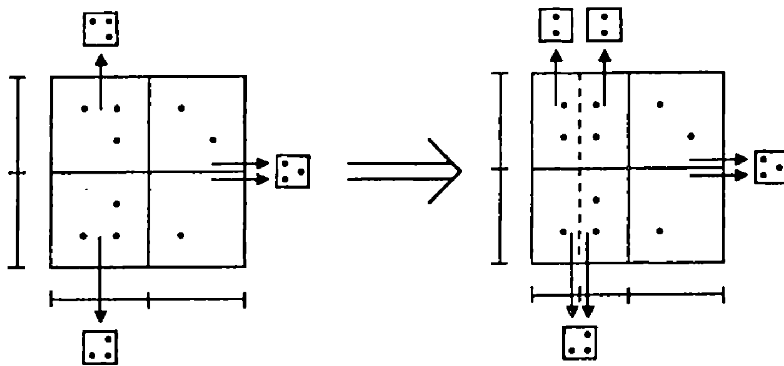

Fig. 1: Splitting a bucket refines the space partition.

The grid directory is likely to be large and must therefore be kept on disk, but the scales are small and can be kept in central memory. Thus the grid file realizes the *two-disk-access principle* for single point retrieval (exact match query): by searching the scales, the k coordinates of a data point are converted into interval indices without any disk accesses; these indices provide direct access to the correct element of the grid directory on disk, where the bucket address is located. In a second access the correct data bucket (i.e. the bucket that contains the data point to be searched for, if it exists) is read from disk.

The grid file performs proximity queries of arbitrary shape efficiently, as shown in Fig. 2. The query region Q is matched against the scales and converted into a set of index tuples that refer to entries in the directory. Only after this preprocessing do we access disk to retrieve the correct pages of the directory and the correct data buckets whose regions intersects Q.

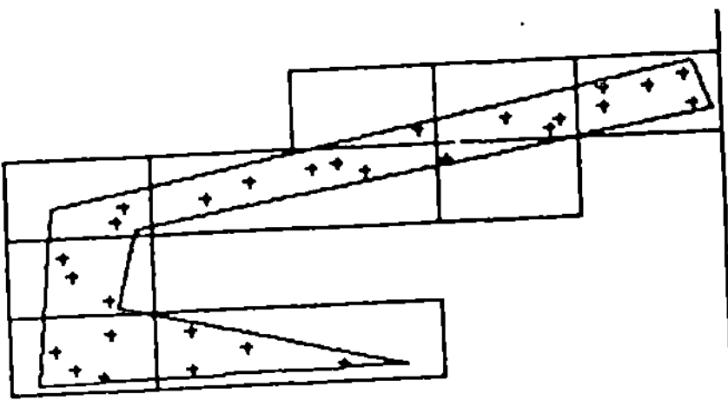

Fig. 2: Region query in a grid file.

In order to determine the *nearest neighbor* of a given data point the grid cells surrounding the data point are processed in order of increasing distance. This is done as long as there exist grid cells which could contain a point that is closer to the given data point than the nearest neighbor found so far. Whether a grid cell could contain such a data point can be determined with the aid of the scales without any disk accesses. If a grid cell could contain such a data point then the corresponding data bucket must be accessed and the points stored in it must be examined.

A *join query* is a generalization of the join operator known from relational data bases; it is performed on multiple grid files f_1, ..., f_n in parallel and retrieves tuples $(r_1, ..., r_n)$ of records which fulfill certain conditions. In a join query the Cartesian product of the grid files f_1, ..., f_n involved, i. e. the file of all tuples $(r_1, ..., r_n)$ of records $r_i \in f_i$, need not be computed explicitly. The scales of the grid files f_1, ..., f_n define a grid on the Cartesian product of the underlying data spaces. Those cells of this Cartesian product grid that could contain points representing tuples of records to be searched for can be determined with the aid of the scales of all grid files involved without any disk accesses. If such a grid cell could contain points representing tuples of records to be searched for then the corresponding data buckets must be accessed and all possible tuples of points stored in this tuple of data buckets must be computed and examined.

The grid file is implemented in Modula-2 as a portable data management package. Portability has been achieved by using the host interface described in 5 which isolates the machine-dependent part of the software. The interface towards client programs provides several utility and query procedures:

- creating, deleting, opening and closing a grid file;
- inserting and deleting records in a grid file;
- modifying non-key information in a record;
- point query: find all records with given key values $x_1, \dots, x_k$;
- range query: find all records whose key values x_i lie in given intervals $[l_i, u_i]$ $(1 \leq i \leq k)$;
- user defined region query: the user has to write a procedure which is called by the grid file system and determines whether a grid cell (given by intervals $[l_i, u_i)$ $(1 \leq i \leq k)$) intersects the search region defined by the user;
- nextabove, nextbelow: given key i with key value x_i, find the records with key values above or below x_i and next to x_i; this gives the user the possibility to process the records sequentially with respect to any key;
- join query: the user has to write some procedures which are called by the grid file system and guide the join query;
- counting: all queries can be performed by only counting the records, without retrieving them.

2.2 Prolog

Prolog has become so well known that we can limit ourselves to mentioning the special characteristics of our interpreter, *Modula-Prolog*. It is completely accessible to Modula-2 programs, with all details of the implementation hidden from the Modula-2 programmer. The basic Prolog functions, such as the parser, the prover, or the unification and backtracking algorithms are isolated and can be called separately as library procedures.

The programmer's interface of Modula-Prolog allows structured access to Prolog terms and in particular permits the construction and execution of Prolog queries by Modula-2 programmers. The same interface also allows access to Prolog variables, which contain the results of queries, and lets the Modula-2 program affect backtracking. The advanced interface of Modula-Prolog makes writing a simple, personalized Prolog interpreter a simple task, and also allows the implementation of more elaborate interpreters that can use several windows or accept input from a mouse or other graphic input devices. Last but not least, new built-in predicates can easily be defined in Modula-Prolog to implement functions that would be inefficient or impossible in Prolog, such as accessing system variables (the system clock or the file directory) and drawing graphic objects.

The details of the implementation are hidden from the programmer, i. e. a Prolog expression is represented by an equivalent hidden Modula-Prolog expression. The programmer's interface provides two sets of procedures for accessing Modula-Prolog expressions. The first allows the construction of an expression out of the basic components (atoms, functors, numbers, variables), the second is used to separate the basic components of an expression for further use in Modula-2. A Prolog query may be represented in a textual form, if desired, and converted to a hidden Modula-Prolog expression by the parser. The parser of course takes into account the precedences of user-defined and built-in operators. For symmetry, Modula-Prolog also provides an 'unparser' which accepts a Prolog structure as input and produces a sequence of characters which may be printed, output to the screen, stored on a file or otherwise used as required.

The communication with Modula-Prolog usually consists of the following three steps: a query expression is built by a call to the parser or explicitly using the construction procedures; this expression is given as an argument to the Prolog prover which tries to deduce a solution, and finally the results of the proof are passed to a user-supplied 'Answer Procedure' which can freely use the values of instantiated variables and tell the prover whether to look for another solution.

Modula-Prolog is upward compatible from the standard described in [CM 81], and is largely machine-independent, thanks to the fact that it uses only functions from a standard machine-interface-package to access system objects and to perform input/output.

2.3 Easy

User interfaces are mostly developed on a case-by-case basis, in that each application program has its own independent user interface, partly because of a lack of general-purpose and machine-independent user interfaces. Easy is a software package that can be used by application programs to simplify, standardize and improve their user interface. It is application- and machine-independent and provides support for many common types of input, generalized as commands and parameters, and for many common output requirements, such as screen refresh. Existing programs can be adapted to use Easy with little effort, since Easy implements most user interface requirements. New programs can best be designed with Easy as a user interface, thus relieving the implementor of this otherwise nontrivial task.

The user interfaces of even well-designed programs suffer from being different from each other, since each program has its own user interface, with commands that may be similar to those in other applications but invoked differently, with different parameters or defaults, and different side effects. Additionally, the user can 'get lost' if the state of the system is not continously visible or at least available to the user. Having the state of the system means being able at all times to answer the questions [Ni 82] "Where am I?" (what data can be accessed), "What can I do now?" (what commands are available) and "How did I get here?" (what were my last few actions?). This feature is not normally found in application programs that have their own user interface, partly because making the state of the system available at all times requires considerable design and implementation effort. With a user interface package such effort is worth while, whereas for any given application the effort required for implementation is often disproportionate to the benefit the end-users would incur.

What most applications require of a user interface is a mechanism for obtaining commands and data from the user and a mechanism for conveying information and feedback to the user. The difference between commands and parameters is more significant to the user than to the application program and could even be eliminated completely, as in XS-2 [St 84]. From the user's point of view the input mechanism must provide for the correction of incorrectly entered input and easy default selection, as well as offering guidance in providing parameters and shorthand notations for specifying complex sets of parameters; these considerations are irrelevant to the application, which simply needs to be given a command and its parameter values (data). As far as output goes, the application needs to be able to output to the screen and to write messages showing the state of the computation. Screen output as required by the application should be very simple for normal usage, but provide full power (window handling, graphics of different types, window-size dependent refresh etc.) if required. The user should be able to shift and change window sizes and to scroll or zoom within a window, all independent of the specific application.

In addition to input and output, a good user interface must present the user with the state of the system and allow its interactive modification. Since also the application can modify the state of the system, in particular the data and the available data sets (files, directories etc.), user and application access of the system state must be synchronized carefully: the application expects its data to remain unchanged while it is operating on it, the user must at all times have an up-to-date picture of the available data. One advantage of user access to the system state is that many commands (such as copy, delete data) can be implemented by the user interface instead of the application program, thus further simplifying the design and implementation of the latter. The advantage of these commands being in the common user interface package is that they are available no matter what application the user is working with.

The user and application requirements are orthogonal to one another and can therefore be implemented in a single package. Easy satisfies most of the requirements described above, even though it is only a prototype and could still be improved. The output functions in particular are still rather primitive, being limited to random-access as well as sequential alphanumeric output, plus refresh facilities. Integration of all the above features would only be a question of time, however, and the new features would easily fit into the existing software.

Easy is related to the interactive systems XS-1 [Be 82] and XS-2 [St 84, BNSS 85]. Like these systems, Easy divides the screen into several non-overlapping *windows*, one of which is reserved for exclusive use by the application. Also like XS-1 and XS-2, Easy displays the state of the system in the form of *trees*, and displays one tree in each *system window* (so-called to distinguish them from the *application window*). The *site tree*, in the *site window*, displays the data available to the user as well as to the application; this data corresponds to the data files and directories found in many operating systems. The site window is always visible to the user, but can be shrunk or enlarged any time if a larger application window is desired or if a larger display of the data environment is desired. A number of *universal commands* is defined on the site window: these commands are generally classified into *viewing* commands, which affect the status display, *selection* commands, which affect the data available to the application, and *editing* commands, used to actually change the application's data. The viewing commands include a help facility (which presents a different *view* of a selected node), the editing commands include backing up the entire tree onto disk and reloading it as well as simple copying and deleting of subtrees. The site window constantly reminds the user of *where* he is, i.e., of the current data environment.

All of the above applies to the *operation window* as well as to the site window. The only difference lies in the fact that the operation window displays the *commands* and *parameters* available to the user, rather than the *data*. Selecting a command executes it, selecting a parameter lets the user enter a new value for that parameter. The viewing and editing commands are the same as in the site window and have exactly the same effect. The operation window constantly reminds the user of *what* he may do, i.e., of the current command environment.

The *trail windows* display trees which record the selections of sites and operations. There is one trail window for sites and one for operations. The same commands defined on the other two windows are also available in the two trail windows The trail windows constantly reminds the user of *how* he reached the current state, by displaying the dialog history.

Typically, a user of an application with an Easy front end proceeds by selecting a site as a data environment (also known as *path* or *default directory* on many systems), then entering all the parameters for a given command before selecting the command itself. In general for different applications most of the action will be in either the site or the operation window, rather than in both; in any case, all universal commands are available on both windows at all times.

The application calls Easy whenever it is ready to accept a command, Easy returns control every time a command or a new data environment is selected. In-between, control rests with Easy, i.e. with the user. This arrangement insures that Easy and the application do not interfere with each other and helps keep the interface between the two as simple as possible. Control returns to the application whenever the user enters a command, so Easy always returns a record identifying the command entered by the user and the values of all the parameter that belong with that command, whether strings, numbers, options (menus) or site tree identifications (files). The application need not concern itself with how the parameters were entered, Easy does not concern itself with the actions appropriate to each command.

The interface between Easy and the application program is provided by the single module that most Modula-2 programs will use to call Easy. In addition to this module, Easy provides the application writer with two other basic (but still optional) functionalities, each defined in a different module:

- access to the trees that represent and store the system's data, where each node is available and may have any amount of data (up to hardware and compiler restrictions) and any number of descendants (subject to the same restrictions); these trees are the same that are displayed in the site window and may be manipulated by the user.

- facilities for output onto the application window. Only alphanumeric access (both scrolling and positioning, of course) is implemented, graphic output is defined but not implemented at this time.

The machine- and application-independent user interface Easy brings substantial advantages to both users and application programmers. The user is in full control of the data and command input, is able to refer to the system state at all times, and can at all times answer the critical questions Where, When, How. The application need not know about any of the user's specific actions, it obtains its inputs in a compact and well-structured form. The application can call the command interpreter whenever it is ready to execute a new command, even deep in a recursion. The machine-independence of Easy facilitates porting applications to machines other than the one on which they were developed and shows that a good user interface does not require elaborate hardware. The hardware requirements of Easy are limited to a video terminal or screen with character-positioning capability and a keyboard or pointing device capable of moving a cursor on this screen (arrow or function keys are satisfactory). A single module (in addition to the standard interface described below) needs to be implemented to provide the small set of input and output functions used by Easy, the remainder of the package is machine-independent.

3 Interplay of building blocks

The integration of the three building blocks Grid File, Prolog and Easy leads to the Smart Data Interaction package: Easy handles the dialog between a user and the Prolog interpreter, which in turn provides access to the Grid File System:

$$\text{Easy} \quad \longleftrightarrow \quad \text{Modula-Prolog} \quad \longleftrightarrow \quad \text{Grid File System}$$

The arrows correspond to small control programs which call the right procedures from the different interfaces at the right time. None of the three building blocks had to be adapted or changed for this integration.

User interaction with Easy-Prolog is substantially different from user interaction with a conventional Prolog interpreter - the user communicates in terms of structured objects, rather than strings. The site tree of Easy is available to the user for storing Prolog facts, rules and queries as subtrees, so that they can be edited using Easy's built-in tree editor. A database or a query stored as a subtree has the following structure:

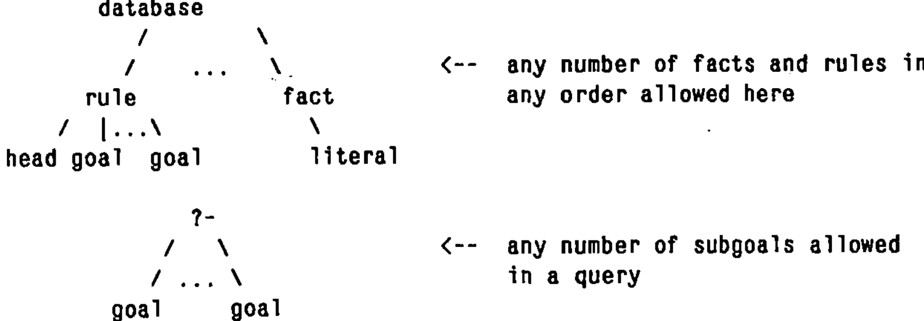

```
        database
        /       \
       /   ...   \.           <--  any number of facts and rules in
    rule           fact       any order allowed here
   / |...\           \
head goal  goal       literal


          ?-
         /  \                 <--  any number of subgoals allowed
        / ... \               in a query
     goal    goal
```

head, goal and literal are Prolog literals represented as trees. The following tree (indented) shows an extract of a Prolog database that contains facts of the form city(City,Country), followed by two queries over this database:

```
* Site Root
   database
     fact
       city
          zurich
          switzerland
     ...
     fact
       city
          rome
          italy
queries                        <-- structural nodes allowed anywhere
   ?-
     city
       City                    /* ?- city(Country,switzerland). */
       switzerland
   ?-
     city
       City
       Country
       write(City)             /* ?- city(City, Country), write(City),
       write(' in ')                write(' in '), write(Country), nl, fail. */
       write(Country)
       nl
       fail
```

Modula-Prolog itself does not directly access the tree: when the user indicates that a subtree should be used for a query or added to the database, Easy-Prolog parses it, builds a corresponding Prolog term and calls the appropriate procedure from Modula-Prolog. Having a Prolog database accessible in structured form, and being able to access queries *as data*, instead of having to type them in every time, represents a considerable improvement over conventional Prolog implementations. Prolog programs stored in files can also be loaded, and queries may also be typed in directly from the keyboard.

A grid file can be considered as a relation in a relational data base. A collection of Prolog facts with the same predicate name and the same number of arguments has also the structure of a relation. The grid file name and the predicate name are equivalent to the name of the relation. A single grid file record and a single fact in Prolog correspond to a tuple in the relation. The keys of the record and the arguments in the fact are the attributes of the tuple. These equivalences show that the grid file is suitable for the implementation of relational data bases and Prolog is useful for querying relations. In contrast to most existing query languages, Prolog allows the retrieval of answers that require deductive reasoning with the facts stored in a data base. This is the reason we have chosen Prolog as query language for the grid file system.

The Modula-Prolog programmer's interface has been used to implement built-in predicates which make all operations provided by the grid file system accessible, such as: open, close, create, or delete a grid file; insert, delete or change records in a grid file; initialize exact match queries, partial match queries, range queries or join queries. Retrieval of records which match the specified query pattern involves the Prolog backtracking mechanism; as a consequence, a query on a grid file behaves in the same way as a query on the internal Prolog database.

Prolog makes it easy to improve the user-friendliness of the query language, as the following example shows. The meaning of a data base attribute in Prolog and in the Grid File is defined by its position in the relation, but users often prefer to identify attributes by name rather than by position. A Prolog program that evaluates queries specified by expressions involving attribute names and properties of attributes allows the formulation of complex queries over data stored in a grid file [Ar 85]. As an example consider the grid file called 'cities' which stores for each city the corresponding country and population. In order to formulate a query involving attribute names we must assign a symbolic name to each attribute in the relation. This is done by a call to the built-in Prolog predicate 'define' which has two arguments: the name of the grid file and an ordered list of attributes:

?- define(cities, [city, country, population]).

A typical query over our example grid file could be: "Give me all the cities in Switzerland with a population between 50000 and 100000". In Prolog, this query is initialized as follows:

?- queryGF(cities, ((country ='Switzerland') and (population >= 50000) and (population < 100000))).

The first argument is the name of the grid file and the second one a description of all the tuples that are to be retrieved. 'and' is a user-declared operator recognized by the parser. The Prolog question

?- getnextrecord(cities, X).

matches X with all the tuples in our grid file that satisfy the expression in the initialization of the query, using the normal Prolog backtracking mechanism.

4 Software engineering aspects

The development of the SDI package has been an instructive exercise in software engineering. Among the many lessons it has taught us we would like to mention the following three:

Building blocks as opposed to turn-key systems: Separation of functions

Our previous projects were aimed at developing turn-key systems for well-defined tasks to be performed by a homogeneous class of users. The advantage of this monolithic program approach is that a workable system can be produced relatively quickly; the disadvantage, that adaptations rapidly escalate into redesign of a new system. If the designer knows the application very well, a monolithic program may be the fastest road to success; in an experimental situation it is more likely to turn into a dynosaur.

The open systems approach we have followed in designing the building blocks of the SDI package has the disadvantage that long discussions about interfaces precede the moment at which the total package can be demonstrated. Once this proof of existence has been achieved, continued progress is rapid. Adaptations of the total system are relatively simple to achieve by means of small control programs that interface the unmodified building blocks in new ways.

Naturally, the success of the building blocks approach hinges on a good choice of the interfaces. Experience with interactive systems had taught us long ago to aim at application-independent human-computer interfaces that separate dialog control from the functional aspects of an application. Since I/O towards the end-user is the most hardare-dependent type of software, an immediate benefit of this separation is that the application program (without user interface) becomes much easier to port. Having decided to separate the user interface, the next logical cut is between storage and access on one hand, and deduction on the other.

Compatibility: Internal interfaces

Control programs. Both the Prolog-Easy and the Prolog-Grid File combination consist of a relatively small main program which uses functions from the component packages and combines them as required. Such control programs determine which procedures to activate at what time. They implement simple control functions that activate complex algorithms from the packages, are typically compact and therefore easy to understand and change.

A control program is a dispatcher: it reads input (usually in structured form from one of the packages) and based on this input calls one or more functions, the results of which it then outputs (usually also in structured form). The Prolog Easy program accepts input from Easy, starts the relevant Prolog query, then outputs the result in Easy's application window. If a sequence of operations is required, the interface makes available a start procedure and a continuation procedure, and lets the caller do the looping. In this way the caller can to do something else between successive executions of the operation in the sequence.

Another useful technique in designing interfaces for compatibility is to assume that at most one package will be responsible for any given logical object. The Grid file is alone in operating on Grid Files, Easy is the only package that does any interaction with the user. The latter is especially important because one of the problems in getting programs to work together is the disciplining of error messages or status output among the various packages. The SDI software has been carefully designed to insure that only components that must output on the screen actually do so: all other packages may return a string describing the error or status. It is then the caller's responsibility to display the string where the user will see it and be able to respond appropriately.

Portability: Interface towards the host

Portability by design. Today's programming languages cannot guarantee portability of a sizable program from one machine to another. Modular programming languages such as Ada, Modula-2 or C support portability by isolating machine-dependent features in a standard subroutine library. The designer can enhance portability significantly by the pedantic discipline of never assuming more than absolutely necessary about the hardware.
Host interface as a virtual machine. All three building blocks use a single standard interface to the host machine and operating system, which turns the target machine into a virtual machine. The interface offers a sizable collection of low-level and input/output functions - in our implementation it requires about 20 Kbytes of code.

5 Implementation, statistics, experience

The implementation of the SDI package has required an estimated 3-4 man-years of programming, spread over two years of part time work. The grid file required most of the work, mainly of a conceptual nature: what functions to offer to the user, how to interface it to different host operating systems. Modula-Prolog went through about three major versions: a first Prolog interpreter written in UCSD Pascal for Apple-2, a second one written in Modula-2 with a rudimentary interface to Modula-2, followed by a complete redesign to get the Modula-2 interface right. Easy was written in four months, thanks to the experience gained with our earlier prototypes of human-computer interfaces. Several demonstration programs show that the interplay between the components of SDI works, for example the geographic data base described in section 4.

Modularity and portability were major design goals, and we have tested our software on different machines. We use Lilith graphics workstations as our development system, and have been able to port the software easily to any system that offers a Modula-2 environment. The grid file has been ported to several workstations based on the Motorola 68000 CPU, to the DEC VAX machines under VMS, and we are now working on a Unix version. Modula-Prolog has been transferred to the IBM PC and, under the name McLogimo, to the Apple McIntosh. [Br 85] describes the use of Modula-Prolog for the automatic construction of objects in a geometric modeler. A few statistical indicators of ths SDI package follow.

Gridfile:

Module	lines of source	compiled code
GFBase (data structures and basic access routines):	1100	4 Kbyte
GFSplit Merge (operations on directory):	1500*	9 Kbyte
GridFile System (exports 30 procedures for client):*	2800	15 Kbyte

Prolog:

Module	lines of source	compiled code
MPLib (programmer's interface):	1000	5 Kbyte
MPProve (unification & backtracking):	600	2 Kbyte
MPPred (built-in predicates):	1800	9 Kbyte
MPParse (parser):	900	4 Kbyte
MPKern (implementation utilities):	1400	8 Kbyte

Easy:

Module	lines of source	compiled code
EasyCmd (main programmer's interface)	500	2 Kbyte
EasyAlpha (window-oriented output)	400	2 Kbyte
EasyTerm (sequential output)	200	1 Kbyte
UCMachine (universal command interpreter)	1300	8 Kbyte
ParEntry (user input handler)	700	3 Kbyte
Trails (trail and storage for universal commands)	500	3 Kbyte
TreeView (tree display package)	500	3 Kbyte
TreeNodes (tree storage and operations)	1000	4 Kbyte
DataFiles (basic data handling)	500	2 Kbyte

Acknowledgement

We are grateful to Gernot Heiser and Massimo Arnoldi for contributions to the SDI package. This software was developed at ETH Zurich with partial support of the Brown Boveri Research Laboratory.

References

[Ar 85] M. Arnoldi, *Integration of the Grid File System in the programming language Prolog*, Diploma thesis, ETH Zurich, August 1985.

[Be 82] G. Beretta, H. Burkhart, P. Fink, J. Nievergelt, J. Stelovsky, H. Sugaya, J. Weydert, A. Ventura, *XS-1: An integrated interactive system and its kernel*, 340-349, Proc. 6-th International Conference on Software Engineering, Tokyo, 1982, IEEE Computer Society Press.

[Bi 85] E. S. Biagioni, *EASY - A front end for interactive programs*, Diploma thesis, ETH Zurich, Feb 1985.

[BNSS 85] E. S. Biagioni, J. Nievergelt, J. Stelovsky, H. Sugaya,
Can an operating system support consistent user dialogs? Experience with the prototype XS-2,
to appear Proc. ACM 85, Denver, CO.

[Br 85] B. Brüderlin, *Using Prolog for constructing geometric objects defined by constraints*, Proc. Eurocal Conf. on Computer Algebra, Linz, April 1985, Lecture Notes in Computer Science, Springer Verlag.

[CM 81] W. F. Clocksin and C. S. Mellish, *Programming in Prolog*, Springer-Verlag, 1981.

[Hi 85a] K. Hinrichs, *The grid file system: implementation and case studies of applications*, Diss. ETH No. 7734, 1985.

[Hi 85b] K. Hinrichs, *Implementation of the grid file: design concepts and case studies*, to appear in BIT.

[Mu 85] C. Muller, *Modula-Prolog User Manual*, Report 63, Informatik ETH, July 1985.

[NHS 84] J. Nievergelt, H. Hinterberger and K. C. Sevcik, *The Grid File: an adaptable, symmetric multikey file structure*, ACM Trans. Database Systems, 9, 1, 38-71, Mar 1984.

[NH 85] J. Nievergelt, K. H. Hinrichs, *Storage and access structures for geometric data bases*, 335-345, Proc. International Conf. on Foundations of Data Structures, Kyoto, May 1985.

[St 84] J. Stelovsky, *The user interface of an interactive system*, ETH Dissertation 7425, 1984.

PREDICT: Ein wissensbasiertes Data Dictionary

P. Pagé

P. Mossack

Software AG, Darmstadt

I. Einführung

In diesem Beitrag versuchen wir, das Thema zukunftsorientierter Data Dictionary Systeme zu behandeln. Dies wird in zwei Phasen geschehen:

Die erste bezieht sich auf die funktionellen Anforderungen an ein solches System, die zweite befaßt sich mit den minimalen technischen Voraussetzungen, die geschaffen werden müssen, um die Implementierung eines solchen Systems zu ermöglichen.

II. Anforderungen

Die funktionalen Anforderungen an ein Data Dictionary System gliedern sich in diverse und zum Teil sehr unterschiedliche Aspekte der Datenverarbeitung. Wir unterscheiden dabei:

a) Entwurf und Wartung von kommerziellen Datenverarbeitungssystemen;

b) Herstellung, Optimierung, Überwachung und Steuerung der Laufzeitumgebung von Datenbankverwaltungssystemen;

c) Intelligente Auswertung bestehender Daten.

Entwurf und Wartung von kommerziellen Datenverarbeitungssystemen

Es ist klar, daß dieser Aspekt durch ein umfangreiches Werkzeug unterstützt werden muß. Hier gibt es bestimmte Funktionen, die als Mindestanforderungen gelten müssen:

- Datenunabhängige Programmierung: Während der Entwurfsphase eines Softwaresystems soll die Datenstrukturanalyse so erfolgen, daß die Beschreibung der Informationselemente so abgespeichert wird, als bestünden diese nur aus Relationen. Das heißt, man macht ein logisches Datenstrukturdesign, ohne Rücksicht auf die physikalische Abspeicherung der Daten zu nehmen. Sinn der Sache ist natürlich, die dritte Normalform des Konzeptes zu gewährleisten, wobei das Werkzeug auch in dieser Richtung die entsprechende Unterstützung zu leisten hat. Selbst während der Programmierphase wird nur Bezug auf die logische Datenspeicherung genommen.

In der Realität sieht es aber meist so aus, daß aus Performance-Gründen Kompromisse zwischen dem reinen Design und der tatsächlichen Abspeicherung der Daten gemacht werden müssen, die dann unter Umständen dazu führen, daß redundante Daten abgespeichert werden.

Aufgabe des Data Dictionaries ist es hier zum ersten, die Verbindung zwischen den logischen und den physikalischen Zugriffen herzustellen, und zweitens die Datenintegrität zu gewährleisten, indem solche aus Leistungs- und Handhabungsgründen redundanten Daten automatisch gepflegt werden (z.B. durch automatisch generierte und im Dictionary abgespeicherte Validationsregeln, die wiederum automatisch aktiviert werden).

- Ein weiterer Punkt ist die maschinengestützte Hilfe bei der Integration von getrennten und bereits existierenden (unter Umständen sehr großen) Datenverarbeitungssystemen in einer Organisation.

Ein Beispiel dafür wäre die Aufdeckung von Datenredundanzen, sowie die Erkennung von nicht redundanten Daten, die aber auf der Oberfläche als redundant erscheinen (dieses Phänomen wird von James Martin 'Semantic Disintegrity' genannt).

- Die intelligente Beratung und Führung durch das Werkzeug beim Entwurf und bei der Implementierung von informationsbearbeitenden Systemen ist eine weitere Anforderung für die Zukunft. Dies steht im Gegensatz zu den heutigen Werkzeugen, wo die Initiative fast ausschließlich vom Benutzer ergriffen werden muß.

Die Laufzeitumgebung von Datenbankverwaltungssystemen

Die tatsächliche DBMS-Umgebung muß völlig vom Data Dictionary überwacht und aktiv gesteuert werden: Vom Design der physikalischen Datenbank und File Layouts (aus Informationen, die aus dem logischen Design stammen) bis zu dessen Erzeugung und Wartung.

Die Wartung bzw. Steuerung der Laufzeitumgebung untergliedert sich in:

- Früherkennen von Grenzsituationen und daraus folgende Beratung des Wartungspersonals, z.B. wenn eine bestimmte Datei voraussichtlich bis zu einem bestimmten Zeitpunkt zum Überlauf kommen wird.

- Automatische Fehlerdiagnose und -beratung zwecks zu ergreifender Maßnahmen, sowohl bei systembedingten als auch durch den Benutzer erzeugten Fehlern. Diese Beratung muß ebenfalls 'intelligent' sein.

- Erhaltung und Nutzung aller Kenntnisse der Netzwerkarchitektur bei verteilten Datenbanken.

- Feststellung von Leichensätzen ('garbage collection').

- Automatische Aufnahme und Auswertung von statistischen Daten bezüglich des Laufzeitverhaltens der Datenbank, um auf der einen Seite Tuningmaßnahmen durchführen zu können, und auf der anderen Vorschläge für ein geändertes physikalisches Layout der Informationen zu machen.

- Ermittlung der Daten und Kontrolle des Systems bezüglich Datensicherheit.

Intelligente Auswertung bestehender Daten

Ein sehr wichtiger Aspekt, dessen Bedeutung in der Zukunft ständig wachsen wird, ist die Gewinnung von neuen Erkenntnissen aus bereits vorhandenen Daten durch wissensbasierte Auswertungen, die unter Umständen ursprünglich garnicht beabsichtigt waren.

Eine solche intelligente Auswertung stellt wiederum Anforderungen an das Data Dictionary nicht nur bezüglich der physischen, sondern vielmehr der semantischen Struktur der existierenden Informationen und setzt die Kenntnis der Regeln, mit denen. die Information bearbeitet werden soll, voraus.

III. Voraussetzungen

Es gibt gewisse systematische Voraussetzungen, ohne die eine Implementierung der oben angedeuteten Anforderungen nicht gewährleistet werden kann.

Zum ersten benötigt man eine Datenspeicherungs- und abfragemethode, die es erlaubt, sehr komplexe Datenstrukturen zu definieren und zu verwalten (entity types und entities) und die Verknüpfungen (relations) zwischen diesen entities müssen ebenfalls frei definiert und abgefragt werden können.

Ein solches Entity-Relationship-Modell muß zwangsläufig in die jeweilige Datenverarbeitungsumgebung integriert sein, d.h. es darf kein isoliertes Produkt sein. Dies ist absolut notwendig, weil es sonst nicht akzeptable Funktionseinschränkungen gäbe, hervorgerufen durch konzeptuelle und physikalische Schnittstellenprobleme.

Das Modell muß so integriert sein, daß es in transparenter Weise aus der gleichen Sprache der vierten Generation betrieben werden kann, in der auch die aus dem Design resultierenden

Programme implementiert werden.

Ein weiterer wichtiger Punkt ist die Adaptierbarkeit bestehender Projektdaten (entities) an neue bzw. geänderte Entity-Typen, so daß eine einheitliche Entwicklung von Systemen möglich ist.

Da das Entity-Relationship-Datenbankverwaltungssystem nicht an irgendwelche vordefinierten Datentypen gebunden ist, und da es online aus der Sprache der vierten Generation verwaltet werden kann, ist es ferner möglich, das Knowledge Engineering und das daraus resultierende Wissen in einheitlicher Weise abzuspeichern und weiter zu verwenden.

IV. Zusammenfassung

Um eine zukunftsorientierte Datenverarbeitungsumgebung zu gestalten, ist es unerläßlich, daß eine zentrale Steuerung des gesamten Systems existiert, die das Wissen über die Komponenten und deren Querbezüge enthält und intelligent nutzt. Der Kern einer solchen Steuerung muß ein intelligentes und integriertes Data Dictionary System sein, welches über eine einheitliche Benutzeroberfläche die konzeptuelle Integrität mit realistischen und performanceorientierten Design-Lösungen verbindet, und zusätzlich in der Lage ist, bestehende Informationen optimal zu nutzen.

Entwicklungen der Software AG tendieren in diese Richtung und haben dieses als Ziel.

WISSENSBASIERTE SYSTEME ALS BESTANDTEILE VON PRODUKTEN
UND SYSTEMEN DER ELEKTRO-INDUSTRIE
K. Pasedach
Philips GmbH Forschungslaboratorium Hamburg,
D-2000 Hamburg 54, Vogt-Kölln-Str. 30

Zusammenfassung

Informatik ist seit vielen Jahren schon eine Schlüsseldisziplin der
Elektro-Industrie. Besonders schnell wächst die Bedeutung des Teil-
bereichs der wissensbasierten Systeme. Das wird an den Beispielen der
Automation im Büro, in der Fabrik und im Krankenhaus erläutert. Die
Gründe für den Einsatz wissensbasierter Systeme sowie die Trends für
die Zukunft werden aufgezeigt, und auf die besondere Rolle, die der
Industrieforschung hierbei zukommt, wird eingegangen.

Die Situation wissensbasierter Systeme

In den letzten Jahrzehnten ist die Informatik in eine Schlüsselrolle
für viele Wirtschaftsbereiche hineingewachsen. Besonders auffällig ist
das in der Elektro-Industrie, wo die Informatik neben der Rolle als
verwendetes Werkzeug auch zum entscheidenden Bestandteil vieler herge-
stellter Produkte und Systeme geworden ist. Allein im kleinen Europa
hat der Markt der Informationstechnik heute schon pro Jahr ein Volumen
von 25 Milliarden US-Dollar und wächst mit stattlichen 15%. Das rechtfertigt die Aussage, daß unsere Industriegesellschaft sich momentan in
eine Informationsgesellschaft transformiert.

Die künstliche Intelligenz ist ein Teilbereich der Informatik, der besondere Aufmerksamkeit verdient. In den drei Dekaden seit Entstehen
dieser Disziplin /1/ war der Anfang durch die Suche nach einem "General Problem Solver" geprägt, dessen Leistungsfähigkeit die Komplexität
realer Probleme aber nicht meistern konnte. Es folgten Jahre grund-
legender Forschungsarbeiten an Systemen mit mehr Wissen, beispielsweise für maschinelles Sehen und Verstehen natürlicher Sprache. Erst
die letzten Jahre haben durch die Entwicklung leistungsfähiger Spe-
zial-Hardware sowie durch Entwicklung und erfolgreiche Erprobung von

Experten-Systemen zu einem Durchbruch geführt. Das war verbunden mit einem rasch wachsenden Anteil dieser Teildisziplin an der Gesamt-Informatik.

Warum wissensbasierte Systeme?

Es stellt sich die Frage, warum wissensbasierte Systeme für viele Anwendungen heute so attraktiv werden. Immer stärker hat die Geschichte der Informatik gezeigt, daß viele Aufgabenstellungen der Praxis entweder extrem komplex sind oder aber vielen und häufig wandelnden Randbedingungen unterworfen sind. Die explizite Entwicklung des Kontrollflusses zur Lösung solcher Probleme in Form herkömmlicher Computer-Programme kann dann extrem aufwendig oder gar unmöglich werden. Es bietet sich daher an, in ein wissensbasiertes System nur die Regeln einzubringen, die das Ganze beschreiben; der eigentliche Kontrollfluß wird dann erst zum Zeitpunkt der Programm-Ausführung aus diesen Regeln zusammengestellt und durchlaufen. Neue oder geänderte Regeln in der Wissensbank des Systems führen zu gänzlich anderen Abläufen, ohne daß das System deshalb geändert werden müßte. Diese Entwicklung wissensbasierter Systeme führt aber keineswegs dahin, daß die klassische, algorithmische Datenverarbeitung abgelöst wird; vielmehr wird das bisherige Software-Konzept in entscheidenden Bereichen durch die neuen Methoden ergänzt und geht mit ihnen eine fruchtbare Symbiose ein.

Die Situation in der Elektro-Industrie

Beim Einsatz wissensbasierter Systeme ist in der Elektro-Industrie eine sehr deutliche zeitliche Unterscheidung von drei Etappen möglich, nämlich wissensbasierte Systeme erstens als Werkzeuge in Entwicklung und Produktion, zweitens in Systemen und drittens in den Einzelprodukten.

Zwei einfache Gründe gibt es für diese klare zeitliche Abfolge. Der heute noch hohe Entwicklungsaufwand von wissensbasierten Systemen ist bei den Werkzeugen (z.B. einem CAD-System, das ein Entwickler benutzt) und Systemen (z.B. einem medizinischen Diagnosesystem) leichter zu finanzieren als etwa für die "intelligente" Schreibmaschine; zudem ist der Hardware-Aufwand an Prozessor- und Speicherleistung für die Wissensverarbeitung so groß, daß erst bei weiterem Preisrückgang der

Mikroelektronik auch einzelne Produkte mit ihr ausgestattet werden können, ohne für ihre Märkte zu teuer zu werden.

Japans Stärken

Beeindruckend und für die restliche Industriewelt geradezu bedrohlich sind die Japaner, die schon seit zwanzig Jahren mit einer Folge von staatlich geförderten industriellen Kooperationsprogrammen die Transformation zur Informationsgesellschaft konsequent vorantreiben: Super-Computer, Mustererkennung, Integrierte Schaltungen, Grundlagentechnologie, Optoelektronik, intelligente Roboter und Computer der 5. Generation. Insbesondere beim letzten dieser Programme, in dessen Zentrum die wissensbasierten Systeme stehen, beeindrucken die klaren Perspektiven, mit denen die vier System-Ebenen VLSI-Architektur, Hardware, Software und Benutzeroberfläche über die drei Säulen Datenbank, Problemlösen und intelligente Schnittstellen aufgebaut werden. Beachtlich sind die Leistungen des ICOT (Institute for new COmputer Technology) /2/ nach drei seiner zehn Programmjahre von der persönlichen, sequentiellen Schlußfolgerungsmaschine PSI (mit 20-30 klips) und der relationalen Datenbankmaschine DELTA über die Systeme KAISER zur Wissensdarstellung bis hin zu einem System zur Unterstützung des logischen Schaltungsentwurfs und dem System DUALS für "discourse understanding".

Die Antwort an Japan

Auffällig am japanischen Vorgehen ist die Pragmatik und der starke Praxisbezug, während die Aktivitäten in den USA und in Europa auf den Gebieten der künstlichen Intelligenz und der wissensbasierten Systeme häufig Forschung im Elfenbeinturm waren. Das hat sich allerdings seit einigen Jahren sichtbar geändert. Von den Programmen in USA, nämlich DARPA, MCC und SRC sowie in Europa von den nationalen Programmen, z.B. in Großbritannien, Frankreich und Deutschland und von den gemeinschaftlichen Programmen ESPRIT und EURECA, sind schon deutliche Impulse für praktisch nutzbare, wissensbasierte Systeme zu sehen beziehungsweise sicher zu erwarten. Als besonders günstig erweist sich hier die offene Kooperation verschiedener Firmen und Universitäten im "field of precompetitive research".

Verteilung der Rollen

Für die Elektro- und Elektronik-Industrie erweist es sich als günstig,
den Universitäten und staatlichen Forschungsinstituten wo immer möglich die Grundlagen-Untersuchungen für die wissensbasierten Systeme zu
überlassen, in den industriellen Forschungslaboratorien dann für die
Umsetzung und Ergänzung dieser Egebnisse - orientiert an den konkreten
industriellen Fragestellungen - zu sorgen und den Übergang in den Ent-
wicklungsbereich zu bewirken. Universitäre Forschung ist hier eine Basis, Industrie-Forschung Brücke und industrielle Entwicklung das Ziel.

Die treibenden Kräfte

Drei Faktoren sind bei den wissensbasierten Systemen als entscheidend
auszumachen: Die Hardware, die Software und die "expert ware". Unumg-
gänglich ist auf jeden Fall eine neue Art von Software, die auf einer
leistungsfähigen Schlußfolgerungsmaschine und einer gut organisierten
Wissensbank aufbaut. Dies kann auf herkömmlichen Computern geschehen,
jedoch sind wissensbasierte Systeme dort ausgesprochene "Ressourcen-
fresser", was Speicherplatz, vor allem aber Prozessorleistung angeht.
Große Bedeutung kommt daher spezieller Hardware zu, die das schnelle
Arbeiten regelbasierter Systeme unterstützt. Als eigentlichen Engpaß
für die praktische Nutzung wissensbasierter Systeme hat sich allerdings die "expert ware" erwiesen, also das in den Computer eingegebene
Expertenwissen. Das gilt zum einen für den Experten des Anwendungs-
gebiets, dessen Wissen mühsam vom System-Experten und mit einer Wis-
senserwerb-Komponente für den Computer aufbereitet werden muß. Zum anderen gibt es zur Zeit noch viel zu wenig Experten für wissensbasierte
Systeme, um alle interessanten Anwendungen zu bearbeiten, und das wird
noch lange - wenn nicht sogar immer - so bleiben.

Die Benutzeroberfläche

Ein besonders sichtbarer Fortschritt wissensbasierter, informations-
verarbeitender Systeme - verglichen mit den herkömmlichen - ist die
Gestaltung der Benutzeroberfläche des Systems, die durch drei Eigenschaften geprägt ist: Natürlich, wissend, selbsterklärend.

Natürlich heißt die Benutzeroberfläche, die den Erfordernissen und Erwartungen des Benutzers optimal angepaßt ist. Diesem Aspekt wird beispielsweise vom japanischen Programm der Computer der 5. Generation großer Nachdruck verliehen.

Es gehört hierzu, daß die natürliche Ausdrucksweise mit den Begriffen der Anwendung verstanden wird, und eine Codierung in formalisierter, formatisierter oder chiffrierter Weise entfällt; wissensbasierte Systeme können diese technisch oft nötige Umsetzung dann regelbasiert intern ausführen. Solch ein System kommuniziert mit dem Benutzer stärker über Graphiken und Bilder, nicht nur über Zahlen und Text. Leistungsfähige, wissensbasierte Mustererkennung erlaubt zum Beispiel die Kommunikation über die gesprochene /3/ - auch kontinuierlich gesprochene - Sprache und Eingabe von Texten und Graphiken mit einem elektronischen Schreibstift.

Schließlich ist für die Natürlichkeit des Systems noch die Kohärenz der Benutzer-Aktionen entscheidend. Das System sorgt durch schnelle Verarbeitung, Multi-Media-Ein/Ausgabe und Window-Technik dafür, daß logisch und/oder zeitlich zusammengehörige Benutzer-Aktivitäten nicht aufgetrennt werden.

Wissend wird die Schnittstelle zum Benutzer dadurch, daß das wissensbasierte System nicht nur die Daten und Regeln der Anwendung speichert, sondern zugleich ein Modell vom jeweiligen Benutzer aufbaut und ständig updatet. Bei diesem Benutzer-Modell werden die momentane Absicht, das Wissen und die Fertigkeit des Benutzers in der Bedienung des Systems berücksichtigt. Solche Daten werden aber nur dort, wo absolut unumgänglich, explizit erfragt; im Regelfall werden sie durch system-interne Beobachtung des Dialogs mit dem Benutzer, z.B. verwendete Funktionen, Häufigkeiten, Eingabe-Abfolgen, Fehleingaben usw. gewonnen.

Schließlich werden die Benutzeroberflächen der Systeme selbsterklärend gestaltet. Bei einem CAD-System und in etlichen Jahren auch bei einem Fernsehgerät, kann dem Benutzer die Information über den momentanen Funktionsumfang ständig oder auf Anfrage in einem separaten Informationsfenster des Bildschirms so angeboten werden, daß er vom Stand Null aus die Bedienung eines Geräts am Gerät selbst erlernt. Voraussetzung hierfür ist die Integration eines gemeinsam mit dem System entwickelten Computer-Aided Instruction (CAI)-Moduls. Eine Gebrauchsanweisung oder ein Handbuch werden dann überflüssig und sinnlos.

Der synergetische Ansatz

Um eine breite Palette von wissensbasierten Systemen unterstützen zu können, ist im Hamburger Forschungslaboratorium von Philips ein synergetischer Ansatz gewählt worden. Aufbauend auf früheren Arbeiten im Datenbankbereich /4/ wird eine Datenbank zu einer Wissensbank ausgebaut. Über eine "Cluster Engine" erlaubt sie die effiziente Verarbeitung zusammengehöriger Informationsgebilde unter Optimierung des Verkehrs mit dem Hintergrund-Plattenspeicher. Dieses "Knowledge-Base Management System" residiert im Arbeitsplatz-Rechner selbst und ist so ausgelegt, daß es komplexe Dokumente verarbeitet. Das Konzept der komplexen Dokumente ist dabei so weit angelegt, daß eine Synergie für eine Reihe von Anwendungsgebieten entsteht, denen allen gemeinsam ist, daß sie mit solchen komplexen Dokumenten arbeiten. Speziell gehören hierzu die drei Bereiche der Automatisierung im Produkt-Entwicklungsbereich, im Krankenhaus und im Büro. Als besonders wirkungsvoll für die Wissensdarstellung haben sich hier semantische Netze erwiesen, vor allem in ihrer Ausprägung der Methode KL-ONE /5/.

Wissensbasierte Systeme für die Fabrik

Wissensbasierte Systeme sind im gesamten Bereich des CAE (Computer-Aided Engineering) ein vielversprechender Ansatz. Im Engineering geht es darum, nicht-formale, unvollständige und widersprüchliche (also vage) Produkt-Ideen in ein formales, vollständiges und widerspruchsfreies Produkt-Modell überzuführen. Das ist eine notwendige Voraussetzung für eine spätere Produkt-Fertigung. Diese Produkt-Modellierung läßt sich deshalb so wirkungsvoll durch wissensbasierte Systeme unterstützen, weil die Regeln im technischen Entwicklungsprozeß häufig leichter vom Wissensingenieur beim Feld-Experten ermittelt werden können, als das auf anderen Gebieten der Fall ist. Zur Unterstützung des mechanischen, dreidimensionalen Entwurfs entsteht zur Zeit im Philips-Forschungslaboratorium Hamburg ein System, dessen Wissensbank die Regeln der Konstruktion enthält und so einen entscheidenden Schritt in Richtung des maschinellen geometrischen Schlußfolgerns geht /6/.

Von der Produkt-Entwicklung spannt sich dann der logische und reale Bogen hin zur Fertigung, wo in einem anderen Projekt desselben Laboratoriums ein wissensbasiertes Echtzeit-Überwachungssystem für CIM (Computer-Integrated Manufacturing) entsteht.

Wissensbasierte Systeme für die Medizin

Wissensbasierte Systeme sind vielversprechende Ansätze zur Unterstützung des medizinischen Bereichs. Am bekanntesten ist unter ihnen MYCIN von E. Shortliffe, das mit etwa 400 bei Experten ermittelten Regeln und seinem interessanten Konzept der "Certainty Factors" die ärztliche Diagnose und Therapie von Infektionskrankheiten unterstützt. Daneben gibt es eine Reihe anderer bemerkenswerter Systeme, z.B. ABEL für Störungen im Säurehaushalt des Körpers, CADUCEUS für die Differential-Diagnose der Inneren Medizin, CASNET zur Behandlung des grünen Stars, ONCOCIN für Chemotherapie bei Krebs, PUFF bei Lungenerkrankungen und VM für die Behandlung auf der Intensiv-Station sowie einige andere (s. z.B. /7/). Aufbauend auf diesen Ergebnissen und im Rahmen der Forschungsarbeiten im Bereich der patienten-schonenden Kernspin-Tomographie (NMR) entsteht im Hamburger Forschungslaboratorium von Philips ein wissensbasiertes System zur Unterstützung der Diagnose von NMR-Bildern. Diese NMR-Bilder sind eine spezielle Ausprägung komplexer Dokumente für das schon erwähnte "Knowledge-Base Management System".

Wissensbasierte Systeme für das Büro

Ganz zentral und auch umgangssprachlich gebraucht wird der Begriff des Dokuments bei Bürosystemen. Die Komplexität des Dokuments ist dabei weniger in der Vielfalt möglicher Layouts begründet, sondern mehr in der Kombination der Informationsformen Daten, Text, Bild und insbesondere die Einbeziehung der logischen Dimension, also der Bedeutung der Inhalte (z.B. Datum, Rechnungssumme, Autor, Bestätigungsvermerk etc.). Mit den Arbeiten der Philips-Forschung und -Entwicklung werden heutige Integrationskonzepte wie SOPHOMATION weiterentwickelt zu Büro-und Kommunikationssystemen, die um die Bedeutung ihrer Dokumente wissen und dadurch höherwertige Bürofunktionen, wie z.B. Entscheidungsunterstützung anbieten können.

Die Situation bei Philips

Bei Philips stehen die Arbeiten an wissensbasierten Systemen auf dem
Boden eines Unternehmens, das gleichzeitig auf professionellen und
Verbraucher-Märkten aktiv ist. Dies ist deshalb ein großer Vorteil,
weil aus den schon erläuterten Gründen, z.B. der Kosten von Produkten
und Systemen, die wissensbasierten Systeme zuerst im professionellen
Bereich der Werkzeuge und Systeme Einzug finden, diese Erfahrungen
aber andererseits für die Produkte der Verbraucher-Märkte entscheidend
genutzt werden können. Philips' weiterer Vorteil ist das umfangreiche
Anwendungs-Know-how in der großen Anzahl von Gebieten, auf denen das
Unternehmen tätig ist.

In Zusammenarbeit mit den Produkt-Bereichen des Unternehmens arbeiten
die Forschungslaboratorien von Philips in Europa und USA an dem indu-
striellen Einsatz wissensbasierter Systeme. Schwerpunkte im Hamburger
Laboratorium sind einerseits Wissensdarstellung, Wissenserwerb und
"Knowledge-Base Management System", andererseits der Einsatz für vor-
wiegend professionell zu nutzende Produkte und Systeme, und zwar für
Dokumenten-Verarbeitung, Varianten-Entwurf (Mechanik), Spracherken-
nung, zerstörungsfreie Materialprüfung, analytische Instrumentierung,
NMR-Bilddiagnose, Echtzeit-Überwachung für CIM, benutzer-freundliche
Bild-Datenbank.

Ein gleichzeitiges Angehen einer so großen Palette von Anwendungen ist
nur durch den geschilderten synergetischen Ansatz und intensive Zusammenarbeit mit den Entwicklungsbereichen und mit Universitäten möglich.

Ausblick

Für die Forschung bietet auch die Zukunft noch ein breites Spektrum
wissenschaftlich interessanter Herausforderungen: Genannt sei hier das
angemessene Behandeln unterschiedlicher Wissenskategorien vom Tat-
sachenwissen über Allgemeinwissen, "Common Sense"-Wissen zum heuristischen Wissen und Meta-Wissen, also Wissen über Wissen, Fragen des unvollständigen Wissens, widersprüchlichen Wissens, und fast noch keiner
praktischen Lösung nähergebrachte Probleme wie unscharfes Wissen
(z.B. /8/). Vieles ist in der praktischen Umsetzung der theoretischen
Ergebnisse noch völlig offen. Sicher ist aber, daß ein schnell wachsender Markt von AI-Produkten und Dienstleistungen, der heute 200

Millionen US-Dollar, bis 1990 etwa 2.5 Milliarden Dollar und bis 2000 über 10 Milliarden Dollar haben soll /9/, viel dafür tun wird, das Interesse von Forschung und Industrie an wissensbasierten Systemen wachzuhalten.

Literatur

/1/ Savory, E. (Hrsg.): Künstliche Intelligenz und Expertensysteme. Forschungsbericht der Nixdorf Computer AG. Oldenbourg, 1985, S. 14

/2/ Proc. of the internat. conf. on Fifth Generation Computer Systems, Tokyo, November 1984

/3/ Sickert, K. (Hrsg.): Automatische Spracheingabe und Sprachausgabe. Markt & Technik, 1983

/4/ Fischer, W. E.: Datenbanksystem für CAD-Arbeitsplätze. Informatik-Fachberichte, Springer, 1983

/5/ Schmolze, J. G., Brachman, R. J.: Proc. of the 1981 KL-ONE Workshop, Fairchild Techn. Rep. No 618, 1982

/6/ Aldefeld, B.: Rule-based approach to variational geometry. Lecture for 7th internat. conf. and exh. on Computers in Design Engineering, Brighton, UK, April 1986

/7/ Michie, D. (Ed.): Introductory readings in expert systems. Gordon and Breach, 1982, p. 8 ff.

/8/ Fox, J.: Inferences about beliefs and values. Inference Workshop, September 1984

/9/ Japan Times, Tokyo, 14. November 1984

ERFAHRUNGEN AUS DREI ANWENDUNGSPROJEKTEN MIT MED1

Frank Puppe
Universität Kaiserslautern
Fachbereich Informatik
Postfach 3049
675 Kaiserslautern

Zusammenfassung: MED1 ist ein Werkzeug zur Entwicklung von heuristischen Diagnosesystemen. Wir fassen hier Erfahrungen aus drei Anwendungsprojekten zusammen: Diagnose von defekten Automotoren auf dem Prüfstand, von Computerhardwarefehlern und von Laufzeitproblemen bei Datenbankanwendungen. Der Schwerpunkt liegt auf der Beurteilung der Nützlichkeit der eingebauten Mechanismen und auf durchgeführten Erweiterungen sowie Schwächen von MED1.

1. Einleitung

MED1 [Puppe 83] ist ein Werkzeug zur Erstellung von regelbasierten Diagnostik-Expertensystemen. Es wurde zunächst an zwei Wissensbereichen erprobt: medizinische Diagnostik des Leitsymptoms Brustschmerz [Puppe 84] und Motoren-Diagnostik im KFZ-Kundendienst [Borrmann 83]. Das Ergebnis beider Anwendungen sind nicht-kommerzielle Prototypen, die die Machbarkeit von Expertensysten im jeweiligen Bereich demonstrieren.
Diese Erfahrungen ermutigten uns, Projekte mit dem Ziel des industriellen Einsatzes zu beginnen. Dazu gehören:

- IXMO: Motoren-Diagnostik auf Prüfständen der Serienproduktion (Innovationsgesellschaft für fortgeschrittene Produktionssysteme in der Fahrzeugindustrie mbH, Berlin)
- Hardware-Diagnostik bei Ausfall einer Rechenanlage (Siemens)
- Datenbank-Tuning bei intolerablen Laufzeitverhalten (Siemens)

Wir geben einen Zwischenbericht über den Status dieser Projekte, der folgende Aspekte betont:

- notwendige Erweiterungen von MED1
- Nützlichkeit der Mechanismen von MED1
- Mängel von MED1

Zur Zeit (Juli 85) ist noch keines der Projekte soweit fortgeschritten, daß eine Evaluation des betrieblichen Einsatzes mit Kosten/-Nutzen Abschätzung möglich wäre.

2. Das Werkzeug MED1

Eine grobe Charakterisierung von Werkzeugen entsprechend eines Kompromisses zwischen ihrer Nützlichkeit (Zeitersparnis bei der Entwicklung von Expertensystemen) und ihrer Spezialisierung (Beschränkung möglicher Einsatzgebiete) zeigt Fig. 1.

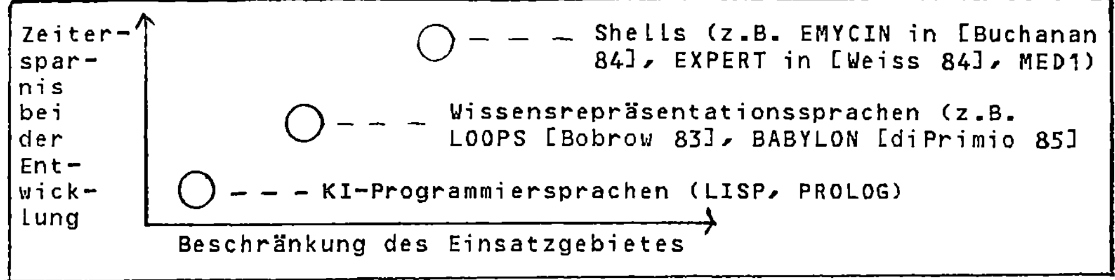

Fig. 1: Klassifizierung von Werkzeugen für Expertensysteme

Das Einsatzgebiet des Shells MED1 ist die heuristische Diagnostik, d.h. das Wiedererkennen bekannter Muster (Diagnosen) aus Symptomen und Meßwerten. Dazu gehört auch die Kostenminimierung bei der Erhebung der Symptome, falls nach Symptomen gesucht werden muß.
Die Entwicklung eines Expertensystems mit MED1 erfordert "nur" den Aufbau der Wissensbasis. MED1 unterstützt diesen Prozeß mit einem eigenen Wissenseditor. Die folgende kurze Beschreibung von MED1 betont die Sichtweise des Experten, der sein Wissen in für MED1 geeigneter Weise strukturieren muß. Eine ausführliche Beschreibung von MED1 einschließlich Wissenseditor und Erklärungskomponente gibt [Puppe 83].

2.1.   Architektur von MED1

MED1 löst diagnostische Probleme mit der Hypothezise-and-Test Strategie (Fig. 2).

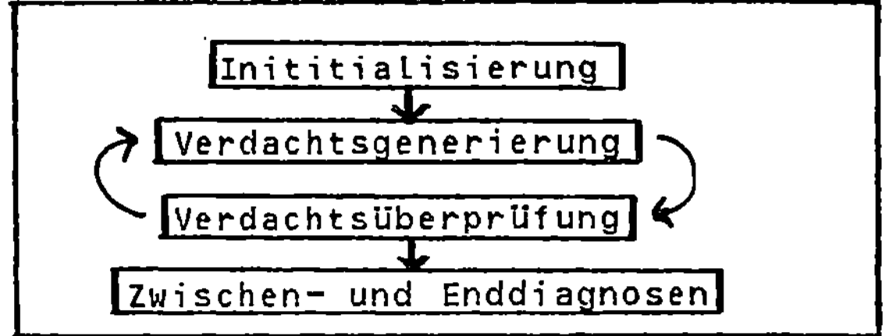

Fig. 2: Hypothezise-and-Test Strategie

Eine Sitzung beginnt mit einer Reihe von Übersichtsfragen, die mit Forwardregeln* zur Generierung von Verdachtshypothesen ausgewertet werden. Nach Abschluß dieser Initialisierungsphase werden in der "Agenda" die Hypothesen entsprechend der Stärke ihres Verdachtes geordnet. Die verdächtigste Hypothese wird jetzt gezielt mit Backward-Regeln* evaluiert. Falls dazu notwendige Symptome unbekannt sind, werden sie hergeleitet oder vom Benutzer erfragt. Diese neu erfaßten Symptome können über Forward-Regeln andere Verdachtshypothesen generieren. In geeigneten Intervallen wird eine Zwischenbilanz gezogen und die Agenda auf den neusten Stand gebracht. Dabei wird überprüft, ob der bisherige Spitzenreiter etabliert, weiteruntersucht oder zugunsten einer anderen Hypothese zurückgestellt werden soll. Der Zyklus von Verdachtsgenerierung und -überprüfung terminiert, wenn eine Enddiagnose etabliert wurde, die Agenda leer ist oder der Benutzer es wünscht.

---

* Forward-Regeln feuern, sobald alle ihre Vorbedingungen erfüllt sind. Backward-Regeln werden nur zielgerichtet aktiviert, nämlich wenn ihre Konklusion, eine Hypothese, untersucht wird.

2.2.   Wissensrepräsentation

MED1 enthält sechs Datentypen: Fragen, Zwischenvariablen, Regeln,
Diagnosen, Prozeduren und technische Untersuchungen. Die Bedeutung der
ersten vier Typen ergibt sich aus dem Diagnostikmodell in Fig. 3.

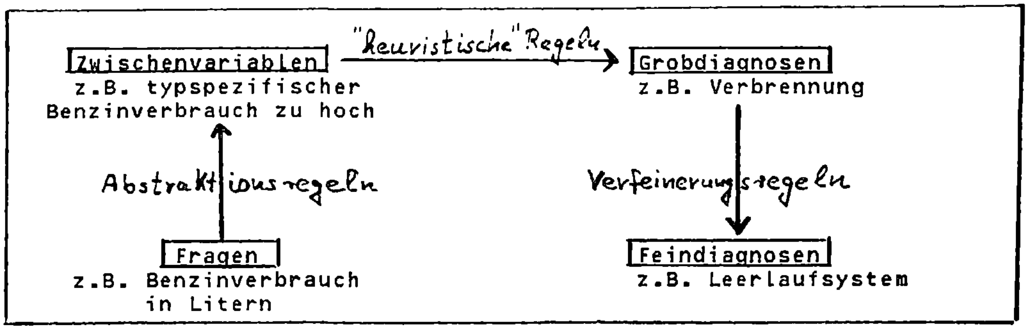

Fig. 3: Diagnostikmodell nach [Clancey 84]; Beispiele aus [Borrmann 83]

Es besagt, daß die Zuordnung von initialen Symptomen zu Enddiagnosen
typischerweise über Zwischenstufen erfolgt, die in MED1 Zwischenvariablen und Grobdiagnosen genannt werden. Prozeduren und technische Untersuchungen dienen zur Dialogsteuerung und werden im nächsten Abschnitt
"Inferenzstrategie" beschrieben. Fig. 4 beschreibt die wichtigsten
Attribute der Datentypen Frage, Zwischenvariable, Diagnose und Regel.

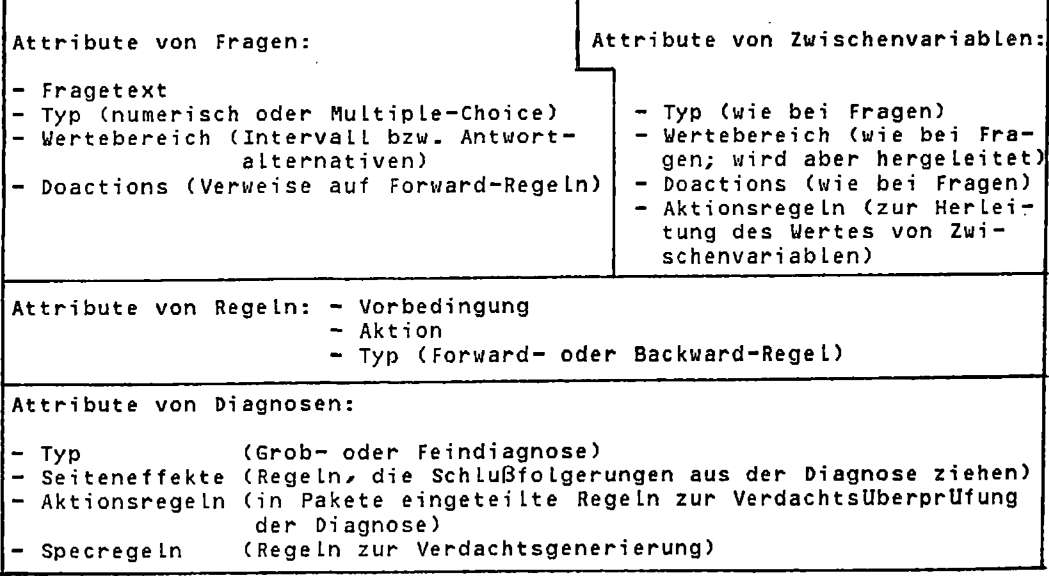

Fig. 4: die Basis-Attribute der Datentypen Frage
        Zwischenvariable, Regel, und Diagnose

2.3   Inferenzstrategie

Außer dem Wissen über Symptom-Diagnose Beziehungen benötigt MED1
auch Wissen, um eine ökonomische Fragestrategie verfolgen zu können.
Dazu gehören:

(1) Frage-Hierarchie

Überflüssige Fragen können vermieden werden, wenn die Fragen hierarchisch organisiert sind: bevor Detailfragen zu einem Symptom gestellt
werden, erfragt MED1 zunächst, ob das Symptom überhaupt vorhanden ist.
Zur Repräsentation solcher Symptomhierarchien haben Fragen zwei spezielle Attribute:

- Askfirst: Welche Bedingungen müssen erfüllt sein, bevor die Frage
             sinnvoll gestellt werden kann?
- Weiterfragen: Welche Folgefragen sollen sofort zur Präzisierung
             einer Antwort gestellt werden?

(2) Prozedur-Konzept und Technische Untersuchungen

Die Verdachtsüberprüfung im Hypothezise-and-Test Kreislauf soll ab-
gebrochen werden, sobald die Verdachtshypothese stark an Plausibilität
verloren hat, ohne daß weitere Untersuchungen durchgeführt werden.
Dazu kann der Experte die Menge der Backward-Regeln einer Diagnose in
verschiedene Pakete (Prozeduren) aufteilen, nach deren Abarbeitung
jeweils eine Zwischenbilanz gezogen wird. Dieser Mechanismus ist
besonders wichtig bei der Indizierung aufwendiger technischer Untersuchungen. Vor ihrer Anforderung führt MED1 eine Kosten/Nutzen Analyse
durch, mit dem Ziel, technische Untersuchungen solange aufzuschieben,
wie noch günstigere Alternativen zur Fortsetzung der Diagnostik zur
Verfügung stehen.
Die Kosten/Nutzen Analyse ist durch das Attribut "Aktivierungspunkte"
des Datentyps technische Untersuchungen realisiert. Positive Indika-
tionspunkte kommen von Diagnosen, die technische Untersuchungen anfordern; negative Punkte von Regeln, die allgemeine und fallspezifische
Kosten und Risiken repräsentieren.

2.4.   .   Umgang mit Unsicherheiten

Unsicherheiten bei der Diagnostik entstehen durch

- Symptomerhebung (Toleranzen von Meßgeräten, subjektiver Eindruck von
  Beobachtern)
- Symptombewertung (ungenügendes Wissen, Vieldeutigkeit von Symptomen)

und verstärken sich durch das Verrechnungsschema (dies gilt auch für
statistische Verfahren, da die Voraussetzungen zu deren Anwendung
nicht eingehalten werden können).

Zur Abstufung von Unsicherheiten bei der Symptomerhebung gibt es
in MED1 die Kategorien: Symptom vorhanden, Symptom fraglich vorhanden,
Symptom unbekannt, Symptom nicht vorhanden.

Die Symptombewertung in Regeln erfolgt mit positiven oder negativen
Punktzahlen, die der Experte abschätzt.
Die Punktzahlen aus verschiedenen Regeln werden für jede Diagnose auf
ein Konto addiert. Deren Summe wird durch eine auf die Diagnose
zugeschnittene Intervalleinteilung in eine von sieben Wahrscheinlich-
keitsklassen (ausgeschlossen .. gesichert) abgebildet. Ein spezieller
Mechanismus sind "rekursive Regeln", deren Punktzahl nur dann einer
Diagnose gutgeschrieben wird, wenn ihre bisherige Punktzahl einen
Schwellwert übersteigt.

3.   IXMO: Motorendiagnostik auf dem Prüfstand

3.1.   Ausgangssituation

In der Automobilproduktion werden Motoren vor der Endmontage auf
Prüfständen getestet. Werden dabei Mängel festgestellt, wird der
defekte Motor in die (räumlich getrennte) Nacharbeit transportiert, wo
die Beanstandung behoben wird. Die Dauer der Nacharbeit hängt entscheidend von der Qualität der Diagnose ab. Sie wird durch folgende Probleme
beeinträchtigt:

(1) Da der Motor im Prüffeld in Funktion getestet wird, bestehen
     dort erheblich bessere diagnostische Möglichkeiten als in der
     Nacharbeit. Andererseits haben die Werker dort die meiste diagno-
     stische Erfahrung.
(2) Auf dem Motorenprüfstand gibt es verschiedene Erhebungsverfahren
     für Symptome:

     - automatisch erhobene Meßdaten
     - durch einen Menschen wahrgenommene subjektive Symptome (z.B.
       Geräusche)

     Es ist für die Werker im Prüfstand in der Regel nicht möglich,
     die automatisch erhobenen Meßwerte zu interpretieren. Die Integra-
     tion beider Wissensquellen ist daher ungenügend.
(3) Weniger auffällige Symptome bemerkt der Mensch häufig erst dann,
     wenn er einen entsprechenden Verdacht hat. Deswegen sollten auf dem
     Prüfstand nicht nur Symptome erhoben, sondern diese sofort inter-
     pretiert werden.

3.2.   Ziel

Zur optimalen diagnostischen Auswertung aller Wissensquellen wurde
das Expertensystem IXMO auf der Basis des Werkzeuges MED1 entwickelt.
Die Wissensbasis befindet sich in einem ständigen Wachstumsprozeß
(Juni 85: über 1000 Regeln).

Zur Integration von IXMO in die Produktion waren folgende Probleme
zu lösen:

(1) Ein Teil der Symptome wird von einem Prüffeldrechner automatisch
     erfaßt. Deren Einlesen erfordert eine Rechnerkopplung von MED1 zum
     Prüffeldrechner und eine Umwandlung der Daten in MED1-Format.
(2) Um einen Kompromiß zwischen der Ökonomie einer automatischen
     Interpretation von vorgegebenen Daten ohne Rückfragemöglichkeit
     und der verbesserten Diagnostik durch gezielte Suche nach relevan-
     ten Symptomen im Dialog zu finden, sollte MED1 in beiden Modi
     einsatzbereit sein. Das erfordert einen flexiblen Dialogmodus mit
     wechselseitiger Initiative.
(3) Die Benutzerschnittstelle von MED1 ist relativ umständlich zu
     bedienen.

3.3.   Erweiterungen an MED1

Um die drei genannten Probleme zu lösen, wurde MED1 entsprechend
erweitert:

(1) Rechnerkopplung und Vorverarbeitung der Daten

Die Meßdaten werden vom Prüffeldrechner über eine V24-Schnittstelle an
den IXMO-Rechner übertragen. Bei der Aufarbeitung der Daten in MED1-
Format wurde die Fülle der Rohdaten, die pro Meßwert aus mehreren
Einzel-Messungen und Angabe der erlaubten Toleranzen bestehen, sofort
in eine der drei Kategorien: "zu hoch", "im Normbereich", "zu niedrig"
eingeordnet. Diese numerische Vorverarbeitung vereinfachte den Aufbau
der Wissensbasis erheblich.

(2) wechselseitige Initiative im Dialog

In MED1 ist der Benutzer passiv und beantwortet nur die ihm gestellten
Fragen. Eine aktive Symptomeingabe durch den Benutzer setzt voraus:

- eine Kontrollstruktur, die flexibel auf neue Daten reagieren kann
- ein einfach zu bedienender und dem Benutzer geläufiger Eingabemodus

Da die Hypothezise-and-Test Strategie die Möglichkeit vorsieht, über
Forward-Regeln neue Verdachtshypothesen zu generieren, bedurfte es
"nur" einer Anpassung der Benutzerschnittstelle. Dieses im allgemeinen
sehr schwierige Problem (die allgemeinste Lösung ist natürlichsprachliche Eingabe) wurde durch die Entwicklung eines hierarchisch aufgebauten Fehlercodes gelöst. Die Eingabe des Fehlercodes entspricht dem
Menü-Selektionsverfahren in BTX, wo man mit allgemeinen Angaben beginnt
und diese stufenweise präzisiert. Der Fehlercode hat insbesondere zwei
Vorteile:

- allgemeine Symptome werden einfach angegeben, indem man die Präzisie-
  rungen wegläßt.
- bei Vertrautheit mit dem Fehlercode erfolgt die Symptomeingabe
  sehr schnell.

(3) Benutzerschnittstelle

Die Benutzerschnittstelle von MED1 war auf einen einfachen Bildschirm zugeschnitten. Sie wurde verbessert unter Einbezug des Window-Konzeptes zur automatischen Präsentation von Erklärungen (insbesondere zur Darstellung der aktuellen Verdachtshypothesen in der Agenda) und der Maus zur Selektion von Alternativen in einem Menü durch Anklicken.

3.4. Bewertung von MED1

3.4.1. Wissensrepräsentation

Bei der Wissensrepäsentation haben sich die Mechanismen von MED1 besonders bewährt, mit denen Hierarchien von Fragen und Diagnosen aufgebaut werden können. Damit wird zum einen die Anzahl der notwendigen Fragen reduziert, zum anderen kann die Genauigkeit der Diagnosen gut an die Präzision bei der Symptomerhebung angepaßt werden (Fig. 5).

	Symptom	Diagnose
zunehmende Verfeinerung	S2000 Laufeigenschaft — —	┣ → D6000 Verbrennung
	S2500 Motor setzt aus — —	— → D6400 Einspritzanlage
	S2530 Motor setzt beim — ┥ Beschleunigen aus	— → D6420 Einspritzpumpe

Fig. 5: Abstimmung der Hierarchiekonzepte bei Symptomen und Diagnosen

3.4.2. Inferenzstrategie

Zur Zeit läuft MED1 überwiegend im passiven Modus (vom Standpunkt des Systems aus): Der Benutzer bzw. die Meßgeräte liefern Daten, die von MED1 ausgewertet werden. Damit wird die Fähigkeit von MED1, Vorschläge zur weiteren Vorgehensweise zu machen, noch kaum genutzt. Sie wird allerdings gebraucht, wenn es von der Prüfstandtechnologie her möglich sein wird, gezielt Spezialuntersuchungen zur Abklärung eines bestimmten Verdachtes durchzuführen, die dann von MED1 als technische Untersuchungen indiziert werden.

3.4.3. Umgang mit Unsicherheiten

Experten können wesentlich besser die wenn-dann Beziehung einer Regel festlegen, als ihr eine Punktzahl zuzuweisen, die ihre Wahrscheinlichkeit repräsentiert. Deswegen haben wir bei IXMO ein einfaches Schema mit wenigen Abstufungen zur Gewichtung der Regeln benutzt, mit dem wir bis jetzt gut ausgekommen sind. Bei der Symptomerhebung reichen die Abstufungen ja/nein/unbekannt aus, die Option "fraglich vorhanden" wurde nicht gebraucht.

3.4.4.   Benutzerschnittstelle

IXMO kann derzeitig mit zwei verschiedenen Benutzerschnittstellen
eingesetzt werden: der alten einfachen und der neuen Schnittstelle
mit Window und Maus. Dem Vorteil des zusätzlichen Komforts der
neuen Schnittstelle steht der Nachteil einer längeren Laufzeit gegenüber. Unsere Messungen ergaben bei interpretiertem LISP-Code für vier
Fälle mit unterschiedlichem Diagnoseaufwand folgende CPU-Zeiten:

Fall	untersuchte Diagnosen	gefeuerte Regeln	CPU-Zeit ohne Windows	CPU-Zeit mit Windows
F1	21	38	0.48 min	1.50 min
F2	29	55	0.52 min	2.32 min
F3	38	58	0.58 min	3.39 min
F4	48	78	1.07 min	4.25 min

Die Daten zeigen, daß die Benutzerschnittstelle (Aufbau und Update der
Windows) die Gesamteffizienz des Systems bestimmt.
Die wichtigste Kritik an der Benutzerschnittstelle besteht darin,
daß die Lokalisation von Symptomen (die betroffenen Bauteile) codiert
eingegeben werden müssen, anstatt daß sie graphisch auf dem Bildschirm
dargestellt und mit der Maus angeklickt werden.

3.4.5.   Probleme mit MED1

MED1 ist ein reines Diagnosesystem. Die wichtigste zusätzliche Forderung ist die Erweiterung, daß es Empfehlungen zur Reparatur gibt und -
noch wichtiger - die Ergebnisse von Reparaturversuchen erfassen und bei
notwendiger weiterer Diagnostik berücksichtigen kann.

4.   Projekt Hardwarediagnostik

4.1.   Ausgangssituation und Ziel

Die Behebung von Fehlern einer großen Rechenanlage ist meist eine
sehr zeitkritische Angelegenheit. Ziel des geplanten Expertensystems
ist es, den Techniker vor Ort bei der Fehlerbehebung zu unterstützen.
Wegen der großen Komplexität von Rechenanlagen wurde von Siemens
zunächst ein Projekt gestartet, das durch Entwicklung eines einfachen
Prototyps die Machbarkeit eines entsprechenden Expertensystemproduktes
ermitteln sollte. Dazu wurde MED1 als Shell benutzt. Der jetzige
Prototyp umfaßt:

- 93 Fragen
- 122 Regeln
- 33 Diagnosen

Im folgenden beschreiben wir die Schwierigkeiten, die bei seiner
Entwicklung aufgetreten sind.

4.2.   Probleme beim Wissenserwerb

Beim Wissenserwerb lassen sich zwei Phasen unterscheiden:

(1) inhaltliche Strukturierung des Wissens
(2) formale Ausarbeitung

MED1 setzt für die erste inhaltliche Phase Rahmenbedingungen durch
die Möglichkeiten und Beschränkungen der verschiedenen Datentypen.
Sein Wissenseditor unterstützt nur die zweite Phase. Die inhaltliche
Strukturierung stellte sich als das Hauptproblem für das Projekt
heraus, bedingt durch folgende Faktoren:

- Größe des Gebietes
Die Größenordnung des Bereichs läßt sich aus der Existenz von zahlreichen Diagnose- und Wartungshandbüchern ermessen. Eine Beschränkung auf
ein gut isolierbares Teilproblem war nicht möglich.

- Probleme bei der Einarbeitung in die Anwendung
Die Projektmitarbeiter hatten wenig eigene Erfahrungen in der Hardware-
diagnostik. Der Kontakt mit den sehr beschäftigten Experten beschränkte
sich auf wöchentliche Treffen.

- Probleme bei der Einarbeitung in MED1
Die Projektmitarbeiter hatten keine vorherigen Erfahrungen mit MED1.
Die Existenz mancher Strukturierungsmöglichkeiten (insbesondere die
Relevanz des nicht benutzten Datentyps "technische Untersuchungen" zur
Steuerung des Diagnostikprozesses) stellte sich erst im Verlaufe des
Projektes heraus.

- unübersichtliche Listings der Wissensbasis
Das wichtigste Hilfsmittel, um Übersicht über die wachsende Wissensbasis zu behalten, sind Computerausdrücke. Dabei sollte für jeden
möglichen Strukturierungsaspekt ein eigener Ausdruck angefertigt werden
können. In MED1 fehlte vor allem die Möglichkeit, die Abhängigkeiten
zwischen den Fragen übersichtlich darzustellen.

4.3.   Bewertung von MED1

Wegen der Schwierigkeiten beim Aufbau der Wissensbasis wurden kaum
Versuche unternommen, um MED1 zu erweitern. Bei der Benutzung der
Originalversion gab es u.a. folgende Probleme:

- Zur Eingabe von Fehlermeldungen der Rechenanlage als Symptome ist
   das Menü-Selektionsverfahren von MED1 ungeeignet, da es zuviele
   Fehlermeldungen gibt. Angemessener wäre eine Eingabe als String, die
   von MED1 vorverarbeitet und in sein internes Format umgewandelt

wird.

- Eine wesentliche diagnostische Informationsquelle ist das testweise
Austauschen von Bauteilen mit der anschließenden Abfrage:

(1) Fehler behoben
(2) Fehler unverändert
(3) neuer Fehler aufgetreten

Zur Darstellung längerer Sequenzen von Tauschaktionen ist die Repräsentation von MED1 umständlich zu handhaben.

- Insbesondere zur Diagnostik von sporadisch auftretenden Fehlern
sind Mehrfachsitzungen nötig. Dazu sollte MED1 das Wissen von
früheren Sitzungen zur Verfügung haben, um die Symptomeingabe zu
verkürzen und Wissen von früheren Sitzungen auswerten zu können.

5.   Projekt Datenbank-Tuning

5.1.   Ausgangssituation und Ziel

Zu lange Laufzeiten bei Datenbankanwendungen sind häufig bedingt
durch unzureichendes Wissen der Anwender über die zweckmäßigste Benutzung des Datenbanksystems. Deren Ursache läßt sich häufig mit den
Kenngrößen, die der Datenbankmonitor liefert, diagnostizieren. Ziel des
geplanten Einsatzes eines Expertensystems ist es, dem Datenbankanwender
dieses Wissen zur Verfügung zu stellen. Dazu wurde auf MED1-Basis ein
Prototyp erstellt, der zur Zeit (Juli 85)

23 Fragen
44 Regeln
11 Diagnosen

enthält. Der Prototyp arbeitet überwiegend so, daß er die Kennwerte
des Datenbankmonitors in verschiedener Weise verknüpft und die Resultate mit Sollwerten vergleicht, welche von der Leistungsfähigkeit der
Rechenanlage abhängen.

5.2.   Erweiterungen an MED1

Die durchgeführten Erweiterungen an MED1 bezogen sich vor allem
auf zwei Bereiche:

- Regelformat
- Benutzerschnittstelle

Die Änderungen im Regelformat ergaben sich aus der Notwendigkeit, in
großem Umfang numerische Berechnungen durchzuführen, was in MED1

umständlich ist, da es viele Zwischenvariablen erfordert. Dazu wurde
das Regelformat [Puppe 83, S. 60] so erweitert, daß sowohl im
Bedingungs- als auch im Aktionsteil komplexe arithmetische Operationen
möglich sind.
Die Änderungen der Benutzerschnittstelle umfaßten:

- Hervorhebungen von Text (invers, unterstrichen, blinkend)
- variable Textausgabe (Möglichkeit zur Angabe von Variablen im Text)
- Einführung eines neuen Datentyps, der nur zur Textausgabe dient

5.3.   Bewertung von MED1

Bei dem Prototyp handelt es sich um eine kleine Anwendung, bei der
es nicht auf die effiziente Abarbeitung großer Suchräume, sondern
auf die vollständige Auswertung der zur Verfügung stehenden Fakten
ankommt, und die numerische Verarbeitung von Daten im Vordergrund
steht. Die Hypothezise-and-Test Strategie von MED1 wurde in der Weise
adaptiert, daß mittels Regeln zur Verdachtsgenerierung immer alle
Hypothesen vollständig überprüft werden. Obwohl sich für solche Anwendungsgebiete auch herkömmliche Programmierverfahren eignen, ergaben
sich aus der Verwendung des Expertensystem-Shell MED1 Vorteile:

- kurze Entwicklungszeit
- schnelles Feedback für die Experten
- Möglichkeit, unterschiedliche Expertenmeinungen in verschiedenen
  Wissensbasen zu implementieren
- Erklärungsfähigkeit des Systems

6.   Zusammenfassung

Ein Vergleich der Erfahrungen mit MED1 aus den drei stark unterschiedlichen Anwendungsprojekten erlaubt folgende Schlußfolgerungen und Verbesserungsvorschläge für ein Diagnostik-Expertensystem-Shell, die wir
bei dem Nachfolgesystem MED2 [Puppe 85] berücksichtigen:

(1)   Die in MED1 realisierte Hypothezise-and-Test Strategie eignet sich
      gut für diagnostische Problembereiche, da sie flexibel genug ist,
      verschiedene Vorgehensweisen zu unterstützen (hierarchische Diag-
      nostik, Interpretation vorgegebener Daten, ökonomische Datensuch-
      strategien).
(2)   In allen Anwendungsgebieten waren spezielle Erweiterungen von MED1
      notwendig. Zur Vereinfachung deren Implementierung sollte ein
      Expertensystem-Shell offene Schnittstellen zur Programmiersprache
      bereitstellen.
(3)   Die Benutzerschnittstelle von MED1 war für alle Anwendungen
      unzureichend. Wegen der unterschiedlichen Möglichkeiten zu ihrer
      Verbesserung auf verschiedenen Rechnern sollte sie besonders modu-
      lar und änderungsfreundlich implementiert sein.

(4) Ein Diagnoseprogramm ist erheblich attraktiver für den Anwender,
wenn es Vorschläge zur Fehlerbehebung macht und die Ergebnisse der
Durchführung zur eventuell notwendigen weiteren Diagnostik auswer-
tet. Das erfordert vor allem eine explizite Repräsentation der
zeitlichen Dimension.

Darüber hinaus bestätigte sich wiederum die überragende Rolle des
Wissenserwerbs. Der bisherige Erfolg des IXMO-Projektes war entscheidend durch die Mitarbeit eines erfahrenen "KnowlegdeEngeneer" bedingt,
der sowohl mit dem Werkzeug MED1 als auch dem Anwendungsgebiet vertraut
war und den schwierigen Prozeß der Strukturierung und Aufarbeitung des
Expertenwissens geleistet hat.

Danksagung: Die Projekte wurden und werden durch die Einsatzbereit-
schaft der "Knowledge-Engeneers" Horst-Peter Borrmann (InWare GmbH,
Berlin im IXMO-Projekt) und Irmgard Büttel (Siemens) sowie aller
anderen der über zwanzig beteiligten Mitarbeiter getragen. Weiterhin
danke ich den beteiligten Firmen Innovationsgesellschaft, Siemens und
InWare für ihre Bereitschaft zu dieser Veröffentlichung.

7.   Literaturverweise

[Bobrow 83] D. Bobrow, M. Stefik: The LOOPS Manual, Xerox Corporation,
    1983.
[Borrmann 83] H.-P. Borrmann: MODIS - ein Expertensystem zur Erstellung
    von Reparaturdiagnosen fuer den Otto-Motor und seine Aggregate,
    Diplomarbeit, Memo-Seki-83-05, Kaiserslautern 1983.
[Buchanan 84] B. Buchanan, E. Shortliffe: Rule-Based Expert Systems:
    The MYCIN Experiments of the Stanford Heuristic Programming
    Project, Addison Wesley, 1984.
[Clancey 84] W. Clancey: Classification Problem Solving, Proceedings
    of AAAI-84 S. 49-55, 1984.
[diPrimio 85] F. di Primio: BABYLON as a Tool for Building Expert
    Systems, GI-Kongreß "Wissensbasierte Systeme" 1985.
[Puppe 83] F. Puppe: MED1: Ein heuristisches Diagnosesystem mit
    effizienter Kontrollstruktur, Diplomarbeit, Memo-Seki-83-04, Kai-
    serslautern 1983.
[Puppe 84] B. Puppe: Die Entwicklung des Computereinsatzes in der
    medizinischen Diagnostik und MED1: ein Expertensystem zur Brust-
    schmerz-Diagnostik, medizinische Dissertation, Universität Frei-
    burg, 1984.
[Puppe 85] F. Puppe, B. Puppe: MED2: How Domain Characteristics Induce
    Expert System Features, eingereicht zur GWAI-85.
[Weiss 84] S. Weiss, C. Kulikowski: A Practical Guide to Designing
    Expert Systems, Rowman & Allanheld Publishers, 1984.

Expertensys<u>teme für Praktiker heute und morgen</u>
Dr. Markus Rauh
Philips Kommunikations Industrie AG
Unternehmensbereich Philips Data Systems
Weidenauer Straße 211-213
5900 Siegen

Sehr verehrte Damen und Herren,
erlauben Sie mir, daß ich als Einleitung nicht eine Definition eines
Expertensystemes vortrage, wie Sie vielleicht erwartet haben, sondern
diejenige eines Praktikers, eines Verantwortungsträgers in Wirtschaft
und Verwaltung also. Neben vielen Problemen muß sich doch der Praktiker bei der Analyse des Istzustandes und der Projektion der erkennba-
ren Entwicklungen in seinem Verantwortungsbereich mit folgenden Fragen
auseinandersetzen:

- Mit welchen unbürokratischen und innovativen Methoden und Prozeduren
  gelingt es, das operationelle Geschehen besser zu verstehen und vor-
  hersagen zu können?

- Wie können bessere, transparentere, schneller verfügbarere und auf
  Alternativen aufbauende Entscheidungsgrundlagen beschafft werden?

- Wie kann die - teilweise fatale - Abhängigkeit von den meist unver-
  ständlichen Gesetzmäßigkeiten der historisch gewachsenen EDV-Syste-
  men reduziert werden, ohne einen Leistungsabbau oder gar einen
  Systemzusammenbruch befürchten zu müssen?

- Wie kann die unvorhersehbare, aus internen und externen Quellen
  stammende Informationsflut für die vorgebenen Zielsetzungen erfolg-
  versprechend ausgewertet werden? (Wir alle wissen, daß intern heute
  schon mehr Daten und Berichte produziert werden, als irgendwer lesen
  und verarbeiten kann.)

- Wie gelingt es, eine höhere Motivation der Mitarbeiter zu erreichen,
  vom eskalierenden Taylorismus, d.h. der Scheuklappen tragenden Spezialisierung wegzukommen und ein Verständnis für die Gesamtzusammen-
  hänge auf allen hierarchischen Ebenen zu schaffen?

- Eng mit dem Taylorismus verbunden ist die Frage nach der Abhängigkeit von Spezialisten. Denn wir wissen, daß die allgemeine Leistung
  eines Unternehmens oft eingeschränkt oder sogar bedroht wird durch
  die Tatsache, daß nur wenige Mitarbeiter hochwertiges Spezialwissen
  besitzen, das schwer weitergegeben werden kann. Dazu kommt noch, daß
  diese Spezialisten in der Regel nicht nur schwer erreichbar sind,
  sondern auch oft hohe Schwankungen ihrer Leistungen hingenommen werden müssen. Die Besten leisten oft zehn mal mehr als die Schlech-
  testen, wobei fallbezogen nicht von vornherein feststeht, welche der
  Primadonnen zu den Guten oder Schlechten gehört.

- Eine weitere Frage, auf die ich etwas näher eingehen möchte, ist
  diejenige nach der Vermehrung und der Erosion des Wissens. Obwohl
  wir es selten und ungern aussprechen, wissen wir, daß mitunter jeder
  arbeitende Mensch in einer wettbewerbsfähigen Umgebung ein Wissens-
  Arbeiter ist. Denken Sie nur an unsere Sekretärinnen, Telefonistin-
  nen, Portiers, nicht zu reden von den Verkäufern, Entwicklern, Konstrukteuren und Bedienungskräften. Sie sind deshalb besonders wertvoll, weil sie über ein bestimmtes Wissen verfügen.

Angesichts der Bedeutung des Wissens muß es das zentrale Anliegen
jeder erfolgreichen Organisation sein, Prozesse der Wissensvermehrung und -verbreitung zu fördern. Wissen ist lebendig, es wächst
langsam durch Erfahrung in den Köpfen und verkümmert schnell. Die
Weitergabe von Wissen ist schwierig, weil es dazu keine sicheren
Methoden gibt. Spezialistenwissen besteht aus den drei Komponenten:
* terminologisches Wissen, d.h. relevante Sprache
* Allgemeinwissen
* und fachspezifisches Wissen.

Vor allem letzteres ist einem immer schnelleren Wandel und einer
dramatischen Vermehrung unterworfen. Die Geschwindigkeit, mit der
neues Wissen entwickelt wird, erhöht sich ständig und die Zeit, während der ein bestimmtes Wissen gültig bleibt, verkürzt sich. Auch
wird das Umfeld, in dem sich Organisationen bewegen müssen, ständig
komplizierter. Man denke nur an die vielen Gesetze und Vorschriften,
aber auch an die neuen Geräte und Maschinen, die immer raffinierter

werden und deshalb ständig höheres Wissen erfordern, was die Konstruktion, die Fertigung, die Wartung, aber auch den Einsatz beim Kunden betrifft. Nur durch gezielte Prozesse, wie Trial and Error, training on the job, job rotation oder externe Beratung, sind Institutionen bis heute in der Lage, mit dieser Herausforderung zu leben. Dem entgegen steht die Bedrohung durch die Wissenserosion, die für die betroffene Organisation nicht wiedergutzumachende Auswirkungen haben kann.

Die Verkürzung der wöchentlichen Arbeitszeit in Verbindung mit der Gleitzeit und der zunehmenden Urlaubsdauer läßt nicht mehr genügend Zeit für Wissensvermehrung oder -erhaltung, weil es nur noch schwer möglich wird, kognitiv zu kommunizieren. Wir wissen auch, daß es bis heute unmöglich ist, einen wissensintensiven Arbeitsplatz auf mehrere Menschen aufzuteilen, wie es mit einer gewissen Berechtigung von Arbeitslosen gefordert wird. Es fehlen uns einfach die Werkzeuge, die die Gedächtnisse dieser Menschen verlängern und die Kenntnisse, die von einer Person erworben sind, anderen verfügbar machen. Der Umstand, in das Erwerbsleben später einzusteigen und es früher zu beenden, verbunden mit einem fatalen Konservativismus und einem verbesserungsbedürftigen öffentlichen Bildungs- und Ausbildungswesens erhöht die Gefahr, daß eine Organisation die Fähigkeit verliert, ihren Aufgaben gerecht zu werden, d.h. daß ein Unternehmen seine Wettbewerbsfähigkeit verliert und daß staatliche Funktionen versagen. Die Wissenserosion führt nicht nur zum Niedergang bestehender Institutionen. Die Erschließung innovativer Industriezweige, d.h. die Entwicklung von Wissen in völligem Neuland erfordert einen Ressourcen-Überschuß. Wenn es aber schon problematisch ist, bestehendes Wissen zu erhalten, ist es unrealistisch anzunehmen, daß Ressourcen für die Entwicklung neuen Wissens zur Verfügung stehen würden.

Vor diesem Hintergrund hören wir als Praktiker über den Abschluß der ersten Phase des japanischen Projektes der fünften Computergeneration. Neben Grundlagen und Prototypen einer seriellen Inferenzmaschine, hören wir, daß die grundlegenden Mechanismen von Wissensbanken erforscht wurden. Ein auf der Sprache "Prolog" aufbauendes Softwaresystem konnte entwickelt werden, das der Mensch/Maschine-Schnittstelle, vor allem den Aspekt des Dialoges mit natürlicher Sprache und symbolisch-graphischer Darstellung beachtet.

Nicht nur aus Japan vernehmen wir solche Bestrebungen, die Medien berichten auch über das Strategic Computing Programm des US-Departe-

mentes of Defense, über das ALVEY Programm in Großbritannien sowie
über das CNRS und das INRIA in Frankreich. Unter ESPRIT läuft das
Projekt über Advanced Information Processing und aus der Bundesrepublik sind einige Programme des BMFT und vor allem der GMD bekannt
geworden. Von den meisten technischen Universitäten, vor allem den-
jenigen im nördlichen und südwestlichen Raum sowie den hierzulande
forschenden Computerlieferanten, wie IBM, Philips, Nixdorf und weiteren weiß man, daß sie sich mit Fragen der künstlichen Intelligenz
auseinandersetzen.

Meine Damen und Herren, ein so definierter Praktiker, der über diesen
beschriebenen Wissenstand verfügt - und ich hoffe, daß viele davon
hier sind - wird sich einige Fragen stellen, auf die ich versuche, anschließend Antworten zu geben.

1. Was ist ein Expertensystem?

Ein Expertensystem ist im wesentlichen ein interaktives Softwareprodukt, das in einer Wissensbank Fakten und Regeln über einen ein-
grenzbaren, weitgehendst konsolidierten Anwendungsbereich enthält
und das beim Lösen von Problemen in diesem Bereich helfen soll. Expertensysteme unterstützen also Fachleute gleichen Gebietes kreativ
mit unscharfem Wissen und im wesentlichen unformalisierten Abläufen
umzugehen.

Drei Haupteigenschaften kennzeichnen Expertensyteme:

- Sie führen mit den Anwendern einen Dialog in natürlicher, in der
  Regel geschriebener Sprache und entwickeln durch laufende Rückkopplung von Hypothesenvalidierungen problemspezifische Lösungsstrategien.

- Sie sind in der Lage, die Schlußfolgerungen und Ergebnisse wie
  auch die als Zwischenschritte gestellten Fragen bei Bedarf zu begründen.

- Sie sind lernfähig, denn durch gelöste Aufgaben und neue Erkenntnisse kann die Wissensbank neue Regeln aufnehmen, respektiv bestehende anpassen.

Expertensysteme stellen, wie Abbildung 1 zeigt, den Übergang von
klassischer Datenverarbeitung mit Entscheidungstabellen zur künstlichen Intelligenz dar und eignen sich zur Bearbeitung einfach-for-
maler Systeme. Robotics, Musterkennung und Deduktionssysteme unterstützen die höheren Formen des intelligenten Verhaltens.

**Beziehung zwischen intelligentem Verhalten und
künstlicher Intelligenz** (Abb. 1)

Stufen des intelligenten Verhaltens	Anwendungsgrad der künstlichen Intelligenz
nicht formales Verhalten	Deduktionssystem
komplex-formale Systeme	Mustererkennung
einfach-formale Systeme	Robotics
assoziatives Verhalten	Expertensysteme / klassische DV

2. Wo können Expertensysteme produktiv eingesetzt werden?

Einfach-formale Systeme sind in der Regel vorhanden, wenn es darum
geht, zu interpretieren, zu prognostizieren, eine Diagnose zu stellen, zu konstruieren, eine Planung oder eine Überwachung vorzunehmen, Fehlersuchen oder Reparaturen durchzuführen, zu instruieren
oder zu steuern.

Die heute erfolgreich eingesetzten Expertensysteme stammen denn
auch ausschließlich aus dem technisch-naturwissenschaftlichen Bereich und unterstützen Anwendungen wie die

- Analyse modularer Strukturen
- Auswertung von Bohrlochmessungen bei der Suche nach Erdöl und
  Mineralien
- Fehlerdiagnose und Vorgehen zur Fehlerbehebung
- Konfiguration komplexer Systeme
- Aufklärung und Mitteloptimierung im militärischen Bereich.

Aber auch im Umfeld der Medizin, der Rechtswissenschaften, der Beratung bei Banken, Versicherungen und der Anwendung von Chemikalien sind erfolgversprechende Ansätze zu erkennen. Die Kombination von Expertensystemen und Bildschirmtext könnte Kunden, die oft auch Spezialisten sind, auf sehr kompetente Weise beraten, um Wettbewerbsvorteile zu schaffen.

Ob Anwendungen in der Unternehmensführung sinnvoll sind, kann noch nicht mit Bestimmtheit gesagt werden. Es gibt Anzeichen dafür, daß Expertensysteme der in letzter Zeit eher in Verruf geratenen strategischen Planung zu einer Renaissance verhelfen könnten. Wie es in der komplex-formalen Büroumgebung aussieht, wird unter anderem ein vor Jahresfrist begonnenes Forschungsprojekt der Philips-Unternehmungen aufzeigen, über das wir hier von Herrn Dr. Pasedach noch weiteres hören werden.

3. Gehören Expertensysteme in den Bereich der heutigen ORG/DV?

Eigentlich sollte diese Frage mit einem klaren Ja beantwortet werden und langfristig muß das sicher auch so sein. Denn Expertensysteme und künstliche Intelligenz allgemein können sich nur durchsetzen, wenn sie die Applikationen, in die Milliarden investiert wurden, ergänzen. Allerdings müssen die heutigen Anlagen in den 90er Jahren durch Inferenzmaschinen, die 10 - 50 mal schneller sind, erweitert werden.

Die Erfahrung zeigt aber, daß die heutigen EDV-Spezialisten mit ihrem prozeduralen Weltbild aus Flow Charts und Integer Values nur schwer in der Lage sind, das deterministische Umfeld der Expertensysteme zu begreifen und mit Werten wie "Wahrscheinlichkeit", "möglich", "vielleicht" sowie unvollständigen und inkonsistenten Regeln zu leben.

Um Expertensysteme zu realisieren, brauchen wir Wissensingenieure,
die in der Lage sind, das zu bearbeitende Problem zu definieren und
die erforderlichen Regeln und Objekte in Gesprächen mit Experten
herauszuschälen. Für Wissensingenieure gibt es leider weder Lehr-
gänge noch Anforderungsprofile. Sie werden noch während langer Zeit
Mangelware bleiben. Sie gehen recht in der Annahme, daß wir die
Schaffung einer neuen Spezies von "freischaffenden Künstlern" mit-
erleben. Der mühsame Prozess der Normalisierung und Eingliederung,
den wir nach zwanzigjähriger Leidensgeschichte soeben mit den
Systemanalytikern und Programmierern abschließen, wird also von
neuem beginnen. Wir sind gut beraten, wenn wir uns frühzeitig
darauf vorbereiten, denn auch diese Spezialisten werden uns hohe
Investitionen beantragen und werden unsere Wettbewerbsfähigkeit
entscheidend mit beeinflussen.

4. Können Expertensysteme gekauft werden?

Wie es zu Beginn der Datenverarbeitung nicht möglich war, Buchhal-
tungs- oder Auftragsabwicklungssysteme zu kaufen, wird es vorläufig
auch nicht möglich sein, fertige Expertensysteme zu kaufen. Die Anforderungen sind noch zu individuell und die rechtlichen Probleme
noch nicht lösbar.

Hingegen verfügen wir über schon recht komfortable Werkzeuge zur
Erstellung von Expertensysteme. Hauptsächlich handelt es sich um
Software, die von spezialisierten, meist amerikanischen Häusern,
die oft Universitäten nahestehen, angeboten wird. Vermehrt bieten
auch etablierte Computerhersteller Software für Expertensysteme
an. Da die klassische John von Neumann'sche Datenverarbeitungs-
Hardware für leistungsfähige Expertensysteme nicht geeignet ist,
gibt es auch spezielle Hardwareangebote, die allerdings für einen
produktiven Einsatz noch recht kostspielig sind, und die in der
Regel Insellösungen bleiben müssen.

5. Wie soll beim Einsatz eines Expertensystems vorgegangen werden?

Als erstes muß zwischen dem Management, dem Wissensingenieur und
dem Experten die Zielsetzung des Projektes definiert werden. Diese
Aufgabe ist schwieriger als bei klassischen DV-Projekten, aber umso
wichtiger. Die meisten Fehlschläge sind denn auch auf mangelhafte
Zieldefinition zurückzuführen.

Nach der Definitionsphase muß sich das Management über folgende Er-
folgsfaktoren im klaren sein:

- Expertensysteme benötigen sehr viel Speicherkapazität und Prozessorleistung.

- Für alle Beteiligten, auch den Wissensingenieur ist ein hohes Maß
  an Schulung und Erfahrungsaustausch erforderlich.

- Die Wissensakquisition ist ein mühsamer und langwieriger Prozess,
  dem die Experten auch wirklich zur Verfügung stehen müssen. Die
  Gefahr ist groß, daß nach einer mühsamen Anlaufsphase die Wissensingenieure die Rolle der Experten übernehmen, was als erstes
  Todeszeichen eines Projektes erkannt werden muß.

- Schnell verfügbare Prototypen, mit denen oft eindrückliche Vor-
  führungen gemacht werden können, bedeuten nicht, daß das Projekt
  kurz vor dem Abschluß steht, die extrem schwierige Phase der Einbettung des Systems in bestehende Abläufe steht jeweils noch bevor.

Expertensysteme benötigen also einen hohen Mitteleinsatz, qualifi-
zierte Ressourcen und vor allem große Beachtung durch das Management während der ganzen Laufzeit.

6. Wie sieht der Markt für Expertensysteme aus?

Die Komplexität der Wissensbereiche erfordert enorme Rechner-Res-
sourcen bezüglich Speicherkapazität und Durchsatzraten. Hier rechne
ich mit deutlichen Verbesserungen in der Zukunft. Heutige Rechner

bewältigen Softwaremodelle mit etwa 2.000 Regeln zur Problemlösung. Aufgrund der Weiterentwicklung der Computersysteme ist davon auszugehen, daß etwa Anfang der 90er Jahre preisvergleichbare Systeme bis zu 20.000 Regeln beherrschen. Auch werden die Rechnerleistungen dann parallel zum Benutzerdialog die Ergebnisse vorhergesagter Lösungen simulieren und können deshalb die Vorhersagegenauigkeit und damit die Akzeptanz für weitere Benutzerkreise erhöhen. Heute muß die Korrektheit der Lösungen im Prinzip durch die Regelbasis bewiesen werden.

Deshalb bin ich auch der Meinung, daß erst die jetzt langsam beginnenden Pilotanwendungen eine genauere Bewertung der Chancen und Risiken erlauben werden. Sie sind aber in jedem Falle unerläßlich, um eine Entfremdung von der praktischen Benutzerumgebung zu vermeiden. Zuviele an sich gute Entwicklungen sind unter anderem oder hauptsächlich daran gescheitert, daß sie zu lange ausschließlich unter Experten, unter Ausschluß der potentiellen Benutzer oder Ignoranz ihrer ersten Erfahrungen, durchgesetzt werden sollten. Letztlich waren aber die Märkte für die erarbeiteten Lösungen nicht aufnahmefähig, weil die Nachfrage nach der spezifischen Art der Lösung nicht bestand oder die angebotenen Systeme zu komplex und im täglichen Gebrauch zu unhandlich und unübersichtlich waren.

Bei meinem Versuch, die weitere Entwicklung zu prognostizieren, gehe ich davon aus, daß sich die Expertensysteme erst dann in nennenswertem Maße durchsetzen werden, wenn es gelingt, sie in die betriebliche Einsatzumgebung einzubinden. Für einen sehr kleinen und eher isolierten Anwendungsbereich werden sich nach meiner Einschätzung weder die hohen Entwicklungsvorleistungen lohnen noch der anwenderseitige Nutzen einen ausreichenden Anreiz zur Arbeit mit dem System bieten.

Um zu einem raschen Durchbruch mit Expertensystemen zu kommen, sind m.E. zwei wesentliche Voraussetzungen noch nicht erfüllt. Es fehlen heute und auf mittlere Sicht die erforderlichen Spezialisten, d.h. Wissensingenieure, um auf der Anwender- und Anbieterseite praxisgerechte Systeme zu konzipieren, ihren Einsatz zu optimieren und neue Formen der Wissensakquisition und des Benutzerdialoges zu realisieren. Heutige Soft- und Hardware-Spezialisten werden nach wie vor dringend in den angestammten Bereichen gebraucht und die erforderlichen Ausbildungskapazitäten im universitären und Forschungsbereich sind noch nicht vorhanden. Die gegenwärtig für Experten-

systeme <u>erforderliche Hard- und Software</u> ist entweder noch nicht in
ausreichender Leistungsfähigkeit vorhanden oder - soweit sie es in
Ansätzen ist - zu den in der betrieblichen Praxis vorherrschenden
Computersystemen, Softwarepaketen und der gesamten Infrastruktur
zum Informationsaustausch nicht kompatibel und bildet deshalb noch
auf längere Sicht eine Insellösung.

Nach unseren bisherigen Einschätzungen rechnen wir mit einem eher
geringen Marktwachstum für diese Systeme in Europa. Wir glauben
vielmehr, daß die heutigen Computersysteme und vor allem die
eingesetzten und bereits praxisbewährten Softwarepakete und Tools
wesentlich weiterentwickelt werden und einen großen Teil der
bestehenden Akzeptanzprobleme beseitigen. Dadurch werden wir in
einigen Bereichen teilweise expertensystemähnliche Lösungen, jedoch
mit dem Vorteil einer vollen Integration in die betriebliche Praxis
und Infrastruktur bieten können.

Die Schwelle, ab der dann reine Expertensysteme mit eindeutig
höherer Leistung erforderlich und sinnvoll sind, wird dadurch an-
gehoben.
Hinzu kommt, daß das Preis-/Leistungsverhältnis bei den immer
leistungsfähiger werdenden microcomputerbasierten, netzfähigen Computern immer günstiger wird und ein nach unserer Meinung großer
absoluter Abstand zu den Expertensystemen entstehen wird.

7. <u>Welche Unterlassung begehe ich, wenn ich mich nicht mit
Expertensystemen auseinandersetze?</u>

Sicher kann durch Nichtstun vorläufig Geld und Ärger gespart
werden.

Ob aber Expertensysteme nun zum Durchbruch kommen oder nicht, ganz
sicher ist, daß wir durch die Erfahrung mit Expertensystemen unser
Wissen über das Wissen gewaltig vergrößern.

<u>Produktionsfaktoren respektiv Management Ressourcen</u> (Abb. 2)

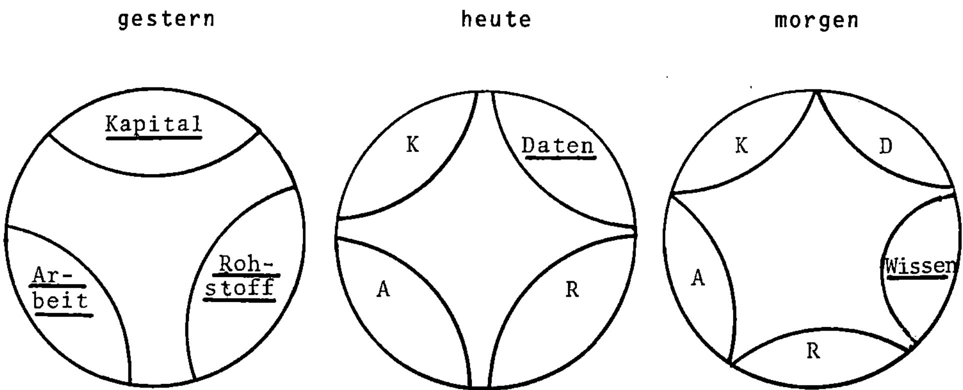

Dadurch wird, wie Abb. 2 zeigt, Wissen zu einem Produktionsfaktor,
der gleichberechtigt neben den klassischen Produktionsfaktoren
Kapital, Arbeit und Rohstoffe und der neuen Management-Ressource
Daten steht.

Als Praktiker müssen wir uns sehr wohl überlegen, ob wir es uns
leisten können, uns heute nicht mit den Management-Ressourcen von
morgen auseinander zu setzen.

Wissen ist Macht, so akut wie heute standen wir noch nie vor dieser
Tatsache. Selbst wenn unsere eingangs erwähnten Probleme durch
Expertensysteme nicht gelöst werden können, sind wir gut beraten,
nichts zu unterlassen, was uns dem Wissen über das Wissen näher
bringen könnte.

A METHODOLOGY FOR THE DEVELOPMENT OF GENERAL KNOWLEDGE-BASED VISION SYSTEMS

Edward M. Riseman and Allen R. Hanson
Computer and Information Science Department
University of Massachusetts
Amherst, Massachusetts 01003

ABSTRACT

Expert system technology has been successfully applied to many practical problems, but there has been little evidence of transfer to computer vision. In this paper we discuss some of the problems confronting computer vision, and present an approach to the development of general knowledge-based vision systems. Our approach involves the building of an intermediate symbolic representation of the image data using knowledge-free segmentation processes. From the intermediate level data, a partial interpretation is constructed by associating an object label with selected groups of the intermediate primitives.

The primary mechanism for generation of initial object hypotheses is a rule-based approach applied to the attributes of the lines, regions, and surfaces in the intermediate symbolic representation. Simple rules are defined as ranges over a feature value which are converted to a vote for an object label; complex rules are constructed via a functional combination of the output from the simple rules. The rules are constructed interactively with visual feedback as part of the knowledge engineering process.

The object hypotheses are used to activate portions of the knowledge network related to verifying or more completely extracting the hypothesized object. Once activated, the procedural components of the knowledge network direct additional more expensive extraction of object features, as well as further grouping, splitting and labelling processes at the intermediate level to construct intermediate events which are in closer agreement with the stored symbolic object description. We conclude with some principles which could be used to guide knowledge-based vision research.

I. INTRODUCTION

Expert system technology, especially techniques for rule-based knowledge engineering, has been successfully applied to many practical problems. Although there are inherent limitations in the complexity and power that can be achieved [1], particularly when the number of rules are not constrained, there has been little evidence of its application to image interpretation. Typically, vision systems [e.g. 2 – 17] are highly system or application dependent and consequently it has been difficult to transfer them to different task domains. This paper will discuss some of the problems that are specific to computer vision and describe one general methodology for the development of knowledge-based vision systems. The focus is on the initial iconic to symbolic mapping, a portion of the problem of identifying objects and constructing a 3D representation of the physical environment.

I.1. Complexity of Vision

The complexity of visual tasks can be made explicit by examining almost any complex image. While this initial discussion is qualitative, we believe the conjectures are intuitive and reasonable even though it is very difficult to be introspective of one's own visual processing. Human beings are rarely aware of any significant degree of ambiguity in local portions of the sensory data, nor are they aware of the degree to which they are employing more global context and stored expectations derived from their collective experience. However, if the visual field is restricted so that only local information is available about an object or object-part, interpretation is often difficult or impossible. Increasing the contextual information so that spatial relations to other objects and object-parts are present makes the perceptual task seem natural and simple. Consider the scenes in Figure 1 and the closeup images in Figure 2. In each case we have selected subimages of objects which show:

a) "primitive" visual elements — image events which convey limited information about the identity of the objects or of their decomposition into parts (this is of course at least partly a function of resolution) and

b) absence of context — there is limited information about other objects which might relate to the given object in expected ways.

In Figure 2 as some of the surrounding context of the shoes and the head are supplied, the perceptual ambiguity disappears and the related set of visual elements is easily recognized. In each of the above cases the individual local hypothesis is inherently unreliable and uncertain and there may be little surface information to be derived in a bottom-up manner. It appears that human vision is fundamentally organized to exploit the use of contextual knowledge and expectations in the organization of the visual primitives. However, it may be impossible to associate object labels with these ambiguous primitives until they are grouped into larger entities and collectively interpreted as a related set of object or scene parts. Thus, the inclusion of knowledge-driven processes at some level in the image interpretation task, where there is still a great degree of ambiguity in the organization of the visual primitives, appears inevitable.

We conjecture that image interpretation initially proceeds by forming an abstract representation of important visual events in the image without knowledge of its contents. The primitive elements forming this representation are then collected, grouped, and refined to bring their collective description into consistency with high-level semantic structures that represent the observer's knowledge about the world.

II. ISSUES FACING KNOWLEDGE-BASED VISION SYSTEMS

The development of knowledge-based vision systems has been hampered by several factors: lack of agreement on what constitutes an adequate representation of image events, lack of low-level processes that can reliably extract relevant image features, lack of satisfactory three-dimensional representations which can capture the inherent variability in the structure of physical objects and scenes, lack of adequate mechanisms for utilizing knowledge during the interpretation process, and finally by the necessity of a tremendous investment in software development before the capability for even simple interpretation experiments can be achieved. Most of the systems in the current literature only address some of these issues and, perhaps even more discouraging, there do not appear to be ways in which these systems can be easily generalized. This paper does not attempt to carefully survey the literature in knowledge-based vision systems. However, a partial review of image interpretation research can be found in [5,18,31] and a few of the individual research efforts are listed here [2 – 17].

Early attempts to interface stored knowledge to image data at the pixel level met with only limited success and little possibility of generalization [15]. For example, blue pixels could immediately be hypothesized to have "sky" labels and appropriate constraints could be propagated, but such an approach to interfacing visual knowledge seems rather futile in the face of increasing numbers of objects and increasing complexity of the task domain. Instead, vision systems must confront the problem of dynamically forming from the large number of individual pixels more useful entities to which propositions will be attached; (in an image of reasonable resolution there are $512 \times 512 \cong 1/4$ million pixels). Transforming the data into a much smaller set of image events is the goal of segmentation processes. However algorithms for extracting primitives such as 2D regions of homogeneous color and texture, straight lines, simple geometric shapes, and/or local surface patches have proven to be complex and quite unreliable, suggesting that substantial further processing is required before one can expect this intermediate representation to support a globally consistent interpretation.

For a variety of reasons one must expect the data at the level of representation of this first stage of segmentation to be distorted, incomplete, and sometimes meaningless. Segmentation of an image into regions, each of which is composed of a spatially contiguous set of pixels, is a very difficult and ill-formed problem [34]. The sensory data is inherently noisy and ambiguous and this leads to segmentations that are unreliable and vary in uncontrollable ways; for example, regions and lines are often fragmented or merged. In the case of the familiar problem of character recognition, this would be akin to being given joined letters and split letters at a very high frequency. In fact this is one of the major problems in automatic cursive script recognition that makes it much harder than recognition of printed or typed characters. Rather than being concerned only with the classification of a highly variable set of objects (the cursive characters), the system is also faced with the accompanying problem of organizing the input data into the appropriate segments that form the entities to be classified. Of course general vision is far more complicated than interpretation of handwriting, with a much larger number of more complex objects in task domains that are interesting.

In addition, the effect of occlusion leads to the difficult problem of partial pattern matching, where a strong match with part of the pattern is the desired result, as opposed to a weak match of the whole pattern. One must also expect many region and line samples which do not belong to any of the classes because they may be shadow regions, portions of occluded objects which cannot be identified, objects that have not been included in the set of object classes in the knowledge base, or object parts which are only identifiable in the context of the object hypothesis. While there has been some success [17] in applying a Bayesian classification viewpoint to these problems, difficulties abound and we believe standard statistical approaches generally lead to insoluble problems. The classical pattern recognition techniques are not powerful enough by themselves to produce effective classifications in the domains we wish to consider.

Scene interpretation requires processes that construct complex descriptions, where many hypotheses are put forth and a subset that can be verified and which satisfy a set of relational constraints are accepted. AI systems are often faced with fitting a set of very weak but consistent hypotheses into a more reliable whole. This usually is a complex process that requires a great reliance on stored knowledge of the object classes. This knowledge takes the form of object attributes and relations between objects, particularly relations between parts of objects which leads to a part-of hierarchy in the knowledge base.

It has been suggested that 2D regions and lines are not appropriate descriptions of the initial image data and that they should be replaced with local estimates of surface orientation, reflectance, depth, and velocity [15, 18, 19]. In this case the descriptive elements are surface patches which directly capture aspects of the three-dimensional world from which the image was obtained. The implication is that the interpretation task will be far simpler when the surface description is used since it is a representation of the actual physical world that is to be interpreted, and therefore a broader spectrum of domain constraints can be brought to bear upon the information. Although the claim is undoubtedly correct to some degree, reliable extraction of surface range, reflectance, and orientation from monocular image data has yet to be demonstrated except in highly constrained domains or under very unrealistic constraints on the type of surfaces making up the objects in the scene.

On the other hand, even if a very reliable description of this type could be obtained, the complexity of the natural world will leave us facing many of the same representation, grouping, and interpretation issues. Let us assume for the moment, that in addition to the original spectral information at each pixel, the distance to the corresponding visible surface element at each pixel was also available. Consider the problem of interpreting a complex environment such as a typical crowded city street scene, even if one had such a perfect depth map. How should one partition the information into meaningful entities such as surfaces, parts of objects, and objects? And then how could this be interfaced to the knowledge base so that control of the interpretation process is feasible? Given that many initial local hypotheses are inherently uncertain and unreliable, how do we achieve globally consistent and reliable integration of the information? This, in fact, is exactly the set of problems that we face with 2D data of regions and lines. We believe that the principles and approaches presented here will be applicable not only to the 2D events extracted from static monocular color images presented in this paper, but also to the interpretation of 3D depth data recovered from stereo and laser ranging devices, and 2D and 3D motion data derived from a sequence of images.

At the other end of the spectrum is the problem of representing the complexity of the 3D physical world in a form which is useful to the interpretation process [6]. The 3D shape, color, texture, and size of an object class, as well as spatial and functional relations to other objects, often have a great deal of natural variation from object to object and scene to scene. This problem is compounded by the fact that the 2D appearance of these objects in the image are affected by variations in lighting, perspective distortion, point of view, occlusion, highlights, and shadows. These difficulties ensure that the transformation processes for grouping intermediate symbols and matching them to knowledge structures will produce highly unreliable results. The interpretation processes will require general mechanisms for dealing with this uncertainty, detecting errors, and verifying hypotheses.

Figure 1. Original images. These images are representative samples from a larger data base. All are digitized to 512 × 512 spatial resolution, with 8 bits in the red, green, and blue components.

Figure 2. Closeups from original images. In many cases, the identity or function of an object or object part cannot be determined from a small local view. Only when the surrounding context becomes available can the objects be recognized.

In summary, there are a variety of issues which must be addressed and resolved before substantial progress in computer vision can be achieved:

a) An effective intermediate symbolic representation must be obtained to serve as the interface between the sensory data and the knowledge base.

b) Knowledge representations must be defined which are capable of capturing the tremendous variability and complexity in the appearance of natural objects and scenes, particularly 3D shape representations.

c) Techniques must be developed for flexibly organizing the intermediate symbols under the guidance of the knowledge base.

d) Mechanisms must be developed for integrating information and data from multiple sources.

e) Inference mechanisms must be available for assessing the indirect implications of the direct evidence.

f) Mechanisms must be developed for coping with the great degree of uncertainty which exists in every stage of data transformation that is part of the interpretation process.

III. OVERVIEW OF THE VISIONS SYSTEM APPROACH TO THESE ISSUES

Over the past ten years, the VISIONS group at the University of Massachusetts has been evolving a general system for knowledge-based interpretation of natural scenes, such as house, road, and urban scenes [8, 25, 33–36]. The goal of this effort is the construction of a system capable of interpreting natural images of significant complexity by exploiting the redundancies and general constraints expected between and within scene elements.

The general strategy by which the VISIONS system operates is to build an intermediate symbolic representation of the image data using segmentation processes which initially do not make use of any knowledge of specific objects in the domain. From the intermediate level data, a partial interpretation is constructed by associating an object label with selected groups of the intermediate primitives. The object labels are used to activate portions of the knowledge network related to the hypothesized object. Once activated, the procedural components of the knowledge network direct further grouping, splitting and labelling processes at the intermediate level to construct aggregated and refined intermediate events which are in closer agreement with the stored symbolic object description. Figure 3 is an abstraction of the multiple levels of representation and processing in the VISIONS system. Communication between these levels is by no means unidirectional; in most cases, recognition of an object or part of a scene at the high level establishes a strategy for further manipulating the intermediate level primitives within the context provided by the partial interpretation, and for feedback for goal-directed resegmentation.

Let us consider some of the stages of processing in a bit more detail.

1) Segmentation processes [20, 21, 22] are applied to the sensory data to form a symbolic representation of regions and lines and their attributes such as color, texture, location, size, shape, orientation, length, etc. Figures 4 and 5 show sample results from two segmentation processes applied to the images in Figure 1. The region and line representations are integrated so that spatially related entities in either can be easily accessed [23]. Two-dimensional motion attributes can also be associated with these entities.

2) Object hypothesis rules are applied to the region and line representation to rank-order candidate object hypotheses [24]; this initial iconic to symbolic mapping provides an effective focus-of-attention mechanism to initiate semantic processing. A simple rule is defined as a range over any scalar feature of the lines or regions. If the attribute of the line/region has a value in the range it will be

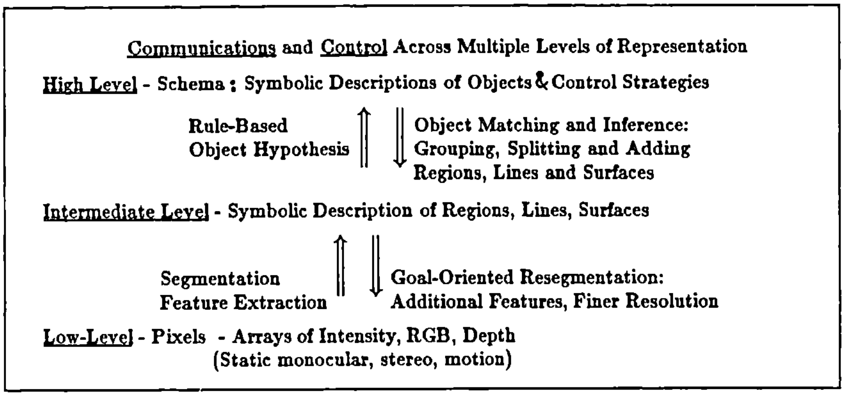

Image Interpretation

Figure 3. Multiple levels of representation and processing in the VISIONS system.

considered as a "vote" for a particular object label. More complex rules are formed via a logical or arithmetic combining function over several simple rules. The rules can also be viewed as sets of partially redundant features, each of which defines an area of feature space which represents a vote for an object. The region features could include color, texture, size, location in image, simple shape, and motion; line features could include location, length, width, contrast and motion. To the degree that surface patches have been formed, rules can be applied to surface features such as depth, size, location, orientation, reflectance, curvature, and motion.

3) More complex object-dependent interpretation strategies are represented in a procedural form in knowledge structures called schemas [8,25,28]; these strategies represent control local to a schema node and top-down control over the interpretation process. One interpretation strategy that utilizes the output of the rule set involves the selection of reliable hypotheses as image-specific object exemplars. They are extended to other regions and lines through an object-dependent similarity matching strategy [24]. Thus, as in the HEARSAY paradigm, partial interpretations begin to extend from "islands of reliability" [26]. At this point in the continuing evolution of the VISIONS system, we are concentrating on the development of intermediate grouping strategies for merging and modifying region and line elements to match expected object structures [28]. For this purpose, general knowledge of objects and scenes is organized around the relationships that would be found in standard 2D views of 3D objects. Verification strategies exploit particular spatial relationships between the hypothesized object and other specific expected object labels or image features. In cases of simple 3D shapes, such as the planar surfaces forming a "house" volume, 3D models and associated processing strategies are employed, and we hope to evolve similar intermediate grouping strategies for complex 3D shape representations in the future.

4) Feedback to the lower-level processes for more detailed segmentation can be requested in cases when interpretation of an area fails, when an expected image feature is not found, or when conflicting interpretations occur. Both the region and line algorithms have parameters for varying the sensitivity and amount of detail in their segmentation output. However, the control of such strategies and the integration of their results is an open problem that is under examination.

5) Due to the inherent ambiguities in both the raw image data and the extracted intermediate representations, a method for handling uncertainty is required if there is to be any possibility of combining this information into a coherent view of the world [29,30,31]. Some of the limitations of inferencing using Bayesian probability models are overcome using the Dempster-Shafer formal-

ism for evidential reasoning, in which an explicit representation of partial ignorance is provided [32]. The inferencing model allows "belief" or "confidence" in a proposition to be represented as a range within the [0,1] interval. The lower and upper bounds represent support and plausibility, respectively, of a proposition, while the width of the interval can be interpreted as ignorance.

IV. RULE-BASED OBJECT HYPOTHESIS STRATEGIES

We propose a simple approach to object hypothesis formation, relying on convergent evidence from a variety of measurements and expectations. In the early interpretation phase, when little is known about the scene or its contents, the approach is primarily bottom-up and involves the generation of a few reliable hypotheses about prominent image events. The object hypothesis system provides the first link between the image data and the knowledge structures. Control can then shift to a more top-down orientation as

Figure 4. Region segmentations. Regions partition the image into areas which are relatively uniform in some feature (in this case intensity). Mapped into a symbolic structure with a rich set of descriptors, they provide one form of link between the image data and the interpretation system.

Figure 5. Extraction of straight lines. The straight line algorithm uses a local estimate of gradient orientation to group pixels into regions. A straight line and an associated set of features is extracted from each region. The resulting line image (which contains many lines not shown here) can be filtered in various ways. The two images on the left show all lines whose gradient magnitude exceeds 10 gray levels per pixel; the right images represent a second filtering on the basis of length. The short, high contrast lines in the images in the left images are used as the basis of a texture measure.

context and expectations allow the use of further knowledge-dependent processing to validate and extend the initial hypotheses.

Our goal, therefore, is to develop methods for selecting specific image events that are likely candidates for particular object labels, rather than the selection of the best object label for each region and line. For example, given a set of regions in an outdoor scene (and assuming a standard camera position), we might choose to select a few bright blue areas, with a low degree of texture, near the top of the image which are likely to be "sky". Similarly, in an outdoor scene one could select grass regions by using the expectation that they would be of medium brightness, have a significant green component, be located somewhere in the lower portion of the image, etc.* For each object, these expectations can be translated into a "rule" which combines the results of many measurements into a confidence level that a region (or small group of regions) represent that object.

IV.1. Knowledge as Rules

Simple rules are defined as the ranges over a scalar-valued feature which will map into a vote for an object label. Typically a feature will be the mean or variance of a property of the pixels or edges composing the regions or lines, respectively. Complex rules involve a combination of simple rules, and they allow fusion of information from a variety of different types of measurements.

We will now develop a simple rule which captures the expectation that grass is green using a feature which is a coarse approximation to a green-magenta oppenent color feature by computing the mean of 2G-R-B for all pixels in this region. In order to demonstrate the actual basis and form of knowledge embodied in the rule, in Figure 6 we compare histograms of the green-magenta feature distribution of grass pixels to the distribution of the same feature for all pixels. This data was obtained by hand-labelling segmentations from 8 sample images of outdoor house scenes.

The basic idea is to construct a mapping from a measured value of the feature obtained from an image region, say f_I, into a vote for the object. One approach is to define this mapping as a function of distance in feature space between the measured value and a stored prototype feature vector which captures the feature properties of the object.

Let $d(f_P, f_I)$ be the distance between the measured feature value f_I and the prototype feature point f_P. The response R of the rule is then (see Figure 7):

$$
R(f_I) = \begin{cases}
1 & \text{if } d(f_P, f_I) \leq \theta_1 \\
\dfrac{\theta_2 - d(f_P, f_I)}{\theta_2 - \theta_1} & \text{if } \theta_1 < d(f_P, f_I) \leq \theta_2 \\
0 & \text{if } \theta_2 < d(f_P, f_I) \leq \theta_3 \\
-\infty & \text{if } \theta_3 < d(f_P, f_I)
\end{cases}
$$

The thresholds θ_1, θ_2, and θ_3 represent a coarse interpretation of the distance measurements in feature space. When the measured and expected values are sufficiently similar (less than θ_1 units apart), the object label associated with the rule receives a maximum vote of 1. Since small changes in a feature measurement should not dramatically alter the system response, the voting function is linearly ramped to 0 as the distance in feature space increases from θ_1 to θ_2.

---

* Note that a camera model and access to a 3D representation of the environment could dynamically modify the value of these location limits in the image; thus, the use of rules on relative or absolute environmental location in a fully general system would involve modification of expectations about image location as the system orients the camera up or down relative to the ground plane.

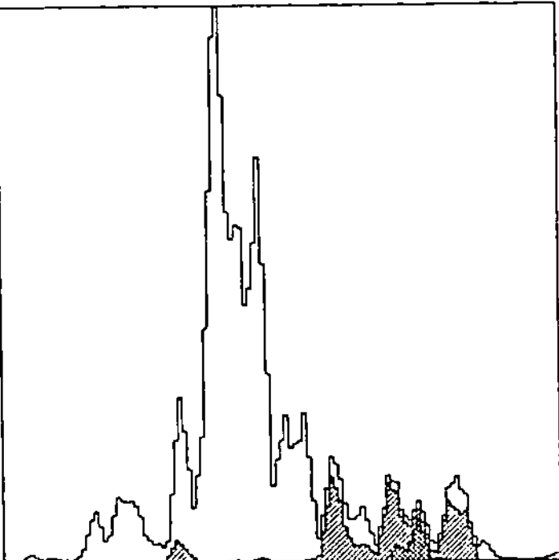

Figure 6. Image histograms of an "green-magenta" feature (2G-R-B). The unshaded histogram represents the global distribution of the feature across all pixels in the eight sample images. The intermediate diagonal shading represents the feature distribution of all grass regions in the eight images, obtained by hand labelling the image regions. The darkest cross hatched histogram is the feature distribution of grass regions in a single image.

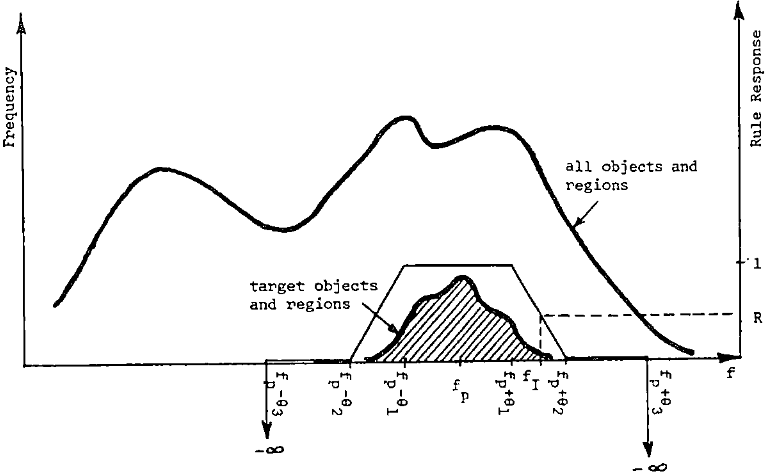

Figure 7. Structure of a simple rule for mapping an image feature measurement f_I into support for a label hypothesis on the basis of a prototype feature value f_P obtained from the combined histograms of labeled regions across image samples. The object specific mapping is parameterized by four values, $f_P, \theta_1, \theta_2, \theta_3$, and stored in the knowledge network. The use of six threshold values allows an asymmetric response function.

θ_3 allows a "veto" vote if the measured feature value indicates that the object label associated with the prototype point cannot be correct. For example, a certain range of the green-magenta oppenent color feature implies a magenta, red, or blue color which should veto the grass label. Thus, certain measurements can exclude object labels; this proves to be a very effective mechanism for filtering the summation of several spurious weak responses. Of course there is the danger of excluding the proper label due to a single feature value, even in the face of strong support from many other features. A natural extension to the mechanisms presented here would generalize the rule form to be parameterically varied from the fixed form that we have defined. Thus, the ranges could be dynamically varied so that fewer or larger numbers of regions are in the positive voting range of a particular rule. In a further generalization of this rule form, an assymmetric rule form is applied to feature space; thus θ_1, θ_2, and θ_3 are replaced with six values. Figure 8 shows the structure of a simple rule based on the "green-magenta" color feature superimposed on the histogram of Figure 6.

A simple rule is a specification of a constraint on the value of a feature which should be satisfied if the object is present. A complex rule is defined as a (partially redundant) set of simple features that is assembled into a composite rule via a combining function which can take any logical or arithmetic form; this is an extension of the functional form of hypothesis rules in Nagao et al [12]. The premise is that by combining many partially redundant rules, the effect of any single unreliable rule is reduced.

It is useful to provide a hierarchical semantic structure on the set of simple rules. In this paper each object is organized into a composite rule of 5 components which provide a match of color, texture, location, shape, and size of the object. This allows some flexibility in combining several highly redundant features (e.g., several color features) into a composite rule which is somewhat more independent of the other composite rules (e.g., color vs. location); one should recognize however, that this is only one alternative for imposing a hierarchical structure on the set of simple rules. Each of the five composite rules is in turn joined into a composite rule; Any rule might have a weight of 0, which means that the rule will have no effect on the weighted response of the composite rule except that the veto range of the rule can reject a region as a candidate for the object in question. The structure of the composite rule for grass is shown in Figure 9 with two levels of hierarchy; it consists of a normalized weighted average of the five components C_j:

$$grass\ score = \frac{1}{N} \sum_{j=1}^{5} W_j C_j$$

where the W_j are the weights and $N = \sum_{j=1}^{5} W_j$. Each of the components is in turn a weighted sum of a set of individual rules:

$$C_j = \sum_{k} V_k R(f_k)$$

where $R(f_k)$ is the response from an individual feature rule based on feature f_k and the V_k are the weights.

The weights shown in Figure 9 reflect the heuristic importance of each of the contributions to the rule response. The weights are integers from 0 to 5, and reflect an expectation that only a few levels of relative importance are needed ("weak" $\equiv 1$, "medium" $\equiv 3$, "strong" $\equiv 5$ in importance). The intention is to avoid twiddling of numbers, but to allow obvious relative strengths to be expressed. Since the composite rule response is used only to order the regions on the basis of their similarity to the stored feature templates, rather than classifying them as an instance of a specific class, the expectation is that the rule response is relatively insensitive to small changes in the weights.

IV.2 Relationship to Bayesian Theory Classification

It will be instructive to briefly consider the relationship to the standard statistical approaches used in Bayesian pattern classification. If one considers the pattern recognition paradigm of classification of the jth region R_j as one of a fixed set of object classes C_i, i = 1,...,N on the basis of a feature vector $\bar{X}_j = (X_1, \ldots X_K)$ extracted via measurements on region R_j. Using Bayes rule and noting that $P(\bar{X}_j)$ is constant across classes, the optimal decision process for a given region R_j is to choose class C_i such that

$$MAX\ P(\bar{X}_j \mid C_i)\ P(C_i)$$

Under an assumption of statistical independence of features, the joint conditional probability of features will be a product of the class condition probabilities of individual features.

In contrast, we have modified the classification strategy to become a "focus-of-attention" process since it is not feasible to initially classify all image events. The organization of the input data is not sufficiently well-defined to pose the classical pattern recognition goals in our domain. Thus, rather than the selection of the best object label for each region and line, we are looking for good region and line candidates for a particular object label.

Now, instead of the measurement vector $P(\bar{X}_j)$ being held constant across samples, the a priori class probability $P(C_i)$ is constant across regions to be classified. While there is a common set of features measured on each region, the measurement vector $\bar{X}_j$ may be different for each (i.e. a different set of feature values). This changes the optimal decision rule via a Bayes formulation to

$$\underset{j}{MAX}\ \frac{P(\bar{X}_j \mid C_i)}{P(\bar{X}_j)} j$$

which will decompose into the product of individual feature terms under an assumption of independence.

It should now be clear to the reader that our simple piecewise-linear rule form is more than just an approximation to $P(x_j \mid C_i), j = 1,...,K$. What it also must balance is the relation to $P(x_j)$, which appears in the denominator of the Bayesian focus-of-attention ratio. This term is important because it brings in the degree of <u>discrimination</u> of each feature measurement x_j for class C_i. For example, there would be little value in a feature which exhibited a very tight range (i.e., very low variance) for some object class, if in fact it also exhibited the same distribution for all classes. In the application of our rule methodology presented in Section IV, the vision system designer/knowledge engineer was responsible for the selection of the features introduced in the object rules. To the degree that a rule developed by

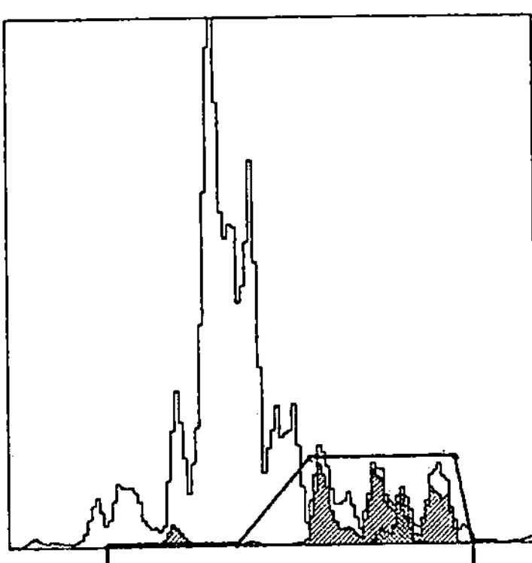

Figure 8. An example grass rule, showing an asymmetrical structure, superimposed on the histogram of Figure 6.

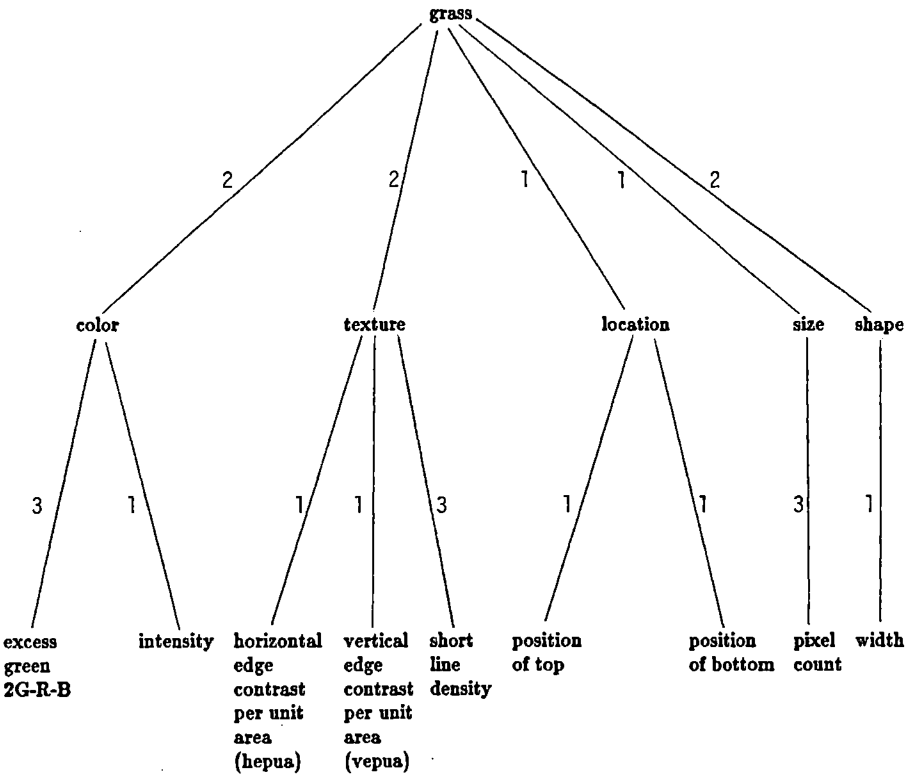

Figure 9. Structure of the grass rule. The rule response is the normalized weighted sum of the responses of five component rules, each of which is in turn a normalized weighted sum of the responses from simple rules associated with a single feature. Table I describes each of the features at the bottom of the tree. Note that a weight could be 0, thereby allowing the veto range for that feature to be propagated

this expert covered $P(x_j \mid C_i)$ and excluded $P(x_j \mid C_k)$, *for all* $k \neq i$, that rule would be effective. Of course there is still the problem of the usually invalid assumption of feature independence, and therefore our heuristic hierarchical combination of features may be just as reasonable. In fact the use of the veto range for individual features has the same effect as a ratio of zero in the product of probabilities under the assumption of independence.

IV.3. Results of Rule Application

Figure 10 shows the results of applying selected simple rules for grass to the region segmentation from Figure 4c. For each rule there are two images. The left image of each pair is a composite feature histogram showing the feature distribution across all pixels (the unshaded curve) in a set of images, and the distribution for grass pixels (the cross hatched curve) across the same set of images. The histograms were computed from a set of eight hand-labelled images and smoothed. The right image of each pair shows the strength of the rule response for each region coded as a brightness level: bright regions correspond to high rule output.

The rule that was developed interactively by the user is superimposed on the histograms in piecewise linear form. In the upper left "Target" refers to the object associated with the rule, in this case grass, while "Other" refers to all objects other than the object. The first row of numbers shows the weighted average response of grass pixels and other pixels to the rule function (100 is maximum), while the lower numbers tabulate the percentage of target pixels and other pixels vetoed. Thus, the ideal rule is one which responds maximally with a value of 100 to the target pixels, while vetoing 100% of all other pixels. In practice, there is almost always a tradeoff and optimal settings are not at all obvious. In some cases rules for the target object were set to exclude regions associated with other objects, while in other cases the goal was to maximize the response for the target object regions. There is no intent here to put forth these specific rules as a significant contribution or even as a satisfactory set; in fact some of these rules probably need modification.

Figure 11 shows the rule response for three of the five components and the final result via the composite rule. For each rule the region response is shown superimposed over the image in two complementary formats. The left image of each pair shows the strength of the rule response coded in the intensity level of each region; bright regions correspond to good matches. The right image shows the vetoed regions in black (with all others uniformly grey). Figure 12 shows the final results for the foliage, grass, and sky rules in the house image in Figure 1b (vetoed regions not shown).

The effectiveness of the rules can be seen by examining the rank orderings of the regions on the basis of the composite rule responses. For the grass results shown in Figure 11, for example, the two top ranked regions are actually grass. For the grass results shown in Figure 12, the top six regions are grass and 8 of the top 10 regions are grass; the two non-grass regions were actually sidewalk and driveway. For the foliage responses shown in Figure 12b, the top 21 regions were some form of foliage (tree, bush, or undergrowth); of the 30 regions not vetoed, there were only 7 non-foliage regions. These 7 regions were actually grass and were among the lowest ranked of the non-vetoed regions (7 of the last 9). For the sky results in Figure 12c, only four regions were not vetoed and the top three were sky. The fourth region, with a significantly lower rule response, was actually foliage with some sky showing through. Figure 13 shows the highest ranked regions for each of the three object hypothesis rules when applied to the three example images. In Section V we discuss how these initial object hypothesis results may be used as the basis of a strategy to produce a more complete interpretation.

IV.4 A Language Interface for Knowledge Engineering

Knowledge engineering of rules is facilitated by an interactive environment for rule construction. A user can get an immediate sense of their effectiveness by displaying the rating of each symbolic candidate in intensity or color. Thus, rule development is a dynamic process with a natural display medium for user feedback.

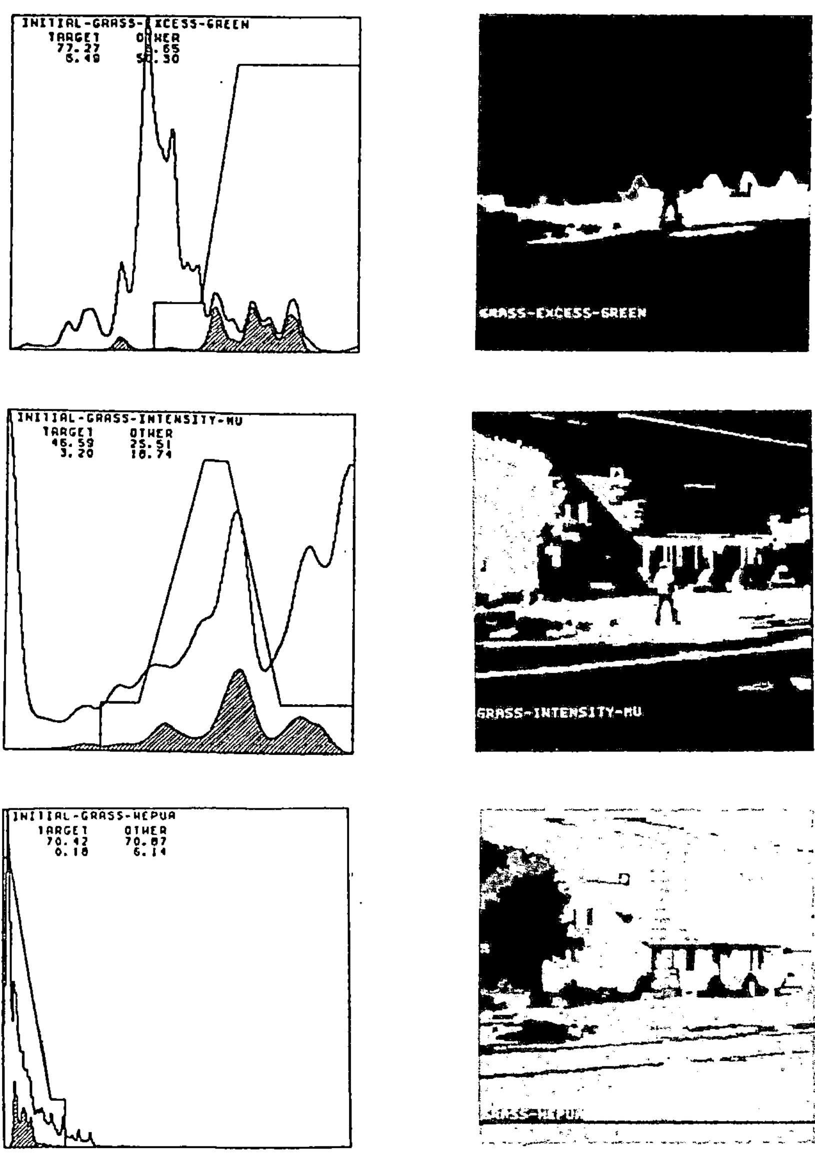

Figure 10. (caption on next page)

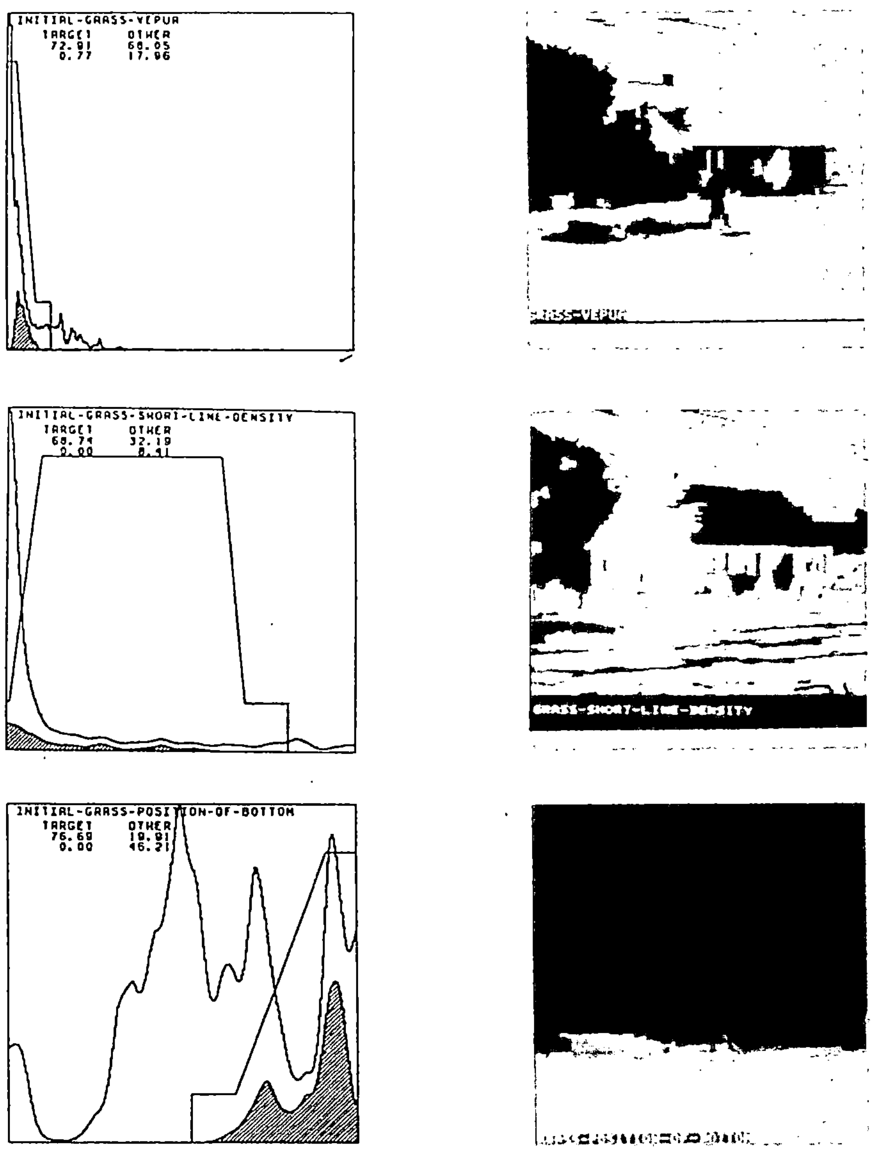

Figure 10. Results from the simple grass rules. In each image pair, the left image is a composite feature histogram showing the feature distribution across all pixels in a set of images, the distribution of grass pixels in the same set, and the rule. The right image shows the brightness encoded strength of the rule response when applied to all regions in the segmentation of Figure 4c; bright regions correspond to a high rule response. See text for a discourse of the discussion of the four numbers in the upper left corner of the histograms.

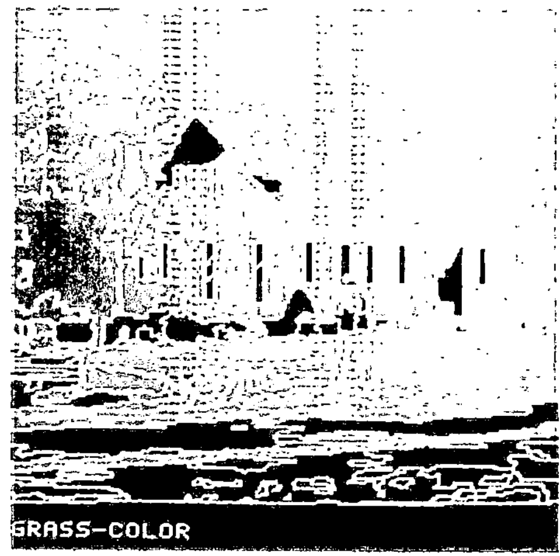

(a)

(b)

Figure 11. (caption on next page)

(c)

(d)

Figure 11. Rule responses for the grass component rules and the final composite rule. In each pair of images, the left image shows the brightness encoded (bright $\equiv$ high) rule response. The right image shows regions vetoed by the rule in black; all others (non-vetoed regions) are uniformly gray. (a) color component rule; (b) texture component rule; (c) location component rule; (d) final result from grass composite rule.

a

b

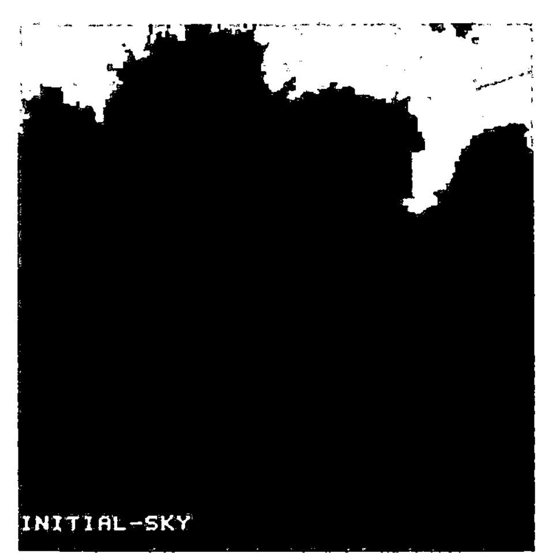

c

Figure 12. Composite rule responses applied to Figure 1b for grass, foliage, and sky rules, encoded in brightness. (a) grass, (b) foliage, (c) sky.

In addition to receiving an immediate visual response to a proposed rule or rule set, the knowledge engineer must not be forced into a "parameter twiddling" mode. The rules should be robust enough so that a fairly crude specification of the rule parameters generates reasonable results. The specification can then be interactively refined, if necessary. As a first step toward an interactive specification facility, a simple language interface has been constructed so that rules can be specified on any feature in terms of five intervals of the dynamic range of a feature – "very low", "low", "medium", "high", "very high" [24,36] These labels induce a partition on the range of the feature; for each interval, the user specifies whether the rule response is "ON", "OFF", or "VETO".

The results obtained from the linguistically defined rules are quite good and are comparable to the results obtained in the previous section using the more carefully defined rules. The linguistically defined

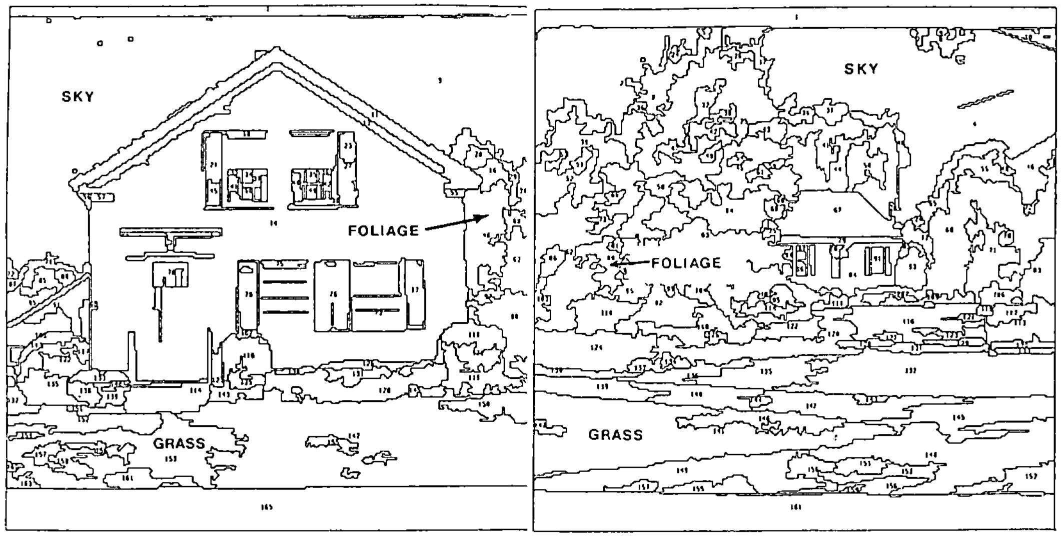

Figure 13. Highest ranked object hypothesis for the three examples images.

rules offer the knowledge engineer the opportunity to quickly develop and assess a rule set without detailed examination of feature statistics. It may be possible, in some cases, to completely develop the rule base using semantic terms that are intuitive to the user, including the structure of the composite rules and the relative weights, as well as the setting of the individual rule values.

V. SCHEMAS AND THEIR INTERPRETATION STRATEGIES

V.1. Introduction

In the VISIONS system, scene independent knowledge is represented in a hierarchical schema structure organized as a semantic network [8,24,25,33]. The hierarchy is structured to capture the decomposition of visual knowledge into successively more primitive entities, eventually expressed in symbolic terms similar to those used to represent the intermediate level description of a specific image obtained from the region, line, and surface segmentations. Each schema defines a highly structured collection of elements in a scene or object; each object in the scene schema, or part in the object schema, can have an associated schema which will further describe it. For example, a house (in a house scene hierarchy) has roof and house-wall as object-parts, and the house-wall object has windows, shutters, and doors as object-parts. Each schema node (e.g. house, house wall, and roof) has both a declarative component appropriate to the level of detail, describing the relations between the parts of the schema, and a procedural component describing image recognition methods as a set of hypothesis and verification strategies called *interpretation strategies*.

The contextual verification of hypotheses via consistency with stored knowledge leads to a variety of interpretation strategies that are referred to as data-directed (or bottom-up), knowledge-directed (or top-down), or both. In addition these strategies can be domain and object-dependent, or uniform across domains. A rich set of possibilities opens up which unfortunately has not been sufficiently explored by the research community carrying out knowledge-directed vision processing. The first type of interpretation strategy discussed uses the rule system to select "exemplar" regions as candidates for partial objects, and then extends them to similar regions. A second class of strategies uses geometric information to direct the grouping of intermediate events to better match the expected model. A third strategy involves the detection and correction of errors in the interpretation process as shown in an example in the section on final results.

V.2. Exemplar Selection and Extension

Once the output of the rule-based feature system is available, the most reliable object hypotheses obtained by applying the object hypothesis rules to the intermediate level data (e.g. regions, lines, and surfaces), can be considered object "exemplars" and viewed as a largely incomplete kernel interpretation. There are a variety of ways by which the exemplar regions can be used to extend and refine the partial interpretation [24,28] and we will briefly present one specific implementation for an exemplar extension strategy.

For those objects with spectral characteristics that are reasonably uniform over the image, the similarity of region color and texture can be used to extend an object label to other regions. The image-specification variation of a feature of an object is expected to be much less than the inter-image variation of that feature for the same object (see Figure 6). In many situations another instance can be expected to have a similar color, size, or shape. The shape and/or size of a region can be used to detect other instances of multiple objects, as in the case when one shutter or window of a house has been found [27], or when one tire of a car has been found, or when one car on a road has been found, perhaps using the expected spatial location and relative spatial information in various ways to restrict the set of candidate regions examined. It is our hope that this permits reliable hypotheses to be formed even with high degrees of partial occlusion.

We have made a basic assumption that exemplar extension will in fact involve a knowledge engineering process that will use different strategies for each object. In some cases, however, color and texture may be more reliable than shape and size (as in a sky exemplar region), while in other situations shape and size might be very important (as in the shutters). Spatial constraints may be used very differently in each case. One possibility is to utilize the object-specific set of simple features that were associated with the object hypothesis rules. In fact the same rule system presented earlier can be used to weight the feature differences to form the similarity rating in terms of feature differences. Similarity extension rules can be implementations of distance metrics or functions, with values of feature differences used to determine the rule response for each. It might be appropriate in one case to employ a piecewise-linear distance function, with high values for small differences and low values for large differences; in another case, a rule might provide a uniformly high response within some threshold. It is also easy to use the veto region for large differences, or for spatial constraints to restrict the spatial area over which region candidates for exemplar extension will be considered.

For the similarity results shown in Figure 14, the full object hypothesis rules discussed earlier were used to measure the similarity between the exemplar region and each candidate region. The rule response was converted into a distance metric and bright regions correspond to small differences. Each of the rules contained location and size components which enter into the final distance measurement, but in general, there are more intelligent ways of using these features in the interpretation strategy responsible for grouping regions. Our goal here was simply to rank order the regions that were candidates for extension; and again, the specific results shown in the figures are not as important as the overall philosophy.

Figure 14 shows the similarity rating of regions obtained using the features of the grass rule (Figure 9) and comparing them to the exemplar region (see Figure 13). In addition to the final grass similarity response, the similarities obtained from the color component rule and two of its constituent simple rules (green-magenta and intensity) are also shown.

It is interesting to compare the region rankings produced by the image independent initial grass rule and the rankings obtained from the exemplar matching strategy. The original grass rule applied to the same image as Figure 14 (these results are shown in Figure 12) vetoed all but 27 regions; of these, 15 were grass and the 6 highest ranked regions were grass. By way of comparison, of the 27 regions most similar to the grass exemplar region, 18 were actually grass, and the 8 highest ranked regions were grass. Of the 16 regions most similar to the exemplar, all but two were grass. Again, the confusion was between grass, sidewalk, and driveway. The exemplar matching strategy produces more reliable results than the initial hypothesis rule since it takes into account image-dependent characteristics of the object's appearance.

VI.3. Interpretation Strategies for Intermediate Grouping

In this section we briefly motivate the types of additional top-down strategies that will be necessary for properly interpreting the primitives of the intermediate representation in terms of the hypothesized higher level context. The work presented here is taken from Weymouth [28], and is the subject of active exploration within the vision group at the University of Massachusetts.

The basic idea will be sketched using as an example the problem of grouping and interpreting a house roof from a fragmented intermediate representation. Figure 15 shows a number of intermediate stages in the application of a house roof interpretation strategy associated with the house roof schema. Figure 15a, b portray a pair of region and line segmentations that exhibit difficulties expected in the output of low-level algorithms; figure 15a also shows the initial roof hypothesis. In this example the region segmentation algorithm was set to extract more detail from the image by producing more regions; the result, which is typical of a class of segmentation problems, is the fragmentation of the roof, so that the shadowed left portion was broken into several regions separate from the main roof region. (It should be noted that the segmentation in this example is different from the segmentation used to present the interpretation results in other sections.) When examined carefully, the line extraction results show line segments that are fragmented into pieces, multiple parallel lines, and gaps in lines.

Figure 14. Similarity between grass exemplar region and all other regions for Figure 1b. (a,b) similarities associated with green-magenta and intensity. (c) similarities based upon the color component of the composite rule of intensity and color; (d) similarities from the whole composite object hypothesis rule; In all cases, similarity is encoded as brightness.

The goal is to use typical segmentation results to produce the trapezoidal region (which is almost a parallelogram) representing the perspective projection of a rectangular roof surface, as well as the orientation in 3D space of that surface. The top-down grouping strategy that we employ here is organized around evidence of the almost parallel lines forming the two sets of sides of the trapezoid. There are alternate strategies for other typical situations where some of this information is missing. Thus, this roof grouping strategy expects some evidence for each of the four sides, and in particular uses the long lines bounding the putative roof region. Figure 15c shows the long lines along the region boundary; "long" is determined as a relative function of the image area of the roof region, here 1/3 of the square root of the roof region area. Figure 15d illustrates the result of merging similar regions which are partially bounded by the long lines. Figure 15e shows the lines bounding the extended roof region, after removing shorter, parallel, almost-adjacent lines, joining co-linear nearby segments, and then fitting straight lines to the boundaries to form a partial trapezoid (almost a parallelogram). Finally, Figure 15f shows the complete hypothesized roof trapezoid. The three-dimensional geometry of the roof can then be computed (up to some possibly non-trivial degree of error) based upon either the location of the pair of vanishing points of the two sets of image lines that are parallel in the physical world, or one pair of parallel lines and an assumption of perpendicular angles to a third line.

The point of this discussion is that the interpretation process required a flexible strategy for grouping and reorganizing the lines and regions obtained from imperfect segmentation processes. At this point in our understanding we are developing each strategy independently, but we hope to begin to define some standard intermediate grouping primitives that would form the basis of a variety of general top-down strategies.

VI.4. RESULTS OF RULE-BASED IMAGE INTERPRETATION

Interpretation experiments are being conducted on a large set of "house scene" images. Thus far, we have been able to extract sky, grass, and foliage (trees and bushes) from many of these images with reasonable effectiveness, and have been successful in identifying shutters (or windows), house wall and roof in some of them. Object hypothesis and exemplar extension rules as described in previous sections, were employed. Additional object verification rules requiring consistent spatial relationships with other object labels are being developed. The features and knowledge utilized vary across color and texture attributes, shape, size, location in the image, relative location to identified objects, and similarity in color and texture to identified objects. In the following figures, we show isolated intermediate and final results from the overall system.

The interpretation results shown were obtained from a version of the VISIONS system that used a different (somewhat coarser grained) set of initial segmentations than those presented earlier, and a set of object hypothesis and exemplar extension strategies that differed in structure (but not in principle) from those presented earlier. Figure 16 shows selected results from the object hypothesis rules after exemplar extension and region merging. Figure 17 illustrates typical interpretations obtained from a house scene schema interpretation strategy that utilizes a set of object hypothesis rules for exemplar selection, extends the partial model from the most reliable of these hypotheses, and which employs relational information for verifying hypotheses and predicting image location of object parts and related objects. The image areas shown in white in Figure 17 are uninterpreted either because the object did not exist in the knowledge network (and hence no label could be assigned) or because the object varied in some way from the rather constrained set of alternate descriptions of the object stored in the knowledge base.

Figure 17d illustrates a problem which may be expected to occur quite frequently. The original interpretation was produced using a fairly coarse segmentation, which is desirable from the standpoint of computational efficiency since fewer regions are involved. However, the sky and house wall are merged into one region since the difference between the two areas was below the resolution of the segmentation process. This is the disadvantage of using a coarse segmentation. Parameters of the segmentation processes can be set to produce a finer grained segmentation but, many more regions are produced. On the other hand, the

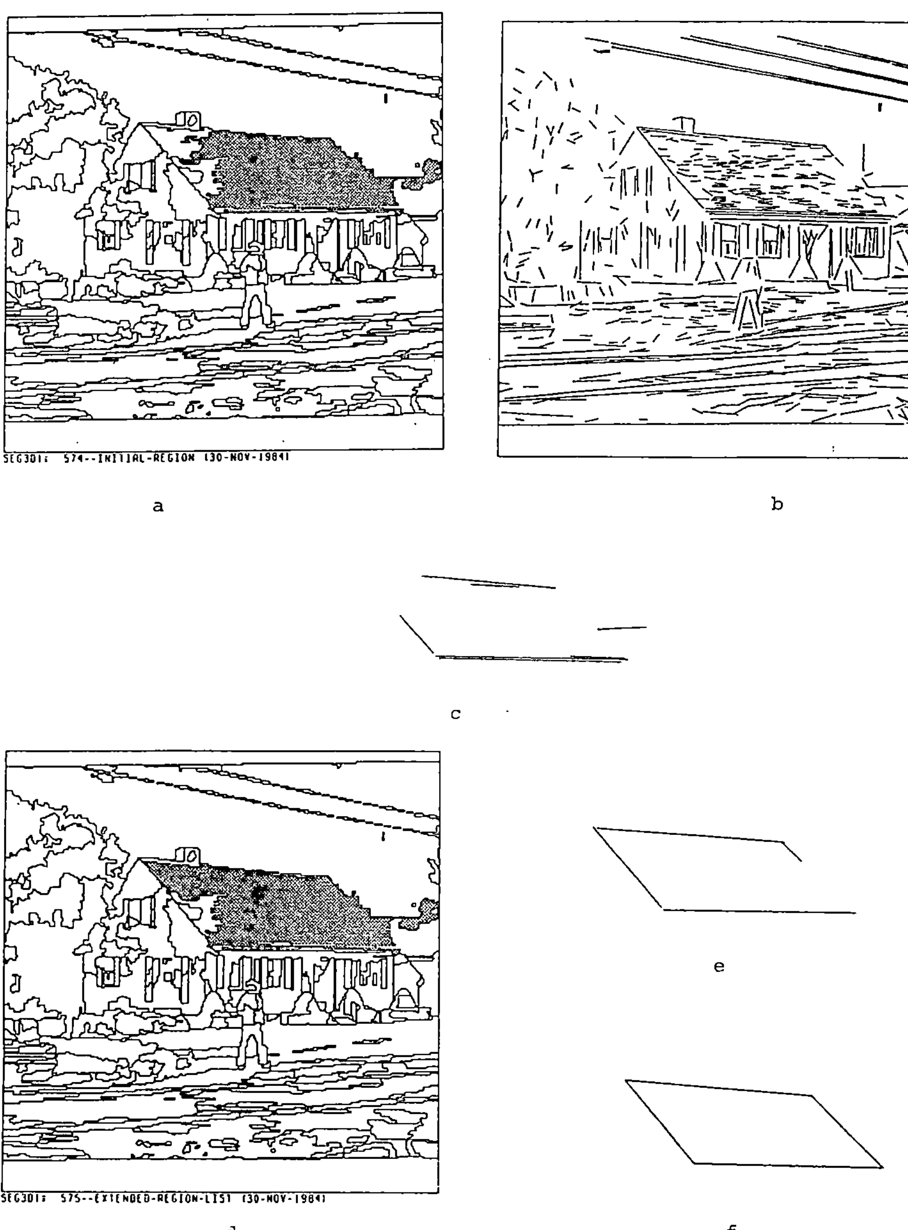

Figure 15. Steps in the schema directed interpretation of a roof. (a,b) region and line representations; the initial roof hypothesis region is crosshatched. (c) long lines bordering the roof hypothesis region boundary. (d) new roof hypothesis after merging regions which are partially bounded by the long lines in the previous image. (e) after joining colinear, nearby segments and filling a straight line to the joined boundaries. (f) the completed hypothesized roof trapezoid (almost a parallelogram).

smaller regions can be expected to find more of the desired boundaries and sometimes better match the object descriptions in the knowledge base, at the risk of overfragmentation. Because of these conflicting constraints, we believe it is extremely important to closely couple the lower level processes responsible for constructing the intermediate representation and the interpretation processes which operate on the intermediate and higher level representations. The interpretation processes should have focus-of-attention mechanisms for correction of segmentation errors, extraction of finer image detail, and verification of semantic hypotheses.

An example of the effectiveness of semantically directed feedback to the segmentation processes is shown in Figure 18. The missing boundary between the house wall and sky led to competing object hypotheses (sky and house wall) based upon local interpretation strategies. The region is hypothesized to be sky by the sky strategy, while application of the house wall strategy (using the roof and shutters as spatial constraints on the location of house wall) leads to a wall hypothesis. There is evidence available that some form of error has occurred in this example: 1) conflicting labels are produced for the same region

Figure 16. Results of schema interpretation strategies. Results of (a) roof rule – based on roof features and spatial relation to shutter; (b) grass – exemplar selection and similarity extension; (c) results of shutter rule.

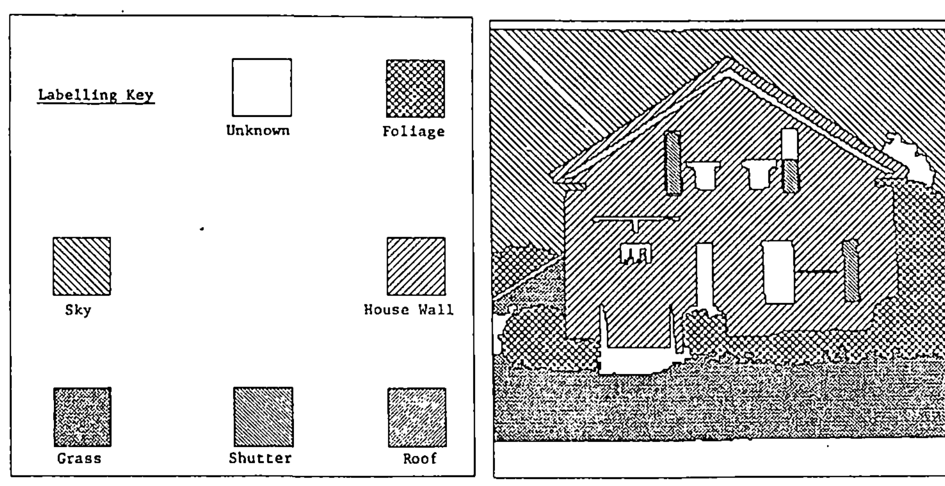

Figure a.

Figure b.

Figure c.

Figure d.

Figure 17. Final interpretations. These images show the final results obtained by combining the results of the interpretation strategies under the constraints generated from the knowledge base. (a) interpretation key; (b-d) interpretation results. In (d), the missing boundary between sky and wall results in a labelling conflict (the identification shown is sky; a second interpretation has this region labelled house wall).

a

b

c

Figure 18. Resegmentation of house/sky region from Figure 17d. (a) the original segmentation showing the region to be resegmented; (b) the regions resulting from the resegmentation of the selected region; (c) final interpretation of the house scene in Figure 1c, after inserting resegmented house/sky regions and reinterpreting the image. process to the cross-hatched area in (a).

by local interpretation strategies; 2) the house wall label is associated with regions above the roof (note that while there are houses with a wall above a lower roof, the geometric consistency of the object shape is not satisfied in this example); and 3) the sky extends down close to the approximate horizon line in only a portion of the image (which is possible, but worthy of closer inspection).

In this case resegmentation of the sky-housewall region, with segmentation parameters set to extract finer detail, produces a reasonable segmentation of this region (Figure 18b). It should be pointed out that in this image there is a barely discernable boundary between the sky and house wall. However, once the merged region is resegmented with an intent of overfragmentation, this boundary can be detected. Now, the same interpretation strategy used earlier produces the quite acceptable results shown in Figure 18c. We note that this capability (of detecting labelling conflicts and resegmentation) is not automatic in the current version of the system.

Future work is directed towards refinement of the segmentation algorithms, object hypothesis rules, object verification rules, and interpretation strategies. System development is aimed towards more robust methods of control: automatic schema and strategy selection, interpretation of images under more than one general class of schemata, and automatic focus of attention mechanisms and error-correcting strategies for resolving interpretation errors.

VI. PRINCIPLES TO GUIDE
KNOWLEDGE-BASED VISION RESEARCH

In summary, we list some of the principles of our work on knowledge-based vision systems that might provide guidance to other researchers. We do caution the reader, however, that in no way are we asserting that this is the "only" or "correct" or "complete" approach to high-level vision. Rather, the problem domain has been so difficult that there has been little work of any generality. Thus, our statements at this time are distilled from the experience of a partially successful approach to general knowledge-based vision that is continuously evolving as we understand the visual domain more thoroughly.

1) An integrated symbolic representation of 2D image events such as regions and lines, and 3D world events such as surface patches, should be used as the symbolic interface between sensory data and world knowledge. In particular it is the attributes of these elements, potentially including depth (3D) and motion (2D and 3D) information, that provides linkages to stored knowledge and higher-level processing strategies.

2) In the initial stages of bottom-up hypothesis formation, focus of attention mechanisms should be used to selectively group elements of the intermediate representation and construct tentative object hypotheses. The interpretation should be extended from such "islands of reliability". The choice of object classes for initial consideration can be controlled (top-down) via context or expectation.

3) A simple initial interface to knowledge can be obtained via rules defined over a range of the expected values of the attributes of the symbolic events that have been extracted. These rules can be organized around the most likely events or the easiest events to extract when highly structured situations are expected.

4) Knowledge of the physical world should be organized around scene schema and object schema that can be represented as a structured collection of parts. This allows the contextual relationships to guide the further processing of partial interpretations. In places where 3D shape and spatial relations are complex, the general relationships between image events in typical 2D views can be used to interface to the bottom-up 2D symbolic representation. However, long-range progress is dependent upon more effective 3D shape representations.

5) More complex strategies will be needed for matching salient aspects of the ambiguous, incomplete, and sometimes incorrect intermediate data representation to the object models stored in

the knowledge base. They involve a diverse collection of goals, and given our understanding at this time, it may be easier to represent them as procedural knowledge. These strategies include knowledge-directed grouping, deletion, and manipulation of intermediate symbolic entities, as well as goal-oriented feedback to low-level processes.

6) Inference mechanisms for utilizing distributed fine-grained and weak hypotheses will be needed. These inference mechanisms must deal with the issues of high degrees of uncertainty and of pooling a variety of sources of information in order to control processes for extending partial interpretations.

7) Highly interactive user-friendly environments for visually displaying results of knowledge application are very important. The vision domain provides a natural medium for user feedback and interaction.

Acknowledgements

This work has been supported by the Air Force Office of Scientific Research under contract AFOSR-85-0005 and the Defense Advanced Research Projects Agency under contract N00014-82-K-0464. The authors wish to acknowledge the many members of the VISIONS research community, particularly Robert Belknap, Joey Griffith and Terry Weymouth, who have contributed to the technical ideas developed in this paper and the software that produced the results. Our thanks also to Janet Turnbull and Judy Rose for their patience and perseverance in producing this manuscript.

VI. REFERENCES

[1] R. Davis, *Expert Systems: Where are We? And Where Do We Go From Here?*, AI Magazine 3 (Spring 1982), 3 - 22.

[2] R. Bajcsy and M. Tavakoli, *Computer Recognition of Roads from Satellite Pictures*, IEEE Transactions on Systems, Man, and Cybernetics SMC-6 (September 1976), 623 - 637.

[3] D. Ballard, C. Brown and J. Feldman, *An Approach to Knowledge-Directed Image Analysis*, Computer Vision Systems (A. Hanson and E. Riseman, eds.) (1978), Academic Press.

[4] H. Barrow and J. Tenenbaum, *MSYS: A System for Reasoning About Scenes*, Technical Note 121 (April 1976), AI Center, Stanford Research Institute.

[5] T. Binford, *Survey of Model Based Image Analysis Systems*, International Journal of Robotics Research 1 (1982), 18–64.

[6] R. Brooks, *Symbolic Reasoning Among 3-D Models and 2-D Images*, STAN-CS- 81-861 and AIM-343 (June 1981), Department of Computer Science, Stanford University.

[7] O. Faugeras and K. Price, *Aerial Images Using Stochastic Labeling*, IEEEPAMI 3 (November 1981), 638–642.

[8] A. Hanson and E. Riseman, *VISIONS: A Computer System for Interpreting Scenes*, Computer Vision Systems (A. Hanson and E. Riseman, eds.) (1978), 303 - 333, Academic Press.

[9] T. Kanade, *Model Representation and Control Structures in Image Understanding*, Proc. IJCAI-5 (August 1977).

[10] M. Levine and S. Shaheen, *A Modular Computer Vision System for Picture Segmentation and Interpretation*, IEEE PAMI 3 (September 1981), 540 - 556.

[11] A. Mackworth, *Vision Research Strategy: Black Magic, Metaphors, Mechanisms, Miniworlds, and Maps*, Computer Vision Systems (A. Hanson and E. Riseman, eds.) (1978), Academic Press.

[12] M. Nagao and T. Matsuyama, A Structural Analysis of Complex Aerial Photographs (1980), Plenum Press, New York.

[13] Y. Ohta, *A Region-Oriented Image-Analysis System by Computer*, Ph.D. Thesis (1980), Information Science Department, Kyoto University, Kyoto, Japan.

[14] K.E. Price and R. Reddy, *Matching Segments of Images*, IEEE PAMI 1 (June 1979), 110-116.

[15] J.M. Tenenbaum and H. Barrow, *Experiments in Interpretation-Guided Segmentation*, Technical Note 123 (1976), AI Center, Stanford Research Institute.

[16] J. Tsotsos, *Knowledge of the Visual Process: Content, Form and Use*, Proceedings of 6th International Conference on Pattern Recognition (October 1982), 654– 669, Munich, Germany.

[17] Y. Yakimovsky and J. Feldman, *A Semantics-Based Decision Theory Region Analyzer*, Proceedings of IJCAI-3 (August 1973), 580–588.

[18] D. Marr, Vision (1982), W.H. Freeman and Company, San Francisco.

[19] M. Brady, *Computational Approaches to Image Understanding*, Computing Surveys 14 (March 1982), 3–71.

[20] P.A. Nagin, A.R. Hanson and E.M. Riseman, *Studies in Global and Local Histogram- Guided Relaxation Algorithms*, IEEE PAMI PAMI-4 (May 1982), 263–277.

[21] R. Kohler, *Integrating Non-Semantic Knowledge into Image Segmentation Processes*, Ph.D. Dissertation and COINS Technical Report 84-04 (1984), University of Massachusetts at Amherst.

[22] J.B. Burns, A.R. Hanson and E.M. Riseman, *Extracting Linear Features*, Proc. of the Seventh International Conference on Pattern Recognition (July 30 – August 2, 1984), Montreal, Canada.

[23] G. Reynolds, et al., *Hierarchical Knowledge-Directed Object Extraction Using a Combined Region and Line Representation*, Proc. of the Workshop on Computer Vision: Representation and Control (April 30–May 2, 1984), 238–247, Annapolis, Maryland.

[24] T.E. Weymouth, J.S. Griffith, A.R. Hanson and E.M. Riseman, *Rule Based Strategies for Image Interpretation*, Proc. of AAAI-83 (August 1983), 429–432, Washington, D.C. A longer version of this paper appears in Proc. of the DARPA Image Understanding Workshop (June 1983), 193–202, Arlington, VA.

[25] C.C. Parma, A.R. Hanson and E.M. Riseman, *Experiments in Schema-Driven Interpretation of a Natural Scene*, COINS Technical Report 80-10 (April 1980), University of Massachusetts at Amherst.

[26] V.R. Lesser and L.D. Erman, *A Retrospective View of the Hearsay-II Architecture*, Proc. IJCAI-5 (1977), 790–800, Cambridge, MA.

[27] L. Erman, et al., *The Hearsay-II Speech-Understanding System: Integrating Knowledge to Resolve Uncertainty*, Computing Surveys 12(2) (June 1980), 213–253.

[28] T.E. Weymouth, *Using Object Descriptions in a Schema Network for Machine Vision*, Ph.D. Dissertation, under development, Computer and Information Science Department, University of Massachusetts at Amherst.

[29] J.D. Lowrance, *Dependency-Graph Models of Evidential Support*, Ph.D. Dissertation and COINS Technical Report 82-26 (September 1982), University of Massachusetts at Amherst.

[30] L. Wesley and A. Hanson, *The Use of an Evidential-Based Model for Representing Knowledge and Reasoning about Images in the VISIONS System*, Proc. of the Workshop on Computer Vision (August 1982), 14–25, Rindge, New Hampshire.

[31] A. Hanson and E. Riseman, Computer Vision Systems (1978), Academic Press.

[32] G. Shafer, A Mathematical Theory of Evidence (1976), Princeton University Press.

[33] A. Hanson and E. Riseman, *A Summary of Image Understanding Research at the University of Massachusetts*, COINS Technical Report 83-35 (October 1983), University of Massachusetts at Amherst.

[34] A. Hanson and E. Riseman, *Segmentation of Natural Scenes*, Computer Vision Systems (A. Hanson and E. Riseman, Eds.), Academic Press (1978), 129–163.

[35] E. Riseman and A. Hanson, *The Design of a Semantically Directed Vision Processor*, COINS Technical Report TR 71C-1, University of Massachusetts (February 1975), Revised version COINS Technical Report 75C-1.

[36] E. Riseman and A. Hanson, *A Methodology for the Development of General Knowledge-Based Vision Systems*, Proc. of the IEEE Workshop on Principles of Knowledge-Based Systems (December 1984), Denver, Colorado.

T W A I C E : Die Expertensystem-Shell von Nixdorf

(c) Stuart E. Savory Ph.D

Nixdorf Computer AG
D-4790 Paderborn

TWAICE ist das erste einer Reihe von Produkten der Nixdorf Computer
AG im Bereich der "Kuenstlichen Intelligenz". Wie Henry Bergson
schon 1907 sagte :- "Intelligenz ... ist die Faehigkeit kuenstliche
Objekte zu erzeugen, insbesondere Werkzeuge um Werkzeuge herzustellen."

Nun, TWAICE ist ein generisches Werkzeug, um Expertensysteme bauen
zu koennen. Als vollportables Rumpfsystem konzipiert, bedarf es
(lediglich) der Zugabe von anwendungsspezifischem Wissen, um ein
zugeschnittenes Expertensystem zu erhalten. TWAICE ist seit Ende
1984 auf Nixdorf 32-bit Rechnern kommerziell erhaeltlich und seit
Mitte 1985 auf Fremdrechnern (zB. VAX unter VMS, IBM & Amdahl unter
VM/SP usw.).

Expertensysteme lassen sich kurz in folgenden vier Saetzen
definieren :-

Expertensysteme sind "intelligente" Computersysteme, in denen die
fachliche Kompetenz von Experten in Form von Sachwissen und
Erfahrungswissen gespeichert wurde. Sie benutzen neben Fakten- und
Regelwissen Heuristiken und vages Wissen. Expertensysteme sind
imstande ueber Regeln aus dem vorgegebenen Wissen selbststaendig
Schluesse zu ziehen, d.h. Problemloesungen anzubieten. Sie koennen
an jeder Stelle des Loesungsprozesses Auskunft darueber geben,
warum sie einen eingeschlagenen Loesungsweg gewaehlt haben, zu
welche Schlussfolgerungen sie bereits gelangt sind und wie sie zu
diesen Schlussfolgerungen kamen.

Am Beispiel der Nixdorf Computer AG moechte ich nun zwei sinnvolle
Anwendungsgebiete der Expertensysteme skizzieren, denn neben
mehrjaehriger Entwicklungsarbeit im eigenen Hause und enger nation-
aler wie auch internationaler Kooperation mit fuehrenden
Universitaets- und Industriepartnern haben wir bei Nixdorf selbst
Expertensystem fuer unsere spezielle Belange aufgebaut.

Als erstes Beispiel dient FAULTFINDER mit REPPLAN (zur Fehlerdiagnose und zur Erzeugung von Reparaturanweisungen), vgl. [Savory
1984] in [Bernhold und Albers 1985]. Die Aufgabe dieses Systems
ist die Erkennung und Lokalisierung von Fehlern (durch den
Bediener, ohne unnoetige Hilferufe an das technische Kundendienst)
sowie die Erzeugung von Reparaturanweisungen fuer beliebige komplexe Geraete und Anlagen (Rechner, Fotokopierer, Autos, Flugzeuge,
chemische Anlagen, Kraftwerke, Stromnetze, usw.).

* TWAICE ist ein eingetragenes Warenzeichen
  der Nixdorf Computer AG.

Das Expertensystem enthaelt sowohl das Wissen des Konstrukteurs als
auch das des Kundendienst-Ingenieurs und kann auch Nichtfachleute
bei der Reparatur anleiten. Wir bei Nixdorf wenden FAULTFINDER z.B.
bei der Fehlerdiagnose des Systems 8832 an. Besondere Eigenschaften des Systems FAULTFINDER sind sowohl die generelle Anwendbarkeit
im Bereich der Fehlerdiagnose, denn FAULTFINDER ist ein allgemeiner
Mechanismus zum Schlussfolgern, Erklaeren, Begruenden im Bereich
der Fehlerdiagnose (der Benutzer kann FAULTFINDER auf eine
beliebige, von ihm selbst zu erstellende Wissensbasis anwenden);
als auch die leicht handhabbarer Dialog, denn die Bedienung in
Fehlersituationen ist einfach. Zehn Eingaben, die dem Benutzer zu
Beginn jeder Sitzung angezeigt werden (und die er auch waehrend des
Dialogs jederzeit abrufen kann), genuegen, um den Dialog zu
fuehren. REPPLAN ist ein allgemeiner Mechanismus, der nach der
Diagnose eines Fehlers durch FAULTFINDER die Ausgabe einer detail-
lierten Reparaturanleitung veranlasst. Bei einer entsprechenden
Anzahl von Reparaturen kann der Nutzen allein dieses Expertensys-
tems einige Millionen Mark betragen. Alle Wartungsorganisationen
koennten diese Methode einsetzen.

Als zweites Beispiel dient CONAD (Configuration advisor = Konfigurationsberatung). CONAD ist ein Expertensystem zur Konfiguration
von komplexen Geraeten, Anlagen, Angeboten und Dienstleistungen
(Computer, Prozessanlagen, Maschinen, Netzwerke, finanztechnische
Beratung, Versicherungspakete, usw.) CONAD wird bei Nixdorf fuer
die Konfigurationsberatung eingesetzt. Anwendungsziel ist, den
Vertrieb computergestuetzt in die Lage zu versetzen, auf der Basis
der Preislistenstruktur aus spezifischen Kundenwuenschen die
bestellungsgerechte Hardware-Konfiguration zu erzeugen. Hardware-
Komplexitaet fuehrt oft zu unvollstaendigen Angaben bei Bestellung,
was zu unnoetigen Belastungen bei unseren Kunden und im eigenen
Hause fuehren kann. Die CONAD zugrundeliegende Wissensbank
enthaelt alle fuer jede Geraetezusammenstellung notwendigen Informationen. Auf dieser Basis kann der Benutzer im Dialog und regel-
gesteuert die vollstaendige und konkrete Konfiguration seines Com-
putersystems vornehmen. Ist einmal eine Beratungssitzung "zur
Zufriedenheit" von CONAD beendet, so ist fuer eine weitere Bestellung eines Nixdorf-8864-Bankencomputers sichergestellt·, dass sie
fehlerfrei ist, kein Teil vergessen wurde und alle Teile zusammen-
passen. Besondere Eigenschaften von CONAD sind sowohl die
allgemeine Anwendbarkeit in allen Bereichen, wo in Form von Beratung Produkte oder Dienstleistungen unter Beruecksichtigung indivi-
dueller Kundenwuensche und -Gegebenheiten zu einem sinnvollen Ganzen zusammengefuehrt werden muessen; als auch die Erk-
laerungsfaehigkeit.

Die Erklaerungskomponente sorgt dafuer, das der Benutzer bei ihm
nicht sofort einleuchtenden Schritten oder Vorschlaegen des Systems
die Wissensbank analysieren kann. Auf Kommandos wie Warum?, Fakten?, Wie? Wissen?, Regel?, Rat? usw. erklaert das Expertensystem,
aufgrund welchen Wissens Schlussfolgerungen gezogen und
Vorschlaege gemacht wurden, was das Loesungsverstaendnis und die
Systemakzeptanz beim Benutzer unterstuetzt.

Die Entwurfsziele fuer TWAICE waren u.a. :-

- TWAICE soll als fachgebietsunabhaengige Expertensystemshell
  konzipiert werden.

- TWAICE soll den Aufbau von Expertensystem fuer komplexe
  Entscheidungssysteme (Decision Support Systems) stark unterstuetzen.

- Der Wissenserwerb soll einfach sein, insbesondere sollen die Wissensbanken auf Leichter Weise inkrementell modifizierbar sein.

- TWAICE soll seine Ergebnisse rechtfertigen und seine Fragen begruenden koennen.

- TWAICE soll auch durch Computer-Laien als Beratungs bzw. Lehrsystem benutzbar sein.

- Es darf nicht begrenzt sein auf ein "Ein-Benutzer" Rechner wie z.B. einen Xerox 1108, Symbolics oder Lisp Maschine, denn wenn die TWAICE Kunden expandieren wollen und mehrere Leute sollen gleichzeitig ihre Expertensystem benutzen, moechten Sie auf eine Familie von Rechner (ueber ein weites Leistungsspektrum (1, 10, 40 oder 100 Benutzer)) mit dasselbe Software und dasselbe Wissensbank arbeiten koennen.

- Es muss auf jeder normale Rechner Laufen, unter Verwendung von billige dumme Terminals, integriert mit ihre bestehende Anwendungen und mit Zugriff auf ihre bestehenden Datenbanken.

- Der Benutzerdialog muss eine schmale Schnittstelle haben, sodass er ggf. ueber einer breitverteilte Datenfernuebertragungsnetz betrieben werden kann; soll heissen − die Waehlnetze der Bundespost mit 2400 Baud ; Konsequenz, keine schoene breitbandig Grafiks Schnittstellen.

- Es muss in die jeweilige Landessprache kommunizieren koennen, und nicht sein Benutzer zwingen z.B. Amerikanisch zu lernen; denn nicht jeder der in Genuss der Leistung des Expertensystems kommen soll ist unbedingt bereits Fremdsprachenexperte.

- ein explizites Taxonomie-Modell fuer die Wissensbasis muss vorhanden sein,

- interaktive Formulierung von Wissen in Form von Produktionsregeln, sowie die Gewinnung taxonomischer Strukturen im Dialog soll unterstuetzt sein,

- einen Regel-Compiler fuer beschleunigtes Laufzeitverhalten (sowie Pruefung der Wissensbasis auf Konsistenz und Vollstaendigkeit) ist noetig,

- mehrere Inferenz-Mechanismen fuer verschiedene Logik-arten soll enthalten sein. Die Interferenz-Mechanismen enthalten die Rueckwaertsverkettung und die Vorwaertsverkettung von Produktionsregeln sowie die Vergabe von Sicherheitsgraden (confidence factors) bei der Verwendung von nicht exaktem (= vages) Wissen.

- eine Leicht zu bedienende Dialog-Schnittstelle soll enthalten sein. Der Dialog soll demnach wie folgt aussehen :- Vor dem Einstieg in das konkrete Problem werden vom System zunaechst Informationen zum Problemfeld gesammelt. Ein "spelling corrector" korrigiert kleinere Tippfehler. Dann erfolgt die Pruefung von Eingaben auf semantische Zulaessigkeit. Fehlen dem System an einer bestimmten Stelle zur Loesung des Problems Informationen, die nur von aussen kommen koennen, erzuegt das Expertensystem automatisch Fragen an den Benutzer. Lautet die Benutzerantwort auf eine Frage des Systems "Das weiss ich nicht.", versucht das Expertensystem die Antwort anderweitig aus seinem Wissen heraus zu finden.

Dem erfahrenen Benutzer stehen fuer die Dialogfuehrung
Kurzkommandos zur Verfuegung. Ueber jederzeit verfuegbare
Help-Funktionen werden die zu einem bestimmten Zeitpunkt moe-
glichen Eingaben angezeigt und erklaert.

Bei der Problemloesung kann es vorkommen, dass Wissen erforderlich ist, das nicht explizit in der Wissensbasis steht. Die
Inferenz-Komponente des Expertensystems kann solches fehlendes
Wissen logisch ableiten. Dieses abgeleitete Wissen kann als
Ganzes oder in Teilen betrachtet und untersucht werden. Zum
Beispiel die Taxonomie kann als Ganzes oder in Ausschnitten
untersucht werden. Die Gesamtheit der Regeln, Teile davon
oder einzelne Regeln koennen gezielt betrachtet und untersucht
werden.

- Das Rumpfsystem soll seine Ausgaben quasi in der natuerlichen
  Sprache formulieren, d.h. die Schlussfolgerungen der
  Inferenz-Komponente werden fuer den Benutzer verstaendlich
  aufbereitet. Nicht sofort einsichtige Fragen des Expertensystems koennen auf Wunsch erlaeutert oder begruendet werden.
  Das Kurzzeitgedaechtnis des Benutzers wird entlastet, indem er
  sich jederzeit den bisher beschrittenen Loesungsweg im Zusammenhang darstellen lassen kann.

- Eine starke Erklaerungskomponente schliesst die Moeglichkeit
  ein, das Expertensystem jederzeit zu fragen, zum Beispiel
  warum es eine bestimmte Frage stellt, oder mit welchen Regeln
  neues Wissen abgeleitet wurde, oder welche Regeln auf ein vor-
  gegebenes Objekt anwendbar sind, oder in welcher Beziehung ein
  Objekt zu seiner Wissensumgebung steht, usw.

- Je nach Bedarf muss die Moeglichkeit bestehen, direkt in der
  Wirtssprache des Rumpfsystems geschriebene benutzerspezifische
  Prozeduren einzubinden (ueblicherweise ist dies LISP oder bei
  neuere Systeme PROLOG). Das System muss in der Lage sein,
  mehrere hundert Regeln, zahlreiche Datentabellen usw. zu
  nutzen. Fuer den Wissenserwerb soll ein leistungsfaehiger
  Texteditor zur Verfuegung stehen. Fuer eine spaetere Analyse
  durch den Knowledge Engineer sollen ganze Beratungssitzungen
  abgespeichert werden koennen. Alle Schlussfolgerungen sollen
  in allen Schritten nachvollzogen werden koennen (damit kann
  der Knowledge Engineer in Zusammenarbeit mit dem Experten die
  Wissensbasis begutachten und auf sachliche Korrektheit
  pruefen. Erkannte Fehler in der Wissensbasis (Fakten oder
  Regeln) koennen direkt beseitigt werden. Zur Ueberpruefung der
  (geaenderten) Wissensbasis steht eine Falldatenverwaltung zur
  Verfuegung.

TWAICE hat alle diese Anforderungen erfuellt und ist nach
zweijaehrigem internen Test zum stabilen, kommerziell erfolgreichen
KI-Produkt geworden. Der Platz reicht hier nicht aus, um die
Architektur von TWAICE zu beschreiben. Dies ist aber hier auch
nicht noetig, denn die Architektur von TWAICE ist in [Mescheder
1985] detailliert dargestellt. Zusammenfassend kann gesagt werden,
dass TWAICE ein hervorragendes Werkzeug zum Wissenserwerb und zur
Wissensformalisierung fuer den kommerziellen Einsatz ist (Fr.
Schachter-Radig beschreibt ihren Anforderungskatalog hierfuer auch
in diesem Heft), mit dem Nixdorf bereits viel praktische Erfahrung
gesammelt hat. Ferner sind Konfigurierungsprobleme (wie Dr.Lehmann
ebenfalls in diesem Heft skizziert) bereits seit 1984 erfolgreich
mit TWAICE geloest worden (z.B. CONAD).

Weitere Informationen ueber TWAICE, sowie Vorfuehrungen usw., werden von Nixdorf Expert Systems Centre, Abt. VLD/VE, Berlinerstrasse
95, D-8000 Muenchen 40 angeboten.

Literaturverweise

[1] Bernold und Albers (Hrsg) Artificial Intelligence
     Towards Practical Application. North-Holland 1985

[2] Mescheder, B. Funktionen und Arbeitsweise der
     Expertensystem-Shell TWAICE.   In : Savory 1985a.

[3] Roesner, H. Expertensysteme fuer den kommerziellen
     Einsatz.   In : Savory 1985a.

[4] Roesner,H. und Savory,S.   Anforderungen der Praxis
     an Expertensysteme. In State-of-the-Art Herbst 1985
     Oldenbourg Verlag.

[5] Savory, S. :1983: The Prototype Nixdorf Expert
     System.   In : Angewandte Informatik 11/83.

[6] Savory, S.(Hrsg.) :1985a: Kuenstliche Intelligenz
     und Expertensysteme. Oldenbourg Verlag, Muenchen
     1985.   ISBN 3-486-29281-1

[7] Savory, S. :1984 : FF; A Nixdorf Expert System for
     Fault-Finding and Repair Planning - An Outline
     Description. In Bernold und Albers pp119 bis 128.

LARGE-SCALE KNOWLEDGE SYSTEMS

John Miles Smith

Computer Corporation of America
4 Cambridge Center
Cambridge MA 02142 USA

Abstract

AI technology has produced a variety of tools for generating knowledge-based systems ranging from Programming Languages to Expert System Shells. When used for large-scale applications, these tools suffer from several significant limitations. First, virtual memory size limits the volume of knowledge that can be handled. Second, there are no facilities for allowing the knowledge base to be shared among several applications. Third, inference mechanisms are computationally intractable when large knowledge bases are resident on secondary storage. Fourth, there are no facilities for distributing the knowledge base across multiple workstations to achieve better performance and reliability. Database technology, when properly integrated with these AI tools, has the potential for overcoming these limitations. However, the solution requires more than just coupling a DBMS as a back-end storage system to an AI tool. To achieve the best functionality and performance, the tool's knowledge representations and inference engines must be designed to operate in cooperation with those of the DBMS. Knowledge processing must be modularized to provide a stable "working set" for the tool inference engine. Inferences that can be performed efficiently by the DBMS alone must be separated by the tool inference engine and delegated to the DBMS. Furthermore, DBMS facilities must be extended to provide more efficiency and flexibility in knowledge processing. A lot of design and experimentation will be required before the full integration of AI Knowledge Tools and DBMS technology is fully understood. This paper takes a first step towards this integration by identifying approaches and principles in the design of large-scale knowledge systems.

1. Introduction

This paper characterizes a class of computer systems to be called here "Large-scale Knowledge Systems". A Large-scale Knowledge System (LKS) involves a combination of Database Management System (DBMS) and Knowledge System (KS) technology. KSs are used to intelligently process data being stored in, or retrieved from, a shared repository maintained by a DBMS. The knowledge used by the KSs may also be stored in the repository.

This combination of technology is required in an increasing number of applications, including office automation, CAD/CAM and military command and control. Today, the integration of KS and DBMS technology is an emerging research area seeking to develop general-purpose LKS engines. By the 1990's, it is expected that these LKS engines will have left the research laboratories and become important tools for commercial software development.

The paper focusses on identifying system architectures, key technical problems and design principles to meet application requirements for LKS engines.

Performance is expected to be a key challenge in the development of LKSs. Two factors are involved. First, both DBMSs and KSs are powerful search engines, and their combination has the potential to create a multiplicative explosion in computation time. Second, an LKS seeks to provide higher-level functionality for application development than either a DBMS or a KS alone. This higher-level functionality will require novel optimization techniques to identify efficient execution strategies.

Section 2 examines two applications of LKSs to motivate technical requirements and performance considerations. The first application involves CAD/CAM for the production of maps. Multiple intelligent processes are required to extract feature and terrain information from raw image data. The extracted information, together with the raw data, is stored in a database. Real-time delays in availability of extracted information are acceptable, but a long backlog in unprocessed data must be avoided. The second application is command and control in either a military context (naval situation assessment) or civilian context (airport traffic control). Automatic sensors update a database of contact information which is intelligently analyzed by multiple processes to determine threatening situations and suggest possible courses of action. In this application, response must be fast and occur within bounded real-time constraints.

Section 3 investigates architectural approaches to providing the technology required in these LKS applications. The separate limitations of current KS and DBMS systems are discussed and four paradigms for integrating these systems are introduced. The first paradigm is to treat the DBMS merely as an extended storage manager for a KS. Once data has been down-loaded to a KS, all other LKS functionality is provided by the KS. The second paradigm is to treat the DBMS as a persistent knowledge manager. In this role, the DBMS can support knowledge sharing across KSs. The third paradigm is to treat the DBMS as an inference engine for persistent knowledge. In this role, inferences can be executed directly by the DBMS when it is more efficient to do so. The fourth paradigm is to treat the DBMS as a distributed inference engine for persistent knowledge. The DBMS now can provide the increased performance and reliability achievable with distributed processing. These paradigms suggest quite different decompositions of LKS functionality across the KS and DBMS engines. The last paradigm offers the best opportunity for meeting the functionality and performance requirements of LKSs.

Section 4 investigates a key technical problem underlying the third and fourth architectural paradigms. This problem is concerned with delegating subinferences from the KS to the DBMS. As a step towards a solution, a comparison is made between inference in KSs and query evaluation in DBMSs. It is concluded that query evaluation can provide some, but not all, of the inference capabilities of a KS. However, in many cases, the DBMS can provide inference capabilities more efficiently than the KS. In essence, the DBMS is sacrificing flexibility in exchange for performance. The role of recursive view definitions in increasing the inferential power of a DBMS is clarified. It is argued that the DBMS component in an LKS be able to support recursive views to offload expensive inferences from a KS, and to give the DBMS more scope for optimization and exploitation of parallel processing.

Section 5 briefly examines two fundamental problems in designing an LKS based on the ideas of Sections 3 and 4. The first problem is concerned with making the DBMS engine extensible enough to handle a variety of knowledge representations. Abstract data types can be used for new scalar representations, but are insufficient for new structured representations. This problem occurs predominantly with dimensional (space and time) representations of objects. A solution is proposed which involves the introduction of dimensional semantics directly into the data model. The second problem is concerned with the language environment for developing applications over the LKS engine. The key question is how the combined DBMS/KS facilities should be presented to the knowledge engineer. It is suggested that a preprocessor be used to provide the engineer with a fully integrated application development language. This language would then be used to build a complete application development environment.

2. LKS Applications

An LKS is an application development tool intended for applications that involve intelligent processing of data being stored in, or retrieved from, a shared information repository. Two examples of such applications will be examined in this section to motivate technical requirements. These requirements will be used in the next section to evaluate generic LKS architectures.

2.1 Cartographic CAD/CAM

This application is an automated map production system as illustrated in Figure 2.1. The DBMS must maintain a model of the world's surface which reflects changes over time. The surface model is being continuously updated on the basis of raw image data received from satellites. The raw images must be analysed to extract information about significant features and terrain elevation. This structured information is then used to update the surface model. On the output side, the surface model is used to automatically generate (hardcopy or softcopy) maps according to given map specifications. The potential size of the Knowledge Repository is on the order of 10**19 bytes. It will contain all knowledge involved in the application including raw data, the structured surface model, schema descriptions, information extraction rules and procedures, and operational rules and constraints.

The arrival rate of raw image data is so great that human analysts cannot keep up with it using manual methods. Each human analyst must be aided by a KS for feature analysis. Given a raw image, the KS must interpret the image and identify features. Typically, when the KS is forming hypotheses about certain features, related information must be retrieved from the existing surface model for correlation. When features have been extracted, the KS must update the surface model accordingly. Up to one thousand human analysts with various areas of expertise may each be simultaneously using the system.

Since feature extraction and map production operations can take an extended period of time, multiple versions of images, surface models and maps may be in process at any time. An Integrity Subsystem is required to ensure that proper control is exercised over versions, changes and map releases. The Knowledge Repository must maintain data about who is using which versions for what purpose, as well as the operational integrity rules themselves. The Integrity Subsystem then invokes these rules whenever an analyst checks information into, or out of, the Knowledge Repository.

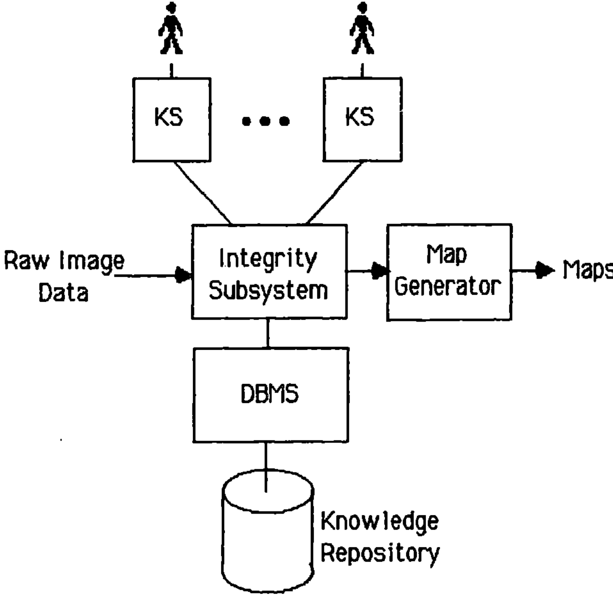

Figure 2.1: Automated Cartography System

The performance of the automated cartography system in Figure 2.1 will be determined by how the system components are distributed across hardware devices. It is appropriate to have each KS resident on a powerful workstation under the control of a single analyst. In addition, it will be necessary to use a mainframe to support map production, and possibly to act as a file server for the workstations. An important question is how the Knowledge Repository, the DBMS and the Integrity Subsystem should be distributed across the workstations and the mainframe.

A key fact is that, when a workstation is processing a particular raw image, all relevant database information comes from a localized geographical area. The information associated with this area will be small enough to be held by the workstation ... either in virtual memory, or in secondary storage. Moving the information to the workstation will significantly reduce the time to process an image. This suggests that the Knowledge Repository should be distributed, and partially replicated, across the mainframe and workstations. The location, or locations, of knowledge will change with the processing requirements of the KSs.

To provide query processing, integrity control and recovery for knowledge resident on the workstations, the DBMS and Integrity Subsystem must also be distributed across the workstations and mainframe. In fact, each workstation will need its own copy of the DBMS and Integrity Subsystem. These DBMS copies should be able to operate over data in either virtual memory or secondary storage. In effect, a new form of distributed DBMS is required which supports dynamic redistribution of data, virtual memory query processing, and uses the Integrity Subsystem for concurrency and recovery control.

Within a session at a workstation, the KS will need to retrieve knowlege (from its local DBMS node) to help with hypothesis formation and also to corroborate hypotheses already formed. For high performance, these retrievals should return as little information as possible into the inference cycle of the KS. As much information filtering as possible should be done by the DBMS. In addition, the DBMS should receive retrieval requests at a high level of abstraction so that maximum optimization can be performed. These objectives can only be achieved if the DBMS query language captures the principal semantics of the application. In this case, it is the semantics of space and time that dominate the application. It is important that the DBMS query language support these semantics.

In summary, the new technical requirements for an LKS in this automated cartography application are a new form of distributed DBMS which supports:

- dynamic redistribution of data,

- virtual memory query processing,

- an integrity subsystem providing consistency and recovery,

- a query language and data model with space and time semantics.

2.2 Real-time Situation Assessment

This application is a real-time situation assessment system as occurs in military command and control and in airport traffic control. Figure 2.2 presents an architecture for such a system in a naval command and control context. The system is for tactical situation assessment on board ship. The Knowledge Repository must store both static and dynamic information. The static information includes maps, charts, ship characteristics and weapon characteristics. Dynamic information includes real-time "contact" reports describing the positions and actions of other ships and aircraft in the vicinity. The change over time of the dynamic information is important as well as the current state.

On the data input side, the DBMS must be able to rapidly receive, store, and commit contact reports. The reports are received at high and bursty rates. Each report must be made available to users within some real-time period after it is received. On the data output side, there is situation display showing the current disposition of contacts. In addition, there are multiple KSs for analysing the various kinds of threats. The KSs must identify contacts, try to determine their intentions, analyse the threats they pose, alert users, and suggest alternative courses of action. The inferences produced by the KSs are stored in the Knowledge Repository, and also appear on the situation display.

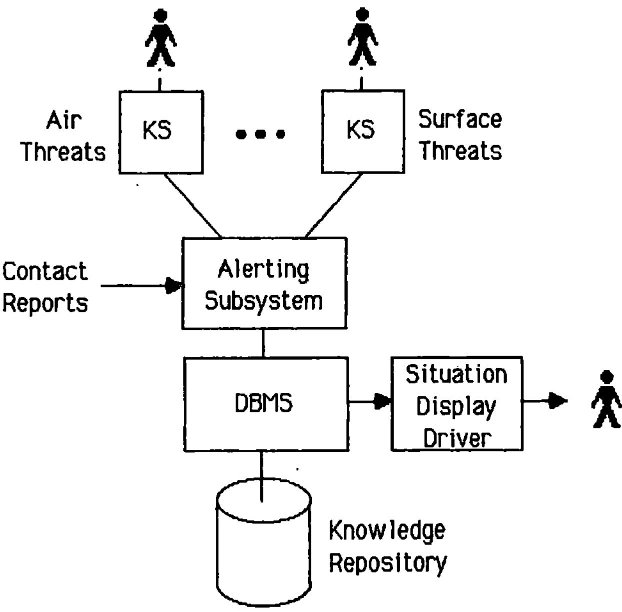

Figure 2.2: Tactical Situation Assessment System

The key problem in this application is alerting users to impending threats in real-time. As soon as the DBMS commits data relevant to a threat, the appropriate KSs must act on it. It does not make sense for the KSs to repeatedly poll the DBMS to see if relevant new information has arrived. Instead, the DBMS should alert the appropriate KSs when they need to respond to a situation. The Alerting Subsystem is responsible for doing this. The Alerting Subsystem is informed by the KSs which situations to detect at any given point of time. Incoming data and KS inferences are then monitored to detect when these situations arise. On detecting a situation, the Alerting Subsystem must notify the appropriate KS and supply it with sufficient information for it to take charge of the situation.

The performance of the Situation Assessment System of Figure 2.2 will depend heavily on how quickly the Alerting Subsystem can operate. In general, the Subsystem may need to check several hundred situation predicates over the Knowledge Repository whenever new contact reports or KS inferences arrive. To do this in real-time, innovative hardware and software techniques must be used.

It will be necessary to spread the predicate checking across multiple hardware devices by using a special-purpose distributed DBMS. Each node of the distributed DBMS is assigned a number of predicates to check. A node retains the smallest view of the Knowledge Repository required for checking its predicates. New information is broadcast to all nodes in parallel. When new information arrives, a node updates its view and reevaluates its predicates. This approach requires a distributed DBMS which supports dynamic data redistribution, update broadcasting and view update.

Typically, after a KS has taken charge of a potential threat situation, it will start analysing the situation in higher-level terms than the information actually stored in the Knowledge Repository. These higher-level terms would usually be defined using logic rules. Now consider what should happen when the KS needs to retrieve some additional information from the database.

For efficiency reasons, these additional queries should return as little information as possible back into the inference cycle of the KS. This means that the queries should be expressed to the DBMS in the higher-level terms used by the KS. The relevant KS logic rules should therefore be captured in the DBMS in the form of view definitions. In this way, queries are expressible directly in the higher-level terms. However, it is particularly important to capture recursive logic rules as these are computationally the most expensive to process. This will require an extension of DBMS view processing to efficiently handle recursive view definitions.

In summary, the new technical requirements for an LKS in this situation assessment application are a new form of distributed DBMS which supports:

- dynamic redistribution of data,

- view update,

- an alerting subsystem,

- recursive view processing.

3. LKS Architectural Paradigms

The previous section introduced two applications to illustrate the requirements for "Large-scale Knowledge Systems". This section focusses on the architecture of a generic LKS engine which is applicable to a class of applications. The general characteristics of this class are given, and four architectural paradigms for LKSs are presented. These paradigms are compared on the basis of the application characteristics they support.

3.1 Application Characteristics

The Automated Cartography System and the Tactical Situation Assessment System are intended as representative examples of LKS applications. Generalizing from these examples, Figure 3.1 illustrates the characteristics for a class of applications that, it is expected, will become of increasing importance over the next decade. The characteristics are broken down into those of the knowledge repository and those of knowledge processing. The entries in Figure 3.1 will be discussed in turn.

The volumes of knowledge can be extremely large as illustrated by the $10{**}19$ bytes of the Automated Cartography example. These volumes are beyond the capacity of the virtual memories in available computer systems. This means that knowledge must be kept on secondary (or tertiary) storage devices and brought into virtual memory on an as needed basis.

	large volumes	Knowledge volumes can be extremely large (up to 10**19 bytes). Orders of magnitude larger then the capacity of available virtual memories.
knowledge	persistent	The lifespan of knowledge exceeds the invocation of particular procedures which use that knowledge.
	shared	The knowledge is shared by multiple processes which may be simultaneously reading and writing knowledge.
	stratified	The knowledge is segmented into many different types (fact, procedure, constraint, definition) at multiple levels (object, meta, meta-meta).
	dimensional semantics	The semantics of space and time is a dominant aspect of knowledge representation both internally and at the user interface.
processing	distributed	The sources and/or users of knowledge are only loosely coupled and provide opportunities for distributed (parallel) processing.
	intelligent	The processing goes beyond routine clerical functions to provide intelligent advice and assistance to decision-makers.
	predefined	Many aspects of processing are pre-defined and change slowly, or not at all, over the lifespan of the application.
	high performance	High performance is required to intelligently process large knowledge volumes within a short, possibly real-time constrained, window.

Figure 3.1: LKS Application Characteristics

Knowledge is persistent in that its lifespan exceeds the duration of processes which are using the knowledge. For example, information about the world's surface in the Automated Cartography System may be used by many map generation, and many feature extraction, processes. This means that knowledge must be protected from corruption by the normal, or abnormal, execution of processes.

Knowledge is shared by several processes which are simultaneously reading and writing knowledge. In particular, the knowledge repository is often being updated in the background while inferences are drawn using that knowledge. This means that the knowledge repository must provide a concurrency control scheme to prevent interference between processes.

Knowledge in the repository is stratified into different types at different levels. The use of knowledge within a type and level is circumscribed by the application. For example, in the Automated Cartography System: operational integrity rules are used by the Integrity Subsystem to exercise version, change and release control; feature extraction procedures are used by a KS to process raw image data; factual surface knowledge is used by the Map Generator to create maps; meta-knowledge about data representations is used by the DBMS to efficiently access object knowledge. There is no requirement that all knowledge be uniformly accessible to a general purpose inference engine.

Space and time semantics are a dominant aspect of knowledge, particularly in military command and control and in engineering applications. Dimensional qualities arise in dealing with spatial objects like maps or manufactured parts, in exercising version control, in enforcing real-time constraints, and in archiving changes over time. Specialized knowledge representations and algorithms are required to efficiently process many kinds of spatial and temporal data.

The generators and users of knowledge are loosely-coupled. For example, images of different geographic regions can be processed with relative independence, decisions about version control do not affect on-going feature extraction, and the analysis of different kinds of battle situations can proceed with little coordination. This provides opportunities to use distributed processing techniques to increase performance and reliable operation.

The objective in these applications is to provide support for human decision-making. This means that expert knowledge, involving heuristic and approximate reasoning, may be required. It may also be necessary to capture administrative rules and procedures. Such knowledge may be difficult to specify and debug, and furthermore may evolve over time as improved decision-making procedures are understood. In this case, it is desirable to capture knowledge using rule-based methods rather than conventional programs. Special inference processors will be required to process knowledge of this kind. In addition, intelligent processing may require smart algorithms for speeding up potentially time-consuming operations.

Many, but not all, aspects of knowledge processing are predefined and change slowly, or not at all, over the lifespan of the application. Examples include the representation and use of knowledge, coordination between simultaneous users, the user interface and key algorithms. These "invariants" make it possible to use precompilation techniques to speed up system performance.

High performance is mandated by the combination of intelligent (heuristic) processing and large knowledge volumes. In addition, some applications will require very rapid response, possibly within real-time constraints. In general, powerful optimization procedures must be used to prevent unnecessary effort, and parallel processing must be used to complete the necessary effort in the shortest time.

3.2 LKS Architecture

This section begins by identifying the limitations of existing KS and DBMS engines with respect to the LKS application characteristics of Figure 3.1. Four architectural approaches are then introduced for creating an LKS engine from the integration of KS and DBMS engines. These four approaches are compared and evaluated.

A commercial DBMS engine today supports application requirements for large volumes of shared, persistent knowledge and optimization of predefined knowledge representations. Experimental DBMS engines have demonstrated methods for the distributed processing of partitioned and/or replicated knowledge. Some experiments have also been done in using abstract data types to handle aspects of stratified knowledge. The key limitations of DBMS engines for LKS applications are lack of support for dimensional semantics, rule-based processing and high performance.

A commercial KS engine today supports application requirements for rule-based processing. Some engines utilize multiple knowledge representations which contribute to the handling of stratified knowledge. In addition, some experiments have been done to exploit compilation of knowledge structures to improve performance. KS engines are oriented towards sophisticated, single-purpose, single-user applications. Their key limitations are lack of support for large volumes of shared knowledge, high performance, optimization and distributed processing.

Between them, KS and DBMS engines support most of the required application characteristics. The integration of the two engines is therefore an important technical goal.

The basic mode of integration is illustrated in Figure 3.2. KSs typically operate within virtual memory. Inference operations are applied to knowledge within a part of virtual memory called "working memory". However, in an LKS, all knowledge will be stored in the knowledge repository maintained by the DBMS. The DBMS must therefore transfer knowledge into working memory as it is required by the KS. This is done by anchoring a buffer in the physical part of working memory, and using it to transfer knowledge to and from the DBMS.

Two modifications are required of the KS. First, the KS must generate calls to the DBMS when knowledge is to be transferred. The KS must determine, as part of its overall operation, when new knowledge is needed, and/or old knowledge is no longer needed, in working memory. The KS must then formulate calls in the DBMS interface language to execute the appropriate transfers. Second, the KS must be modified so that it can interpret the format of the knowledge transferred to the buffer. If necessary, the KS must translate the knowledge and place it into its own internal format.

It is important that the KS be very economical in generating calls to the DBMS. There is a large overhead associated with a DBMS call and typically a DBMS can only process a few transactions per second. The KS should minimize the number of calls to the DBMS and ensure that any call transfers a relatively large block of knowledge. This allows the DBMS to spread the retrieval overhead across many knowledge items. In effect, the KS must identify a current "working set" of knowledge blocks and attempt to keep this working set in physical memory. To achieve this, the KS must have some way of

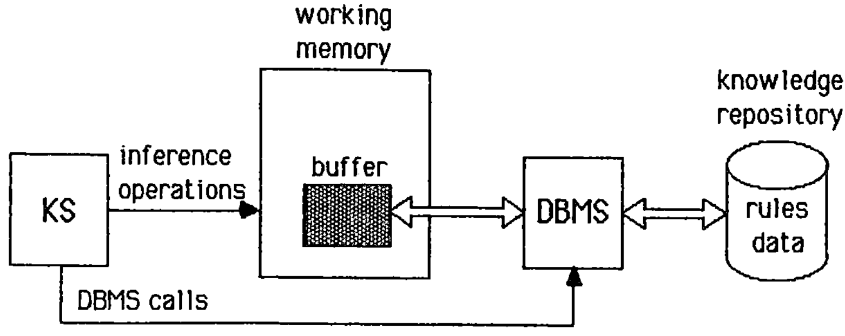

Figure 3.2: KS - DBMS Integration

Paradigm	DBMS calls:	Additional DBMS facilities used:
Type 1	block transfer	storage capacity data transfer
Type 2	transactions	concurrency control recovery system
Type 3	view query/update transactions	query processing view processing
Type 4	distributed transactions	distributed processing reconfiguration

Figure 3.3: LKS Architectural Paradigms

modularizing knowledge, and associated working data, into various contexts. These contexts should have the property that much more processing time is spent within a context, than in changing contexts. A notion of context, or logical knowledge module, is available for some KS engines.

Given the basic mode of integration in Figure 3.2, there are at least four different architectural paradigms for an LKS engine. These paradigms differ in the nature of the DBMS calls and in the DBMS facilities which are used in the LKS. These paradigms are listed in Figure 3.3 in order of increasing numbers of features.

The simplest paradigm is called "Type 1". In this case, the DBMS calls are simply requests for contiguous blocks of knowledge from the knowledge repository. This approach is intended for a single-user configuration. The knowledge engineer need not be aware of the existence of the DBMS. The role of the DBMS is merely to give the illusion of a virtual memory with a very large storage capacity. Most of the facilities of the DBMS are either unused, or used in only a rudimentary way. All semantic processing of knowledge is done by the KS. The Type 1 paradigm is basically a way of improving the storage capacity of existing KS engines.

The Type 2 paradigm goes a step further by supporting multiple users sharing the same knowledge repository. In this case the DBMS calls are full transactions with provision for concurrency control and failure recovery. Knowledge is tranferred not only for increased storage capacity but also to deposit knowledge which can be seen by other users. To maintain consistency of the knowledge repository, knowledge must be deposited in increments which preserve integrity constraints. In general, it is not possible for the KS to deduce these increments during knowlege processing. Instead they must be explicitly introduced by the knowledge engineer. This means that the knowledge engineer must be aware of the existence of the DBMS. Further, the knowledge representation language of the KS must be extended to include a construct for commiting knowledge so that others can see it in the repository. This approach uses more of the facilities of the DBMS. However, all semantic processing of knowledge is still being done in the KS. The Type 2 paradigm is a way of sharing knowledge between multiple KSs.

The Type 3 paradigm exploits the ability of the DBMS to do semantic processing. In this case, the DBMS is regarded as a special purpose inference engine which can directly, and efficiently, perform certain kinds of inference. The DBMS calls now may include queries over extensional (stored) knowledge, requests to process intensional (view) knowledge, and requests to monitor the truth of specific (alert) conditions. Again, it is unreasonable to expect that the KS engine can itself deduce which inferences should be assigned to the DBMS and which to itself. The knowledge engineer must make this determination as part of the engineering process. This means that the knowledge engineer must have full awareness of the semantic knowledge representations provided by the DBMS. Ideally, the knowledge engineer should have an integrated view of all KS and DBMS facilities. The Type 3 paradigm provides a way of efficiently delegating knowledge processing within a large-scale application. As indicated by the applications of Section 2, such delegation can lead to major performance improvements.

The Type 4 paradigm provides the performance and reliability advantages of distributed processing. In this case a distributed DBMS is used, and the knowledge repository is distributed and/or replicated across multiple hardware devices. Typically, each user workstation will have its own DBMS node which is tightly coupled with the KS engine. In addition, other DBMS nodes may be used for special purposes such as checking alert conditions. When a user starts a new session at a workstation, its DBMS node must be loaded with the knowledge required to support that session. In some circumstances, the KS will be able to predict what view of the knowledge repository is required. However, in general, it is desirable to include a new "session" construct in the knowledge representation used by the KS. The knowledge engineer will then be able to specify the view required for a session, and also to determine how the view is to be updated. Parts of the view under version control may be allowed to age as new knowledge enters the repository. Other parts of the view (for example, status information) may need to be updated dynamically. Given a suitable hardware environment, the Type 4 paradigm provides the basis for a high-performance distributed LKS engine.

Since the Type 4 paradigm includes the features of the previous paradigms and comes closest to meeting all the characteristics of Figure 3.1, it will be the focus of the remainder of the paper.

A lot of investigation is required to fully determine the requirements, functionality and design for a generic Type 4 LKS engine. However, much of the underlying technology is already available in the KS and distributed DBMS areas. There seem to be three fundamental research problems to be solved. The first problem is how to delegate inference responsibilities between KS and DBMS as discussed in the Type 3 paradigm. This problem is investigated more deeply in Section 4. The second problem is how to introduce appropriate dimensional semantics into KS and DBMS engines. The third problem is how to provide the knowledge engineer with a suitably structured view of the integrated KS and DBMS engines. The last two problems are treated briefly in Section 5.

4. Inference versus Query Evaluation

Inference is the fundamental process underlying KSs and a key aspect of DBMSs. The inference mechanisms of KSs vary significantly depending on the knowledge representation which is used. It can range from mechanisms based on the formal deduction systems of logic to forward and backward chaining mechanisms with no formal logical counterpart. The inference mechanism of DBMSs is equivalent to a form of logical deduction called query evaluation. The objective of this section is to compare KS inference mechanisms with query evaluation to understand how the two should coexist in an LKS engine.

Given the wide variety of KS inference mechanisms, it is impractical to perform a comparison with them all. So deductive inference in first order logic will be used as a representative KS inference mechanism. Similarly, query evaluation in DBMSs varies depending on the underlying data model. In this case, relational query processing will be used as the representative method. Deductive inference will be characterized first, then relational query evaluation, and then the two will be compared.

4.1 Deductive Inference

In deductive inference, knowledge is represented in the language of logic as a set of formulae (axioms) A. A query is another formulae $Q(v)$ with free variables v. The result of a query is the set of free variable instantiations s, such that $Q(s)$ is provable from A.

Consider the example in Figure 4.1 which is concerned with the positions of ships as in naval tactical situation assessment. There are two axioms. The first asserts that the Kennedy is positioned at either point_V or point_W. The second asserts that the Kennedy is not at point_W. The query asks for the position of the Kennedy. Since position(Kennedy, point_V) is provable from the axioms A, but position(Kennedy, point_W) is not, the result is point_V.

Let's use the standard symbols $\vdash$ and $\models$ to mean "is provable" and "is a logical consequence of" respectively. Deductive inference can be characterized by the search required to demonstrate that $A \vdash Q(s)$. By using well-known metatheorems of logic, $A \vdash Q(s)$ is equivalent to $\models A \Rightarrow Q(s)$. Deductive inference can then be characterized as the search required to demonstrate that $A \Rightarrow Q(s)$ is true under every possible

<u>Axioms</u>

1. position(Kennedy, point_U) ∨ position(Kennedy, point_W)
2. ¬ position(Kennedy, point_W)

<u>Query</u>

?position(Kennedy, p)

<u>Inference</u>

Find **p**'s such that **position(Kennedy, p)** is provable
from the axioms

<u>Results</u>

p = point_U

Figure 4.1: Deductive Inference

interpretation of the predicate symbols. An interpretation of an n-ary predicate symbol is
an n-ary relation over a given set.

Notice that deductive inference involves a "second-level" demonstration. It is not
sufficient to demonstrate on the first level that **A ⇒ Q(s)** holds for a specific
interpretation. Instead, it is necessary to demonstrate that **A ⇒ Q(s)** holds for all
possible interpretations. It is this second level demonstration that makes deductive
inference computationally expensive, and potentially non-terminating.

4.2 Query Evaluation

In query evaluation, knowledge is represented by a set of definitions **D** and by an
interpretation **I**. **I** gives an interpretation to the set of primitive predicate symbols. **D**
defines derived predicate symbols in terms of the primitive symbols. A query is a formula
Q(v) with free variables **v**. Let **Q(v)/D** be the result of substituting definitions for the
derived symbols in **Q(v)**. The result of a query is the set of free variable instantiations **s**,
such that **Q(s)/D** evaluates to **true** under interpretation **I**.

The example in Figure 4.2 represents the same knowledge as in Figure 4.1. The
derived predicate symbol "position" is defined by a (rather lengthy) formula over the
primitive predicate symbol "report", which, in turn, has the given relation as its
interpretation. Reports are of two types: positive reports and negative reports. Positive
reports state that a ship might be at a given position. Moreover, among positive reports
with the same id* and ship, the ship is in exactly one of the given positions. Negative
reports state that the ship is not in the given position. The id*'s for negative reports
occur only once.

Definition

position(x, y) is

range r1: report, type(r1) = positive
r2: report, r1 ≠ r2, id#(r1) = id#(r2)
r3: report, type(r3) = negative

(∃r1)(∀r2)(∃r3)(ship(r1) = x &
position(r1) = y &
position(r2) = position(r3) &
ship(r2) = ship(r3))

Interpretation

report

id#	type	ship	position
b-2	positive	Kennedy	point_U
b-2	positive	Kennedy	point_W
f-4	negative	Kennedy	point_W

Query

?position(Kennedy, p)

Evaluation

Find **p** such that **position(Kennedy, p)** evaluates to
true under the interpretation

Result

p = point_U

Figure 4.2: Query Evaluation

As far as an LKS user is concerned, the knowledge content of this representation is indistinguishable from the one in Figure 4.1 on the basis of the answers to queries. Moreover, the syntax and semantics of predicate logic is used for both representations. Nevertheless, the representations appear very different.

Query evaluation can be characterized by the search required to find the truth-value of Q(s)/D under the interpretation I. Only one level of demonstration is required: the evaluation of one query under one interpretation. The search is guaranteed to terminate since the interpretation is finite.

4.3 A Comparison of Inference Mechanisms

Deductive inference will be compared with query evaluation.

The search in query evaluation is much simpler than the search in deductive inference. Only one interpretation needs to be searched as opposed to an arbitrarily large number of them. On the other hand, the formula $Q(s)/D$ involved in query evaluation is usually more complex than the formula $A \Rightarrow Q(s)$ involved in deductive inference. In most cases, formula complexity is a minor factor in comparison to the number of interpretations. In general, query evaluation can be expected to be orders of magnitude faster than deductive inference.

The knowledge representation for deductive inference is more powerful than the knowledge representation for query evaluation. Specifically, there are sets of axioms which cannot be captured by the combination of an interpretation and a set of definitions. To see this, notice that the interpretation I is a specific encoding of the axioms A. The definitions D determine a particular strategy for searching the encoded axioms to determine whether or not $Q(s)$ is provable. While any axioms can be encoded as an interpretation, predicate logic is not powerful enough to express the required definitions D.

Deductive inference is more flexible than query evaluation. Specifically, with deductive inference, any new knowledge can be added to the representation without impacting knowledge already represented. With query evaluation, the addition of new knowledge in the form of new tuples in the relations of I may invalidate the definitions D. In the example of Figure 4.2, adding a negative report, with the same id* as one already stored, will invalidate the definition of "position". In DBMS parlance, constraints on I to maintain the validity of D are called "integrity constraints".

The flexibility of deductive inference is an unneeded luxury in many applications. Usually, there is some knowledge which will never change for the lifetime of the application. It is best to exploit knowledge stratification and build this knowledge into the LKS as constraint knowledge. By limiting the complexity of inference, constraint knowledge can produce a side benefit in the form of improved performance. In deductive inference, knowledge is not stratified, integrity constraints are not distinguished from other forms of knowledge and, as a result, the inference engine cannot take advantage of them. In many applications, integrity constraints are used for detecting and/or correcting errors in input knowledge. In this situation, there is no alternative to distinguishing constraint knowledge.

An important quality of a knowledge representation is that it support "explanations" of query results. Query evaluation and deductive inference have comparable qualities in this respect. In deductive inference, explanation involves backtracing the proof tree. In query evaluation, it involves backtracing the query evaluation tree. However, due to the additional complexity of $Q(s)/D$ over $A \Rightarrow Q(s)$, the evaluation tree may be larger than the proof tree. As a result, the query evaluation explanation may have to deal with a lower level of detail than is required with the deductive inference explanation. This can be handled easily by exploiting intermediate definitions.

It is reasonable to assume that users understand all defined terms, both top-level and intermediate, and so an explanation can be given by describing the evaluation tree at the next lowest intermediate level. For example, consider the addition of the following intermediate definitions to the knowledge representation of Figure 4.2. Two reports are "from the same source" if they both have the same id*. A negative report "cancels" a positive report if they both have the same ship and position. The top-level predicate "position" can then be defined in terms of these intermediate-level predicates as follows: position is given by a positive report when all other reports from the same source are cancelled. The response to the explanation request "Why is the Kennedy shown at point-V" might be "There is a positive report for point-V, and all other reports from this source are cancelled". Intermediate definitions can be informative, control the level of detail in an explanation, and fit naturally into the query evaluation approach.

The above observations have been cast in model-theoretic terms. It is informative to also provide a proof-theoretic viewpoint. It is generally known that a more efficient deductive search is possible if the axioms are restricted to conjunctions of simple predicate clauses (i.e. no negations, disjunctions, or existential quantifiers). Disregarding some minor complications, the tuples in an interpretation I can be regarded as axioms in this form. The effect of moving from a knowledge representation for deductive inference to one for query evaluation is to transform the axioms to a simpler form. However, queries are correspondingly transformed to a more complex form. The overall effect is to transfer complexity from the axioms to the queries. Such a transfer would be pointless, if it were not for the fact that it allows a more efficient deductive search mechanism to be employed.

4.4 LKS Design Considerations

This section draws some conclusions about how KS and DBMS inference mechanisms should coexist in an LKS.

It is dangerous to apply observations about deductive inference to other KS inference mechanisms. However, the discussion of Section 4.3 does highlight the strengths and weaknesses of relational query evaluation. The key strengths of query evaluation are that it provides good performance through an efficient search mechanism, and exploitation of stratification for predefined constraint knowledge. The key weaknesses are that the knowledge representation is of limited representation power, and is constrained in the freedom of adding new knowledge. In effect, relational query evaluation is trading off power and flexibility in exchange for performance.

It is possible to get an even better tradeoff by going beyond relational query evaluation to allow recursively defined predicates in the definitional part D of the knowledge representation. Recursive definitions provide a dramatic increase in knowledge representation power without increased performance overhead. This is a principal source of the power in the programming language PROLOG.

The DBMS engine in an LKS should be delegated all the inferences over knowledge in the repository that can be handled with query evaluation. In general, it is expected that this will be a large percentage of total inferences. The DBMS inference mechanism will handle these inferences as efficiently as it is possible to do them. The only alternative is to transfer a superset of the relevant knowledge to the KS engine, and have the KS engine perform the inferences instead. This approach has several drawbacks. First, it precludes the use of fast access paths in the repository for knowledge processing. At best the KS engine will have to rebuild these access paths outside the repository. Second, much more knowledge may be transferred than would otherwise be necessary. This is a wasted effort and may require the creation of secondary storage files to hold intermediate results. Third, the KS engine may be inherently far less efficient for this class of inference than the DBMS engine.

It can be argued that the DBMS engine in an LKS should be able to handle recursive query evaluation so that a larger class of inferences can be processed efficiently. This argument is sound provided that the DBMS engine can actually exploit this increased scope for optimization. Otherwise, the recursive processing can be done just as well within the KS engine, or even some external application program, and little would be gained. The optimization of recursive processing within a DBMS is the subject of active research [DAYA85a, DAYA85b].

Initial results suggest that several, frequently occurring, forms of recursion can indeed be highly optimized by a DBMS. Typically, the knowledge engineer will need to supply the DBMS with certain facts about the nature of the recursion involved. Armed with these facts, the DBMS can intelligently select, from a predefined repertoire, the most efficient algorithm for executing the recursive computation. Such a DBMS engine can lead to orders of magnitude performance improvement in LKS applications.

5. Research Directions

This section discusses research topics in two areas: the ability of the DBMS to support multiple knowledge representations, and the integration of KS and DBMS facilities into an applications environment.

Consider the first topic. The DBMS engine in an LKS must be capable of storing a wide variety of knowledge representations. These representations include traditional data records, logic rules, situation-action rules, raw image data, programs, historical archives, graphics data and meta-information. The fixed repertoire of representations supported by existing DBMSs cannot efficiently capture all these forms of knowledge. It is essential that the DBMS be able to support an extensible set of knowledge representations. Two kinds of extensibility must be considered. First, there is extensibility of representations which do not need to be interpreted by the DBMS. This kind of extensibility is relatively easy to provide. Second, there is the extensibility of representations which must be interpreted by the DBMS. This kind of extensibility is more difficult to provide.

Consider the first kind of extensibility. In general, a DBMS engine will not need to interpret all the knowledge representations which are stored in the knowledge repository. Some of them can be stored as large file structures which can be passed as a unit to some specialized processor. For example, the DBMS will not need to interpret situation-action rules stored in the repository if these rules are merely passed to a KS for processing. Abstract data types can be used to provide this kind of "scalar" extensibility. The basic approach is to embed a construct for defining abstract data types in the DBMS data model. When the DBMS encounters data of an abstract type, it simply calls operations defined on the type.

Now, consider the second kind of extensibility. To make inferences over a knowledge representation, the DBMS must be able to interpret all, or part, of that representation. This means that the representation must appear as a collection of related objects in the DBMS data model. Further, the DBMS must know how to how to optimize inferences over these objects. In particular, the DBMS must know the logical properties of these objects and how to exploit available physical data structures. In conventional DBMSs, this knowledge is hard-wired. It seems like a very difficult task to develop an efficient DBMS that has an open, fully extensible, data model.

Fortunately, for the LKS applications considered in Figure 3.1, a fully extensible DBMS is not required. The DBMS engine only needs to handle those inferences that can be optimized over secondary storage structures. All other inferences can be handled by the KS engine. The key requirement is that the DBMS be sufficiently extensible to handle a variety of structured space and time representations. Most applications involve space and/or time, and efficient representations have been developed for many of them. It is essential that the DBMS be able to take advantage of the representations to optimize performance.

The ideal solution would be an extended data model with the ability to:

- capture the logical semantics of space and time in a simple way,

- structure space-time knowledge so that the DBMS can optimize inferences,

- allow alternative physical data structures to be used,

- treat time, and 1, 2, and 3-dimensional space uniformly.

Such a model could provide much more efficiency in processing dimensional knowledge.

There is active work at CCA to develop an extended data model to meet the above requirements [DAYA85b]. Early results have been promising. The basic idea is to introduce a class of space-time (s-t) objects with special semantics. These s-t objects relate to traditional database objects by serving as the values of attributes such as "shape" or "boundary". The semantics of s-t objects is based on "point sets" which have been used as mathematical abstractions in 2 and 3-dimensional modelling. The same semantics can be restricted to support time as a special 1-dimensional case. The semantics is relatively simple, allows structured representations, and does not constrain the choice of physical data structures.

Now consider the second topic of an applications development environment. Several widely-used database application development environments are in existence and there are a growing number of knowledge engineering environments. The environment for developing LKS applications will require an integration of these two kinds of environment. To date, there has been little or no work on this topic. The LKS environment requires a language for writing applications, a repository to hold versions of applications under development, and an integrated collection of development tools.

The application writing language is the key to the whole environment. This language will need to integrate and rationalize the diverse features of the DBMS and KS engines and support software. In particular, the language must unify the knowledge representations of the KS and DBMS engines. One approach might be to treat the DBMS as having three key facets: persistence, distribution and inference. Persistence and distribution should be qualities which are applicable to any knowledge representation. However, inference, in the forms of query evaluation, view processing and predicate alerting, would only be available to certain knowledge representations (i.e. those interpretable by the DBMS).

Given the application writing language and a collection of tools, the environment itself could be written as an application in the language. In this case, the knowledge repository will contain all knowledge about an LKS under development. This might include schedules for managing the development, knowledge modules under design, dependencies between modules, database designs, and debugging results. In addition, an important piece of knowledge will be the operational rules to enforce version, release and change control over the knowledge engineering process. These rules would be maintained by an integrity subsystem as engineers check knowledge modules into, and out of, the repository. Distributed knowledge engineering is a good example of an LKS application.

<u>References</u>

[DAYA85a]
Dayal, U., and J. M. Smith, "PROBE: A Knowledge-Oriented Database Management System", <u>Proc. Islamorada Workshop on Large-Scale Knowledge-Base and Reasoning Systems</u>, Feb. 1985, pp.103-138.

[DAYA85b]
Dayal, U., A. Buchmann, D. Goldhirsch, S. Heiler, F. A. Manola, J. A. Orenstein, and A. S. Rosenthal, "PROBE -- A Research Project in Knowledge-Oriented Database Systems: Preliminary Analysis", Technical Report CCA-85-03, Computer Corporation of America, July 1985.

Wissenserwerb und -formalisierung für den kommerziellen Einsatz Wissensbasierter Systeme

M.-J. Schachter-Radig
SCS Organisationsberatung und Informationstechnik GmbH
Hamburg

Einleitung

Jede technologische Entwicklung, so auch die Software Technologie, ist charakterisiert durch den Übergang von einer extrem kreativen Aktivität mit Ausnutzung aller ad-hoc möglichen Mittel hin zu einem strukturierten, kontrollierbaren und somit planbaren Prozeß. Wenn diese Phase erreicht ist, sind die Vorbedingungen für einen sicheren und breit gefächerten kommerziellen Einsatz einer Technologie gegeben. Ein Rückblick auf die Einsatzgeschichte der Daten- und Informationsverarbeitung zeigt, daß der Applikationsdruck für Software-Technologie einen vorzeitigen Einsatz bei fehlenden methodologischen Grundlagen erzwungen hat. Der Schlüssel zu einem fundierten Fortschritt in der Software-Technologie liegt in einem Blickwinkelwechsel: vom Softwareprodukt zur Analyse des Entstehungsprozesses des Produktes Software. Dieser neue Aspekt fördert das Entstehen einer Software-Methodologie. Die IFIP Working Group 8.1 (Information Systems Design Methodologies) hat einen Anforderungskatalog für eine Methodologie vorgeschlagen [1] :

- Überdecken des gesamten Entwicklungsprozesses
- Verstärkung der Kommunikation der Beteiligten am Entstehungsprozeß
- Unterstützung folgender Punkte:

    ◇ Problemanalyse und -verstehen
    ◇ `top-down´ und `bottom-up´ Entwicklung
    ◇ Validation und Verifikation
    ◇ Einhalten von Randbedingungen des Entwurfs und der Performanz
    ◇ Organisation der Software-Entwicklung
    ◇ Koordinierte Weiterentwicklung des Systems während des gesamten Lebenszyklus
    ◇ Konfiguration der Software

- Möglicher Einsatz rechnergestützter Werkzeuge
- Erlernbarkeit der Methodologie
- Offenheit der Methodologie zur Integration neuer Erkenntnisse und Entwicklungen.

Viele der hier beschriebenen Forderungen hat SCS mit der Entwicklung des Projekt-
abwicklungs- und Dokumentationssystems PRADOS [2] für konventionelle Softwaresysteme integriert und realisiert. Deshalb ist es nur konsequent, sich vor dem Einsatz
Wissensbasierter Systeme in der Kundenpraxis nicht nur mit den generischen Methoden
und Verfahren der Künstlichen Intelligenz, sondern auch mit dem Entwicklungsprozeß
Wissensbasierter Systeme auseinanderzusetzen. Da für diese Technologie der Übergang
vom wissenschaftlichen Labor in die industrielle Praxis erst seit kurzer Zeit vollzogen
wird, kann die für die Retrospektion notwendige Erfahrung beim Bau Wissensbasierter
Systeme nur durch das Zusammenführen mehrerer Erfahrungsquellen in einem Projektteam erbracht werden. Zu diesem Zweck haben sich mehrere Industriefirmen und zwei
Forschungseinrichtungen aus dem universitären Bereich im Rahmen des ESPRIT-
Programmes zusammengetan, um eigene Erfahrungen und Vorarbeiten in einem Projekt
zusammenzuführen mit dem Ziel, eine einheitliche und werkzeugunterstützte Methodologie für die Entwicklung Wissenbasierter Systeme zu schaffen [3,4].

Erfahrungshintergrund

Wissensbasierte Systeme sind die Umsetzung der Forschungsergebnisse der Künstlichen
Intelligenz für die Anwendungspraxis. Die veröffentlichte Erfahrung legt einen experimentellen Entwicklungsweg nahe, beispielsweise [5]. Drei der möglichen Gründe für ein
solches Vorgehen sind:

- Die Problemfelder, die mit Wissensbasierten Systemen bearbeitet werden
  sollen und die Natur der dazu verwendeten Software sind so beschaffen, daß
  nur ein experimentelles Vorgehen möglich ist.

- Die neuen Methoden und Verfahren der Künstlichen Intelligenz   (z.B.
  Sprachen, Integrierte Werkzeuge) erleichtern den Implementationsprozeß
  derart, daß Entwicklungsfreiheit preisgünstig und somit nützlich ist.

- Andere Vorgehen könnten möglich sein, derzeitige Systeme sind mit ad-hoc
  Systematiken erfolgreich entstanden.

Dem großen Vorteil des experimentellen Vorgehens akademischer Labors, dem Entwickler
keine Vorschriften vorzugeben und somit keine Schranken für das Erarbeiten grundlegend
neuer Erkenntnisse aufzubauen, steht der Nachteil eines unstrukturierten Wiederauf-
setzens des Entwicklungsprozesses entgegen. Unstrukturiert ist das Wiederaufsetzen
deshalb, weil allein das Ergebnis des Entwicklungsprozesses bewertet wird und nicht
vorgegebene Schritte des Entwicklungsprozesses zum Anlaß genommen werden.
Entwicklungspfade werden verlassen oder Prototypen aufgegeben, ohne daß wiederver-
wertbare, allgemein gültige Erkenntnisse über die Entwicklung entstehen.

Vorgehensmodelle sind eine strukturierte Abstraktion der Entwicklungsrealität. Sie
regeln das Wiederaufsetzen im Fehlerfall oder wenn neue Erkenntnisse bei der Proto-
typen-Entwicklung gewonnen wurden. Die Entwicklung ist eingebettet in eine Hierarchie

von Modellen, die eine jeweils verfeinerte Abstraktion der Problemrealität beinhalten.

Die berechtigte Forderung nach Kontrollierbarkeit und Planbarkeit der Entwicklung konventioneller Softwaresysteme hat zum Entstehen verschiedener Vorgehensmodelle geführt, die entweder **tätigkeitsorientiert** oder **ergebnisorientiert** sind [6,7]. Beide Ansätze sind unzureichend, sie werden der Realität nicht gerecht. **Iterative Vor-gehensmodelle** beschreiben sowohl die Ergebnisse als auch die Tätigkeiten, die notwendig sind, um diese Ergebnisse zu erreichen. Tätigkeiten sind im System-entwicklungsprozeß nicht streng sequentiell, sondern nach ihrer Bedeutung für die Ergebnisse geordnet. Iterative Vorgehensmodelle werden der Realität besser gerecht. Sie liefern genau den roten Faden für die Entwicklung, geben aber dem Systementwickler den benötigten Freiraum. Sie standardisieren die Ergebnisse so, daß die Kommunikation im Entwicklungsteam erhöht wird. Die Abbildungen 1a,b zeigen die Wiederaufsetzpfade wie von PRADOS für konventionelle Software vorgeschlagen. Iterative Vorgehensmodelle sind aus den aufgezeigten Gründen gute Kandidaten, um ein Gerüst für eine Methodologie der Entwicklung Wissensbasierter Systeme zu bilden.

Spezifische Anforderungen

Experimentelle Naturwissenschaften sind in ihrem Vorgehen von neopositivistischen, wissenschaftstheoretischen Grundlagen geprägt. Die Sammlung von Informationen (Daten) über einen Forschungsgegenstand dient dem Falsifizieren einer vorgefaßten Theorie. Wesentliche Voraussetzung ist also die Existenz einer vorformulierten Theorie, die die Realität vollständig beschreibt und somit durch gezielte Experimente zu Fall gebracht werden kann. Eine Theorie kann somit experimentell nicht bewiesen werden, sie besteht aber so lange, wie sie experimentell nicht in einzelnen Phänomenen falsifiziert werden konnte.

Dieser Exkurs soll die wissenschaftheoretischen Grundlagen der Wissensverarbeitung verständlich machen. Die Korrektheit der Schlußfolgerungsfähigkeit eines Experten-systems kann nicht bewiesen werden, jedoch ist es möglich, durch gezielte Problem-stellungen die Funktionsweise zu falsifizieren. Im Software Engineering, aber auch in Kognitiven Wissenschaften (einschließlich der Künstlichen Intelligenz), ist das angemes-sene Vorgehen zum Unterschied zu den klassischen, empirischen Wissenschaften (z.B. Physik) das Verbessern (Korrigieren) vorgefaßter Konzepte. Die naheligende Folgerung wäre, daß die Entwicklung Wissensbasierter Systeme durchgehend von Problemanalyse und -verstehen bis zur vollständigen Implementation durch inkrementelle Verbesserung und Korrektur geschieht. Die Sammlung von Daten dient also nicht der Falsifikation einer vorgefaßten Theorie, sondern dem Zusammensetzen einer **guten** Theorie (in diesem Fall ein System).

Um diese Vorgänge effizient unterstützen zu können, muß ein ausreichend reichhaltiger interpretativer Rahmen für die Analyse der `Daten´ vorgegeben sein. Die `Daten´ sind in diesem Fall die Informationen über das Fach (`domain´) und das Expertenwissen, die im System repräsentiert werden sollen. Ist das interpretative Rahmenwerk zu einfach, z.B.

ein assoziativer oder 'regelbasierender' Formalismus, so ist die Wahrscheinlichkeit sehr groß, daß die Komplexität der zu den 'Daten' gehörenden 'Realität' nicht erfaßt wird [4]. Das Verbessern wird dann zu einer unkontrollierbaren und nicht nachvollziehbaren Konfigurationsaufgabe. Der zugrundeliegende Formalismus – die Regeln – gibt nur eine schwache Unterstützung bei der Strukturierung der Daten, insbesondere auf einer globalen, strategischen Ebene. Der Entwickler wird von der Informationsmenge über- flutet. Ihm stehen zuwenig Randbedingungen zur Strukturierung zur Verfügung. Dies ist der Fall beim **Schnellen Prototypisieren** insbesondere dann, wenn zwischen ursprüng- licher Konzeptualisierung und Implementationssprache ein zu großer Formalisierungs- unterschied existiert.

Eine angemessene und nützliche Methodologie muß deshalb vor allen Dingen Mittel zur Interpretation zur Verfügung stellen, so daß Problemanalyse und -verstehen konti- nuierlich und nachvollziehbar durchgeführt werden können. Dies geschieht über Model- lierungsverfahren, die eine Repräsentation des Wissens auf verschiedenen Abstraktions- ebenen und unter verschiedenen Blickwinkeln erlauben. Diese Verfahren übernehmen eine ähnliche Funktion für die Entwicklung Wissensbasierter Systeme wie 'Structured Analysis and Design' [8,9] oder SADT [2,10] für die Entwicklung konventioneller Systeme. Für die Wissensanalyse erweist sich ein **Interpretationsmodell,** insbesondere zur Strukturierung verbaler Daten, als sinnvoll [6].

Voraussetzungen für eine strukturierte Methodologie

Die Entwicklung von Software ist eine besondere Instantiierung von Problemlösungs- verhalten und kann im allgemeinen Kontext der Analyse methodologischen Vorgehens betrachtet werden. Ein Vorgehensmodell besteht aus einem Lösungsmuster (Paradigma) für die Konzeptualisierung und Problemspezifikation und einem Musterzyklus, der die Ordnung von Aktivitäten beschreibt [18]. Die Erfahrung zeigt, daß der Entwicklungsprozeß Wissensbasierter Systeme sich in diskrete Aktivitäten partitionieren läßt [5], diese bestimmten Phasen je nach Intensität der jeweiligen Aktivität zuzuordnen sind und Iterationen zwischen den Phasen möglich und zulässig sind. Die Abbildungen 2a,b fassen diese Erkenntnis in zwei SADT-Diagrammen zusammen, die zwei Abstraktionsebenen veranschaulichen und die Sicht eines 'knowledge engineer' berücksichtigen. Ein Angebot unterstützender ad-hoc Methoden, Verfahren und Werkzeuge für die einzelnen Phasen enthält Abbildung 2c. Abbildung 3 zeigt darüberhinaus das Phasenmodell aus der Sicht eines Systemanalytikers, für den ein Wissensbasiertes System eine Teilkomponente ist, die in einem funktionierenden Ganzen integriert werden muß.

Eine weitere Annahme, die als Voraussetzung für die Entwicklung eines Vorgehens- modells notwendig ist, beschreibt die Tatsache, daß Wissensbasierte Systeme sich in verschiedenen Abstraktionsebenen entsprechend den Ergebnissen der verschiedenen Entwicklungsphasen modellieren lassen. Dies ist eine kühne Annahme, gemessen an der Praxis der Entstehung insbesondere von Expertensystemen. Hierbei ist die Systemspezi- fikation gleich dem kodierten und ablauffähigen Wissen.

Die von SCS mitgetragene Forschung zeigt jedoch einen Fortschritt in Richtung einer implementationsunabhängigen Repräsentation in Form von Verfahren für die Dokumentation der Ergebnisse der Analysephase [8,13,14]. Weitere Forschung im Rahmen dieses Projektes beschäftigt sich mit dem Umsetzen dieser Erkenntnisse für die Entwurfs – und Implementationsphase wie auch mit der Formalisierung der Übergänge von einer Phase zur anderen.

Die rechnergestützten Werkzeuge, die dieser Methodologie entstammen, sind in einem **Wissensakquisition- und Dokumentationssystem (KADS- Knowledge Acquisition and Documentation System)** integriert worden. KADS hat einen prototypischen Reifegrad erreicht und wurde zur Unterstützung der Methodologie in verschiedenen Fällen eingesetzt. Methodologie und Werkzeugkasten sind sehr nützlich, denn sie erlauben eine effiziente Ausnutzung der menschlichen Ressourcen – Fachexperte und Systementwickler (`knowledge engineer´). Die Ergebnisse der durchgeführten Analyse beschreiben die grundlegende Architektur des Expertensystems, indem sie die Wissensquellen (Regelsätze), die Wissensobjekte und deren Beziehungen zueinander aufzeigen [8,13,15,16,17].

Verglichen mit dem mehr experimentellen Ansatz beim Bau von Expertensystemen unterstützt dieses Vorgehen eine wesentlich strukturiertere Systemarchitektur mit erhöhter Transparenz der Funktionsweise, einer verbesserten Kontrolle und gesteigerter Wartungsfähigkeit.

Beschreibung der Methodologie

Der hier vorgestellten **KADS**-Methodologie liegt das Bemühen zugrunde, einen Mechanismus zum Aufdecken und Aufzeichnen der Struktur des Wissens im betrachteten Fachgebiet (´domain´) zu liefern. Die Methodologie schlägt als Vorstufe zum Expertensystem die Bildung zweier Komponenten vor:

- eine Hierarchie aller Konzepte die dem Fachgebiet immanent sind, als Auswirkung der **Konzeptualisierung des Wissens**;

- ein Interpretationsmodell, welches die Verknüpfung der Konzepte im Hinblick auf den Gebrauch oder die Anwendung des Fachwissens darstellt; dieser Teil ist Ergebnis der **erkenntnistheoretischen Analyse**.

Abbildungen oder Transformationen zwischen diesen Konzepten werden durch Wissensquellen repräsentiert, die die `Expertise in Aktion´ darstellen. Dieser Satz von Abbildungen bildet das Interpretationsmodell. Ein Satz von Interpretationsmodellen könnte gebildet werden, wobei die einzelnen Modelle jeweils generische Aufgaben wie Diagnose, Entwurf, Beratung usw. erfassen. Spezielle, mit Fachwissen versehene, Instantiierungen sind dann die Expertensysteme [3]. Zusätzlich zu den beiden Komponenten ist eine volle Beschreibung des Fachgebiets notwendig, die

- die Definition von Strategien als globale Kontrolle der Anwendung von Wissensquellen,
- die Modelle zur Beschreibung der Relationen zwischen Konzepten und
- andere Typen von Strukturen außer der Verallgemeinerungshierarchie

beinhalten.

Dieses wird erreicht in der Phase der Wissensakquisition, in der zwei Aktivitäten zu unterscheiden sind:

- **die Erhebung der Daten der Expertise** und

- **die Analyse der (verbalen) Daten.**

Der Interpretationsprozeß während der Wissensakquisitionsphase versucht, eine Abbildung zwischen verbalen Daten — gewonnen z.B. in Arbeitsgesprächen mit dem Experten — und den Wissensstrukturen herzustellen. Diese Abbildung kann auf verschiedenen Ebenen abhängig von den Konstrukten geschehen, die zur Darstellung des Wissens verwendet wurden.

Für die Abbildung verbaler Daten in Wissensstrukturen eignen sich die fünf Ebenen, die eine Vereinigung zwischen Slomans [18] Klassifikations- und Brachmans [19] Darstellungsebenen sind:

Wissensidentifikation
Die Aussagen eines oder mehrer Experten werden in einer der Originalaussage des jeweiligen Experten am nächsten liegenden, wenn auch formalisierten, Form aufgezeichnet.

Wissenskonzeptualisierung
Ziel ist die Formalisierung des Wissens in Form von Beziehungen, Primitivkonzepten und Konzeptuellen Modellen. Das Wissen mehrerer Experten oder aus verschiedenen Untergebieten werden in einem Modell vereinigt.

Erkenntnistheoretische Analyse
Ein erkenntnistheoretischer Rahmen faßt verschiedene Arten von Konzepten, Arten von Wissensquellen, strukturierenden Beziehungen (wie hierarchische Relationen, Vererbungnetze usw.) und Arten von Strategien zusammen.

Logische Analyse
Der Formalismus für die Strategien wird festgelegt, der die Schlußfolgerungsmechanismen determiniert.

Implementationsanalyse.
Die Representationsprimitiven aus dem Repertoire der Programmierungsmethoden der Künstliche Intelligenz (z.B. 'matching, testing, slot-filling')

werden ausgewählt.

Operationalisierung der Methodologie

Die Wisssensakquisition besteht aus dem Sammeln und Verarbeiten von Daten über das
Funktionieren von Expertise in einem ausgewählten Fachgebiet, um Wissensbasierte
Systeme zu entwerfen, zu realisieren, zu erweitern, anzupassen und zu verändern.
Wissensakquisition ist ein permanenter Prozeß, der alle Phasen des Entwurfs, der
Implementation und der Wartung eines Wissensbasierten Systems begleitet. Da das
spätere System etwa als Expertensystem in einer operationellen Umgebung arbeiten soll,
muß nicht nur Information über die Expertise an sich, sondern auch über die Interaktion
mit der Einsatzumgebung sowie über den zukünftigen Systemnutzer gesammelt werden.

Einige der offensichtlichen Vorteile des Einsatzes der Methodologie liegen in folgenden
Punkten:

- Die Funktionalität des Systems in der Einsatzumgebung wird im Vorhinein,
  das heißt vor der Implementation festgelegt. Die funktionale Analyse, die der
  Anforderungsdefinition vorangeht, erlaubt einen angemesseneren und kreati-
  veren Einsatz eines Expertensystems als den bloßen Ersatz eines menschlichen Experten.

- Die Machbarkeit der angestrebten Lösung kann frühzeitig eingeschätzt werden, bevor allzuviel Aufwand, insbesondere in die Implementation, investiert
  wurde.

- Die Aufteilung der Wissensakquisition in eine Erhebungsphase und eine
  systematische Aufarbeitungs- und Dokumentationsphase macht die Ergebnisse zugänglich und transparent für Dritte. Dieses erlaubt eine Realisierung
  von Expertensystemen unter industriellen Bedingungen, d.h. Arbeitsaufteilung
  in einem Team, welches mindestens aus einem Wissensträger (Experten) aus
  dem gewählten Fachgebiet und den Konstrukteuren des Systems besteht.

- Fachexperten sind selten und deshalb kostspielig. Durch Verwendung gut
  planbarer Verfahren für die Wissenserhebung und Analyse kann die Bele-
  gungszeit eines Fachexperten extrem reduziert werden.

Die wesentlichen Funktionen der Wissensakquisition sind die **Wissenserhebung,** die
Identifikation der Wissensquellen und die **Interpretation der gesammelten
Daten über die Expertise.** Die Abbildung 4 zeigt die Funktionen und die Struktur der
Beziehungen zu den angesprochenen Zielen.

Die Wissensakquisition selbst verläuft in zwei Phasen mit unterschiedlichen Arten von
Ergebnissen. Die erste Phase soll vor allen Dingen die Rolle des zukünftigen Wissensbasierten Systems festlegen. Dafür muß ausreichend Information über das Fachgebiet

und die Einsatzumgebung gesammelt werden, um bei Betrachtung der jeweiligen Paare,
Komplexität – Kosten und Funktionalität – Nutzen, zwischen möglichen Alternativen der
Automatisierung von Expertise wählen zu können.

Nachdem die Funktionalität des späteren Systems und die zukünftigen Nutzer festgelegt
worden sind, setzt die zweite Phase der Wissensakquisition ein. Deren Ziel ist die
detaillierte Spezifikation der Aufgaben, die das System erfüllen soll. Diese Spezifikation
schließt das Wissen und die Strategien ein, die in der Expertise verwendet werden. Die
Ausarbeitung des gesammelten Wissens geschieht in dieser Phase durch die Bildung
eines Interpretationsmodells. Folgende Tabelle faßt die Teilaufgaben der beiden Phasen
und deren jeweiligen Ergebnisse zusammen:

1. Phase: Orientierung, Fachanalyse und Machbarkeit

Teilaufgabe	Ergebnis
Orientierung	– Wissensquellen
	– Initialvokabular
	– Fachcharakteristiken
	– globale Machbarkeit
Fachanalyse	– Struktur der Fachkonzepte
	– Glossar
Problemdefinition	– Problemdefinition
Funktionale Analyse	– Agenten, Objekte, Funktionen
	– Funktionale Diagramme
	– Engpässe und Probleme
	– Anwendungsgebiete für Expertensysteme
	– Abschätzung der Machbarkeit

2. Phase: Expertise in Aktion

Teilaufgabe	Ergebnis
Analyse des Umfeldes	– zusätzliche Aufgaben
	– Performanzkriterien
	– Problembeispiele
Analyse des Nutzers	– Charakteristiken des Nutzers
	– Aufgaben des Nutzers
Analyse der Aufgaben	– Struktur der Konzepte
	– Interpretationsmodelle
Analyse der Expertise	– Korrektur des Interpretationsmodells
	– Vollständige Spezifikation des Modells

Die Operationalisierung der Methodologie beinhaltet auch die möglichen **Verfahren und
Techniken der Wissenserhebung** [14]. Deren jeweilige Anwendung deckt verschiedene
Aspekte des erhobenen Wissens ab. Eine einfache Aufzählung der Kategorien von Verfah-

ren beinhaltet folgende Bereiche [11]:

- Fokussierte Interviews
- Strukturierte Interviews
- Introspektion
- Selbstbeobachtung
- Lösungsprotokolle
- Dialog- und Simulationsprotokolle
- Rückblick.

Innerhalb dieser Kategorien steuern verschiedene Strategien den Erhebungprozeß und erlauben eine flexible Anpassung an den jeweiligen Partner.

Systembeschreibung

Um den Übergang von Wissensakquisition – Erhebung und Analyse – zur Implementation zu erleichtern, müssen formale Mittel zur Beschreibung der Analyseergebnisse bereitgestellt werden . Am geeignetesten sind Werkzeuge, die durch eine graphische Oberfläche die Visualisierung der Ergebnisse ermöglichen und deshalb auch in den Erhebungssitzungen mit dem Fachexperten eingesetzt werden können. Graphische Mittel haben sehr häufig den Vorteil, auch dem methodologischen Laien verständlich zu sein. Sie erlauben ihm, am Formalisierungsprozeß seiner Expertise zu partizipieren, ohne deshalb generische Sprachen oder Werkzeuge der Künstlichen Intelligenz erlernen zu müssen. Dadurch wird eine Vermischung der Rollen der zwei beteiligten Gruppen – Fachwissenträger und Systementwickler – vermieden.

Der Werkzeugkasten – **KADS** – wird folgende Unterstützungsfunktionen dem Systementwickler anbieten :

Formalisierung
Die Ergebnisse jeder Aktivität sind beschrieben und ein formaler Rahmen für die Einbettung ist gegeben.

Führung
Der Systementwickler kann den Werkzeugkasten als Quelle für weitere Handlungsanweisungen verwenden. Er kann die Folge von Aktionen erfragen, herausfinden, welche Fragen noch gestellt werden müssen und wie die gewonne Information interpretiert werden kann.

Dokumentation
Eine Stuktur der Dokumentation, insbesondere für das Fachwissen, wird vorgegeben, um somit die Pflege des Bestandes zu erleichtern.

Konsistenzprüfung
Die während der Analyse entstandenen Daten werden auf Konsistenz geprüft,

insbesondere im Hinblick auf die verwendete Terminologie (Vokabular).

Informationsgewinnung
Der Werkzeugkasten wird die Interpretation verbaler Daten unterstützen,
indem Module aus seinem Inhalt Fragen nach Konzepten, deren Beziehungen
untereinander, ihren Definitionen, den formalen Umsetzungen usw. beantworten
können.

Die Komponenten des Wissensaquisitions- und Dokumentationssystems, **KADS**, die diese
Fähigkeiten ermöglichen, sind:

die **Wissensbasis** ,
die Wissen über die Analyse enthält, einige vom Fachgebiet unabhängige Konzepte und das Wissen des aktuellen Fachgebietes;

das **Lexikon** ,
das lexikalische Einträge über das Fachgebiet mit Verweisen zu den Konzepten
in der Wissensbasis und auch Ableitungswissen über die jeweiligen Einträge,
wie zum Beispiel Synonyme, Abkürzungen, Pluralbildung usw. enthält;

die **Analysekomponente** ,
die die interaktive Analyse des Fachgebietes durch Instantiierung und Aktualisierung der Wissensstrukturen unterstützt;

der **Editor** ,
der die Veränderung und Aktualisierung der Wissensbasis ermöglicht und eine
graphische Interaktionsschnittstelle bereitstellt, die der Analysekomponente
ebenfalls zur Verfügung steht;

der **Dokumentengenerator** ,
der die Dokumente erzeugt, die den Inhalt der Wissensbasis und des Lexikons
für ein aktuelles Fachgebiet beschreiben.

Schlußwort

Weder Methodologie noch Werkzeugkasten haben den Reifegrad erreicht, um sie in ein
kommerzielles Produkt umzusetzen. Der Weg dahin hat aber unser Verständnis für die
Problematik des Entstehens Wissensbasierter Systeme verstärkt und zu gleicher Zeit
— wie die Umsetzungspraxis gezeigt hat — unsere Effizienz und Produktivität beim Entwickeln Wissensbasierter Systeme erhöht.

Literaturhinweise

[1] Wasserman et al.: "Characteristics of Software Development Methodologies", in Olle, Sol und Tully: "Infomation Design Methodologies: A Feature Analysis", North-Holland 1983

[2] "PRADOS Projektabwicklungs- und Dokumentationssystem der SCS", SCS GmbH 1983

[3] ESPRIT-Projekt 12/304/1098: "A Methodology for the Development of Knowledge Based Systems", 1983, 1984, 1985

[4] Breuker, Hayward, Wielinga: "Structering of Knowledge Based Systems", Contribution of the Polytechnic of the Southbank, London, Scicon Ltd., London, SCS GmbH, Hamburg, STC PLC, London, University of Amsterdam, Amsterdam, to ESPRIT Technical Week, 1985

[5] Hayes-Roth:, Waterman, Lenat (Eds.): "Building Expert Systems", Addison-Wesley, Reading / Mass. 1983

[6] Schachter-Radig: "Braucht Knowledge Engineering Software Engineering?", KI-Frühjahrsschule 1985 in Dassel, Solling

[7] Schachter-Radig: "Einsichten und Ansichten zum Entstehungsprozeß von Wissensbasierten Systemen", DEC-College, Frankfurt a.M., 1985

[8] Breuker, Wielinga: "Interpretation of Verbal Data for Knowledge Acquisition", Report 1.4 ESPRIT-Project 12, 1984

[9] Grover: "A Progmatic Knowledge Acquisition Methodology", Proc. 8th Intern. Joint Conf. Artificial Intelligence, Karlsruhe 1983

[10] Dignan: "Strategy for Knowledge Based IPSE Development", Alvey Directorat, 1984

[11] Radig:"Expertensysteme", KI-Frühjahrschule Dassel, Solling 1985

[12] Sloman: "The Computer Revolution in Philosophy", Harvester, Brighton 1980

[13] Breuker, Wielinga: "Initial Analysis for Knowledge Based Systems an Example, the Acquisition of Expertise", Report 1.3a ESPRIT-Project 12, 1983

[14] Breuker, Wielinga: "Techniques for Knowledge Acquisition, the Acquisition of Expertise", Report 1.5 ESPRIT-Project 12, 1984

[15] Clancey: "The Epistemology of a Rule Based Expert System — A Framework for Explanation", Artificial Intelligence 20, 1983, pp. 215-251

[16] Starzun et al.: "A KADS Case Study in Airconditioning Design (ACE)", Report 1.6 ESPRIT-Project 304/12, 1984

[17] Starzun et al.: "A KADS Case Study in Exhibition Planning (APE)", Report 1.6 ESPRIT-Project 304/12, 1984

[18] Partridge: "What's in an AI Program?: A Concept Learning Cognitive Language Understander by Any Other Name will Behave the Same", Proc. 6th Europ. Conf. Artificial Intelligence, Pisa 1984

[19] Brachman: "On the Epistemological Status of Semantic Networks", in Finder (Ed.): "Associative Networks", Academic Press, New York 1979

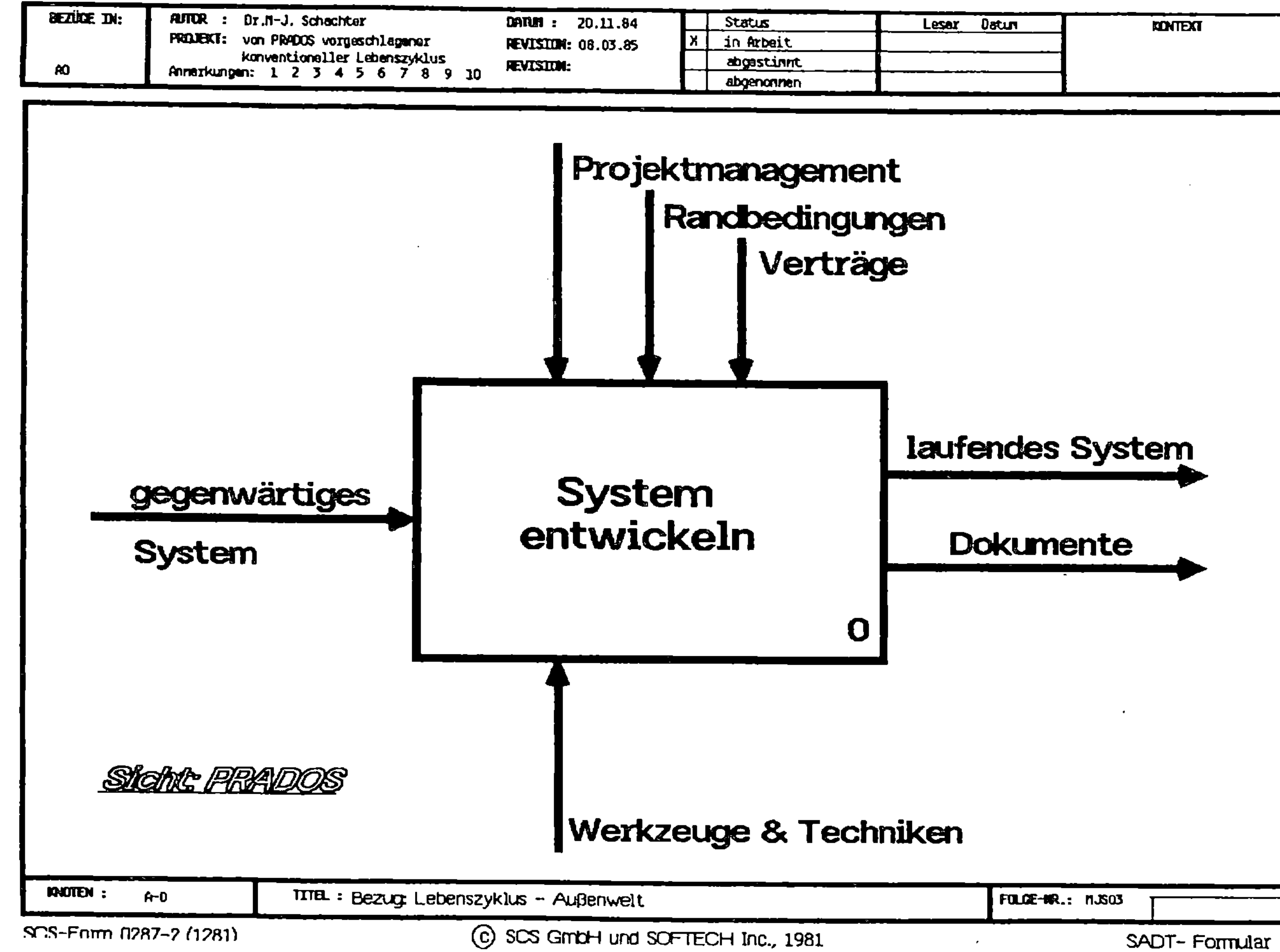

Abbildung 1a

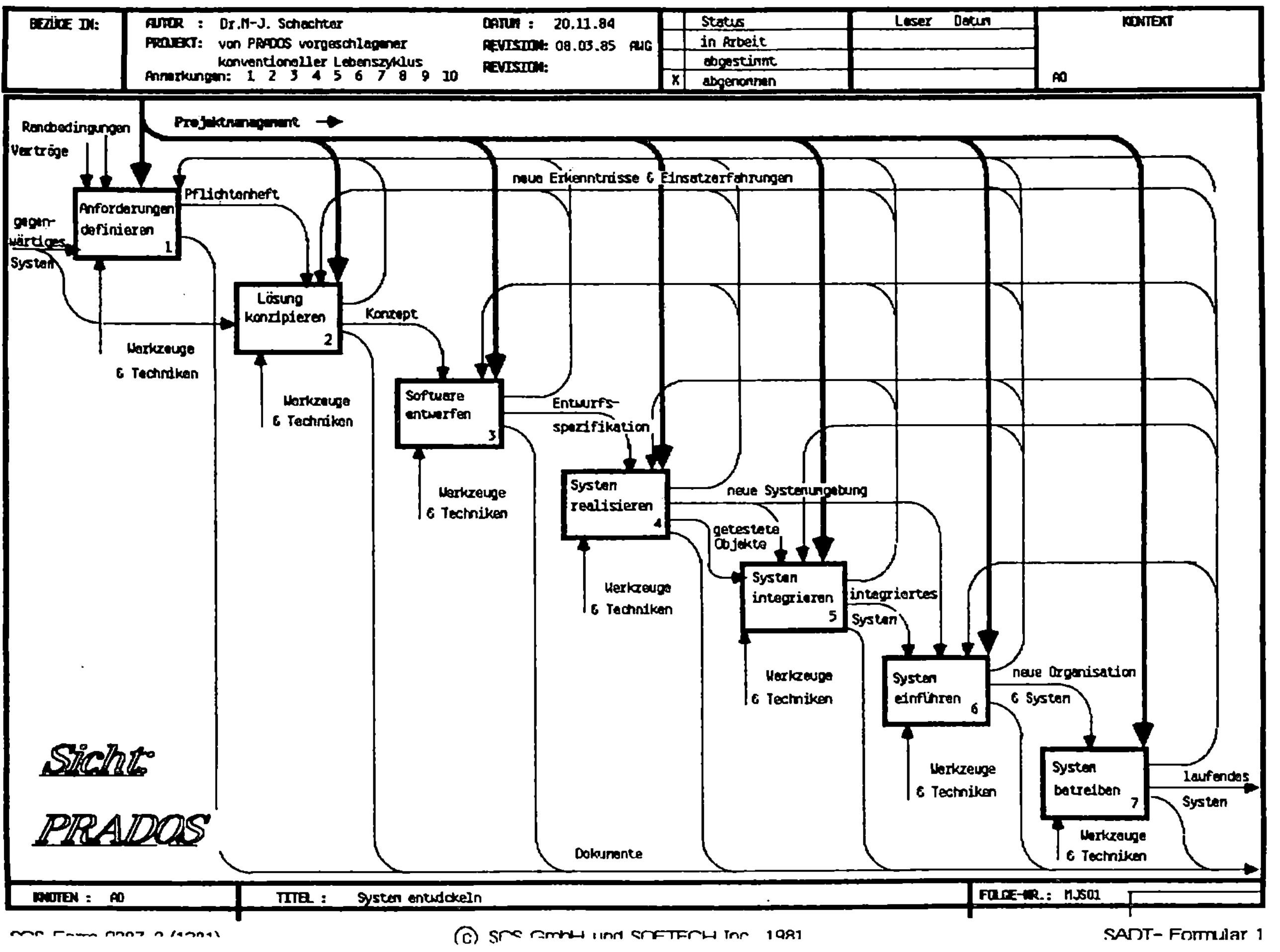

326

Abbildung 1b

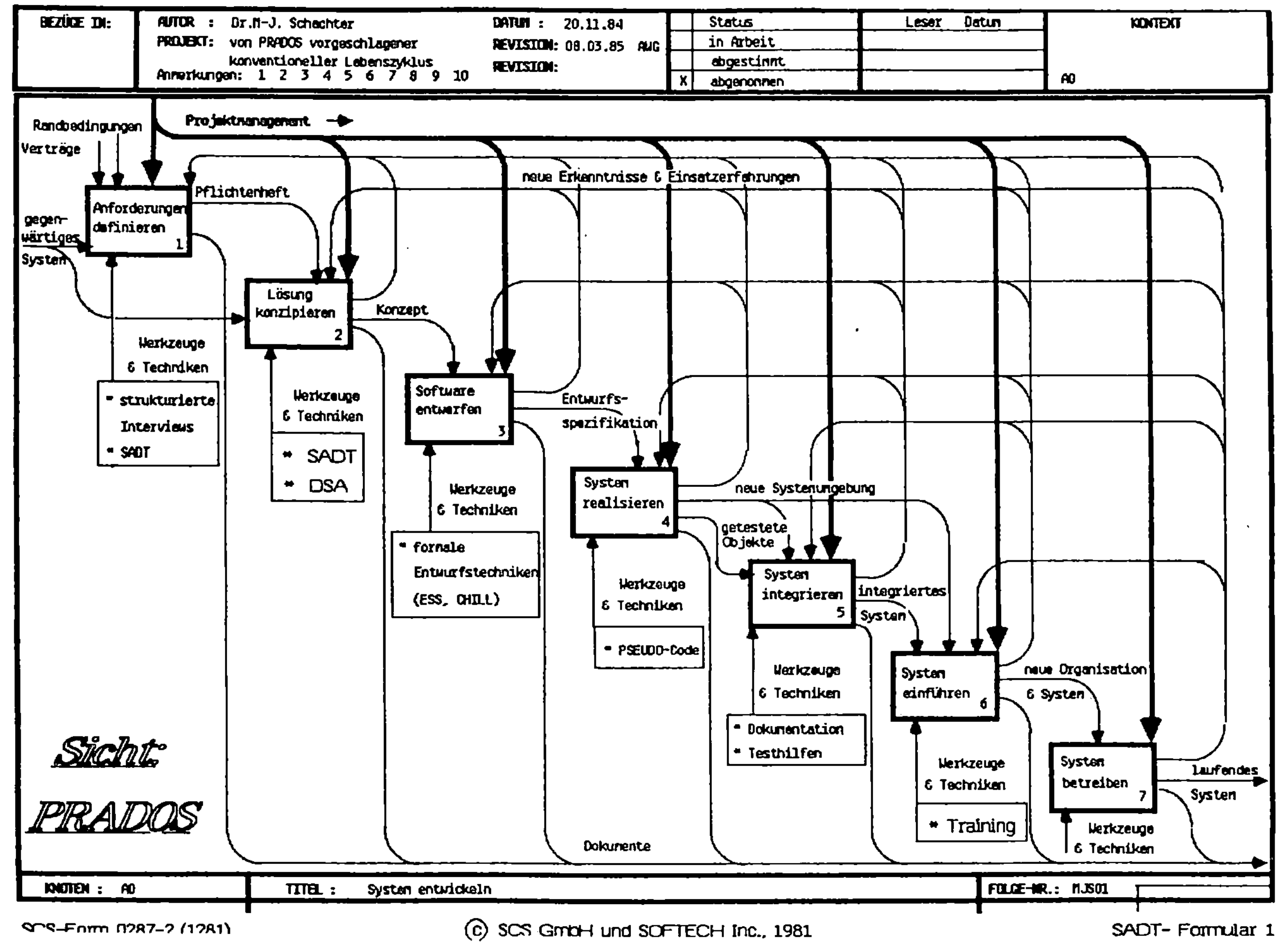

Abbildung 1c

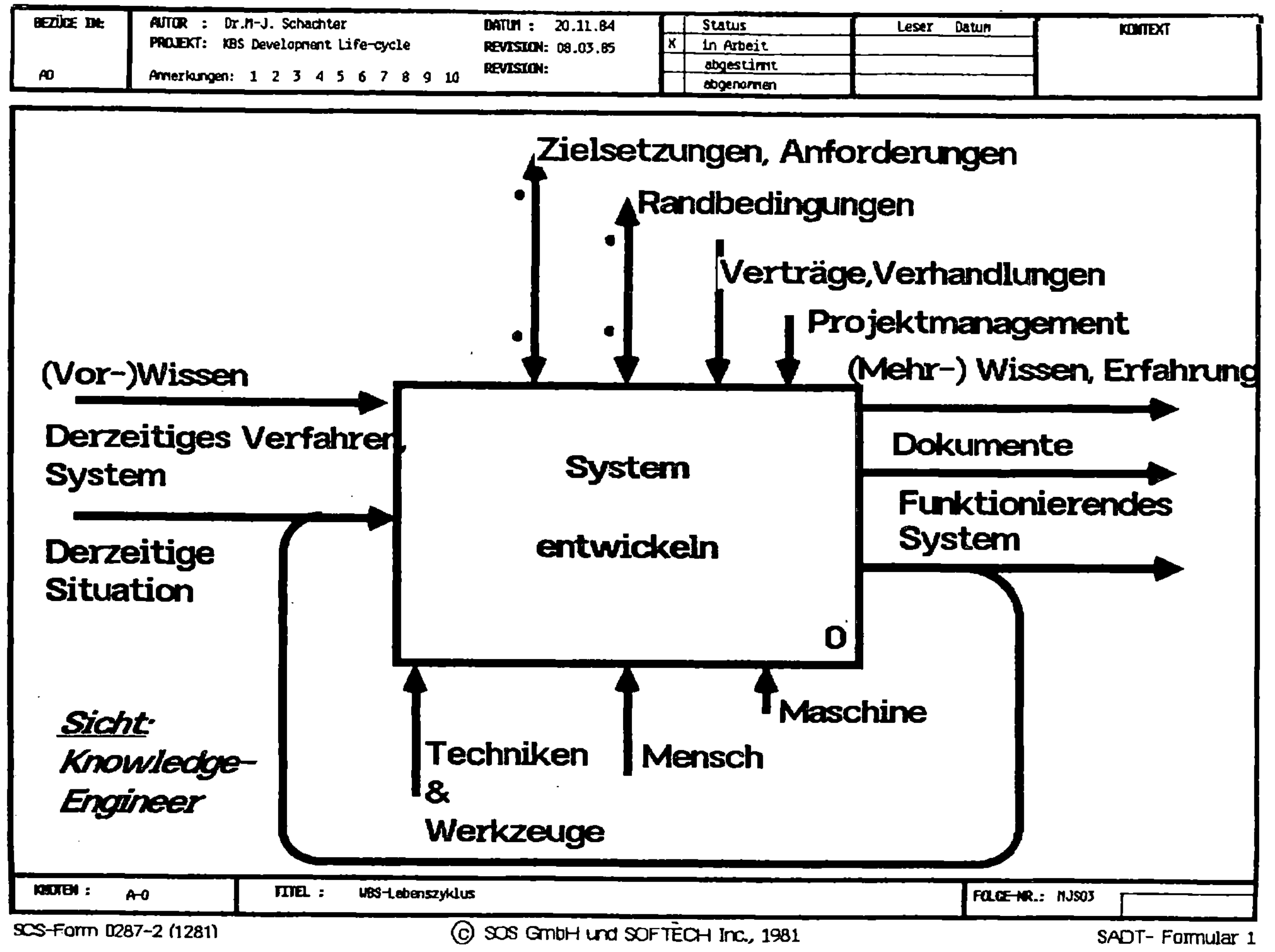

Abbildung 2a

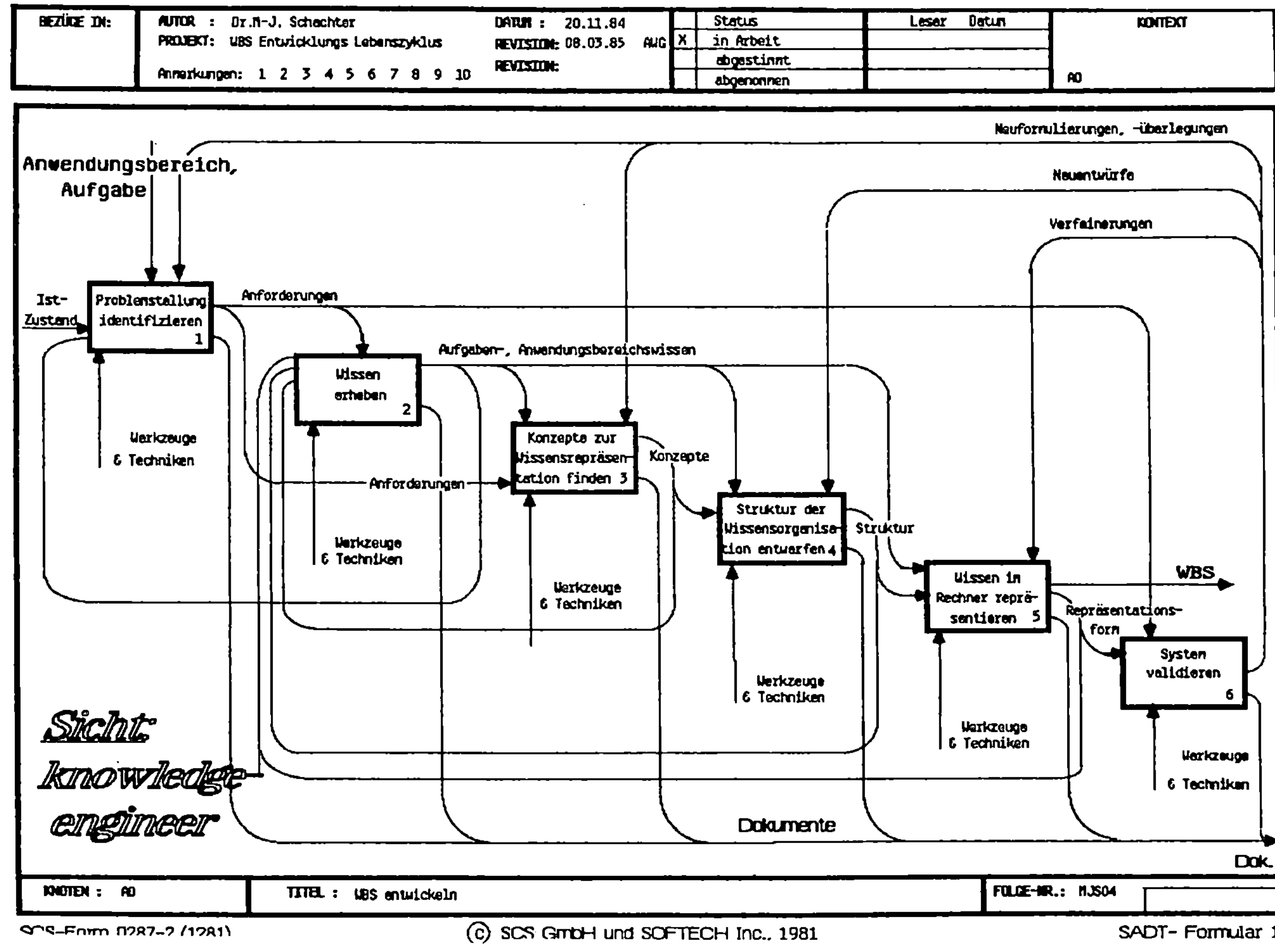

Abbildung 2b

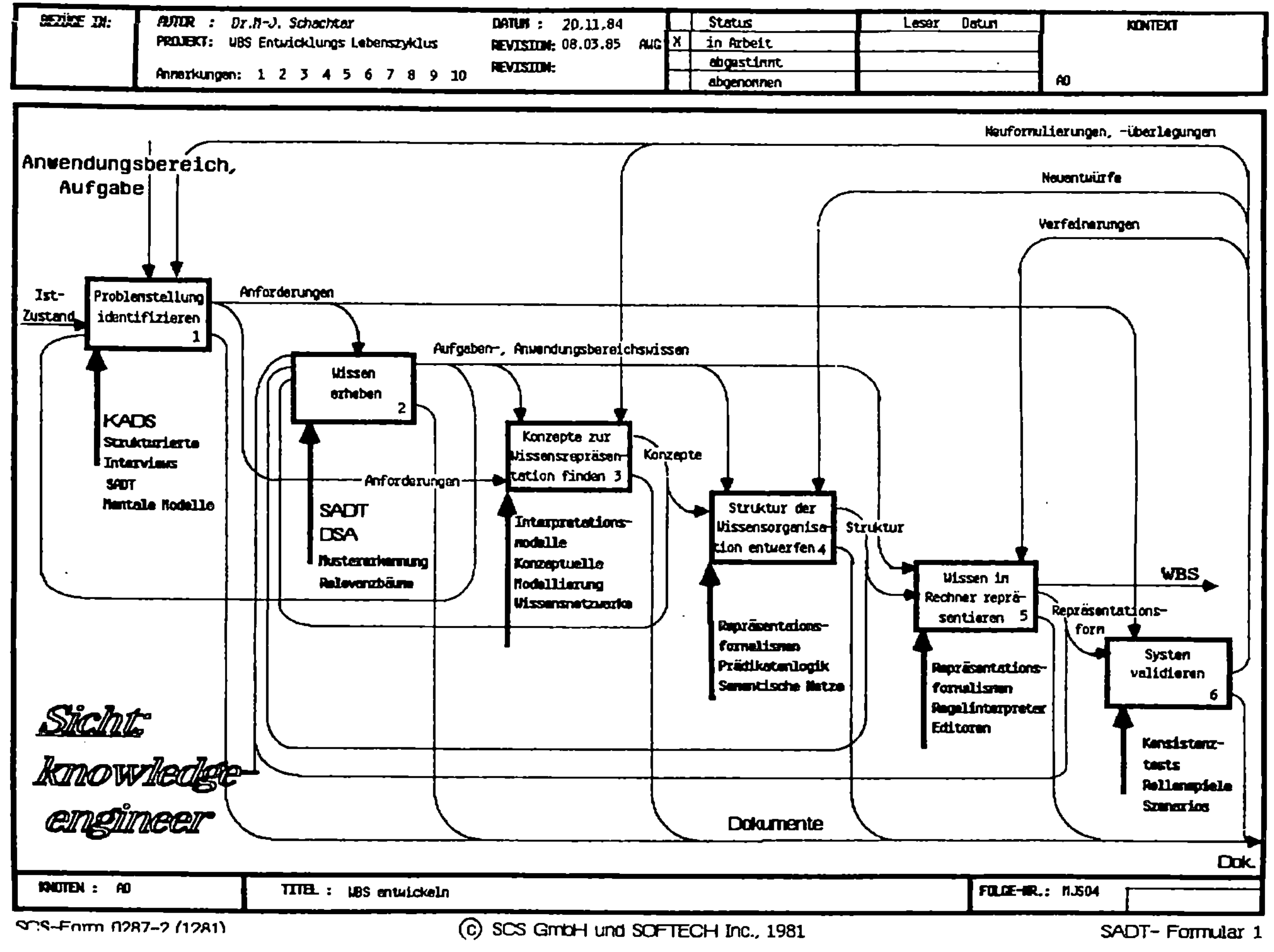

Abbildung 2c

BEZÜGE IN:
AUTOR : Dr.M-J. Schachter
PROJEKT: WBS Entwicklungs Lebenszyklus
Anmerkungen: 1 2 3 4 5 6 7 8 9 10
DATUM : 20.11.84
REVISION: 08.03.85 AUG
REVISION:
Status
X in Arbeit'
abgestimmt
abgenommen
Leser Datum
KONTEXT
A0
Randbedingungen
Verträge
Projektmanagement
Ist-Zustand
Anforderungen bestimmen 1
Anforderungsspezifikationen
neue Ergebnisse und Erfahrungen
Werkzeuge & Techniken
System-struktur entwerfen 2
neue Systemumgebung
Werkzeuge & Techniken
WBS entwerfen und imple-mentieren 3
WBS
Werkzeuge & Techniken
WBS einbinden 4
Gesamtsystem
Werkzeuge & Techniken
System einführen 5
neue Organisation
neues System
Werkzeuge & Techniken
System betreiben 6
System in Betrieb
Werkzeuge & Techniken
Dokumente
Dok.
Sicht System-analytiker
KNOTEN : A0
TITEL : WBS entwickeln
FOLGE-NR.: MJS02
SCS-Form 0287-2 (1281)
(C) SCS GmbH und SOFTECH Inc., 1981
SADT- Formular 1

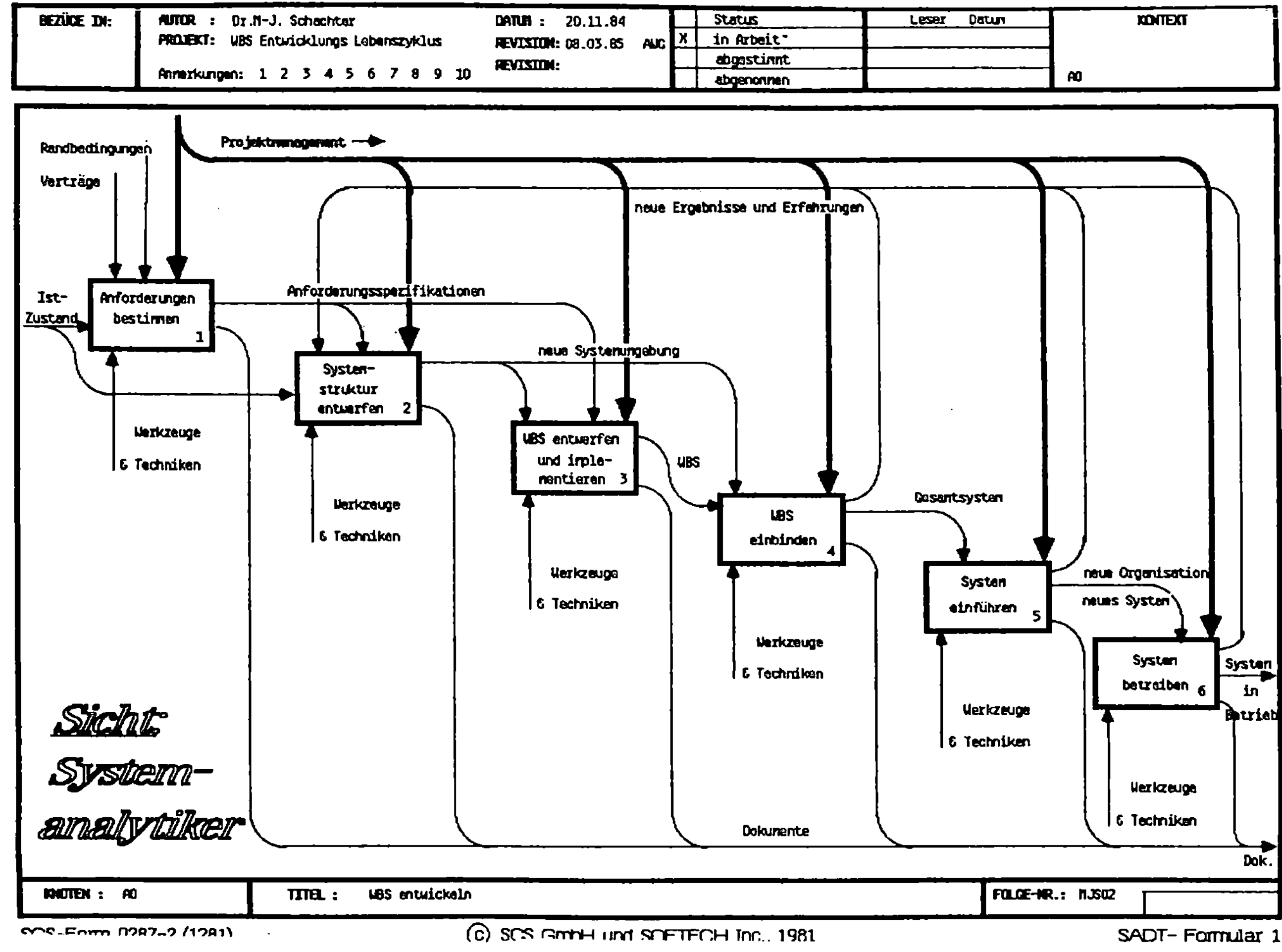

Abbildung 3

Konstruktion eines
Wissensbasierten Systems
Auswahl
Entwurf
Implementation
Verstehen
operationelles
Wissensbasiertes
System
Aufbereitung des Wissens
Identifikation
Interpretation
Wissenserhebung
Sammlung von
Information
Dokumentation
Wartung

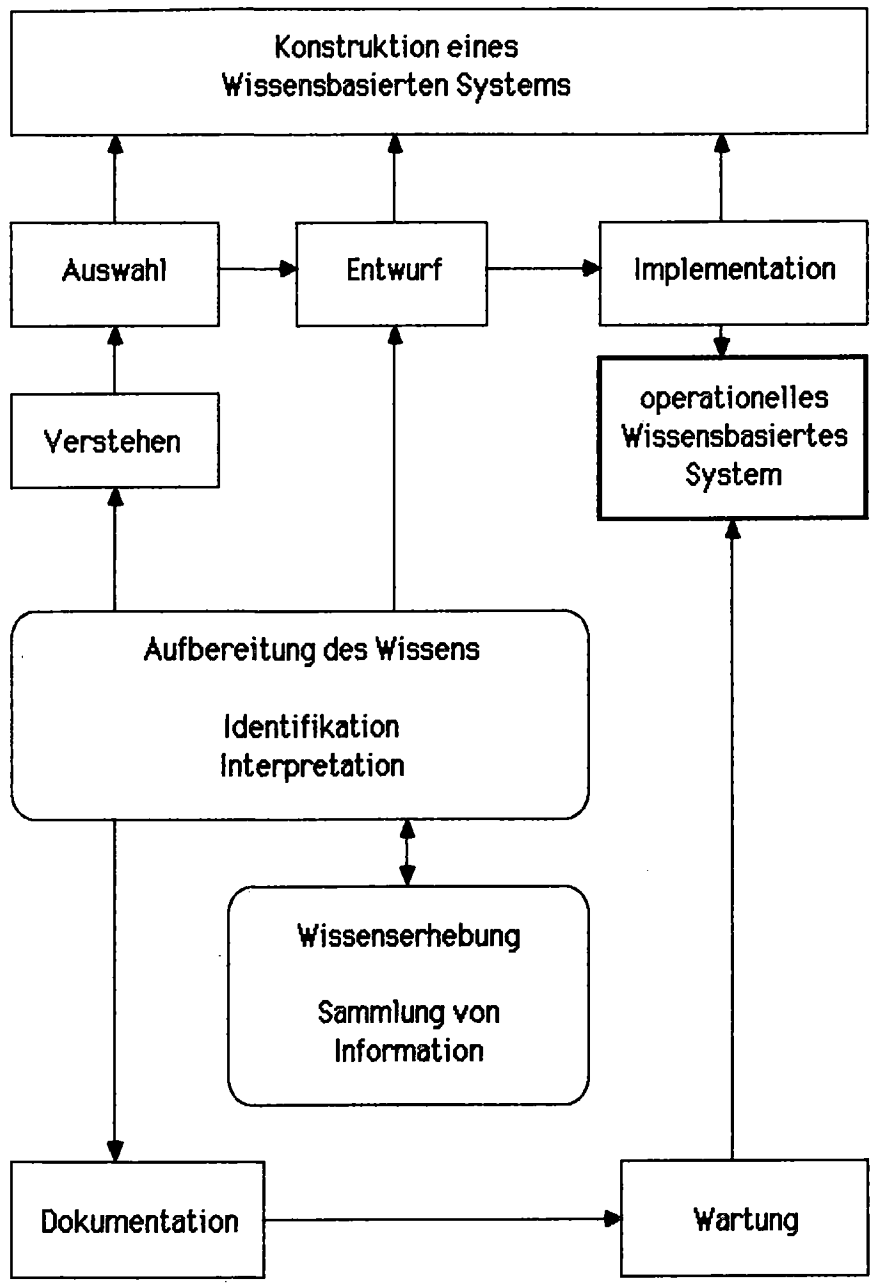

Abbildung 4

ERFAHRUNGEN BEIM EINSATZ VON EXPERTENSYSTEMEN
UND DER INTEGRATION IN DIE GESAMTORGANISATION EINES UNTERNEHMENS

****

D. Schieferle
Digital Equipment GmbH
München

I. DIE EINFÜHRUNG NEUER TECHNOLOGIEN

Die Erfahrung hat gezeigt, dass die Einfuehrung neuer Technologien in drei aufeinanderfolgenden Phasen vonstatten
geht. Man könnte sie beschreiben als:

1. Test auf Funktionalitaet
2. Kosten-Nutzen-Betrachtungen
3. Integration in die bestehende Organisation

Die Entwicklung der "Kuenstlichen Intelligenz" und besonders
des Teilgebiets "Expertensysteme" zeigen als neue Softwaretechnologie genau denselben Verlauf.

Waehrend die Phase 1, der Test auf Funktionalitaet, die
grundsaetzliche Anwendbarkeit einer Technologie ueberprueft
und dieses Ergebnis dann als allgemein verwertbare Erkenntnis betrachtet wird, koennen die in Phase 2 und Phase 3
erworbenen Erfahrungen nur fuer die individuellen Gegebenheiten des Anwenders und die jeweiligen Applikationen Guel-
tigkeit haben.

In der Praxis heisst das, daß eine kleine Anzahl von Innova-
toren die Phase 1 durchlaufen und, vorausgesetzt die Resultate sind positiv, damit den Weg freimachen fuer die sogenannten "fruehen Adaptoren", die jetzt ebenfalls beginnen,
sich mit der neuen Technologie auseinanderzusetzen. Ihnen
bleibt jedoch der Aufwand erspart die grundsaetzliche
Anwendbarkeit zu ueberpruefen; sie koennen somit sofort in
die Phase 2 eintreten.

Waehrend der Phase 1 kristallisieren sich in der Regel aus den vielfaeltigen Moeglichkeiten, die Wissenschaft und Forschung andeuten, anwendungsfaehige Methoden, Verfahren, Techniken und damit verbunden geeignete Standardwerkzeuge heraus.

Basierend auf diesen Erkenntnissen lassen sich nun anhand ausgewaehlter Anwendungen Nutzen und Kosten fuer die neue Technologie ermitteln.

In dieser Phase kommt es vornehmlich darauf an, die richtigen Anwendungsbereiche auszuwaehlen. Applikationen also, in denen sich die neue Technologie besonders optimal einsetzen laesst.

Da der Nutzen der einfachen Berechenbarkeit wegen sehr gern in "eingesparten Kosten" angegeben wird, besteht an dieser Stelle haeufig die Gefahr, neue Technologien in erster Linie fuer Rationalisierungsmassnahmen einzusetzen.

Eine weitere Moeglichkeit, naemlich Einsatz der Technologie fuer erweiterte Funktionalitaet, ist weitaus schwieriger und wird daher meistens gescheut. Die Profitabilitaet ist schwer zu ermitteln, und das Kreieren solcher neuer Funktionen setzt fundierte Kenntnisse der Technologie mit all ihren Moeglichkeiten voraus - und die Bereitschaft, Veraenderungen vorzunehmen.

Nach der Phase 2, die den oekonomisch sinnvollen Einsatz der Technologie anhand ausgewaehlter Pilotprojekte bewiesen hat, muss die Integration in die Gesamtorganisation erfolgen. Damit können weitreichende Veraenderungen oekonomischer, technischer und operationaler Art verbunden sein. Dieser Vorgang, soll er erfolgreich ablaufen, ist daher sorgfaeltig zu planen.

II. <u>EXPERTENSYSTEME BEI DIGITAL EQUIPMENT</u>

1. VOM EXPERIMENT ZUM INTEGRALEN BESTANDTEIL

Als 1979 die Arbeiten zum Expertensystem R1 - heute XCON - begannen, war durch andere Projekte wie Dendral und MYCIN bereits die Ueberlegenheit der Methoden der KI (Kuenstliche Intelligenz) in sehr komplexen Anwendungen gegenueber konventionellen Softwaretechniken nachgewiesen.

Allerdings waren bis zu diesem Zeitpunkt die Anwender von Expertensystemen ausschliesslich in Forschung und Wissenschaft zu finden. R1 sollte erstmals eine Aufgabe uebernehmen, die die Leistungsfaehigkeit der KI-Methoden und ihre oekonomische Verwertbarkeit im industriellen Umfeld unter Beweis stellt, naemlich die Konfiguration von Rechnersystemen.

Digital Equipment fertigt Rechnersysteme nach den individuellen Wuenschen seiner Kunden. Die Konfiguration solcher Systeme ist ein aeusserst komplexer und langwieriger Vorgang. Haeufig kommt es zu Missverstaendnissen und Konfigurationsfehlern, die erst waehrend der Endmontage oder im Test festgestellt werden. Dies fuehrt zu zeitraubenden Nachfragen, kostspieligen Nachruestungen und Lieferverzoegerungen.

Digital Equipment hatte bereits drei vergebliche Versuche hinter sich, das Konfigurationsproblem mittels traditioneller Softwaretechnik zu loesen, als man Prof. McDermott von der Carnegie Mellon Universitaet, einen namhaften Forscher auf dem Gebiet der Expertensysteme, um Hilfe bat.

Schon drei Monate spaeter gab es einen vielversprechenden
Prototypen mit 250 Regeln, und als Digital Equipment im
Jahre 1980 das mittlerweile auf 750 Regeln angewachsene R1
uebernahm, war es bereits in der Lage, die meisten Konfigurationen richtig zu erstellen. Digital Equipment hat R1 mit
einer eigens dafuer an der Carnegie Mellon Universitaet
ausgebildeten Mannschaft kontinuierlich unter der Bezeichnung XCON weiterentwickelt.

XCON beherrscht mittlerweile ueber 5.000 Regeln und ist
damit das groesste existierende Expertensystem. Rings um
XCON haben sich neue Expertensysteme fuer weitere Aufgaben
angesiedelt, die alle miteinander verbunden sind und gemeinsam ein Wissensnetzwerk darstellen.

Dazu gehoeren:

XSEL   Expert Sales Assistent
            Dialogsystem zur Konfigurationsunterstuet-
            zung fuer den Vertriebsbeauftragten

XSITE   Expert Site Preparation
            Auslegung von Rechnerraeumen

ISA   Intelligent Scheduling Assistent
            Materialplanung

IMACS   Intelligent Management Assistent
            for Computer Systems Manufacturing

ILOG   Intelligent Logistic Assistent

MATCHER   Vergleich von Auftraegen mit dem Lagerbestand

XTEST   Expert for System Testing
            Generierung systemspezifischer Testprogramme

2. DER NUTZEN VON EXPERTENSYSTEMEN

Der gesamte Nutzen von Expertensystemen, und das ist eine der interessantesten Erfahrungen mit dieser neuen Softwaretechnologie, laesst sich zu Beginn eines Projektes nie in vollem Umfang erahnen. XCON beispielsweise hatte zum Ziel, die Zahl der inkorrekten und missverstaendlichen Auftraege zu reduzieren, da sonst in absehbarer Zeit die begrenzte Zahl der verfuegbaren Konfigurationsspezialisten zu einem Engpass in der Fertigung gefuehrt haetten. Der wahre Nutzen wurde erst spaeter sichtbar. Die schnelle und genaue Arbeitsweise von XCON hat den Materialfluss, die Logistik und Lagerhaltung erheblich vereinfacht und letztlich bewirkt, daß auf den Bau eines neuen FA&T-Werkes (Final Assembly and Test) in USA verzichtet werden konnte.

Die meisten der von Digital Equipment heute ausgelieferten Systeme werden, dank XCON, nicht mehr im Werk zusammengebaut und getestet, sondern direkt beim Kunden. XCON hat die Fertigungsverfahren des Unternehmens grundlegend veraendert.

Die durch XCON erzielten Einsparungen belaufen sich derzeit auf insgesamt rund 54 Millionen Mark. Ein zusaetzlicher Nebeneffekt ist die Möglichkeit der Weiterverarbeitung durch XCON erzeugter Informa-tionen im Bereich der Fertigungsplanung und -steuerung mit Hilfe weiterer Expertensysteme oder durch neu geschaffene Programme in konventioneller Technik ausgefuehrt.

Darüber hinaus ist waehrend der Entwicklung von XCON ein aeusserst leistungsfaehiges Softwareprodukt entstanden, die Programmiersprache OPS5 fuer regelbasierende Expertensysteme, die Digital Equipment seit Jahren erfolgreich vermarktet.

3. INTEGRATION IN DEN BETRIEBLICHEN ABLAUF

Die Entwicklung von XCON war ein typischer Fall von Technologietransfer direkt aus der Forschung in eine konkrete
Anwendung hinein. XCON wird als sehr gelungenes Projekt
beurteilt, doch sind sich alle Beteiligten, sowohl die
Forscher als auch Digital Equipment, darueber im klaren,
dass eine Reihe gluecklicher Umstaende zum Erfolg beitru-
gen, die nicht notwendigerweise auch bei Folgeprojekten gegeben sein muessen. Um die Risiken zu minimieren, aber auch
um einen kontinuierlichen und raschen Transfer neuester
Forschungsergebnisse in die praktische Anwendung zu gewaehr-
leisten, hat Digital Equipment ein eigenes Technologietrans-
ferkonzept entwickelt.

Der Transfer einer Technologie vom Forschungsgegenstand zur
angewandten Technik ist ein aeusserst aufwendiger Prozeß,
der von vielen Randbedingungen beeinflusst wird und anfael-
lig ist gegenueber unvermittelt auftretenden Schwierigkeiten und externen, kaum bestimmbaren Parametern. Diesen Prozess in einem einzigen Schritt zu vollziehen, erscheint als
Standardverfahren zu komplex und zu wenig stabil, um sich
darauf abstuetzen zu koennen. Da DEC jedoch auf den Einsatz
neuester Technologien angewiesen ist, muessen Wege gefunden
werden, um Technologietransfer erfolgreich, ungestoert und
kontinuierlich ablaufen zu lassen.

4. DIGITAL EQUIPMENT'S TRANSFERKONZEPT, DIE OPERATIONALE INTEGRATION

Die Implementation des neuen Transferkonzeptes wurde im Jahre 1982 begonnen und bedeutete den ersten Schritt zur Integration von KI und Expertensystemen in den organisatorischen
Ablauf des Unternehmens. In Anlehnung an das 3-Phasenmodell -
1. Funktionalitaet pruefen, 2. Kosten und Nutzen betrachten
und 3. Integration in den betrieblichen Ablauf - wurden Aufgaben definiert und verschiedenen Teilen der Organisation
uebertragen.

4.1 Phase 1: Das External Research Programm

Fuer den direkten Kontakt zu den Universitaeten und Forschungseinrichtungen ist die zentrale Forschungs- und Entwicklungsabteilung verantwortlich. Im Rahmen des sogenannten "External Research Program" werden Forschungsprojekte unterstuetzt, ohne dabei auf Projektentwicklung und Projektziele Einfluss zu nehmen. Neueste Forschungsergebnisse aus diesen Projekten stehen der zentralen Entwicklungsabteilung zur Verfuegung und dienen als Entscheidungshilfe fuer die Entwicklung von Standard-Hard- und Softwarewerkzeugen sowie zur Identifizierung von Anwendungsbereichen und Entwicklungsmethoden. Die zentrale Entwicklungsabteilung ist verantwortlich fuer die Einfuehrung genereller Konzepte und deren Verwirklichung in den Basisprodukten, sowohl hinsichtlich Hardware wie auch Software.

Hier wurde z.B. die Unterscheidung von "Funktion" und "Form" in der Software definiert und fuehrte zur Trennung der Benutzeroberflaeche von der eigentlichen Funktion eines Programms. Die Schnittstellen sind so definiert, dass die Auswahl von beliebigen "Formen" bei ein und derselben "Funktion" moeglich wird. Damit ist sichergestellt, dass "Funktionen", zu denen neben konventionellen Programmen auch die Expertensysteme, Roboterplanungssysteme, automatisches Beweisen und automatisches Programmieren gehoeren, Benutzerschnittstellen je nach Bedarf einsetzen und vor allem je nach Machbarkeit spaeter eventuell austauschen koennen. So kann ein Expertensystem heute mit konventioneller Menuetechnik betrieben und dasselbe System morgen mit einer natuerlichsprachlichen Schnittstelle, einem bildverstehenden System oder gar mit beidem versehen werden. Funktion und Form koennen im Extremfall auf unterschiedlichen Rechnern ablaufen und ueber eine traditionelle Kommunikationseinrichtung miteinander kommunizieren.

Anhand dieses Beispiels erkennt man deutlich zwei zentrale
Aufgaben der Entwicklungsabteilung im Technologietransfer-
Prozess, die neben der Realisierung in der Praxis anwendba-
rer Werkzeuge stehen:

1. Zukuenftige Entwicklungen, wie die Implementierung natuerlicher Sprache und bildverstehen der Systeme, muessen
   beruecksichtigt werden

2. Die Integration von KI auf technischer Ebene muß gewährleistet sein. Das umfaßt Softwarewerkzeuge mit standardi-
   sierten Schnittstellen, Anknuepfung an konventioelle
   Module, Verteilung auf mehrere Rechner mit den dazugehoerigen Kommunikationseinrichtungen.

Zusammenfassend kann man die Aufgaben der zentralen Ent-
wick-lungsabteilung wie folgt beschreiben:

1. Unterstuetzung zukunftsweisender Forschungsprojekte
2. Sichten der Ergebnisse und Prüfung auf Anwendbarkeit
3. Entwicklung praxisnaher und im industriellen Umfeld
   einsetzbarer Werkzeuge

Der Wissenstransfer erfolgt bei diesem Konzept allerdings
nicht nur ausschliesslich von den Universitaeten in die
Entwicklungsabteilungen. Auch umgekehrt wird Erfahrungsaustausch betrieben. Die Forscher erhalten Feedback ueber
die Anwendbarkeit ihrer Forschungsergebnisse und damit
Unterstützung bei der Auswahl neuer Forschungsthemen, ohne
jedoch gleichzeitig mit den Zwaengen, die bedingt durch die
kommerzielle Ausrichtung in einer industriellen Umgebung
normalerweise vorhanden sind, konfrontiert zu werden.

Der naechste Schritt im Sinne eines Technologietransfers
findet zwischen "zentraler Entwicklung" und "zentraler Funktion" statt.

4.2 Phase 2: Die ökonomische Integration

Die "zentralen Funktionen", hierzu gehoeren beispielsweise
Fertigung, Service, Vertrieb, Marketing, Personalwesen,
Entwicklung usw., haben die Aufgabe, einheitliche Verfahren, Techniken und Methoden fuer ihre jeweiligen Funktionen zu definieren, die notwendigen Werkzeuge und Hilfsmittel zur Verfuegung zu stellen, die neuen Methoden einzu-
fuehren und die Aktivitaeten ihrer ausfuehrenden Organe in
den verschiedenen Betriebsteilen zu unterstuetzen und zu
koordinieren.

So entwirft die zentrale Fertigungsabteilung z.B. ein fuer
alle Fertigungsbetriebe anwendbares CIM Konzept, definiert
konkrete Projekte, in denen die verschiedenen Einzelmodule
entwickelt werden, waehlt die Anwender aus, die die Realisierung vor Ort vornehmen sollen und koordiniert all diese
Aktivitaeten. Hierzu gehoert insbesondere die Ausbildung
der Mitarbeiter, die Ernennung von "Programm Managern", die
Organisation gemeinsamer Besprechungen zum Erfahrungsaustausch und die Ueberwachung der Einhaltung gegebener Design-
regeln.

Im Falle der Expertensysteme werden in der Fertigung Anwen-
dungsnischen, die ausgesprochen komplex erscheinen, einem
Gremium von Experten uebergeben. Es entscheidet, ob ein
Versuch unternommen werden soll, das Problem mit KI-Methoden zu loesen. Wenn ja, wird ein Betriebsteil gesucht, der
die Realisierung uebernimmt, und ein Programm Manager
ernennt. Ressourcen werden in Form von KI- und Applikation-
sexperten und der erforderlichen Rechenleistung zur Verfuegung gestellt. Als Softwarewerkzeuge kommen ausschliesslich die von der zentralen Entwicklung freigegebenen Stan-
dardprodukte, die gleichzeitig extern vermarktet werden,
zum Einsatz. Kein Verantwortlicher im Betrieb liesse sich
auf unausgegorene oder gar fehlerhafte Softwarewerkzeuge
ein, denn er ist einzig und allein am Erfolg seiner Funktion, nicht aber am Austesten von Software interessiert.

Die Aufgaben der zentralen Entwicklung und der zentralen Funktionen sind vergleichbar mit den Rollen des Innovators und eines fruehen Adaptors im ueblichen Technologie transfer-Prozess. Bei DEC bieten die zentralen Entwicklungsabteilungen den zentralen Funktionen seit mittlerweile drei Jahren KI-Methoden und die dazugehoerigen Werkzeuge neben den traditionellen Hilfsmitteln gleichrangig an.

Ein weiterer wichtiger Schritt zur Integration von Kuenstlicher Intelligenz als Standard Technologie.

4.3 Phase 3: Die technische Integration

Die Realisierung eines Expertensystems selbst liegt in den Haenden der eigentlichen Anwender. Nur direkt vor Ort kann ueber den Sinn und die Notwendigkeit neuer Funktionen oder Hilfsmittel zur Verbesserung der bestehenden Verfahren kompetent geurteilt werden. Und nur hier wird der Nutzen einer neuen Anwendung sichtbar.

Wie bereits erwaehnt, werden nur ausgetestete Standardwerkzeuge verwendet. Das einzelne zu realisierende Projekt muss sich in das Gesamtkonzept der Informationsverarbeitung eingliedern. Applikationen werden meist dort realisiert, wo traditionell ein Mensch Informationen und Daten von einem Rechnersystem geliefert bekommt, diese auf der Basis seiner Expertise "weiterverarbeitet", zu bestimmten Resultaten kommt und diese dann wiederum als Eingabe fuer ein weiteres EDV-gestuetztes System benutzt. D.h. ganz konkret, dass Expertensysteme bei DEC keine Automatisierungsinseln entstehen lassen, sondern die Luecken zwischen den bereits in konventioneller Technik existierenden Automatisierungsinseln schliessen.

Folglich haben alle Expertensysteme entweder direkten Zugriff auf die benachbarten traditionellen Programme oder zumindest auf deren Datenbestaende und bedienen sich entsprechender Kommunikationseinrichtungen. Expertensysteme muessen mit traditionellen Systemen kooperieren. Expertensysteme und KI sind die konsequente und logische Weiterentwicklung der Informationsverarbeitung zur Wissensverarbeitung und setzen den Trend fort, mit Hilfe noch besserer Werkzeuge noch komplexere Probleme zu loesen.

So wie die Datenbanktechnologie in der Lage war, Applikationen wie z.B. die Platzreservierung bei Fluggesellschaften zu realisieren, so koennen Expertensysteme in Anwendungsbereiche vordringen, die fuer die traditionellen Techniken zu komplex sind. Aber genau so wie Datenbanken nicht traditionelle Programmiersprachen ersetzen, ersetzt auch KI nicht die konventionelle EDV.

III. <u>ZUSAMMENFASSUNG</u>

Die Erfahrung von Digital Equipment aus rund 120 Projekten beweist darueber hinaus, dass selbst die Expertensysteme intern nicht auf traditionelle Techniken verzichten koennen. Benutzerdialog, arithmetische Funktionen, Statistik, Grafik, Prozessanschluss und vieles mehr wird besser in den auch bisher dafuer benutzten Sprachen geschrieben. Ein sogenanntes Expertensystem besteht in der Praxis aus etwa 20 Prozent KI und 80 Prozent traditioneller EDV. Diese Tatsache soll allerdings keineswegs die Ueberlegenheit der KI-Methoden herunterspielen. Die 20 Prozent KI sind der Kern des Systems, ohne den die Gesamtloesung inklusive des achtzigprozentigen EDV-Anteils nicht moeglich waere.

Diese Zahlen deuten an, dass

1. die Produktivitaet eines KI-Entwicklers auch von seinen Kenntnissen ueber den Umgang mit konventionellen Techniken abhaengt, und

2. die technische Integration der KI gleichzeitig die Verwendung der unter der Software liegenden Hardware fuer KI, konventionelle Software, den Zugriff auf traditionelle Datenbanken und die Verwendung gegebener Kommunikationseinrichtigungen erfordert.

Und genau in diesen Punkten liegt der eigentliche Grund, warum Digital Equipment so schnell und so erfolgreich so viele Expertensysteme zum Einsatz bringen konnte. Denn das Rechnerkonzept der VAX-Familie ist so ausgelegt, daß all diese Forderungen bereits beruecksichtigt werden. Alle DEC-Expertensysteme laufen auf VAX-Rechnern mit dem Betriebssystem VMS und benutzen Standard-Softwarewerkzeuge wie VAX-LISP und OPS5.

Das Zusammenspiel zwischen zentraler Funktion und ausfuehrendem Anwender ist, ebenso wie die Kommunikation der anderen am Technologietransfer-Prozess beteiligten Gruppen keine Einbahnstrasse. Aus den Erfahrungen vor Ort erhaelt die zentrale Funktion Anregungen zur Verbesserung ihrer Konzepte und Verfahren, die ihrerseits wieder weitergegeben werden an die zentrale Entwicklung, um eventuelle Produktverbesserungen vorzunehmen.

Durch die Dreiteilung des Technologietransfers bei Digital Equipment sind verschiedene Ziele erreicht worden:

1. Der Prozess ist transparenter
2. Ein kontinuierlicher Fluss von neuen Technologien kommt zustande
3. Wissenschaftler sind von kommerziell bedingen Zwaengen entlastet
4. Dem Anwender stehen stabile Werkzeuge zur Verfuegung
5. Die Integration in die Organisation auf operationaler, oekonomischer und technischer Ebene ist gewaehrleistet.

Integration in den betrieblichen Ablauf bedeutet

Operational: Festlegung von Verfahrensprozeduren, von der
                  Identifikation eines geeigneten External Re-
                  search Programms bis hin zur Durchfuehrung von
                  KI-Projekten in Form von standardisierten
                  Richtlinien.

Oekonomisch: Beruecksichtigung der KI-Methoden beim Entwurf
                  neuer Fertigungs-, Engineering-, Service, Ve-
                  triebs- und Marketing-Konzepte

Technisch: Einbindung aller KI-Produkte in eine einheit-
                  liche VAX-Rechnerarchitektur

Allerdings gibt es zwei Voraussetzungen, die unabdingbar sind
und die Integration von KI erst moeglich machen.

1. Ein Unternehmen muss die bisher zur Verfuegung stehenden
   traditionellen Softwaretechniken einschließlich Datenbanken,
   Netzwerke, usw. beherrschen. KI kann nicht dazu dienen, einen
   Rueckstand in diesem Bereich wieder auszugleichen.

2. Die Mitarbeiter müssen entsprechend ausgebildet werden. KI-
   Technologie kann man nicht fix und fertig kaufen. Training
   oder Consulting ist notwendig, um die eigenen Mitarbeiter und
   im Unternehmen beschaeftigten "Experten" zu sensibilisieren
   und selbst kreativ Anwendungen identifizieren zu lassen.

Seit 1979 - dem Jahr, in dem Digital Equipment erstmals als Anwender von KI in Erscheinung trat - sind intern rund 200 Mitarbeiter in KI-Techniken geschult worden. Die Schulung dauert zwischen 15 Wochen und 15 Monaten. Im Laufe der Jahre ist intern an
ueber 120 Projekten gearbeitet worden. 60 Projekte, die mit KI-
Methoden oder KI-Werkzeugen realisiert wurden, wuerde man heute
nicht mehr zu den Expertensystemen zaehlen, entweder weil der
KI-Anteil zu klein ist oder weil im Verlauf des Projekts ein
Loesungsalgorithmus entwickelt wurde. Von den restlichen 60
"echten" Expertensystemen befinden sich ca. 40 im taeglichen
Einsatz und 20 in einem Stadium, das den Einsatz zwar noch nicht
rechtfertigt, aber schon weit ueber den Prototyp hinausgeht.

Zusammenfassend kann man feststellen, dass Expertensysteme ein
integraler Bestandteil des DEC-Informationsverarbeitungskon-
zepts sind - sowohl bei den internen Anwendungen als auch bei
den Produkten. Endziel der Entwicklung wird es sein, nicht mehr
zu unterscheiden zwischen Entwicklern von KI-Software und traditioneller Software und zwischen Expertensystemen und konventioneller EDV. Die Grenze zwischen beiden wird verwischt und
jeder Softwareentwickler wird in der Lage sein, sowohl KI als
auch traditionelle Methoden und Werkzeuge zu verwenden.

Industrielle Nutzung wissensbasierter Systeme

Egbert Lehmann, Heinz Schwärtzel, Heinz Schweppe

Siemens AG
Zentralbereich Forschung und Technik
München

1. Einleitung

Noch vor wenigen Jahren war der Begriff "Wissensverarbeitung" (knowledge processing) außerhalb der Artificial Intelligence (AI)-Forschung praktisch unbekannt. Heute befinden wir uns an der Schwelle zum praktischen Einsatz dieser Technologie in einer Vielzahl von Anwendungsfeldern, vornehmlich im technisch-naturwissenschaftlichen Bereich.

Ansätze zur Modellierung von "intelligenzerfordernden" Tätigkeiten werden seit Mitte der 50er Jahre im Rahmen der AI entwickelt. Trotz ihrer beschränkten praktischen Einsetzbarkeit haben sie schon in den vorangegangenen Jahrzehnten - manchmal recht unkonventionelle - Beiträge zur Weiterentwicklung der Informatik und zur Erschließung neuer Anwendungsmöglichkeiten von Computern geleistet.

Ende der 70er Jahre erreichte die Computertechnologie - insbesondere auch das Preis-Leistungs-Verhältnis der Hardware - einen Stand, der Methoden und Hilfsmittel der AI-Forschung unter dem Gesichtspunkt industrieller Nutzbarkeit interessant erscheinen ließ. Namentlich auf dem Gebiet der Expertensysteme sind prototypische Lösungen für eine reichhaltige Palette von Aufgaben inzwischen zu wirkungsvollen und benutzerfreundlichen Anwendungssoftwaresystemen herangereift (vgl. etwa Lehm 83,, SrJo 85). Diese sind aber nur als Spitze des Eisberges softwaretechnologischer Innovationen zu betrachten, die im Zusammenhang mit der weiteren Entwicklung und Verbreitung wissensbasierter Systeme im nächsten Jahrzehnt zu erwarten sind.

Im folgenden Beitrag wird zunächst der Begriff des wissensbasierten Systems erläutert. In den Kapiteln 3 und 4 werden Vorzüge und Einsatzperspektiven der im AI-Bereich entstandenen Softwaretechnologie und der vielfältigen Interaktionsformen wissensbasierter Systeme erläutert. Nach Klärung des Unterschieds zwischen Programmieren und automatischem Problemlösen (Kapitel 5) werden in Kapitel 6 Expertensysteme als wissensbasierte Problemlöser für sehr spezielle reale Einsatzbereiche behandelt, wobei unter dem Gesichtspunkt industrieller Nutzbarkeit auf die Vielzahl unterschiedlicher Anwendungsfelder und technischer Einsatzumgebungen , auf Kriterien für die Auswahl von Entwicklungsprojekten und die erhofften Auswirkungen solcher Entwicklungen eingegangen wird. Kapitel 7 enthält Betrachtungen zur Marktentwicklung bei wissensbasierten Systemen. Abschließend werden einige organisatorische Probleme beim industriellen Neuaufbau eines eigenen Entwicklungspotentials diskutiert.

2. Wissensbasierte Systeme

Gegenwärtig stehen wissensbasierte Systeme erst an der Schwelle des routinemäßigen industriellen Einsatzes, d.h. die bei Entwicklung und Einsatz solcher Systeme gewonnenen Erfahrungen sind noch nicht sehr umfangreich. Außerdem erschwert das Fehlen allgemein anerkannter Kriterien für die definitorische Abgrenzung wissensbasierter Systeme gegenüber anderen Systemtypen sowie die Heterogenität ihrer Einsatzgebiete und Einsatzbedingungen die Verallgemeinerung einzelner Erfahrungen. Angesichts der vielen unbefriedigenden Erklärungsversuche muß eingangs gesagt werden, in welchem Sinne im folgenden von wissensbasierten Systemen gesprochen wird.

Im Sinne einer Arbeitsdefinition lassen sich *wissensbasierte Systeme* folgendermaßen charakterisieren:
1. Als primäres architektonisches *Gliederungsprinzip* wird nicht mehr die algorithmische Struktur operationaler Abläufe sondern eine die betroffenen *statischen Gegebenheiten* (Objekte, Eigenschaften und Beziehungen) *modellierende Wissensbasis* bei hinreichend detaillierter *begrifflicher Klassifizierung* und *Charakterisierung* zugrundegelegt.
2. Die *dynamischen (prozedural realisierten) Anteile* des Gesamtsystems sollen möglichst stark *eingeschränkt* und *vereinfacht* werden, und zwar a) durch Ersetzung expliziter Handlungsvorschriften durch *generelle Interpretationsmechanismen*, etwa zur gezielten logischen Verknüpfung von Einzeltatsachen und regelhaften (allgemeinen) Aussagen,
b) durch Beschränkung der verbliebenen speziellen *prozeduralen Anteile auf lokale Systembereiche* und stärkere Bindung an einzelne Elemente der Wissensbasis, was eine stärkere *Modularisierung* ermöglicht.

Wissensbasiertheit ist damit keine Eigenschaft, die man einem System klar zu- oder absprechen kann, sondern eher das deutliche Vorherrschen der o.g. *Tendenz in Entwurfsprozeß und Architektur* eines Systems.

Zum Ausgliedern deskriptiver Elemente (Mengen gleichartig strukturierter Einzeldaten) kam es bereits im Verlaufe der Entwicklung der Datenbanktechnik. Der *Übergang von der Datenverarbeitung zur Wissensverarbeitung* ist vor allem ein Übergang von der Speicherung einfach strukturierter *Einzelaussagen* zur Speicherung wesentlich komplexer strukturierter, *genereller Aussagen*. Solche Aussagen stellen gewöhnlich Gültigkeitsbeziehungen zwischen mehreren Aussagen bestimmter Form oder Klassenzugehörigkeit dar. Sie können oft in natürlicher Weise als Wenn-Dann-Regeln formuliert werden, die durch Schlußfolgerungsprozesse (Inferenz) mit Einzelaussagen verknüpfbar sind.

Die technische Fähigkeit, komplexe Informationsbestände darzustellen und zu bearbeiten, rechtfertigt es allein noch nicht, von Wissensverarbeitung zu sprechen. Vielmehr ist es darüber hinaus notwendig, daß die dargestellten Informationsstrukturen nach einheitlichen Prinzipien interpretierbar sind oder - anders ausgedrückt - einen semantisch klar definierten Status besitzen, also nicht erst durch die sie verarbeitenden speziellen Programme ihre Bedeutung erhalten. Diese Eigenschaft ist eine wesentliche Voraussetzung für die Fähigkeit, Problemlösungen mit Hilfe gebietsspezifischen, meist umfangreichen Wissens herbeizuführen oder zumindest zu unterstützen. Die meisten heute existierenden Systeme genügen allerdings dieser letzten (in die Zukunft weisenden) Forderung höchstens sehr unvollkommen.

Die Entwicklung der AI-Forschung ist ganz wesentlich durch die Suche nach wissensbasierten Gestaltungsprinzipien qualitativ leistungsfähiger ("intelligenterer") Informationsverarbeitungssysteme gekennzeichnet. Bei genauer Betrachtung der Nutzungsmöglichkeiten von Ergebnissen der AI kann man drei Aspekte unterscheiden :

*   Programmiersprachen für Symbolverarbeitung (LISP, PROLOG) mit komfortablen Programmierumgebungen (typischerweise auf sogenannten AI-workstations) als Beitrag zur Softwaretechnologie für schnelle Prototyperstellung

*   Methoden für die formale Strukturierung und Lösung nichtnumerischer Problemen (ohne bekannte, geschlossene Lösungsalgorithmen) sowie entsprechende anwendungsspezifische Systeme und entwicklungsunterstützende Software-Tools.

*   Generelle Methoden zur theoretisch fundierten Aufbereitung und Repräsentation größerer Wissensbereiche sowie Verfahren zur flexiblen, zielgerichteten Verknüpfung und zur erfahrungsabhängigen Erweiterung solcher 'Wissensbasen'.

Während der dritte Aspekt noch weitgehend Vorfeldcharakter hat und noch lange Zeit eines der zentralen Themen der AI-Forschung sein wird (vgl. Bobr 85), liegen die Hauptakzente der industriellen Nutzung auf den erstgenannten Bereichen.

3. Softwaretechnologische Aspekte

Die Entwicklung praktisch nutzbarer, wissensbasierter Systeme ist nicht zuletzt durch Programmierwerkzeuge und eine Programmiermethodik begünstigt worden, die sich von der klassischen Softwareerstellung beträchtlich unterscheidet. Sowohl die typischen verwendeten Programmiersprachen (LISP bzw. PROLOG) als auch die hochkomfortablen Softwareentwicklungsumgebungen ermöglichen rasche Pilotentwicklungen, die dem Endbenutzer einen unmittelbaren Eindruck vom funktionalen Verhalten eines Systems vermitteln. Dieses unter dem Schlagwort 'Rapid Prototyping' bekannte Verfahren reduziert die bei der Anwendungssoftwareentwicklung bestehende Gefahr, daß das Endprodukt trotz korrekter Implementierung gemäß vereinbarter Systemspezifikation nicht den Vorstellungen des Endbenutzers entspricht.

Drei Aspekte sind für eine Softwareentwicklungsumgebung typisch, die schnelle Prototypentwicklungen erlauben.
*	Arbeitsplatzrechner mit grafikfähigem Bildschirm, Fenstertechnik, Maus o. ä. und Anschluß an lokale Netze
*	interaktive, für die Symbolverarbeitung geeignete Programmiersprachen
*	problemloses Zusammenspiel leistungsfähiger Programmier- und Testwerkzeuge.

Arbeitsplatzrechner mit den genannten Eigenschaften gehören heute zum 'state-of-the-art', z.B. das SIEMENS System EMS 5815. In Kürze werden auch leistungsfähige Personal Computer mehr und mehr mit der entsprechenden Technik ausgestattet sein.

Eine mindestens ebenso große Rolle wie die Hardwarekonfiguration spielt die gewählte Programmiersprache. So erlaubt z.B. die Sprache PROLOG (CIMe 81) idealerweise eine nahezu vollständig deskriptive Problemformulierung in Form von Regeln, die weitgehend unabhängig von der Art der Programmausführung ist.

Beispiel: Bekanntlich ist die Ableitung einer Summe von Funktionen gleich der Summe ihrer Ableitungen. In einem (aus wenigen Zeilen bestehenden) Programm zur symbolischen Ableitung von Funktionen würde diese Regel wie folgt formuliert sein:

abl(F + G, X, F1 + G1):- abl(F, X, F1), abl(G, X, G1)

d.h. die Ableitung der Funktion F + G nach X ist F1 + G1, wenn F1 die Ableitung von F nach X und G1 die Ableitung von G nach X ist (das gesamte Programm findet sich z.B. in CIMe 81.).

Während die Entwicklung von PROLOG auf das logische Theorembeweisen und ei- speziellen Anwendungsfall, nämlich die ausführbare Definition von Regeln natürlichsprachlichen Grammatik zurückgeht, wurde LISP (siehe etwa GöSt **84,** vornherein als allgemeine symbolverarbeitende Sprache für die KI-Forschung entwo und implementiert. Der einfache Aufbau komplexer Datenstrukturen und mächtige Konstrukte zu deren Manipulation bilden den Kern der Sprache, die durch Zugrundelegung der Berechenbarkeitstheorie rekursiver Baumfunktionen auch theoretisch gut begründet werden konnte.

Die Anwendung einer Funktion auf Argumente ist die zentrale Operation eines LISP-Systems (man spricht deshalb auch von einer funktionalen bzw. applikativen Sprache). Die symbolischen Daten von LISP sind beliebig modifizierbare und wachstumsfähige Listenstrukturen, was durch eine vollautomatische dynamische Speicherplatzverwaltung ermöglicht wird. Ein weiteres wesentliches Merkmal ist die Uniformität, mit der Daten und Programme (genauer: Funktionen) in LISP behandelt werden. Die einheitliche Behandlung von Programmen und Daten, die z.B. auch die dynamische Modifikation von Funktionen erlaubt, ist ein mächtiges Hilfsmittel zur Formulierung von symbolverarbeitenden Prozessen.

Die heutige Bedeutung von LISP als Implementierüngssprache für wissensbasierte Systeme beruht ganz wesentlich mit auf der mustergültigen Programmierumgebung mit hoher Funktionalität (ca. 10000 eingebaute Funktionen!) ausgereifter LISP-Systeme wie ZetaLisp oder INTERLISP-D, die für *exploratorische Programmierung* (Shei 84, Shei 83) prädestiniert erscheinen.

Was ist darunter zu verstehen?
Die heute dominierende Programmiermethodologie geht von einer klaren Trennung von Problemspezifikation, Programmentwurf und Implementierung aus, um die gefürchteten, da sehr arbeitsintensiven Etappen der Implementierung (d.h. Programmentwurf, Kodierung, Testung, Fehlersuche, Korrektur usw.) auf das unvermeidlich notwendige Maß zu beschränken. Diese Methodologie hat sich in vielen Programmierprojekten bewährt, bei denen die Aufgabenstellung präzise vorgegeben und keinen oder nur geringen Änderungen während der Realisierung unterworfen ist.

Es gibt jedoch Anwendungen, bei denen der Auftraggeber nicht in allen Punkten präzise Vorstellungen vom gewünschten Systemverhalten haben kann und für die deshalb eine vollständige Anforderungsspezifikation vor Implementationsbeginn unmöglich ist. Ursachen können die extreme Komplexität des Problems oder die kontinuierlich sich ändernden Anforderungen sein. Auch haben die unvermeidlichen Korrekturen einzelner Komponenten meist nichtlokale Auswirkungen, die ebenfalls nicht im Detail vorzuplanen sind. Die Entwicklung wissensbasierter Systeme ist in hohem Maße mit all diesen Problemen behaftet.

Durch Implemetationsmöglichkeiten auf einem hohen deskriptiven Niveau können Umfang und Arbeitsaufwand für die bisher zeitaufwendigsten Implementationsetappen wesentlich reduziert werden, nicht zuletzt auch die zahlenmäßige Stärke des Entwicklerteams. Hingegen wird die Spezifikation des gewünschten Systemverhaltens auf einer globaleren Ebene zunehmend zu einem nur rechnerunterstützt und schrittweise experimentell lösbaren Entwurfsproblem. Spezifikation, Programmentwurf und Implementierung sind nicht mehr streng von einander trennbar.

Eine wichtige Voraussetzung für explorative Programmierung ist die Verfügbarkeit aller Hilfsmittel innerhalb einer einheitlichen Arbeitsumgebung: die Fehlerlokalisierung mit einem Debugger, die Programmkorrektur im Editor und das definierte Wiederanlaufen finden aus Sicht des Programmierers in einer Systemumgebung ohne explizite Betriebssystemintervention statt. Alle Änderungen müssen automatisch protokolliert und gegebenenfalls wieder rückgängig gemacht werden können; die schrittweise

Systemerweiterung ist zu unterstützen (inkrementeller Compiler, Interpreter); der Editor orientiert sich an Programmobjekten, z.B. den zentralen Datenstrukturen, nicht an den vom Ausgabemedium vorgegebenen Randbedingungen, z.B. der Zeilenpositionierung (syntaxgesteuerter Editor); die Korrektur von Schreibfehlern, die in klassischen Programmentwicklungssystemen nicht selten Anlaß zu aufwendiger Fehlersuche sind, wird meist automatisch vorgenommen und protokolliert; der Programmzustand kann auf verschiedenen Ebenen und in unterschiedlichem Detaillierungsgrad parallel sichtbar gemacht werden (Fenstertechnik), Benutzereingaben werden unmittelbar auf Konsistenz geprüft. Die Liste ließe sich noch bedeutend erweitern. Sie charakterisiert moderne, arbeitsplatzorientierte Softwareentwicklungsumgebungen. Diese sind keinesfalls nur in wissensbasierten Systemen anzutreffen; sie beruhen allerdings entscheidend auf den Erfahrungen, die bei der Entwicklung von AI-Systemen gemacht wurden.

Wenn Programme eine akzeptable Funktionalität erreicht haben, erweist sich manchmal die Effizienz als unbefriedigend. Für das Ziel einer schnellen Prototypentwicklung muß dies nicht tragisch sein, solange nur die Überführung in eine Produktversion effektiver durchgeführt werden kann. Auch hierfür sind Werkzeuge erforderlich, etwa zur Transformation des Systems in effizienten Maschinencode der Zielmaschine oder zur Analyse und Verbesserung des Leistungsverhaltens.

Trotz der Bedeutung der für wissensbasierte Systeme so typischen Softwaretechnologie bedarf es noch erheblicher Anstrengungen, um diese einer breiteren industriellen Nutzung zugänglich zu machen. Schon allein die Kosten eines mit einer leistungsfähigen personal workstation ausgerüsteten Arbeitsplatzes für Softwareentwicklung liegen noch bedeutend über denen eines Programmierterminals zur Benutzung eines Zentralrechners, werden aber kontinuierlich weiter sinken. Auch Bedürfnisse nach Vielfachnutzung der Systeme, nach Wartung durch Dritte anstatt durch den Entwickler oder die Erstellung sehr großer Softwaresysteme werfen Probleme auf, deren Lösung die Bedeutung der AI-orientierten Softwaretechnologie über den engen Bereich der wissensbasierten Systeme hinaus entscheidend beeinflussen wird.

Allerdings kann und soll exploratorisches Programmieren nicht als Universalrezept empfohlen werden, zumal wenn es sich um wohldefinierte Programmieraufgaben handelt, wie sie für die kommerzielle Datenverarbeitung auch heute noch typisch sind.

4. Interaktionsformen wissensbasierter Systeme

Als Folge wissensbasierter Systemgestaltung entstehen nicht nur neue Bedürfnisse nach engerer Interaktion des Benutzers mit dem System, sondern auch interessante Möglichkeiten zum Inspizieren und Modifizieren der Wissensbasis und zum schrittweisen Überprüfen der ablaufenden Schlußfolgerungsprozesse. Dabei kann, zumindest bei

Benutzung von komfortablen personal workstations, die Mensch-Maschine-Interaktion durch graphische Visualisierungs- und Zeigemöglichkeiten und Multi-Window-Technik bedeutend vereinfacht und effektiviert werden: Es ergibt sich eine natürlichere Interaktionsform, die der menschlichen Neigung zum "anschaulichen Denken" entgegenkommt. Typische Funktionsklassen hierbei sind:

Wissensinspektion: Betrachtung von Definitionen bestimmter Begriffe und Funktionen, von Eigenschaften und Bestandteilen bestimmter Objekte

Browsing: übersichtliche Visualisierung größerer Zusammenhänge zwischen Elementen einer Wissensbasis

interaktive Wissenseingabe: Editieren und Ergänzen von Bestandteilen einer Wissensbasis

Benutzerführung: Dialog-Assistenz und automatische Hilfestellung (HELP-Funktion) zur Bedienungsunterstützung bei unzureichender Systemkenntnis

Erklärungsfähigkeit: (argumentative Erläuterung der automatisch abgeleiteten End- und Zwischenergebnisse bei mehrstufigen Entscheidungs- und Klassifikationsprozessen)

Gleichzeitig wird der *Interaktionsstil* dadurch *komplexer,* daß der Benutzer in einer gegebenen Situation (etwa auf eine vom System gestellte Frage) in prinzipiell unterschiedlichen Weisen reagieren kann (die Antwort eingeben, sich nach den Antwortmöglichkeiten erkundigen, die Antwort verweigern bzw. die Frage übergehen, Rückfragen stellen, die Berechtigung der Frage anzweifeln oder sich nach deren Zweck erkundigen, auf frühere Antworten oder Fragen Bezug nehmen, das Dialogprotokoll inspizieren oder den Dialog abbrechen). Gegenüber einem rein reaktivem Interaktionsstil ergeben sich hier *natürlichere Dialogformen,* die Assoziationen zur zwischenmenschlichen Konversation nahelegen. Natürlich werden subtilere Reaktionsweisen eines Systems auf derart vielgestaltige Benutzeräußerungen notwendig, das System muß das natürliche Dialogverhalten des Benutzers verstehen, dabei möglichst auch individuelle Eigenarten des Benutzers berücksichtigen und selbst geeignete Dialogstrategien zur Befriedigung seines Informationsbedarfs besitzen.

Eine weitere Dimension eröffnet sich durch Einbeziehung (eingeschränkter Formen) der *natürlichen Sprache.* Die menschliche Sprache (auch in ihrer schriftlichen, über Tastatur eingebbaren Form) besitzt eine nahezu unbegrenzte Ausdruckskraft, die sie auch als Metasprache für alle spezielleren (z.B. formalen) Sprachen prädestiniert und steht über ihr umfangreiches Begriffssystem in engster Wechselbeziehung zum menschlichen Wissen. Leider ist das Verstehen natürlichsprachlicher Äußerungen (die in der Regel mehrdeutig und fragmentarisch sind) sehr kompliziert und zudem stark kontext- und situationsabhängig. Trotz beachtlicher Fortschritte auf dem Gebiet der inhaltsorientierten automatischen Sprachverarbeitung (Wahl 82) ist auf absehbare Zeit nicht mit einer vollen Sprachbeherrschung automatischer Systeme zu rechnen, da hierfür nahezu die volle menschliche Intelligenz und Erfahrung nachgebildet werden müßten. Hingegen sind für spezielle technische Anwendungen zweckmäßige Formen partiellen Sprachverstehen entwickelbar, die die Mensch-Maschine-Interaktion wie auch die Bedeutungsanalyse natürlichsprachlich fixierten Wissens in bestimmten Situationen weiter erleichtern können. Natürlichsprachliche Benutzerschnittstellen zur Abfrage von Datenbanken stellen heute eine besonders anwendungsnahe Klasse solcher Systeme dar (Lehm 83a). Bei vielen wissensbasierten Systemen wird der Darstellungsaspekt der natürlichen Sprache (gegenüber dem Kommunikationsaspekt) eine vorherrschende Rolle spielen.

Eine weitere Dimension (bei gleichzeitig hinzutretenden zusätzlichen Schwierigkeiten und Effizienzproblemen) stellt die Fähigkeit zum automatischen *Verstehen und Erzeugen gesprochener menschlicher Sprache* dar. Hier ist zunächst an sehr restringierte Sprachen (z.B. Kommandosprachen) oder Wortschätze zu denken, die von der natürlichen menschlichen Sprachkommunikation noch weiter entfernt sind als im Falle der o.g. natürlichsprachlichen Dialogsysteme mit Tastatureingabe. Dagegen spielt bei technischer Ausnutzung dieser Möglichkeiten die Erschließung des akustischen Kanals mit seinen vom Herkömmlichen weitgehend abweichenden (vor- und nachteiligen) Eigenschaften für die Mensch-Maschine-Kommunikation eine wesentliche Rolle.

Obwohl die Annäherung natürlichsprachlicher Dialogfähigkeiten heute vielen Anwendern als das Nonplusultra auf dem Gebiet der Mensch-Maschine-Kommunikation erscheint, muß von Fall zu Fall sorgfältig geprüft werden, ob für den angestrebten Zweck nicht ein anderes Modell als das der (symmetrischen) zweiseitigen menschlichen Konversation angemessen ist. Als Alternativen kämen etwa das Modell des Werkzeuggebrauchs oder des Navigierens durch eine Wissensbasis in Betracht, was vielfach auch zu einfacheren und kostengünstigeren Lösungen führen könnte. Über die Kombinationsmöglichkeiten und -probleme verschiedener Eingabeformen, etwa Tastatureingabe, grafische Eingabe über die Maus und Benutzung gesprochener Sprachkommandos, gibt es noch kaum Erfahrungen.

5. Problemlösefähigkeit

Unter *Programmieren* im herkömmlichen Sinne versteht man die genaue *Ausarbeitung eines Ablaufplanes* für die in einer algorithmischen Sprache spezifizierbaren, vom Rechner ausführbaren Operationsfolgen. Als *"automatisches Problemlösen"* bezeichnet man demgegenüber die Fähigkeit, ausgehend von einer global und vorwiegend deskriptiv spezifizierten Anforderungssituation (gegeben als Ausgangszustand und Zielspezifikation) *durch Such- oder Deduktionsprozesse* unter Einsatz zulässiger Elementarhandlungen, die in geeigneter Reihenfolge ausgeführt werden, *einen gangbaren Lösungsweg und damit das gewünschte Resultat zu finden.* Dies geschieht durch (in gewissem Sinne nichtdeterministische) Such- und Deduktionsprozesse, die zulässige Elementaroperationen in geeigneter Weise anwenden. Wegen der vielfach enormen Anzahl von Kombinationsmöglichkeiten solcher elementaren Transformations- oder Verknüpfungsschritte kommt es beim Problemlösen darauf an, sukzessive durch geschickte

Auswahl zwischen den jeweiligen Handlungsalternativen einen möglichst geradlinig zum Ziel führenden Weg unter Vermeidung häufiger Schleifen und Sackgassen einzuschlagen. Im einzelnen sind hierzu *unterschiedliche Problemlösemodelle* (etwa unter Zugrundelegung heuristisch gelenkter Graphensuche, des prädikatenlogischen Theorembeweisens oder der interpretativen Abarbeitung von Produktionensystemen) entwickelt (Nilsson 80, Rich 83) und an exemplarischen Anwendungsbeispielen untersucht worden. Vor dem Hintergrund dieser Problemlösemodelle wurden *generelle Lösungsstrategien* definiert, deren Effizienz durch Einbeziehung *problemspezifischer Heuristiken* noch weiter gesteigert werden kann.

Der Aufwand für die Spezifikation des *"Wie"* der Informationsverarbeitung soll hier also wesentlich gesenkt werden, jedoch müssen dazu für die Spezifikation des *"Was"*, also für die Repräsentation anwendungs- und anforderungsspezifischen Wissens, qualitativ höhere Techniken verfügbar sein. Das Problem des Findens einer adäquaten Repräsentation des zur Lösung benötigten anforderungsspezifischen Wissens wird allerdings durch die o.g. Problemlösemodelle kaum berührt.

Problemlösefähigkeiten machen einen wesentlichen Teil der besonderen Qualifikation eines Fachexperten aus und werden daher auch *als Kernbereich der Funktionsweise eines Expertensystems* betrachtet. Soweit ein spezielles Anwendungsgebiet also nur das Abfragen explizit gespeicherter Fakten oder die Abarbeitung vollständig spezifizierter deterministischer Handlungsvorschriften erfordert, wäre hierfür kein wirkliches Expertensystem erforderlich.

Eine in ihrer Struktur relativ einfach erfaßbare und daher von existierenden Expertensystemen vorrangig nachgebildete Problemklasse ist das (meist mehrstufige) *Klassifizieren von Objekten* anhand vorliegender Merkmale bzw. das *Entscheiden* zwischen einer Anzahl vorgegebener Alternativen in einer bestimmten Situation. Diesem als besonders *statisch* zu betrachtenden Problemtyp lassen sich im Prinzip bereits existierende *logische oder wahrscheinlichkeitstheoretische Entscheidungsverfahren* zugrundelegen, die nach Bedarf zur Berücksichtigung *unvollständigen, unsicheren und vagen Wissens, spezieller Berechnungsvorschriften* und unterschiedlicher *Bewertungskriterien* zu modifizieren sind. Im Prinzip werden dabei jedoch lediglich aus einer vorgegebenen Charakterisierung eines Objekts (oder Zustandes) bestimmte (u.U. eingeschränkt) gültige Aussagen über das fragliche Objekt abgeleitet (deduziert), ohne daß dieses selbst dabei verändert würde. In der Auseinandersetzung mit dieser Problemklasse entstand übrigens der Begriff einer generellen "Inferenzmaschine", die die Schlußfolgerungsfähigkeit eines wissensbasierten Systems inkorporieren und durch schrittweises Verknüpfen geeignet ausgewählter Elemente einer Wissensbasis die gewünschten Lösungen erzeugen soll.

In den Bereich der Klassifizierungsprobleme fallen beispielsweise Anforderungen der Katalogauswahl, der Mustererkennung, Signalverarbeitung und Meßwertinterpretation sowie vereinfachte Modelle der (techn. oder medizin.) Diagnose, wirtschaftlichen oder finanziellen Variantenentscheidung und der juristische Entscheidungsfindung.

Ein Beispiel für klassifizierende Expertensysteme ist das bei Siemens entwickelte prototypische Diagnosesystem ABDIA für die Diagnose akuter Bauchkrankheiten. Das allgemeine diagnostische Wissen von ABDIA (ABdomen-DIAgnose) ist in einer Menge von Wenn-Dann-Regeln enthalten, die Zusammenhänge zwischen Krankheitsanzeichen (Symptomen, physischen und technischen Untersuchungsergebnissen und Labortests) und Krankheitshypothesen beschreiben und mit abgestuften Gültigkeitsgraden versehen sind.

Andere Anforderungsklassen besitzen demgegenüber einen ausgeprägt *dynamischen* Charakter wie z.B. das *Entwerfen* neuer Gebilde aus vorgegebenen Grundelementen oder das *Planen* (komplex aufeinander bezogener, zeitlich koordinierter Handlungsabläufe). Hier werden alternative Möglichkeiten des *schrittweisen Aufbauens und Veränderns* von Objekten und Strukturen in Richtung auf bestimmte Zielanforderungen verfolgt. Dabei müssen die vergleichend zu beurteilenden möglichen *Gestaltungsalternativen sorgfältig auseinandergehalten* und in separierbaren Teilen der Wissensbasis gespeichert werden.

Zu diesem Typ gehören etwa Aufgaben wie Systemkonfigurierung, Entwurf und Konstruktion technischer Gebilde, Planung komplexer zeitlicher Abläufe, Steuern und Regeln von Prozessen, Simulation des Zeitverhaltens physikalischer, ökologischer oder wirtschaftlicher Systeme.

Zur Illustration diene etwa das bei Siemens entwickelte Expertensystem SICONFEX (Lehm 85a, Lehm 85b) zur Konfigurierung von Betriebssystemen für SICOMP-Prozeßrechner. Es besitzt heterogene Architektur unter starker Berücksichtigung einer objektorientierten Repräsentation und ein für den praktischen Einsatz ausgelegtes grafisches Benutzerinterface.

Die theoretische Basis für die Beherrschung dieser Problemklassen ist z.Zt. noch unzureichend entwickelt, könnte aber in den nächsten Jahren stärker ausgebaut werden. Für die allmähliche Einbeziehung kreativer menschlicher Tätigkeiten werden in noch stärkerem Maße dynamische Modelle benötigt, die die Alternativen der zeitlichen Entwicklungsmöglichkeiten bestimmter Strukturen zu repräsentieren und zu manipulieren gestatten und zusätzlich mit einer gewissen Lernfähigkeit ausgestattet sind. Es scheint klar, daß die hier zugrundezulegenden Fähigkeiten entsprechender wissensbasierter Systeme *nicht allein auf Schlußfolgerungsvermögen* (Deduktion, Inferenz) *zurückführbar* sein können, sondern vielfältigere Intelligenzleistungen (*Kombinationsfähigkeit, räumliches Vorstellungsvermögen, Analogiebildung, begriffliches Denken, Abstraktion, induktives Schließen*) beinhalten. Infolgedessen ist in diesem Bereich nicht damit zu rechnen, daß durch Bereitstellung eines einzigen generellen Mechanismus (oder - technisch gesprochen - einer *shell*) diese höchst unterschiedlichen Fähigkeiten nachgebildet werden können.

Vielmehr müssen Funktionsmodelle für eine größere Anzahl typischer Intelligenzleistungen entwickelt werden, was schon allein ein umfangreiches Pensum an Vorlaufarbeiten beinhaltet, und sodann den Erfordernissen bestimmter Aufgaben gemäß angepaßt und kombiniert werden. Dies erfordert noch umfangreiche Vorfeldarbeiten, ohne die langfristig eine Verbreiterung der kommerziellen Einsatzgebiete dieser Technologie nicht möglich ist.

6. Expertensysteme

6.1. Begriffsbestimmung

Obwohl in letzter Zeit unübersehbar viel über Expertensysteme geschrieben wurde, fehlt immer noch eine allgemein akzeptierte Begriffsbestimmung, was den Stellenwert globaler inhaltlicher Aussagen (etwa über Besonderheiten, Vorteile, Schwierigkeiten oder Marktchancen von Expertensystemen) wesentlich schmälert. Wir sollten uns daher nicht auf eine zu einseitige Begriffsbestimmung festlegen, aber auch nicht in das andere Extrem der beliebigen Neudefinition durch eigenwillige Auslegung des Wortsinnes verfallen, sondern der historischen Entwicklung gemäß diejenigen Aspekte als definitionsrelevant herausarbeiten, durch die sich in der Vergangenheit die unter dieser Bezeichnung subsumierten Systeme von anderen (innerhalb und außerhalb der AI entwickelten) Systemtypen unterschieden. Dies führt uns zur Berücksichtigung von drei unterschiedlichen Aspekten bei der Begriffsbestimmung, die möglichst alle erfüllt sein sollten (Lehm 83):

i) Expertensysteme sind *wissensbasierte Programmsysteme* zur automatischen oder interaktiven *Lösung spezieller Symbolmanipulationsprobleme,* kurz gesagt: *wissensbasierte Problemlöser,* die auf der Basis einschlägigen Fachwissens durch gezieltes schlußfolgerndes Verknüpfen unter Einbeziehung problemspezifischer heuristischer Methoden bearbeitbar sind *(methodischer Aspekt)* .

ii) Die zu lösenden Probleme entspringen aus *realen Bedürfnissen existierender Tätigkeitsbereiche* (z.B. Naturwissenschaften, Medizin, Technik) und sind von echter *praktischer Bedeutung* für das entsprechende Gebiet (*pragmatischer Aspekt*).

iii) Die zu lösenden Probleme sind von *beträchtlicher Schwierigkeit* und erfordern zu ihrer Bearbeitung normalerweise hochqualifizierte und *erfahrene Experten* (*qualitativer Aspekt*).

Expertensysteme sind also *nicht* Systeme für Experten oder von Experten, sind nicht mit Theorembeweisern, deduktiven Datenbanken oder beliebigen LISP- oder PROLOG-Programmen gleichzusetzen, sind nicht benutzerfreundliche Programmierumgebungen oder Dialogsysteme zur (u.U. natürlichsprachlichen) Wissensabfrage, sie sind auch nicht mit regelbasierten Systemen deckungsgleich und stellen keinesfalls ein Synonym für den gesamten Bereich der anwendungsorientierten AI dar.

Expertensysteme sollen bestimmte Bereiche bereits *vorhandenen* Expertenwissens *nachbilden* und zu speziellen Problemlösungen heranziehen, nicht jedoch noch fehlendes menschliches Expertenwissen ersetzen. Sie übernehmen damit *Routineaufgaben hochqualifizierter Fachleute* und führen diese u.U. schneller, billiger oder zuverlässiger aus, sicher auch oft weniger flexibel und umsichtig als Menschen.

Expertensysteme, die auf das Wissen einer ganzen Fachdisziplin zugreifen können, sind derzeit noch nicht in Sicht. Der Grund hierfür liegt ganz eindeutig nicht in der mangelnden Einbeziehung von Massenspeichern und der unzureichenden Effizienz heutiger Inferenzverfahren, sondern primär im Fehlen hinreichend universeller Repräsentationsmittel und im enormen Aufwand, den die vollständige formale Durcharbeitung schon von sehr kleinen Wissensbereichen verursacht.

De facto läßt sich zusätzlich feststellen, daß Expertensysteme zwar in gewissem Sinne die Lösung bestimmter anspruchsvoller Probleme in einem Anwendungsgebiet übernehmen können, ob dies jedoch als ein "Ersetzen des menschlichen Experten" bezeichnet werden darf, ist zu bezweifeln. Expertensysteme sind immer nur dann erfolgreich, wenn sie innerhalb eines fachlich strikt begrenzbaren schmalen Wissensbereiches operieren, ohne dafür menschliches Alltagswissen zu benötigen. Ein menschlicher Fachexperte - Arzt, Ingenieur oder Jurist - und sei er noch so spezialisiert, könnte ohne seine vielfältigen, genuin menschlichen Fähigkeiten wohl kaum beruflich erfolgreich sein!

6.2. Unterschiedliche Einsatzumgebungen

Der bei Expertensystemen anzutreffende außerordentlich hohe Diversifikationsgrad äußert sich nicht nur in unterschiedlichsten Systemarchitekturen und Anwendungsfeldern, sondern auch im Benutzerinterface und in der Einsatzumgebung. Expertensysteme können interaktiv sein oder auch ohne menschliche Eingriffsmöglichkeit arbeiten, die Spezifikation des Problems und die Einflußnahme auf das Lösungsverhalten kann über Menüs, eine Kommandosprache, graphische Eingabeformen oder (quasi-)natürlichsprachlich erfolgen, wobei die Dialoginitiative entweder (meist) beim System liegt, mitunter aber auch zeitweise an den Benutzer übergehen kann. Viele Systeme haben keine Erklärungsfähigkeit, die meisten können nicht interaktiv belehrt werden; in bestimmten Einsatzumgebungen wären solche Fähigkeiten auch kaum sinnvoll oder wünschenswert.

Während die ersten Expertensysteme experimentelle Programmsysteme waren, die als Forschungsvehikel dienten, und sich daraus teilweise selbstständige Softwarepakete als praktisch einsetzbare Prototypen entwickelten, wird sich mit der Zeit die Tendenz zur kostenoptimalen speziellen Implementierung einerseits und zur Kopplung und Integration bzgl. vorhandener Systeme andererseits verstärken. Als Endprodukt einer Expertensystem-Entwicklung erscheint vielfach ein minimiertes, auf preisgünstigen Mikroprozessoren ablauffähiges Programmsystem (etwa als Anwendersoftware für PC's) oder sogar eine spezielle Hardwareimplementation (als "hand held expert system oder zum Einbau in

Geräte, Fahrzeuge und Anlagen) wünschenswert. Solchen Endstadien einer über mehrere Etappen führenden Entwicklung wird man oft das für Expertensysteme Typische kaum mehr ansehen. Allein der Gebrauchswert und nicht die Behauptung, daß es sich hier um ein AI-Produkt handelt, sollten die Marktchancen eines solchen Systems bestimmen.

Mit fortschreitender Entwicklung wird sich aber auch das Bedürfnis nach Kopplung mehrerer Expertensysteme verstärken. Expertensysteme könnten durchaus die Rolle einer intelligenten Dialogkomponente für ein größeres konventionelles Softwaresystem übernehmen oder als Supervisor für das Zusammenspiel der einzelnen (bereits vorhandenen) Softwarekomponenten eines komplexen Systems dienen.

6.3. Anwendungsfelder

Für ein großes Elektrotechnik-Unternehmen wie Siemens untergliedern sich die Einsatzmöglichkeiten von Expertensystemen zunächst grob in
i) solche für den *internen Bedarf* (zur Unterstützung von Entwicklung, Fertigung, Kundendienst und Verwaltung) und
ii) solche, die in die diversen *Produkte* (vom Telefon bis zum Großkraftwerk) eingehen.
Außerdem sind reine *Anwendungssysteme* von *Entwicklungswerkzeugen* zu unterscheiden.

Ein Vorzug eines großen Unternehmens besteht bei der Erschließung neuer Anwendungsgebiete zweifellos darin, daß unterschiedlichste Systeme zunächst *im internen Einsatz erprobt* werden können, bevor sie nach ihrer firmeninternen Bewährung auf dem Markt erscheinen.

Im folgenden sollen mögliche *Anwendungsfelder für den industriellen Einsatz* von Expertensystemen skizziert werden.

a) *Selbständig vermarktbare Anwendersoftware* für AI-workstations, mainframes und PCs, die u.U. auch über öffentliche Rechnernetze oder BTX zur Verfügung gestellt wird, kann zur Unterstützung von Diagnose, Konfigurierung, Entwurfs- und Planungsprozessen dienen oder auch den Zugang zu umfangreichen Softwaresystemen (z.B. Betriebssystemen, CAD-systemen, Programmbibliotheken) erleichtern. Ein vielseitiges Aufgabengebiet liegt sicher im Bereich der Marktberatung (Vergleich spezifizierter Käuferwünsche mit vorliegenden Angeboten). Hierbei ist auch an einfache Beratungssysteme für Telefonbenutzer zu denken (etwa an einen "yellow page assistent").
b) *Hardwaremäßig realisierte Expertensysteme* im Taschenrechnerformat (für Wartungsingenieure, Steuerberater, Versicherungsagenten) oder als Bestandteile größerer technischer Systeme (Fahrzeuge, Präzisionsmeßgeräte) dürften am ehesten in großen Stückzahlen vermarktbar sein, auch wenn durch sie nur relativ einfache Aufgaben bearbeitet werden.
c) Bedeutende technische Einsatzmöglichkeiten für Expertensysteme sind bei der *technischen Fehlerdiagnose* in den verschiedensten Bereichen zu erwarten.

d) Bei der *Steuerung und Überwachung technischer Prozesse* (z.B. in Kraftwerken, Schaltwarten, in der chemischen Industrie) sind die real-time-Anforderungen an Expertensysteme und deren Anteil numerischer Operationen oft recht hoch, daher spielt die Effizienz der Implementierung (u.U. in der Endversion in konventionelleren Programmiersprachen) eine große Rolle.

e) Ebenfalls ein sehr umfangreiches Einsatzgebiet eröffnet sich im Bereich der *Fertigungsautomatisierung* (Einsatzplanung, Fertigungsplanung, Maschinenbelegung, Einsatzvorbereitung und Wartung von Industrierobotern).

f) Auf dem bereits stark automatisierten Gebiet der Entwicklung von *Digitalschaltungen* und *Computer-Hardware* ist ein allmähliches Vordringen wissensbasierter Verfahren zu erwarten, da diese ein höheres Maß an Flexibilität zulassen. Allerdings befindet sich das Expertenwissen hier teilweise so rasch im Fluß, daß dessen Nachbildung durch ein Expertensystem auf prinzipielle Schwierigkeiten stoßen kann. Auch bei der technologischen Überwachung der Chip-Fabrikation und der Ursachenforschung beim Auftreten von Fabrkationsfehlern können Expertensysteme eine wesentliche Rolle spielen.

g) Die *Software-Entwicklung* wird ohnehin ganz unmittelbar durch die Methodik für die Schaffung wissensbasierter Systeme bereichert. Ein besonders interessantes Forschungsgebiet stellen Verfahren der globalen interaktiven Programmspezifikation und automatischen Programmerzeugung dar. Hierzu werden die unterschiedlichsten Ansätze verfolgt. Gut vermarktbar dürften auch benutzerfreundliche wissensbasierte Zugangssysteme zu Datenbanken, Betriebssystemen, Bürosystemen und Programmbibliotheken sein. Ein weiteres Spezialgebiet könnten wissensbasierte Lehr- und Trainingssysteme für das Erlernen von Programmiersprachen sein. Längerfristig erscheinen wissensbasierte Beratungssysteme mit sehr komfortablen Formen des Mensch-Maschine-Dialogs recht verheißungsvoll, die sich an die Besonderheiten der individuellen Benutzer anpassen können.

6.4. Kriterien für die Auswahl von Anwendungsfeldern

Bei den zahlreichen definitorischen Einschränkungen (vgl. 6.1.) und ungelösten Forschungsproblemen (Davi 82, Bobr 85) stellt die richtige Auswahl von Einsatzgebieten und Aufgabenstellungen für Projekte zur Entwicklung von Expertensystemen eine sehr anspruchsvolle und in ihrer Tragweite für den weiteren Projektverlauf kaum zu überschätzende Aufgabe dar (vgl. auch Prer 85). Die folgenden Stichworte und Fragen sollen als Hinweise auf die dabei zu berücksichtigenden Kriterien und Randbedingungen betrachtet werden.

Fachgebiet
Wieweit gibt es eine spezielle Fachterminologie, ein feststehendes fachspezifisches Begriffssystem? Wird das Gebiet bereits zufriedenstellend verstanden? Gibt es bereits eine gut entwickelte Theorie (für das gesamte Gebiet oder für Teilgebiete)? Kann man sich durch Literaturstudium gut in das Gebiet einarbeiten? Welche Literatur ist zur Einarbeitung geeignet?

Technisch-methodische Charakteristika des Anwendungsbereichs
Welche Rolle spielen Berechnungen, Tabellen, große Datenbanken, logische Darstellungsmittel, empirisch gewonnene Einzeltatsachen, plausibles Schließen, statistische Verfahren, Meßwerte und Meßfehler, interaktiv einzugebende Problemspezifikationen, natürlichsprachige Eingabeformen, graphische Darstellungsmöglichkeiten, Forderungen nach Lernfähigkeit?

Aufgabenstellung
Ist die Aufgabenstellung klar? Ist die Aufgabe gegenüber benachbarten Aufgaben gut abgrenzbar? Müssen Entscheidungskriterien aus umfangreichem empirischen Material abgeleitet werden? Existieren schriftliche Unterlagen? Wieweit sind diese aufbereitet und für den Außenstehenden verständlich ? Ähnelt die Aufgabenstellung der anderer in der Literatur beschriebener Expertensysteme? Gibt es objektivierbare Bewertungskriterien für die Güte der gefundenen Lösungen? Gibt es eine Sammlung instruktiver Fallbeispiele? Gibt es andere konkurrierende Lösungsansätze?

Quantitative Anforderungen
Welcher zeitliche Rahmen für die Projektbearbeitung ist vorgesehen? Wie umfangreich ist das zu berücksichtigende Wissen? Ist die verfügbare Speicherkapazität begrenzt? Wie stark verändert sich das Anwendungswissen voraussichtlich während der Bearbeitungszeit? Gibt es zeitkritische Anforderungen? Sind gelegentliche Systemabstürze tolerierbar? Wie zuverlässig muß das System sein?

Qualitative Anforderungen
Schwierigkeitsgrad, Komplexitätsgrad, Innovationsgrad, sind neue Forschungsresultate erforderlich?

Was soll durch Entwicklung und Einsatz des projektierten Expertensystems bewirkt werden?
Hohe Qualität von Entscheidungen, hohe Zuverlässigkeit, ständige Verfügbarkeit (24 Stunden pro Tag), geringer Programmieraufwand, geringer Rechenaufwand, hohe Reaktionsgeschwindigkeit, zweitrangiger Ersatz für zu knappe oder zu teure hochspezialisierte Experten, know-how-Sicherung und Tradierung von Expertenwissen, terminologische Vereinheitlichung, Vereinheitlichung individuell stark differierender Vorgehensweisen, Objektivierung von Verfahrensweisen und Heuristiken, Bewältigung einer höheren Komplexität, Kumulation des Wissens verschiedener Experten für aneinander grenzende Aufgabenbereiche, Entlastung menschlicher Experten von relativ monotonen Routineaufgaben, Substitution menschlicher Arbeitskräfte, Einsatzfähigkeit an unzugänglichen, gefährlichen oder unwirtlichen Orten.

Verfügbarkeit und Kompetenz der Anwendungsexperten
Welche Qualifikation (d.h. Ausbildung und Erfahrung), unbestrittene Autorität in ihrem Tätigkeitsbereich haben diese? Welche Fähigkeiten zur Verbalisierung oder sonstigen Vermittlung ihres Wissens haben die Experten? Wie genau ist die jeweils vorhandene Expertise abgrenzbar? Wieweit sind die Experten für die Mitwirkung an dem Projekt verfügbar (etwa durch zeitweilige Freistellung von ihren sonstigen Aufgaben)? Wieweit sind sie dem Anliegen des Projekts gegenüber aufgeschlossen, verständnisvoll und kooperativ? Fühlen sich die Experten in ihrer beruflichen Existenz, ihrem Ansehen oder ihrem Selbstwertgefühl durch das Projekt bedroht? Sollen mehrere Experten oder nur ein einziger als Wissenslieferant herangezogen werden?

Spezifika des Entwicklungsteams
Wieviele Mitarbeiter stehen zur Verfügung? Wie ist deren Qualifikation? Welche AI-Erfahrungen besitzen diese (Vertrautheit mit bestimmten Problemklassen, Methoden, Programmiersprachen, AI-Tools)? Welche für die Aufgabenstellung relevanten technischen Vorkenntnisse sind vorhanden? Gibt es einen fachlichen Konsens oder ständige Verständigungsprobleme und Rivalitäten?

Weitere zu berücksichtigende Gesichtspunkte betreffen die Vorgeschichte (Wurden schon mehrfach fehlgeschlagene Anstrengungen unternommen?), die Projektverantwortung und Steuerung (Wer wünscht das Projekt? Wer wählt die Aufgabenstellung aus? Wer legt die Projektlaufzeit und die Kosten fest? Wer kontrolliert den Projektfortschritt? Wer beurteilt das erreichte Ergebnis?), die Erwartungshaltung der Auftraggeber und Anwender (unkritische oder überkritische Attitüden) und die Vorstellungen über Nutzen und Bedeutung des Projekts.

Gegenwärtig muß es als normal betrachtet werden, daß die meisten Projektvorschläge für die Entwicklung eines Expertensystems einer sorgfältigen Prüfung nicht standhalten und daher eine Weiterverfolgung unter den gegebenen Umständen als wenig aussichtsreich erscheint. Das bedeutet, daß die heutige Technologie der Expertensysteme noch in keiner Weise flächendeckend ist, was angesichts der unterschiedlichsten Anwendungsbereiche und Einsatzumgebungen sowie des hohen Stellenwerts schwer zu beurteilender subjektiver Faktoren nicht verwundern kann.

Zur Verringerung des Risikos kann sicher die Auswahl solcher Aufgabenstellungen beitragen, die in ähnlicher Weise bereits früher erfolgreich gelöst worden sind oder dem Entwicklungsteam gut vertraut sind. Andererseits kann es sehr wertvoll sein, sich auf technisches Neuland vorzuwagen und neue methodische Ansätze zu erproben. Dies sollte jedoch ohne massiven Zeitdruck und Erfolgszwang geschehen und dem Entwicklungsteam die Möglichkeit zur Reflexion und Weitergabe der gewonnenen Erfahrungen geben.

Besonders sollte darauf geachtet werden, daß im Rahmen eines einzigen im Anfangsstadium befindlichen Projektes, das sich immer zunächst intensiv um das Verstehen der Aufgabenstellung und die Strukturierung von Wissensbasis und Problemlösefähigkeit zu bemühen hat, nicht eine große Zahl zusätzlicher softwaretechnischer Anforderungen (wie extreme Effizienz, Mehrfachbenutzung, Recovery, Portabilität, spezielle Programmiersprachen, Integration in komplexe existierende Systeme) hineingetragen wird, die von den zentralen Problemen ablenken. Als erste Aufgabe ist immer die prinzipielle Funktionsweise des zu entwickelnden Systems zu klären. Erst wenn dies gelungen ist (was keinesfalls selbstverständlich ist), muß man sich erforderlichenfalls einer Reihe weiterer technischer Probleme zuwenden. Bis zur Integration in einen umfassenderen Betriebsablauf oder ein komplexes Informationssystem und zur Akzeptanz durch den echten Anwender ist dann freilich noch ein weiter Weg zurückzulegen.

6.5. Erhoffte Auswirkungen eines industriellen Engagements

Die Entwicklung von Expertensystemen führt nicht nur zu einer ganzen Pallette neuer Anwendungssysteme und Software-Werkzeuge, sondern auch zu neuen Entwicklungsverfahren im Bereich der Softwaretechnik, darüber hinaus in verschiedenen Fachdisziplinen zu neuen Methoden des Erkenntnisgewinns und der weiteren Objektivierung und Akkumulation von Fachwissen. Bei der Gesamtbewertung des Nutzens eines industriellen Engagements in diesem Bereich ist vielleicht der technologische Aspekt wichtiger als die möglichen Endprodukte. Schon allein die routinemäßige Beherrschung hochmoderner Softwareumgebungen und unkonventioneller Programmierstile kann wesentlich zu innovativen Ergebnissen beitragen.

7. Marktlage und Perspektiven industrieller Nutzung

Die wissensbasierte Informationsverarbeitung gilt heute als eine der wesentlichen zukünftigen Hochtechnologien. Besonders das japanische Forschungsprogramm "Fifth Generation Computer Systems", dessen Ziel die Entwicklung einer Basistechnologie für die Wissensverarbeitung und damit für einen sehr viel breiteren Einsatz von Computern ist, hat international große Beachtung erfahren und damit einen neuen Forschungswettlauf ausgelöst. Die Erfolge einzelner Expertensysteme - besonders hervorzuheben ist hier das

Konfigurierungssystem R1/XCON der Firma DEC - haben hohe Erwartungen an die Marktwirksamkeit dieser Technologie erzeugt.

Die in der folgenden Tabelle (Wiig 84) aufgrund nicht unrealistischer Betrachtungen vorausgesagte Umsatzentwicklung von AI-Produkten zeigt, auch bei Berücksichtigung erheblicher Vorhersageunsicherheit, auf jeden Fall eine ganz enormes Wachstumspotential innerhalb der nächsten zehn Jahre, was weitreichende Auswirkungen nach sich ziehen wird.

	AI Umsatz (Mrd.$)	Gesamtumsatz d. Computerindustrie	prozentualer Anteil
1984	0,15	148	0,1
1985	0,25	158	0,16
1990	11,8	267	4
1995	67	348	20
2000	113	422	26

Bei den heute auf dem Markt angebotenen AI-Produkten stehen die auf eine AI-Sprache spezialisierten Hardwaresysteme einschließlich der entsprechenden, meist LISP-basierten Softwareentwicklungsumgebung im Vordergrund. Die Anzahl der (seit 1981) bis Mitte 1985 weltweit ausgelieferten LISP-Maschinen dürfte bei 3000 bis 4000 liegen, ist also noch recht gering. Jedoch befindet sich der Markt in raschem Wachstum.

Bei Expertensystemen ist eine gewisse Vorsicht bei Betrachtungen zur heutigen und mittelfristigen Marktsituation angebracht. Der Anteil "erfolgreicher" Expertensysteme unter den bisher abgeschlossenen oder noch laufenden Projekten ist noch nicht besonders hoch. Als erfolgreich kann man zunächst ein System betrachten, das seine Fähigkeiten nachgewiesen hat, für anspruchsvolle Leistungsanforderungen auf einem praxisrelevanten Gebiet prinzipiell vernünftig einsetzbar zu sein. Beispiele hierfür sind etwa die bekannten Systeme MYCIN (Shor 76) und PROSPECTOR (Camp 82). Nur bei sehr wenigen Systemen ist der nächste Schritt gelungen, der den routinemäßigen und ökonomischen Einsatz in einem Anwendungsbereich und die Integration in die jeweilige Anwendungsumgebung beinhaltet. Diese Systeme sind jedoch so stark auf den speziellen Einsatz und den Auftraggeber hin entwickelt, daß es wenig sinnvoll erscheint, diese auf dem Markt anzubieten. Ein nennenswertes Angebot anwendungsspezifischer Expertensysteme scheint es heute nicht zu geben, zumal über wirkliche Verkaufserfolge praktisch keine zuverlässigen Informationen vorliegen. Solche Systeme erscheinen am ehesten vermarktbar, wenn sie "praktische Lebenshilfe" in speziellen Situationen (Einkommensteuer, Autopanne, Finanzierungsberatung) für einen Benutzerkreis, u. U. auch in Unterhaltungs- und Hobbybereich anbieten oder (hochtechnisch realisiert) etwa in Fahrzeugen oder technischen Geräten integriert sind. Vermutlich werden auch in den nächsten Jahren anwendungsspezifische Expertensysteme vorwiegend individuell entwickelt werden (vom Anwender selbst oder von einer AI-Firma im Kundenauftrag). Mittelfristig muß man allerdings neben der Vermarktung von Expertensystemen auch damit rechnen, daß Beratungsleistungen bestimmter Expertensysteme kommerziell verfügbar gemacht werden.

Wesentlich größer sind die derzeitigen kommerziellen Aktivitäten bei der Vermarktung von Software-Tools und Entwicklungssystemen, die den Anwender beim Aufbau maßgeschneiderter wissensbasierter Systeme unterstützen sollen. Manche Tools können sehr einfach (z.B. für PCs), andere sehr komplex sein. Sie sind zur Zeit für den Kaufinteressenten äußerst schwierig zu beurteilen und zu vergleichen. Für den Anbieter von AI-Workstations stellt die Verfügbarkeit einer breiten Palette solcher Tools derzeit ein gewichtiges Verkaufsargument dar.

Vielfach fallen solche Werkzeuge im Zuge der durchgeführten Entwicklungsarbeiten mehr oder weniger von selbst an, wobei seitens der Entwickler ein verständliches Interesse an einer über den ursprünglichen Einsatzbereich hinausgehenden Ergebnisnutzung besteht. Falls jedoch ein potentieller Nachnutzer nicht ohnehin mit weitgehend ähnlichen Anwendungsproblemen beschäftigt ist, ist schwer zu sagen, wieweit das angebotene Werkzeug für seine Zwecke nützlich sein kann. Mit diesen Bemerkungen soll natürlich keinesfalls die Brauchbarkeit oder die Notwendigkeit solcher Werkzeuge generell angezweifelt werden. Die Leistungsfähigkeit der Werkzeuge kann tatsächlich entscheidend für den Erfolg eines Projektes sein.

Eine höhere Modularität der Werkzeuge, die die bessere Anpassung an die jeweilige Aufgabenstellung ermöglichen, ist anzustreben. Ein solcher 'Werkzeugkasten' kann beispielsweise unterschiedliche Repräsentationssysteme für die Wissensbasis oder verschiedenen Anwendungsklassen angepaßte Inferenzverfahren enthalten. Die Heterogenität der mit wissensbasierten Methoden bearbeitbaren Anwendungen erfordert im Gegensatz zu manchen Lösungen der klassischen Datenverarbeitung ein hohes Maß an Flexibilität. Dieser Aspekt stellt den Schwerpunkt der Forschungs- und Entwicklungsaktivitäten im Hause Siemens dar.

Ein weiterer Aspekt der derzeitigen Marktsituation sind neu entstandene kleinere Softwarefirmen, die sich neben der Entwicklung von AI-Tools auf bestimmte Anwendungsgebiete von Expertensystemen, z.B. Ölsuche, technische Diagnose, Bankberatung, Molekulargenetik, spezialisiert haben. Sie erbringen vorwiegend Schulungs- und Beratungsleistungen oder entwickeln im Kundenauftrag spezielle Expertensystemlösungen.

Insgesamt gesehen werden Expertensysteme noch immer ganz überwiegend für den Eigenbedarf entwickelt. Der Grund hierfür ist leicht einzusehen: wegen des hohen Spezialisierunsgrades der Expertentätigkeiten, die durch Expertensysteme übernommen werden sollen, konzentriert sich die Entwicklungstätigkeit zunächst auf die Untersuchung von Bedarf und Realisierbarkeit eines solchen Systems in einem ganz konkreten Falle und versucht hierfür ein geeignetes Inferenzmodell auszuwählen und das Expertenwissen entsprechend aufzubereiten. Da der Diversifikationsgrad der im Einsatz befindlichen Experten besonders hoch ist, gilt dies auch für die heute existierenden Expertensysteme. Im allgemeinen dürfte sich erst in einem späteren Stadium herausstellen, wie Systeme für einen breiteren potentiellen Benutzerkreis (Wiederholfaktor!) beschaffen sein müssen. Welche Anteile bei der Entwicklung von Expertensystemen in Zukunft auf Eigenentwicklung, Einzelentwicklung im Auftrag des potentiellen Benutzers bzw. auf dem Markt angebotene Systeme entfallen wird, läßt sich heute noch schwer voraussagen.

Momentan gibt es noch kaum einen "Markt von Expertensystemen" (im Sinne von Softwareprodukten), auf dem hinsichtlich bestimmmter Anforderungsspezifikationen mehrere Anbieter miteinander konkurrieren, während auf dem Gebiet der AI-Maschinen und AI-Tools die Zahl der Anbieter ständig wächst. Prinzipiell ist auch nicht zu erwarten, daß sich früher oder später neben anderen Märkten ein neuer Markt etabliert, der ausschließlich auf Expertensysteme spezialisiert ist. Vielmehr dürften auf den verschiedenen Anwendungsgebieten Expertensysteme mit herkömmlichen Systemen konkurrieren (Hart 84). Sicher wird ein System nicht deswegen gekauft werden, weil es als Expertensystem bezeichnet werden kann, sondern nur dann, wenn es gegenüber herkömmliche gestalteten Softwaresystemen überlegene Gebrauchswerteigenschaften bezüglich eines bestimmmten Einsatzzweckes aufweist. Expertensysteme für verschiedene Einsatzbereiche (z.B. medizinische Diagnose und Schaltungsentwurf) können natürlich nicht miteinander konkurrieren. Marktwirksame wissensbasierte Systeme werden oftmals den Charakter intelligenter Assistenten haben, die in ein umfangreicheres System eingebettet sind. Daneben ist damit zu rechnen, daß gerade auf Anwendungsgebieten, die bisher dem Computereinsatz weitgehend verschlossen blieben (z.B. für biomedizinische Anwendungen oder für den Ausbildungsbereich) bei Angebot sinnvoll konzipierter Expertensysteme schnell eine lebhafte Nachfrage und damit Marktchancen entstehen.

Die für den Eigenbedarf realisierten Systeme sind softwaretechnisch meist noch wenig ausgereift (Durchsichtigkeit, Wartbarkeit, Dokumentation, Schnittstellen), so daß die Voraussetzungen für den Einsatz "außer Haus" auch von dieser Seite fehlen. Auch bezüglich des "Knowledge Engineering" muß sich erst noch herausstellen, wieweit es sich hier um einen relativ homogenen im großen und ganzen nach dem gleichen Schema ablaufenden Tätigkeitsbereich handelt. Andererseits darf die grundsätzliche und langfristige Bedeutung von wissensbasierten Systemen für die Informationstechnologie nicht unterschätzt werden.

Vermutlich werden langfristig die indirekten Auswirkungen auf die Herstellungstechnologie von Software, die Rechnerarchitektur, aber auch Vorgehensweise bei der Gestaltung anderer komplexer Systeme (und vielleicht sogar Organisationen) bedeutender sein als die zu kurzfristig vermarktbaren Software-Paketen führende unmittelbare Nutzanwendung.

7. Organisatorische Aspekte

Für die industrielle Nutzung ist entscheidend, ob und wie die Technologie wissensbasierter Systeme in klassische Produktionsbereiche eingebracht werden kann. Dabei gilt es nicht nur, den Fachexperten mit den neuen Techniken vertraut zu machen, sondern ebenso den AI-Spezialisten mit der oft rauhen Wirklichkeit der täglichen Praxis zu konfrontieren.

Der Aufwand für Know-how-Erwerb bzgl. des Basiswissens ist für Mitarbeiter ohne speziellen Erfahrungen auf dem Gebiet der Wissensverarbeitung beträchtlich. Daher gewinnt neben der objektiv schwierigen Heranführung erfahrener AI-Experten die gezielte externe und interne Weiterbildung vorhandener Mitarbeiter immer mehr Bedeutung. Ein wesentliches Erfordernis bei der Entwicklung spezieller Expertensysteme wird immer die ständige Verfügbarkeit exzellenter menschlicher Fachexperten des jeweiligen Anwendungsfeldes sein. Daher ist es als erstrebenswerter Idealfall anzusehen, wenn im Entwicklungsteam selbst ein gediegenes Know-how über das jeweilige Fachgebiet existiert.

Eine Entscheidung über die technischen Lösungswege und Hilfsmittel kann erst getroffen werden, wenn die fachspezifische Problematik im großen und ganzen inhaltlich klar geworden ist. Es zeichnen sich daher zwei Wege für die Entwicklung spezieller Expertensysteme ab:

Spezialisten für Artificial Intelligence haben bestimmte Techniken für Wissenrepräsentation, Inferenz usw. entwickelt und begeben sich auf die Suche nach einem geeigneten Anwendungsgebiet für Experimente und Demonstrationen

Spezialisten eines bestimmten Fachgebietes erwerben AI-Kenntnisse und -Werkzeuge, z.B. durch Konsultationen oder Kooperation mit AI-Spezialisten, und bauen im wesentlichen in eigener Regie ein Expertensystem auf, meist nach einem bewährten Vorbild.

Eine erfolgversprechende Lösung für den *Know-how-Transfer* zwischen Fachexperten und AI-Spezialisten ist die Etablierung eines *AI-Centers*. Den interessierten Fachleuten wird eine Infrastruktur zur Verfügung gestellt, die erste eigene Erfahrungen mit der Technologie ermöglicht. Das gilt sowohl für die *technische Ausrüstung* als auch für die *fachliche Starthilfe und Betreuung* durch erfahrene Spezialisten. In *gemeinsamen Pilotprojekten* werden Fachwissen und AI-Know-how zusammengeführt. Dadurch wird die Basis für die Nutzung der Technologie wissensbasierter Systeme für praktische Anwendungsfälle verbreitert. Im Endeffekt soll im Laufe einer solchen Entwicklung die Initiative und Verantwortung immer mehr auf die beteiligten Anwendungsspezialisten übergehen, während sich die AI-Spezialisten der Verallgemeinerung der in verschiedenen Projekten gewonnenen Erfahrungen und der Schaffung technologischen Vorlaufs durch Methoden- und Tool-Entwicklung widmen müssen. Dieser Weg wird bei der Siemens AG beschritten.

Auf die Schwierigkeiten der Auswahl erfolgversprechender Projekte für zu entwickelnde Expertensysteme wurde bereits in Abschnitt 6.4 hingewiesen. Die vielseitige, aber keineswegs universelle Einsetzbarkeit dieser Systeme, die durch eine Vielzahl von Randbedingungen eingeschränkt wird, und die weitverbreiteten Fehleinschätzungen der Spezifik und Leistungsfähigkeit dieser Technologie machen eine sorgfältige und *fachkundige Projektauswahl* nach vorangegangener Studienphase unbedingt notwendig. In der Tat sollten Expertensysteme nur für solche Zwecke entwickelt werden, wo man mit einfacheren, konventionelleren Methoden nicht zum Ziel gelangt. Dabei sollten die verfügbaren Ressourcen (vor allem auch bzgl. der Qualifikation des vorhandenen Personals) realistisch eingeschätzt und die Ziele anfangs nicht zu hoch angesetzt werden. Es ist davor zu warnen, die Projektauswahl einseitig nach der Wichtigkeit des Vorhabens oder der Zahlungsfähigkeit des Anwenders zu treffen oder den Projektrahmen von vornherein zu groß anzusetzen, solange nicht die prinzipielle Realisierbarkeit des Projekts nachgewiesen ist. Erfolgreiche Systeme wie DECs R1/XCON haben sich oftmals *schrittweise* aus fast zufälligen, aber erfolversprechenden Einzelaktivitäten heraus entwickelt (vgl. McDE 81, McDe 84, Poli 85). Wegen des beträchtlichen Entwicklungsrisikos sollten besonders zentrale oder dringliche Aufgabenstellungen nicht vorrangig bei der Projektauswahl berücksichtigt werden.

Während die Möglichkeit des rapid prototyping auf eine Verkürzung bisheriger Entwicklungszeiten hinzielt, muß beachtet werden, daß die Entwicklung eines anspruchsvollen AI-Systems die konzeptuelle Auseinandersetzung mit tiefer liegenden Problemen eines Anwendungsgebietes beinhaltet, als dies bei der herkömmlichen Programmierung der Fall ist. So ist es realistisch, eher mit einer deutlich geringeren Gesamtzahl von Mannjahren bei einem solchen Entwicklungsprojekt zu rechnen als mit kurzen Entwicklungszeiten.

9. Zusammenfassung

Zusammenfassend bleibt festzuhalten, daß wissensbasierte Systeme ein enormes Innovationspotential für weite Bereiche der Informationstechnologie und darüber hinaus für die Entwicklung derjenigen Fachdisziplinen und Tätigkeitsbereichen haben, die sich solcher Systeme bedienen. Derzeit erleben wir erst den Beginn einer vielfältigen industriellen Nutzung. Es zeichnet sich ein dynamisches Wachstum ab, dessen Grenzen noch nicht deutlich sichtbar werden, durch das neue Anwendungsfelder erschlossen und herkömmliche softwaretechnische Lösungen verbessert werden können. Im Einsatz bewährte AI-Verfahren werden mit dem Hauptstrom der Informatik verschmelzen, so daß es auf längere Sicht fraglich ist, ob dann noch von AI-Produkten und dem Volumen des AI-Marktes gesprochen werden kann (bzw. was damit gemeint ist).

Gegenwärtig muß man sowohl vor einer Unterschätzung der Bedeutung wissensbasierter Systeme als auch vor übertriebenen Erwartungen warnen, wie sie marktschreierisch oder gesellschaftskritisch durch Werbung und Presse genährt werden. Viele Grundprobleme der AI-Forschung sind noch ungelöst und etliche davon wohl auch unlösbar. Von einer "übermenschlichen Maschinen-Intelligenz" werden wir auch in der nächsten Zeit weit entfernt bleiben. Auch für den menschlichen Erkenntnisprozeß ("knowledge acquisition") gibt es noch kein Patentrezept und die vollkommene rationale Durchdringung und Rekonstruktion nichttrivialer Wirklichkeitsbereiche ("knowledge engineering") wird weiterhin zumindest mühevoll und kostspielig, vielfach auch erfolglos sein. Für die sinnvolle Weiterentwicklung wissensbasierter Systeme sind viel Sachverstand, Behutsamkeit, Kreativität und Geduld erforderlich. Hoffnungen auf rasche Gewinne bei geringem Einsatz werden wohl - wie anderswo auch - meist enttäuscht werden. Langfristige Forschungs-anstrengungen zur Verfeinerung und Bereicherung des derzeitigen methodischen Repertoires und eine Kumulation praktischer Erfahrungen sind erforderlich. Sie werden sich selbst dann bezahlt machen, wenn manche der ursprünglich anvisierten Ziele nicht erreicht werden sollten.

10. Literatur

Bobr 85   Bobrow, D.G.; Hayes, P.J.: Artificial Intelligence - Where Are We? Artificial Intelligence 25 (1985), 375-415

Camp 82   Campbell, A.N.; Hollister, V.F.; Duda, R.O.; Hart, P.E.: Recognition of a Mineral Deposit by an Artificial Intelligence Program. Science 217(1982), 927-929

ClMe 81   Clocksin, W.F.; Mellish, C.S.: Programming in Prolog, Springer Verlag, Berlin, 1981

Davi 82   Davis, R.: Expert Systems: Where Are We? And Where Do We Go From Here? AI Magazine 5 (1982)3, 21-32

GöSt 84   Görz, G., Stoyan, H.: Lisp - eine Einführung in das Progammieren, Springer, Berlin 1984

Hart 84   Hart, P.: Artificial Intelligence in Transition, The AI Magazine 5 (1984) 3, 17-20

Haug 85   Haugeneder, H.; Lehmann, E.; Struss, P.: Knowledge-Based Configuration of Operating Systems - Problems in Modelling the Domain. Proc. International GI Congress '85 on Knowledge-Based Systems, Munich, Oct. 1985 (in this volume)

Lehm 83   Lehmann, E.: Expertensysteme: Überblick über den aktuellen Entwicklungs-stand (1983). Siemens, Zentralbereich Technik, München

Lehm 83a   Lehmann, E.: ISAR - ein experimentelles deutschsprachiges Faktenabfrage-system. In J.M.Schmidt (Hrsg.), *Sprachen für Datenbanken*, Springer, Berlin 1983, 11-25

Lehm 85   Lehmann; E.; Enders; R.; Haugeneder, H.; Hunze, R.; Johnson, C:; Schmid, L.; Struß, P.: SICONFEX - ein Expertensystem für die Konfigurierung eines Betriebssystems. 15. GI-Jahrestagung 1985, Springer 1985

McDe 81   McDermott, J.: R1: The Formative Years. AI Magazine 2 (1981)2, 21-29

McDe 84   McDermott, J.: R1 Revisited: Four Years in the Trenches. AI Magazine 5 (1984)3, 21-32

Nils 80   Nilsson, N.J.: Principles of Artificial Intelligence. Tioga, Palo Alto, Calif. 1980

Poli 85   Polit, St.: R1 and beyond. AI Technology Transfer at DEC. AI Magazine (1985)

Prer 85   Prerau, D.S.:Selection of an Appropriate Domain for an Expert System. AI Magazine 6(1985)2, 26-30

Rich 83   Rich, E.: Artificial Intelligence. McGraw-Hill 1983

Shei 83   Sheil, B.: Environments for Exploratory Programming, Datamation, Febr. 1983

Shei 84   Sheil, B.: The Artificial Intelligence Tool Box, in: *Artificial Intelligence Applications for Business* (ed.: W. Reitmann) Ablex Publ. Corp., Norwood, N.J., 1984

Shor 76   Shortliffe, E.H.: Computer Based Medical Consultations: MYCIN North Holland, Amsterdam, 1976

Smit 84   Smith, R.: On the Development of Commercial Expert Systems. AI Magazine 5 (1984) 3, 61-73

SmBa 83   Smith, R.; Baker, J.: The Dipmeter Advisor System - A Case Study in Commercial Expert System Development. Proc. IJCAI-83, 1983, 122-127

SrJo 85   Sriram, D.; Joobbani, R. (eds.): Special Issue AI In Engineering. SIGART Newsletter, Number 92 (April 1985), 38-127

Wahl 82   Wahlster, W.: Natürlichsprachliche Systeme. In *Künstliche Intelligenz.* Springer,Berlin 1982, 202-283

WIIG 84   Wiig, K.: Market Trends in Artificial Intelligence in the United States and Japan. Fifth Generation Computer Systems 1, 1984, 113-118

THE CENTRALISED SCHEDULER VS. THE DISTRIBUTED SPECIALISTS : TOWARDS A FLEXIBLE CONTROLLER IN PROLOG FOR EXPERT SYSTEMS

Raf Venken
B.I.M.
Everberg - Belgium

Maurice Bruynooghe, Luc Dekeyser, Bruno Krekels
Katholieke Universiteit Leuven
Leuven - Belgium

Abstract

The main problem in the development of expert systems or knowledge based systems is the construction of the knowledge base. Not only the elicitation of the human knowledge is a crucial problem but also the codification of this knowledge into a consistent and easily modifiable and extensible knowledge system. In this paper we analyse two possible strategies to build a knowledge system. We describe how they can be implemented in Prolog and investigate their usability and their flexibility for building expert systems. The two architectures are used to build an expert system for symbolic integration. Finally we describe how the technique of partial evaluation could be used to derive an expert system of the second architecture from an expert system written using the centralised scheduler.

1. Introduction

For the past 15 years, applied work in the domain of artificial intelligence has focused mainly on the development of "expert systems". Recent publications (e.g. <Reit83>) concerning the application of artificial intelligence mostly discuss some kind of expert system or knowledge based system in some particular domain.

These systems already achieve acceptable levels of performance in relatively complex tasks, sometimes, e.g. in very clerical or computational directed tasks, even better than human experts.

In <Haye83> the history of artificial intelligence is summarized as follows :

- Conception (1956), symbolic computing on very powerful general purpose computers was hoped to solve all problems.
- Redirection (1968), most workers redirected their efforts towards knowledge based reasoning and heuristic methods.
- Success (1977), the knowledge based methods were judged successful.
- Recognition (1980), official certification of the technology as crucial and relevant by scientific and political authorities.
- Initiative (1981), the fifth generation computer project challenges the artificial intelligence community.
- Industrialization (1982), application of artificial intelligence techniques for solving concrete problems.

There are some important lessons one has learned during this history. The major lesson is that knowledge plays a central role in artificial intelligence applications. The structure of the human know-how, which experts use to solve their problems, and the mechanisms to manipulate it, are unfortunately not completely understood and are difficult to codify in machine-oriented terms. Therefore knowledge engineers must interrogate human experts to elicit this know-how, reformulate it, codify it, refine it and assemble it in a consistent system. These knowledge systems usually consist of a set of rules, each rule expressing an elementary part of the human know-how.

The central issue in building expert system applications is the problem of structuring these rules into a consistent knowledge base, which is easy to maintain, to modify, to extend and to manipulate. This problem becomes very severe with large rule bases. In general, the interactions between the different rules become very complex and it is not only very difficult to modify such large knowledge bases, but also to see the limits of the expertise described in the system.

Mastering this complexity is a typical software engineering problem. Specific features of this particular task however are : that the system is always incomplete and that it should be easy to extend or modify the system.

In this paper we will discuss two possible architectures for building expert systems. We describe how to realize them in Prolog and discuss the advantages and disadvantages of both approaches, especially concerning their extensibility and their behaviour in the handling of problems outside the domain of expertise. Both approaches are tested for the application domain of symbolic integration.

2. Two ES Architectures

In this section we give a brief description of two possible architectures for building an expert system which will be used to solve an example application. The first approach is called the centralised scheduler, the second the distributed specialists.

2.1 The centralised scheduler

Schematically one could code the centralised scheduler as follows :

```
Scheduler (Data, Meta) <-
        Advice (Data, Meta, "stop", ""),
        ! ,
        Report(Data, Meta).

Scheduler (Data, Meta) <-
        Advice (Data, Meta, Task, Meta-relevant-to-task),
        Execute (Task, Data, Meta-relevant-to-task,
                            Result, Happened),
        Evaluate (Data, Result, Happened, Meta, Newdata,
                            Newmeta),
        Scheduler (Newdata, Newmeta).
```

The first parameter "Data" denotes the object under study by the expert system ; e.g. in an expert system for symbolic integration, this "Data" would be the formula to be integrated.

The second parameter "Meta" of the scheduler is the meta-knowledge needed to execute the problem. It describes the state of the problem solving activity, i.e. the methods which were already tried, how the initial problem has been split up in subproblems and the outcome of the different attempts to solve the different subproblems.

The "Advice"-step plays a central role in the problem solving activity : it advices on how to proceed using the contents of the knowledge base and the outcome of the previous execution steps. "Advice" consults a rule base before advicing to fire a particular task. These rules describe the conditions needed before a particular task can be executed and can depend on the pattern of the input as well as on the history of the already executed tasks. Although the order of doing tasks can be very important, the ordering can be very implicitly stated in the description of the conditions in the rules and this "Advice"-task can become very complex.

The "Execute"-step executes a basic step in the solution of the problem, it uses the advice of the scheduler to apply a specific mechanism to the input data and gives back eventually partial solutions and a report on how successfully the problem has been treated. The "Executer" can be very complex, e.g. a finite element analysis system, therefore, to reduce the complexity of the scheduler the "Execute"-part can become a system on its own, with its own separate control architecture and internal structure.

"Evaluate" uses the output of "Execute" to construct a new subproblem and metaknowledge to be provided recursively to the scheduler, so that it can proceed with the next subtask. In general this new meta-knowledge includes the old knowledge and the output-report of the execute step, although a filter can reduce the amount of knowledge to be kept.

Finally "Report" is the step where the expert system in interaction with the user, gives explanations about how the problem has been treated and what the final results are. In general this step will start with a general overview of the execution : i.e. the initial problem and its solutions. The user can then ask for more information on how this solution has been reached (the "Why"-explanation) or eventually why no solution has been found ("Why-not"-explanation).

These explanations can include a "trace" of the execution and background information to clarify concepts of the application domain.

2.2 The distributed specialists

In this approach the expert system consists of a limited set of "specialists" which can invoke each other. Each specialist is able to receive requests (messages), handle them and reply to them. The system is activated by the user sending a request to one particular specialist.

In handling a request, a particular specialist can activate other specialists, it knows about, by sending appropriate messages. A specialist is defined in terms of the kinds of messages it can handle and the kind of replies it can. give. For each type of message a program (or script) to handle it has to be defined.

Schematically a definition of a specialist could be as follows :

```
            Spec1 (Message-in, Message-out).


            Spec1 (Mess1 (...), Out) <-
                  Cond11 (Mess1 (...)),
                  ! ,
                  ScriptM1 (..., Out).
            Spec1 (Mess2 (...), Out) <-
                  Cond12 (Mess2 (...)),
                  ! ,
                  ScriptM2 (..., Out).
                  .

                  .

            Spec1 (Mess, "cannot handle").


            ScriptM1 (..., Out) <- .....
                  .

                  .

                  SpecN (Mess, Answer),
                  Evaluateanswer ( Answer, Out).
```

The different specialists can be organised as desired to solve particular problems. They can include facilities for storing lemma's in order to avoid large recomputations, they should include facilities to provide explanations about their own behaviour, eventually parameterized according to different types of users.

The "Scripts" describe the actions to be taken by the specialist, the tasks it has to activate and the replies to be sent. This means a.o. that any particular specialist has knowledge about the other specialists which it needs for executing the eventual subtasks. This implies that the knowledge about the capabilities of the different specialists is distributed over the system, not every specialist has complete knowledge about every other specialist, so that duplication of knowledge is restricted to a minimum. The ordering of the tasks is more explicitly described in the script than it is in the first approach.

3. An example application

As an example application we will take the domain of symbolic integration. We will use both architectures to build a minimal system for symbolic integration and, doing so, pinpoint some problems concerning maintenance and extensibility.

3.1 The distributed specialists

The development of the distributed specialists approach of the expert system for symbolic integration is at first sight straigthforward. The top level specialist could look like :

```
        Spec1 (Integrl (F, X), R) <-
            ! ,
            Script1 (F, X, R).
        Spec1 (Mess, "cannot handle").

        Script1 (F, X, R) <-
```

```
Spec3 (Simplify (F), FS),
Spec2 (Integrf (FS, X), IF),
Spec3 (Simplify (IF), R).
```

This specialist takes the input function, calls for a specialist to
apply a simplification to it, invokes the specialist for the
integration of simplified functions and simplifies the result, which
is given back to the invoker of the specialist.

Let us make abstraction of specialist 3, which is responsible for
simplifying the input formula, and proceed to sketch the specialist 2,
which handles simplified formulas :

```
1) Spec2 (Integrf (C, X), C*X) <-
        Cond21 (C, X),
        ! .
   Cond21 (C, X) <-
        Independent (C, X).


2) Spec2 (Integrf ( - F, X), - IF) <-
        ! ,
        Script22 (F, X, IF).
   Script22 (F, X, IF) <-
        Spec2 (Integrf (F, X), IF).


3) Spec2 (Integrf (F+G, X), IF+IG) <-
        ! ,
        Script23 (F, G, X, IF, IG).
   Script23 (F, G, X, IF, IG) <-
        Spec2 (Integrf (F, X), IF),
        Spec2 (Integrf (G, X), IG).


4) Spec2 (Integrf (F-G, X), IF-IG) <-
        ! ,
        Script23 (F, G, X, IF, IG).


5) Spec2 (Integrf (F, X), C*IG) <-
        Cond25 (F, X, C, G),
        ! ,
        Script25 (G, X, IG).
   Cond25 (F, X, C, G) <-
        Getconstant (F, X, C, G).
```

```
      Script25 (G, X, IG) <-
            Spec3 (Simplify (G), SG),
            Spec4 (Integrc (SG, X), IG).


   6) Spec2 (Mess, "cannot handle") <-
            ! .
```

This specialist 2 calls itself recursively until it has all terms
isolated, then these elementary terms are forwarded to specialist 4,
which can treat some standard integrations. This specialist 4 consists
of two parts : the first part treats some elementary functions like :

```
      Spec4 (Integrc (X, X), X**2/2) <-
            ! .
      Spec4 (Integrc (X**C, X), X**(C+1)/(C+1) ) <-
            ! .
      Spec4 (Integrc (sin(X), X), - cos(X) ) <-
            ! .
      etc.
```

The second part treats the multiplication of two functions and invokes
another   specialist,   which   knows   about   the   method   of   partial
integration.

```
      Spec4 (Integrc (F/G, X), R) <-
            ! ,
            Script41 (F, 1/G, X, R).
      Script41 (F, G, X, R) <-
            Spec5 (Partintegr (F, G, X), R).
      Spec4 (Integrc (F*G, X), R) <-
            ! ,
            Script41 (F, G, X, R).
```

And finally :

```
      Spec4 (Mess, "cannot handle") <-
            ! .
```

To finish the system, we still have to define the specialist 5 which
implements the method of partial integration :

```
      Spec5 (Partintegr (F, G, X), F*IG-IR) <-
```

```
        Script51 (F, G, X, IG, IR).
   Script51 (F, G, X, IG, IR) <-
        Spec1 (Integr1 (G, X), IG),
        Spec6 (Differt (F, X), DF),
        Spec3 (Simplify (IG*DF), IGDF),
        Spec1 (Integr1 (IGDF, X), IR).
```

We suppose that a specialist 6 for differentiating functions is available and the solution is very straightforward. This implementation of an expert system for symbolic integration works fine for a number of formulas. But there are a few problem cases which illustrate very well the limitations of the distributed specialists approach.

3.2 The centralised scheduler

But let us first show how the same application can be solved using the centralised scheduler approach. We take the scheduler of 2.1 as starting point and show how the "Advice" and "Execute" function can be built on the basis of an appropriate knowledge base. We will not develop the "Report" function here, more details about explanation can be found e.g. in <Haye83b>.

The top level rule of the "Advice" knowledge base could be as follows :

```
    Advice (int(Formula, X), "", simplify(Formula), var(X) ).
```

This advice-rule is read : if the metaknowledge is empty (nothing has been done yet) and the input has the specified format, the first task to be executed is the simplification of the input formula, knowing that X is the integration variable.

The corresponding execution rule in the "Execute" knowledge base is :

```
    Execute (simplify(Formula), int(Formula,X), var(X),
    intf(SFormula,X), simplification ) <-
        simplify (Formula, X, SFormula), ...
```

The "Evaluate" step in the scheduler constructs a new meta-knowledge
to restart the scheduler again, which consists of the history of the
execution :

```
        Evaluate (Data, Result, Happened, Meta, Result,
                                        Happened(Data).Meta).
```

A few other "Advice" and "Execute" rules :

```
        Advice (intf(Formula,X), simplification(...),
                                        splitterm(Formula), var(X) ).
        Advice (Formula, splitterm..., intc(SubFormula), var(X))<-
                findsimple (Formula, Meta, SubFormula, X).
        Advice (Formula, Meta, part(F*G), var(X) ) <-
                findproduct (Formula, Meta, F*G, X).


        Execute (splitterm(F), intf(F, X), var(X), NFormula,
                                        splitterm(F) ) <-
                integrf (F, X, NFormula).
```

Where integrf :

```
        integrf (C, X, C*intc(1)) <-
                independent(C,X),
                !.
        integrf (-F, X, -IF) <-
                !,
                integrf (F, X, IF).
        integrf (F+G, X, IF+IG) <-
                !,
                integrf (F, X, IF),
                integrf (G, X, IG).
        integrf (F-G, X, IF-IG) <-
                !,
                integrf (F, X, IF),
                integrf (G, X, IG).
        integrf (F, X, C*intc(G)) <-
                getconstant (F, C, G),
                !.
```

The next rule solves elementary formulas, which are selected in the second "Advice" :

    Execute (intc(F), F, var(X), NFormula, simple(F)) <-
            integrc (F, X, NFormula).

Where integrc :

    integrc (X, X, X**2/2).
    integrc (X**C, X, X**(C+1)/(C+1)).
    integrc (sin(X), X, -cos(X)).
    etc.

For this rule and the next the "Evaluate"-part is a bit more complicated as before : "Evaluate" should replace in the original formula the simple integral by the result of the "Execute" step and include information concerning this step in the metaknowledge.

    Execute (part(F*G), F*G, Meta, F*IG-intc(DFIG), part(F*G))<-
            integrc (G, X, IG),
            differt (F, X, DF),
            simplify (DF*IG, X, DFIG).

4. The behaviour of the two approaches

The approach of the centralised scheduler is a typical example of an interpreter : the scheduler accepts a problem to be solved from the user and tries to apply different rules. The scheduler uses metaknowledge to judge on which rule to use first, to evaluate the results of previous steps and to explain the behaviour of the system to the user. We can distinguish different knowledge bases in this approach : we have a first knowledge base containing a set of rules which can be applied to different subproblems of the application, a second knowledge base to describe the conditions on which particular rules can be applied and a last one with more common sens knowledge to be able to explain the system's behaviour to the user (this base was not included in the example application). The types of knowledge are clearly separated in different knowledge bases and relate to different conceptual parts of the scheduler.

The second approach is more procedurally oriented, the system is split up in different specialists, which have only a limited amount of knowledge, related to the execution of a very specialized task, which is a combination of fragments of each of the three knowledge bases described above. There is no overall knowledge base anymore, but the same knowledge, relevant to the task to be executed, is available at the right place.

4.1 Problems with distributed specialists

The approach of the distributed specialists is very close to the normal writing of Prolog programs and is very straigthforward, at first sight. While using the system for a few examples we noticed some problems with partial integration : some formulas diverge if partial integration is not effectuated appropriately (e.g. X*sin(X) will be solved correctly, but sin(X)*X not). This problem can be solved by keeping track of the history of the integration taking place and reorder the input formula when diverging. But this requires a substantial modification in the implementation : each specialist has to be modified, although the problem occurs only within the partial integration. Other infinite loops are possible : when the result of an integration contains the input formula, the integral may not be solvable or is trapped in an infinite loop which can be broken by moving this formula to the left hand side, again a history of the problem solving process is needed to detect this problem. In general the distributed specialist are more difficult to maintain and to modify, since overall knowledge about the system is not readily available. The control structure, i.e. when to invoke which rule, is distributed over the system and therefore difficult to master.

If an explanation facility is needed, the distributed specialist could be the input of an expert system shell (as in <Nibl85>). But the explanation given to the user by such shells is very closely connected to the rules themselves and therefore not manageable. It is easier to take advantage of a history of the calculation (which is apparently needed anyway in this example application) and develop a customized explanation facility enriched with some common sense knowledge. Moreover, the performance is degraded heavily when using an expert system shell, and performance is the only advantage of the specialists in comparison with the scheduler.

4.2 The benefits of the scheduler

It was much easier to adapt the application to the changing requirements that infinite loops in partial integration should be detected. Not only because a history is kept anyway for reporting purposes, but also because the decision process is strictly separated from the calculation process and thus clearer specified and easier modified. The task to be performed is described in different conceptual levels : in terms of high level advice, medium level execute and low level Prolog code for the effective manipulations to take place.

The only disadvantage of the centralised scheduler is the fact that it is a meta-interpreter and therefore rather slow for practical computations. For an average application a meta-interpreter degrades performance by a factor of 10 in comparison with a more procedurally oriented approach, such as the distributed specialists.

4.3 Partial evaluation

The relationship between the two different approaches resembles very much the relationship between partially evaluated programs and their sources as shown in <Komo81>. In a partial evaluation system, programs are converted to semantically equivalent programs by evaluating what can be evaluated at compile time, in the case of Prolog by unification, by opening calls and executing builtins whenever possible (see also <Venk84> for more details in relation with a practical implementation in Prolog).

In <Gall84> it has been suggested that a technique related to partial evaluation could be used to specialise meta-interpreters to a specific task by taking into account its input (i.e. the program it has to execute and some associated knowledge or data bases). The idea is to generate more performant Prolog code for different input patterns. In this view the centralised scheduler could be specialised using the "Advice" and "Execute" knowledge bases to obtain code with a performance similar to the distributed specialists for different subproblems of the application. Further investigation should point out whether the specialisation of the centralised scheduler results indeed into programs which are close, what concerns format and performance, to the distributed specialists.

5. Conclusion

We discussed two possible architectures for building expert systems and demonstrated them in the example application of symbolic integration. We commented on their behaviour and suggested the use of partial evaluation to convert automatically expert systems from one approach to the other. We would like to thank the SPPS, IRSIA and CEC for their ongoing support for several research projects, from which this paper reflects some results.

References

<Gall84>   Gallagher, J., Transforming Logic Programs by specialising Interpreters, University of Dublin, 1984.

<Haye83>   Hayes-Roth, F., The Industrialization of Knowledge Engineering, in <Reit83>.

<Haye83b>   Hayes-Roth, F., Waterman, D.A. and Lenat, D.B., Building Expert Systems, Addison-Wesley Publishing Co., 1983.

<Komo81>   Komorowski, H.J., A Specification of an abstract Prolog Machine and its Application to Partial Evaluation, Linkoping Studies in Science and Technology Dissertations No 69, Linkoping University, 1981.

<Nibl85>   Niblett, T., Yet another Prolog Expert System, The Journal for the Integrated Study of Artificial Intelligence, Cognitive Science and Applied Epistomology, Vol 2, nr. 2, Rijksuniversiteit Gent, 1985.

<Reit83>   Reitman, W. (ed.), Artificial Intelligence Applications for Business, Ablex Publishing Corp, 1983.

<Venk84>   Venken R., A Prolog Meta-Interpreter for Partial Evaluation and its Application to Source to Soutrce Transformation and Query-Optimisation, in Proc. ECAI '84, Pisa, 1984.

Expertensysteme in der Prozeßleittechnik

Thies Wittig
Krupp Atlas Elektronik
2800 Bremen

Zusammenfassung:

Ausgehend von einer kurzen Einführung in die Prozeßleitsysteme und in
die Aufgaben von Expertensystemen in der Prozeßleittechnik wird ein
kurzer Überblick über die Klassifizierungsmöglichkeiten und die Einsatzgebiete existierender Expertensysteme gegeben. Die besonderen Anforderungen an Expertensysteme in der Prozeßleittechnik werden insbesondere gekennzeichnet durch   die automatische Datenübernahme (also nicht dialogorientiert), die große Menge an zu verarbeitenden
Daten und die Forderung nach zeitabhängigen Schlußfolgerungsver-
fahren. Ferner werden unterschiedliche Anwendungsaspekte von Expertensystemen in diesem Bereich skizziert, wie z.B. Behandlung von
Notsituationen, Automatisierung im Routinebetrieb oder kostengünsti-
gere Entwicklung "klassischer" Prozeßleitwarten.

1. Einleitung

Bis auf wenige Ausnahmen leiden bis heute Expertensysteme noch unter
dem Ruf, sich überwiegend mit Demonstrationsproblemen (toy-problems)
zu befassen und noch ein ganzes Stück von einem praktischen, d.h.
wirtschaftlichen, Einsatz entfernt zu sein. Dies lag - und liegt -
sicherlich einerseits daran, daß einige Anwendungsgebiete nur bedingt
praktisch relevant sind, anderseits wohl daran, daß wirkliche praktische Anwendungen oft um Größenordnungen komplexer sind als Spielan-
wendungen. Hinzu kommt für viele KI-Forscher das Problem, daß sie mit
dem Anwendungsgebiet zu wenig vertraut sind und Gefahr laufen, die
eigentliche Problematik zu übersehen. Dieser Aufsatz befaßt sich mit
dem Thema der Expertensysteme in der Prozeßleittechnik, einem Thema
dessen praktische Relevanz sicherlich außer Frage steht. Die Gefahr,
durch Spiellösungen die Realität aus den Augen zu verlieren, ist in

diesem Bereich geringer als in vielen anderen. Selbst einfache Prozesse oder in sich geschlossene Teilprozesse einer großen Anlage bergen noch ausreichend Komplexität für ein ernstzunehmendes Anwendungsgebiet in sich. Ein anderes Problem - und damit natürlich auch der besondere Reiz dieses Themas - liegt darin, daß auch auf der KI-Seite Neuland betreten wird. Die temporale Logik z.B., die hier eine wichtige Rolle spielt, steckt noch weit in der Theorie (Allen,1983, McDermott,1982) , und wie man eine Wissensbasis mit mehreren tausend Regeln noch auf ihre Konsistenz überprüfen kann, ist noch völlig offen.

Dieser Beitrag soll zum Verständnis der Rolle der Expertensysteme im Prozeßbereich beitragen, die besonderen Probleme aufzeigen und einige Lösungsansätze vorstellen.

2. Aufgaben der Leitwartentechnik

Zunächst werden die Aufgaben und die Lösungsprinzipien der Leittechnik erläutert, ohne auf die Unterstützung dieser Lösungen durch Expertensysteme einzugehen. In den folgenden Kapiteln wird auf die spezielle Problematik dieser Anwendung eingegangen. Als Leittechnik läßt sich das Gesamtgebiet der übergeordneten überwachung, Steuerung und Regelung ganzer Systeme zusammenfassen. Es existieren vielfältige, räumlich oft ausgedehnte Versorgungsnetze, die sehr unterschiedlichen Aufgaben dienen. Die Leittechnik befasst sich primär nicht mit den Zustandsänderungen, Transport- oder übertragungsfragen selbst, sondern mit der Koordinierung der Informationen, also z.B. den Meldungen, Meßwerten, Stellbefehlen und ihrem Zusammenhang. Typische Anwendungsfälle, die hier näher betrachtet werden sollen, sind die Meßwerterfassung und Steuerung von Versorgungsanlagen im Bereich der kommunalen Energie, Gas und Wasserversorgungsunternehmen.

Als Grundaufgaben von Leitsystemen sind zu nennen:

- Verbesserung der technischen Sicherheit
  Dies wird erreicht durch verbesserte übersicht, geringere Gefahr von Fehlbedienungen, rechtzeitige Warnung vor kritischen Zuständen. Nicht zuletzt läßt sich die Sicherheit durch verbesserte Arbeitsbedingungen, wie sie die Leittechnik mit sich bringt, erhöhen.

- Erhöhung der Wirtschaftlichkeit
  Diese wird erzielt durch geringere Ausfallzeiten der überwachten
  Anlage, geringerer Wartungsaufwand und kürzere Reaktionszeiten.
  Die Wirtschaftlichkeit zeigt sich außerdem unter anderem im spezi-
  fischen Material- und Energieaufwand, im Personalbedarf und im
  Aufwand zur Ermittlung von Kenngrößen.

Zur Lösung dieser Grundaufgaben sind drei Prinzipien anwendbar:

- Istwert-Erfassung
  Hier geht es nicht nur um die einfache Erfassung von Meßwerten,
  sondern auch um ihre Bewertung, wie Berücksichtigung von Faktoren,
  Kennlinien, Nullpunktwanderungen usw. Dabei können die Zeitpunkte
  der Erfassung in weiten Grenzen vorgewählt werden oder von Zuständen bzw. Meßwerten selbst abhängen.

- Zentrale Steuerungssysteme
  Sie ermöglichen einen Informationsfluß in beiden Richtungen (Meßwerterfassung und Steuerung des Prozesses). Ein Wirkungskreis wird
  über den Menschen geschlossen.

- Regelungssysteme
  Wesentlich hierfür ist die Führung des Prozesses ohne ständige
  Mitwirkung des Menschen. Zentrale Regelungssysteme sind im allge-
  meinen voneinander unabhängigen Regelkreisen übergeordnet. Ein
  Zweck kann die selbsttätige Optimierung der Wirkung der Gesamtan-
  lage sein.

Versorgungsunternehmen wie Elektrizitäts-, Gas- und Wasserwerke bieten einige Besonderheiten. Allgemein besteht, um Netzzustände wiederzugeben und zu bewerten, die Aufgabe darin, zwei Gruppen von Informationen zusammenzuführen. Dies sind einerseits die wenig zeitabhängigen Daten (Topologie des Netzes, vorhandene Betriebsmittel und ihre
Bemessung, Regeln des Betriebes, Vorgeschichte) und andererseits die
Daten des Betriebszustandes (Meßwerte, Schaltzustände, usw.). Hinzu
kommen häufig Rechnungen, die sich auf den Betriebsverlauf der nächsten Minuten oder Stunden beziehen.

3. Aufgaben von Expertensystemen in der Leittechnik

Expertensysteme sollen nicht - und das sei hier ganz deutlich betont
- die Aufgaben übernehmen, die von den Leitwarten der heutigen Generation erfüllt werden. Nicht nur deswegen, weil die schnelle Verarbeitung vielkanalig abgetasteter Signale kein typisches Anwendungsgebiet für Expertensysteme ist, sondern auch weil die Prozeßrechner-
technologie inzwischen mit einem sehr hohen Entwicklungsaufwand
einen hohen Standard erreicht hat. Diesen mit KI-Methoden nachent-
wickeln zu wollen, ist sicherlich kein sinnvolles Unterfangen. Dennoch gibt es eine Reihe von Problemen und Aufgaben, die über das
hinausgehen, was heutzutage Bestandteil der Leitwartentechnik ist und
was mit der aktuellen Leitwartentechnologie schwer oder gar nicht zu
lösen ist. Solche Probleme sind z.B.

- Optimierung von Netzauslastungen aus technischer Sicht
- Optimierung aus tariflicher Sicht
- Einsatzplanung von Kraftwerkzuschaltungen in Versorgungsnetzen
- Behandlung von Notsituationen

Probleme dieser Art werden zur Zeit immer noch einem möglichst erfahrenen Bediener überlassen, wobei der Optimierungsgrad oft zu wünschen
übrig läßt. In modernen Leitwarten wird zwar bereits versucht, auch
Aufgaben dieser Art mit Hilfe klassischer Methoden zu integrieren,
doch handelt es sich dabei immer um maßgeschneiderte Lösungen, die
sehr viel Entwicklungsaufwand erfordern und nicht übertragbar sind.
Einzelerfolge sind dabei in der tariflichen Optimierung zu verzeich-
nen, da hier das Wissen vollständig vorliegt, und zwar in Form der
Tarifverträge der Versorgungsunternehmen. Einen geschlossenen Algorithmus daraus zu entwickeln ist aber aufgrund der vielen Ausnahme-
und Sonderregelungen nicht möglich. Außerdem ändern sich Tarifbe-
stimmungen laufend, was einen nicht unerheblichen Programmänderungs-
dienst erfordert. Die Kraftwerkseinsatzplanung bei Versorgungsunternehmen ist aber im Gegensatz dazu weit schwieriger, da hier das
Wissen nur in der Erfahrung der Bediener vorliegt.
Aus diesen Beispielen lassen sich zwei Anwendungsaspekte für Expertensysteme herleiten:

- Unterstützung bei der Entwicklung von Leitwarten
  Wissensbasierte Methoden zur Integration tariflicher Bestimmungen

ermöglichen neben einer kostengünstigen Erstentwicklung auch eine
schnelle Modifizierung bei sich ändernden Verträgen. Nicht zu vergessen sind in diesem Zusammenhang Konfigurierungsprobleme einer
jeden neuen Leitwarte. Hier bieten sich Expertensysteme zur Unterstützung natürlich an. Da diese Probleme aber keine leitwartenty-
pischen sind, werden sie hier nicht weiter diskutiert.

- Unterstützung beim Betrieb von Leitwarten
  Systeme, die auf den Erfahrungsschatz der Bediener zurückgreifen
  können, sind viel eher in der Lage, Abläufe zu optimieren oder den
  Bediener in Notsituationen zu unterstützen.

4. Realisierungsmöglichkeiten

Um einen besseren Einblick in die Problematik von Expertensystemen in
der Prozeßleittechnik zu bekommen, sollen im folgenden einige typische Einsatzgebiete mit den sich daraus ergebenden besonderen Anforderungen an Expertensysteme aufgeführt werden. Um Klarheit über die
dabei verwendeten Termini zu schaffen, wird zunächst eine grundsätzliche Klassifizierung von Expertensystemen versucht. Das Hauptaugenmerk wird dabei auf die Einheit von Anwendungsgebiet, Benutzer und
Expertensystem gerichtet. Nur durch diese gesamtheitliche Betrach-
tungsweise läßt sich eine adäquate Klassifizierung vornehmen.

4.1 Der allgemeine Problemlösungsprozeß

Es wird im folgenden der verallgemeinerte Problemlösungsprozeß des
Menschen betrachtet, wie er in Bild 1 schematisch dargestellt ist.
Das Augenmerk wird dabei auf die drei Wissensgebiete, nämlich Beob-
achtungswissen, Inspektionswissen und Diagnosewissen gerichtet sein.
Die als zyklisch dargestellte Beobachtung irgendeines Vorganges setzt
ein bestimmtes Wissen über diesen Vorgang voraus, wenn sie - wie hier
angenommen - zur Entdeckung von Problemen führen soll. Dieses Wissen
kann sich im allgemeinen auf das nach außen sichtbare Verhalten des
fehlerfrei ablaufenden Vorganges beschränken. Es ist also kein Wissen über kausale Zusammenhänge notwendig.
Sobald nun ein Problem auftritt, d.h. eine Abweichung von einer
vorgegebenen Norm, beginnt der Prozeß der Problemlösung. Diese Problemlösung läßt sich unterteilen in zwei Bereiche, nämlich die Inspektion, d.h. das Sammeln von Fakten über den fehlerhaften Zustand,

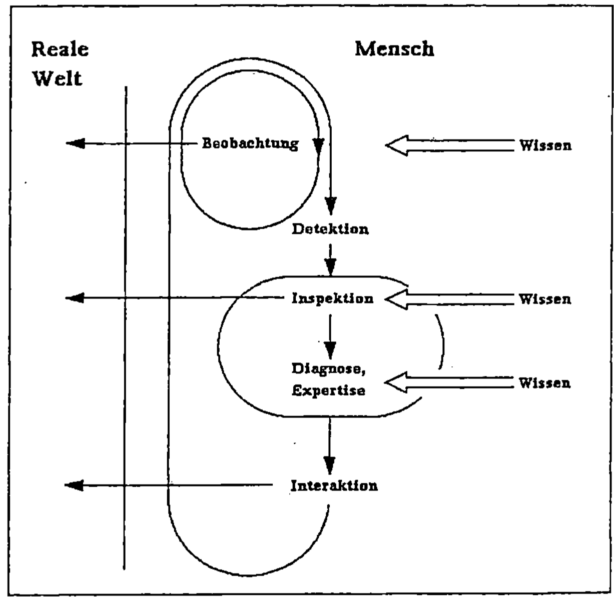

Bild 1: Verallgemeinerter Problemlösungszyklus

und die Diagnose, d.h. das Ziehen von Schlüssen aus diesen Fakten, um einen Fehler zu erkennen und einen Plan für dessen Behebung zu entwickeln.

Dieser Diagnose schließt sich dann die Interaktion an, nämlich die Behebung des Fehlers. Danach beginnt wieder die Phase der Beobachtung.

Wenden wir uns nun den beiden für die Problemlösung notwendigen Bereichen zu. Zweck der Inspektion ist es, ein genaues Bild von der Wirklichkeit zu bekommen, das dann bei der Findung der Expertise als Modell fungiert. Das wesentliche dabei ist, daß es sich bei diesem Modell um ein abstrahiertes und bereits in bestimmter Richtung interpretiertes und bewertetes Abbild der äußeren Welt handelt. Es stellt eine Zusammenfassung der Situation dar, die möglichst alle relevanten Fakten beinhaltet. Dieses Modell ist somit Grundlage der eigentlichen Diagnose, d.h. der Ermittlung von Ursachen, die zu diesem Zustand geführt haben sowie von Maßnahmen, um diesen fehlerhaften Zustand zu beheben.

4.2 Klassifizierung von Expertensystemen

Die hier angegebene Trennung von Inspektion (Faktensammlung), Abstraktion (Situationserfassung, Modellbildung) und Diagnose tritt beim menschlichen Problemlösungsprozeß nicht offen zutage, weil beide Schritte iterativ miteinander verknüpft sind. Wichtig ist diese Trennung aber bei der Entwicklung und der Klassifizierung von Expertensystemen. Zwei Klassen von Expertensystemen lassen sich aus dieser Sicht feststellen:

Klasse 1:
Hierzu zählen Expertensysteme, bei denen die Inspektion und damit auch die Abstraktion und die Interpretation außerhalb des Systems, nämlich beim Benutzer, erfolgt. Systeme dieser Art verlangen einen Benutzer, der mit dem Anwendungsgebiet vertraut ist und im Dialog mit dem System in der Lage ist, Auskunft über die zu untersuchende Problemsituation zu geben. Er wird vom System dabei zwar geführt, muß aber das Modell in seiner Vorstellung bilden. Nur so kann er zu der üblicherweise vom System geforderten Bewertung seiner Beobachtungen kommen. Systeme dieser Klasse verdienen eher den Namen "Expert Assisting Systems".

Klasse 2:
Expertensysteme dieser Klasse beinhalten die Inspektion (Datenerfassung) und sind somit auch gezwungen, die Abstraktion und die Modellbildung selber durchzuführen. Der Dialog mit dem Benutzer beschränkt sich hier allenfalls auf Zusatzinformationen, die nicht vom System direkt erfaßt werden können, sowie auf die Mitteilung der Diagnoseergebnisse. Systeme dieser Art erwarten vom Benutzer weit weniger Expertenwissen als die oben genannten.

4.3 Einsatzgebiete

Nachdem nun die grundsätzlichen Kriterien zur Beurteilung von Expertensystemen erläutert wurden, sollen jetzt einige typische Einsatzgebiete mit den sich daraus ergebenden Anforderungen vorgestellt werden. Sie werden einerseits anhand der soeben dargelegten Kriterien wie Inspektion, Interpretation und Abstraktion (Modellbildung) sowie Diagnose charakterisiert, als auch anhand der Besonderheiten des Anwendungsgebietes (wie z.B. Zeitabhängigkeit) unterschieden.
Das klassische Anwendungsgebiet von Expertensystemen ist die medizi-

nische Diagnose (Shortliffe, 1976). Dieses Gebiet läßt sich folgendermaßen beschreiben:

- zeitunabhängige Daten
- Abstraktion außerhalb des Expertensystems
- wenige Datenquellen, geringe Datenmenge
- umfangreiches Expertenwissen (Lehrbuchwissen)

Betrachtet man im Gegensatz dazu Systeme wie Dipmeter-Advisor (Smith,1983), die zur Analyse von Daten, die z.B. bei Bodenuntersuchung gewonnen wurden, dann kann man folgendes feststellen:

- zeitunabhängige Daten
- Inspektion und Abstraktion automatisch, aber noch außerhalb des eigentlichen Expertensystems
- wenige Datenquellen, umfangreiches Datenmaterial
- umfangreiches Lehrbuchwissen

Ein dritter Bereich ist hauptsächlich für den militärischen Einsatz (wie z.B. Gefechtsfeldaufklärung) relevant. Hier kommt es darauf an, aus einer Vielzahl von teils widersprüchlichen Informationen aus sehr unterschiedlichen Quellen, ein Bild von der aktuellen Situation zu erhalten. Dies läßt sich folgendermaßen charakterisieren:

- zeitabhängige Daten
- wenig Klarheit über ihre Sicherheit
- Inspektion und Abstraktion sind Hauptaufgabe des Systems, nicht die Diagnose (situation assessment, data fusion)
- viele Datenquellen, große Datenmenge
- wenig Lehrbuchwissen

Der letzte zu betrachtende Bereich ist die Prozeßsteuerung, für das als Beispiel das PICON-System genannt werden kann. Dieser Bereich läßt sich so beschreiben:

- zeitabhängige und zeitkritische Daten
- Inspektion/Abstraktion und Diagnose innerhalb des Expertensystems
- eine Datenquelle, sehr große Datenmenge (max. 20000 Signale)
- viel Wissen über Normalbetrieb, sehr wenig über Störfälle

Je größer also die Datenmenge wird, die von einem Expertensystem verarbeitet werden soll, desto stärker wird die Forderung nach einer im

System liegenden Inspektions- und Interpretationskomponente. Diese
Forderung gewinnt noch mehr an Gewicht, wenn die Interpretation bzw.
die Diagnose die Zeitabhängigkeit der Daten berücksichtigen muß. Die
Eingabe von Daten im Dialog mit dem Bediener wird sowohl ab einer
bestimmten Datenmenge unpraktikabel als auch bei zeitabhängigen Daten
unmöglich. Es ist eine Rollenverschiebung festzustellen von der reinen Diagnose (d.h. der Schlußfolgerung von Symptomen, die auf ein wie
immer geartetes Fehlverhalten deuten, auf ihre Ursachen) hin zum
Erfassen und Verstehen einer Situation, nämlich dem sog. situation
assessment. Bei diesem Verstehen kommt es zunächst gar nicht so sehr
auf die Detektion von Fehlerverhalten an, sondern auf ein Verstehen
der zeitlichen und ursächlichen Zusammenhänge in dem zu beobachtenden
Vorgang. Der Sinn eines solchen Systems liegt darin, dem Benutzer ein
klares Bild aus einer großen Menge von unstrukturierten und im einzelnen schwer zu bewertenden Informationen zu vermitteln. Erst in
einem weiteren Schritt (je nach Anwendungsgebiet) wird die Detektion
von Fehlverhalten und eine Diagnose erforderlich.

4.4 Die spezielle Problematik in der Leitwarte

Im vorangegangenen wurde eine Rollenverschiebung von der reinen Diagnose zur Situationserfassung festgestellt. Im Bereich der Leittechnik bedeutet dies, daß das Expertensystem ein genaues Bild der aktuellen Situation des zu überwachenden Prozesses haben muß. Nun ist
dies aber ebenfalls eine Aufgabe der Leitwarte selbst, denn sie
stellt dem Bediener auf den Bildschirmen ja nicht einfach nur die
Meßwerte dar, sondern bereits außerdem eine Interpretation dieser
Werte, indem z.B. abgeleitete Werte dargestellt werden, Werte unter
bestimmten Kriterien zusammengefaßt als Kurve angezeigt werden usw.
Der wesentliche Unterschied bei der Situationserfassung durch die
Leitwarte und durch ein Expertensystem liegt darin, daß der Leitwarte
das Verständnis für die kausalen Zusammenhänge fehlt. Ihm sind zwar
funktionale Zusammenhänge bekannt - z.B. in Form der Algorithmen zur
Steuerung -, es fehlt ihm aber symbolisches und argumentatives Wissen, um daraus weitergehende Schlüsse zu ziehen. Das wichtigste Ziel
für eine Leitwarte ist die Vollständigkeit der Information. Im Gegensatz dazu ist beim Expertensystem das Verständnis das wichtigste.
Ohne dises kann es keine Schlüsse aus den vorliegenden Informationen
ziehen. Die Vollständigkeit der Informationen bis ins kleinste Detail
ist dabei gar nicht gefordert, solange sichergestellt ist, daß De-
tailinformationen im Bedarfsfall von der Leitwarte zur Verfügung
gestellt werden können. Betrachtet man nun noch einmal Bild 1 und

bildet die unterschiedlichen Schritte auf den Bereich der Leitwarten und Expertensysteme ab, ergeben sich die Bilder 2 und 3. In der klassischen Leitwarte ohne intelligente Unterstützung ist lediglich der erste Wissensbereich, nämlich das algorithmisierbare Wissen enthalten. Aus dem Bild 3 wird deutlich, daß das Expertensystem als Zusatz zur Leitwarte gesehen wird, indem es seine Informationen von dort bezieht und sich auch der durch die Leitwarte bereits vorgenommenen Interpretation bedient. Der Dialog mit dem Bediener beschränkt sich im Idealfall auf die Mitteilung von Expertisen und Diagnosen einerseits und das Erfragen von Zusatzinformationen, die außerhalb der Prozeßwelt liegen, andererseits. Vom Bediener wird dann nur noch die Interaktion, also das Eingreifen in den Prozeß über die Leitwarte gefordert.

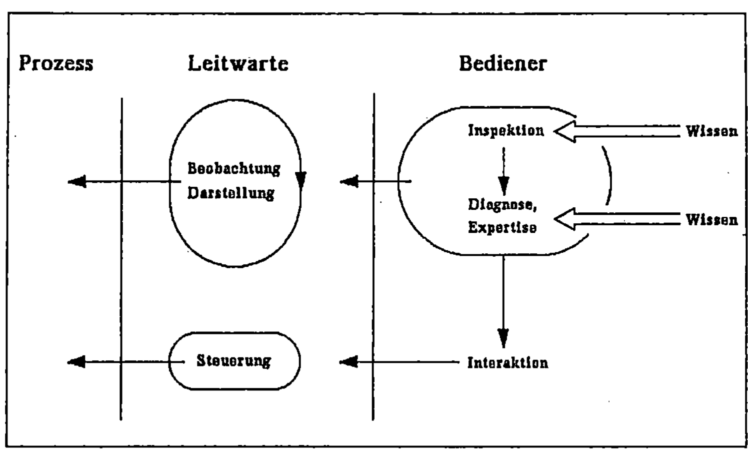

Bild 2:   Die klassische Leitwarte

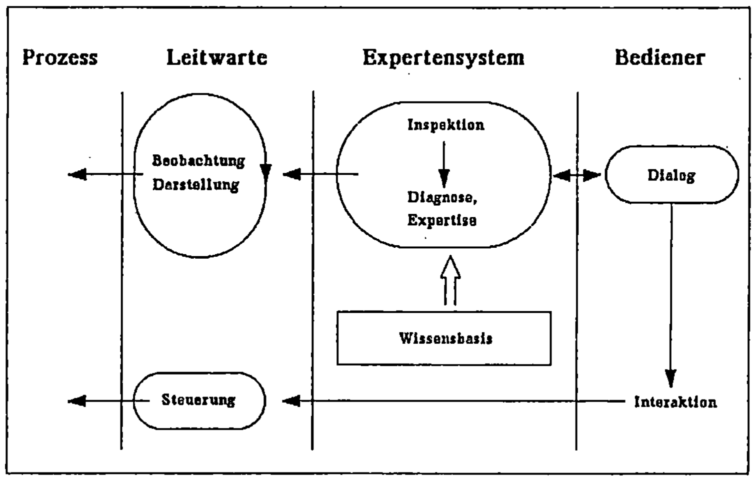

Bild 3:   Die Leitwarte mit einem Expertensystem

Kern eines jeden Expertensystems ist seine Wissensbasis. Neben der
bekannten Aufteilung von Faktenwissen und Regelwissen ist bei Expertensystemen im Leitwartenbereich noch eine andere Unterteilung wichtig:

- Wissen über den Prozeß selbst

- Wissen darüber, wie der Prozeß kontrolliert wird.

Wissen über den Prozeß bezieht sich auf seine Organisationsstruktur,
seine funktionalen Elemente, deren Zusammenwirken, die Zahl und Art
der Meßwerte mit ihren Grenzen, Kriterien für Gefahrensituationen
usw. Wissen über die Kontrollmechanismen bezieht sich darauf, welche
Eingriffsmöglichkeiten es gibt und wie sich diese auswirken. Da sich
ein Expertensystem, wie hier vorgeschlagen, an eine Leitwarte an-
schließt, bedeutet dies vor allem Wissen über die Funktion der Leitwarte mit ihren Einwirkungsmöglichkeiten auf den Prozeß.
Folgende Aspekte bilden die Schwerpunkte bei der Entwicklung von
Expertensystemen in der Prozeßleittechnik:

- Große Datenmengen

Obwohl das Expertensystem nach der oben skizzierten Konzeption nicht
direkt auf den Prozeß zugreift, und somit von der reinen, zeitgebun-
denen Datenabtastung befreit ist, muß es, um einen umfassenden Überblick des Prozeßgeschehens zu erhalten, auf eine große, im allgemeinen vorverarbeitete Menge von Daten aus der Leitwarte zugreifen
können.

- Zeitabhängigkeit

Abgesehen von dem statischen Faktenwissen (Topologie des Versor-
gungsnetzes, Art der Umspannstationen etc.) sind sämtliche Daten des
dynamischen Faktenwissens zeitabhängig. Jeder Meßwert ist ohne seinen
Zeitbezug bedeutungslos. Ebenso muß jede aufgrund einer Fehlerdiagnose empfohlene Aktion einen festen Zeitbezug hinsichtlich ihrer
vorgesehenen Ausführung haben.
Diese Zeitabhängigkeit ist nicht zu verwechseln mit einer Echtzeit-
forderung. Natürlich muß eine Expertise rechtzeitig vorliegen, damit
sie überhaupt noch einen Einfluß auf das Geschehen haben kann. Die
Reaktionszeit eines Expertensystems zu verkürzen ist im wesentlichen

eine Frage der Programmoptimierung, die zeitabhängige Schlußfolgerung
ist dagegen ein prinzipielles Problem.

- Datenübernahme, Situationserfassung

Einerseits durch den Zwang, Daten automatisch , also nicht im Bedie-
nerdialog, zu erfassen, andererseits durch die Forderung ein stets
aktuelles Bild vom Prozeßgeschehen zu haben, anhand dessen etwa der
Bediener in kritischen Situationen geleitet werden kann, ergibt sich
die Forderung nach integrierter Dateninterpretation und -abstraktion.

- Komplexität

Die Komplexität der zu überwachenden Prozesse zwingt zu entsprechend
komplexen Interaktionsmethoden mit dem Bediener. Eine rein textuelle
ist sicherlich ungeeignet, vielmehr wird der Schwerpunkt auf graphische Interaktion - wie bei den Leitwarten ohnehin schon vorhanden -
liegen.

4.5 Lösungsansätze

Es gibt bereits eine Reihe von Systemen, die man dem Bereich der
industriellen Prozesse zuordnen kann. Obwohl ihre speziellen Ziel-
richtungen sehr unterschiedlich sind, weisen sie bestimmte Gemeinsamkeiten auf, die auch für die Anwendung in der Prozeßleittechnik
interessant sind.
Diese Gemeinsamkeiten sind die Situationserfassung durch das Expertensystem mittels Vorwärtsschlußweise und die Diagnose mittels Rück-
wärtsschlußweise. In dem REACTOR-System sind beide Verfahren getrennt, d.h. zunächst läuft die Beobachtung des Prozesses und wenn
ein Fehler entdeckt worden ist die Diagnose. Während der Diagnose ist
die Beobachtung ausgeschaltet. Im DELTA-System (Bonissone) laufen
beide Verfahren parallel, d.h. während der Diagnose ist die Beobachtung weiter aktiv. Dies bedingt am Ende der Diagnose eine Überprüfung
der aktuellen Situation, die sich inzwischen verändert haben kann, um
festzustellen, ob das Diagnoseergebnis überhaupt noch relevant ist.
Im PICON-System (Moore, 1985), das speziell für die Prozeßsteuerung
entwickelt wurde, wird ein Teil der Situationserfassung von einem
Preprozessor abgewickelt, wobei das System selbst entscheidet, auf
welche Teilbereiche des zu beobachtenden Prozesses sich der Preprozessor konzentrieren soll. Auf diese Weise wird eine Fokussierung

auf wesentliche Aspekte erreicht, die es wesentlich erleichtert, aus der Vielzahl der zur Verfügung stehenden Daten die relevanten auszuwählen. PICON unterscheidet sich von dem hier vorgeschlagenen Konzept dadurch, daß es direkt mit den Sensoren des Prozesses verbunden ist, und nicht an eine existierende Leitwarte angeschlossen ist.
Ein wichtiger Punkt, der sehr unterschiedlich gehandhabt wird, ist die Art des Wissens, das die Grundlage dieser Systeme bildet. Hier gibt es zwei grundsätzlich verschiedene Ansätze.
Der erste ist modellorientiert, indem hier ein Modell der realen Welt, auf die das System angewendet werden soll, enthalten ist. Im DART-System (Genesereth, 1982), das zur Fehlersuche in elektronischen Systemen gedacht ist, existiert ein hierarchisches Modell über die physikalischen und funktionellen Eigenschaften elektrischer Komponenten, sowie eine formale Beschreibung, wie einzelne Komponenten zu größeren Modulen zusammengeschaltet werden können. Durch diesen Ansatz lassen sich zwar Fehler sehr gut lokalisieren, aber es können keine Fehler gefunden werden, die nicht auf die Modellbeschreibung zurückzuführen sind, wie z.B. Brücken über Leiterbahnen.
Der zweite Ansatz ist heuristisch orientiert. Im CRIB-System (Hartley, 1984), gedacht zur Fehlersuche in Rechnern, wird davon ausgegangen, daß es nicht notwendig und auch nicht möglich ist, die komplette Theorie elektrischer Schaltkreise zu inkorporieren. Die Fehlersuche beschränkt sich hier auf die Detektion fehlerhafter Module, aber nicht auf die in ihnen enthaltenen Komponenten. Daher konzentriert man sich hier auf die Diagnose des Ein-Ausgabeverhaltens einzelner Module. Die Heuristik der Vorgehensweise ist in Metaregeln zur Diagnoseablaufsteuerung enthalten.

Diese Lösungsansätze sollen nur einen groben Überblick geben. Ein detaillierter Vergleich existierender Systeme findet sich in Bigham, 1985. Grundsätzlich kann man feststellen, daß es zwar eine Reihe von Ansätzen für die Entwicklung von Expertensystemen im Prozeßsteuerungsbereich gibt, aber bisher noch keine in der Praxis einsetzbare Lösung existiert. Dies wird die Aufgabe für die nächsten Jahre sein, die unter anderen von verschieden Projekten im Rahmen des ESPRIT-Programmes und der deutschen Verbundvorhaben intensiv verfolgt wird.

5. Literaturverzeichnis

Allen, J.F. (1983): Maintaining Knowledge about Temporal Intervals.
    In: CACM 26, No. 11, p. 832 - 843

Bigham, J. (1985): Existing Knowledgebased Systems - An Overview.
    Technical Memo 2, ESPRIT-Project KRITIC, Krupp Atlas
    Elektronik, Bremen (In Vorb.)

Bonissone, P.P.: Expert Systems for Fault Diagnosis in Diesel
    Electric Locomotives. Internal Report, General Electric

McDermott, D. (1982): A Temporal Logic for Reasoning about Plans and
    Actions. In: Cognitive Science, 6, p. 101-155

Genesereth, M.G. (1982): Diagnosis Using Hierarchical Design Model.
    Proceedings of AAAI-82, Pittsburg, p. 278-283

Hartley, R.T. (1984): CRIB: Computer Fault-Finding Through Knowledge
    Engineering. IEEE Computer, März 1985, p. 76-83

Moore, R.L., Hawkinson L.B., et al. (1985): A Real Time Expert
    System for Process Control. LISP Machine Inc.

REACTOR: An Expert System for Diagnosis and Treatment of Nuclear
    Reactor Accidents. In: Proceedings of AAAI-82,
    Pittsburg,
    p. 296-301

Shortliffe E.H. (1976): Computer-Based Medical Consultations:
    MYCIN. Elsevier Computer Science Library.

Smith, R.G., Baker, J.D. (1983): The Dipmeter Advisor System.
    In: Proceedings 8th IJCAI, Karlsruhe, p. 122-129

A Formalization of Commonsense Reasoning Based on Fuzzy Logic[*]

L.A. Zadeh

Computer Science Division
University of California
Berkeley, CA 94720

Abstract

The basic idea underlying the approach outlined in this paper is that commonsense knowledge may be regarded as a collection of dispositions, that is, propositions which are preponderantly, but not necessarily always, true. Technically, a disposition may be interpreted as a proposition with implicit fuzzy quantifiers, e.g., *most, almost all, usually, often,* etc. For example, a disposition such as *Swedes are blond* may be interpreted as *most Swedes are blond.* For purposes of inference from commonsense knowledge, the conversion of a disposition into a proposition with explicit fuzzy quantifiers sets the stage for an application of syllogistic reasoning in which the premises are allowed to be of the form Q A's are B's, where A and B are fuzzy predicates and Q is a fuzzy quantifier. In general, the conclusion yielded by such reasoning is a proposition which may be converted into a disposition through the suppression of fuzzy quantifiers.

1. Introduction

In recent years, it has become increasingly clear that further advances in AI require a better understanding of how to represent and infer from commonsense knowledge. The problem with such knowledge - exemplified by *snow is white, a loaf of bread costs about a dollar, students are young,* etc. - is that it does not lend itself to representation within the framework of traditional logical systems, although some progress toward this end has been achieved through the employment of variants of predicate logic involving circumscription (6), default reasoning (12), truth-maintenance (1), non-monotonic reasoning (8) and related techniques.

In an alternative approach which is outlined in this paper,[*] a key idea is that commonsense knowledge may be viewed as a collection of dispositions, that is, propositions which are preponderantly, but not necessarily always, true. Commonplace examples of dispositions are: *glue is sticky, slimness is attractive, overeating causes obesity,* Maria is very straightforward, big planes are safer than small planes, etc.

Techically, a disposition may be interpreted as a proposition which contains implicit fuzzy quantifiers such as *most, almost always, usually, often,* etc. For example, *Maria is very straightforward* may be interpreted as *usually Maria is very straightforward.* The process of conversion of a disposition into a proposition is·referred to as *explicitation.* An important aspect of explicitation is that it is interpretation-dependent in the sense that the manner in which the suppressed quantifiers in a disposition are restored is determined by the intended meaning of the disposition. For example, *slimness is attractive* may be understood as *most of the slim are attractive,* but it may also be interpreted as *most of the attractive are slim.* Similarly, *heavy smoking causes lung cancer* may be interpreted in many ways, among them: *most of the heavy smokers develop lung cancer, most of those who have lung cancer are heavy smokers,* and *among those who have lung cancer, the number of heavy smokers is much larger than the number of non-smokers.*

Explicitation sets the stage for the representation of the meaning of a disposition through the use of fuzzy logic and, more specifically, test-score semantics (16). A brief exposition of test-score semantics is presented in the following.

2. Test Score Semantics

In test-score semantics, a proposition is regarded as a collection of elastic, or, equivalently, fuzzy constraints. For example, the proposition *Kathryn is tall* represents an elastic constraint on the height of Kathryn. Similarly, the proposition *Charlotte is blonde* represents an elastic constraint on the color of Charlotte's hair. And, the proposition *most tall men are not very agile* represents an elastic constraint on the proportion of men who are not very agile among tall men.

In more concrete terms, representing the meaning of a proposition, p, through the use of test-score semantics involves the following steps.

1. Identification of the variables $X_1, \ldots, X_n$ whose values are constrained by the proposition. Usually, these variables are implicit rather than explicit in p.

2. Identification of the constraints $C_1, \ldots, C_m$ which are induced by p.

3. Characterization of each constraint, C_i, by describing a testing procedure which associates with C_i a test score τ_i representing the degree to which C_i is satisfied. Usually τ_i is expressed as a number in the interval $[0,1]$. More generally, however, a test score may be a probability/possibility distribution over the unit interval.

4. Aggregation of the partial test scores $\tau_1, \ldots, \tau_m$ into a smaller number of test scores $\bar{\tau}_1, \ldots, \bar{\tau}_k$, which are represented as an *overall vector test score* $\tau = (\bar{\tau}_1, \ldots, \bar{\tau}_k)$. In most cases $k = 1$, so that the overall test scores is a scalar. We shall assume that this is the case unless an explicit statement to the contrary is made.

It is important to note that, in test-score semantics, the meaning of p is represented not by the overall test score τ but by the procedure which leads to it. Viewed in this perspective, test-score semantics may be regarded as a generalization of truth-conditional, possible-world and model-theoretic semantics. However, by providing a computational framework for dealing with uncertainty and dispositionality — which the conventional semantical systems disregard — test-score semantics achieves a

Research supported by NASA Grant NCC2-275 and NSF Grant IST-8420416.
[*] A more detailed exposition of fuzzy logic and its application to commonsense reasoning may be found in (18).

much higher level of expressive power and thus provides a basis for representing the meaning of a much wider variety of propositions in a natural language.

In test-score semantics, the testing of the constraints induced by p is performed on a collection of fuzzy relations which constitute an *explanatory database*, or *ED* for short. A basic assumption which is made about the explanatory database is that it is comprised of relations whose meaning is known to the addressee of the meaning-representation process. In an indirect way, then, the testing and aggregation procedures in test-score semantics may be viewed as a description of a process by which the meaning of p is composed from the meanings of the constituent relations in the explanatory database. It is this explanatory role of the relations in *ED* that motivates its description as an *explanatory database*.

As will be seen in the sequel, in describing the testing procedures we need not concern ourselves with the actual entries in the constituent relations. Thus, in general, the description of a test involves only the frames of the constituent relations, that is, their names, their variables (or attributes) and the domain of each variable. When this is the case, the explanatory database will be referred to as the *explanatory database frame*, or *EDF* for short.

As a simple illustration of the concept of a test procedure, consider the proposition $p \triangleq$ *Maria is young and attractive*. The *EDF* in this case will be assumed to consist of the following relations:

$$EDF \triangleq POPULATION \ [Name; Age; \mu Attractive\,]$$

$$+ \ YOUNG\,[Age; \mu] \ . \tag{2.1}$$

in which + should be read as "and."

The relation labeled *POPULATION* consists of a collection of triples whose first element is the name of an individual; whose second element is the age of that individual; and whose third element is the degree to which the individual in question is attractive. The relation *YOUNG* is a collection of pairs whose first element is a value of the variable *Age* and whose second element is the degree to which that value of *Age* satisfies the elastic constraint characterized by the fuzzy predicate *young*. In effect, this relation serves to calibrate the meaning of the fuzzy predicate *young* in a particular context by representing its denotation as a fuzzy subset, *YOUNG*, of the interval $[0,100]$.

With this *EDF*, the test procedure which computes the overall test score may be described as follows:

1. Determine the age of Maria by reading the value of *Age* in *POPULATION*, with the variable *Name* bound to Maria. In symbols, this may be expressed as

$$Age \ (Maria) = {}_{Age} POPULATION \ [Name = Maria] \ .$$

In this expression, we use the notation $_YR[X = a]$ to signify that X is bound to a in R and the resulting relation is projected on Y, yielding the values of Y in the tuples in which $X = a$.

2. Test the elastic constraint induced by the fuzzy predicate *young*:

$$\tau_1 = {}_\mu YOUNG[Age = Age\,(Maria)] \ .$$

3. Determine the degree to which Maria is attractive:

$$\tau_2 = {}_{\mu Attractive} POPULATION[Name = Maria] \ .$$

4. Compute the overall test score by aggregating the partial test scores τ_1 and τ_2. For this purpose, we shall use the min operator $\wedge$ as the aggregation operator, yielding

$$\tau = \tau_1 \wedge \tau_1 \ . \tag{2.2}$$

which signifies that the overall test score is taken to be the smaller of the operands of $\wedge$. The overall test score, as expressed by (2.2), represents the compatibility of $p \triangleq$ *Maria is young and attractive* with the data resident in the explanatory database.

In testing the constituent relations in *EDF*, it is helpful to have a collection of standardized translation rules for computing the test score of a combination of elastic constraints $C_1, \ldots, C_k$ from the knowledge of the test scores of each constraint considered in isolation. For the most part, such rules are *default* rules in the sense that they are intended to be used in the absence of alternative rules supplied by the user.

For purposes of commonsense knowledge representation, the principal rules of this type are the following.**

Rules pertaining to modification

If the test score for an elastic constraint C in a specified context is τ, then in the same context the test score for

(a) *not C* is $1 - \tau$ (*negation*)

(b) *very C* is τ^2 (*concentration*)

(c) *more or less C* is $\tau^{\frac{1}{2}}$ (*diffusion*) .

Rules pertaining to composition

If the test scores for elastic constraints C_1 and C_2 in a specified context are τ_1 and τ_2, respectively, then in the same context the test score for

(a) C_1 *and* C_2 is $\tau_1 \wedge \tau_2$ (*conjunction*), where $\wedge \triangleq min$.

(b) C_1 *or* C_2 is $\tau_1 \vee \tau_2$ (*disjunction*), where $\vee \triangleq max$.

(c) *If* C_1 *then* C_2 is $1 \wedge (1 - \tau_1 + \tau_2)$ (*implication*) .

Rules pertaining to quantification

The rules in question apply to propositions of the general form $Q \ A\text{'s are } B\text{'s}$, where Q is a fuzzy quantifier, e.g., *most, many, several, few*, etc, and A and B are fuzzy sets, e.g., *tall men, intelligent men*, etc. As was stated earlier, when the fuzzy quantifiers in a proposition are implied rather than explicit, their suppression may be placed in evidence by referring to the proposition as a *disposition*. In this sense, the proposition *overeating causes obesity* is a disposition which results from the suppression of the fuzzy quantifer *most* in the proposition *most of those who overeat are obese*.

To make the concept of a fuzzy quantifer meaningful, it is necessary to define a way of counting the number of elements in a fuzzy set or, equivalently, to determine its cardinality.

There are several ways in which this can be done (15). For our purposes, it will suffice to employ the concept of a *sigma-count*, which is defined as follows.

Let F be a fuzzy subset of $U = \{u_1, \ldots, u_n\}$

expressed symbolically as

$$F = \mu_1/u_1 + \ldots + \mu_n/u_n = \Sigma_i \mu_i/u_i$$

or, more simply, as

$$F = \mu_1 u_1 + \ldots + \mu_n u_n \ ,$$

in which the term μ_i/u_i, $i = 1, \ldots, n$, signifies that μ_i is the grade of membership of u_i in F, and the plus sign represents the union.

The sigma-count of F is defined as the arithmetic sum of the μ_i, i.e.,

$$\Sigma Count \ (F) \triangleq \Sigma_i \mu_i, i = 1, \ldots, n \ ,$$

** A more detailed discussion of such rules in the context of PRUF may be found in (16).

with the understanding that the sum may be rounded, if need be, to the nearest integer. Furthermore, one may stipulate that the terms whose grade of membership falls below a specified threshold be excluded from the summation. The purpose of such an exclusion is to avoid a situation in which a large number of terms with low grades of membership become count-equivalent to a small number of terms with high membership.

The *relative sigma-count*, denoted by $\Sigma Count(F/G)$, may be interpreted as the proportion of elements of F which are in G. More explicitly,

$$\Sigma Count(F/G) = \frac{\Sigma Count(F \cap G)}{\Sigma Count(G)} .$$

where $F \cap G$, the intersection of F and G, is defined by

$$\mu_{F \cap G}(u) = \mu_F(u) \wedge \mu_G(u) , \quad u \in U .$$

Thus, in terms of the membership functions of F and G, the relative sigma-count of F in G is given by

$$\Sigma Count(F/G) = \frac{\Sigma_i \mu_F(u_i) \wedge \mu_G(u_i)}{\Sigma_i \mu_G(u_i)} .$$

The concept of a relative sigma-count provides a basis for interpreting the meaning of propositions of the form Q A's are B's , e.g., *most young men are healthy*. More specifically, if the focal variable (ie., the constrained variable) in the proposition in question is taken to be the proportion of B's in A's, then the corresponding translation rule may be expressed as

$$Q \; A\text{'s are } B\text{'s} \to \Sigma Count(B/A) \text{ is } Q$$

As will be seen in the following section, the quantification rule together with the other rules described in this section provide a basic conceptual framework for the representation of commonsense knowledge. We shall illustrate the representation process through the medium of several examples in which the meaning of a disposition is represented as a test on a collection of fuzzy relations in an explanatory database.

3. Representation of Meaning of Dispositions

To clarify the difference between the conventional approaches to meaning representation and that described in the present paper, we shall consider as our first example the disposition

$$d \; \triangleq \; snow \; is \; white \; .$$

The first step in the representation process involves a restoration of the suppressed quantifiers in d. We shall assume that the intended meaning of d is conveyed by the proposition

$$p \; \triangleq \; usually \; snow \; is \; white \; ,$$

and, as an *EDF*, we shall use

$$EDF \; \triangleq \; WHITE[Sample; \mu] + USUALLY[Proportion; \mu] .$$

in which   (3.1) .

$\tau_i, \; i = 1, \ldots, m$, denotes the degree to which the color of S_i matches white. Thus, τ_i may be interpreted as the test score for the constraint on the color of S_i which is induced by *WHITE*.

Using this notation, the steps in the testing procedure may be described as follows:

1. Find the proportion of samples whose color is white:

$$\rho = \frac{\Sigma Count(WHITE)}{m}$$

$$= \frac{\tau_1 + \ldots + \tau_m}{m}$$

2. Compute the degree to which ρ satisfies the constraint induced by *USUALLY*:

$$\tau = {}_\mu USUALLLY[Proportion = \rho] . \qquad (3.2)$$

In (3.2), τ represents the overall test score and the right-hand member signifies that the relation *USUALLY* is particularized by setting Proportion equal to ρ and projecting the resulting relation on μ. The meaning of d, then, is represented by the test procedure which leads to the value of τ.

To illustrate the use of translation rules relating to modification, we shall consider the disposition

$$d \; \triangleq \; Frenchmen \; are \; not \; very \; tall \; .$$

After explicitation, the intended meaning of d is assumed to be represented by the proposition

$$p \; \triangleq \; most \; Frenchmen \; are \; not \; very \; tall \; .$$

To represent the meaning of p, we shall employ an *EDF* whose constituent relations are:

$$EDF \; \triangleq \; POPULATION[Name; Height] +$$
$$TALL[Height; \mu] +$$
$$MOST[Proportion; \mu] .$$

The relation *POPULATION* is a tabulation of *Height* as a function of *Name* for a representative group of Frenchmen. In *TALL*, μ is the degree to which a value of *Height* fits the description *tall*; and in *MOST*, μ is the degree to which a numerical value of *Proportion* fits the intended meaning of *most*.

The test procedure which represents the meaning of p involves the following steps:

1. Let $Name_i$ be the name of ith individual in *POPULATION*. For each $Name_i, i = 1, \ldots, m$, find the height of $Name_i$:

$$Height(Name_i) \; \triangleq \; {}_{Height} POPULATION[Name = Name_i] .$$

2. For each $Name_i$, compute the test score for the constraint induced by *TALL:*

$$\tau_i = {}_\mu TALL[Height = Height(Name_i)] .$$

3. Using the translation rules, compute the test score for the constraint induced by *NOT.VERY.TALL:*

$$\tau'_i = 1 - \tau_i^2 .$$

4. Find the relative sigma-count of Frenchmen who are not very tall:

$$\rho \; \triangleq \; \Sigma Count(NOT.VERY.TALL/POPULATION)$$

$$= \frac{\Sigma_i \tau'_i}{m} .$$

5. Compute the test score for the constraint induced by *MOST:*

$$\tau = {}_\mu MOST[Proportion = \rho] . \qquad (3.3)$$

The test score given by (3.3) represents the overall test score for d, and the test procedure which yields τ represents the meaning of d.

4. Inference

In what follows, we shall restrict our attention to dispositions which, after explicitation, are expressible in the canonical form QA's are B's, where Q *is a fuzzy quantifier*, e.g., *most, almost all, usually,* etc., and A and B are fuzzy predicates such as *small, tall, slim, young,* etc.* Fuzzy logic provides a basis for inference from dispositions of this type through the use of *fuzzy syllogistic seasoning* (19). As its name implies, fuzzy syllogistic seasoning is an extension of classical syllogistic seasoning to fuzzy predicates and fuzzy quantifiers. In

---

* A more general treatment of inference in fuzzy logic may be found in (15).

its generic form, a fuzzy syllogism may be expressed as the inference schema

$$Q_1 A's \text{ are } B's \tag{4.1}$$
$$\underline{Q_2 C's \text{ are } D's}$$
$$Q_3 E's \text{ are } F's$$

in which A, B, C, D, E and F are interrelated fuzzy predicates and Q_1, Q_2 and Q_3 are fuzzy quantifiers.

The interrelations between A,B,C,D,E and F provide a basis for a classification of fuzzy syllogisms. The more important of these syllogisms are the following. ($\wedge \triangleq$ conjunction, $\vee \triangleq$ disjunction).

(a) *Intersection/product syllogism*: $C=A \wedge B, E=A, F=C \wedge D$

(b) *chaining syllogism*: $C=B, E=A, F=D$

(c) *Consequent conjunction syllogism*: $A=C=E, F=B \wedge D$

(d) *Consequent disjunction syllogism*: $A=C=E, F=B \vee D$

(e) *Antecedent conjunction syllogism*: $B=D=F, E=A \wedge C$

(f) *Antecedent disjunction syllogism*: $B=D=F, E=A \vee C$.

In the context of expert systems, these and related syllogisms provide a set of inference rules for combining evidence through conjunction, disjunction and chaining (17).

One of the basic problems in fuzzy syllogistic seasoning is the following. Given A, B, C, D, E and F, find the maximally specific (i.e., most restrictive) fuzzy quantifier Q_3 such that the proposition $Q, E's$ are $F's$ is entailed by the premises. In the case of (a), (b) and (c), this leads to the following syllogisms.

Intersection/product syllogism

$$Q_1 A's \text{ are } B's \tag{4.2}$$
$$\underline{Q_2 (A \text{ and } B)'s \text{ are } C's}$$

$$\vdots$$

$$(Q_1 \otimes Q_2) A's \text{ are } (B \text{ and } C)'s$$

where $\otimes$ denotes the product in fuzzy arithmetic (4). It should be noted that (4.2) may be viewed as an analog of the basic probabilistic identity

$$p(B,C/A) = p(B/A)p(C/A,B) .$$

A concrete example of the intersection/product syllogism is the following

$$most \text{ students are } young \tag{4.3}$$
$$\underline{most \text{ young students are single}}$$
$$most^2 \text{ students are } young \text{ and } single$$

where $most^2$ denotes the product of the fuzzy quantifier $most$ with itself.

Chaining syllogism

$$Q_1 A's \text{ are } B's \tag{4.4}$$
$$\underline{Q_2 B's \text{ are } C's}$$

$$(Q_1 \otimes Q_2) A's \text{ are } C's .$$

This syllogism may be viewed as a special case of the intersection product syllogism. It results when $B \subset A$ and Q_1 and Q_2 are monotone increasing, i.e., $\geq Q_1 = Q_1$, and $\geq Q_2 = Q_2$, where $\geq Q_1$ should be read as *at least* Q_1, and likewise for Q_2. A simple example of the chaining syllogism is the following:

$$most \text{ students are } undergraduates$$
$$\underline{most \text{ undergraduates are single}}$$
$$most^2 \text{ students are } single$$

Note that *undergraduates* $\subset$ *students* and that in the conclusion $F = single$, rather than *young and single*, as in (4.3).

Consequent conjunction syllogism

The consequent conjunction syllogism is an example of a basic syllogism which is not a derivative of the intersection/product syllogism. Its statement may be expressed as follows:

$$Q_1 A's \text{ are } B's \tag{4.5}$$
$$\underline{Q_2 A's \text{ are } C's}$$
$$Q A's \text{ are } (B \text{ and } C)'s .$$

where Q is a fuzzy quantifier which is defined by the inequalities

$$0 \otimes (Q_1 \oplus Q_2 \ominus 1) \leq Q \leq Q_1 \otimes Q_2 \tag{4.6}$$

in which $\otimes, \oslash, \oplus$ and $\ominus$ are the operations of $\vee$ (max), $\wedge$ (min), $+$ and $-$ in fuzzy arithmetic.

An illustration of (4.5) is provided by the example

$$most \text{ students are } young$$
$$\underline{most \text{ students are single}}$$
$$Q \text{ students are } single \text{ and } young$$

where

$$2most \ominus 1 \leq Q \leq most . \tag{3.17}$$

This expression for Q follows from (4.6) by noting that

$$most \otimes most = most$$

and

$$0 \otimes (2most \ominus 1) = 2most \ominus 1 .$$

The three basic syllogisms stated above are merely examples of a collection of fuzzy syllogisms which may be developed and employed for purposes of inference from commonsense knowledge. In addition to its application to commonsense reasoning, fuzzy syllogistic reasoning may serve to provide a basis for the development of a system of rules for combining uncertain evidence in expert systems (17).

REFERENCES AND RELATED PUBLICATIONS

[1] J. Doyle, "A truth-maintenance system." *Artificial Intelligence 12*, pp. 231-272, 1979.

[2] D. Dubois and H. Prade, *Fuzzy Sets and Systems: Theory and Applications*. New York:Academic Press, 1980.

[3] J.A. Goguen, "The logic of inexact concepts," *Synthese 19*, pp. 325-373, 1969.

[4] A. Kaufmann and M.M. Gupta, *Introduction to Fuzzy Arithmetic*. New York:Van Nostrand, 1985.

[5] E.H. Mamdani and B.R. Gaines, *Fuzzy Reasoning and its Applications*. London:Academic Press, 1981.

[6] J. McCarthy, "Circumscription: A non-monotonic inference rule," *Artificial Intelligence 13*, pp. 27-40, 1980.

[7] D.V. McDermott and J. Doyle, "Non-monotonic logic. I." *Artificial Intelligence 13*, pp. 41-72, 1980.

[8] D.V. McDermott, "Non-monotonic logic, II: non-monotonic modal theories." *J. Assoc. Comp. Mach. 29*, pp. 33-57, 1982.

[9] R.C. Moore and J.R. Hobbs, (eds.), *Formal Theories of the Commonsense World.* Harwood, NJ:Ablex Publishing, 1984.

[10] C.V. Negoita, *Expert Systems and Fuzzy Systems.* Menlo Park:Benjamin/Cummings, 1985.

[11] N. Nilsson, *Probabilistic logic,* SRI Tech. Note 321, Menlo Park, CA, 1984.

[12] R. Reiter and G. Criscuolo, "Some representational issues in default reasoning," *Computers and Mathematics 9,* pp. 15-28, 1983.

[13] M. Sugeno, "Fuzzy measures and fuzzy integrals: a survey," in *Fuzzy Automata and Decision Processes.* M.M. Gupta, G.N. Saridis and B.R. Gaines, (eds.), Amsterdam:North-Holland, pp. 89-102, 1977.

[14] R.R. Yager, "Quantified propositions in a linguistic logic," in: *Proceedings of the 2nd International Seminar on Fuzzy Set Theory.* E.P. Klement, (ed.), Johannes Kepler University, Linz, Austria, 1980.

[15] L.A. Zadeh, "A theory of approximate reasoning," *Electronics Research Laboratory Memorandum M77/58,* University of California, Berkeley, 1977. Also in: *Machine Intelligence 9.* J.E. Hayes. D. Michie and L.I. Kulich, (eds.), New York:Wiley, pp. 149-194, 1979.

[16] L.A. Zadeh, "Test-score semantics for natural languages and meaning-representation via PRUF," *Tech. Note 247, AI Center, SRI International,* Menlo Park, CA, 1981. Also in *Empirical Semantics.* B.B. Rieger, (ed.), Bochum:Brockmeyer, pp. 281-349, 1981.

[17] L.A. Zadeh, "The role of fuzzy logic in the management of uncertainty in expert systems," *Fuzzy Sets and Systems 11,* pp. 199-227, 1983.

[18] L.A. Zadeh, "A theory of commonsense knowledge," in *Issues of Vagueness.* H.J. S. Skala Termini and E. Trillas, (eds.), pp. 257-296, Dordrecht:Reidel, 1984.

[19] L.A. Zadeh, "Syllogistic reasoning in fuzzy logic and its application to usuality and reasoning with dispositions," to appear in the *IEEE Trans. on Systems, Man and Cybernetics,* 1985.

[20] M. Zemankova-Leech and A. Kandel, *Fuzzy Relational Data Bases - A Key to Expert Systems.* Cologne: Verlag TUV Rheinland, 1984.